Corey Urband

2062453895

WHY FREUD WAS WRONG

WHY FREUD WAS WRONG

SIN, SCIENCE, AND PSYCHOANALYSIS

Richard Webster

BasicBooks
A Division of HarperCollins*Publishers*

Heinrich Heine's "Grenadiere" reprinted from *Poetry and Prose*, ed. Jost Herman and Robert C. Holub, trans. Louis Untermeyer (New York: Continuum, 1982), by permission of the publisher.

Copyright © 1995 by Richard Webster.
Published by BasicBooks, A Division of HarperCollins Publishers, Inc.

Also published in the United Kingdom in 1995 by HarperCollins Publishers.

Library of Congress Cataloging-in-Publication Data
Webster, Richard, 1950–
    Why Freud was wrong : sin, science, and psychoanalysis / Richard
  Webster.
      p. cm.
    Includes bibliographical references and index.
    ISBN 0–465–09579–8
    1. Freud, Sigmund, 1856–1939.   2. Psychoanalysis—History.
I. Title.
BF109.F74W33   1995
150.19'52'092—dc20   95-22640
                                            CIP

95 96 97 98 ❖/HC 9 8 7 6 5 4 3 2 1

Contents

A Note to the Reader   vii

INTRODUCTION: The Legacy of Freud   I
PROLOGUE: Images, Myths and Legends   13

I: THE CREATION OF A PSEUDO-SCIENCE

 I   From Caul to Cocaine   33
 2   Hypnotism and Hysteria   52
 3   Charcot's Mistake   71
 4   Anna O. and the Birth of Psychoanalysis   103
 5   Freud's First Case   136
 6   More Medical Mistakes   155
 7   Mysterious Mechanisms   168
 8   Sex, Masturbation and Neurasthenia   182
 9   The Seduction Theory   195
10   Freud, Fliess and the Theory of Infantile Sexuality   214
11   Exploring the Unconscious: Self-Analysis and Oedipus   241
12   Dreams and Symptoms   259
13   Developing the Doctrine   278

II: THE CHURCH AND
THE PSYCHOANALYTIC GOSPEL

14   'Freud, who was my Christ!'   299
15   Freud, Satan and the Serpent   320
16   Priests, Penitents and Patients   334
17   Critics and Dissidents   356
18   Jung: Crown Prince and Beloved Son   368
19   The Secret Committee: From Formation to Failure   390
20   Anna Freud: Daughter and Disciple   402

III: PSYCHOANALYSIS, SCIENCE AND THE FUTURE

21   Psychoanalysis, Science and Human Nature   437
22   The Ghost in the Psychoanalytic Machine   457
23   The Behaviour of the Body   477
24   Beyond Psychoanalysis   489

AFTERWORD: Freud's False Memories:
          Psychoanalysis and the Recovered Memory
          Movement   511
APPENDIX I: The Diagnosis of 'Hysteria'   529
APPENDIX II: Babinski's Test for 'Hysteria'   549

Notes and References   553
Bibliography   629
Index   647

A Note to the Reader

THE TITLE OF THIS BOOK, bold though it may seem to some, is not intended simply as another stinging rebuke to Freudians. It is true that if I did not believe that Freud could be unseated, and unseated in an even more comprehensive and conclusive manner than he has been yet, I would not have thrown down my gauntlet in quite this way. But throughout the pages that follow I have tried to bear in mind the common claim that 'we are all Freudians now'. Because I believe there is some truth in this claim, I have tended to treat the founder of psychoanalysis as the embodiment of *our* ideas rather than simply as the propagator of his own. My ultimate goal is not to humiliate Freud or to inflict mortal injury either on him or his followers. It is to interpret and illuminate his beliefs and his personality in order that we may better understand our own culture, our own history and, indeed, our own psychology. It is to this *constructive* attempt to analyse the nature and sources of Freud's mistakes that my title primarily refers.

Why Freud Was Wrong has taken me a long time to write and I would like to thank all those people who have encouraged me along the way. Many years ago the philosopher and Freud scholar Professor Frank Cioffi helped to light the slow fuse which would eventually lead to this book when he responded generously and enthusiastically to a paper I had sent him about Freud and Fliess. He, in turn, was one of the first people to read the earliest draft of this book and I remain grateful for his encouragement and for his constructive criticism. It was only when he had read my first draft that this book began to seem real to me. As a result I promptly rewrote it. My friend Ruth Whittaker then undertook to read again a book she had already read once. Her comments and criticisms were, as usual, immensely valuable. Another early reader was Professor Raymond Tallis whose critique of modern literary theory, *Not Saussure*, I have long admired. As a medical doctor with a special interest in neurology who had strayed into literary criticism, he seemed the ideal reader for a book written by a literary critic who had strayed into neurology, psychiatry and the history of medicine. Such was the warmth and enthusiasm of his response that for some time I felt that any further audience for this book would be entirely redundant. If my feelings about this have gradually changed, my gratitude for his response, and for his helpful comments and criticisms, remains undiminished.

Seeking an agent who would not be daunted by my subject matter, I sent the early part of my book to David Godwin. I am particularly grateful to him for responding so promptly and so positively and for his continued help since. I am no less grateful to his wife, Heather Godwin, who made off with the completed manuscript as soon as I delivered it, started to read it, and refused to relinquish it until she had finished. She thus became my first real reader and her unsolicited enthusiasm meant a great deal to me.

Equally valuable were the reactions of two other people who read the manuscript at this stage – Dr Morton Schatzman and Allen Esterson. As a practising psychotherapist and a Freud scholar Morton Schatzman gave both encouragement and constructive criticism, while Allen Esterson, whose own book on Freud had recently been published, combed through my manuscript with immense care, spotted one glaring error which everyone else had missed and made many helpful suggestions.

Professor Frederick Crews in the United States also generously undertook to read my manuscript. Since I end this book by disagreeing with him I must begin it by thanking him for responding to my arguments so fully. Only as our correspondence developed did it become clear that our enthusiastic agreement about many aspects of Freud's work, and about other forms of 'grand theory', had obscured underlying differences on issues which are, I believe, even more important. Frederick Crews's sharp disagreement with the view of cultural history expressed in an earlier draft of this book, and with my reading of the history of modern science, has not affected the overall direction of my arguments. But his response has been immensely helpful. For while agreement strengthens convictions, it is generally only disagreement which helps to strengthen arguments. The third part of this book has been completely rewritten in the light of his comments and for any resulting improvements he must take a large part of the credit. But the issues which divide us are extremely important, and I do not think any good purpose would be served were I to suppress criticisms of his position which I feel ought to be made. While my disagreement with

Professor Crews, deeply felt and vigorously expressed here, compli-
cates my feelings of gratitude to him, it does not in any way extinguish
them. Indeed my admiration for many aspects of his work remains as
strong as ever. I will certainly always remain grateful for his help and
for his robust dissent from some of the positions I have chosen to
maintain. If, as a result of his help, my arguments succeed in persuading
him after all, I shall be doubly in his debt.

A number of my other debts are more straightforward. This would
not make them any easier to discharge if they really were debts. But
market forces have evidently not triumphed completely and goodwill
has not been entirely privatised. For nobody has yet sent me an invoice
for the time they have spent talking to me on the phone – a practice
recently recommended in all seriousness by one author to his fellow
members of the Society of Authors. Instead a great many people have
given help freely and generously. I am particularly grateful to those
members of the medical profession, hard-pressed by other commit-
ments, who have found time to answer my queries. For during the
writing of this book I have bothered practically every doctor that I
know – and a good many that I don't – with questions about everything
from rheumatism to rhinitis. I am particularly grateful to Dr Gerald
Townsley who used the rare moments of leisure afforded by a bout of
flu to help me rediagnose one of Charcot's cases of 'hysteria' – that
of the patient Le Log–. I am also grateful to the neurologists with
whom I have discussed this and other cases. I must specially thank two
leading experts on epilepsy, Professor Alan Richens of the University of
Wales College of Medicine and Dr Colin Binnie, Consultant Clinical
Neurophysiologist at the Maudsley Hospital, for advice on the diagnosis of epilepsy and for reading and commenting helpfully on portions
of my manuscript. I am also grateful to G. Neil-Dwyer, Consultant
Neurosurgeon at the Wessex Neurological Centre for advice on the
case of Le Log–, and to Malcolm Robson Parsons, Consultant Neurologist at the University of Leeds School of Medicine, who, at an early
stage in my research, gave me valuable advice on the case of Anna O.
In the midst of all this advice some difficulties of interpretation remain
and I alone am responsible for any misconceptions.

The entire world of neurology might have remained closed to me
but for the work of E. M. Thornton. With the notable exceptions of
Frederick Crews and Carol Tavris, most scholars have failed to appreciate the value of her arguments. I am grateful to Elizabeth Thornton
both for her two books and for a number of discussions I have had

with her about the history of medicine. It would have been difficult to follow any of the paths she sent me down without the unfailing helpfulness of the librarians at the Wellcome Institute for the History of Medicine and the Royal Society of Medicine, and I am grateful to them for all they did to make my research both easier and more pleasant.

I must also thank Peter Swales who kindly sent me copies of some of his articles together with a recording of a seminar he had conducted in New York. A great many other Freud scholars helped me unawares simply by writing their books. From two such scholars, Frank Sulloway and Paul Roazen, I have learned so much that it would seem wrong not to thank them here, even though I take issue with both of them in the main argument of this book.

Only when my book was nearing completion did it gradually become apparent to me that for a number of years I had, quite inadvertently, been writing a book not only about Freud and psychoanalysis but also about the pre-history of a movement of whose existence I was barely aware – the recovered memory movement which has flourished in the United States in the last decade. Towards the end of 1994 I visited America in order to find out more about this movement and I was able to talk to a number of psychiatrists, therapists, psychologists and feminists about the problem of 'false memory'. Some of the conclusions which I drew from these discussions will be found in the Afterword to this book, 'Freud's False Memories'. This Afterword is much more closely related to the central argument and structure of my book than its designation may suggest and I am grateful to all those American friends and contacts who helped me with it.

My last two debts are, in a sense, the most important. Authors depend upon their publishers for far more than advances and I would like to thank mine – in particular Stuart Proffitt and Philip Gwyn Jones – for all their help. Their enthusiasm for, and belief in, this book have been heartening and I am immensely grateful to them. Finally, and most importantly of all, I would like to thank my wife. Without her help and support this book would not have been written or even contemplated.

Southwold, March 1995

WHY FREUD WAS WRONG

INTRODUCTION

The Legacy of Freud

'MURDER IS A CRIME. Describing murder is not. Sex is not a crime. Describing it is.'[1] These words of Gershon Legman express well something of the confusion, fear and anxiety which have surrounded the subjects of sex and violence for very many centuries.

This confusion clearly affects individuals at the most intimate and private level. But it is also significant in intellectual terms. For to think at all about subjects which are hedged round by such powerful taboos requires not simply lucidity of intellect, but emotional fluency of the kind we do not normally associate with the scientific mind. To think clearly requires even more unusual capacities. It also calls for a degree of intellectual rebelliousness which is rare among those trained in the natural sciences.

Sigmund Freud is frequently held to have possessed all of these qualities. The American writer Lucy Freeman begins her popular study of Freud and the psychoanalytic movement by observing that nearly twenty-one centuries have passed since Plato wrote, 'the life that is unexamined is not worth living', and advised man to 'Know thyself'. She goes on to describe the birth of psychoanalysis in the following terms:

> For close to two millenniums Plato's celebrated dictum seemed to pose an impossible challenge to mankind. Then, at the dawn of the twentieth century, a lone doctor in Vienna, Sigmund Freud, conducted what Alexander Pope, in 1733, called 'the proper study of mankind'. Freud made startling discoveries that were to revolutionise the thinking of the world about the mind of man. Five centuries before Christ, Heraclitus had said, 'The soul of man is a far country, which cannot be approached or explored.' But one man, Sigmund Freud, not only crossed the frontier of that far country, but penetrated its heartland, and through his writings and personal influence made the inner landscape available to all who dared follow.[2]

I

Lucy Freeman's journalistic fluency, and the seemingly naive assurance with which she disposes of more than two millennia of intellectual history, make it very tempting to dismiss her words as yet another example of the myth-making which has always surrounded the figure of Freud. Yet the most striking feature of Freeman's brief conspectus of Western thought is just how much truth it contains. For one of the simplest but most startling facts of intellectual history is that, until the beginning of the twentieth century, European thinkers made virtually no significant contribution to the scientific study of human nature and human behaviour. For at least half a century after Charles Darwin published *The Origin of Species* we possessed no systematic theory which even attempted to explain the exceptionally violent nature of our own species, the extraordinary range and complexity of our non-reproductive sexual behaviour or the depth and power of some of the most ordinary human emotions. The fierce taboos and the atmosphere of religious unreason which surrounded nearly every form of intimate human relationship for centuries, had, it would seem, triumphed over science itself. Here, at least, the advance of human knowledge, which in almost all other areas had proved irresistible, had been held back.

That Freud eventually challenged many of these ancient taboos cannot be disputed. As the intrepid intellectual adventurer he was, he led an assault on the highest peak of human knowledge in a manner which has seemed to many observers not simply impressive, but in some respects magnificent. Yet the view that his expedition was triumphant – that Freud actually succeeded in solving the enigma of human nature – is one which, in the last twenty years or so, has been questioned or rejected by a series of increasingly hostile critics.

Indeed the sheer volume of such attacks has sometimes led to the mistaken impression that psychoanalysis is already a defeated force. Freud, however, has proved more difficult to vanquish than many of his opponents have calculated. As Walter Kendrick has written, 'How can you simply kill the Father who taught you that his death must be your desire?'[3] Although some psychoanalysts themselves now profess a degree of defensive agnosticism about Freud's theories, the movement which he founded continues to show many signs of vigorous life. If the figure of Freud no longer bestrides the intellectual landscape in triumph, it seems at times that he still lies across it like Gulliver, diminishing his critics by the sheer scale and grandeur of his enterprise, and shrugging off as pin-pricks the lances which they hurl against him. 'Why,' asks Phyllis Grosskurth in a recent study of Freud's inner circle, 'has Sigmund Freud's life and work commanded such undiminished interest? Today – as we approach the end of the century – he appears to have been its leading intellectual force, a far more tenacious influence than Karl Marx.'[4] More recently still, in a book which sets out to answer some of Freud's critics, the American historian Paul Robinson expressed optimism about the future of psychoanalysis:

> Unless I am seriously mistaken ... Freud's recent critics will do him no lasting damage. At most they have delayed the inevitable process by which he will settle into his rightful place in intellectual history as a thinker of the first magnitude. Indeed the very latest scholarly studies of Freud suggest that the anti-Freudian moment may already have begun to pass.[5]

Robinson goes on to quote the view of Harold Bloom that 'No twentieth-century writer – not even Proust or Joyce or Kafka – rivals Freud's position as the central imagination of our age.'[6] The fact that such views as these can still be seriously advanced is a mark of the status psychoanalysis continues to enjoy in at least some quarters of intellectual culture.

One of the reasons that psychoanalysis has proved so resilient in the face of recent attacks is that Freud's theories were themselves formulated in an environment of hostility. Those who follow Freud are thus able to account for the continuing scepticism about his ideas by invoking the same arguments which he deployed against his original detractors. One of the arguments resorted to most frequently is that which explains all criticism of psychoanalysis as a product of 'resistance'. Like many of Freud's ideas this notion contains an element of truth. For there can be no doubt that some people do reject his theories because of a conscious or unconscious aversion to their sexual content. But what defenders of psychoanalysis rarely if ever acknowledge is that theories about sexual behaviour which are wrong are just as likely to be met with resistance as theories which are right. The argument about unconscious resistance is therefore a diversion from the main issue. What is far more important about some recent criticism of Freud is that a number of scholars who do not regard the subject-matter of psychoanalysis as offensive or indelicate remain genuinely doubtful about the validity of psychoanalytic theory. They are dissatisfied with it because it fails to do the only thing we ultimately have a right to demand of explanatory theories – it fails to explain.

I share this dissatisfaction. Psychoanalysis is, I believe, one of the most subtle of our many attempts to use reason in a 'magical' rather than in a scientific manner – to use reason, that is to say, not in order to provide a genuine solution to an intellectual problem, but in order to provide a defence against the forces which we fear, and against aspects of our own nature which arouse anxiety. Freud saw himself as the rational foe of religion. Significantly, however, far from setting out radically to subvert the values of Judaeo-Christian asceticism which were deeply internalised in his own culture, Freud made the Lamarckian assumption that such asceticism had become part of our biological inheritance, so that it now belonged to our very nature. It is for this reason that his notion of therapy contains an implicit endorsement of the oldest of all ascetic ideals – the glorification of the spirit at the expense of the body:

> We liberate sexuality through our treatment, but not in order that man may from now on be dominated by sexuality, but in order to make a suppression possible – a rejection of the instincts under the guidance of a higher agency . . . We try to replace the pathological process with rejection.[7]

Driven by what some have construed as fierce intellectual honesty, Freud declined to excise sexuality from human nature completely. To some extent at least we have benefited from his attitude. But throughout the twentieth century, from the time of D. H. Lawrence to the time of Gershon Legman, Nancy Friday and their successors, there have been many who have rebelled against Victorian primness with far more gusto and far more enthusiasm for the realm of the obscene than can ever be glimpsed in the writings of any psychoanalyst. In the climate of explicitness which these latter-day rebels have helped to create it is now possible to see that psychoanalysis is far less adventurous and far less open than we once thought. Significantly, the science of sexuality which Freud brought into being is couched in a language purged of obscenity. Not only this, but Freud's own attitude towards some of the commonest forms of sexual behaviour, including masturbation, homosexuality and many aspects of women's sexuality, was one of distaste bordering on disgust. This attitude is reflected in psychoanalytic theories which are, in many respects, a flight away from the very forms of sexual behaviour which Freud claimed fearlessly to confront.

Given this cryptic conservatism it is perhaps not surprising that some writers have regarded Freud's doctrines as being compatible with traditional religious beliefs. One of Freud's earliest and most enthusiastic followers, the Protestant pastor Oskar Pfister, saw psycho-analysis as a gospel of love comparable with that preached by Jesus. More recently both Erik Erikson in his portrait of Luther, and Norman O. Brown in his *Life Against Death* have pointed to the numerous similarities between Luther's view of the human condition and that found in psychoanalysis.[8] The resemblances which Brown and Erikson found between Lutheran Protestantism and classical psychoanalysis can scarcely be disputed. Some of those who are members of a Prot-estant church, or who hold any form of religious belief, may take comfort in discovering that the revealed truths perceived by Luther are in harmony with the analytic hypotheses produced by Freud. Those who possess greater intellectual caution, however, or those who hold no religious beliefs, may well feel some scepticism in the face of such an easy congruence of ancient faith and modern reason. They will be prompted to ask to what extent we should regard psychoanalysis not as a scientific approach to human nature but as a disguised continuation of the Judaeo-Christian tradition.

For if psychoanalysis seems in some quarters to have attained the weight and seriousness of orthodoxy it is perhaps for no other reason than that it is a form of orthodoxy itself – a subtle reconstruction in a challenging and modern form of some of the most ancient religious doctrines and sexual ideologies.

This view of psychoanalysis has sometimes been taken by other writers. But it has not been taken very far. One of the reasons for this is that today, in our sceptical materialism, we tend to be profoundly unfamiliar with the doctrines and eschatology which once lay at the heart of the Judaeo-Christian tradition. So powerful has the ethos of secular rationalism become that we rarely recognise the fundamental role which has been played in history by irrational fantasies – by religious dreams of redemption and world-purification, by miracles, rituals and magic, by the belief in angels, demons and witches, by visions of cosmic struggles between the forces of light and the forces of darkness, by the fear of Satan and the belief in the eternal punish-ment of the wicked.

Such fantasies were once the very essence of religious orthodoxy, and it was in the white-hot religious zeal which was associated with them up to and beyond the time of the Reformation that our modern rational conscience was originally forged. But one of the effects of our

internalisation of the rational Protestant conscience has been actually
to obscure the conditions in which that conscience was created. Out
of its very severity the Protestant mind has tended progressively to
repudiate the very supernaturalism which originally licensed its strict-
ness, together with all those aspects of Christianity which no longer
seem compatible with its modern rational form. As a result, although
the doctrines of Heaven and Hell, of Original Sin and of the Last
Judgement may have some nominal significance for us, they are no
longer part either of our imaginative or of our intellectual reality. The
fantasies which were once expressed in Christian demonology and in
Christian visions of hell have been progressively relegated to the thriv-
ing sub-cultures of Satanism and science fiction, of horror comics and
pornography. In the dissociated post-religious culture which has in
this way been brought into being, Christians and rational humanists
alike are often unable to bring themselves to believe that the very
forms of fantasy they have been conditioned to revile once lay at the
orthodox heart of the religious tradition which our culture tends still
to revere. Our modern cultural predicament has been most succinctly
and poignantly expressed by the novelist John Updike: 'Alas we have
become, in our Protestantism, more virtuous than the myths which
taught us virtue; we judge them barbaric.'[9]

Our culturally orthodox lack of familiarity with our own culture
has not only brought about the virtual destruction of our historical
consciousness, but it has also profoundly affected every area of contemporary intellectual life. Above all it has determined our reaction to
modern theories of human nature. In considering such theories what
must always be borne in mind is that it is only in the last century or
so that secular theories of human nature have become at all common.
Before that time intellectuals generally felt little need of such theories.
They felt no need of them for the simple reason that they subscribed,
almost without exception, to the creationist theory of human nature
which is contained in Judaism, in Christianity and in Islam. It was only
in the early part of the nineteenth century, as the 'truths' of revealed
religion were increasingly discredited, that an acute need for secular
theories of human nature began to emerge.

The confident assumption which is generally made by modern
rationalist thinkers is that the propositions about human nature which
are contained in such theories as Marxism, psychoanalysis, existentialism, functionalism, and structural anthropology, are of a quite different
order to the propositions about human nature which are contained

within the Judaeo-Christian theory which they effectively replace. Whatever judgement may be passed on particular theories, it is at least generally assumed that modern thinkers have succeeded in freeing themselves from the superstitious and theological modes of thought which dominated those intellectuals who belonged to an era of faith. It is, however, just this assumption which needs to be questioned. For although such secular theories as psychoanalysis and structural anthropology have evidently shed the theism of Christianity, it is not at all clear that they have repudiated the view of human nature which was once associated with creationist theology, and with Judaeo-Christian doctrines of sin and redemption. Modern theorists of human nature, indeed, trapped as they are within a culture which has systematically mystified its own strongest traditions, are rather in the position of the mariner who sets out to sea without a chart. When he lands at a different point on the same continent from which he originally set sail, there is always the danger that he may fail to recognise this, and announce instead that he has discovered a new world.

In the last hundred years such thinkers as Marx, Freud, Sartre and Lévi-Strauss have, I believe, repeatedly made just such a voyage. Setting out from a culture alienated from its traditional beliefs, disconsolately counting the small change of its new spiritual poverty, they have returned richly laden with belief and certainty in order to announce the discovery of the Brave New Worlds of dialectical materialism, of psychoanalysis, of existentialism and of structuralism. Many thinkers have greeted these discoveries with relief and enthusiasm. But because of their profound lack of familiarity with the orthodoxies of their own culture, they have often failed to recognise that the New Worlds in question are in reality but part of the old religious continent which was once their own, and that what they have embraced are not fresh theories of human nature but Judaeo-Christian orthodoxies which have been reconstructed in a secular form, safe from the attacks of science precisely because they are presented *as* science.

Any culture which is founded upon the internalisation of a body of sacred doctrine, but which allows that body of doctrine to fall into obscurity, is always in danger of recreating old errors in new secular forms, and of allowing unexamined forms of irrationalism to determine its very definition of rationality. It is to this danger that our own culture has succumbed over and over again during the past century.

What I have set out to do in this book is to show in detail how the creation of psychoanalysis in the closing years of the nineteenth century and its development and reception during the twentieth century has followed just this pattern. At the same time I have tried to use what amounts to an essay in cultural analysis in order to untie some of the complex intellectual knots which have been tied in our understanding of sexuality and of human nature by Freud and his followers.

I have devoted a whole book to a theory I believe to be mistaken partly because I think it is mistaken in a particularly interesting way, and partly in order to establish the need for an alternative theory of human sexuality and human nature. It is because my ultimate aim is constructive, rather than destructive, that I have not yielded to the temptation to dismiss the psychoanalytic movement out of hand as being without intellectual value or significance. In the past twenty or thirty years there have been a number of attacks on psychoanalysis which have taken such a view. But I believe that one of the great dangers in any critique of Freud is that of underestimating the real achievements of those who have written within the psychoanalytic tradition. For this tradition has every claim to be regarded as richer and more original than any other single intellectual tradition in the twentieth century. Many of Freud's earliest followers were themselves highly creative and the writings of Otto Rank, Ernest Jones, Victor Tausk and Hans Sachs still reward careful reading. In its subsequent development the psychoanalytic tradition has included the original and sometimes heterodox contributions of Wilhelm Reich, Karen Horney, Erich Fromm, Donald Winnicott, John Bowlby, Bruno Bettelheim, Anthony Storr and Nancy Chodorow. Valuable contributions have also been made by many other psychoanalytic writers – I think in particular of the American analysts Lawrence Kubie and Joel Kovel.[10]

The writings of all these analysts make up what is, relatively speaking, an extremely interesting intellectual tradition. But this acknowledgement of the breadth and vitality of the work which Freud has helped to inspire must immediately be qualified. In the first place it is important to bear in mind the larger cultural context in which psychoanalysis grew up. For it might well be claimed that the reasons for the 'success' of the psychoanalytic tradition have been almost entirely negative. If psychoanalysis has attracted some of the most lively intellectuals of the twentieth century it is not, I believe, because of the truth which psychoanalytic theories contain, or their explanatory value. It is perhaps because psychoanalysis is, with the increasingly fragile exception of literary criticism, the only branch of the human sciences which even begins to recognise the existence of the human imagination in all its emotional complexity. In this respect it might well be said that the incorrect theory elaborated by Freud has been infinitely preferable to no theory at all, and in the vast desert of twentieth-century rationalism it is scarcely surprising that many have seen, in the drop of imaginative water which is contained in Freud's theories, a veritable oasis of truth.

But there is another reason why the vitality of the psychoanalytic tradition should not be taken as confirmation of the validity of Freud's theories. This is because a great deal of it is owed not to any intellectual factor but to Freud's own remarkable and charismatic personality and to the heroic myth which he spun around himself during his own lifetime. Freud himself consciously identified with Moses, and the prophetic and messianic dimensions of his character have been noted again and again even by those who have written sympathetically about psychoanalysis. It would be difficult to overestimate the extent to which Freud's messianic personality has profoundly distorted the perception of his theories.

One of the most important roles of the messianic personality has always been that of acting as the fearless transgressor. The messiah is that person who *appears* to have the inner strength openly to attack established authorities or flout laws and taboos in order to further his chosen cause. It is by systematically transgressing taboos that he relieves his followers of the burden of guilt and anxiety they would otherwise feel as a result of pitting themselves against their elders, or against established orthodoxies.

It was in just such a role that Freud cast himself when he created the psychoanalytic movement at the beginning of the twentieth century. The need which he filled by doing this should be clear enough. For in any intellectual culture which is oppressed by rigorous taboos the most powerful though least conscious desire of its members will be to transgress these taboos and in this way seek relief from what Chesterton, in an essay on Freud, called 'our monstrous burden of secrecy'.[11] To suppose that such a transgression may be easily made is to fail to appreciate both the power of taboo and the extent to which intellectuals, simply because they have been selected according to the criterion of academic success, tend to be conformist by nature. Ultimately it is only to authority, whether or not this authority derives from genuine explanatory power, that the majority of intellectuals will defer. If what is at stake is the transgression of some of the most sacred principles of rationalism, then no ordinary authority will suffice. What is needed is nothing less than the authority of a messiah.

Perhaps the most significant of Freud's achievements lay in the way he intuitively perceived this need and went on to use the aura and authority of scientific rationalism in order to create around himself a 'church' whose doctrines sought to subvert the very rationalism they invoked.

The kind of need which was answered in this way is conveyed well by some words of André Gide, who speaks of having found in Freud *'rather an authorisation than an awakening*. Above all he taught me to cease doubting myself, to cease fearing my thoughts, and to let those thoughts lead me to those lands which were not after all uninhabitable since I found him already there.'[12] Gide's experience is one that reflects that of countless other twentieth-century artists and intellectuals. In Germany Thomas Mann spoke admiringly of Freud's heroic achievement and of his insight into human nature. In England W. H. Auden greeted psychoanalysis enthusiastically, writing of Freud:

> To us he is no more a person
> Now but a whole climate of opinion.

In France the novelist Romain Rolland emerged as one of Freud's most enthusiastic admirers. Meanwhile, in America, Freud gained an even wider following both among writers and scholars. After reading some of Freud's work the novelist Theodore Dreiser wrote in the following terms of his achievement:

> Every paragraph came as a revelation to me – a strong revealing light thrown on some of the darkest problems that haunted and troubled me and my work. And reading him has helped me in my studies of life and men ... [H]e reminded me of a conqueror who has taken a city, entered its age-old, hoary prisons and there generously proceeded to release from their gloomy and rusted cells the prisoners of formulae, faiths and illusions which have racked and worn man for hundreds and thousands of years ...
> The light that he has thrown on the human mind! Its vagaries and destructive delusions and their cure! It is to me at once colossal and beautiful![13]

Again and again Freud has been hailed, as he is here by Dreiser, as the bringer of cultural and intellectual liberation. Yet if Freud has indeed established himself as one of the most significant messianic figures in modern intellectual culture this is perhaps itself a reason for preserving our scepticism about his mission. For from the time of Moses to the time of Marx it has been one of the characteristics of messianic prophets that their apparent willingness to attack established authorities has concealed a deeper adherence to orthodoxy than their followers have ever suspected. Frequently, indeed, the movements of liberation which they have led have actually ended by redoubling the very forms of repression they have ostensibly opposed.

If Freud has not often been seen in this light it is perhaps because the very success which he has enjoyed by casting himself in the role of intellectual liberator has brought with it the kind of idealisations and projections to which all messiahs are subject. One of the most fundamental psychological transactions in all religious movements stems directly from followers' feelings of unworthiness in relation to their messiahs. As a result of these feelings they frequently find themselves inwardly compelled to disown not only their own rebelliousness but also their own generosity, their own intuitive sensitivity, their richly humanistic social hope and even their own intellectual originality. Unconsciously all these qualities are denied or minimised and reattributed to the messiah. The image of the messiah is in this way enriched by gifts and talents which followers are either too anxious or too submissive to proclaim as their own. This kind of transaction may frequently be observed within the psychoanalytic movement itself where psychoanalytic theorists with genuine insights into human behaviour have failed to develop them through an inability to challenge Freud's authority. Instead they have sometimes represented ideas which are in fundamental conflict with classical psychoanalytic theory as having been in some way 'derived' from Freud. In consequence their own sensitivity to human motivation – which is sometimes incomparably greater than that shown by Freud himself – comes to be associated with psychoanalysis and thus to increase still further Freud's own authority and cultural status. This has even been the case with some of the best-known psychoanalytic writers, including Erich Fromm, Karen Horney, Erik Erikson and Heinz Kohut, who are regarded within the psychoanalytic movement as highly original or even 'dissident' thinkers. For because their theoretical rebellions against Freud have been conducted within a larger pattern of submission to Freud's authority, these thinkers have never been able to bring about the intellectual revolution which alone might have rescued psychoanalysis from itself.[14]

As a result Freud's own reputation has been preserved and the status of his theories protected. There can be no doubt at all that his work is shot through, in a somewhat random manner, with real insights into human nature. But Freud repeatedly shows that he is unable to organise these insights systematically. Frequently, indeed, his own complex, and sometimes bizarre theories have the effect of strangling the insights which are scattered throughout his writings. Partly because of these sporadic insights the pseudo-science which Freud eventually succeeded in constructing is highly plausible. But it remains a pseudo-science for all that – perhaps the most complex and successful which history has seen.

If the psychoanalytic movement were not important or if it had made little intellectual impact, Freud's pseudo-science could be ignored or briefly rebutted. But Freud's influence on contemporary intellectual life has been so large and his psychological assumptions have proved so enduring that it is difficult to re-examine human sexual behaviour – or any other form of human behaviour – without finding that our very perception of this behaviour is distorted by psychoanalysis.

It is for this reason, I believe, that the task of untangling sexual behaviour from the psychoanalytic theories in which it has become enmeshed is such an important one. For only when this has been done will it be possible to build a genuinely scientific theory of human nature upon the foundations which Darwin laid in the middle of the nineteenth century.

The task I have set myself in this book is more modest. It is to examine in some detail, through the medium of a critical intellectual biography, why Freud, who claimed to have produced just such a theory almost a century ago, was wrong.

PROLOGUE

Images, Myths and Legends

THROUGHOUT COUNTLESS VERSIONS of the early history of the psychoanalytic movement there is one constant image which recurs. It is that of Freud as an isolated hero, a lonely messiah fighting for the cause of truth in a hostile world. One classic version of this image of Freud may be found in the text of an address once given by Thomas Mann:

> Actually we know that Sigmund Freud, that mighty spirit in whose honour we are gathered together, founder of psychoanalysis as a general method of research and as a therapeutic technique, trod the steep path alone and independently, as a physician and natural scientist, without knowing that reinforcement and encouragement lay to his hand in litera-ture . . . By his unaided effort, without knowledge of any previous intuit-ive achievement, he had methodically to follow out the line of his own researches . . . And we think of him as solitary – the attitude is insepar-able from our earliest picture of the man. Solitary in the sense of the word used by Nietzsche in that ravishing essay 'What is the meaning of Ascetic Ideals?' when he characterises Schopenhauer as 'a genuine philosopher, a self-poised mind, a man and gallant knight, stern-eyed, with the courage of his own strength, who knows how to stand alone and not wait on the beck and nod of superior officers'. In this guise of man and gallant knight, a knight between Death and the Devil, I have been used to picture to myself our psychologist of the unconscious, ever since his figure first swam into my mental ken.[1]

The picture which Mann paints is a deeply impressive one. As a rep-resentation of the character of Freud's intellectual achievement it is, however, almost entirely false. For, as some recent scholars have pointed out, this myth of the hero was one which Freud himself con-sciously created, sometimes by destroying or suppressing the evidence which might conflict with it.[2]

The history of Freud scholarship over the past fifty years can perhaps best be understood by considering the degree of reverence or scepticism which various authors have shown towards this heroic myth.

Very little scepticism is in evidence in the first major biography – Ernest Jones's three-volume work on the life of Freud. Indeed the preface to Jones's book makes it clear that it was written, in part at least, in order to defend Freud against his critics and the use they were already making of his occasional self-revelations. 'Ill-natured people,' he wrote in his preface, 'were already at work distorting isolated passages with the object of disparaging his character . . .' He went on to suggest that the only way of rebutting such negative views was to probe even more deeply into the biographical secrets which Freud had sometimes attempted to withhold and to offer 'a still fuller exposition of his inner and outer life'.

The professed object of Ernest Jones's massive biography of Freud, then, was to counter the numerous 'false stories' circulating about his master, which were, in his words, 'gradually accumulating into a mendacious legend'.[3] The problem with the book which resulted, as a number of writers have already observed, was that Jones replaced the hostile legend with a legend of another kind. Jones, like Freud himself before him, did not hesitate to retouch reality wherever it seemed to conflict with the portrait which he sought to create. Certain episodes in Freud's life which might seem to impugn his greatness, certain passages in his letters which might too easily be misconstrued, were silently suppressed. At the same time Jones was happy to endorse many of Freud's own self-estimates and to conduct his researches into Freud's inner life in accordance with these. Freud himself once observed that 'biographers are fixated on their hero in a quite particular way' and suggested that, because of their emotional involvement with their subjects, their work was almost bound to be an exercise in idealisation.[4] That Jones's work conformed to this pattern should not be entirely surprising. For he ended by creating very much the kind of biography one would expect a disciple to write of his master.

What is perhaps rather more surprising is that a work which was in almost all respects an exercise in piety should have been so widely acclaimed on its appearance even by those who were not themselves psychoanalysts. For instead of immediately submitting Jones's book to the kind of clerical scepticism it invited, a number of highly respected cultural critics hailed it as a masterpiece.

Not long after its appearance Lionel Trilling and Steven Marcus embarked on the task of abridging the original work into a single volume. The essay which Trilling wrote as the introduction to this new volume, coming as it does from such a distinguished hand, is a remarkable cultural document. In it Trilling accurately observes that Freud 'overtly and without apology . . . hoped to be a genius, having before that avowed his intention of being a hero'. But rather than inquire into the origins of Freud's extraordinary ambitions and seek to relate these to his supposed achievement, Trilling unsceptically accepts Freud at his own valuation. The myth of solitary greatness, which Freud himself created, which Thomas Mann, Ernest Jones and countless others had faithfully perpetuated, was now endorsed by a literary academic widely regarded as one of the greatest critics of the twentieth century. 'The basic history of psychoanalysis,' writes Trilling, 'is the account of how it grew in Freud's own mind, for Freud developed its concepts all by himself.' This innocently trustful statement is immediately compounded when Trilling goes on to talk admiringly of the 'legendary quality' of Freud's life, even suggesting that Freud, by his own example, refuted the claim of W. B. Yeats that 'a man must choose perfection of the life or of the work'. Not only does he implicitly attribute perfection to Freud, but he goes on to reproduce an account of Freud's attitude to empirical facts which accords with Freud's own self-estimate of his scientific worth but which bears no resemblance to his scientific practice. 'He reached his discoveries,' Trilling writes, 'by means of thought which walked no less humbly than courageously. The humility of the scientist, his submission to facts, is something of which the scientist often boasts, but the facts to which Freud submitted himself were not only hard but human . . .' Applied as it is to a system of thought founded upon an almost complete disregard for empirical facts, Trilling's claim is remarkable indeed.[5]

Lionel Trilling's willingness to bow down uncritically before the monumental statue which Freud erected to himself might be disregarded or registered as a mere curiosity were it not representative of an entire cultural tendency. If Freud has again and again been accorded an almost supernatural pre-eminence by twentieth-century intellectuals, it is perhaps for no other reason than that our intellectual culture is historically the product of an ideology in which the concept of supernatural pre-eminence is fundamental.

The habit of worshipping as a God a supreme being who by his very perfection commands obedience is, I believe, an extremely bad habit. But it is also, because of the very rigour and cruelty with which it has been inculcated into our culture over a period of centuries, one of the habits we are most likely to fall into. Whenever a suitably secular milieu, from which all the obvious paraphernalia of worship have been removed, lulls us into a false sense of security, the old habit of God-worship tends to return. Among those who have achieved positions of immense power and influence as a result of the continuing strength of this cultural reflex may be numbered such figures as Marx, Lenin and Trotsky – and indeed Hitler and Stalin. But in a less obviously destructive way Freud has also been a beneficiary. It is his success in attracting to himself the projections and idealisations which are traditionally associated with divinity, which has made the task of under-standing him as a human being so difficult.

It would be wrong, however, to suggest that this problem has passed completely unnoticed and unaddressed by Freud scholars over the last thirty years. For although Ernest Jones's biography has exercised a huge and sometimes stultifying influence over the study of psychoan-alysis during this time, other more interesting and less orthodox voices have also been heard. One of the first scholars to touch upon the problem was Henri Ellenberger in his study of the history of dynamic psychiatry, *The Discovery of the Unconscious*. Ellenberger observes that one of the difficulties in evaluating Freud's contribution to psychiatry is that 'psychoanalysis has grown in an atmosphere of legend, with the result that an objective appraisal will not be possible before the true historical facts are separated from the legend.' The legendary version of Freud, in Ellenberger's view, has two particular features. The first is 'the theme of the solitary hero struggling against a host of enemies, suffering the "slings and arrows of outrageous fortune" but triumphing in the end'. The second is 'the blotting out of the greatest part of the scientific and cultural context in which psychoanalysis developed', which leads to claims about Freud's 'absolute originality'. Ellenberger argues that the first aspect of the legend rests on an exaggeration not only of the anti-semitism Freud encountered but also of the hostility of the academic world and of the Victorian prejudices which sup-posedly hampered psychoanalysis. Meanwhile the second feature of the legend led to the hero being credited 'with the achievements of his predecessors, associates, disciples, rivals and contemporaries'. More specifically, Ellenberger writes that the current legend . . . attributes to Freud much of what belongs, notably, to Herbart, Fechner, Nietzsche, Meynert, Benedikt and Janet, and overlooks the work of previous explorers of the unconscious, dreams and sexual pathology. Much of what was credited to Freud was diffuse current lore, and his role was to crystallise these ideas and give them an original shape.[6]

Since the publication of Ellenberger's work a number of other scholars have noted the way in which legends have obstructed a full understanding of Freud's work. Paul Roazen opens his book *Freud and His Followers*, which appeared in 1975, with a chapter on 'The Legend of Freud'. He notes that Freud 'knew the power of legend' and observes that if he 'became a living legend in his own lifetime, he himself had contributed to the stories that grew up around him'. Roazen sets out to go beyond this 'legend-weaving' and to present a version of Freud which sees him both as human and fallible. Basing his work on extended interviews with over seventy of Freud's followers he goes on to offer a richly textured portrait of Freud and his movement which focuses on the complex and often conflict-ridden relationships between the first psychoanalysts.[7]

In 1979 another scholar, Frank Sulloway, made a concerted attempt both to analyse the various components of the legend and to excavate the layers of intellectual history which it concealed. 'Over the years,' he writes, 'psychoanalytic devotees have cultivated a complex and politically expedient mythology about their collective past . . .' He takes the view that 'the mythical bubble surrounding Freud's life and achievements is finally beginning to show signs of rupture and gradual deflation.' In his view the time has come when 'these myths can not only be identified and set apart from historical fact, but, more important, they can now be understood in their own right as an integral and fascinating part of the historical process.' As well as carefully anatomising the Freud legend, Sulloway examines in illuminating detail the complex cultural and scientific context in which Freud created the psychoanalytic movement. In demonstrating how, at almost every stage in its development, the psychoanalytic movement has engaged in the 'expedient denial of history' he shows in detail how Freud derived many of his crucial hypotheses from contemporary biological theories. He contends that 'many, if not most, of Freud's conceptions were biological by *inspiration* as well as by implication', and goes on to offer extensive documentation of this claim.[8]

Partly because of the sheer depth and range of their research, both Roazen and Sulloway have made valuable contributions to the study of psychoanalysis. Their contribution, however, has by no means always been appreciated by the guardians of Freudian orthodoxy. Both Roazen and Sulloway have been attacked or slighted on so many occasions that their iconoclasm is sometimes in danger of being perceived as more truly subversive than it actually is.[9] In some quarters they have even been represented as opponents of Freud and psychoanalysis, even though their own books make it quite clear that this is not the case.

In order to place their contribution to Freud studies in perspective it is perhaps worth observing that although we have long been accustomed to associate iconoclasm with those who reject orthodoxy and seek liberation, this conventional appraisal perhaps only indicates once again the extent to which we have allowed the orthodoxies of our own culture to become invisible. For from the story of Moses and the Golden Calf to the bonfires of Savonarola, or the bullet-holes left by seventeenth-century Puritans in the fabric and images of our most ancient churches, iconoclasm has been part of the very essence of orthodoxy. The command to break graven images was enshrined originally not in any revolutionary or subversive manifesto but in the Ten Commandments. It belongs not to any recent, sceptical tradition of reason but to our long heritage of religious rationalism which can be traced back to the very origins of Judaism. Our modern intellectual culture, in so far as its ideals were born among humanists such as Erasmus, nurtured in the Reformation and refined by Puritanism, is founded upon deep hostility towards the entire realm of myth, magic and ritual and to the role played in religion by miracles and legends. It repudiated this realm not in order to seek liberation, but – originally at least – because intellectuals and theologians believed that religious truth was rational and austere and that it could be embraced only by eschewing the carnal adornments which others had draped around it. Interestingly enough, modern Protestant theologians, from Schweitzer and Bultmann onwards, have continued the programme of their seventeenth-century predecessors in attempting to sift out the rational gold of religious belief from the sediment of legends, miracles and myths which has supposedly come to obscure it. The project of 'demythologisation' with which Bultmann is associated amounts to a concerted attack on the 'legend' of Jesus which is made not as part of any radical critique of Christianity, but as part of an attempt to recover the 'true' historical Jesus in order that reverence for him may be rooted in reason and founded upon fact. The modern Protestant attack on legends is thus essentially born out of reverence towards the figure who inspired those legends. It seeks to use scepticism against the sceptics and to uphold the very orthodoxy it appears to be confounding.

The contribution of Roazen, Sulloway and other like-minded scholars to our understanding of psychoanalysis can, I believe, best be understood if it is located in this larger cultural context. For while Roazen has at times been dubbed the *enfant terrible* of psychoanalysis, his attitude towards Freud contains an underlying reverence and respect for his supposed intellectual achievement which conflicts with this reputation. The rationale he gives for his own approach is a complex one:

> To the extent that Freud deserves to be a hero for our time, we have been deprived of his full possibilities as a model. As Freud once lamented, 'thanks to their own discretion and to the untruthfulness of their biographers, we learn little that is intimate about the great men who are our models . . .' Jones unfortunately presented us with such a rationalised version of Freud's struggles that we have seen less of his depths. Yet to minimise what Freud had to overcome only limits the stature of his achievements. And to mythologise Freud as a man in full control of all his emotions is to deprive us of the opportunity of iden- tifying with him as a struggling innovator . . . The Freud of history, with his large mistakes as well as his great intellectual victories, is a far more interesting figure than the Freud of legend, and it can do his memory no service to see him smaller and more life-sized than the courageous genius he was.[10]

Roazen's analysis of his own attitude is a curious one. The problem with the Freud legend is not that it belittles Freud, but that it portrays him as a towering giant among twentieth-century intellectuals. It is Roazen who, in some respects, presents the founder of psychoanalysis as smaller and more life-sized. As he himself makes clear, however, his motive for doing this is not to portray Freud as an ordinary human being. It is to pay homage to Freud as a courageous genius who, by implication at least, has triumphed over his various limitations and thus proved his heroic, even superhuman stature.

The impulse behind Roazen's approach is thus recognisably that of the rational humanist who distrusts the inclination to worship yet who at the same time cannot overcome his own need to revere Freud as a hero. By adopting an attitude of studied irreverence towards certain portions of the Freud legend, and by portraying the hero as mortal and mistaken in at least some respects, he is able to avoid the appearance of hagiography while still upholding the traditional view of Freud as a hero and a genius. The careful reader of Roazen's book thus finds it difficult to avoid the impression that the many criticisms of Freud which it contains are in reality but forms of penance which the rational conscience of the author inflicts upon himself in order to atone for the irrational submission to the myth of Freud which underlies his vision. Criticism and outward disrespect for the Freud of tradition and legend become the price which is paid for inward genuflection. The legend of Freud is not carefully taken apart and analysed so much as refashioned in such a way that it will appeal to a doubting generation embarrassed by the excesses of Freud-worship in the past yet still in thrall to the image of superhuman greatness which was central to such worship.

Frank Sulloway's portrait of the founder of psychoanalysis in his *Freud, Biologist of the Mind: Beyond the Psychoanalytic Legend* is in some respects even more sophisticated than Roazen's. As the sub-title of his book implies, he does undertake an analysis of the Freud-legend, and the account he gives of it is one of the most valuable features of his book. Just as valuable is his immensely detailed survey of the scientific context in which Freud developed his ideas and of the biological and sexological theories which shaped them. Yet, like Roazen's, Sulloway's attempt to recover the historical Freud from the distortions of legend bears a curious and significant resemblance to that adopted by some twentieth-century theologians towards the problem of the historical Jesus. When Albert Schweitzer published his *The Quest of the Historical Jesus* in 1906, one of his main aims was to counter the powerful myth that the teachings of Jesus were wholly original and unmarked by the beliefs of his contemporaries and predecessors. Against this orthodox view he argued that the way in which Jesus expressed his teachings was shaped and determined at practically every point by Jewish apocalyptic and by the simple and realistic expectation of a messiah which was current among his contemporaries. In one respect Schweitzer's argument was boldly unorthodox. For in effect he argued that Jesus had himself succumbed to the fantasies and fallacies current in first-century Palestine. No sooner has he put forward this disturbing proposition, however, than he reasserts his belief in the religious 'genius' of the founder of Christianity, arguing that the ethical message contained within Jesus's doctrines ultimately transcended their eschatological form. Jesus may have been profoundly mistaken in many of his most fundamental beliefs, but he was still, in Schweitzer's view, a divinely inspired saviour.

Sulloway's portrayal of Freud is as unorthodox, in some respects, as Schweitzer's of Jesus. But it is also, ultimately, no less reverent. He too presents Freud as a surprisingly unoriginal thinker who was profoundly influenced by the mistaken, and sometimes bizarre theories of his contemporaries and predecessors. But at the same time he attempts to salvage the image of Freud as a thinker of genius by arguing that Freud's fundamental debt was to Darwin and by presenting him as a precursor of modern sociobiologists, whose theories Sulloway appears to accept. Sulloway's book, like Roazen's, is a curious mixture of sceptical historicism and irrational piety. Once again we are left with the impression that a scholar has unconsciously multiplied the doubting and agnostic portions of his work in order to compensate for a profound impulse to submit to Freud's authority. Ultimately Sulloway, like Schweitzer, seems unable to resist submission to the power of the legend he so lucidly and so productively interrogates. In the final paragraph of his book he suggests that the Freud of legend will survive in spite of all scholarly objectivity: 'After all, Freud really was a hero. The myths are merely his historical due, and they shall continue to live on, protecting his brilliant legacy to mankind, as long as this legacy remains a powerful part of human consciousness.'[11]

In recent years Sulloway has begun to shift away from this position and the view of Freud which he now holds is much more critical. One of the factors which may have helped to bring about this change of view is the influence of two critics who have not felt the need to wrap up their scepticism in the rags and tatters of residual piety – Frank Cioffi and Frederick Crews. In 1970 Frank Cioffi published a penetrating essay in which he argued with much energy and *brio* that psychoanalysis was in reality a pseudo-science. In subsequent papers Cioffi has taken these arguments further and has proved one of the most astringent of Freud's many academic critics. During the 1980s the American literary critic and former devotee of psychoanalysis, Frederick Crews, consolidated his rejection of Freud in a series of striking essays which have received wide attention, particularly in America. In 'The Freudian Way of Knowledge', which was first published in 1984, Crews carefully analyses the 'epistemological quicksand' in which he finds psychoanalysis to consist and looks forward speculatively to the day when our intellectual successors 'will be able to understand more fully how, in the topsy-turvy moral atmosphere of our century, we came to befuddle ourselves with the extraordinary and consequential delusion of Freudian thought.' Some of the arguments put forward by Crews and Cioffi recur in another sharp and interesting critique of psychoanalysis, Ernest Gellner's *The Psychoanalytic Movement* (1985).[12]

In some respects, however, perhaps the most important critiques of Freud which have been produced in the latter part of the twentieth century are those which have either been launched by feminists, or which have come to be associated with the cause of feminism. Simone de Beauvoir's attack on the psychoanalytic denigration of women in her *The Second Sex* (1949) helped to inspire many subsequent critiques, including Betty Friedan's essay on 'The Sexual Solipsism of Sigmund Freud' in *The Feminine Mystique* (1963), Kate Millet's analysis of the reactionary character of psychoanalysis in *Sexual Politics* (1970), and Germaine Greer's scathing irreverence towards Freud and psychoanalysis in *The Female Eunuch* (1970). In his study *Freud and His Critics* Paul Robinson ruefully suggests that the feminist attack on Freud as one of the principal founts of modern misogyny 'provided a firm base of sentiment and opinion – a kind of ideological substructure – upon which the more comprehensive criticisms of the past decade were to build.' Many observers would agree with this estimate of the importance of feminist critiques, but would see their appearance as a matter for celebration rather than regret.

There are two particular contributions to the study of psychoanalysis which, while not explicitly feminist, have sometimes been endorsed by feminists, and which have much more than a passing significance. Both books appeared in America in 1984: E. M. Thornton's *The Freudian Fallacy* and Jeffrey Masson's *The Assault on Truth*.[13] Elizabeth Thornton's book, which was first published in Britain in 1983 under the title *Freud and Cocaine*, is one of the most curious and interesting contributions to Freud studies. The thesis which lies at the heart of her book is that Freud was not merely an occasional user of cocaine, something which was well known, but that he became a cocaine addict and that his theories were actually shaped by his addiction. This argument, however, while it is the most sensational element in Thornton's book, is not the most important. Much more significant is her sceptical treatment of Freud's relationship to Charcot and of the whole concept of hysteria. Thornton's basic contention here is that a great many of the conditions which Freud diagnosed as hysteria were actually organic illnesses which escaped recognition either by Freud himself, or by nineteenth-century medicine as a whole. This argument is pushed to extremes, with Thornton succumbing to a kind of anti-psychological fundamentalism in which she seeks organic causes for everything, arguing, for example, that agoraphobia is invariably caused by disorders of the inner ear which affect the sense of balance. Such excesses tend to discredit the more moderate and reasonable aspects of Thornton's book. It remains the case, however, that a number of her claims are both original and persuasive and that her detailed review of the medical context in which both Charcot and Freud worked contains an abundant crop of insights which Freud scholars in particular, and our intellectual culture in general, have been lamentably slow to harvest.[14]

The hostility towards Freud and psychoanalysis which marks Thornton's book is also a feature of Jeffrey Masson's *The Assault on Truth*. While Thornton wrote her rebuttal of Freud from the perspective of an outsider to the world of psychoanalysis, Masson wrote his critique after a brief but extraordinary career at the very heart of the movement. Having entered psychoanalysis after an earlier career as a successful Sanskrit scholar, Masson so impressed some of the most influential Freudians, including Kurt Eissler and Anna Freud, that he rose in the space of a few years to become projects director of the Sigmund Freud Archive. Masson, however, rapidly became uneasy with his role, especially when his access to some of Freud's unpublished letters led him to the conclusion that Freud had deliberately suppressed his early hypothesis that hysteria was caused by sexual abuse during infancy. It was this position which he outlined in *The Assault on Truth*, in which he suggested that Freud was unable to face up to the reality of child sexual abuse, and suppressed a valid scientific hypothesis out of fear.

Since *The Assault on Truth*, Masson has published a number of other books, including *Against Therapy* and *Final Analysis*, the latter being an account of his own experience of psychoanalysis. These books, I believe, contain a number of significant insights into the limitations of the movement which Freud founded. *The Assault on Truth* itself also makes some interesting contributions to the history of psychoanalysis. Yet the central argument of Masson's book has failed to persuade not only the psychoanalytic establishment but also the majority of Freud's critics. The reasons for this will be examined in due course. What is of more immediate relevance here is Masson's curious ambivalence. For although his book is an attack on Freud's integrity which effectively accuses him of lacking both moral and intellectual courage, its attitude towards Freud remains deeply divided. It rejects unequivocally the particular image of Freud which is worshipped in the psychoanalytic church – a church whose earthly corruptions Masson documents in *Final Analysis*. But at the same time it creates an alternative image of the founder of psychoanalysis, which is in some respects even more elevated. For in it we are introduced to a kind of prelapsarian Freud who, up to 1896 at least, remained a therapeutic genius whose discoveries might really have shaken the world, if only he had not decided to suppress them. Freud may have been wrong at the end, but according to Masson he was profoundly and uniquely right at the beginning. The possibility that Freud was equally mistaken both before 1896 and afterwards is evidently one which Masson cannot bring himself to contemplate.

Masson's most controversial book thus illustrates once again the difficulty many critics of Freud have in overcoming their reverence for the ideas they seek to analyse. One other notable instance of ambivalence is provided by Adolf Grünbaum's philosophical critique of Freud's ideas, *The Foundations of Psychoanalysis*.[15] When this book appeared in 1984 it was widely seen as a landmark in the entire debate about the merits of psychoanalysis and a number of critics of Freud hailed it as a masterpiece. Yet Grünbaum, though deeply critical of some aspects of Freud's thinking, devotes considerable effort to defending Freud against some of his philosophical critics. In effect he denies the charge that Freud was the creator of a pseudo-science. In view of this it is perhaps not surprising that he should have found his own most trenchant critic in Frank Cioffi, whose views about the pseudo-scientific nature of psychoanalysis have already been noted. Cioffi takes exception to Grünbaum's portrayal of Freud as a philosophically astute investigator of human psychology who was 'hospitable to refutation' and 'responsive to adverse findings'. He is particularly offended by Grünbaum's belief that 'Freud "carefully", "brilliantly", "squarely", "unflaggingly", "unswervingly" (though ultimately unsuccessfully) "faced up" to the problem of suggestion.' Although Cioffi's full argument cannot be summarised here, his conclusion deserves to be quoted, both for its sheer rhetorical energy, and for the characterisation of Freud's thought which it offers:

> Citizen Kane in the Orson Welles film responded to refutation in what we would all concur was a non-exemplary fashion. On the eve of the election in which he is running for governor he prepares two headlines.

'Kane Elected' and 'Fraud at the Polls'. Grünbaum thinks it libellous to suggest that Freud characteristically behaved in this fashion, I think it pusillanimous to deny that he did. In attempting a demonstration of his claim that Freud was 'clearly motivated by evidence' and 'alert to the need for safeguarding the falsifiability of his reconstructions and interpretations', and that he dealt 'brilliantly' and 'unswervingly' with the contamination issue, Grünbaum has only succeeded in illustrating how prophetic were Wittgenstein's words of almost half a century ago: 'It will be a long time before we lose our subservience.'[16]

Just as Grünbaum's contribution to the debate has elicited this fierce rejoinder from one of Freud's more robust critics, so Masson's tendentious version of the events which led Freud to abandon his seduction theory has helped to focus scholarly attention on one of the many unsolved mysteries in Freud's intellectual biography. Here once again Frank Cioffi has played a significant role and his scholarly scepticism has been developed in a fascinating and revealing paper by Morton Schatzman and Han Israëls. Meanwhile other studies have appeared in which scepticism about Freud's ideas has been developed on a much larger front. A notable figure in this respect is Malcolm Macmillan, whose *Freud Evaluated* is an indispensable resource which contains perhaps the most detailed close reading of Freud yet to appear. In 1993 Allen Esterson's valuable contribution to the debate appeared in America and was received enthusiastically by Frederick Crews in a significant review published in the *New York Review of Books*. More recently still Robert Wilcocks has offered a number of acute and original critical insights in his book *Maelzel's Chess Player: Sigmund Freud and the Rhetoric of Deceit*.[17]

In view of the accumulating mass of trenchant criticism which has appeared during the past two decades it might well seem that the case against Freud has been proven beyond any reasonable doubt and that he would by now lack any credible or academically respectable defenders. Yet this is very far from being the case. One of the reasons that critics of Freud have failed to persuade his defenders is that they have sometimes tended to ignore both the complexity of psychoanalysis, and the manner in which its assumptions are interwoven with our entire cultural history. Perhaps the most influential of all critics of psychoanalysis in recent years has been Frederick Crews. His essays are both tough-minded and perceptive and almost all the criticisms he has made of Freud's own theories are, I believe, entirely justified. Yet

Crews sometimes seems to imply that psychoanalysis might be cleanly excised from our intellectual culture without any residual damage. The assumption seems to be that such an operation would restore a state of underlying intellectual health which, but for Freud, Marx and the postmodernists (and the residues of religion and romanticism), would never have been in doubt. This kind of rationalist optimism, which appears to go hand in hand with an all but traditional faith in what has been termed 'the heroic model of science', is certainly bracing. But by no means all observers can share it.[18]

One of the difficulties in Crews's view of psychoanalysis is that although he is both eloquent and persuasive in giving reasons why psychoanalysis ought to have been an intellectual failure, he is less convincing when it comes to explaining why it has actually enjoyed such extraordinary success. The same problem sometimes manifests itself in a much more acute form in the writings of some other critics of psychoanalysis. It is formulated well by Walter Kendrick in a review of Masson, Thornton and others which appeared in 1984:

> I mistrust the nostalgia for prelapsarian innocence that pervades these simple-minded campaigns. I'm also wary of their ignorance of history. Masson, Miller and Thornton come at psychoanalysis from different angles and do their demolition work in different ways, but along with a frenzied desire to pulverise Freud, they share the naive belief that they can wipe out the twentieth century in the process. None of them so much as attempts to explain why an egregious card-house like psychoanalysis, ready to crumble at the impact of any feather, was bought wholesale by an entire culture that still dwells in it.

Kendrick goes on to note the manner in which many contemporary psychoanalysts have sought to immunise themselves against criticism by distancing themselves from Freud. 'Ordinarily,' he writes, 'the members of an establishment are willing to acknowledge at least some kinship with its founder, but when the shrinks are accused of fidelity, they retort with proud assertions of faithlessness.'[19] Kendrick's observation is an acute one. It should be noted, however, that the response of the psychoanalytic movement to its critics is not quite as unusual as he suggests. For it is very similar to the response of modern Protestants to the attacks made on Christianity by secularists and scientists over the last two centuries. Like contemporary theologians, many psychoanalysts have internalised the scepticism of their opponents, and have begun to question or even reject elements of the Freudian creed with almost as much energy as their antagonists.[20] Just as liberal Protestant theologians have anxiously repudiated the original, literal understanding of Christian doctrines, so an increasing number of psychoanalysts have rejected any literal reading of the psychoanalytic doctrines which Freud propounded. A characteristic example of this reaction is provided by an 'independent Freudian analyst' quoted in a recent newspaper article about psychoanalytic controversies. Asked if she believed that all male infants wanted to sleep with their mothers and kill their fathers, she glossed Freud to read: 'We all experience being excluded from a couple, typically the intimate married relationship of our parents.' In the same article the feminist psychoanalyst Juliet Mitchell was quoted as calling the Oedipus complex 'a psychic truth not a literal truth'.[21]

The development of a new, sceptical, and at times seemingly agnostic theology of psychoanalysis has been one response of the devotees of Freud to the arguments of their critics. Perhaps even more effective, however, has been the continuing vitality and adaptability of the very Freud legend which underlay the original creation of the psychoanalytic movement. Just as Ernest Jones reacted to some of the early criticisms of psychoanalysis by producing a much more elaborate and sophisticated version of this legend in his authorised biography, so, more recently, the distinguished cultural critic Peter Gay has performed a similar task for a movement which might with good cause regard itself as intellectually beleaguered. In 1988 he published a major new biography, *Freud: A Life for Our Time*, which was announced as 'one of the most important books on Freud ever written'.[22]

Gay's biography draws on the mass of new material which has become available in the years since Jones's book. It is presented very much as an objective exercise in historical scholarship. In the course of his narrative Gay shows himself engagingly ready to entertain negative insights about psychoanalysis, and to probe Freud's mistakes and misapprehensions. Yet Gay writes not simply as a cultural historian but as a fully accredited psychoanalyst, and it soon becomes evident that his surface agnosticism rests, like that of many contemporary analysts, on a bedrock of reverence. Although some details are added or subtracted, the basic outlines of the Freud legend are allowed to remain virtually unchanged. At the same time, in a bibliographical essay which is a small masterpiece of pro-Freudian advocacy, Gay dismisses or subtly denigrates almost all those writers who have made the most forceful objections to psychoanalysis.

Peter Gay's achievement, in what is presented by its publishers as a dispassionate and scholarly biography, is to produce a sophisticated and updated version of Jones's official biography, whose appeal to the devotees of psychoanalysis is that it seems to sound a clarion bell of faith and certainty even in the midst of doubt, and is able to concede the existence of the many objections to psychoanalysis without sacrificing allegiance to its founder or giving up the image of him as a genius and a scientific hero.

The resilience of the Freud legend can perhaps be judged by the fact that, just as Jones's earlier exercise in piety was widely acclaimed on its appearance, so too was Gay's 1988 biography. There were certainly dissenting voices, among them the dissident Freud scholar Peter Swales.[23] Many of the reviews of Gay's book, however, were lavish in their praise. This was particularly true in Britain, where a number of well-known critics hailed the book as a triumph without apparently noticing that it had been written by a psychoanalyst and was clearly the work of a disciple rather than an objective observer of psychoanalysis.

The reception accorded to Gay's renovation of the Freudian legend lends weight to the view of Frederick Crews that, as a culture, 'we remain largely unacquainted with the founder of psychoanalysis, whose steps of reasoning, as opposed to his brilliant but untrustworthy rhetoric, have been glimpsed only by a handful of scholars.'[24] This view is supported by the continual appearance of new positive, deferential and even reverential assessments of Freud's standing in twentieth-century culture.[25] Among younger scholars there can be little doubt that the immense influence achieved by the French psychoanalyst Jacques Lacan has helped to strengthen regard for Freud's ideas. But it would be wrong to underestimate the continuing personal appeal of Freud himself. Reviewing the Freud–Jones letters in a British Sunday newspaper in 1993, the novelist Candia McWilliam gives her own estimate of the founder of psychoanalysis:

> The monumentality and authority of Freud's thought characterise his side of the correspondence . . . If Freud lacks the human fear of truth, he is also without self-righteousness. These wants make him terrifying yet merciful; they give the percipience and cool analytical power that were his genius. His style has a logical penetration and scope that eradicate confusion and distend the reading mind, lifting its capabilities . . .
>
> This magisterial correspondence moves clearly through deep waters, scraping from the most sceptical reader's mind the barnacles of triviality and debasement that have grown upon the study of psychoanalysis.[26]

In expressing, at this late stage of the twentieth century, such a high regard for Freud and for the movement which he founded, there can be no doubt that Candia McWilliam speaks on behalf of many. But the resonance of her words should already be familiar to us, as should the portrait of Freud which she draws. Both belong recognisably to the myth of the hero which Thomas Mann propagated much earlier in the century, and whose origins must be traced back to Freud himself. In this myth the personality of Freud remains both vast and inscrutable, and the figure of Freud, 'terrifying yet merciful', continues to be over-laid with projections which were once associated with the idea of God.

The continuing remoteness of Freud's personality from our intellec-tual grasp is significant. For perhaps the clearest evidence that Freud did not understand us is the fact that we do not understand Freud. In the entire complex body of psychoanalysis he left us no theoretical means by which we might unravel his own deepest motives or analyse his development and his evident sense of mission. As a result Freud himself remains an enigma – a psychologist who is beyond the reach of psychology, the creator of a movement which has encircled the globe but which has formulated no theory which can even begin to account for its own success.[27]

Both the enigma of Freud and the mystery of the movement he founded continue to be protected by the legend of Freud which still dominates our intellectual culture. Since the biographies written by Jones and Gay remain citadels of this legend, the challenge offered to any would-be critic of psychoanalysis is to give an alternative account of Freud's life and his intellectual development. While I have certainly not attempted to write yet another full-scale biography of Freud, what I have tried to do in the pages that follow is to offer a critical and truly sceptical alternative to some of the biographical myths which Freud himself created, which Jones and Gay have perpetuated, and which Roazen and Sulloway have interrogated – interestingly, productively, but on the whole too gently.

I

THE CREATION OF A
PSEUDO-SCIENCE

ONE

From Caul to Cocaine

ONE OF THE MOST striking features of the mythology which has grown up around Freud during the twentieth century is that, in almost all cases, the source of the most powerful myths was none other than Freud himself. For behind the legend of Freud there lies the reality of a man who appears to have been compulsively driven to persuade others to regard him as a hero of almost supernatural proportions. The huge scale of Freud's ambitions has been widely recognised, and I have already cited Lionel Trilling's observation that Freud 'overtly and without apology . . . hoped to be a genius'.[1] Yet although Freud's love affair with fame, and with his own fame in particular, was evidently one of the most important elements in his psychological make-up, his biographers have been reluctant to probe this affair in any depth. There is one particular incident in Freud's life which all his biographers, from Ernest Jones onwards, have related, but whose significance seems far larger than any of them have ventured to suggest.

In April 1885 Freud embarked on a curious programme of destruction. He gathered together the scientific notes he had made over the past fourteen years, together with his letters, scientific excerpts and the manuscripts of his papers, and destroyed them. The motives for what he did might have remained shrouded in permanent obscurity, had not he himself explained them to his fiancée. This action, he wrote to her, was one which a number of 'as yet unborn and unfortunate people' would resent.

> Since you can't guess whom I mean I will tell you: they are my biographers . . . I couldn't have matured or died without worrying about who would get hold of those old papers . . . As for the biographers, let them worry. We have no desire to make it too easy for them. Each one of them will be right in his opinion of 'The Development of the Hero' and I am already looking forward to seeing them go astray.[2]

In relating Freud's act of destruction none of Freud's major biographers has pointed out that it was strangely inept. What was intended as an act of concealment may well have succeeded in hiding some episodes in Freud's external biography. But the act reveals a great deal about Freud's inner biography. Most notable is the startling boldness with which he assumes that his life will be of interest to future generations, and that he will eventually be the subject not simply of one biography but of several. Had Freud used the royal 'we' to express such a conviction fifteen years later, when he had already formulated the fundamental principles of psychoanalysis, it might have seemed strange but not entirely irrational. But in 1885 he had scarcely even glimpsed any of the theories which would one day make him famous. If he had died the day after his act of destruction it seems virtually certain that he would have sunk rapidly from sight and that the waters of obscurity would have closed over him for ever.

This, and not the act itself, is what is so remarkable about Freud's attempt to frustrate future historians. Freud's feelings of certainty about his own eventual fame seem to have been completely independent of his actual achievements. If we are to have any chance of understanding Freud's inner biography we need to consider in some detail what lay behind this appetite for fame, and ask to what extent Freud's compulsive need for fame may have engendered his psychological theories, rather than, as is normally assumed, his theories generating his fame by their own profundity and intellectual acuity.

A number of his biographers have already noted that Freud was affected by the fond hopes his parents had for him when he was a small child. When Freud was born in 1856 in the small Austro-Hungarian town of Freiberg, he appears to have been surrounded by expectations of his future greatness. He had been born in a caul and his mother had immediately taken this as a portent of his future fame and happiness. An old woman she encountered by chance in a shop confirmed her feeling, telling her she had brought into the world a child who would become a great man. There seems little doubt that Freud's mother quickly transmitted to him her anxious and superstitious belief in his future greatness. She called him 'mein goldener Sigi' and, as her oldest child, he was to remain her favourite throughout her life.

In 1860 the family moved to Vienna and it was here that he received his education. Freud's father, like his mother, tended to treat him as special. He taught his son to read and write before sending him to a private school. He gave priority to his education to the degree that the entire household increasingly became subservient to the young Sigmund's need to study. Partly as a result of these attentions he won a place in the *Gymnasium* at the early age of nine and was top of his class for the last six of the eight years he spent at school.

According to some accounts Jakob Freud was not as strict and as rigid as some Jewish fathers. But he did expect his children to honour their parents and did not look kindly on rebelliousness. One day the young Moritz Rosenthal, who later became a famous pianist, was arguing with his father in the street when they met Jakob Freud. He scolded the boy, saying, 'What, are you contradicting your father? My Sigmund's little toe is cleverer than my head, but he would never dare to contradict me!'[3] The comment encapsulates the predicament of the founder of psychoanalysis. For while on the one hand Jakob Freud accorded to his son a quite extraordinary status in return for his intellectual achievements, such distinction was conferred on the understanding that the young Sigmund chose the path of conformity. In his later life Freud would struggle again and again with the terms of this parental 'contract' and would repeatedly seek to cast himself in the role of the rebel. But it would seem that his fear of rejection was such that he took care to secrete an underlying conformity just beneath the surface of his seemingly rebellious science.

Freud himself was in no doubt that his own character had been shaped, to some extent at least, by the attitude of his parents towards him. In one of the most frequently quoted of his remarks, he wrote that 'a man who has been the indisputable favourite of his mother keeps for life the feeling of being a conqueror, that confidence of success which often induces real success.'[4] Superficially the remark seems a perceptive one. But, like many of Freud's psychological insights, its almost aphoristic neatness distracts attention from complexities that it leaves unexplored. Coming from a psychologist who made a point of unmasking the tendency of children to idealise their parents the remark is surprisingly naive. What it leaves out of account is the double-edged nature of the kind of parental adulation which Freud recognised in his own mother. It is quite true that a child's sense that it has been 'chosen' by its parents can lead to the feeling of being one of the 'elect' and that such inner confidence may be one of the preconditions of outward success. But it is also true that children tend to experience their parents' adulation not as an unconditional gift but as something much more complex. For behind such adulation there lies a knot of cultural taboos which binds parents' affection and controls their emotional relationship with their children in a way that almost always remains invisible to parents themselves.

One insight into this knot of taboos is afforded by an observation made by one of Freud's most interesting followers, the psychoanalyst Donald Winnicott. In one of his papers Winnicott discusses the difficulties some mothers have in feeding their children. 'It is relevant here,' he writes, 'to describe a common problem . . . as I see it':

> I mean as I see it *now*, for I have struggled through all the phases all doctors experience, in the heartbreaking attempts to deal with feeding problems along physical lines, altering quantities, intervals, proportions of fat, protein and carbohydrate and switching from one brand of milk to another . . . It took me years to realise that a feeding difficulty could often be cured by advising the mother to fit in with the baby absolutely for a few days. I had to discover that this fitting in with the infant's needs is so pleasurable to the mother that she cannot do it without moral support. If I advise this I must ask my social worker to visit daily, else the mother will wilt under criticism and feel responsible for too much. Obeying a rule, she can blame others if things go wrong, but she is scared to do as she deeply wants to do.[5]

This particular psychoanalytical observation resonates with a larger significance. It should be noted that Winnicott here is not discussing breast-feeding and the guilt which can be aroused in mothers by the specifically sexual or sensual pleasure which they may experience when breast-feeding. He is discussing the kind of psychological problems which are experienced by mothers who elect not to breast-feed. What this passage points to is the immense pleasure which parents can derive from 'giving' to their children in any form – whether by feeding, by physically caressing them, by bestowing affection and praise or, indeed, by supplying them with material goods. But at the same time it suggests the existence of a powerful cultural taboo which makes it extremely difficult for parents to indulge their own most generous impulses unconditionally without being made to feel guilty. Children who are apparently surrounded by unconditional parental generosity tend, indeed, to be sharply stigmatised in our society as 'spoilt'. Although individual parents frequently try to find ways of resisting the massive cultural forces which are brought to bear on them in this way, it is all but impossible for them to do so. In countless subtle or not so subtle ways the affection and approval which parents give to their children tend to be conditional on 'good' behaviour – on obedience and cleanliness and on conformity both with their own family regime and with the demands of school. Affection thus comes to be bestowed in the medium of complex forms of discipline and it is only in this medium that it can be bestowed without guilt.

The profound psychological conflicts which are an essential part of the 'normal' parent–child relationship can perhaps best be illuminated by considering traditional or 'old-fashioned' child-rearing styles in which discipline is overt rather than covert. Parents who follow the axiom 'spare the rod and spoil the child' may like to think of their attitudes as simple and straightforward, but they nevertheless have great emotional complexity. The violence which such parents regularly inflict on their children is perhaps best understood as being motivated by the parents' sense of their own worthlessness and the feeling that they are themselves filled with some kind of essential badness. Their greatest anxiety, born out of the passionate affection and, indeed, the impulses of emotional generosity which they feel towards their children, is that their own 'badness' may be contracted by their children. One of their fears is that if they were to bestow unconditional affection on the children they would effectively be affirming the parts of them that are 'bad' or 'dirty'. Unconditional affection would thus lead to intense feeling of guilt. Punishing the child overtly for 'bad' behaviour is a way of conferring upon themselves a licence to love and to extend their most generous impulses to their children. Many parents clearly believe that, if they are sufficiently 'firm' with their children, they will actually be able to eliminate the 'badness' and the sense of worthlessness which they feel within themselves, and ensure that their children are 'better', more worthy and more successful than they can ever hope to be. Discipline thus becomes the means by which parents unconsciously set out to redeem their children from their own sense of sinfulness. It is the medium in which alone they can express fully the love which they feel for their children.

Although we now like to regard such traditional child-rearing regimes as outdated or alien, a more sceptical appraisal of modern alternative regimes might very well lead to the conclusion that instead of entirely emancipating ourselves from the psychological pattern which I have just described, we have internalised it together with its violence. Driven by feelings of inner failure, middle-class parents who may abjure all violent disciplinary sanctions, still unconsciously 'whip' their children to success, using as the ultimate sanction the oblique threat of withdrawing their love and affection should their children fail to live up to their expectations. Once again, it is only in the medium of intense and exacting demands, of whose severity they are often completely unaware, that such parents feel that they can legitimately bestow affection and love. The most subtle and complex way in which these parents express disapproval for their children's 'badness' is by constantly surrounding them with lofty expectations and with the kind of adulation which is implicitly conditional upon the child's ability to fulfil these expectations. Parental adulation of this kind almost inevitably has the effect of situating children on a terrifying emotional precipice. Their abiding anxiety is that they may prove unworthy of their parents' love, and it is in order to allay this anxiety that they compulsively pursue fame, success, or material wealth. They cannot 'look down' or in any way lower their sights simply because to do so would be to risk losing love and being precipitated into an abyss of obscurity and rejection.

Such children secretly regard the many favours, gifts and material benefits which their parents shower upon them not as unconditional privileges but as conditional 'loans'. They grow up weighed down by the sense of having incurred an essentially unrepayable debt which they must, nevertheless, spend the rest of their lives endeavouring to repay. For if they cannot offer token repayment in the currency of fame, professional achievement or wealth, their fear is that their own essential worthlessness will be detected and they will be rejected as unworthy of love.

For this very reason extreme ambition is almost always related to a sense of resentment – and perhaps above all to a desire for vengeance. Many people are aware of the extent to which their own drive to succeed is related to fantasies of revenge in which all those who have ever wronged them, spurned them, or even simply undervalued them, finally 'get their come-uppance' or are 'put in their place' by being made to recognise that the child they spurned is now more rich, more famous or more successful than they will ever be. It must be suggested, however, that at a deep level of fantasy those who are driven by the fiercest ambitions seek revenge ultimately not simply against contemporaries but against their own family and their own parents. For to the extent that such children experience their parents' adulation for their 'specialness' as a profound negation of their own ordinary, sensual, sexual and affectional identities, to that extent do they experience their parents' love as being itself a form of hurtful rejection

– as constituting the subtlest but most painful of all forms of emotional neglect. When children who have been treated in this way become famous they are at one level merely fulfilling their emotional contract by 'repaying' their debts. But at another level they are settling old scores. For to be revered, to be worshipped, to be loved unconditionally by strangers is to prove to the parents who, by the very intensity of their conditional adulation, made them feel unloved and unlovable, that they were mistaken. At a certain tortured extreme it would seem that it is just such a dream of exchanging intimate rejection for universal acceptance which underlies messianic fantasies. The religious leader who, gripped by the sense of his own specialness, implicitly or explicitly rejects his own family and fantasises that he has become the beloved son of a Holy Family, entitled to demand that his followers worship and revere him, seeks to exact revenge through love. Such dreams of love and vengeance can be extraordinarily destructive. But they have played a fundamental role in Judaeo-Christian culture since its very beginnings.

This account of the psychological content of parental adulation and its relationship to messianic fantasies is very far from Freud's own analysis of his family background. But it provides a much more telling insight into his own remarkable career. Ernest Jones notes in his biography that there are only five incidents in Freud's life between the ages of three and seven of which we have any record. It would seem to be significant that two of these concern Freud's attitude towards fame. In the first incident, which was related by his mother, Freud soiled a chair with his dirty hands. He immediately consoled his mother, however, by promising her that he would grow up to be a great man and that then he would buy her another chair.[6]

Already by the age of three, it would seem, Freud had absorbed the terms of his parents' implicit contract with him, and already he was preparing to pay back their emotional 'loans' in the currency of fame; the disgraced and implicitly rejected persona of the 'dirty child' would be replaced by that of the 'great man'.

Freud himself recalled how, in another incident which took place when he was seven or eight, he had deliberately urinated in his parents' bedroom. His father momentarily forgot his customary pride in his son and exclaimed, 'That boy will never amount to anything.' Freud's own comment on this incident is significant: 'This must have been a terrible affront to my ambition,' he wrote, 'for allusions to this scene occur again and again in my dreams, and are constantly coupled with enumerations of my accomplishments and successes, as if I wanted to say: "You see, I have amounted to something after all." [7]

The pattern which already emerges clearly in these two early incidents was to remain characteristic. For one of the most striking features of Freud's life was his enduring and insatiable hunger for achievement. From his very youngest days as a pupil in the local *Gymnasium*, Freud, it would seem, was precipitated by an acute fear of ordinariness into a headlong pursuit of academic excellence. He seems to have been psychologically incapable of living without wearing the mantle of some extraordinary achievement. He began to read Shakespeare at the age of eight. He not only went to the top of his class but became an accomplished linguist, gaining a thorough knowledge of Greek, Latin, German, Hebrew, French and English and teaching himself the rudiments of Spanish and Italian. Before long family life began to revolve around Freud's studies and the house was organised in order to facilitate these. The young Sigmund was given the *Kabinett*, a long narrow room which was separated from the rest of the apartment and which held a bed, chairs, a bookshelf and a desk. As he grew older the future founder of psychoanalysis spent more and more time in this room and was encouraged to do so in order that he might further his studies. In order that these studies might not be interrupted he took his evening meals in his own room apart from the rest of the family. He had the only oil lamp in the apartment – the other rooms had candles. When he objected to his sister practising the piano, saying that it distracted him from his own studies, his mother had the piano removed from the apartment. [8]

Already, while still in the bosom of his family, Freud was given, in return for his compliance with his parents' 'contract', what was, in effect, his own kingdom. The very severity of the demands which they made upon their son was, it would seem, what enabled them to bestow such a token of their affection without guilt. The kingdom in question was one over which Freud alone presided and which he alone could enlarge. But it had originally been given to him by his parents, and there was always the possibility that it might be taken from him if his diligence ever faltered. Freud's subsequent career was in many respects an extraordinarily determined and prolonged attempt to reconstruct the 'kingdom' of his childhood in the adult world and to do so in terms which would finally free him from any dependence on the intense but wounding love of his own family. To the extent that he would eventually succeed in founding his own 'church' within which he was worshipped as a hero and even a saviour, this attempt was remarkably successful. But the fear that his kingdom might be taken from him never left him. He remained vigilant – restlessly, anxiously diligent – almost to his last days.

Freud left high school in 1873 at the age of seventeen, graduating *summa cum laude*. As a young boy he had entertained dreams of being a great general or political leader but he now had to make a more realistic choice between law and medical science – the latter being seen in nineteenth-century Vienna as a means of becoming a research scientist and not necessarily as a medical apprenticeship. He was inspired to choose a scientific career, he tells us, by hearing a public reading of Goethe's essay on nature – an essay which vividly personifies Nature as a woman and portrays the study of nature as a passionate, romantic affair between the student and an all-generous woman who unstintingly reveals her secrets to those whom she favours.[9]

Before long Freud found that he was not particularly successful either as a student of physics or as a chemist but he did devote more and more time to zoology and eventually in his third year he felt he had found an intellectual home in the physiology laboratory of Ernst Brücke. Brücke's Institute derived its ideals from the Berlin scientific movement which had been inspired by Brücke himself and other scientists such as Emil Du Bois-Reymond and Hermann Helmholtz. The scientific goal which they pursued with a religious, almost Calvinistic zeal, was to eradicate all forms of vitalism from the life sciences and to reduce all scientific descriptions of natural phenomena to the categories of physics and chemistry. To this end the Helmholtz school had already pioneered new instruments of investigation such as the ophthalmoscope and introduced new techniques of microscopy. Freud himself was set to work on problems of comparative anatomy and distinguished himself as a meticulous and exact researcher whose faith in the physicism and mechanism of Brücke's ideals seemed no less fervent than that of his teacher.

In March 1881 he passed his final medical examinations and carried on working in the Brücke Institute following a course which, as his biographers have frequently speculated, might eventually have led him to succeed Brücke to the Chair of Physiology which he held. What complicated Freud's future was that any immediate prospects of academic advance were blocked by the relative youth of Brücke's assistants and of the man destined to be his immediate successor. When this factor was placed alongside Freud's recent engagement to Martha Bernays and the financial responsibilities which marriage would bring, it strongly suggested that the only realistic course was for Freud to abandon his research career and to become instead a medical practitioner. Indeed this course was strongly advised by none other than Brücke himself. In 1882 Freud took his advice and left the Institute which he had for some six years regarded as his intellectual home.

Because of the system of medical instruction which was then in force, Freud had qualified without any of the practical skills needed by a physician. In order to gain such necessary experience he was therefore obliged to spend some time in residence at the Vienna General Hospital. Freud soon concluded that the life of a general physician was not for him. But he did find ways of furthering his own intellectual interests in the hospital, particularly when, in 1883, he went to work in the psychiatric department of the hospital under Professor Theodor Meynert. Freud had already attended Meynert's lectures at an earlier stage in his studies and had spoken then of 'the great Meynert in whose footsteps I followed with such veneration'. Although their later relationship was more complex, Ernest Jones has written that Freud always recalled Meynert as 'the most brilliant genius he had ever encountered'.[10]

Meynert's main interest was in the anatomy of the human brain, a field in which he was one of the leading European authorities. His goal was to apply to the entire field of psychiatry the philosophy of the new clinico-pathological school of medicine. What this meant in practice was that he made extensive use of post mortem examinations of the brains of psychiatric patients in order to correlate groups of symptoms with the cerebral lesions or patterns of brain pathology which corresponded to them. Freud soon discovered that, by turning his attention from the nervous system of lower vertebrates to that of humans, he was able to continue the same kind of laboratory research he had engaged in under Brücke. As a result of these researches he published a number of papers in neuroanatomy and gradually moved towards a career in neurology.

By the time he was thirty Freud had already established himself as a gifted researcher in the field of neurological anatomy and his future seemed secure. Yet if we are to understand the extraordinary personal and intellectual turbulence which surrounded Freud for at least the next fifteen years, we need to judge his career by more intimate criteria.

For although he seemed successful in all outward respects, Freud could not but assess his own achievements in relation to the expectations of his parents. It would be very easy to underestimate the psychological intensity of these expectations and to imagine that they were concerned merely with worldly success. Perhaps the clearest indication that this was not the case is provided by the inscription which Jakob Freud wrote in Hebrew in the Bible he presented to his son on the occasion of his thirty-fifth birthday:

My dear Son,
   It was in the seventh year of your age that the spirit of God began to move you to learning. I would say the spirit of God speaketh to you: 'Read in My Book; there will be opened to thee sources of knowledge and of the intellect.' It is the Book of Books; it is the well that wise men have digged and from which lawgivers have drawn the waters of their knowledge.
   Thou hast seen in this book the vision of the Almighty, thou hast heard willingly, thou hast done and hast tried to fly high upon the wings of the Holy Spirit. Since then I have preserved the same Bible. Now, on your thirty-fifth birthday I have brought it out from its retirement and I send it to you as a token of love from your old father.[11]

What these extraordinary words make clear is that Freud was regarded by his father as 'special' not simply in some worldly manner but in a religious manner. Indeed the literal meaning of Jakob's inscription suggests that, in some sense at least, he saw his son as standing in an intimate relationship to none other than God himself, a relationship which would be consummated through his pursuit of science.

To an age used to viewing scientific research as a purely secular occupation Jakob Freud's exultantly religious view of his son's vocation may well seem extraordinary. It is worth bearing in mind, however, that such a view was by no means unprecedented. Perhaps the most interesting parallel is with a scientist with whom Freud himself has sometimes been compared, Isaac Newton.

Like Freud, Newton seems to have grown up surrounded by expectations of his future greatness which may well have been partly stimulated by a chance circumstance associated with his birth. Newton was born on 25 December and from a fairly early age he attributed special significance to the fact that he had been born on the same day as the son of God. The deeper sources of Newton's feeling of election are not well documented, but they appear to have been connected with

his unusual childhood. His father had died three months before Newton was born. Newton was brought up by his mother who, having no
husband, and no other children, lavished undivided attention upon her
only child. Three years later, however, she suddenly abandoned him
in order to remarry. Newton was now looked after by his maternal
grandmother, and only at the age of eleven was he taken back into the
care of his mother, who had by then been widowed for a second time.
Much of Newton's later career seems to have been an attempt to
reconstruct the self-esteem he had originally enjoyed as his mother's
only and beloved child, while simultaneously seeking revenge for the
emotional injuries she had inflicted on him by seeking worldly fame.
In Newton's own view, such fame was not only a token of the world's
esteem, but an outward confirmation of the special relationship he
believed he enjoyed with God. As his biographer Frank Manuel has
put it, '. . . in his moments of grandeur he saw himself as the last of the
interpreters of God's will in action, living on the eve of the fulfilment of
the times. In his generation he was the vehicle of God's eternal truth
. . . From him nothing had been withheld.' As these words suggest, it
seems possible that Newton, a passionate Christian who believed his
Rules for Interpreting the Apocalyps to be as flawless as his Principia, came
at times to regard himself as the Messiah, chosen to reveal the secrets
of the universe by none other than God himself.[12]

We need have no doubt that Freud, as a proud and sceptical rationalist, never regarded himself in any literal sense as having been chosen
by God. But, particularly in the light of Jakob Freud's inscription,
there seems every reason to suppose that Freud's messianic sense of
his own mission grew directly out of the way in which his parents'
deep and culturally orthodox yearning for the Jewish Messiah had
become interfused with the fond hopes they had for their own favourite
son, and the almost religious awe with which they came to regard his
youthful academic success.[13]

It is in this perspective, I believe, that we need to view Freud's
intellectual and existential predicament as he approached the age of
thirty. For although in all outward respects he was successful, he
remained, in relation to the world-redeeming identity conferred upon
him by his parents, an utter failure. Nor was there any immediate
prospect of relief. For perhaps the most remarkable feature of Freud's
life was the age which he reached before he even began to glimpse
the psychoanalytic 'truths' which were to mean so much to him. Most
scientists of genius make their crucial discoveries early on. Freud,

however, was already forty by the time he began to formulate his theory of infantile sexuality, and almost fifty by the time the theory was published in 1905. As he grew older it would seem that his need for a theoretical 'revelation' became more and more compulsive and he began to despair of ever receiving it.

What is clear is that, just as a man condemned to poverty dreams of sudden riches, so Freud dreamt almost constantly of academic glory throughout his period of scientific training. During his time at the Vienna General Hospital, in addition to the immense psychological pressure he was under, he also had to cope with the financial pressure resulting from his engagement to Martha Bernays. It is perhaps not surprising that he began to look eagerly for any opportunity which might present itself of cutting short his scientific apprenticeship and to cast around anxiously for ways of making his dreams of glory come true. In the spring of 1884 an opportunity presented itself. For he came across a paper by a German army surgeon reporting the remarkable effects he had achieved by administering cocaine to soldiers suffering from exhaustion. Cocaine at that time was a relatively unknown drug whose therapeutic effects had not been documented. Freud immediately sensed the possibility of overnight fame and he began to investigate the existing medical literature. As he wrote to his fiancée, 'We do not need more than one such lucky hit to be able to think of setting up house.'[14]

This was the beginning of what has become known to Freud scholars as 'the cocaine episode'. In an obscure medical journal, the *Therapeutic Gazette* of Detroit, Freud did uncover one paper which described how cocaine had been used to wean morphine addicts from their addiction. Since one of Freud's colleagues, Ernst von Fleischl-Marxow suffered from such an addiction as a result of the therapeutic use of morphine, Freud was particularly interested in this fact and he determined to investigate the drug further.

After purchasing a single gram of the drug at great expense from a pharmaceutical company he immediately took a twentieth of a gram himself and found that his depressed spirits were replaced by a sense of exhilaration. He also proposed to his friend Fleischl-Marxow that he should free himself from his addiction by substituting cocaine for morphine, a proposal which was enthusiastically adopted.

Like the classic 'cocaine convert' Freud now became an evangelist for the drug, singing its praises to his friends and pressing it upon them. As well as concluding that he had succeeded in the case of

Fleischl-Marxow he also believed he had successfully cured a case of gastric catarrh when a dose of cocaine immediately put an end to the pain. Cocaine, he felt, was a 'magical drug' and when he wrote to Martha he could scarcely contain his excitement:

> If it goes well I will write an essay on it and I expect it will win its place in therapeutics, by the side of morphia but superior to it. I have other hopes and intentions about it. I take very small doses of it regularly against depression and indigestion, and with the most brilliant success. I hope it will be able to abolish the most intractable vomiting, even when this is due to severe pain; in short it is only now that I feel I am a doctor, since I have helped one patient and hope to help more. If things go on in this way we need have no concern about being able to come together and to stay in Vienna.[15]

Seized by the prospect of imminent glory Freud now engaged in a quite extraordinary rush to publication. Only a matter of weeks after his first experiment with the drug he had finished his paper on it and the very next day, according to Ernest Jones, half of it appeared in print in Heitler's *Centralblatt für die gesammte Therapie*.

Jones, seeking to salvage some good from one of the most damaging episodes in Freud's career, characterises the tone of the essay as 'a remarkable combination of objectivity with a personal warmth'. The description is a curious one, particularly in view of the examples which he goes on to give. For in the essay, which Freud himself referred to at the time as 'a song of praise to this magical substance', Freud described 'the most gorgeous excitement' that animals display after an injection of cocaine; he also referred to administering an 'offering' of it rather than a 'dose'. He stated that the drug was not addictive and passionately condemned as 'slanders' critical views of cocaine.[16]

What Jones perhaps suspects, but what he seems reluctant to put into words, is that Freud's paper was actually written under the influence of cocaine. There seems little doubt that this was in fact the case, for Freud not only admitted that he was taking the drug 'regularly', but he also referred repeatedly to the way in which the drug enlarged people's capacity to work. In the paper itself he wrote that one of the results of taking cocaine was that 'You perceive an increase of self-control and possess more vitality and capacity for work ... Long intensive mental or physical work is performed without any fatigue.'[17] His paper, produced at such extraordinary speed, was, it would seem, the proof of this observation.

The feelings of exhilaration caused by the drug were short-lived, however. For it soon became clear that Freud, in his rush to publish, had overlooked some of the most significant effects of the drug. Some two months after the publication of Freud's paper, a friend and medical colleague of Freud's, Carl Koller, gained precisely the kind of fame Freud had been seeking when, after making a series of experiments on the eyes of animals, he entered medical history as the discoverer of local anaesthesia by cocaine. Freud had himself made cursory mention of the drug's anaesthetic properties, but in his haste he had failed to pursue the idea.

The publication of Freud's paper was to have a far more serious sequel than this. For although Freud had succeeded in weaning his friend Fleischl-Marxow from morphine onto cocaine, he was now suffering from an addiction to the substitute drug whose effects were even more damaging and were exacerbated further when Fleischl-Marxow began to take both drugs simultaneously. At first Freud sought solace in the notion that Fleischl-Marxow's addiction was a special case. But by 1886 cases of cocaine addiction were being reported from all over the world. With every justification Freud became the target of public criticism and the psychiatrist Erlenmeyer even went so far as to accuse him of having unleashed the 'third scourge of humanity' – the first two being alcohol and morphine. In 1887 Freud offered a disingenuous defence of his role in the whole affair. Having written his original paper expressly in order to claim a share of the credit for the medical discovery of the drug, he now blamed others for bringing the drug to the attention of physicians, even referring specifically to an 'extravagant' article by Walle in the *Deutsche Medicinalzeitung*. Forced to concede the reality of cocaine addiction he claimed, incorrectly, that it was suffered only by those who were already addicted to morphine. He also blamed the practice of subcutaneous injection while omitting to mention that he had himself recommended just such injections in a paper written in 1885. Indeed it would seem that in this regard Freud went even further than mere omission in his attempts to preserve his own reputation. When, in 1899 in *The Interpretation of Dreams*, he referred to the Fleischl-Marxow episode during his account of the dream of Irma's injection, he contrived to shift responsibility for what happened almost entirely onto his friend: 'These injections reminded me of my unfortunate friend *who had poisoned himself with cocaine* [italics added]. I had advised him to use the drug internally [i.e. orally] only, while morphia was being withdrawn; but he had at once given himself cocaine *injections*.' A mere two pages later Freud repeats this account, writing of how he was reminded 'once more of my dead friend *who had so hastily resorted to cocaine injections* [italics added]. As I have said, I had never contemplated the drug being given by injection.'[18] Yet in his 1885 paper, Freud had written: 'I should unhesitatingly advise cocaine being administered in subcutaneous injection.'[19] Since these words were first written at a time when Fleischl-Marxow was still under Freud's care, we may presume that Freud actively falsified his account of what had happened and endeavoured to conceal his own true role. For although it would seem that Fleischl-Marxow may well have taken the initiative in administering cocaine by injection, Freud had unhesitatingly endorsed this method. When, in 1897, Freud was obliged to draw up a list of his publications to submit with his application for the title of Professor, the 1885 paper, which contained the clearest evidence of this endorsement, was not included. Nor was any copy of it found in Freud's collection of offprints of his own articles. It is no enemy of psychoanalysis but Ernest Jones himself who draws the conclusion that 'It seems to have been completely suppressed.'[20]

The 'cocaine episode' has been discussed by all of Freud's biographers and it has also frequently been invoked by Freud's critics. Interpretations of the affair have differed. What cannot be disputed, however, is that the cocaine episode does throw some light on Freud's character and his intellectual style. In the first place it may be suggested that Freud missed the discovery of cocaine as a local anaesthetic simply because he became obsessed by the idea of cocaine as a world-redeeming panacea; because of his compulsive need to discover a forest, he missed the only significant tree. Not only this, but it took Freud a very considerable time to withdraw from his infatuation with the idea of cocaine as a miracle-therapy. So intense was his emotional need for this kind of revelation, that he seems to have suspended all his critical faculties as he set about expounding his new discovery. More generally the cocaine episode points to Freud's willingness to deviate from the narrow path of painstaking scientific research and take short-cuts in order to achieve the fame he had been condemned by parental expectations to seek.

It is conceivable, of course, that Freud's conduct during the cocaine episode represented an aberration in his medical career, or indeed that he learnt lessons from his professional humiliation which would help him eventually to achieve scientific maturity. But we must also consider the less edifying possibility: that Freud's behaviour with regard to cocaine reveals an essential element in his scientific temperament which was *not* destined to disappear with time. We must consider, in other words, the possibility that psychoanalysis itself was born out of emotional needs so great and so urgent that they overpowered Freud's reserves of scepticism. It was, on this view, Freud's terrifying need for fame which blinded him to the explanatory emptiness of the 'science' which he eventually elaborated, just as it blinded him to the deficiencies of his papers on cocaine.

But there is another aspect of the cocaine episode which casts a significant shadow forward over Freud's subsequent career. This concerns the way he reported the case of his friend Fleischl-Marxow in the scientific papers he wrote at the time. Freud first took cocaine himself in May 1884. At about the same time he persuaded Fleischl-Marxow to take the drug too. By 5 June Freud was already preparing his paper on cocaine. This paper was finished on 18 June and appeared in the July number of *Centralblatt für die gesammte Therapie*. At this stage Freud was simply not in a position to assess what effect cocaine had had on Fleischl-Marxow's long-standing morphine addiction. Yet in his paper, he confidently referred to cocaine as an 'antidote' to morphine and cited a case of his own in which 'after ten days' the patient was 'able to dispense with the coca treatment altogether'. Freud, in other words, reported that one of his patients had been cured when no cure had taken place, and at a time when it was still far too early to judge whether any cure *could* have taken place.[21]

Nor was this simply an isolated example of rash therapeutic hope. For Freud later compounded his medical misreporting in a manner which becomes quite invisible in Ernest Jones's biography and which was uncovered only a century after the event by E. M. Thornton. As she points out, and as Jones himself acknowledges, by April 1885 Fleischl-Marxow was consuming enormous quantities of the drug and Freud noted that he had spent no less than 1,800 marks on it in the previous three months. On 8 June Freud wrote in a letter to Martha that huge doses of cocaine had harmed Fleischl-Marxow greatly and warned her against acquiring the habit. Yet in March Freud had read a paper to the Psychiatric Society in which he described a case – clearly that of Fleischl-Marxow – as one of 'rapid withdrawal from morphine under cocaine'. He went on to claim that the habit had been cured in twenty days and that 'no cocaine habituation set in'. It was in this paper that he said that he had no hesitation in recommending subcutaneous injections of cocaine as an effective means of curing morphine addiction. That Freud was able to give such recommendations in March is itself disturbing. But what is even more remarkable is that he held steadfastly to this judgement throughout June and July at the very time that he was warning Martha against acquiring the cocaine habit and witnessing the extremes of misery and physical wretchedness to which Fleischl-Marxow had been reduced by his addiction to cocaine. For Freud's paper, with its confident announcement of an effective cure for morphine addiction, was published in the *Medicinisch-chirurgisches Centralblatt* on 7 August 1885. Not only did Freud allow the publication of this paper to go ahead but he subsequently expressed satisfaction when his highly dangerous work of medical fiction was abstracted in the *Lancet*.[22]

In drawing attention to this remarkable chain of events for the first time E. M. Thornton refers to Freud's 'mendacity'. It is difficult to see how this charge can be rebutted. But at the same time it would be wrong to allow a black-and-white moral reflex to obscure the particular circumstances of the case. Lies may be among the most common of moral sins but they are not the most simple and often spring from complex motives. The scientific lie which Freud told about Fleischl-Marxow is no exception. For there seems every reason to suppose that Freud had persuaded himself that in this case his particular lie hid a general truth – a truth so important that its enunciation should not be muffled by too many moral scruples. Freud, we must recall, had not only administered the drug to his friend, he had also taken it himself. And although he subsequently wrote to Martha that he was taking it 'regularly', he clearly believed that he had not developed any craving for it and that there were no signs of addiction. If he had not become addicted then it followed that cocaine was not inherently addictive. The fact that Fleischl-Marxow had succumbed was therefore due to a peculiarity of his constitution rather than to the properties of the drug itself. If this was so then it would be wrong to deprive humanity of a much-needed therapeutic procedure simply because of the aberrant constitution of an individual; much better to report Fleischl-Marxow's actual addiction as a complete cure.

Unless we are to charge Freud with the most cynical kind of scientific cheating – which would be quite out of character – it would seem that some such process of rationalisation lay behind Freud's behaviour. But what is even more significant is that the cocaine episode provides only the first example of this curious mixture of idealism and expediency in Freud's career.

In order to examine the sequel to this particular incident we need to follow the next crucial stage in Freud's career – his journey to Paris to study hypnosis and hysteria under Charcot. When Freud returned from this journey to Vienna he would, in collaboration with Josef Breuer, begin to develop the techniques of psychoanalysis. As we will see, the first patient to be 'cured' of her hysteria by these techniques, the famous Anna O., has something in common with Fleischl-Marxow. For, as an ingenious piece of historical detective work has shown, she was not cured either. Not only this, but history and medical research have combined to suggest that she was not suffering from 'hysteria' at all.

TWO

Hypnotism and Hysteria

THE COCAINE EPISODE cast a shadow over Freud's medical career. But, partly because a considerable time elapsed before the full seriousness of Freud's misjudgement became clear, it did not interrupt his gradual progress upwards through the academic ranks. In 1885 he was appointed *Privatdozent* in Neuropathology – a position roughly equivalent to that of university lecturer. At about the same time he won a travelling grant which enabled him to become a pupil of Charcot, who had achieved a quite extraordinary pre-eminence in the world of neurology, and whose hospital, La Salpêtrière, had become a place of pilgrimage for physicians throughout Europe and America – 'the Mecca of neurologists', as Ernest Jones put it.[1] In his own estimate Freud's journey to Paris represented no ordinary stage in his career but another alchemical opportunity to create a golden reputation for himself out of the dross of his present relative obscurity. The ecstasy which he felt when he heard the news of his success is conveyed well in the letter he wrote to Martha at the time:

> O, how wonderful it is going to be. I am coming with money and am staying a long while with you and am bringing something lovely for you and shall then go to Paris and become a great *savant* and return to Vienna with a great, great nimbus. Then we will marry soon and I will cure all the incurable nervous patients and you will keep me well and I will kiss you till you are merry and happy – and they lived happily ever after.[2]

Freud's excitement at the prospect of his visit to Charcot was conditioned partly by the romance attached to Paris itself – a city which he had always longed to visit – and partly by Charcot's reputation both as a researcher and as a dazzling and accomplished teacher. This reputation was in many respects well earned. Born in Paris in 1825, Jean Martin Charcot began his medical studies in 1844. He spent his time as an intern at La Salpêtrière, an old hospital which had become a medical pauper house for several thousand old women. He quickly realised that he had stumbled upon a living museum containing numerous specimens of rare neurological diseases which would be an ideal place to conduct clinical research. He kept this in mind and, in 1862, when he qualified for a teaching post, he elected to return to the same hospital in order to carry out the research of which he had long dreamt. Charcot made the unusual decision to return to the Salpêtrière because he wanted to apply the anatomical-clinical method – developed in relation to physical medicine – to the realm of neurology. What this meant was that he undertook a close study of the way in which the distinctive clinical signs of neurological diseases, observable before the patient's death, could be correlated with post mortem findings. Charcot, in short, was the most significant pioneer of the very technique of neurological investigation to which Freud had already been introduced in the early 1880s by Theodor Meynert.

Before he distinguished himself in the field of neurology, Charcot made a number of significant contributions to general medicine. He detected excessive uric acid in cases of gout, recognised the lobular structure of the lung, liver and kidney and introduced routine temperature-taking in everyday hospital practice.[3] But it was to the investigation of diseases of the nervous system that he found himself increasingly drawn. In the middle of the nineteenth century this entire realm remained virtually a *terra incognita*. The organic disorders which lay behind various forms of tremor, tics, paralysis and anaesthesia were simply not known, while the structure of the brain itself remained to a large extent veiled in mystery. By setting up his research with immense care, by attending carefully to the observations of other physicians and by supervising post mortem examinations of patients' brains, Charcot was able to make an impressive series of discoveries. Even before 1860 he was trying to differentiate multiple sclerosis from Parkinson's disease and it was he who, on the basis of Parkinson's monograph of 1817, actually named *paralysis agitans* after the English physician. In 1864 he and a colleague were able to describe the changes in the spinal cord which were characteristic of polio myelitis. A few years later, with the help of another colleague, Félix Vulpian, he carefully pieced together almost the entire pathology of multiple sclerosis, establishing the relationship between the spinal lesions of multiple sclerosis and the tremors and other characteristic symptoms of the disease. He also gave one of the first clinical descriptions of motor neurone disease – which is still called Charcot's disease in mainland Europe.[4] Other major discoveries through which Charcot established himself as the foremost neurologist of his day included his work on locomotor ataxia, cerebral localisation and aphasia. In layman's terms he had become an expert on a number of degenerative diseases of the brain and the spinal cord which affected both people's powers of speech and their ability to co-ordinate their muscular movements. He also contributed to the charting of the human brain, helping to identify the centres which controlled different parts of the body and particular physiological functions. At the same time he used his very considerable artistic and theatrical talents to establish himself as an outstanding teacher. His lectures were dramatic events in which patients were brought onto the stage, engaged in dialogue by the master and diagnosed 'live' in front of a fascinated audience of students, physicians and writers.

The immense reputation which Charcot had created for himself by the end of the 1880s is conveyed well by Léon Daudet, himself a medical student at the time, and the son of the novelist Alphonse Daudet, who had been both a friend and a patient of the master:

> Towards 1890 Professor Charcot was at the apogee of his reputation and his power. He held the Faculty [of Medicine] bent to his grindstone. His doctrines, whose fundamentals had not yet been overturned, gave an impression of solidity and even majesty . . . No one anywhere in the civilized world could publish a book on diseases of the nervous system without seeking his approval, his *imprimatur*, in advance. The structure of the liver and the kidney obeyed him as well as that of the spinal cord. Physicians sent him patients with ataxia and cases of paralysis agitans from North America, the Caucasus, and even China.[5]

The story of Charcot, however, like many tales of overweening ambition, had a tragic end. Léon Daudet himself had seen another side of Charcot's clinical practice at first hand. For after Charcot had (correctly) diagnosed his father as suffering from syphilis he had hastened his death by ordering that he should be suspended by the neck to relieve pain by 'lengthening' the nerves.[6] That Charcot's undoubted clinical genius should be associated so closely with such dubious therapeutic methods was entirely characteristic of his career as a whole. For, as Daudet's own carefully chosen words imply, the solidity and majesty of many of Charcot's theories was *only* an impression, and some of his most important doctrines would be overturned by the very physicians he had once ruled with a rod of iron. The story of Charcot's medical theorising is both tragic and instructive. The fact that it is still not generally known, even though many of its major elements have been in the public domain for well over half a century, makes it, in many respects, even more compelling. The particular story of Charcot's relationship to Freud and of his role in the genesis of psycho-analysis is certainly essential to any understanding of the development of twentieth-century intellectual culture. It is also one of the least understood but most important episodes in the entire history of modern medicine. For modern neurology and modern psychiatry have developed in the way that they have largely because of Charcot's work on hysteria at the end of the nineteenth century, and the way in which it was received and developed by Freud.

There can be little doubt that one of the reasons why the full story of Charcot's later career remains little known is provided by the sheer quantity and quality of his early research. It is by the discoveries which he made during this golden period that he is chiefly remembered by physicians today and many medical students are given no intimation of the scientific vagaries of Charcot's subsequent work. It is generally recognised, however, that Charcot's major discoveries were all com-pleted by the end of the 1870s. From this point onwards it would seem that the fame he had earnt through his genuine scientific achievements encouraged him to give more rein to the less empirically cautious and more boldly speculative side of his personality. Increasingly he maintained his medical pre-eminence in Paris by fear and charisma rather than by making new discoveries. Meanwhile, throughout the 1880s a major part of his research was given over to the problem of 'hysteria', whose mysteries he believed he could unravel just as he had those of the spinal cord.

Charcot found it necessary to develop a theory of hysteria because of a particular group of patients in La Salpêtrière. For while some patients were classified as being purely epileptic, a separate ward had been created before Charcot's arrival in 1862 for patients who were deemed to be suffering from 'hystero-epilepsy'. The ward was filled by women suffering from various kinds of fits. Some of them appeared to be suffering from a combination of epilepsy and mental illness. Others were held to be suffering primarily from hysteria but with an admixture of epilepsy.[7] Faced with the medical conundrum of 'hystero-epilepsy' Charcot was unable to resist his overriding impulse towards classifying. Taking as his invisible premise the assumption that 'hysteria' was a clinical reality – a distinct disease-entity – he set out first to differentiate hysterics from epileptics and then to define what he believed to be the distinctive clinical signs of hysteria, which he termed neurological 'stigmata'. Although Charcot's assumption about the real existence of hysteria was speculative in so far as it was based on no pathological evidence, the fact that 'hysteria' or 'passio hysterica' had been current for centuries made it seem a very natural basis on which to conduct research.

In 1870 a reorganisation which took place inside the Salpêtrière left Charcot in complete charge of all those non-insane patients who were classified as hysterical or epileptic. This chance development greatly increased Charcot's opportunities for research and from this time onwards he was increasingly drawn towards the study of hysteria – 'the great neurosis'.

One of the difficulties which stood in Charcot's way was the lack of any satisfactory definition of hysteria. For this putative disease has been associated with a bewildering variety of symptoms over the centuries. In 1853 the English physician Robert Carter observed that the concept of hysteria had 'an inexactness unparalleled in scientific phraseology'. A little later the American nerve specialist Silas Weir Mitchell called hysteria 'the nosological limbo of all unnamed female maladies' and suggested that 'it were as well called mysteria'. In 1878 a contemporary of Charcot's, the French alienist Lasèque, ruled out the very possibility of defining it: 'The definition of hysteria has never been given and never will be. The symptoms are not constant enough nor sufficiently similar in form or equal in duration or intensity that one type, even descriptive, could comprise them all.'[8]

The situation is complicated still further by the fact that the use of 'hysteria' as a noun was adopted in relatively recent times, being first used in French in 1731 and in English in 1766.[9] Other terms, however, clearly understood to be referring to a single disease, were in use much earlier than this. In 1603 the physician Edward Jorden published 'A Briefe Discourse of a Disease Called the Suffocation of the Mother' in which he made this quite clear, as well as indicating what he understood to be the most common symptoms of the illness:

> This disease is called by diverse names amongst our Authors. *Passio Hysterica, Suffocatio, Praefocatio*, and *Strangulatus uteri, Caducus matricis, &c.* In English the Mother, or the Suffocation of the Mother, because

most commonly it takes them with choaking in the throat: and it is *an affect of the Mother or wombe wherein the principal parts of the bodie by consent do suffer diversely according to the diversitie of the causes and diseases wherewith the matrix is offended.*[10]

What Jorden's words help to clarify is that, in spite of the protean character which some physicians attributed to the disease, there was at least one thread of symptoms which appeared to be continuous and which was related to the traditional explanation of the disease – and indeed to its very name. For, from the time of Plato onwards, physicians had frequently explained a particular set of physical sensations reported by patients by suggesting that it was caused by the womb moving upwards through the body towards the head. This theory derived from the subjective experience of victims of 'hysterical' fits. For a woman suffering from such a fit would experience a sensation as if her womb were rising up through her body. As it travelled towards the head it would cause a feeling of tightness in the chest and on its arrival at the throat it would cause choking as if by a ball – the *globus hystericus.* Sometimes the woman would suffer only a slight lapse of consciousness. Sometimes she would fall down in a convulsive fit.

Charcot, like earlier theorists, held fast to the notion that, in addition to the convulsive forms, there were many non-convulsive kinds of hysteria which did not issue in fits. Some patients supposedly manifested the disease through hysterical paralyses or contractures in which muscles remained permanently tensed. Others showed that they were suffering from hysteria by a variety of losses or distortions of neurological function for which no organic explanation was then available. Others suffered from putatively hysterical movement disorders such as 'Hysterical Chorea' in which they exhibited rhythmical stereotyped movements, or 'astasia abasia' in which, although they could execute all normal movements when examined in bed, they were unable to stand or walk. Still others were afflicted by somnambulisms, ambulatory automatisms or amnesiac fugues, in which they forgot their own identity.[11]

Yet although Charcot's concept of hysteria was, like the traditional concept, swollen with a wide variety of ostensibly quite different disorders, he never relinquished the idea that hysteria was a single disease, and that its most characteristic manifestation was in the 'hysterical' fit. In this respect he was particularly influenced by the theories of Paul Briquet who, in 1859, had published a treatise in which he had in turn revived an idea first proposed in the seventeenth century by Thomas Sydenham. Sydenham had maintained that hysteria was a real clinical entity but that its prime characteristic was that it *simulated* epileptic fits and other organic disorders.[12] In order that he might better distinguish between real epileptic fits and what he took to be 'hysteria', Charcot attempted to produce a meticulous and systematic description of a classic hysterical crisis. This aspect of his thinking has been usefully summarised by A. R. G. Owen:

> Convulsive attacks vary among patients and even within the same individual. But such variation occurs in most diseases and is not peculiar to neuroses. According to Charcot, a typical [hysterical] convulsive attack passed through three distinct stages: First came the *epileptoid stage*, which rarely came on entirely without warning, but was heralded by certain prodromata or premonitory signs. Sometimes there would be mental excitement and agitation and possibly hallucination, or a nervous cough, yawning or tremor. But the most usual 'premonitory aura' consisted of palpitation with a sense of tightness in the head, a feeling of excessive warmth, and the famous 'globus hystericus' – a sensation of obstruction in the throat as of a ball rising there. A fairly common sign was the 'ovarian aura', a sharp pain in the ovarian or some other region of the trunk. The epileptoid stage, usually of a few minutes duration, commenced with the patient falling backward with loss of consciousness, weak breathing, swelling of the neck, and foaming at the mouth. Then came a 'tonic phase', with the arms and legs stretched out and going into short and violent oscillations. This was succeeded by the phase of 'muscular relaxation', in which activity subsided while full respiration was resumed. While these subsidiary phases could often be distinguished, they showed considerable variation in duration and intensity.[13]

The 'epileptoid stage' would be followed by a second stage – the 'period of contortions and *grands mouvements*', otherwise known as 'clownism'. In this stage the body was sometimes bent into improbable postures such as *arc-de-cercle* (sometimes known as *arc-en-ciel*), in which the body was arched upwards supported only by the head and heels. This was followed by a third stage of impassioned poses (*attitudes passionelles*) and in some rare cases by a fourth stage of *post-hysterical derangement* in which, as Edward Shorter has put it, 'anything could happen'.[14]

Given that Charcot's apparently rigid description of what he termed '*la grande hystérie*' was based on a tiny sample consisting originally of only five patients, it is perhaps not surprising that, no sooner had he presented his description, than he felt it necessary to introduce into it a considerable degree of elasticity. For he went on to admit the existence of atypical forms, or variations of these standard phases:

> Perhaps an attack would be entirely dominated by the first period, not progressing further. In another variety, 'demonic behaviour', such as tearing one's blouse from one's breast, might characterise the clownism of the second period. In still another variation, attitudes of ecstasy might preempt all the impassioned poses in the third period. Or hallucinations and delusions might be the chief events of the terminal period.[15]

In many patients only a few features of the *grande attaque* would be observed, such as brief contractions of the hands and arms or legs. Charcot called these attacks *formes frustes* or *hysteria minor* as opposed to *hysteria major*.[16]

Satisfied that he had given rigorous clinical criteria by which it was possible to identify a real disease entity, Charcot proceeded to speculate on its causes. Although he is sometimes seen as the first investigator to understand hysteria as a *psychological* phenomenon, any simple version of this view would be misleading. For in one sense Charcot always remained a neurologist, whose whole conception of neuroses was founded on the idea that they were disorders with a real, if undetectable, organic cause. Because his entire approach to medicine rested on the pathological investigation of the human brain and the nervous system, he habitually correlated the physical signs of neurological disorder with the brain pathology which gave rise to them. Where it was not possible to detect such pathology by examining the brain under a microscope, Charcot sometimes postulated the existence of a hypothetical lesion. He did this, for example, in considering a case of what he had termed 'hysterical' paralysis:

> There is without doubt a lesion of the nervous centres . . . It is, I opine, in the grey matter of the cerebral hemisphere on the side opposite the paralysis, and more precisely in the motor zone of the arm . . . we may believe . . . it is not strictly limited to the motor zone, and that it extends behind the median convolution to the adjacent parts of the parietal lobe. But certainly it is not of the nature of a circumscribed organic lesion . . . We have here unquestionably one of those lesions which escape our present means of anatomical investigation, and which, for want of a better term, we designate *dynamic* or *functional* lesions.[17]

It should immediately be said that in postulating the existence of an invisible and undetectable lesion in order to explain the visible symptoms of his patient, Charcot was not doing anything intrinsically unscientific. For scientists frequently need to assume the existence of hypothetical entities or processes in order to advance their own investigations. An excellent example is provided by the way in which William Harvey made use of the theoretical term 'pore' in his explanation of the circulation of the blood.[18] After making a careful study of the anatomy and functioning of the heart, lungs and blood vessels, Harvey came to the conclusion that the heart pumped a fixed amount of blood through the body. This theoretical account was based for the most part on Harvey's observation of visible anatomical entities and processes. But there was one exception. For the only way in which Harvey could make sense of all his observations was by assuming that an exchange of blood took place between arteries and veins. Since anatomical investigation revealed no route for such an exchange, Harvey was obliged to postulate that the exchange took place through minute openings, or pores, which were too small to be seen. As Malcolm Macmillan has observed, a logical implication of his hypothesis was that the pores would be visible through microscopes more powerful than those available at the time. This proved to be the case. For, as Macmillan writes, 'Some years after his death the smaller vessels were actually observed and the status of the pores changed. Postulated or assumed pores had been transformed into real capillaries; a theoretical term had become a fact.'[19]

In many respects Charcot's strategy of postulating the existence of hysteria-causing lesions, even though no such lesions had been observed, was directly comparable to Harvey's earlier hypothesis. Indeed, as Anne Harrington has noted, underlying his initial theoretical formulation 'seems to have been the implicit hope . . . that once "present methods" of post mortem investigation were sufficiently refined, the putative differences between hysterical and organic disorders might turn out to have been more apparent than real.'[20] As will eventually become clear there is good reason to suppose that, had Charcot waited for the right investigatory techniques to become available, his hypothesis – or a part of it at least – would have been triumphantly vindicated.

The course of scientific patience, however, was not one which he was able to maintain. This was in part, it would seem, because of the sheer scale of the scientific problems by which Charcot was faced as his research developed. For by the middle of the 1880s, just before the time Freud arrived in Paris, Charcot found himself wrestling not with one but with a number of unsolved unscientific problems which were all related to the central enigma of 'hysteria', and which were all extremely difficult to explain in neurological terms. One of the most difficult and long-standing of these problems concerned Charcot's experiments with hypnosis which he had begun in around 1877. At that time the phenomenon of hypnosis was in medical disrepute after the wildly speculative theorising of Franz Anton Mesmer and his ideas of 'animal magnetism' at the end of the eighteenth century. The exact reasons why Charcot started his experiments are not clear. One possibility is that he was influenced by the physiologist Charles Richet, who was one of the few contemporary scientists who had taken the subject seriously, and who had insisted that the phenomenon of hypnotism was a genuine one in which there could be no question of simulation. Another possibility is that Charcot was responding directly to the work of the neo-mesmerist Victor Burq who believed that hysterical patients could be directly influenced by magnets and metal bars and whose work had been authenticated by Charcot himself. A third possibility is that Charcot's interest in hypnotism was a natural outgrowth of his interest in *la grande hystérie*. For a number of his *hystériques* frequently lapsed into spontaneous somnambulism, a state which appeared to be preceded by a definite external stimulus. One patient, for instance, was rendered cataleptic by the brass instruments of a military band; another by the bark of a dog; a third became entranced in the act of pulling on her stockings. It may well be that, noting the apparent susceptibility of his 'hysterics' to external stimuli, Charcot began to experiment with various means of hypnosis in order to bring about altered states of consciousness deliberately.[21]

The states of consciousness which Charcot produced in his *hystériques* by artificially provoking what he called 'hypnosis' were sometimes so bizarre and so extreme that many modern commentators, basing their view on the writings of Charcot's many critics, have assumed that his subjects were consciously or unconsciously simulating these states in order to please him.[22] In a number of cases this is almost certainly what did happen, particularly in the latter stages of Charcot's career. But historians who take the view that *all* Charcot's experiments in hypnosis were nothing but exercises in suggestion are able to sustain this thesis only by ignoring both Charcot's own detailed and expertly observed clinical descriptions and the accounts of numerous impartial eye-witnesses whose powers of clinical observation were sometimes no less acute.

What tends to happen frequently is that modern commentators define the state of hypnosis by reference to the practice of some twentieth-century hypnotists and then assume that Charcot's experiments were of exactly the same order. Charcot himself, however, made it abundantly clear that when he used the term hypnosis he employed it in a very restricted and specific sense. In his view it was a pathological state which could be induced only in subjects who were already suffering from 'hysteria'.

The idea that hypnotism was a neurological phenomenon was not entirely new. James Braid, the English physician who had experimented with mesmerism in the 1840s and who had introduced the term 'hypnosis', had put forward just such a view, suggesting that the hypnotic trance was produced when fixed staring at an object placed just above the normal field of vision produced eye-strain. The continued stare 'by paralysing nervous centres in the eyes and their appendages, and destroying the equilibrium of the nervous system, thus produced the phenomenon referred to'.[23] Braid's own descriptions of the reactions of some of his early subjects seem to bear out this view. For in their clear references to involuntary muscular spasms and convulsive movements they suggest a parallel between a particular kind of hypnotic trance and some minor, neurologically based seizure. Braid, for example, describes his first experiment in the following terms:

> I requested Mr Walker, a young gentleman present, to sit down, and maintain a fixed stare at the top of a wine bottle, placed so much above him as to produce a considerable strain on the eyes and eyelids, to enable him to maintain a steady view of the object. In three minutes his eyelids closed, a gush of tears ran down his cheeks, his head drooped, his face *was slightly convulsed*, he gave a groan, and instantly fell into a profound sleep, the respiration becoming slow, deep and sibilant, the right hand and arm *being agitated by slight convulsive movements*. At the end of four minutes I considered it necessary for his safety, to put an end to the experiment [italics added].

It is notable that not all Braid's subjects react in this way and he often unsceptically accepts 'symptoms' which were clearly the products of suggestion. But when he employs the same method of induction on his wife, he describes a similar convulsive reaction:

In two minutes the expression of the face was very much changed; at the end of two minutes and a half *the eyelids closed convulsively*; the mouth was distorted; she gave a deep sigh, the bosom heaved, she fell back *and was evidently passing into an hysteric paroxysm*, to prevent which I instantly roused her. On counting the pulse I found that it had mounted up to 180 strokes a minute.[24]

In Charcot's experiments the fact that his subjects were chosen only from among patients who regularly experienced fully developed convulsive seizures seems to have exercised a decisive influence over the kind of hypnotic state he was able to induce. The involuntary, convulsive signs described above were found again and again in his experiments, as is shown by a series of eye-witness accounts culled from contemporary journals by Thornton. In 1878 Professor Arthur Gamgee of Manchester University visited the Salpêtrière with a number of medical colleagues and carefully described the physical reactions of Charcot's subjects as they were hypnotised. One young woman, described as a 'hystero-epileptic', was hypnotised by the eye-fixation method:

At 10.6 the eyelids dropped, and, at the same time, began to wink in a rapid, tremulous manner; this phenomenon continued throughout the whole duration of the induced sleep, being, Professor Charcot remarked, constant; at the same time a tonic contraction of the flexors of both forearms occurred, the fists becoming temporarily clenched.

After showing that his patient could still write and sew even in her trance-like state, Charcot blew into her eyes, and she came out of hypnosis. 'The act of awaking, in her case and that of all hystero-epileptics who have been thrown into the mesmeric sleep,' wrote Gamgee, 'is accompanied by a peculiar reflex; there is an automatic and sudden act of expulsion of saliva – as if it were a slight effort to spit.'[25] Similar convulsive or seizure-like reactions were reported by an American medical observer in 1879. In this case the subject of Charcot's experiments was a twenty-one-year-old woman suffering from 'hysteria', who was hypnotised by being required to gaze at a bright light. 'In a few seconds she became cataleptic and completely anaesthetic. The limbs were flexible and assumed any position in which they were placed by the operator.' If the light was removed the subject swallowed convulsively and entered another state in which any slight friction on the skin produced contractions of the underlying muscles.

At the same time it was possible to observe 'a constant motion of the upper eyelid, convulsions of the globe of the eye in various directions, and persisting anaesthesia'.[26]

The state of catalepsy referred to here – a condition in which the subject's limbs assume a characteristic 'waxy rigidity' – was frequently induced in Charcot's 'hysterics'. Freud himself was one of many foreign visitors who witnessed the strange spectacle of patients suddenly being rendered cataleptic by the sound of a gong, and then subsequently being brought out of that state, so that they gave the impression of statues coming to life.

Charcot did not seek to disguise his perplexity in face of these phenomena. His puzzlement, however, did not cause him to cut short his experiments. By putting pressure on his subject's eyeballs, by opening or closing their eyes, or by employing some other physical stimulus, he found that he was able to make his subjects move between different states of hypnosis. That these changes were sometimes neurologically precipitated, rather than being brought about by the will, is suggested by the physical signs which accompanied them. 'A slight sound and movement of deglutition announces the transition,' wrote W. Morton in 1880, 'and perhaps a little foam in the corner of the mouth.'[27]

Some of the more theatrical spectacles witnessed by visitors to Charcot's wards – such as the scenes of group catalepsy – seem almost certainly to have been the products of suggestion. In some other cases too it would appear that patients were reacting consciously or unconsciously to cues given to them by Charcot or his assistants. But, as Thornton has persuasively argued, the physiological reactions which were recorded by a number of trained medical observers suggest that, in some cases at least, the phenomena in question were real. In what Charcot dubbed 'the lethargic state' it was possible to observe a series of reactions which could never have originated through simulation or even suggestion. For by pressing on individual nerves it was possible to produce a lasting contraction of the corresponding muscle *including* muscles which were not subject to voluntary control. The contracture persisted after the pressure was removed and could only be released by stimulation of the opposing muscles. Robertson, writing in the *Journal of Mental Science* in 1892, weighed the evidence carefully and found it persuasive:

> One cannot help agreeing with Charcot, that here there was a very strange nervous state which could not possibly have been simulated, for

not only were the anatomy and physiology of the nerves unknown to these women, but contraction of muscles could be caused, which are, as a rule, more or less involuntary, such as the superior muscle of the ear ... I was impressed with the involuntary nature of the phenomenon.[28]

Charcot also claimed to be able to bring about in certain subjects a state of iron rigidity, completely unlike anything which could be produced by the voluntary stiffening of muscles. Freud himself witnessed one of Charcot's experiments in which the rigid body of a girl under hypnosis was placed on two chairs in such a way that she was supported only by her head and heels. In this particular case it is by no means clear that Charcot was exploiting a neurologically abnormal reaction, as Thornton suggests.[29] For the posture which Freud witnessed can be maintained for some time by people in a physiologically normal state. Freud, however, was deeply impressed. After watching this and other demonstrations, his regard for Charcot was strengthened further. 'I found to my astonishment,' he later reported, 'that here were occurrences plain before one's eyes, which it was quite impossible to doubt, but which were nevertheless strange enough not to be believed unless they were experienced at first hand.'[30]

It was not Charcot's experiments with hypnosis, however, which in themselves provided Freud with the key which he was looking for. For Charcot himself had initially been quite unable to offer any coherent explanation of the curious reactions he had produced. When he was asked to do so he habitually replied by saying that facts should come before theory. It was only around the time that Freud himself arrived in Paris that Charcot began to develop a theory of hysteria which attempted to offer a solution to the enigma of hypnosis. The catalyst which helped to produce this theoretical development was probably the establishment in 1882 of an outpatients' department at the Salpêtrière with wards for short-term patients. This brought Charcot into contact with an entirely new set of patients and he now began to encounter various seemingly 'hysterical' symptoms in patients, usually men, who had been involved in accidents or fights. This particular problem was a topical one mainly because of the number of accidents associated with the recent expansion of railway travel and the insurance claims against railway companies which had resulted. Since many cases of 'railway brain' and 'railway spine' were not associated with any visible physical injury some physicians had argued that convulsive fits, paralysis and anaesthesia – loss of bodily sensation – could be the product of psychological shock alone. In 1883 the English doctor Herbert Page went further in order to point out that the condition of *hemianaesthesia* (loss of sensation in one side of the body), was frequently encountered in these cases just as it was in hysteria itself. He concluded that the condition was therefore essentially hysterical. During the years 1883 and 1884 this view was supported by a number of American physicians.[31]

The question which was now raised was whether 'hysteria' might actually have a psychological cause. Charcot's own training tended to make him extremely resistant to such ideas. Like most forward-looking physicians at the end of the nineteenth century, his orientation was fundamentally organic and almost completely in tune with the revolutionary medical breakthroughs – such as the formulation of the germ theory of disease by Pasteur and Koch – which were taking place around him. But one development which took place around 1885 may have prompted him to reconsider this position. For it was at this time that Charcot was struck by the seemingly dramatic effect of therapeutically isolating women suffering from anorexia from their family and friends. Until this time Charcot had always believed, quite mistakenly, that anorexia nervosa was an organic nervous disease passed on by heredity. The effectiveness of therapeutic isolation, however, suggested that anorexia could be cured by influencing the mind, and that perhaps it was itself a 'psychical' illness.[32]

This development may have encouraged Charcot to adopt a psychological perspective when he came to consider the symptoms suffered by some of the men he was treating for traumatic hysteria. In these cases, although the patients might have fallen from a considerable height, or struck their heads, there was often no sign of physical injury. In seeking to explain the paralyses and convulsive fits which subsequently developed Charcot apparently began to take seriously a curious medical paper by the British physician, J. Russell Reynolds, which had appeared in the *British Medical Journal* in 1869. Reynolds had argued that in certain cases the paralysis of a limb could be produced merely by the patient's continual contemplation of the *idea* of paralysis. Applying the same kind of reasoning to some of his own cases, Charcot gradually developed the view that in these cases too the paralyses of his patients had been caused not by their real accident, but by the idea which they had formed of the accident.

The great advantage of this explanation from Charcot's point of view was that it could simultaneously be invoked as a solution to his other most pressing scientific problem – that posed by the phenomena associated with hypnosis. For here too it might be claimed that physical changes in the body were brought about by suggestion or by the influence of ideas. Charcot, indeed, almost immediately worked out this combined explanation of hypnotism and hysteria in great detail. In the state of hypnosis, he argued, it was possible to bring forth by suggestion or by intimation

> an idea, or a coherent group of associated ideas, which become lodged in the mind in the manner of a parasite, remaining isolated from all the rest and interpreted outwardly by the corresponding motor phenomena. If such is the case one can conceive that an inculcated *idea of paralysis, being of this type, results in an actual* paralysis; and we shall see that in such cases it will frequently appear with as distinct clinical characteristics as a destructive lesion of the cerebral substance.[33]

In Charcot's view an idea could only be translated into a bodily symptom if it was isolated from ordinary consciousness. He suggested that this was precisely what happened both in hypnosis and in traumatic hysteria. For both hypnotism and the nervous shock produced by a trauma led, in Charcot's view, to an 'annihilation of the *ego*'. This enabled a particular idea or complex of ideas to become lodged in a part of the brain where they would not be challenged or worked against by conscious cerebration. In this way the idea 'would be removed from every influence, be strengthened, and finally become powerful enough to realise itself objectively through a paralysis.'[34]

No sooner had Charcot formulated this completely speculative solution to his two major scientific problems than he began to treat it as if it were an established scientific fact, claiming that it was being resisted only because of a reluctance to believe that men, no less than women, could succumb to hysteria. 'That a vigorous artisan,' he wrote, 'well built, not enervated by high culture, the stoker of an engine for example, not previously emotional, at least to all appearance, should, after an accident to the train, by a collision or running off the rails, become hysterical for the same reason as a woman, is what surpasses our imagination.'[35] Charcot went on to argue that, just as hysteria 'simulated' the convulsive fits associated with epilepsy, so cases of 'hysterical trauma' simulated the kinds of paralysis which were otherwise associated with organic lesions of the brain. Charcot did not abandon his fundamentally organic conception of hysteria. For he still saw it as a hereditary disease of the nervous system. In his new theory, however, hysteria was seen as a nervous weakness which could remain latent, and whose overt symptoms were sometimes only triggered by traumatic accidents and the ideas which patients formed of these accidents. In terms which captivated Freud and which would later shape the whole evolution not simply of psychoanalysis but of modern psychiatry as a whole, he talked of 'those remarkable paralyses, paralyses depending on an idea, paralyses by imagination'. He went on to stress that the phrase 'paralyses by imagination' did not mean 'imaginary paralyses' since 'these motor paralyses of psychical origin are as objectively real as those depending on an organic lesion; they simulate them, as you will see, by a number of identical clinical characters, which render their diagnosis very difficult.'[36]

In order to offer experimental 'proof' of what might otherwise seem a highly improbable contention, Charcot had recourse once again to demonstrations undertaken with hysterical patients who had been hypnotised. Having produced an example of a male patient who was suffering from a particular form of paralysis as the result of an accident he would then usher in one of his own hysterical patients, hypnotise her, and, by means of a light tap on her arm or leg, produce exactly the same kind of paralysis in her. Although this paralysis was apparently produced by a purely *physical* stimulus Charcot avoided the implications of this by arguing that this kind of 'slight traumatism' sufficed to produce 'a sense of numbness . . . and a slight indication of paralysis'. This physical indication of paralysis was then supposedly translated into an idea of paralysis and the idea was in turn 'realised' as an actual paralysis.[37]

By this extraordinary chain of reasoning in which layers of conjecture were laid one upon the other in an inverted pyramid of speculation which was quite unlike his earlier theorising, Charcot seems to have convinced himself that he had actually discovered the invisible 'dynamic' lesion whose existence he had postulated. This 'lesion' had no discernible physical form but consisted in effect in a process of unconscious symptom-formation. Freud, who by a curious historical coincidence virtually witnessed the birth of Charcot's 'discovery', received it with uncritical enthusiasm. To use his own remarkable words: '[Charcot] succeeded *in proving, by an unbroken chain of argument* that these paralyses were the result of ideas which had dominated the patient's brain at moments of a special disposition' (italics added).[38] Ideas could themselves, Charcot appeared to be saying, produce bodily changes.

It was this view, seemingly so profoundly subversive of all medical orthodoxy, which struck Freud with the force of a revelation. His attitude towards Charcot's theoretical solution to the problems of hysteria and hypnosis was profoundly conditioned by the deep admiration he had already conceived for him. For it would seem that even before he had imparted his discovery, Freud had already been seduced by the aura of the great man. Only a month or so after he had arrived in Paris Freud had written to Martha of the inner revolution he felt he was undergoing:

> I think I am changing a great deal. Charcot, who is one of the greatest physicians and a man whose common sense borders on genius, is simply wrecking all my aims and opinions. I sometimes come out of his lectures as from out of Notre Dame, with an entirely new idea about perfection . . . Whether the seed will ever bear fruit, I don't know; but what I do know is that no other human being has ever affected me in the same way.[39]

What is perhaps most significant in Freud's words is the way they show his readiness, even at this late stage of his life, to idealise his teachers. Although, as we have seen, Freud himself had been cast in the role of the great man by his parents, it would seem that his continuing intellectual insecurity compelled him to project his own world-redeeming 'messianic' identity onto others and to attribute to them the kind of inhuman greatness he yearned for himself. Brücke and Meynert had already been the recipients of such vast projections. Soon, in the most extraordinary episode in Freud's intellectual development, Wilhelm Fliess would receive similar projections. For the moment, however, it was the turn of Charcot.

We may note that Freud's compulsion to idealise his teachers is so extreme that he comes very near to identifying Charcot the man with the sublime architecture of Notre Dame. This was not the first time that Freud had used such a comparison. Only a few years earlier he had described his colleague Ernest von Fleischl-Marxow, whose intellectual talents he had always admired, as his 'ideal' and had gone on to compare him to a sublime work of architecture: 'I admire and love him with an intellectual passion . . . His destruction would move me as the destruction of a sacred and famous temple would have affected an ancient Greek. I love him not so much as a human being but as one of Creation's precious achievements.'[40]

The tone of these words is that of the diminutive disciple awed by the majesty of his intellectual hero. So great is his sense of awe that he cannot conceive of the object of his idealisation as simply another human being; the hero must be pushed upwards into a superhuman realm and imagined as a god or – as in this case – as sublime architecture. The danger of allowing any intellectual relationship to be coloured by this kind of religious awe is that it implies an attitude of intellectual submission. The god is almost always exempted from the kind of criticism which might be directed against a mere human. In the case of Freud's relationship to Charcot there seems to have been just such a suspension of critical faculties. The possibility that Charcot might be both mortal and mistaken simply does not seem to have occurred to Freud. Instead, deferring to Charcot's scientific authority and taking his insights on trust, Freud would spend the next few years using these insights in order to develop his own theory of hysteria.

THREE

Charcot's Mistake

ONE OF THE MOST INTRIGUING aspects of the history of psychoanalysis is the fact that Freud, following Charcot, worked out some of his most significant concepts in relation to a medical condition which Charcot had termed 'the great neurosis', but which is now rarely encountered. This curious fact has been noted somewhat casually by a number of scholars. Frank Sulloway, for example, mentions what he calls 'the mysterious clinical diminution of hysteria in the course of the twentieth century' and says that it is a disease 'many present-day neurological specialists see only once or twice in a lifetime of medical practice'. More recently Anthony Storr has observed that 'the type of case on which early psychoanalytic theory was originally based, namely, severe conversion hysteria in women, is seldom seen today.'[1] In France Jacques Lacan has noted the same mysterious phenomenon. 'Where have they all gone, the hysterics of yesteryear,' he asked in 1977, 'those extraordinary women, the Anna O.s, the Emmy von N.s? What now has come to replace the hysterical symptoms of a bygone age?' The historian Etienne Trillat expresses a very similar sentiment. 'Hysteria is dead: that is certain,' he writes in his *Histoire de l'hystérie*, 'and it has taken its secrets with it to the grave.'[2]

Amidst their various expressions of surprise and puzzlement, however, none of these writers offers any satisfactory answer to the obvious question: why did a disease which was apparently prevalent not simply in the time of Freud but for centuries previously, suddenly become a great deal less common?

The phenomenon of the 'disappearing disease' is not unknown in the history of medicine. Some diseases – such as smallpox or tuberculosis – diminish for the very simple reason that conditions of hygiene improve or effective antidotes are found. Other diseases disappear because their very existence was the result of a medical misunderstanding – a failure to define a disease-syndrome accurately. When a

71

primitive misdiagnosis is replaced by a more scientific understanding the old medical label gradually falls into disuse with the result that an entire disease may appear to have vanished into medical limbo. One common mistake of this kind springs from a failure to define the boundaries of a disease-entity correctly – the most common tendency being that of identifying as individual afflictions what are in reality but different branches of the same disease tree. A classic mistake of this kind was finally corrected only in 1905 when the German zoologist Fritz Schaudinn discovered the specific microbe of syphilis. Only then did medical science finally recognise that a strangely assorted set of afflictions involving the heart, the nervous system and the aorta were actually different manifestations of the same condition.[3]

There are very good reasons for suggesting that the mysterious diminution in cases of hysteria which has taken place during the present century is due to a similar advance in knowledge. If this is indeed so then Freud, far from building on Charcot's 'scientific' understanding of hysteria, was actually the victim of one of the most significant mis-understandings in the entire history of medicine.

One reason for making this suggestion is provided by the way in which Charcot himself developed his concept of hysteria. For during the 1880s – around the time Freud was in Paris – Charcot had become so confident of his diagnostic powers, and so captivated by the whole concept of hysteria that the term became an elastic one. Before very long it was being required to accommodate and explain a bewildering variety of symptoms. Not only did Charcot apply it to convulsive fits, contractures and paralyses, but he and his followers also concluded that hysteria could produce haemorrhages, lesions in the skin, vesicles, ulceration, superficial gangrene, and fever. Charcot himself was responsible for many of these diagnoses. He even gave the name of 'blue oedema' to a circulatory disorder which he attributed to hysteria. In view of these extraordinary diagnoses it is perhaps not surprising that one of Charcot's more sceptical colleagues, Professor Chaufford, was moved to confess in 1912 that 'we too, under the influence of Charcot, went through a period of hysteria.'[4]

If Chaufford's scepticism represented the prevailing attitude towards Charcot's research, little further analysis would be necessary. Yet resist-ance to the various criticisms of Charcot which have been made since his death runs deep. It is true that the idea that some of Charcot's patients were carefully 'trained' by his assistants to 'act out' particular sequences of symptoms has gained some currency. But much more fundamental objections to Charcot's work on 'hysteria' have been almost completely overlooked. Some practising neurologists and physicians still seem to regard Charcot as a scientist of unalloyed genius, and this view of Freud's most significant mentor has coloured even the most critical accounts of psychoanalysis.

The most serious flaws in Charcot's approach can best be seen if we consider the problem of 'hysterical paralysis', Charcot's elucidation of which so impressed Freud. Although none of Freud's main biographers has ever remarked upon the fact, the most striking feature of Charcot's diagnosis of these cases from today's vantage-point is its almost complete implausibility. For if a man who has been involved in a railway accident, or who has fallen from scaffolding, subsequently develops paralysis or weakness of a limb, or of one side of his body, it is most unlikely that this is due to the emotional shock he has suffered. It is much more probable that there has been an injury either to the spine, or to the cortex of the brain – in the form of what doctors would now call a 'closed head injury'. Such injuries, caused by a severe but blunt impact on the skull, frequently leave no external scar. But, as a result of the impact, the soft tissue of the brain is forced against the inside of the skull, giving rise to bleeding, bruising, scarring or clotting. These invisible internal injuries can be the cause of paralysis or, indeed, of epileptic fits, which follow in about a tenth of the cases. The brain lesions which give rise to the symptoms of closed head injury, however, are often so minute that the crude methods of microscopic investigation used by Charcot would not have been able to detect them during post mortem examinations. Only the subsequent development of new techniques of microscopic staining and of brain-imaging has rendered these lesions observable and it is only in the latter part of the twentieth century that the immensely complex pathology of head injuries has been mapped in any detail. Having no access to modern investigatory techniques, nineteenth-century physicians were for the most part obliged to construct the pathology of head injuries by a process of speculative induction. Such a process of inductive reasoning led many physicians to an imperfect understanding of some aspects of intracranial pathology. But the crudity of the investigatory techniques which were then available, combined with an understanding of neurology which was flawed or misleading, meant that a number of crucial pathological processes remained veiled in almost complete mystery. In these circumstances Charcot's claim that convulsive seizures or certain kinds of paralysis might be caused by a parasitical idea which had lodged and incubated in an unconscious portion of the mind could not be clearly refuted and seemed to some physicians, Freud among them, entirely plausible.

One of the reasons that Charcot's diagnosis of 'traumatic hysteria' has not been questioned more often and more radically is that relatively few of the scholars who have written about his relationship to Freud appear to have taken the trouble to go back to Charcot's original case histories. Where they have done so they have frequently read these case histories through psychogenic eyes informed by little or no knowledge of pathological medicine. As a result their own attempts to summarise them have sometimes been selective and misleading. An extreme example of this process of distortion is provided by the American historian Mark Micale, who has written more extensively about Charcot and the history of hysteria than almost any other modern scholar. In his most recent work Micale has made many valuable contributions to the history of hysteria. Some of his early work, however, illustrates how difficult it has been for modern scholars to free themselves from the tyranny of misconceptions about medicine which were propagated by Charcot and Freud. In his article 'Charcot and the Idea of Hysteria in the Male', Micale discusses the case of 'Le Log–', a twenty-nine-year-old florist's delivery man who came under Charcot's care after an accident which took place in October 1885. The case of Le Log– is in many respects the *locus classicus* of Charcot's theories about traumatic hysteria since it is in the course of relating it that he works out his theories about psychological causation in the greatest detail. Micale summarises the medical aspects of the case in the following terms:

> While crossing the Pont des Invalides with a wheelbarrow one afternoon, 'Le Log' was sideswiped by a passing horsedrawn carriage. The man sustained only minor physical injuries but lost consciousness momentarily. When he appeared at the Salpêtrière several days after the accident, 'Le Log' presented an eccentric panoply of symptoms, including headaches, trembling hands, amnesiac episodes, hypersensitivity of the scalp, and complete tactile and thermal anaesthesias in the lower half of his body except for his toes.[5]

From this summary the non-physician might well conclude that Le Log– suffered a trivial injury and then subsequently developed a series of symptoms which, since they are dismissed as an 'eccentric panoply', are not explicable in medical terms. Yet if we turn to the original account, an entirely different picture emerges. Far from losing consciousness only 'momentarily', Le Log–, after having been thrown down violently onto the pavement, showed no signs of recovery, and was picked up *'absolutely unconscious'*. According to Charcot's own account,

> Le Log– was placed upon his own barrow and was taken in the first place to a chemist's shop, where he remained for about twenty minutes, and was then carried *still unconscious*, to the Beaujon Hospital . . . *where he remained during five or six days without consciousness* [italics added].

Le Log– himself maintained that he had 'struck his head violently upon the ground'. Although Charcot dismissed this as the product of confusion, the course of Le Log–'s subsequent illness was entirely consistent with his claim. For, after being sent home from the Beaujon hospital, Le Log–'s convalescence was interrupted by severe nose-bleeds which could only be stopped by plugging his nose. He eventually suffered a violent seizure, preceded 'by a sensation of a ball rising in his throat'. During the seizure he lost consciousness and was taken on a stretcher to a second hospital, the Hôtel Dieu. He stayed in this hospital for a total of two months and during the first week was in a state of continual coma. After coming out of this coma he was unable to speak for two days. He suffered from frequent severe nose-bleeds and the lower extremities of his body gradually became almost completely paralysed. Far from appearing at the Salpêtrière 'several days after the accident', as Micale writes, Le Log– was transferred to Charcot's hospital in March 1886 – almost exactly six months after the accident happened. On admission his memory and intelligence were 'considerably affected' and he stated that 'at night-time he has flames before his eyes, and terrifying dreams, and all the while beating in the temples and dizziness in the ears.' The left-hand side of his mouth was partly open due to a spasm of the muscles on the left side of the face which was accompanied by a twitching or tremor of the corner of the mouth. Throughout most of this period Le Log– suffered from 'a permanent headache of a constrictive character, producing the sensation of a heavy helmet pressing all parts of the head'.

Micale's bizarre, partial, and completely inaccurate summary of the case is an extreme example of what can happen when complex medical case histories are related from a purely psychogenic point of view. In the case of most Freud scholars we are not even offered a distorted account of Le Log–'s illness; the sin of distortion is replaced by the sin of omission and few medical details are given of any of Charcot's cases. When the full story of Le Log–'s physical symptoms is told, however, and separated out from Charcot's own diagnostic interpolations, the entire case is one which, rather than being a classic example of psychogenesis, is saturated in organicity. Most modern physicians would unhesitatingly recognise in Le Log–'s story a severe case of closed head injury. The long period of unconsciousness would itself be construed not as an indication of emotional trauma but as a sign of the severity of the intracranial injury. This would in turn suggest the likelihood of late epilepsy developing. This evidently happened in the case of Le Log–, and the exceptionally severe seizure he suffered appears to have resulted in further brain damage. The profuse nosebleeds, for which Charcot's psychogenic pathology offers no explanation, would merely confirm the picture, as would the facial spasm and the various other neurological signs which Charcot describes – including the terrifying dreams, the flames before the eyes and the noises in the ear, which are forms of hallucination often associated with epileptic events.

Far from being a clear case of hysteria as Charcot claimed, Le Log–'s illness is entirely consistent with a head injury resulting in lesions or even a basal fracture of the skull. His symptoms, which Micale dismisses as an 'eccentric panoply', would be recognised by most modern physicians as those of brain damage, epilepsy and raised intracranial pressure.[6]*

Not all Charcot's cases of 'traumatic hysteria' present such clear diagnostic errors as that of Le Log–. In a number of cases he appears to have ingeniously sought out trivial accidents which coincidentally preceded attacks of 'spontaneous' epilepsy and then argued that the psychological shock had been responsible for triggering a 'hysterical' attack. Many of Charcot's cases of traumatic hysteria, however, including some of the earlier ones which impressed Freud, follow the same pattern we see in the case of Le Log–. He thus frequently explained cases of organic, neurologically determined paralysis as 'hysterical paralysis' and habitually interpreted the epileptic seizures which sometimes follow head injuries as signs of full-blown 'traumatic hysteria'. Charcot, for instance, describes the case of a baker's apprentice who

---

* For a more detailed analysis of Le Log–'s illness and his subsequent partial recovery, see note 6.

started having fits fifteen days after an attack in the street in which he was knocked unconscious. 'The attack,' he wrote, 'whether spontaneous or provoked, is always preceded by an aura: iliac pain at the level of the hysterogenic point, a sensation as of a ball rising from the epigastrium up to the throat, buzzing sound in the ears, and beating of the temples. The attack commences; the eyes are turned upwards in their sockets, the arms become stiff and extended, and the patient, if standing, falls to the ground with complete loss of consciousness.'[7] Although modern neurologists would, almost without exception, assume that the case described here was one of focal epilepsy, following focal brain damage, Charcot used this case, as he did later the case of Le Log–, in an attempt to substantiate his own theory of unconscious symptom-formation and 'traumatic hysteria'.

So simple is it to identify Charcot's most glaring medical mistake that it seems surprising that none of Freud's major biographers – Ernest Jones, Henri Ellenberger, Ronald Clark, Frank Sulloway or Peter Gay – so much as hints at the possibility that perhaps the most significant of all his medical mentors was fundamentally mistaken.[8] The credit for first formulating the argument which I have developed here goes once again to one of Freud's most interesting critics – E. M. Thornton. Not only does she argue that Charcot diagnosed cases of closed head injury as hysterical, she also contends that Charcot's entire concept of hysteria was based on a medical misunderstanding. What she suggests, in effect, is that behind this misunderstanding there lay the long failure of medical scientists to recognise that epilepsy was not a discrete phenomenon with a constant pathology and symptomatology, but a cluster of related disorders of the brain which might manifest themselves in a variety of quite different seizure patterns.

It would, in fact, be misleading to give to modern neurologists the whole credit for making this recognition. One of the most interesting early insights into the diversity of epileptic phenomena was made by Bernard of Gordon in the fourteenth century:

> Sometimes the paroxysm is very long and violent, sometimes short. I have often seen it so short that the patient had only to lean against a wall or the like, rub his face and it ceased. Sometimes he did not need a support, but there came to him a dizziness in the head, and blindness in the eyes, and he himself, sensing it, recited the Hail Mary, and before he finished it, the paroxysm had passed off, and he spat once and the whole thing passed off, and it used to come often during the day. There are some who after a paroxysm remember absolutely nothing about the

attack, nor their affliction, and there are some who remember and feel ashamed.[9]

Bernard's clinical acumen, however, was the exception rather than the rule, and it was not until the latter part of the nineteenth century that knowledge about different forms of epilepsy began to be systematically accumulated. Between 1861 and 1902 the British neurologist John Hughlings Jackson pioneered the clinical investigation of epilepsy. He rejected talk of 'genuine epilepsy' and in 1879 made the crucial observation that

> there are numerous epilepsies, under the definition that any epilepsy is, on its anatomical side, a 'discharging lesion' of some region of the *cortex cerebri*. The kind of paroxysm differs according to the particular region of the cortex affected; and since many regions, if not any region, of it may be affected, the number of different epilepsies, scientifically regarded, is great.[10]

Whereas previously the term epilepsy tended to be applied to generalised seizures which originated in the central core of the brain, involved the whole body in convulsions, and suddenly caused the patient to fall down unconscious, Hughlings Jackson described other forms of epileptic fit which were not so serious but which could lead to convulsive fits, automatic movements, rigid contractures or episodes of 'dazed' behaviour. These 'focal attacks' originated in a particular area of the cortex and only subsequently spread to the rest of the brain. Depending on the part of the brain in which they originated they would give rise to a sequence of sensations which began in a particular part of the body and then sometimes travelled through other parts of the body, becoming progressively more generalised.

Before the discovery of cerebral localisation it was assumed that every painful sensation which was experienced as being located in a particular part of the human body was actually a sign of a disorder in that part of the body. Thus, if a convulsive fit apparently originated in a patient's right leg, it was assumed to be a disease of the leg, and in certain cases the entire limb might be amputated in an attempt to cure the disease. More significantly still, it was assumed that, because the classical 'hysterical' fit was experienced subjectively as originating in the area of the womb and then rising upwards through the body, then it was actually a disorder of the womb. This ancient theory was still held by many medical practitioners in the nineteenth century and, with the advent of new anaesthetic techniques, many women were subjected to quite unnecessary operations to remove their ovaries and their wombs.

The close observation of focal epileptic fits, of the kind pioneered by Hughlings Jackson, would eventually lead to another quite different explanation of these phenomena – namely that the sensations located by the patient in different parts of their body were actually produced by epileptic discharges in the corresponding areas of the brain. Charcot himself was familiar with Jackson's work and it was he who introduced the term 'Jacksonian fit' to refer to a pattern of gradually spreading convulsions (which might, for example, begin with twitching in a hand, then spread to arm, face and then down to leg and foot). But Hughlings Jackson himself was unable to solve the problem of the more complex fits originating in the temporal lobes, with their strange, seemingly psychical symptoms, and their unusual premonitory aura. Indeed, Charcot's own massive authority, and his insistence that such fits were 'hysterical' made it virtually impossible for neurologists of the time to 'see' temporal lobe epilepsy at all. Only in the 1940s, after the introduction of the electroencephalogram, was temporal lobe epilepsy finally defined.

Because of the connections between the temporal lobes and the 'visceral brain', the 'aura' which ushers in the seizure often begins in the abdomen – or even the vagina – and travels upwards.[11] To make clear the relevance of this fact to Charcot's researches into hysteria, Thornton quotes Charcot's own description of the aura which preceded the 'hysterical' fit of one of his patients:

> These sensations, springing from the ovarian region, successively attain: Firstly the epigastrium; secondly the neck or throat – manifesting themselves in these regions by a more or less considerable oppression, the well known sensation of a ball or globe (*globus hystericus*); thirdly the head, where the irradiation is characterised by buzzing and whistling in the left ear, by cephalgia with throbbings, which the patient compares to so many hammer-strokes on the left temple, and finally to an obnubilation of sight in the corresponding eye.[12]

This description corresponds closely to the classical hysterical aura which had been described by physicians for many centuries, and Charcot himself always treated the presence of such an aura as a sign that any subsequent convulsions were *not* epileptic. Alongside Charcot's description of a 'hysterical' aura, however, Thornton sets a description of a temporal lobe aura written in 1954 by the distinguished neurosurgeon Murray Falconer:

> A very common [aura] is an epigastric sensation which may be likened to 'the stomach turning over' or some similar feeling. Sometimes the sensation may be situated instead in the lower chest or even in the umbilical and rectal regions. A common sequence, however, is for the epigastric sensation to rise up quickly to the throat where a choking feeling ensues.[13]

As Thornton notes in her earlier study, *Hypnosis, Hysteria and Epilepsy*, other neurologists have confirmed the prevalence of the visceral aura in temporal lobe epilepsy. Henner, for example, describes the aura in terms which are almost identical to the old accounts of the hysterical fit. The patient experiences a feeling of constriction in the epigastrium, he writes, often accompanied by anxiety:

> This spasmodic sensation travels upwards through the thorax, into the throat and is then followed by unconsciousness or by psychomotor automatism. The symptoms described by the patients correspond exactly with Charcot's *boule hystérique* or *globus hystericus*.

Henner himself goes on to suggest that one of the tasks of modern neurology should be to correct traditional interpretations of *globus hystericus*, 'for I presume that in these cases one is nearly always dealing with an epileptic seizure.'[14]

In view of these arguments it is difficult to resist the conclusion that, in those cases where they were not simulated (as may sometimes have been the case), the 'hysterical' fits of Charcot's patients were not caused by emotional traumas or by unconscious ideas. Like the other fits which had been misdiagnosed as 'hysterical' throughout the centuries, they were epileptic seizures caused by minute lesions of the brain which, even if any case had come to autopsy, would not have been discernible by Charcot's relatively primitive laboratory techniques.

The fact that Charcot was apparently able to induce abnormal states in his 'hysterical' patients by hypnotising them, is, Thornton suggests, far from being at odds with this view. For hypnotism is not a mystical or magical process. It can take a number of forms and medical science has as yet no completely adequate explanation for hypnotic trances in which EEG readings remain normal. Thornton suggests, however, that the particular form of 'hypnosis' used by Charcot was itself an essentially neurological phenomenon. It worked by exploiting the fact that epileptic states can be reflexly precipitated in subjects who are already organically predisposed to them by a number of sensory stimuli. Fits can be precipitated, for example, by the stroboscopic effect of rapidly flashing lights, by loud rhythmical noises, sudden sounds or even by touching or stroking the body. It is Thornton's contention that the paralyses, contractures and other abnormal states which Charcot succeeded in producing in his patients through hypnosis were not caused by ideas, any more than those which took place spontaneously without hypnosis. They too were caused by organic factors which Charcot and his contemporaries had been unable to observe because of the limitations of their investigatory techniques.

The argument put forward by E. M. Thornton, which I have very briefly summarised here, offers an intriguing solution to the enigma of Charcot's later research. The explanation which she offers of Charcot's experiments in hypnosis is a particularly interesting one. These experiments were frequently attacked in Charcot's own lifetime, most notably by Hippolyte Bernheim, Professor of Medicine at the University of Nancy. Bernheim had himself learnt a technique of hypnotism from a charismatic country doctor, Auguste Liébeault. He believed that hypnosis was a purely psychological state. It brought about a heightened state of suggestibility which he defined as 'the aptitude to transform an idea into an act'. Shortly after Charcot read a paper about hypnotism to the Académie des Sciences in 1882 in which he presented it as a *physiological* phenomenon, Bernheim revealed the existence of Liébeault's work and soon afterwards embarked on a bitter struggle against Charcot in an attempt to prove that hypnotism itself was nothing more than an effect of suggestion. Bernheim pursued his campaign against Charcot's ideas with such zeal that, by the time Charcot died in 1893, his opponent had effectively carried the day.

Because of Bernheim's persistence it is common to encounter attempts to explain away all of Charcot's research into hypnotism as a delusion. Pierre Marie has described how Charcot's assistants would often pre-hypnotise patients for him before his morning lectures:

Thus the patients passed from hand to hand during the morning; in the afternoon the interns, and frequently as well the externs, begged by their colleagues from other hospitals or by friends, would again repeat once or several times the experiments from the morning, without thinking anything of it. The result of all these attempts is easy to imagine: at Charcot's behest a series of suggestions were produced in these patients, unconsciously resulting in actual coaching [*un véritable dressage*] of which Charcot was entirely unaware. In consequence, all of his research on hypnotism was vitiated from the beginning.[15]

In view of the fact that Marie worked closely with Charcot there is undoubtedly some truth in the account he gives. But it seems reasonably clear that the story of Charcot's research is much more complex than Marie's version allows. Credulous believers in the power of the mind over the body were evidently prepared to take seriously Bernheim's attempts to use hypnotism in an attempt to cure pneumonia, emphysema, and cirrhosis of the liver. Once it was conceded that the mind might have such unlimited powers then any conceivable physiological phenomenon could be 'explained' by invoking the power of unconscious suggestion. Some of Charcot's clinical habits support the view that the Salpêtrière became at times a hothouse of unconscious suggestion in which physicians unwittingly planted ideas in the minds of their patients, who then exhibited the very symptoms or behaviour which elicited the greatest medical attention. But precisely because 'suggestion' could be invoked to provide an explanation of everything, the idea has frequently been overused. As the case of Le Log– demonstrates, many of the physiological reactions of Charcot's patients were quite genuine. It is also significant that some of those who observed the kinds of hypnosis produced both by Charcot and by Bernheim noted a marked difference. In Bernheim's subjects physical signs that hypnosis had been induced, such as slight muscular spasms, were notable by their absence. The neuromuscular hyperexcitability which was revealed in Charcot's experiments was not observed at Nancy and the catalepsy which Bernheim claimed to be able to produce by suggestion was not like true catalepsy; according to one observer it 'was much more like voluntary posturing'.[16]

The great advantage of Thornton's solution to the enigma of Charcot's research is that it *does* offer an explanation of a number of the strange-seeming phenomena produced by Charcot's experiments, as well as accounting for the presence of the spasms, twitches and other focal neurological signs which, as we have seen, marked the induction of hypnosis in Charcot's subjects. On this latter subject Thornton quotes Hughlings Jackson to the effect that a 'dreamy state', which he himself compares to somnambulism, could often be brought about by a minor epileptic fit and was actually a *post*-seizure phenomenon. Sometimes this fit could be so slight that its symptoms were scarcely noticed:

> We may occasionally be consulted because a person suddenly acts strangely, violently, or passes into a state which resembles somnambulism, and nothing will be volunteered as to epileptic attacks. Unless we have very carefully studied the phenomena of very slight seizures of epilepsy we shall misinterpret these cases; we shall dwell with exaggeration on the striking, and neglect the essential; the thing is to ferret out the quasi-trifling signs of a transitory fit.[17]

The signs which Jackson went on to enumerate were transient pallor, movements of mastication, and turning up of the eyes. Elsewhere in his writings, as Thornton observes, Jackson describes other signs, including the fixed, vacant stare, slight spasms of face, hand or eyes, spasm of the glottis, ejaculation of saliva and rapid blinking. As we have already seen, just such signs were frequently observed at the Salpêtrière at the moment that Charcot's subjects entered into the hypnotic state, and one contemporary observer actually commented that certain signs suggested 'the faintest possible approach to an epileptoid seizure'.[18] Thornton also notes that the state of catalepsy, or 'waxy rigidity' which Charcot frequently induced in his patients by what he termed 'hypnotism' is a distinct *physical* state, and that W. G. Lennox, one of the foremost twentieth-century experts on epilepsy, subsumed catalepsy under the 'akinetic seizures' of temporal lobe epilepsy.[19] In Thornton's view, 'the key to the understanding of Charcot's work both in hypnotism and hysteria is to regard them as two different faces of temporal lobe epilepsy, both representing seizurcs of the different types found in this condition.'[20]

Thornton's theoretical model of Charcot's research is not complete and some elements of it may need to be refined or revised. But precisely because it possesses genuine explanatory power, and is able to locate within the framework of modern neurological knowledge a number of otherwise inexplicable phenomena, it should, I believe, be recognised as one of the most important of all the contributions which have been made to the pre-history of psychoanalysis.

This argument should certainly not be taken to imply that all cases which have been diagnosed as 'hysterical' throughout the centuries necessarily have organic rather than emotional causes. There can be no doubt that there are and always have been cases where patients have consciously or unconsciously simulated convulsive fits in order to gain care and attention. It also seems clear that some patients genuinely mistake imaginary symptoms for real ones and claim to be ill without any deliberate attempt to deceive. Just as importantly, any non-dualistic account of the human organism is bound to recognise that all emotional experiences are actually *physiological* events and can therefore sometimes give rise to a limited range of physical symptoms. But Thornton's argument does explain the 'mysterious diminution' in cases of hysteria during the twentieth century. Indeed it would seem quite reasonable to suggest that, if the relevant clinical, psychological and pathological evidence were available to us, all of Charcot's presumed hysterics could be explained without having recourse to Charcot's own highly specific and completely conjectural model of 'hysteria'. To the extent that extreme 'conversion hysteria' has disappeared, it has done so largely because Charcot's mistaken diagnosis of 'hysteria' has been replaced by accurate diagnoses of a range of neurological disorders unrecognised in Charcot's own time.[21]

This argument does not in itself, of course, invalidate psychoanalysis. But it does effectively sweep away the particular ground upon which Freud was to construct his first proto-psychoanalytic theories of hysteria. Yet Thornton's arguments have been almost completely ignored not only by the psychoanalytic establishment, but also by the vast majority of Freud scholars. One reason may well be that Thornton herself tends to claim too much for them, situating them in a polemic which seems at times to be hostile not simply to psychoanalysis but to almost all forms of psychological explanation. Ironically her own explanatory style sometimes resembles that of Freud himself in that she tends to favour single-factor solutions to problems when more complex and diverse explanations seem to be required. In many cases it seems highly probable that Charcot failed to recognise the symptoms of temporal lobe epilepsy and used them to bolster his own theories of hysteria. This suggestion, indeed, was made quite independently, long before E. M. Thornton incorporated it into her critique of psychoanalysis. She herself quotes the words not only of Henner, but also of the French neurologist Henri Gastaut. Writing in 1954, he claimed that: 'It is now an established fact, well-recognised by a large-number of epileptologists, that the "hystero-epileptics" of the last century almost certainly consisted of patients with lesions in the perifalciform region, the hippocampal gyrus or the inferior surface of the temporal lobe.'[22] In view of the state of neurological knowledge at the end of the nineteenth century, this kind of mistake was all but inevitable. But there were also countless other organic conditions which Charcot and his contemporaries were either unaware of or did not fully understand. Many obscure neurological syndromes long thought to be 'hysterical' or psychogenic have been recognised as having an organic basis only in the latter part of the twentieth century. At the same time the diagnostic poverty of medical science at the end of the nineteenth century meant that ante mortem diagnosis of many common diseases was difficult or uncertain. It was impossible, for example, to discriminate reliably between paralysis caused by multiple sclerosis and other forms of paralysis. Only in 1896, with Joseph Babinski's discovery of the 'cutaneous plantar reflex' and his recognition that an upward-turning toe indicated the presence of an upper-motor neurone lesion, did it become easier to make a reliable diagnosis of multiple sclerosis. Edward Shorter is almost certainly right when, noting this fact, he observes that 'hysteria was vastly overdiagnosed in the past, as many young women with that diagnosis probably had multiple sclerosis.' More recently Mark Micale, in what is by far the most valuable of all his discussions of hysteria, has pointed out how large a role was played in nineteenth-century medicine by the failure to recognise some of the more complex symptoms of syphilis. As soon as the aetiology and course of syphilis began to be understood in the twentieth century it rapidly became known as 'the disease which has everything' or, just as hysteria once had been, as 'the great imitator'. Since the symptoms of syphilis include epileptic seizures, double-vision and loss of pain sensation in scattered areas of the body there can be little doubt that, as Micale suggests, a significant number of supposed 'hysterics' were actually suffering from syphilis at a time when this disease was epidemic in urban Europe.[23]

If E. M. Thornton's argument is modified by taking such factors into consideration, however, it can scarcely be said that it is undermined as a result. Indeed it is very considerably strengthened. Evidence which has become available since has further reinforced her position. In the same year that Thornton's book first appeared a clinical paper was published in the journal *Neurology*. In this paper R. P. Lesser and his colleagues presented the case of a man with a history of alcoholism and depression who began to have recurrent seizures at the age of fifty-eight. For some time these fits appeared to respond to anticonvulsant drugs, but they eventually began again. The seizures consisted in a feeling of weakness or numbness that lasted for about a minute. The numbness mainly affected the left shoulder, arm, and leg, but sometimes involved the right leg and occasionally spread to the rectal area. Brain scans revealed some mild abnormalities but nothing which satisfactorily explained the fits. The patient was therefore treated as if the fits were hysterical. Anti-convulsant medicine was stopped and the diagnosis of hysteria appeared to be confirmed when two subsequent EEGs were normal. At this point an attempt was made to induce one of these spells by suggestion. A minute after this procedure had begun the man had a typical seizure. This seizure, however, was accompanied by an abnormal EEG reading over the left temporal lobe. Seven more seizures then occurred spontaneously, all accompanied by the same abnormal EEG reading. Anti-convulsant medication was resumed and the seizures were controlled. However, during the next few months the patient began to have difficulty speaking and developed right-sided paralysis. A scan revealed a mass in the left temporal area, which proved to be a malignant brain tumour. As a result of this salutary clinical experience Lesser and his colleagues recommend that the fact that seizure-like symptoms can be induced by suggestion should not be used in order to confirm a diagnosis of hysteria.[24] What is perhaps most interesting about their findings is that they precisely invert the lesson which Charcot derived from his similar experiences in the Salpêtrière – the very lesson which so impressed Freud and led him to construct his own theory of unconscious symptom-formation. In this respect, as in many others, the case history significantly strengthens the case put forward by E. M. Thornton.

An even more impressive piece of corroborative evidence became available only in 1988 with the publication of a case history by the neurologist Colin Binnie. He describes a twenty-two-year-old woman who suffered from frequent attacks which were characterised by screaming, dropping to the floor without injury and by the assumption of 'a classical arc-de-cercle posture, often with rhythmic pelvic thrusting'. Binnie himself notes that this patient attracted some interest, as her attacks resembled those described by Charcot. Partly because of this resemblance, and partly, it would seem, because of the apparently sexual content of her attacks, the woman was treated as suffering from hysteria or 'pseudoseizures' only. This diagnosis seemed to be confirmed when numerous EEGs taken between her seizures had shown no neurological abnormalities. As a result of this view of her illness the woman had repeatedly been admitted into mental hospitals over the previous twelve years. Intensive monitoring *during* seizures, however, eventually revealed epileptic activity in the right frontal part of the brain. This finding was confirmed by the insertion of electrodes into the brain. The affected area of tissue was surgically removed and the patient, after suffering from twelve years of supposedly psychogenic attacks, became seizure free. Commenting on the general problem of distinguishing real epileptic seizures from putative 'pseudoseizures', Binnie makes the following observation:

> It has only recently been realised that partial epilepsies of mesial frontal origin in particular can give rise to a florid symptomatology previously thought to typify pseudoseizures, including bilaterally symmetrical flapping movements, arc de cercle, and obscene or aggressive utterances ... The conclusion [that such attacks are epileptic] sometimes comes as a considerable surprise to those concerned with the patient's management ... [for] the attacks may be so grotesque as to invite a psychiatric interpretation. Indeed, patients presenting this problem often also have psychosocial difficulties which have not been helped by the insistence of their medical advisers that their attacks were psychogenic.[25]

There can be very little doubt that the discovery of frontal lobe epilepsy and its bizarre seizure-patterns in the latter part of the twentieth century will eventually be recognised as having made a quite crucial contribution to our historical understanding of 'hysteria'.

A third intriguing piece of evidence which has recently come to light is also a product of Colin Binnie's work. During a study of pattern-sensitivity among photosensitive epileptics, Binnie and his fellow researchers noticed that a surprisingly high number of their experimental subjects were in the habit of inducing paroxysmal activity or even fully developed seizures in themselves. A significant feature of all thirteen subjects who did this 'was that they made repeated slow eyeclosure movements *with simultaneous upward deviation of the eyes*'. The finding is a striking one in view of the fact that, as we have seen, James Braid's favoured technique for inducing hypnosis involved his subjects focusing their eyes on an object placed just above their normal field of vision – which would itself produce an upward deviation of the eyes. Binnie seeks to explain the phenomenon by citing two sets of research – one which shows that eye-closure has the effect of increasing alpha activity in the brain and another which indicates that the same is true of *forced* upward deviation of the eyes – the latter form of alpha-enhancement being known as the 'Evans–Mulholland effect' after the two researchers who first described it. Binnie suggests that his subjects may have been using the same process of alpha-enhancement in order to induce epileptic seizures. The same argument might reasonably be applied to James Braid's experiments in hypnotism.[26] Even though Thornton herself does not discuss James Braid specifically or his methods of inducing hypnotism, Binnie's findings would appear to offer an interesting corroboration of her general views on hypnotism and epileptic phenomena.

In view of the merits of Thornton's argument it is extremely difficult to explain why it has received so little recognition by scholars and critics of psychoanalysis. It is particularly interesting that Peter Gay in his 1988 biography of Freud, writing in full knowledge of Thornton's book, does not modify the conventional version of Freud's encounter with Charcot, or suggest that Charcot's understanding of hysteria was unscientific in any way. Even more recently Paul Robinson has maintained a similar course. For while reviewing Freud's relationship with Charcot during the course of his critique of Frank Sulloway, he does not for a moment intimate that any doubt might surround Charcot's research.[27]

It is difficult to avoid the impression that some supporters of psychoanalysis have ignored the problem posed by Charcot's attitude to hysteria simply because they are unable to contemplate the possibility that Freud might have been the victim of such an elementary and momentous medical misunderstanding. Yet the resistance to the various criticisms of Charcot which have been made since his death perhaps runs even deeper than this, and suggests that there is a powerful, culturally conditioned reluctance to forego scientific heroes. The most likely explanation is that we have become addicted as a culture to the idea of science as a repository of superhuman (or inhuman) knowledge, and tend to regard scientists themselves as in some way inhuman or superhuman. Determined to categorise those who profess systematic knowledge as either scientists or charlatans, we find it difficult to believe that any thinker who makes a genuine contribution to scientific knowledge can, either simultaneously or subsequently, become the propagator of folly, error and misjudgement. Yet the most cursory acquaintance with the history of science should be sufficient to remind us that scientists are pre-eminently human, that many 'great' scientists have gone on to create significant pseudo-sciences, and that sometimes the prestige and authority which they have earnt through their genuine contributions to science has both encouraged them along the path of folly at the same time that it has silenced or eclipsed their critics.

Perhaps the clearest example of a significant medical researcher who began his career as a scientist and ended it as a pseudo-scientist was Franz Joseph Gall. Gall was a brilliant neuroanatomist, whose skill at dissecting brains in their semi-fluid natural state led him to make some of the most fundamental discoveries of modern medicine. He distinguished between the grey and white matter of the brain, recognised the role of the cerebral cortex and traced, in its grey matter, the origins of the nerves. Although Hippocrates had long ago identified the brain as the most important organ of the human body and characterised it as 'the interpreter of consciousness', his view had not found universal acceptance and some physicians still regarded the brain as almost functionless – a kind of cranial appendix. Gall's work transformed this situation almost at a stroke. The modern science of neuro-anatomy was, to a very large extent, his creation.

Yet Gall did not rest content with precise investigations of the anatomical structure of the brain. His familiarity with this organ, and his recognition of the crucial role it played in human consciousness, led him to assume that he could create an entire science of human life based upon these observations. The theory which he went on to develop held that the mental powers of individuals consist of separate faculties, each of which has its organ and location in a definite region of the surface of the brain. Since the size and shape of these organs indicated the degree to which the faculty had been developed, Gall maintained that it was possible to read a person's character by studying the external configuration of the cranium. Gall, in short, was a medical researcher of genius who ended by creating phrenology. Although phrenology is now widely recognised as a pseudo-science, many of Gall's followers, knowing his genius as an anatomist of the human brain, could not bring themselves to believe that phrenology was anything other than a momentously important contribution to medical science.[28]

Charcot's theories of hysteria, which are no less a tissue of error, folly and partial truth than Gall's science of phrenology, have, on the whole, been protected even better by the carapace of science than Gall's nineteenth-century pseudo-science. Yet if we are to understand the full significance of Charcot's theories both in Freud's personal biography and in the development of psychoanalysis we need to pause for a moment in order to consider how it was that a researcher of Charcot's undoubted genius allowed himself to be lured so completely from the path of organic medicine into the byways of unfounded psychogenic speculation.

This question is all the more intriguing in view of the fact that Charcot appears to have begun his research into hysteria by viewing this putative disease from a thoroughly organic point of view. We have already seen how he postulated the existence of invisible, 'dynamic' lesions of the brain in order to account for hysterical symptoms. If we accept that what Charcot viewed as symptoms of hysteria were in most cases actually symptoms of temporal lobe epilepsy, we are bound to recognise how close Charcot's hypothesis was to the truth. For temporal lobe epilepsy is caused by lesions of the brain which are, in a sense, 'dynamic' and which would certainly not have been detected by the investigatory techniques which Charcot employed. Yet Charcot was unable or unwilling to hold to this initial hypothesis. The reasons which caused him to abandon not simply the hypothesis but his entire orientation towards an exclusively organic neuropathology will never be known exactly. But it is possible, I believe, to construct a speculative explanation which does not only throw light on the development of modern psychiatry and neurology but which also helps to explain why Charcot's ideas were taken up so enthusiastically by Freud – who by training was steeped almost as deeply in neuropathology as Charcot himself.

I have already suggested that the key to Charcot's intellectual development may be found in the manner in which he allowed his immense and well-earned reputation as a scientist of genius to distract him from proper scientific scepticism and to persuade him to stray from the paths of normal scientific research. At times Charcot seems to have come to believe that he could solve some scientific problems by the sheer force of his personality. Because he evidently came to rule with absolute authority within his own domain at the Salpêtrière, where he maintained his position by a combination of fear and intolerance of criticism, he seems to have concluded that he was immune to criticism and that he could tread with impunity in areas where many researchers were afraid to venture for fear that they might entirely destroy their scientific reputation.

There was, perhaps, an element of just this kind of recklessness in Charcot's decision to investigate the phenomenon of hypnosis. Even more reckless than this, however, had been his involvement with Victor Burq, a fifty-four-year-old doctor who, rather in the manner of Mesmer, used metallic discs and magnets in order to produce medical cures. His specific claim was that he could cure 'hysterical hemianaesthesia' by applying discs to whichever side of the patient's body was affected. After battling for some twenty-five years against the disparagement of medical critics, Burq had managed to persuade the Société de Biologie in Paris to appoint a commission to investigate and pass judgement on his work. Charcot was one of the three members of this commission and he invited Burq to the Salpêtrière where he carried out a series of experiments. At first it would seem that Charcot remained sceptical about the value of Burq's work. But one day he was holding forth to a group of English physicians who had expressed doubts about the occurrence of anaesthesia in hysterical patients. In an attempt to overcome their scepticism, he suddenly pricked the arm of a nearby patient whom he believed to be permanently anaesthetic. Instead of showing no reaction as he had expected, she cried out with pain. Charcot's guests could not suppress their amusement at seeing his massive confidence so easily confounded. On inquiring into the reasons why his demonstration had failed, Charcot discovered that Burq had applied a gold plate to this particular patient's arm, and claimed to have restored its sensibility. According to one report, this incident changed Charcot's entire attitude towards Burq's work and he soon afterwards became a believer in the virtues of 'metallotherapy'.[29]

The emotional factors which contributed to this change of attitude are not recorded but they may be imagined. Used to having his views treated with exaggerated seriousness and respect by his own students, it seems likely that Charcot had felt deeply humiliated by the incident with the English physicians. One way out of his dilemma would have been to confront the possibility that the hemianaesthesia he thought he had detected was not real. Since for Charcot anaesthesia was almost always a symptom which the doctor presented to his patient, and not a symptom which the patient presented to his doctor, it seems quite likely that many of the hemianaesthesias 'discovered' by Charcot were purely imaginary. For by actively searching for a symptom of which patients rarely or never complained Charcot may often have generated the symptom himself.[30]

Charcot, however, had always regarded hemianaesthesia as one of the essential symptoms of hysteria. If he had been obliged to confess that this symptom was sometimes only imagined he would have lost one of the cornerstones of the entire elaborate architecture of his theory. In the short term at least, the only way in which he could preserve intact his immense scientific *amour-propre* was by uncritically accepting Burq's extraordinary therapeutic claims. Not only did he do this but he actively supported Burq as he subjected his initial theory to a series of increasingly fantastic elaborations. Before long Burq was claiming that he could use magnets and metal discs to 'transfer' symptoms from one side of a patient's body to another. In the most bizarre twist of all Joseph Babinski eventually proposed that symptoms could be transferred in this manner from one *patient* to another.

In that Burq may have been responsible for interesting Charcot in the much more substantial phenomena associated with hypnotism, his influence may not have been entirely negative. In 1882, indeed, when Charcot triumphantly presented a paper on hypnosis to the Académie des Sciences, it seemed that his prestige had succeeded in carrying all before it. For as his pupil, Pierre Janet, would later put it, it was a *tour de force* for Charcot to command respectful attention for a report on hypnosis from the same academy which had already condemned the phenomenon three times in the last century under the name of animal magnetism.[31]

Yet if Charcot's immense scientific reputation was responsible for bringing about this response, it was precisely this reputation which he had placed in jeopardy by becoming involved with Burq's experiments in metallotherapy. For by embracing Burq's research in an apparent effort to protect a small part of his ideas about hysteria, Charcot was running the risk that all his work on hypnotism and hysteria, even that which was more securely based, would be brought into scientific disrepute.

It was just such a reaction which began to develop in 1883 when Hippolyte Bernheim published his own first work on hypnotism in which he revealed the existence of Liébeault's work and began to formulate the principle of suggestion. At first Bernheim did not reject the work of Charcot and his disciples. But from 1885 onwards he subjected the entire phenomenon of metallotherapy to a barrage of increasingly severe criticism. Speaking at first before the Société de Biologie, and following up this presentation with a number of articles, Bernheim accused Charcot and his followers of conducting their experiments in an atmosphere laden with explicit or implicit cues which indicated to patients what kind of reaction they were expected to produce. This criticism was extended to Charcot's experiments in hypnosis, and the states which Charcot claimed to be able to produce in his *hystériques* were dismissed as 'artefacts'.

In the long term the effect of Bernheim's criticisms was, in the words of Janet, 'that of a thunderbolt', leading to dissent among Charcot's followers and a widespread feeling that Charcot's experiments were in some way fraudulent.[32] There is, however, every reason to suppose that in the short term Bernheim's criticisms, and the principle of suggestion which he began to work out in 1883, had a significant effect on Charcot's own attitudes towards his work. Up until 1882, Charcot had had the entire field of hypnosis almost to himself, and what is interesting is the extent to which he refrained from theorising about the phenomena he had managed to produce. Charcot's dictum that facts should come first and theories afterwards is often cited as an example of his scientific attitude. But in uttering this principle, Charcot was actually misrepresenting his own practice. For throughout his work Charcot had, up until now at least, effectively inverted the relationship between empirical facts and scientific theory which he himself idealised. By treating as axiomatic the entirely theoretical and unsubstantiated proposition that hysteria was a real disease entity, he had sought out, and where necessary conjured into existence, only those facts which were compatible with this proposition. The problem with his subsequent experiments in hypnosis and with the phenomenon which he chose to call 'traumatic hysteria' was that they appeared to stand outside his theoretical framework. The only satisfactory way of resolving this problem would have been to dismantle the entire elaborate edifice which he had spent so long constructing, and start again. At this point, however, Charcot was trapped once again by the rigid authoritarianism with which he maintained the 'laws of hysteria' which he himself had formulated. Unwilling to transgress these laws, he had placed himself in a position where his own initial theoretical constructs effectively prevented him from offering any adequate theoretical account of the very phenomena on which his research now concentrated.

Charcot's theoretically determined inability to theorise had serious consequences. For the proper function of a theory in scientific research is not to subordinate the facts to an abstract model but to bring observed facts into an even sharper relief, and, by offering a coherent explanation of these facts, to ensure that their reality and significance are adequately acknowledged. When Harvey postulated the existence of minute pores which allowed an exchange of blood between arteries and veins, he was not subjugating observation to theory. He was actually providing a framework in which a whole series of phenomena which had previously been dismissed as insignificant or even unreal, could be fully acknowledged for the first time.

Seen in this way the scientist's obligation to theorise is actually a part of a duty which is owed to the realm of empirical facts. For in a strongly rationalistic culture such as our own any unusual phenomena which cannot be satisfactorily explained are likely to be discounted as mere anomalies or even denied. By repeatedly refusing to offer any theoretical explanation of the phenomena of hypnosis, Charcot risked just such a reaction to his experiments. At first he was able, instead of justifying his research through theory, to rely upon his immense scientific prestige to confer credibility on his work. But when Bernheim, the leader of the 'Nancy school' who himself had a considerable medical reputation, first advanced his own theory of hypnotism and then subsequently subjected Charcot's work to criticism, the entire precarious structure of Charcot's work on hysteria was threatened at its insecure foundations. The 'iron laws' of hysteria which he had elaborated so confidently in his role as 'the Napoleon of the neuroses' began to appear to some more like the whims of an autocrat than the pronouncements of a serious scientist.

Once again Charcot was threatened with humiliation and this time what was called into question was not simply a detail, as it had been in the original incident involving Burq, but the entire structure of what Charcot himself undoubtedly regarded as his most important scientific achievement. The physician who entertained royalty and fraternised with the aristocracy on the strength of his scientific reputation now seemed, partly because of his support for Burq's therapeutic charades, to be poised on the brink of ignominy, shame and ridicule.

The acuteness with which Charcot himself experienced his predicament is perhaps indicated by the sudden change in his entire scientific orientation which took place from 1885 onwards. Whereas previously he had apparently been content to rest upon his authority, and to refrain from what he regarded as over-hasty generalisations, he seemed now to see his major unsolved scientific problems – and above all the phenomena of hypnotism – as standing in urgent need of a theoretical solution.

Yet, as in the earlier incident with Burq, Charcot showed no inclination to reconsider any of his most fundamental propositions about hysteria. Just as at that point he had compounded his scientific problems by endorsing Burq's bizarre experiments, so now he took a similar course. He constructed a new model which would appear to have been specifically formulated in order that it might be compatible with the series of unsubstantiated hypotheses he had already embraced. This model was not so much a genuine scientific theory as an exercise in scientific confabulation. Its primary function, it would seem, was to protect Charcot's intellectual *amour-propre* and to ward off humiliation and ridicule.

It was for these complex, and ultimately vainglorious reasons, I would suggest, that Charcot quite suddenly, in about 1885, abandoned his purely organic orientation towards neurology, and began to work out the mixed organic and psychogenic theory of hysteria which we have already examined. It may well be that his observations of the effect of isolation on women suffering from anorexia played a catalytic role in bringing about this theoretical change. But it seems highly probable that Bernheim's theory of suggestion and his incipient critique of Charcot was also a significant factor.

The terms in which Bernheim worked out his own theory of hypnotism seem to have been influential. For although Charcot still saw hypnotism as a physiologically determined state, he now combined this view with a new psychological perspective. This perspective is conveyed extremely well in the following words:

> An idea induced during artificial somnambulism becomes a fixed idea and remains unconscious after awakening ... One sees it pursue its course despite the usual thinking activity with an impetus nothing can stop. More than that, while the mind is occupied with the daily actions of normal life which the subject accomplishes consciously and of his own free will, some of the ideas suggested in that former passive state continue their hidden movement. No obstacle can hinder them in their fatal course ...[33]

These words, however, are not Charcot's, but are taken from Liébeault's treatise on psychology, which was originally published in 1873, and which Bernheim had rescued from oblivion. So closely do they resemble some of Charcot's own formulations that it seems quite possible that he succumbed to the same kind of process we have already observed in another context, and ended by internalising the scepticism of his opponents. In short, when Charcot argues that hysterical symptoms are implanted by suggestion in patients' minds, and sees ideas as being 'realised' in the form of bodily symptoms, he is replying to his critics by incorporating their own psychological theories into his new theoretical model. Towards the end of his life, Charcot even published an article on faith-healing in which he suggested that there were special kinds of tumours and ulcers which were analogous to 'psychical paralyses' and which could be removed by suggestion.[34] When Charcot died in 1893, Charles Féré maliciously suggested that he had become 'the star pupil of the Nancy school'.[35] In view of the manner in which he had adopted some of the key assumptions of Liébeault and Bernheim, it would seem that Féré's remark was not only malicious, but also true.

If the purpose of a scientific theory is to accommodate and explain a series of observable phenomena without distorting their character, then Charcot's theory was profoundly unscientific. For its principal aim, according to the account I have offered here, was to protect his own scientific reputation. To this end it set out to accommodate not facts but theories which had already been formulated – both Charcot's own theory of hysteria, and, to some extent at least, the theories of suggestion and auto-suggestion put forward by Bernheim and his followers. So far as the actual observed phenomena of hysteria and hypnosis were concerned, Charcot's new theory either ignored crucial facts completely or entirely re-shaped them in order to conform with the psychological model which he had now adopted. Thus, to take but one example, we might consider the various reflex mechanisms which Charcot had used in order to bring about different hypnotic states in his patients – such as tapping them on the shoulder. When in 1882 he had read his report on hypnotism to the Académie des Sciences, Charcot had quite properly stressed that he was able to manipulate hypnotic states by purely *physical* means. Yet once he had adopted his new psychological model he found it necessary, as we have already seen, to invent a complex and entirely hypothetical mental process whereby these physical stimuli were supposedly interpreted by patients as psychological suggestions. In a bizarre feat of reasoning Charcot can thus be seen referring to physical stimuli as though they were themselves ideas.

For these, and for many other reasons, Charcot's 'theory' provided only an illusion of explanatory power. What may seem remarkable is that a scientific confabulation such as his should have been embraced so enthusiastically by Freud. Yet to suggest that Freud was in a better position than Charcot to recognise the folly and error which he had woven into his theory of hysteria would, I believe, be to misunderstand the true nature of the relationship between them. For, as should already be apparent, Freud did not come to Paris in the spirit of a sceptical scientist in order to assess the ideas of a colleague. He came as a deferential student who had already completely accepted Charcot's own implicit idealisation of himself as the greatest of all neurologists. His strongest inclination, as indicated by the letters he wrote at the time, was not to criticise Charcot's formulations but to worship him as an approximation to scientific divinity.

Some measure of the deeply personal nature of the regard which Freud had for Charcot is provided by the fact that he named his own eldest son 'Jean Martin', after Charcot. Another curious manifestation of this regard is offered by the fact that Freud's study, packed as it eventually became with oriental antiques and curios, appears to have been modelled directly on Charcot's study, which Freud described in an admiring letter to Martha Bernays written from Paris in January 1886. It is a psychoanalyst, Kurt Eissler, who, on the basis of these and other facts, draws the conclusion that Freud actually identified with Charcot.[36]

Given Freud's immense idealisation of Charcot, it must be suggested that Charcot's exercise in scientific confabulation was almost as crucial to Freud as it was to Charcot himself. For Freud was no more able to relinquish his image of Charcot's infallibility than the master himself. At the same time it would seem that there were many aspects of Charcot's new confabulatory scientific style which actively appealed to Freud. Trained as a cautious empirical neurologist to keep theoretical speculation to a minimum, Freud now discovered in Charcot an example of a kind of neurological theorising in which speculation about hidden mental events was licensed in the name of science. In future years, as we will see, the example which Charcot set in his confabulations and flights of speculative fancy is one which Freud enthusiastically followed. At the same time, trained as he was in the tradition of scientific materialism, it seems likely that Freud found Charcot's teaching that the mind could influence and control bodily processes strangely attractive.

Contrary to one of the most powerful of all current myths about the history of medicine, this view of the relationship of the mind to the body was very far from being a modern innovation. In many respects it was deeply traditional. From the time of Hippocrates onwards many physicians had put forward the idea that emotions not only influenced bodily functions but sometimes acted as causative, pathogenic factors. Galen, for example, included the passions among the causes of bodily disease and the medical historian L. J. Rather has suggested that, as a result of Galen's influence on European medicine down to the nineteenth century, physicians had given a great deal of attention to theories postulating the psychological causation of a variety of diseases.[37] Such theories were particularly attractive in the era preceding the formulation of the germ theory of disease when physicians remained unaware of the pathogenic role of microbes and viruses. In these essentially pre-scientific conditions some extremely crude psychogenic theories of disease remained highly plausible. That such theories frequently embraced both contagious and epidemic diseases is made clear in a passage from Archer's *Every Man His Own Doctor*, published in 1673: 'The observation I have made in practice of physick these several years, hath confirmed me in this opinion, that the original, or cause of most men and womens sickness, disease, and death is, first, some great discontent, which brings a habit of sadness of mind . . .'[38] With the advent of new knowledge about the aetiology of disease brought by such researchers as Pasteur and Koch, such crude psychogenic theories had been rapidly eclipsed, and most physicians in the latter part of the nineteenth century were quite able to see them for what they were – ancient medical fallacies based on superstition and ignorance.* Yet in some quarters of the medical profession, particularly those associated with exorcism and faith-healing, simplistic ideas about psychogenesis had been preserved. Such ideas were certainly held by the mesmerists and by later 'miraculous' healers such as Liébeault. Now similar ideas seemed to have been scientifically legitimated in the theories of Charcot. Since Freud had himself fantasised, as he did in the letter to Martha which has already been quoted, that he would return from Paris able to 'cure all the incurable nervous patients', these traditional ideas about healing may have had a particular appeal. It would seem, however, that Freud himself was never aware of their true provenance. As would happen again on subsequent occasions, Freud became smitten by ideas which were actually traditional and pre-scientific while all the time regarding them as daringly modern and even revolutionary.

As a result of his historical innocence and his credulous acceptance of the authority of Charcot, Freud thus took back to Vienna from Paris a whole series of ideas about the relationship of the mind to the body which, because they were based on a combination of misdiagnosis and theoretical confabulation, were mistaken. Most importantly of all

---

* Some (though by no means all) modern concepts of psychosomatic medicine are much more subtle and my strictures on Freud and Charcot should certainly not be construed as a repudiation of *all* psychosomatic medicine.

he returned to Vienna believing in Charcot's doctrine that ideas could lodge in an unconscious portion of the mind where *they could actually be transformed into bodily symptoms*. In spite of the entirely false foundations on which this doctrine rested, he would subsequently use it in order to help shape the entire course of twentieth-century psychiatry.

Although Freud would eventually reject some of the particulars of Charcot's theories, he never questioned Charcot's authority in any radical way, either in the immediate aftermath of his visit to Paris or in the long years of reflection that supervened. Indeed so high a regard did he conceive for Charcot that, partly in an attempt to force the great man to take notice of him, he wrote to him while he was in Paris and offered his services as translator for the third volume of *Leçons sur les maladies du système nerveux* – the very volume in which Charcot expounded his theory of traumatic hysteria. Charcot accepted, with the result that Freud immediately became, in an almost literal sense, Charcot's apostle to the German-speaking medical world. Nor did Freud's missionary activities on behalf of Charcot stop here. For in October 1886, soon after his marriage to Martha and the opening of his own private medical practice, Freud read a paper entitled 'On Male Hysteria' to the Viennese Society of Physicians. In his enthusiasm about Charcot's 'discoveries', Freud was anxious to make these known among his colleagues; he was particularly keen to convert them to Charcot's theory of hysteria. To this end his paper consisted of an account of his activities in Paris, in the course of which he outlined Charcot's theories. He then went on to focus on the case of a man whom he had seen at the Salpêtrière whose arm was paralysed and who had been diagnosed as suffering from 'traumatic hysteria' caused by his recent fall from a scaffold.

Although the history of psychoanalysis is full of strange incongruities, few are as strange as the discrepancy between Freud's own account of this meeting and the accounts which appeared in medical journals at the time. According to Freud his paper was met with incredulity and hostility which ran so deep that it initiated his slow but certain expulsion from the Viennese medical establishment. In reality it would seem that the paper was received in an almost routine manner. A few sceptical comments were made from the floor which included some reasoned objections to Charcot's theories. Among these were the remarks of Professor Leidesdorf, who suggested that in cases of paralysis caused by accidents caution should be exercised before ruling out organic causes. But Freud was certainly not hounded for proposing revolutionary theories. On the contrary, some of the physicians present seemed disappointed that he had dealt at such length with the problem of 'male hysteria', which was familiar to them, and with Charcot's theories, of which they were aware already. Yet it was to this somewhat low-key meeting that Freud traced the beginnings of a profound alienation from his medical colleagues.

The first person to question Freud's version of events was Ernest Jones, who notes that Freud referred to his 'bad reception' at this meeting and that he was in the habit of indicating how much this hurt him. But as Jones goes on to observe, 'there seems to have been nothing very remarkable in the reception'.[39] The episode was subsequently investigated in a great deal more detail by Henri Ellenberger whose findings have been developed by Frank Sulloway and E. M. Thornton. These writers amplify Jones's original judgement and imply that Freud's own reaction to the meeting was profoundly irrational. The question which must be asked is why Freud reacted in the manner that he did.

One way of answering this question is to suggest that behind his reaction to the meeting there lay a huge disproportion between the expectations brought to it by Freud himself and by his medical colleagues. From his colleagues' point of view the meeting was simply another routine event at which they were exposed to the latest enthusiasm of a very gifted neuroanatomical researcher who seemed to have strayed somewhat beyond his own field of competence. But for Freud, the occasion had an altogether greater significance. His experience in Paris had had a profound effect on him and he returned not so much as a student reporting on a study-trip as a zealot who had undergone a religious conversion. The new gospel which he brought with him, based as it was on the idea that physical illnesses could have a purely psychological origin, was profoundly subversive of all the old beliefs which had once united Freud with his colleagues. His old 'aims and opinions' had indeed, by his own confession, already been 'wrecked'. Freud's new religious zeal thus went hand in hand with the perilous insecurity of the convert. As we will see, Freud would eventually compare himself not only to Moses but also to St Paul and he certainly returned to Vienna as one who had been vouchsafed a revelation. At this point in his life his most compelling psychological need – like that of many a religious convert, including Paul himself after his return from Damascus – was to silence his own inner doubts by persuading others to share his new beliefs.

Freud, according to this view, would have brought to the meeting not only the burning zeal of the convert, but also the expectation that his paper would make a great impression. In Paris, after all, not only physicians but also writers, intellectuals and even royalty attended to the pronouncements of the great Charcot. Freud had returned from Paris, moreover, in no ordinary capacity, but as one of Charcot's intellectual intimates, bearing a gospel of which every neurologist seemed to stand in need. In view of all this, and in view of the dream of greatness by which he was himself driven, it seems likely that Freud looked upon the crucial meeting of the Viennese Society of Physicians as the beginning of his own 'real' career – an occasion when, for the first time, his colleagues would be forced to recognise his intellectual superiority.[40]

When a somewhat routine reality replaced this glorious dream it is scarcely surprising that Freud experienced bitter disappointment. For, true to the prophecy he had made to Martha, he had gone to Paris, he had become a great *savant* and then he had returned to Vienna with a great, great nimbus. His colleagues, however, had not only failed to recognise his genius, they had suggested that Charcot might be mistaken. In making their very reasonable criticisms of Charcot's theories, Freud's colleagues no doubt felt that they were commenting quite impersonally on the views of a third party who was not even present. Freud, however, was committed to these theories with a kind of passion which amounted to an almost total psychological identification. What Martin Luther once said of Paul's Letter to the Galatians – 'I have betrothed myself to it, it is my wife!' – probably represents Freud's own feelings at that time towards Charcot's theory of hysteria. Only if we understand this can we grasp how personally wounded Freud must have felt when his colleagues subjected this theory so casually to criticism.

The choice by which Freud was now faced was either to risk further scepticism from his colleagues or to give up a precious gospel which had already given him a sense of intellectual redemption and a feeling of imminent glory. In choosing the former path he was certainly not committing himself, as is frequently maintained, to a proud state of intellectual isolation. He was in reality throwing himself into an even greater dependence on Charcot's scientific authority and in particular on his theory of hysteria.

Freud's massive idealisation of Charcot was, as we have seen, by no means the first instance of his seemingly compulsive need to engage in intellectual love-affairs and to throw himself in a state of utter dependence at the feet of his intellectual heroes. It is nevertheless instructive to compare his conduct with regard to Charcot to the attitude he had displayed only a year or so earlier when he was writing his papers about cocaine. For one of the most interesting features of the cocaine episode is the degree of intellectual independence he showed in it. In 1884, when he wrote his first paper on cocaine, he had certainly lived up to his own description of himself as 'a *conquistador* – an intellectual adventurer'. For he had evidently felt confident enough of his own medical insight and intellectual powers to leave behind the safe waters already charted by his earlier intellectual heroes Meynert and Brücke, and to sail alone into more perilous seas. According to the 'psychoanalytic legend', Freud may have been mistaken on this first voyage but he would continue to make a series of yet more heroic and dangerous voyages in order to create psychoanalysis. The reality, however, was very different. For if the 'cocaine episode' was the first occasion on which Freud showed true intellectual independence, relying solely upon his own intellectual judgement, it was also, in some respects, the last. So disastrous was the outcome of this bout of intellectual self-reliance that Freud seems to have lost at least a part of the self-confidence which had led him to announce so boldly his first medical 'discovery'. From this point onwards he continued to show many signs of rebelliousness and intellectual originality. But this apparent originality was almost always sustained by a profound and sometimes credulous acceptance of the theories of others.

Freud's intellectual infatuation with the ideas of Charcot, and his deep and almost craven dependence on these ideas when he returned from Paris, was merely the first instance of such intellectual submissiveness. He would subsequently place almost as much intellectual trust in the ideas both of Josef Breuer and of Wilhelm Fliess. The great tragedy for Freud was that, in all three cases, the ideas which he took from his intellectual mentors were mistaken. The further tragedy was that he chose to use these scientific mistakes as the cornerstones on which he built the entire theoretical edifice of psychoanalysis.

FOUR

Anna O. and the Birth of Psychoanalysis

FREUD'S VISIT TO PARIS proved to be the great turning-point in his life. Until this time he had regarded himself and been regarded by others primarily as a physician. Now, however, seduced into sharing Charcot's assumption that all the important discoveries in the field of neurology had been made, he moved increasingly towards the field of psychology.

If Charcot in Paris was the prime cause of this change of direction, another important factor was Freud's friendship with the Viennese physician, Josef Breuer. Breuer was, after Charcot, the second direct begetter of some of the key concepts in psychoanalysis. Freud first met Breuer at Brücke's physiological Institute in the late 1870s. The two men discovered that they had many interests in common and soon became close friends, with Freud looking to his older and more established colleague for advice and guidance. As Freud would later write in his *Autobiography*, '[Breuer] became my friend and helper in my difficult circumstances. We grew accustomed to share all our scientific interests with each other. In this relationship the gain was naturally mine.'[1]

Like Charcot, Breuer enjoyed a high medical reputation which he had earned through orthodox anatomical research. In 1868 he had discovered the role played by the vagus nerve in the mechanism of breathing (the 'Hering–Breuer reflex'), and in 1873 he discovered the role played in the sense of balance by the semi-circular canals in the ear. Breuer declined to follow the career in medical research which was open to him and went into private medical practice. He continued his orthodox physiological researches but, following a career pattern similar to that of Charcot and Forel, he began to move towards neuro-pathology, which was at that time becoming a fashionable specialism.

He developed a particular interest in hysteria, and this became the subject of his collaboration with Freud.

Freud was especially interested in the most unusual of all Breuer's cases which concerned a twenty-one-year-old patient – the celebrated 'Anna O.', whom Breuer had treated in 1881. Anna O. was a young woman who had fallen ill while nursing her father, who was suffering from a subpleuritic tubercular abscess. Not long before her father died she developed a severe cough and Breuer was called in to help. Subsequently she developed rigid paralysis of the extremities of the right side of her body, a convergent squint, disturbances both in her vision and in her hearing. At a very early stage of her illness she had begun to experience brief lapses of consciousness or 'absences'. During these spells she would stop in the middle of a sentence, repeat her last words and then, after a short pause, go on talking. Gradually these spells of confused behaviour grew longer and more severe, and during her 'absences' she would hallucinate and behave in a disturbed manner, shouting abusively, throwing cushions at people and tearing buttons off her clothes. If anyone came into the room during these states, Anna would complain of having 'lost' some time and would remark upon the gap in her train of conscious thoughts. Attempts at reassurance were often construed as attempts to deceive or trick her. She also developed a number of disorders of speech; eventually she lost her ability to speak her native language and would converse in English instead, apparently without realising what she was doing.

Breuer diagnosed Anna O.'s illness as a case of hysteria. During the course of almost two years, in which it would seem that Breuer and Anna O. became emotionally dependent on one another, he gradually developed a form of therapy which he believed was effective in relieving Anna of her symptoms. First of all he came to the conclusion that when Anna could be induced to relate to him during the evening the content of the hallucinations or day-dreams she had had during the day, she became calm and tranquil. Breuer saw his role as that of 'relieving' Anna of the 'psychical stimuli' which had 'accumulated' during the day. He also described the evening talks as an 'unburdening process' and suggested that if the 'products' of Anna O.'s 'bad self' had not been 'continually disposed of . . . we should have been faced by a hysteric of the malicious type'. Anna O. herself referred to this method as her 'talking cure' and it was this very general process of what might be called 'confessional soothing' which would become one of the prototypes of psychoanalytic therapy.[2]

It should be noted, however, that Breuer never claimed that this simple process in itself could bring about the removal of any of the physical symptoms of Anna's illness. It was about a subsequent refinement of the original 'talking cure' that this claim would be made. According to Breuer's published account, this second, more specialised form, was developed in relation to a time when Anna O. found it impossible to drink. Breuer writes that 'she would take up the glass of water she longed for, but as soon as it touched her lips she would push it away like someone suffering from hydrophobia ... She lived only on fruit, such as melons etc., so as to lessen her tormenting thirst.' Breuer's account continues in the following manner:

> This had lasted for some six weeks, when one day during hypnosis she grumbled about her English lady companion whom she did not care for, and went on to describe, with every sign of disgust, how she had once gone into that lady's room and how her little dog – horrid creature! – had drunk out of a glass there. The patient had said nothing, as she had wanted to be polite. After giving energetic expression to the anger which she had held back, she asked for something to drink, drank a large quantity of water without any difficulty and woke from her hypnosis with the glass at her lips.[3]

'And,' writes Breuer, 'thereupon the disturbance vanished, never to return.'

This single event became the model on which Breuer devised what he called a 'therapeutic technical procedure'. In this 'technical procedure', according to his 1895 account, each of Anna's symptoms was taken individually and all the occasions on which it had appeared were described in reverse chronological order. He went on to claim that, as soon as the event which had led to its first occurrence was described, 'the symptom was permanently removed.'[4]

The case of Anna O. made a great impression on Freud when it was first related to him in 1882. His period of study under Charcot only served to heighten its apparent importance, and Freud attempted, unsuccessfully, to interest Charcot himself in the case. When he returned to Vienna he tried out Breuer's 'technical procedure' on a number of women patients, some of whom had been referred to him by Breuer himself. He and Breuer constantly discussed the results of such treatment and, after publishing an initial joint paper in 1893, Freud eventually prevailed on Breuer to publish his story of Anna O., making this the first case in their jointly written *Studies on Hysteria* (1895).

Perhaps the most interesting, though least remarked feature of *Studies on Hysteria* is just how unoriginal many of its crucial ideas are. The central argument, namely that the physical symptoms of 'hysteria' were actually caused by some traumatic event which lay in the patient's past, was taken directly from Charcot. The contribution made by Freud and Breuer in this regard was not to import any new theory of medical causality, but to broaden the conception of the kind of trauma which might precipitate hysterical symptoms. The therapeutic procedure which they advocated departed quite radically from Charcot's own practice. But it too was derivative rather than original. The notion that some kind of 'catharsis' could be used to offer relief from *emotional* distress was a very old one indeed, going back to the ancient Greeks and beyond. Indeed, many years before Breuer treated Anna O., Jacob Bernays, the uncle of Freud's future wife, had written about the Aristotelian concept of catharsis, engendering a widespread interest in the subject in Vienna.[5] Even before Bernays's publications, the idea of cathartic relief was far from novel, being commonly adopted both by creative writers and by priests and penitents in the Catholic Church. Both these areas were actually pointed to by contemporary reviewers of *Studies on Hysteria*. The *Neue Freie Presse*, while welcoming the book, suggested that it contained 'nothing but the psychology used by poets'. The writer Alfred Berger compared the cathartic cures described by the authors with Orestes' cure in Goethe's play *Iphigenie auf Tauris*. He went on to hail the book as 'a piece of ancient writers' psychology'.[6] Meanwhile, writing in the journal *Brain*, Michell Clarke pointed out that Anna O.'s talking cure 'had long been recognised in the Roman Church by the institution of confession'.[7]

The fact that the cathartic strategy which seemed to lie at the heart of *Studies of Hysteria* was, in its broad outlines, old and familiar rather than new and revolutionary is one of the main sources of the book's enduring appeal. For this ancient strategy now became one of the ingredients of the theory of hysteria which was presented by Freud and Breuer. They had discovered, they wrote, that

> each individual hysterical symptom immediately and permanently disappeared when we had succeeded in bringing to light the memory of the event by which it was produced and in arousing its accompanying affect, and when the patient had described that event in the greatest possible detail and had put the affect into words.[8]

According to Freud and Breuer the underlying aetiology of hysterical symptoms was extraordinarily simple. If somebody suffered a fright or 'psychical trauma' and at the time suppressed their affective reaction to it, the 'strangulated affect' which resulted would remain and might engender hysterical symptoms. The therapeutic procedure which they adopted allowed the 'strangulated affect' to 'find a way out through speech' and thus freed patients from the tyranny which had previously been exercised by a particular idea or complex of ideas.

Though the terms in which they expressed it were different, the theory of emotional dynamics put forward by Breuer and Freud was in some respects similar to that of the poet Tennyson, who wrote of one grief-stricken victim that 'she must weep or she will die', or of William Blake, who described in his poem 'A Poison Tree' ('I was angry with my friend . . .') how anger which is secretly nurtured or 'hoarded', rather than being communicated, can become a destructive psychological obsession.[9]

Partly because it seemed that they were translating into the register of modern science a common psychological theory – namely that strong emotional reactions to an event can, if 'bottled up', engender distress, Breuer and Freud found a reasonably receptive audience for their new therapeutic procedure. Their notion of catharsis certainly exercised a significant influence over the development of twentieth-century psychiatry. The extent of their influence in this regard should not be underestimated. Even William Sargant, the orthodox British psychiatrist who frequently advocated surgical or drug-based therapies for psychiatric patients, acknowledged this influence. In his book *Battle for the Mind* he notes that abreaction, the term used by Breuer and Freud to describe their cathartic cure, was used frequently and success-fully as a therapy for 'war neuroses' in both world wars. By the 1930s this particular kind of therapy had a secure place in psychiatric text-books; in one such work W. S. Sadler defined abreaction as 'a process of reviving the memory of a repressed unpleasant experience and expressing in speech and action the emotions related to it, thereby relieving the personality of its influence.'[10]

During the Second World War psychiatrists used barbiturates or ether in order to disinhibit patients and supposedly to help them release their 'repressed memories', and the emotional reactions associated with these. The use of this kind of drug-abreaction sometimes seemed to be extremely effective at restoring emotional vitality to patients suffer-ing from 'war-neurosis'. It is important to recognise, however, that the psychiatrists who used these methods were often not in a position to determine whether the 'memories' released by drugs were authentic or not. In this respect it is interesting and significant that psychiatrists did not always find it essential to make a patient recall the precise incident which had supposedly precipitated the breakdown. As Sargant writes:

> Some neurotic patients are clearly helped towards recovery when forgotten memories are brought back to consciousness . . . Yet our experience in World War II suggested that the arousing of crude [emotional] excitement might often be of far greater curative virtue than the reliving of any particular forgotten or remembered experience.[11]

In other areas of psychiatry, abreaction, whether or not it has been referred to by this term, has been in almost constant use throughout the twentieth century. There can be little doubt that 'confessional' as opposed to drug-induced abreaction is one of the commonest of all the ingredients which are to be found in modern psychotherapy.

Breuer and Freud undoubtedly made a significant contribution to bringing about this state of affairs. Whether or not their influence has been salutary, however, is a matter of considerable debate. For although it seems reasonably clear that helping people to express 'frozen' emotional reactions can be psychologically beneficial *in some circumstances*, the 'ventilationist' approach to psychotherapy has been cogently and interestingly questioned in recent years, most notably by the social psychologist Carol Tavris.[12]

If we are to understand the most significant contribution which Breuer and Freud made to the evolution of modern psychiatry, however, we must be careful to avoid making anachronistic assumptions about their enterprise. Above all it would be quite wrong to assume that they were merely giving formal expression to folk-wisdom about the consequences of suppressing emotional reactions. For what helped to secure for their book its position of influence was not the traditional ideas of emotional catharsis it contained, but the extraordinary theoretical apparatus which was draped around these, and the extreme and quite unjustifiable claims which it put forward. It should be emphasised above all that Breuer and Freud themselves never understood their book as a contribution to psychotherapy. As practising physicians whose overriding concern was with tracing the pathology of physical symptoms and conquering the illnesses which gave rise to them, they offered it as a contribution to *medicine*. It may well be that traditional ideas about emotional catharsis gave their book much of its psychological resonance. But the purpose of their book was not to expound such ideas in their traditional form. Whereas the claim that repressed *emotions* could engender psychological distress would have been traditional and in some cases perhaps true, the claim made by Freud and Breuer was of a quite different order. For what they believed they had discovered was an aetiological theory which could explain the origins of a particular *disease* and cure this disease by uncovering repressed *memories*.

In this respect too Freud and Breuer, far from being innovators, were following a well-beaten, if relatively recent, path. In *The Discovery of the Unconscious*, Henri Ellenberger shows how, during the nineteenth century, the idea of unburdening oneself by confessing a shameful secret was gradually transferred from religion to medicine. He notes that, although Protestant reformers abolished the ritual of confession, a new practice arose in Protestant communities – the 'Cure of Souls' or *Seelsorge*. This had many facets, but of particular interest is the fact that 'certain Protestant ministers were considered as being endowed with a . . . spiritual gift that enabled them to obtain the confession of a disturbing secret from distressed souls and to help those persons out of their difficulty.'[13] At the beginning of the nineteenth century, under the influence of Mesmer and his theory of 'animal magnetism', this notion was progressively lifted from the sphere of religion and re-applied to medical therapeutics. The entirely reasonable proposition that a disturbing secret might engender emotional distress was thus progressively displaced by the quite unsubstantiated claim that such a secret might engender physical illness or disease. This theory of disease was actually worked out in some detail by the Viennese physician Moritz Benedikt who, in a series of publications which appeared between 1864 and 1895, claimed that the cause of many cases of 'hysteria' and other illnesses was a painful secret, mostly pertaining to sexual life. His further claim was that patients could be cured by the confession of 'pathogenic secrets'.[14] In the 1880s Pierre Janet in France also claimed to have produced medical cures by uncovering such a secret. The most striking of these supposed cures was first described by Janet in a book published in 1889, four years before Freud and Breuer published their own preliminary communication.[15]

Even the specific pathogenic emotional process which Breuer and Freud believed they had discovered had actually been introduced into medical theorising at least a century earlier. For it was in a medical treatise published in 1763 that Gaub had spoken of the harmful effects on the body both of overt and suppressed anger, grief, terror and unrequited love. He writes of grief, for example, that when it is not 'discharged in lamentation and wailing, but instead remains seated firmly within and is for a long time repressed and fostered, the body no less than the mind is eaten up and destroyed'.[16]

When Breuer and Freud published their *Studies on Hysteria* they were thus following an established trend, in which a series of physicians, working in an essentially pre-scientific manner, had taken up interesting and popular psychological theories and used them in order to produce medical aetiologies which were entirely speculative, and whose acceptability was directly related to the under-developed state of nineteenth-century medicine in general and nineteenth-century neurology in particular.

It is because they saw themselves as physicians dealing with real diseases, and not as psychotherapists, that their book did not focus on conditions which were transparently emotional, such as depression or anxiety, but on complex and impressively physical symptoms displayed by patients such as Anna O. She, after all, had suffered long and severely from a remarkable series of disorders, including rigid paralysis and loss of sensation in the extremities of the right side of the body, severely disturbed ocular movements, double vision, sporadic deafness, hallucinations and the loss of ability to speak her native tongue. That she should be cured of all these symptoms completely and almost at a single stroke was no ordinary therapeutic triumph. It was little short of a miracle, a miracle which conferred immense medical prestige both on Breuer and on Freud, who had now associated himself so closely with it.

In view of the role played by Anna O. in the history of psychoanalysis, the revelations concerning Anna O.'s illness which have gradually come to light in the past hundred years are of very considerable significance. The version of events which Breuer put forward in 1895 suggested that, after a climactic session in which Anna O. recalled a frightening hallucination of a snake, her final and most debilitating symptom – her inability to speak her native tongue – at last disappeared:

> In this way too the whole illness was brought to a close ... On the last
> day ... she reproduced the terrifying hallucination which I have

described above and which constituted the root of her whole illness . . .
Immediately after its reproduction she was able to speak German. She
was moreover free from the innumerable disturbances she had previously exhibited. After this she left Vienna and travelled for a while;
but it was a considerable time before she regained her mental balance
entirely. Since then she has enjoyed complete health.[17]

For as long as this version of events remained unchallenged, Anna O.'s
case was regarded as the perfect prototype of a cathartic cure and a
worthy precursor of the therapeutic successes which would eventually
be claimed on behalf of psychoanalysis. The first person to question
Breuer's account publicly was Jung. In a seminar in Zurich in 1925,
Jung claimed that this celebrated case, 'so much spoken about as an
example of brilliant therapeutic success, was in reality nothing of the
kind . . . There was no cure at all in the sense of which it was originally
presented.'[18] Within the psychoanalytic movement Jung's remarks
could easily be dismissed as the envious words of an apostate. But in
1953 Ernest Jones conceded that there was at least an element of
truth in Jung's claim, writing that 'the poor patient did not fare so well
as one might gather from Breuer's published account.' Jones also
related the story that Breuer had fallen in love with his young patient
and had eventually been driven by his wife's jealousy to bring the
treatment to an abrupt end. At this point Anna O. had supposedly
fallen into the throes of an imaginary childbirth, and Breuer,
having calmed her down by hypnotising her, 'fled the house in a cold
sweat'.[19]

Because he believed Anna O. should be recognised as the real discoverer of the cathartic method, Jones also took the unusual step of
revealing the identity of Breuer's patient. She was Bertha Pappenheim,
who later became well known as a pioneer social worker. The mystery
of Anna O. was not brought any nearer to a solution until Henri
Ellenberger used this clue to take up the trail almost a century after
Breuer's famous patient had first fallen ill. After failing to track down
a non-existent sanatorium in Gross Enzersdorf, to which Jones mistakenly claimed she had been sent, Ellenberger came across a photograph of Bertha Pappenheim which had appeared in a biography of
her, and which, if the date ascribed to it was correct, actually belonged
to the period of her illness. He now managed to obtain the original
of this photograph from the author. The date, 1882, was clearly visible,
but it was no longer possible to make out the name and address of
the photographer. Instead of abandoning the trail, Ellenberger now

enlisted the help of the Montreal City Police. When examined under a special light in the police laboratory the inscription on the photograph became partially visible, revealing the name Konstanz. The trail now became clearer. For on the shores of Lake Constance in the Swiss town of Kreuzlingen there was a famous sanatorium. It was there, almost ninety years after the event, that Ellenberger eventually unearthed a series of records which documented Bertha's admission on 12 July 1882 and which included a copy of Breuer's original case notes and a report subsequently written by one of the staff doctors. This report made it quite clear that Anna O.'s symptoms had *not* all disappeared as Breuer had claimed. For although she had apparently recovered from some of the specific disorders enumerated by Breuer, she remained extremely ill. She was still suffering from trances and hallucinations and she had developed convulsions. She was also still afflicted by a severe facial neuralgia which Breuer had supposedly cured and by a recurring loss of ability to speak German – another of the symptoms whose specific and permanent cure was claimed in Breuer's published case history. Perhaps most seriously of all, Anna O. had arrived at the sanatorium suffering from severe addiction to morphine, which Breuer had prescribed in an attempt to relieve the pain of her neuralgia. The details of the report confirmed, in the forthright words of Ellenberger, that 'the famed "prototype of a cathartic cure" was neither a cure nor a catharsis.'[20]

This revelation, shattering though its implications may be for one of the foundation myths of psychoanalysis, is by no means the end of the story. For the question which has too rarely been asked throughout the hundred years which have elapsed since Bertha Pappenheim's parents first consulted Breuer is whether his diagnosis of 'hysteria', a diagnosis later to be endorsed by Freud, is medically sound.

Some of the reasons for doubting any nineteenth-century diagnosis of hysteria have already been considered in the last chapter in relation to Charcot. The argument developed there gives some grounds for regarding Breuer's diagnosis with considerable scepticism, scepticism which is not likely to be diminished by pondering upon what Anna O.'s individual symptoms actually were. For, even from a layman's point of view, many of these symptoms seem unlikely to be the product of psychological factors. The first serious symptom of her illness, on account of which Breuer made his initial examination of her, was 'a very severe cough'.[21] Breuer does not discuss the various diagnoses which could have been made at this point but writes simply that 'it was a typical *tussis nervosa*'. Shortly after her severe cough started, Anna O. developed a convergent squint, which in turn gave rise to double-vision. This is a relatively common disorder to which most physicians would immediately ascribe a physical cause. This was as true in Breuer's time as it is today, and Breuer himself writes that 'an ophthalmic surgeon explained this (mistakenly) as being due to paresis of one abducens.'[22] Breuer offers no reason for so brusquely dismissing the diagnosis made by this specialist. If the symptoms which subsequently evolved had made the diagnosis of an emotionally induced illness certain or even probable his attitude to the early symptoms would be understandable. But, as Breuer's words themselves so clearly convey, even Anna O.'s erratic behaviour took place in the context of a marked physical disability. The severity and complexity of this disability can best be illustrated by quoting directly from Breuer's case history as it appeared in *Studies on Hysteria*:

> There developed in rapid succession a series of severe disturbances which were apparently quite new; left-sided occipital headache; convergent squint (diplopia), markedly increased by excitement; complaints that the walls of the room seemed to be falling over (affection of the obliquus); disturbances of vision which it was hard to analyse; paresis of the muscles of the front of the neck, so that finally the patient could only move her head by pressing it backwards between her raised shoulders and moving her whole back; contracture and anaesthesia of the right upper, and, after a time, of the right lower extremity. The latter was fully extended, adducted and rotated inwards. Later the same symptom appeared in the left lower extremity and finally in the left arm, of which, however, the fingers to some extent retained the power of movement. So, too, there was no complete rigidity in the shoulder-joints. The contracture reached its maximum in the muscles of the upper arms. In the same way, the region of the elbows turned out to be most affected by anaesthesia when, at a later stage, it became possible to make a more careful test of this. At the beginning of the illness the anaesthesia could not be efficiently tested, owing to the patient's resistance arising from feelings of anxiety.[23]

It must be said that, in spite of the careful allusions to the patient's excitable and anxious state, the details which Breuer gives do not unequivocally suggest a condition with emotional origins. It would seem on the contrary that Anna O. was in very severe physical distress. Given the fact that contractures, anaesthesias and double-vision are commonly encountered in neurological disorders it is difficult to understand the basis on which first Breuer and then Freud were able to rule out the possibility that Anna O.'s symptoms had their origin in damage to the brain or the nervous system caused either by physical trauma or by a cerebral infection.

The suggestion that some of the patients treated by Breuer and Freud were suffering from organic disorders is seldom given serious consideration by the most zealous supporters of psychoanalysis.* But it has been made in general terms on a number of occasions. For the most detailed and ambitious exposition of this point of view we are obliged to turn once again to Freud's most neglected and undervalued critic – E. M. Thornton. In her chapter on 'The Famous Case of Anna O.' in *The Freudian Fallacy* she points out that almost all the symptoms which are described by Breuer can be correlated with specific lesions of the brain. This applies not only to the most straightforward physical symptoms, such as Anna O.'s contractures, anaesthesias and paralyses, but also to many of her more subtle symptoms, including the disturbances in her vision and her speech.

The most prominent of Anna O.'s visual disorders was the diplopia or double-vision caused by her convergent squint. With regard to this, Thornton is in agreement with the ophthalmic surgeon cited by Breuer and she provides a gloss on his diagnosis of 'paresis of the abducens':

> The abducens is the sixth cranial nerve supplying the motor fibres of the external rectus muscle of the eye. A lesion of this nerve makes it impossible to turn the eye outward and the unopposed pull of the internal rectus causes the eye to turn in, producing squint. Since images then do not fall on the corresponding parts of the left and right retinae, they cannot be fused and the result is diplopia, or double vision, a symptom complained of by Bertha. There is no way that such a paralysis could be produced psychogenically, since the voluntary motor pathways operated by the upper motor neurons govern entire movements and not individual muscles.[24]

Thornton also comments on a more unusual disorder by which Anna O. was afflicted. 'There was,' Breuer writes in his case history of 1895, 'a high degree of restriction of the field of vision: in a bunch of flowers which gave her much pleasure she could only see one flower at a time.'[25] While implicitly acknowledging that this disorder was not well

* This is partly, no doubt, because Freud himself effectively immunised psychoanalysis against such objections by developing mixed aetiological models such as the theory of somatic compliance. See below, Chapters 5 and 6.

known in Breuer's day, Thornton points out that it has been recognised since as one of the characteristic symptoms which can result from a lesion of the parietal lobes. She also writes that Macdonald Critchley's pioneering work, *The Parietal Lobes*, 'actually contains the description of a similar patient who could only see one flower at a time in a bouquet'.[26]

The various speech disturbances suffered by Anna O. might well seem to stand in the way of this kind of neurological diagnosis. Breuer's published description of the illness contains the following account of the relevant symptoms:

> Alongside the development of the contractures there appeared a deep-going functional disorganisation of her speech. It first became noticeable when she was at a loss to find words, and this difficulty gradually increased. Later she lost her command of grammar and syntax; she no longer conjugated verbs, and eventually she used only infinitives, for the most part incorrectly formed from weak past participles; and she omitted both the definite and indefinite article. In the process of time she became almost completely deprived of words. She put them together laboriously out of four or five languages and became almost unintelligible. When she tried to write (until her contractures entirely prevented her from doing so) she employed the same jargon. For two weeks she was completely dumb and in spite of making great and continuous efforts to speak she was unable to say a syllable.[27]

Anna O. eventually recovered her speech and this coincided with a return of the power of movement to the extremities of the left side of her body, and the virtual disappearance of her squint. She was now able to support her head once again and in general her recovery was so marked that she was able to leave her bed for the first time. The difficulties of speech, however, persisted and took a new form, with Anna O. able to speak only in English, occasionally lapsing back into a complete inability to speak any language.

Breuer has no hesitation in interpreting these complex disorders of speech in psychogenic terms, even though he makes no attempt to explain their specific psychological origin. It is likely that many medically sophisticated readers of the early editions of *Studies* will have accepted this view uncritically for the simple reason that it conformed to one of the orthodoxies of early twentieth-century neurology. For, as Laurence Miller has written:

By Freud's day it was accepted . . . that if someone knows more than one language, brain-damage will affect the later-learned or less familiar language to a greater degree than the native tongue. This later came to be known as *Ribot's law*, after the French neurologist who in 1883 first formulated the 'rule of primacy' with respect to memory, including memory of languages. According to this rule any damage to memory functioning will affect the oldest material less than that which has been acquired later. Actually it was Pitres (1895) who applied this principle specifically to the recovery from aphasia seen in polyglots. Such a multilingual patient, said Pitres, usually first regains comprehension of his native tongue, next his ability to speak it, and, finally, the ability to comprehend and then speak other languages he has acquired. It is this 'last hired, first fired' model of language recovery that has come to be associated with Ribot's law.[28]

The fact that Ribot's Law was applied to disturbances of language-function at exactly the time Breuer's case history was published meant that many of his medical colleagues would be strongly inclined to join him in ruling out organic dysfunction as a possible cause for Anna O.'s difficulties. Yet as Miller goes on to point out, in clinical reality 'Ribot's law has proven to be not much of a law at all.' In many cases where people who speak more than one language have suffered from neurological disorders of speech or comprehension (aphasia), they do recover one language earlier than another. But this is not always the first-learned one. 'In some patients,' writes Miller, 'one language recovers, but the others never do while still other patients enjoy temporary recovery of one language only to have it regress as another takes its place. And in a few cases the same patient shows a different type of aphasic syndrome in each of the different languages.' Anna O.'s own language difficulties are thus consonant with modern neurological findings, and Miller himself refers to her case in this context.[29]

E. M. Thornton makes a number of similar observations. She begins by noting that Breuer's account of Anna O.'s initial disorder, in which she loses command of grammar and syntax and omits definite and indefinite articles is 'an almost classic description of the "telegrammatism" encountered in the expressive dysphasias resulting from a lesion in Broca's area or its connections'.[30] She goes on to discuss the disappearance of Anna O.'s native tongue. In this connection she refers to a case reported in 1977 in which a patient whose first language was Chinese, but who learnt English after settling in the United States at the age of seven, suffered a stroke. As a result of the damage this caused to the brain, he partially lost his ability to speak Chinese, making most spontaneous utterances in English. Investigations carried out subsequently on two different bilingual patients by the Seattle neurosurgeon George Ojemann suggested that although sites in the centre of the language area of the brain were common to both first and second languages, there were also peripheral sites which were involved in only one language. 'The strange vagaries of Bertha's aphasia,' writes Thornton, 'so incomprehensible to Breuer's generation, are thus explained on an anatomical basis.'[31]

Thornton's review of Anna O.'s illness is intriguing. The difficulty which remains, however, is that of accounting for the simultaneous presence of such a bizarre cluster of apparently neurological symptoms in one patient. Thornton's solution to this problem is ingenious. She notes that the early stages of Anna O.'s illness bear some resemblance to the pattern of tuberculous meningitis, a disease which is almost always associated with paralysis, contractures and diplopia. She further observes that meningitis could easily have been contracted from infecting organisms present in a subpleuritic tubercular abscess, the condition through which Anna O. was nursing her father at the time she fell ill. If this had happened then the initial symptom would have been a severe cough – the symptom on account of which Breuer first examined his patient. On the basis of these undeniable points of resemblance, Thornton draws the conclusion that Anna O.'s illness was 'an almost classic example' of tuberculous meningitis.

One objection which might be raised against this conclusion is that a trained physician such as Breuer would at least have suspected meningitis had Bertha really been suffering from it. Interestingly, Thornton is able to show that he did entertain just such a suspicion. For, profiting from the detective-work of Ellenberger, Thornton obtained a photocopy of Breuer's earlier case history of 1882.[32] From this it became clear that at one stage Breuer considered the possibility of 'a tubercle in the pons, chronic meningitis or such like extending into the left sylvian fossa'. He himself rejected these diagnoses on the grounds that the illness had begun with 'a clear *tussis nervosa*' and 'a circumstance to be described'. This circumstance, Thornton writes, 'was none other than the introduction of the famous cathartic method (and Breuer's confidence in its validity)'.[33] Dismissing this cathartic method as a complete illusion, Thornton holds fast to her own retrospective diagnosis of meningitis.

Thornton's argument is detailed, and in some respects seems

plausible. Unfortunately for the sceptical case against Freud and psychoanalysis, however, her claim that Anna O.'s illness was 'almost a classic case' of tuberculous meningitis is simply not true. The first objection to this claim is that, before the introduction of modern drug therapies, tuberculous meningitis was almost invariably fatal. Yet Anna O. appears to have made a complete recovery from her illness with no signs of serious residual damage. It is certainly true that some cases of spontaneous recovery have been documented but they are very rare indeed and most neurologists would take the view that untreated tuberculous meningitis is almost always a fatal condition. The second objection to Thornton's claim is that, while some of Anna O.'s symptoms do occur frequently in meningitis, others do not. The loss of a native language and the simultaneous retention of an acquired language is an unusual symptom which is rarely found in association with meningitis. The same can be said of Anna O.'s tendency to fluctuate between languages on a daily basis or swap languages in mid-sentence. While the evidence available does not allow us to rule out meningitis definitively, most physicians would probably agree with the verdict of the neurologist Malcolm Robson Parsons, an authority on tuberculous meningitis: 'To say that *one patient* recovers from a disease which is normally lethal, has a disorder of speech which is incredibly uncommon, and develops an extremely rare disorder of parietal function, is stretching the limits of credibility to breaking-point.'[34]

The medical implausibility of Thornton's specific rediagnosis of Anna O. was one of the factors which enabled reviewers to dismiss her book so easily when it appeared. In doing this, however, such critics were making exactly the kind of hasty and over-confident generalisation of which they accused Thornton. It may well be that the hypothesis of tuberculous meningitis is one which most physicians would reject. But her account points to a series of anomalies which demand an alternative explanation.

For what cannot be denied is that almost all the behavioural and physiological manifestations of Anna O.'s illness, including the most bizarre, *are* found in neurological disorders. On the evidence which is now available many trained physicians and neurologists, while they might well be extremely sceptical about the possibility of meningitis, would suspect that somewhere at the bottom of Anna O.'s symptoms there lay an organic problem. Without the benefit of a formal history, unbiased observation, or the possibility of undertaking a clinical examination of the patient, no responsible physician would be likely to support any single diagnosis without reservations. But there are a number of organic conditions which, in exceptional circumstances, might have led to symptoms of the kind which Anna O. had. In 1983, for example, in the *Journal of the Royal Society of Medicine*, the psychiatrist Lindsay Hurst suggested that Anna O. had been suffering from sarcoid. Another suggestion which has been made is that she was suffering from encephalitis, a diffuse non-suppurative disorder of the brain which can cause severe and widespread damage (sometimes associated with disturbed behaviour) and from which some patients make a good recovery. Still other suggestions include multiple sclerosis, and a complex form of temporal lobe epilepsy.[35]

This latter possibility is developed in detail in an extremely impressive paper by the American psychiatrist Alison Orr-Andrawes. Writing in 1985, apparently without knowledge of Thornton's work, Orr-Andrawes independently points to the unexplained presence of 'focal neurological signs and symptoms' in Anna O.'s illness. Although her solution to this problem is somewhat different from Thornton's, there is a striking overlap between her argument and the general thesis which Thornton expounds with regard to Charcot and 'hysteria'. Anna O.'s focal neurological symptoms, she writes, 'first developed in conjunction with discrete episodes of altered consciousness, suggesting local paroxysmal dysfunction of the cerebral cortex':

> In searching for an etiology to explain these symptoms, Breuer was handicapped by the scientific limitations of his day. Nevertheless, I believe he accurately described in Anna O. the clinical features of complex partial seizures, and correctly identified their area of spread along the para-Sylvian cortex of the left hemisphere. The idea that Anna O. may have suffered from a seizure disorder is not without precedent. Many of the early cases of hysteria and 'hystero-epilepsy' described by Charcot, Janet and others, were cases of psychomotor epilepsy (Gastaut, 1954), and the prevailing definition of hysteria did not make a clear distinction between the two conditions.[36]

Complex partial seizures are a particular form of temporal lobe epilepsy and Orr-Andrawes goes on to observe that most of the symptoms Breuer describes are typical components of such seizures as described in the relevant neurological literature. Characteristic symptoms include blurred vision, double-vision, feelings of de-personalisation and de-realisation, visual illusions which include the misidentification of objects, macropsia, and distortions of angulation in which upright objects appear tilted, or the walls of the room appear to bend. All of these symptoms appear both in modern neurological discussions, meticulously referenced by Orr-Andrawes, and in Breuer's case history. Interestingly and impressively, Orr-Andrawes is able to offer specific neurological explanations for symptoms which Breuer, Freud and most subsequent commentators have tended to treat as discrete, un-related entities. She thus notes that the language deficit which Breuer describes resembles a 'nonfluent aphasia', which is related to a lesion in the language-area of the brain (Broca's area) on the left side of the frontal lobe just above the Sylvian fissure. She then relates this to the symptoms affecting the right side of Anna O.'s body by quoting a general neurological principle formulated by Geschwind: 'Because these lesions [in Broca's area] also generally involve the adjacent motor cortex, most patients with nonfluent aphasia suffer from an appreciable hemiparesis which is usually greater in the arm.'[37]

In terms which coincide almost exactly with Thornton's discussion, Orr-Andrawes goes on to consider Anna O.'s inability to recognise faces, a very specific neurological disorder which she, like Thornton, recognises as prosopagnosia. She, like Thornton, suggests that Anna O.'s ability to be carried back into the past by very specific stimuli, such as the holding up of an orange, indicates a form of reflex epilepsy. Finally she even cites a modern neurological parallel for the most extraordinary of all Anna O.'s symptoms – her ability to relive through spontaneous auto-hypnoses the events of exactly one year earlier. Although this phenomenon is exceedingly rare, Orr-Andrawes is able to invoke one comparable report by Hommes of a man with temporal lobe epilepsy who re-experienced in his seizures each night the events of forty-eight hours earlier.[38]

So impressive is Alison Orr-Andrawes's investigation of the symp-toms she deals with, and so comprehensive is her own research into the relevant neurological literature, that it seems to place the neuro-logical basis of Anna O.'s illness beyond all reasonable doubt. It should be noted, however, that the conclusion that Anna O. suffered from temporal lobe epilepsy does not in itself constitute a diagnosis. Epilepsy is a symptom rather than an illness, almost in the same way that vomiting is the sign of a disease rather than an illness in itself. Just as vomiting can be caused by a variety of infections or disorders of the gastro-intestinal tract, so epileptic seizures can be produced by a variety of traumas, infections or disorders which directly affect the brain.

Orr-Andrawes acknowledges that seizures are symptomatic of underlying pathology and observes that the presence of focal signs suggests
a structural lesion 'such as a tumour, aneurysm, or scar'. She goes on
to observe that such lesions may be present but 'clinically silent' until
some factor which lowers the patient's seizure threshold is brought
into play. Medically prescribed drugs can sometimes have this effect,
for withdrawal states are among the factors which can activate previously silent epileptic foci. In this particular case Orr-Andrawes speculates that Anna O., who was certainly sedated with chloral hydrate in
the later stages of her illness, may have become addicted to this drug
earlier on and that this was responsible not only for her seizures, but
also for her daily fluctuations of consciousness. She further speculates
that not all Anna O.'s symptoms are neurologically based but
that some of them are hysterical elaborations of organic symptoms
and that others, specifically the left-sided contractures and neck-
paresis 'arose as [hysterical] conversion symptoms without an organic
origin'.[39]

The more speculative portions of Orr-Andrawes's paper are the
least persuasive. There can be little doubt that the seizure-inducing
qualities of chloral hydrate, which were almost completely unrecognised in the nineteenth century, played an extremely significant role
in producing 'hysterical' seizures. In this respect Orr-Andrawes draws
attention to an aspect of medical history which is perhaps even more
significant than she herself suggests.[40] Whether chloral hydrate was
actually responsible for Anna O.'s initial seizures, however, remains
purely a matter of speculation. Orr-Andrawes's further argument that
some of Anna O.'s physical symptoms were the product of psychological conflict is one for which no persuasive evidence is offered. It is
perhaps best regarded as an example of the same kind of residual piety
towards Freud and psychoanalysis which we have already encountered
in other contexts.

The safest conclusion we may draw is that Anna O. was suffering
from a neurological disorder which almost certainly gave rise to complex partial seizures, but which we are never likely to identify with any
certainty because of the relatively primitive diagnostic tools which were
available to Breuer and the other physicians who treated her in the
closing years of the nineteenth century. Perhaps the most remarkable
feature of the case is not the miraculous cure asserted by psychoanalytic
legend – for this cure, as we have seen, never took place. It is
the misplaced confidence with which Breuer, and after him Freud,

completely ruled out the possibility of organic neurological disease without any proper medical grounds for doing so and relied instead on an unproved and unprovable theory of hysteria.

To offer this account of the case of Anna O. is not to dismiss the 'famous cathartic method' out of hand. For it does seem that certain aspects of Breuer's procedure may have had some palliative effect on his patient. In this regard we should bear in mind that almost all physical illnesses have some psychological consequences and that sometimes these can be severe. Patients suffering from cancer, for example, frequently become depressed and it is not uncommon for them to undergo psychotherapy, which is sometimes effective. It seems quite likely that the therapeutic procedures devised by Breuer played a similar role in relieving Anna O. of some of the psychological consequences of her condition. Indeed one of the most interesting differences between Breuer's original case notes and his published case history bears out this view. In the version which appears in *Studies on Hysteria* Breuer follows his account of how Anna O. had finally been induced to drink a glass of water by observing that 'a number of extremely obstinate whims were similarly removed after she had described the experiences which had given rise to them.'[41] Breuer's account, however, gives no indication of what these whims might be. If we turn to the original case notes, however, one answer to this question soon becomes apparent. For Anna O. had developed a curious habit of going to bed with her stockings on. What is perhaps even more interesting is that in his original notes Breuer's account of how this habit was relinquished immediately *precedes* his account of how Anna overcame her aversion for drinking. Although the chronological relationship between the two incidents is not stated explicitly, Breuer's notes certainly give the impression that it was Anna O.'s 'stocking caprice' which provided the initial model for Breuer's cathartic therapy and not, as he claims in his published case history, her aversion to water. His account of the incident is as follows:

> When she was awoken [from her trance-like state] and put to bed in the evening, the patient could not bear her stockings being removed; only on awaking at 2 or 3 o'clock would she occasionally do this, complaining at the same time of the impropriety of allowing her to sleep with her stockings on. One evening she told me a true story of long ago, how at night times she would creep in to eavesdrop on her father (at that time, night nurses could no longer put up with her), how she

slept in her stockings for this reason, then on one occasion she was caught by her brother, and so on. As soon as she had finished she began to cry out softly, demanding why she was in bed with her stockings on. Then she took them off and that was the last we saw of the stocking caprice.[42]

Unlike some of Breuer's claims, this detailed account of Anna O.'s reactions is entirely plausible. Anna O.'s behaviour with regard to her stockings is of a kind which is sometimes found in patients suffering from dementia or from the confusional states and temporal disorientation which are commonly associated with neurological disorders. By relating her present behaviour to her past it would seem that she was able to unravel her evident cognitive confusion. That this confusion also had an emotional dimension seems clear, for she was still behaving as though her dead father was alive and in the next room. In view of all this it is scarcely surprising that Anna O. benefited from her 'talking cure'. Whether we call the effect cathartic, or whether we merely say that, by 'talking it through', Anna O. was able to re-order both her thoughts and her feelings, is a matter of debate. What does seem evident is that her attempt to communicate had a genuine therapeutic effect which led directly to the disappearance of her 'whim'.

In the light of this it might well seem surprising that the story of Anna O.'s stockings disappears entirely from the case history which was published in 1895. Yet a moment's reflection should reveal the difficulties Breuer would have faced if he had retained this story as the sole or even the joint model for what he called his 'technical procedure'. For Breuer's own description of Anna's behaviour as a 'caprice' or an 'obstinate whim', while unsympathetic, conveys well the relative triviality of the entire episode. However it might be described or construed, a young woman's habit of going to bed with her stockings on could scarcely be seen as an important symptom of a major debilitating disease. To use such an incident as the model on which to base a 'technical procedure' designed to alleviate the multiform and extremely serious physical symptoms supposedly produced by 'hysteria' would be to court incredulity and even ridicule.

What happens instead, as we have already seen, is that the story of the stocking caprice, so prominent in Breuer's initial case notes, is quietly dropped. Its place is taken by the story of Anna O.'s aversion to water, which is lifted from its original context and made to stand on its own. The loss of context is significant. For in the unpublished case notes the story is narrated immediately after the incident with her stockings, in terms which suggest that it too was little more than an 'obstinate whim'. The opening sentence of Breuer's account reads as follows: 'For six weeks during the very hottest period she drank nothing, quenching her thirst with fruits and melons.'[43] While this behaviour may have given rise to anxiety it would seem from these words that it was very far from being life-threatening and might very easily have been construed as a rather more serious product of the same confusional state which gave rise to the earlier incident.

In the version which Breuer wrote some thirteen years later the opening sentence of his account is significantly different: 'It was in the summer during a period of extreme heat, and the patient was suffering very badly from thirst; for, without being able to account for it in any way, she suddenly found it impossible to drink.' Whereas in the early account we are immediately told that she was quenching her thirst with fruit and melons, this detail is held back in the later account and then given only in a negative form: 'She lived only on fruit, such as melons etc., *so as to lessen her tormenting thirst*' (italics added). Not only this, but Breuer now adds a significant descriptive touch which is not found at all in the original. For when Anna O. tried to drink from a glass of water, we are told that 'as soon as it touched her lips she would push it away, *like someone suffering from hydrophobia*' (italics added).[44]

It seems fairly clear that what has happened is that Breuer has intensified the entire episode. Not only this, but he has also *medicalised* it. For what was presented originally as a relatively minor behavioural aberration is now compared to hydrophobia – the most prominent symptom of rabies. Having thus converted the episode into something resembling a symptom – and a very serious one at that – Breuer is now able to shift his attention quite naturally to some of the serious physical disabilities from which Anna O. was suffering.

In all this it would probably be wrong to suggest that Breuer was motivated by the desire to deceive others. For it would seem that what was involved was an act of self-deception whose unconscious aim was to prevent him from coming face to face, in the mirror of his narrative, with the image of his own therapeutic folly. This, as should by now be clear, consisted in his belief that a young woman's own method of releasing herself from her habit of going to bed with her stockings on could be taken over by her physician, designated a 'technical pro-cedure', and then used to bring about the removal of severe, painful and disabling symptoms which in most clinical settings would be construed as manifestations of neurological disease.

The question as to how Breuer subsequently managed to convince both himself and Freud that he *had* cured a large number of Anna O.'s physical symptoms is one of the most interesting and, it might be thought, one of the most difficult, in the entire history of psychoanalysis. Yet if we can reconstruct the objective course of Anna O.'s illness from the highly subjective account which Breuer himself gives of it, one possible answer suggests itself. For although Breuer naturally presents his patient's illness as one whose outcome is ultimately determined by his therapeutic interventions, his own account makes it quite clear that the illness spontaneously progressed through several phases and that some of Anna O.'s symptoms receded or disappeared without any therapeutic intervention at all. We may speculate that, in some cases at least, Breuer's belief that he had removed a symptom grew out of the fact that his therapeutic attention to a symptom coincided with the spontaneous remission of that symptom.

It is not difficult to find evidence which appears to support this hypothesis. For the very first of Anna O.'s chronic symptoms which Breuer claimed he had removed by applying his new therapeutic method was the contracture of her right leg – one of the most serious and long-established of Anna O.'s many physical disabilities. Breuer's own commendably honest account of this therapeutic success is revealing. 'She took a great step forward,' he writes, 'when the first of her chronic symptoms disappeared in the same way – the contracture of her right leg, *which, it is true, had already diminished a great deal*' (italics added).[45] If we turn from Breuer's published case history to the original, unpublished version, the situation is made even clearer, since here Breuer describes the contracture as 'having already diminished spontaneously'.[46] It would seem reasonable to suggest that, in seeking to remove this particular symptom by his cathartic method, Breuer may inadvertently have 'shadowed' a process of spontaneous remission, and then, quite innocently, taken therapeutic credit for the results of a natural process of healing.

We may note that, among the many other symptoms Breuer claims to have removed by applying his 'technical procedure' was Anna O.'s 'convergent squint with diplopia'. He traces the origin of this symptom back to a time when Anna had been sitting by her father's sick bed with tears in her eyes. When her father asked the time she could only read her watch by bringing it close to her face and peering through the welled-up tears. 'The face of the watch now seemed very big,' writes Breuer, 'thus accounting for her macropsia and convergent squint.'[47] One inconsistency in Breuer's account is that it is diplopia (double-vision) which has been associated with Anna O.'s squint, and not macropsia (magnified vision), which is reported elsewhere as a distinct symptom which was disposed of separately. We should not allow this inconsistency, however, to distract us from the most salient feature of Breuer's account – which is its almost complete implausibility. For Breuer's explanation of how Anna O. acquired a complex and frequently encountered neurological disorder is neither psychologically persuasive nor physiologically probable. In view of this it seems particularly significant that, at an earlier stage of the case history in which he makes this unlikely therapeutic claim, Breuer has already reported that Anna O.'s squint had begun to disappear before his 'technical procedure' had even been adopted. 'At this point too,' he writes of one of the early developments in Anna's illness, 'her squint began to diminish, and made its appearance only at moments of great excitement.' Once again it would seem reasonable to suggest that Breuer's therapeutic attention to a particular symptom shadowed a process of natural healing which had begun some time before.

It might seem extremely unlikely, on the face of it, that such coincidences would happen more than once or twice. In any organic disease the spontaneous remission of a symptom is often a slow and gradual process, and the chances of a symptom disappearing of its own accord exactly at the moment an external therapy was being applied to it would seem remote. The only circumstance in which this might happen consistently would be if patient and physician entered into a kind of therapeutic alliance in which they devised a method of treatment which could be protracted almost indefinitely until such a time that a particular symptom disappeared.

One of the most intriguing aspects of the case of Anna O. is that Breuer and his patient appear to have unconsciously entered into just such an alliance. For it would seem that it was Anna O. who evolved the methodical routine of informing Breuer, in reverse chronological order, about every single past appearance of a particular symptom. It was this routine which Breuer then adopted as his 'technical procedure'. According to Breuer this procedure 'left nothing to be desired in its logical consistency and systematic application':

Each individual symptom in this complicated case was taken separately in hand; all the occasions on which it had appeared were described in reverse order, starting before the time the patient became bed-ridden, and going back to the event which had led to its first appearance. When this had been described the symptom was permanently removed.[48]

The question which is raised by this description is how Breuer could know with any certainty that his patient had uncovered the first instance of any particular symptom. The most obvious answer – that he could rely on his patient's memory – must be ruled out. For Breuer himself makes it clear that Anna O. was herself unable to single out in advance the event which supposedly precipitated a particular symptom:

> It turned out to be quite impracticable to shorten the work by trying to elicit in her memory straight away the first provoking cause of her symptoms. She was unable to find it, grew confused, and things proceeded even more slowly than if she was allowed quietly and steadily to follow back the thread of memories on which she had embarked.[49]

Since Anna O. could apparently not identify the precipitating cause of a particular symptom by memory alone, it would seem that the only reliable indicator Breuer had was that of therapeutic effectiveness: if, after Anna O.'s description of a particular occurrence of one of her symptoms, the symptom remitted – or appeared to remit – then he could assume that the relevant traumatic event had been discovered. It would therefore follow that if no remission took place, the first occurrence of the symptom had not yet been reached and Anna O. would have to embark on a yet deeper exploration of her unconscious. If therapeutic success was indeed employed tacitly by Breuer as a criterion of accurate recollection, then in practice his 'technical procedure' could be almost infinitely prolonged. This is especially so since, for quite different reasons, Anna O. herself always remained in a position where she could extend the analysis of a particular symptom. For Breuer tells us that all the events Anna O. related were so clearly differentiated in her memory 'that if she happened to make a mistake in their sequence she would be obliged to correct herself and put them in the right order; if this was not done her report came to a standstill.' The extraordinary laboriousness of Breuer's 'technical procedure' is frequently overlooked by commentators. Yet in his case history Breuer himself goes to some pains to illustrate just this aspect of the case:

An example will show the exhaustive manner in which she accomplished this. It was our regular experience that the patient did not hear when she was spoken to. It was possible to differentiate this passing habit of not hearing as follows:

(a) Not hearing when someone came in, while her thoughts were abstracted. 108 separate detailed instances of this, mentioning the persons and circumstances, often with dates. First instance: not hearing her father come in.

(b) Not understanding when several people were talking. 27 instances. First instance: her father, once more, and an acquaintance.

(c) Not hearing when she was alone and directly addressed. 50 instances. Origin: her father having vainly asked her for some wine.

(d) Deafness brought on by being shaken (in a carriage, etc.). 15 instances. Origin: having been shaken angrily by her young brother when he caught her one night listening at the sick-room door.

(e) Deafness brought on by fright at a noise. 37 instances. Origin: a choking fit of her father's caused by swallowing the wrong way.

(f) Deafness during deep *absence*. 12 instances.

(g) Deafness brought on by listening hard for a long time, so that when she was spoken to she failed to hear. 54 instances.[50]

If we read this extraordinary passage with due scepticism it is difficult not to conclude that the therapeutic alliance which Breuer formed with his patient eventually led to their playing out, without understanding what they were doing, a game of aetiological pass-the-parcel. So long as the symptom of deafness persisted, physician and patient together would carefully remove layer after layer of amnesia in an effort to find the traumatic event which was supposedly hidden inside the unconscious. As soon as the symptom stopped, however, or appeared to stop, then whichever memory had been reached at the time would be retrospectively identified as the traumatic event which had precipitated the symptom. On this reading, Breuer's 'technical procedure' was indeed logically consistent in one respect. For if it were applied with sufficient determination, and with sufficient faith in its therapeutic effectiveness *to a symptom which was already in remission*, then sooner or later a miraculous-seeming cure was almost bound to take place.

Breuer's own account of his therapeutic procedure contains one detail which remains unexplained. For, from his record of how Anna

O.'s sporadic deafness was dealt with, it would appear that what was ostensibly a single symptom was actually subdivided into a number of supposedly different disorders. Breuer and Anna O. therefore had to uncover not one unconscious origin for her difficulty in hearing, but seven different ones. Since Breuer offers no explanation for this curiosity yet intimates that a similar procedure was adopted in the case of other symptoms, we can only speculate as to the reasons for it. Perhaps the most likely explanation is that this practice of subdividing symptoms was evolved by Anna O. and her physician in order to deal with instances of therapeutic disappointment. What it meant was that if a symptom which had supposedly been 'talked away' subsequently reappeared, rather than being treated as an indicator of therapeutic failure, the recurring symptom could be redefined as a new symptom and a fresh origin sought out. The game of aetiological pass-the-parcel could thus be continued until the symptom stopped again. It is interesting in this regard that although Breuer himself writes that 'the first provoking cause was habitually a fright of some kind' many of the causes which are offered for Anna O.'s symptoms seem to be trivial, or to have little or no traumatic content. This may perhaps have been because, if a symptom disappeared during the course of treatment, its disappearance had of necessity to be ascribed to whatever memory Anna O. had most recently unwrapped, however mundane, slight or undramatic the event in question might be.

In any assessment of this reconstruction of the case of Anna O., there are two very important factors which ought to be borne in mind. The first, and by far the most important, is that Anna O. was no passive partner in the therapeutic process which Breuer devised. Not only had she helped to evolve the process but, like any patient, she had an interest in its successful outcome. Moreover, as should by now be clear, it was she who was ultimately in control of the progress of her 'cure'. Patients in this position, suffering from a long and apparently intractable illness, frequently form strong relationships with their physicians and may well go out of their way in order to help them achieve their therapeutic ends not simply out of self-interest but out of a genuine desire to please them. They will sometimes tell their doctors what they believe they want to hear, and may even collude with them in avoiding any painful confrontation with the evidence of therapeutic failure. It seems quite possible that Anna O., who evidently came to believe at some point in a psychogenic pathology for her illness, did her best to make Breuer's therapeutic wishes come true by encouraging him to direct his attention to symptoms which were already receding. She may even have intensified such symptoms in her imagination in order that more therapeutic credit would devolve upon her physician when they eventually disappeared. What does seem clear is that, at a certain point in her illness, both physician and patient came to believe in the effectiveness of the therapeutic rituals which they had jointly devised, and carefully shielded one another from any evidence which might help to destroy this precious illusion.

The second factor which should be borne in mind is that not even Breuer himself claimed to have removed *all* of Anna O.'s symptoms. He merely claimed to have removed those which, in his view, had a 'psychical' origin. He specifically pointed to one group of symptoms which he believed had a different origin – 'the paralytic contractures of her left extremities and the paresis of the muscles raising her head'. Breuer noted that once these symptoms disappeared, they never reappeared even in the mildest form. He therefore suggested that they should be attributed to 'a secondary extension of that unknown condition which constitutes the somatic foundation of hysterical phenomena'.[51] Since these symptoms had disappeared quite spontaneously and completely before Breuer had even adopted his 'technical procedure' he clearly had little alternative but to ascribe them to a different cause. Otherwise it could easily be argued that the disappearance of the symptoms he *did* believe he had cured was due to the same process of spontaneous remission. By claiming that the symptoms which he had supposedly cured had *psychical* origins, and that those which had cured themselves had an *organic* cause, Breuer was effectively fortifying himself in advance against the very kind of objections which I have made here. There is, however, no reason to suppose that he did this with any conscious intention to deceive. The much more likely hypothesis is that he had fallen so much in love with the illusion he had begun to develop of his own therapeutic powers that he was psychologically incapable of crediting any evidence which might threaten to destroy that illusion.

It is for this reason, we may presume, that he reported that one of the most persistent of all Anna O.'s symptoms, her inability to speak German, had been permanently removed, even though he knew full well that the symptom was still present, albeit in a sporadic and reduced form. Given the laxity of his criteria for pronouncing a permanent cure in this instance, there is no reason to suppose that his pronouncements about other symptoms are intrinsically more trustworthy.

Though a good number of Anna O.'s supposedly psychical symptoms undoubtedly did disappear during Breuer's attendance on her, there is no evidence to show that some of them did not recur *after* Breuer had completed the therapeutic ritual which supposedly removed them. In other words if we are to accept the proposition that Breuer's therapy unwittingly shadowed a process of spontaneous remission we do not have to believe nearly as much as his own account would imply.

Frank Sulloway, after discussing the 303 instances of Anna O.'s deafness which Breuer presents in his case history, writes that the medical cure achieved by Breuer 'was nothing short of stupendous'.[52] The account of the case which I have given here suggests that the only thing which is stupendous about it is not the cure which Breuer effected (for there was no cure), but our own credulity in taking seriously for so long a case history which, more clearly than any dream which Freud ever analysed, appears to be an example of wish-fulfilment.

That the question marks which surround the case of Anna O. should have been almost completely ignored by Freud's major biographers is scarcely surprising. For to entertain any serious doubt about the diagnosis of Anna O. would be to deal a devastating blow to the mythology which has traditionally sustained the psychoanalytic church. For, although Anna O. was not one of Freud's own patients, the mystique of her cure rapidly became one of the most important elements in the Freudian legend, and Peter Gay is undoubtedly right when he describes Breuer's encounter with her as 'the founding case of psychoanalysis'.[53]

In some respects, however, the doubt which ought to surround Breuer's diagnosis and his therapeutic claims merely adds piquancy to a question which could well have been asked long before Ellenberger tracked down Breuer's original case notes. The question is as to why Freud endorsed the account of Anna O.'s treatment which appears in *Studies on Hysteria*, when he knew that Breuer's claim to have cured Anna O. was false.

That Freud was well aware of the inaccuracy of Breuer's case history is even conceded by Ernest Jones. For when Jones revealed in his biography that 'the poor patient did not fare so well as one might gather from Breuer's published account' he did so on the basis of a 'fuller account' of the case related to him by Freud. Jones went on to disclose that, a year after Breuer had broken off his treatment of Anna O., he had confided to Freud that the patient he had supposedly relieved of all her symptoms 'was quite unhinged and that he wished she would die and so be released from her suffering'. Anna O. did subsequently improve but a few years later she was still suffering from hallucinatory states in the evening.[54]

It is difficult not to be reminded of the episode which had taken place ten years earlier, when Freud misreported Fleischl-Marxow's cocaine addiction as a complete cure (see above, Chapter 1). Once again it would seem that that we must find Freud guilty of scientific mendacity.

Yet, as in the earlier case, it would be wrong to pass judgement on Freud's scientific dishonesty without taking into consideration the complex circumstances out of which it emerged. Here too there is every reason to suppose that Freud had come to the conclusion that Breuer's particular lie hid a general truth and was therefore excusable. For by 1895, when *Studies on Hysteria* was published, Freud had himself been experimenting with Breuer's cathartic method for some time, and seems genuinely to have believed that he was very close to striking therapeutic gold. If, by collaborating with Breuer's exercise in medical misrepresentation, Freud could promote their new therapy, he would be benefiting humanity as a whole. Since Freud clearly believed that Breuer had been successful in removing *some* of Anna O.'s symptoms it would not be stretching the facts too far to claim that they had *all* vanished.

Given Freud's compulsive need to gain recognition, it seems quite likely that he had private recourse to some such argument in order to justify his second major act of scientific deception. It also seems likely that he took into consideration the particular advantages which would almost inevitably flow from Breuer's fiction. For throughout his professional life Freud was always acutely aware of the role played in medicine by authority. 'People follow only authority, after all,' he wrote to Wilhelm Fliess in 1901, 'and that can only be acquired by doing something that is within their comprehension.'[55] Breuer's imaginary 'cure' clearly helped Freud in his own quest for authority. For by laying his medical rod upon ground which the great Breuer had consecrated through his miracle, Freud now had the opportunity to watch it being transformed into a serpent of therapeutic wisdom – and all this in full view of those he hoped would become his followers. With such mythic power within his grasp it is perhaps not surprising that Freud, who had always aspired to carry Moses's rod, should decline to quarrel with the powerful myth which Breuer had managed to create out of what was, in reality, a therapeutic failure.

What has often seemed surprising to those who have accepted Ernest Jones's account of the case at face value is that Freud should subsequently have made such a frank disclosure of the true facts of the case to Stefan Zweig, to Jones, and, it would seem, to Jung. According to the vivid account of 'what really happened with Breuer's patient' which Freud gave to Zweig, Breuer had been called to his patient one evening and had found her confused and writhing with abdominal cramps. Asked what the matter was, Anna O. had replied, 'Now comes Dr B.'s child.' Freud interpreted this 'phantom pregnancy' as a sign that the underlying cause of Anna O.'s illness had been sexual all along. At that moment, he commented to Zweig, Breuer held 'the key in his hand'. But he did not know how to make use of it and 'dropped it'. 'With all his great mental endowment,' Freud continued, 'he had nothing Faustian about him. In conventional horror he took flight and left the patient to a colleague.'

This account of the manner in which Anna O.'s treatment was brought to a close by Breuer has achieved wide currency. Yet we only have to attend carefully to Freud's own words in order to recognise that his revised version of what 'really' happened was itself no more securely based in reality than the original version. For on three separate occasions, showing at least some signs of a sense of intellectual honesty which is not always recognised by his most extreme critics, Freud scrupulously characterised his account of 'what really happened' as a 'reconstruction'. This term is used not only in his letter to Zweig but also in the less detailed accounts given in *On the History of the Psychoanalytic Movement* and *An Autobiographical Study*.[56] In the letter to Zweig, Freud introduced his story thus: 'What really happened to Breuer's patient *I was able to guess* later on, long after the break in our relations, *when I suddenly remembered something Breuer had once told me in another context . . .*' (italics added).

What has confused the issue is that, having frankly disclosed the entirely speculative nature of his story, Freud attempts to rescue it for the realm of empirical fact. For immediately after he has told the story of how Anna O. had fallen in love with her doctor and gone through the throes of an imaginary childbirth, he writes: 'I was so convinced of this reconstruction of mine that I published it somewhere. Breuer's youngest daughter [. . .] read my account and asked her father about it (shortly before his death). He confirmed my version, and she informed me about it later.'[57]

Freud's claim that his reconstruction had been confirmed might seem to put the matter beyond doubt. Yet, as Albrecht Hirschmüller has pointed out, Freud's claim will not bear examination. For Freud never published his reconstruction in its entirety. The story of Anna O.'s hysterical pregnancy was never told in Breuer's lifetime and so could not have been confirmed by him. The supposed confirmation by Breuer probably refers to the account given in *An Autobiographical Study*, which was published in February 1925, a few months before Breuer's death. This account claims merely that Anna O. had 'developed a condition of "transference love"' – and that Breuer had 'retired in dismay'.

Freud's entire version of the episode thus turns out to be a mixture of scrupulous honesty and careless distortion. All in all it would be difficult to dissent from Albrecht Hirschmüller's conclusion:

> Freud's version is an interpretative reconstruction. With increasing lapse of time after the events, this reconstruction became more and more consolidated and condensed, until the mere suspicion that the analysis had not been advanced far enough became the spectacular picture of Breuer's flight from his patient's hysterical birth.[58]

Freud's underlying motive for creating his careful amalgam of truth and falsity is not difficult to divine. In his letter to Stefan Zweig, and in the similar account which he gave to Ernest Jones, Freud can be seen at work carefully undoing the legend of Anna O. which he had himself encouraged Breuer to propagate. The first version of this legend had portrayed a miraculous and complete cure which had been brought about by an entirely new method of therapy which was Breuer's creation. The great advantage of this legend was, as I have suggested, that it enabled Freud to bask in the reflected light of Breuer's 'miracle' and thus gain credibility for his own therapeutic strategies, which were closely modelled on Breuer's pioneering work. Yet once this aim had been achieved and Freud had emerged from obscurity to head the nascent psychoanalytic movement, there was a very considerable danger that the legend, if left intact, would actually serve to diminish Freud's originality in the eyes of his closest disciples. At both stages of the story we thus find Freud engaged in the entirely characteristic act of refashioning history in order to suit the needs of his own compulsively messianic identity. Whereas in the first place he carefully 'borrows' authority from Breuer, in the second place he claims this authority as his own by revealing (initially to Jung) that the cure Breuer reported never took place, and implying that only a therapist gifted with his unique insight could have brought Anna O.'s case to a successful conclusion.

If it were to be accepted that Anna O. not only was not cured, but that she was not suffering from hysteria in the first place, psychoanalysis would be effectively deprived both of its originating 'miracle', and of Freud's ingenious attempt to appropriate the case retrospectively as the 'miracle-which-might-have-been'.

In view of this it is interesting that, in his recent biography of Freud, Peter Gay does not hesitate to accept Freud's 'revised' version of the legend. He thus portrays Freud conventionally as a heroic adventurer who fearlessly follows paths which Breuer had opened up but which he was himself too timid to explore: 'The psychoanalytic process is a struggle with resistances, and Breuer's rejection of the elemental, shocking truths that this process may uncover is a plain instance of such a maneuver.'[59] The 'truths' to which Peter Gay refers were, of course, those concerned with sex and sexual aetiology. But if the entire quest on which Breuer and Freud had embarked took as its starting-point a misdiagnosis which had itself grown out of the more fundamental medical mistakes of Charcot, then the whole of Freud's argument about the sexual aetiology of neurotic illnesses is itself called into question. It is to the question of sex, and of how it came to assume such a fundamental role in Freud's thinking, that we must eventually turn. Before we do so, however, we must first consider some of the cases of 'hysteria' which Freud himself brought to the attention of his colleagues in 1895 and submit to sceptical examination the manner in which he applied the cathartic technique which Breuer had created.

FIVE

Freud's First Case

FREUD HAD EVIDENTLY been deeply impressed by Anna O.'s supposed cure when Breuer first told him about it in 1882. But when he returned to Vienna from his visit to Paris in 1886 he did so without having succeeded in persuading Charcot to take a personal interest in the case. For the time being this rebuff seems to have moderated Freud's own enthusiasm for the cathartic method. But what Breuer himself would eventually call 'the germ-cell of the whole of psychoanalysis' remained in Freud's mind and would soon exercise a decisive influence on his own therapeutic methods.[1]

When he first established his private practice in April 1886, Freud, whose clinical experience was still extremely limited, seems to have experienced acutely a sense of his own therapeutic impotence. For the first twenty months he followed the current medical fashion and confined himself to administering electrotherapy and other entirely physical treatments such as baths and massages. He eventually came to the conclusion that these methods were producing little or no beneficial effect. In December 1887 he therefore began to use hypnotism on his patients in an attempt to dispel their symptoms by suggestion. This method too proved difficult and unrewarding and Freud eventually decided to apply Breuer's cathartic method, using hypnotism not as a medium for suggestion but in order to explore his patients' past experiences and to seek out the traumatic events which had supposedly precipitated their illness. Finding that some patients were difficult to hypnotise he adapted Breuer's method and eventually arrived at the technique of free-association. Through this technique Freud believed he could explore his patients' *unconscious* memories and uncover pathological material which they had repressed. By using Breuer's method as a prototype he thus evolved some of the basic principles of psychoanalysis.

One of the most widely held misconceptions about the history of psychoanalysis is the belief that Freud's early patients came to him because they were suffering from emotional difficulties or because they displayed symptoms which clearly had a psychological origin. The reality was very different. For a large proportion of the patients whom Freud treated during his early years in private practice had initially sought medical advice because they were suffering from *physical* symptoms; they had enlisted the help of a physician for no other reason than that they believed themselves to be ill. Among their symptoms were headaches, muscular pain, neuralgia, gastric pain, tics, vomiting, clonic spasms, *petit mal*, epileptoid convulsions, and a host of other physical reactions.[2] It was Freud who, by either making or confirming a diagnosis of hysteria, came to the conclusion that the origin of these symptoms was to be found in his patients' emotional lives – and specifically in the traumatic events which had supposedly given rise to their illnesses.

This consideration is extremely important in any assessment of the early history of psychoanalysis. For, whether or not Josef Breuer's case of Anna O. was founded upon a misdiagnosis, it seems likely that some of Freud's own cases were. Freud, indeed, would be unusual among nineteenth-century nerve specialists if he had not misdiagnosed a considerable number of his patients. This is because he practised at a time when medical science had only just begun to emerge from a long period of extreme diagnostic poverty. Many of the most basic diagnostic techniques which are taken for granted by modern physicians had still to be discovered. The lumbar puncture, which is the only way in which Breuer could have tested his momentary hunch that Anna O. was suffering from meningitis, was not developed until 1891, and was not in general use until the early part of the twentieth century. X-rays, which would eventually become one of the most useful of all diagnostic aids, were discovered only in 1895 – the same year in which *Studies on Hysteria* was published. The electroencephalogram, which would revolutionise neurology and psychiatry and lead to the final definition of temporal lobe epilepsy, was not invented until 1929, and was not in general use until the 1940s. Many other basic techniques of neurological investigation would not be developed until even later. The computed tomography scan, for example, which uses X-ray transmission readings to generate an image of the brain and which can display some lesions, tumours and other signs of pathology directly, began to be generally used only in the late 1970s. Not only were these diagnostic techniques unavailable to Breuer, Freud and their contemporaries, but neurology and psychiatry were relatively young and under-organised branches of medicine whose stores of knowledge were only just beginning to be built up.

Both medical historians and modern physicians sometimes underestimate the degree of diagnostic darkness to which their nineteenth-century predecessors had become habituated. This is partly because the direct evidence which might lead to a more realistic assessment is not always available. Doctors tend not to advertise their misdiagnoses any more than they are wont to display the corpses of their patients. Frequently, indeed, they are genuinely unaware of their own mistakes. Indirect evidence usually remains, however, and it is intriguing how often this too tends to be ignored. One of the reasons is that many medical historians are themselves physicians and are interested primarily in a view of medicine which portrays it as a continual progress towards the pinnacle of the present day. By such orthodox commentators 'medicine' tends to be invisibly re-defined as 'successful medicine'. The result is that they end up writing a Whig-history of their own profession, concentrating on real medical breakthroughs. The mistakes, misdirections, deceptions and self-deceptions in which the larger part of medical history consists disappear almost completely.[3]

One of the facets of medical history which tends to be obscured in this way is the manner in which disease-syndromes have frequently been brought into existence by doctors not because they correspond to any real clinical entity, but in order to provide a refuge from diagnostic uncertainty. One example of such a 'syndrome of convenience' is provided by neurasthenia – which was invented in 1869 by the American physician George M. Beard, and which would eventually play a significant role in psychoanalysis (see below, Chapter 8). The possibility which we must consider, however, is that hysteria itself should be understood as just such a syndrome.

This view has been canvassed by a number of psychiatrists and neurologists ever since the time of Charcot – and sometimes as a direct response to the clinical vagaries of Charcot's work. In 1908, for example, Steyerthal predicted that:

Within a few years the concept of hysteria will belong to history . . . there is no such disease and there never has been. What Charcot called hysteria is a tissue woven of a thousand threads, a cohort of the most varied diseases, with nothing in common but the so-called stigmata, which in fact may accompany any disease.[4]

But although agnosticism about the concept of hysteria has received significant support within the psychiatric profession (particularly in the United States), the problem has by no means been completely resolved. In Britain, and in some parts of continental Europe, hysteria is still referred to as though it were a distinct syndrome in a number of psychiatric textbooks, and some neurologists, psychiatrists and physicians still believe that the concept is a useful one. In its current usage the term 'hysteria' bears almost no relationship to its original meaning. For it no longer refers to a disorder of the womb. Instead it is used to refer to any symptom or any abnormal pattern of behaviour for which there is no apparent organic pathology and which is therefore believed to be a product of emotional distress, anxiety or some other psychological cause. Those who propose that hysteria might be an entirely unnecessary concept readily accept that it is sometimes difficult to find an organic pathology behind certain physical symptoms. They merely suggest that, since the term 'hysteria' does not refer to any specific or definable disease, it is a sham-diagnosis rather than a real one. If all patients who appear to be suffering from physical symptoms but who have no detectable organic pathology are to be dubbed 'hysterical' then, they argue, the concept of hysteria becomes so broad and so vague as to be quite meaningless. Hysteria, in effect, ceases to be the very specific disease entity it was always historically considered to be, and becomes merely a negative assertion about the nature of certain symptoms. The adjective 'hysterical' is therefore used as though it were a synonym for 'non-organic' or 'psychogenic'. At the same time, however, quite inconsistently, the noun 'hysteria' is used as though it referred still to a positive disease-entity and patients are actually said to be 'suffering from hysteria'. Since, in the current usage of the concept, this is tantamount to claiming that a particular patient is suffering from physical symptoms which cannot be explained, it would be much better, in the view of some thoughtful psychiatrists and neurologists, if the term 'hysteria' were abandoned completely.

One of the most damaging effects of the term 'hysteria' in the past is that it has encouraged doctors to think they have arrived at a diagnosis of symptoms which, in reality, remain mysterious. This in turn means that it is much easier for doctors to miss real but obscure organic illnesses. The point has been well made by the psychiatrist Eliot Slater:

> The diagnosis of 'hysteria' is all too often a way of avoiding a confrontation with our own ignorance. This is especially dangerous when there

is an underlying organic pathology, not yet recognised. In this penumbra we find patients who know themselves to be ill but, coming up against the blank faces of doctors who refuse to believe in the reality of their illness, proceed by way of emotional lability, overstatement and demands for attention . . . Here is an area where catastrophic errors can be made. In fact it is often possible to recognise the presence though not the nature of the unrecognisable, to know that a man must be ill or in pain when all the tests are negative. But it is only possible to those who come to their task in a spirit of humility.

In the main the diagnosis of 'hysteria' applies to a disorder of the doctor–patient relationship. It is evidence of non-communication, of a mutual misunderstanding . . . We are, often, unwilling to tell the full truth or to admit to ignorance . . . Evasions, even untruths, on the doctor's side are among the most powerful and frequently used methods he has for bringing about an efflorescence of 'hysteria'.[5]

Eliot Slater developed his sceptical attitude towards the diagnosis of 'hysteria' only after a great deal of research. This included a meticulous study of eighty-five young or middle-aged patients who had received the diagnosis of 'hysteria' at the National Hospital for Nervous Diseases in London during the years 1951, 1953 and 1955. The most important and the most surprising findings of this study were, as he himself put it, 'the gravity of the after-history and the frequency of misdiagnoses'. During a follow-up period which averaged only nine years, twelve of the eighty-five patients had died, fourteen had become totally disabled and sixteen partially disabled. Most of these cases of death or disability were due to organic illnesses which had been mistaken for 'hysteria'. Among the conditions which had been misdiagnosed either by neurologists or by psychiatrists – including Eliot Slater himself – were three cases of vascular disease, three of tumour and a number of cases where supposedly hysterical black-outs and fits were subsequently rediagnosed as epileptic. Four of the deaths were due to suicide, but in two of these instances the patient had suffered from organic diseases which had not been diagnosed by doctors at the National Hospital. One was a man suffering from various symptoms, including pain in the legs, unsteadiness of gait and impotence. Although Slater himself had diagnosed 'hysteria', the man was later admitted to another hospital and found to be suffering from disseminated sclerosis. In another case a woman who complained of severe headaches and poor vision was held to be suffering from 'drug addiction and hysteria'. She was transferred to the Maudsley Hospital, from which she discharged herself after two weeks, her illness having been diagnosed as 'conversion hysteria'. Two years later she died of a brain tumour.

After discussing these and many less serious misdiagnoses and placing them in the context of medical history, Slater comes to the conclusion that the diagnosis of hysteria has no validity whatsoever – a conclusion which he states in even more outspoken terms than in the essay cited earlier:

> Looking back over the long history of 'hysteria' we see that the null hypothesis has never been disproved. No evidence has yet been offered that the patients suffering from 'hysteria' are in medically significant terms anything more than a random selection. Attempts at rehabilitation of the syndrome, such as those by Carter and by Guze, lead to mutually irreconcilable formulations, each of them determined by their terms of reference. The only thing that hysterical patients can be shown to have in common is that they are all patients. The malady of the wandering womb began as a myth, and as a myth it yet survives. But, like all unwarranted beliefs which still attract credence, it is dangerous. The diagnosis of 'hysteria' is a disguise for ignorance and a fertile source of clinical error. It is, in fact, not only a delusion but also a snare.[6]*

One of the most interesting features of Slater's views is that they are far from being unprecedented. As early as 1648, Thomas Willis, one of the most creative and discerning of all the early neurologists, was putting forward a strikingly similar view of the way in which his colleagues were employing the diagnosis of hysteria:

> The hysterical passion is of so ill fame among the Diseases belonging to Women, that like one half damn'd, it bears the faults of many other Distempers: for when at any time a sickness happens in a Woman's Body, of an unusual manner or more occult original, so that its causes lie hid, and a Curatory indication is altogether uncertain, presently we accuse the evil influence of the Womb (which for the most part is innocent) and in every unusual symptom, we declare it to be something hysterical, and so to this scope, which oftentimes is only the subterfuge of ignorance, the medical intentions and the use of Remedies are directed.[7]

---

* It would be wrong to imply that Eliot Slater pronounced the last word in the medical debate about 'hysteria'. Even in the United States, where the term 'hysteria' has little or no official psychiatric currency, some reforms seem to be little more than terminological. In Britain the term still has some medical advocates. For further discussion of this issue, see Appendix I, 'The Diagnosis of "Hysteria" '.

The main agent of historical continuity between the seventeenth-century physicians referred to by Willis and the twentieth-century neurologists and psychiatrists who are discussed by Slater was, undoubtedly, Jean Martin Charcot. For it was Charcot who, as we have seen, was chiefly responsible for endowing an ancient diagnostic mistake with new scientific respectability at the end of the nineteenth century.

Charcot believed that, although the cause of hysteria was to be found in psychological trauma, it was nevertheless a genuine illness with a real pathology. Freud developed and adapted this view. Specifically he came to believe in the existence of a neurophysiological mechanism whereby the nervous energy created by emotional traumas could be literally transformed into physical symptoms. This transformed nervous energy could either create 'original' physical symptoms, or, alternatively, it could 'feed' ordinary physical symptoms which pre-existed the trauma.

There are no doubt some psychoanalysts and a few psychoanalytically oriented neurologists who still believe in the reality of the intricate and invisible mechanism which Freud postulated. But medical science has found no evidence for the existence of this mechanism. If Freud's notion of hysteria was indeed a chimaera, as I have implied, it would be surprising if his theoretical enthusiasm did not lead him into some very serious medical mistakes.

Indeed at this point we are able to leave the shifting sands of speculation and step onto the *terra firma* of historical fact. For Freud *did* make a very serious diagnostic error. We know that this is the case for the simple reason that he has told us so. In 1901, in *The Psychopathology of Everyday Life*, Freud described an occasion when he had been unable to remember any details of a patient whose name appeared in his appointment book. Seeking the unconscious motives which he believed lay behind all such absent-mindedness, he later recalled the case:

> M–l was a fourteen-year-old girl, the most remarkable case I had had in recent years, one which taught me a lesson I am not likely ever to forget and whose outcome cost me moments of the greatest distress. The child fell ill of an unmistakable hysteria, which did in fact clear up quickly and radically under my care. After this improvement the child was taken away from me by her parents. She still complained of abdominal pains which had played the chief part in the clinical picture of her hysteria. Two months later she died of sarcoma of the abdominal glands.

The hysteria, to which she was at the same time predisposed, used the tumour as a provoking cause, and I, with my attention held by the noisy but harmless manifestations of the hysteria, had perhaps overlooked the first signs of the insidious and incurable disease.[8]

Freud's admission may well appear, on first reading at least, to be an exemplary act of medical candour. Yet a closer examination of what he actually says reveals it as a curious mixture of candour and self-deception. On the one hand he accepts that he failed to diagnose his patient's tumour and he clearly recognises that this was a serious error. What is extraordinary, however, is that although the patient subsequently died of her undiagnosed sarcoma, Freud still clings to his belief that his diagnosis of hysteria was correct. In support of this conviction he is able to produce no evidence whatsoever. Rather the contrary, for having claimed that the hysteria 'did in fact clear up quickly and radically' under his care he immediately reveals that his patient continued to complain of the abdominal pains which 'had played the chief part in the clinical picture of her hysteria'. The two statements do not add up. Indeed it is difficult not to discern in Freud's account a pattern which we have encountered already. For once again we are presented with the claim that a 'radical' cure has been effected, in spite of the fact that the main symptom of the patient's illness has not disappeared at all. It is of course perfectly possible that M–l was already suffering from some kind of emotional disturbance at the time that her tumour appeared. But this is not what Freud claims. His suggestion is that the abdominal pains caused by the girl's tumour were *simultaneously* the main symptoms of her hysteria, which had made use of the tumour as 'a provoking cause'. The much more likely explanation, of course, is that the 'unmistakable hysteria' which Freud had identified was the result purely of medical fantasy and his own diagnostic *idée fixe*.

Freud presents the case of M–l as though it were exceptional. Yet if, as I have suggested here, and as a number of psychiatrists and neurologists have suggested elsewhere, the term 'hysteria' does not correspond to any single disease entity or syndrome, it follows inexorably that *all* the patients Freud confidently pronounced to be suffering from 'hysteria' were, like countless thousands of nineteenth-century patients, wrongly diagnosed. This would necessarily include the very first patient he treated with Breuer's cathartic method, Frau Emmy von N.[9]

Frau Emmy was a wealthy and well-educated widow of around forty whose illness, according to Freud, had started about fourteen years earlier, shortly after the death of her husband. She came to Freud suffering from depression and insomnia and a strange and prominent disorder which he carefully describes:

> She spoke in a low voice as though with difficulty and her speech was from time to time subject to spastic interruptions amounting to a stammer. She kept her fingers, which exhibited a ceaseless agitation resembling athetosis, tightly clasped together. There were frequent convulsive *tic*-like movements of her face and the muscles of her neck, during which some of them, especially the right sterno-cleido-mastoid, stood out prominently. Furthermore she frequently interrupted her remarks by producing a curious 'clacking' sound from her mouth which defies imitation . . . This 'clacking' was made up of a number of sounds. Colleagues of mine with sporting experience told me, on hearing it, that its final notes resembled the call of a capercaillie [according to Fisher (1955), 'a ticking ending with a pop and a hiss'].[10]

Freud goes on to describe how at other times Frau Emmy would break off from her conversation every two or three minutes and exclaim, 'Keep still! – Don't say anything! Don't touch me!' She would then carry on as though nothing had happened. From these words Freud deduces that 'she was probably under the influence of some recurrent hallucination of a horrifying kind'. In a manner which, as we shall see, was characteristic of his therapeutic technique, Freud immediately treats his deduction as a kind of provisional fact, and embarks upon a search for the traumatic events which will confirm its status as a 'real' fact.[11] According to his own account Freud succeeds in tracing the patient's symptoms back to a series of traumatic experiences in childhood. As a result she is partially cured. Later, however, Freud is obliged to report that his patient relapsed.

Given that the case of Frau Emmy was Freud's first recorded attempt to apply Breuer's method, and given the facts surrounding Anna O.'s supposed cure, it is difficult not to entertain the suspicion that, just as no cure had been effected in her case, no cure was effected in the case of Frau Emmy at any stage of Freud's treatment.[12] Some grounds for entertaining this view are given by Freud's own description of his patient's symptoms. For although Freud reports these symptoms as though they were entirely idiosyncratic, they closely resemble the classic symptoms found in Gilles de la Tourette's syndrome. The onset of this syndrome is usually marked by the appearance of simple motor tics which have been defined as 'sudden, quick, involuntary, and frequently repeated movements of circumscribed groups of muscles, serving no apparent purpose'.[13] These tics usually commence in the face, head and neck, and may later spread to other parts of the body and become more severe. Multiple tics are often accompanied by forced vocalisations. Often these are inarticulate noises or sounds and among the most commonly reported are throat-clearing, grunts, sniffs, coughs, screams, snorts, shouts, barks, high-pitched noises, humming, hissing, clicking, stuttering or stammering. More complex vocal tics include the forced repetition of articulate words, phrases and sentences. In about a third of the cases reported, these words and phrases have an obscene content.[14] Another feature of Tourette's syndrome has been described by Shapiro and Shapiro, who have made an intensive study of the disorder. They have designated as 'sensory tics' a pattern of recurring, involuntary, somatic sensations sometimes experienced by patients. 'The sensation is described by patients as feelings of heaviness, lightness, emptiness, tickle, cold, hot, or other sensations in skin, bones, muscles and joints.' It is interesting in this respect that at one point in her treatment Emmy von N. complains of 'sensations of cold and pain in her left leg' and that she also complains of 'neck-cramps' which she describes as consisting in an 'icy grip' on the back of the neck.[15]

So closely do Freud's patient's symptoms resemble those of sufferers from Tourette's disorder that it is difficult to understand why Freud does not at least discuss this diagnosis during his case history. The question is a particularly interesting one in view of the fact that Gilles de la Tourette was a pupil of Charcot. Freud himself had met him in Paris during the very same year that he was to publish his paper defining the disorder and attributing it to a degenerative process of the brain. One reason why Freud may have rejected the diagnosis is that de la Tourette's original paper contained a number of errors. For example, although he had reported obscene vocal tics in only half of his patients, he treated these as a defining characteristic of the syndrome. He corrected some of his errors in 1899, but a number of misapprehensions were perpetuated. It is conceivable that Freud, following Charcot's notion of hysteria as a cunning but imperfect imitator of other diseases, incorrectly construed the absence of obscenity in Frau Emmy von N.'s vocal tics as a sign that she was not suffering from the syndrome itself.

Some later observers have taken a different view. In a detailed paper published in the *International Review of Psychoanalysis* in 1980, Else Pappenheim argued that there is 'substantial evidence that Frau Emmy von N. suffered from Gilles de la Tourette's disease, not from hysteria'. It should by now come as no surprise that a similar conclusion was arrived at quite independently by Elizabeth Thornton. She states forthrightly that 'Frau Emmy was almost certainly suffering from a variant of Gilles de la Tourette's disease.' She goes on to assert that recent studies have 'confirmed' an organic cause for the disease.[16] Once again it would seem that Thornton is in danger of weakening an excellent case by overstating it. One of the difficulties with the diagnosis of Tourette's syndrome is that an onset in childhood is normally thought of as one of its defining characteristics. If Frau Emmy's tics began only in her mid-twenties, as Freud at one point implies, then her case would be an extremely unusual one. Elsewhere, however, we are told that Frau Emmy had her first 'hysterical spasms' in early childhood. It is not clear whether the term 'spasms' is used in a sense which might cover simple motor tics. Since the real time of onset is thus shrouded in uncertainty, any attempt at retrospective diagnosis should recognise this uncertainty. What is perhaps even more important is that, contrary to Thornton's assertion, the hypothesis that Tourette's disorder has an organic cause has not yet been confirmed. The immensely detailed, impressive and coherent work of Shapiro and his colleagues certainly points towards just that conclusion. But not all reports are consistent with Shapiro's neurological findings, and a significant number of psychiatrists still believe in a psychological origin for the symptoms in question.[17] Until it is possible to identify either the structural brain disorder or the biochemical abnormality which lies behind the syndrome, the question cannot be definitively settled. Premature claims of certainty, such as that made by Thornton, can only weaken the case against a purely psychological aetiology.

What must be recognised, however, is that the uncertainty cuts both ways. At the very least we are in a position to claim that, just as it seems almost certain that Breuer's prototype of a psychoanalytical cure was founded upon a misdiagnosis, so there is a strong possibility that Freud's own first psychoanalytic case was itself little more than a protracted medical mistake. Some of the points of resemblance between the two cases are striking. For if we ask how it was that Freud managed to persuade himself that his simple therapeutic strategies had removed some of Frau Emmy's symptoms we must once again consider the possibility that he, like Breuer before him, shadowed a process of spontaneous remission. Freud's case history itself suggests a pattern of waxing and waning symptoms which might well lead to such a mistake. This would be entirely compatible with the diagnosis of Tourette's disorder, of which Lishman writes: 'The natural history of the disorder, with spontaneous remissions and exacerbations, has made it difficult to examine any therapeutic regime based on a small number of cases . . .'[18] In the case of Anna O., in order to explain how Breuer might have been able to mark therapeutic time while waiting for a symptom to remit, it was necessary to enter the realms of speculation and to suggest that the disappearance of a symptom was actually adopted as a criterion of accurate recollection. In Freud's case of Frau Emmy von N. we do not need to speculate along these lines. For Freud himself boldly tells us that he adopted a very similar strategy. After a particular incident in which Frau Emmy tells him the same story twice, adding a significant detail on the second occasion, Freud draws the conclusion that 'an incomplete story under hypnosis produces no therapeutic effect'. He then adds the following remarkable words: 'I accustomed myself to regarding as incomplete any story that brought about no therapeutic improvement, and I gradually came to be able to read from patients' faces whether they might not be concealing an essential part of their confession.'[19]

Not only could such a principle be used in order to protract the course of therapy, but it could also be used in order to devolve therapeutic responsibility. For, strictly interpreted, it implied that if patients did not get better it was *their* fault for having failed to disclose their past in sufficient detail and with sufficient honesty.

In Breuer's case of Anna O. it was suggested that physician and patient had entered into a kind of alliance in order to shield one another from therapeutic disappointment and to explain the reappearance of symptoms. Without recognising what he was doing, it would seem that Freud entered into a similar relationship with his first psychoanalytic patient. For at a certain point in his case history, after he has gone through the necessary cathartic procedure to remove Frau Emmy's stammering and clacking, it becomes apparent that she still sometimes stammers. Freud subsequently added the following note of explanation:

Her stammering and clacking were not completely relieved after they had been traced back to the two initial traumas, though from then on the two symptoms were strikingly improved. *The patient herself explained the incompleteness of the success as follows.* She had got into the habit of stammering and clacking whenever she was frightened, so that in the end these symptoms had come to be attached not solely to the initial traumas but to a long chain of memories associated with them, which I had omitted to wipe out. This is a state of things which arises quite often, and which *always limits the beauty and completeness of the therapeutic outcome of the cathartic procedure* [italics added].[20]

By incorporating Frau Emmy's helpful rationalisation into his own theories, and by taking advantage of a slight amelioration of her symptoms which was probably spontaneous, Freud is thus able to represent a negative outcome as a partial therapeutic success. A further rationalisation of failure is introduced in his summary of the case when he points out that he has applied two different kinds of therapy to the same illness, making use both of direct suggestion under hypnosis and of the cathartic method – 'psychical analysis'. For this reason, he suggests, the case of Frau Emmy 'cannot strictly be used as evidence for the therapeutic efficacy of the cathartic procedure'. In view of the case's negative outcome, Freud's claim might well be seen as part of an essential defensive strategy. Having secured his defences against any imputation of failure, however, Freud immediately goes onto the attack. 'At the same time I must add,' he writes, 'that only those symptoms of which I carried out a psychical analysis were really permanently removed.' Since Freud has already explained that two of Frau Emmy's symptoms which he had analysed had *not* been permanently removed, it is difficult to understand how this claim can be justified. The difficulty is compounded by the manner in which the case history continues:

> The therapeutic success on the whole was considerable; but it was not a lasting one. The patient's tendency to fall ill in a similar way under the impact of fresh traumas was not got rid of. Anyone who wanted to undertake a definitive cure of a case of hysteria such as this would have to enter more thoroughly into the complex of phenomena than I attempted to.[21]

Read with a degree of scepticism, Freud's words can begin to seem like a deliberately planned strategy of contradiction in which the truth of therapeutic failure is boldly and openly laid upon the table only so that no objections can be raised when it is subsequently trumped by the lie of therapeutic success. That is certainly one way of interpreting

Freud's words. Yet to read them in this way would, I believe, be to underestimate the complexity of Freud's mind, and the internal consistency of the pseudo-science which he created. It might also imply that Freud was deliberately attempting to deceive his readers by persuading them of the effectiveness of a therapeutic technique which he himself knew to be completely ineffective. To take this latter view would, I believe, be misleading. For while it is true that Freud was in possession of a great deal of negative evidence about his therapeutic technique, the very fact that he communicates this evidence to his readers so openly suggests that he himself was unable to appreciate its significance. Perhaps the only way we can understand Freud's attitude is if we assume that his faith in the correctness of his therapeutic theory was so huge, and so necessary to the sense he had of his own identity, that he was unable to weigh the evidence for and against his theory with any objectivity. Freud, on this view, discounted negative evidence not because he was dishonest or because he was deliberately seeking to avoid refutation, but because the very possibility of refutation was all but inconceivable to him.

Where he does sometimes seem less than straightforward is in his preference for approximate and vague therapeutic claims over specific and limited ones. When Freud claims that *some* of Frau Emmy's symptoms have disappeared he is careful not to specify which symptoms. Since his impressive-sounding claim is empty of any specific content, those of his readers and followers who wish to be impressed are in a position to fill it with just as much therapeutic glory as they deem appropriate. Freud himself was probably aware that his words might have this kind of effect. But since he genuinely believed (not for the first time) that he was on the point of striking therapeutic gold, he had a positive, idealistic motive for allowing his reputation to run ahead of his actual discoveries. Since one or two of Frau Emmy's symptoms *had* apparently disappeared, and since this was in any case his first attempt at the cathartic method – or 'psychical analysis' – he is able to justify his large and capacious-seeming claim on these minimal grounds. Furthermore, although he goes on to admit that his patient was still ill some years later, he appears to have convinced himself that this illness was not the same as the one she had previously suffered. Rather she had fallen ill again 'in a *similar* way under the impact of *fresh* traumas'. By performing a series of strange and ingenious rationalisations, Freud, it would seem, had found a way of incorporating counter-instances into the very structure of his theory. The description which resulted was one which maximised his own thera-peutic credit and minimised his responsibility for the fact that the patient he had 'cured' was still ill. But it was not, in the ordinary sense of the word, a dishonest description. For to characterise it in this way would be to make the mistake of attributing to Freud a degree of objectivity and clear-sightedness which he was psychologically unable to achieve. When Freud contemplated in Frau Emmy signs of what he thought were therapeutic success, he did not do so through the lens of scientific objectivity. He viewed them through the telescope of his own theoretical ecstasy, with the result that signs which were small, insignificant or illusory seemed weighty and substantial. Since he was unable to examine counter-instances to his theory without first inverting this same telescope, these almost always appeared to him tiny and insignificant. When Freud went on to give a tendentious account of the case which gave an exaggerated impression of his own therapeutic powers, he was merely reporting honestly what he saw – or what he thought he saw.

The way in which psychoanalysis developed suggests that Freud eventually succumbed to this kind of self-deception on a vast scale, building a larger and larger theoretical structure upon foundations of empirical evidence which became smaller and smaller until, at a certain point, they disappeared altogether. One of the most interesting aspects of the case of Frau Emmy is that it enables us to observe the early stages of this process at first hand and thus to see how slight was the clinical evidence from which Freud started and how perilously insecure were the very first diagnostic and therapeutic theories he attempted to construct upon it.

One feature of Freud's later theorising which appears in his first case almost fully formed is his adoption of a mixed aetiological theory to explain his patients' symptoms. For just as Breuer had divided Anna O.'s illness in two, pronouncing some of her symptoms to be organic, so Freud did something similar. Whereas most of Frau Emmy's physi-cal symptoms were deemed to be purely the products of hysteria, Freud decided that 'others of the patient's somatic symptoms were not of a hysterical nature at all.' In particular Freud suggested that Frau Emmy's neck-cramps should be regarded as a modified form of migraine and that 'as such were not to be classed as a neurosis but as an organic disorder'. Freud then went on to introduce a further theoretical refinement by suggesting that hysteria might 'attach' itself to an exist-ing physical symptom. In his view 'Frau von N.'s neck-cramps, for instance, were employed for the purpose of hysterical attacks, whereas she did not have the typical symptomatology of hysterical attacks at her disposal.'[22] This mixed aetiological theory would play a crucial role throughout Freud's early experiments in psychoanalysis. It reappears, as we shall see, in the case of Elisabeth von R. and we find it restated in a slightly different form as the theory of 'somatic compliance' in his account of his treatment of Dora.[23]

There can be no doubt that in Freud's own view this mixture of aetiological viewpoints was justified by the nature of the disease he was studying. But its pragmatic function appears to have been the same as it was in Breuer's treatment of Anna O. What it meant was that Freud's aetiological theories were effectively immunised against the very kind of counter-instances which were most likely to arise in the course of treating patients. If a symptom which had not been analysed spontaneously disappeared, as happened in the case of Anna O., its organic origins could be conceded without modifying the existing aetiological theory. Similarly if patients would not co-operate with the attempt to analyse one of their symptoms, as happened in the case of Frau Emmy's neck-cramps, the physician could insure himself against the counter-instance offered by any future remission by defining that particular symptom *out* of the patient's main illness and attributing it to a subsidiary organic disorder. More significantly still, Freud's theoretical innovation, whereby he held that 'genuine' organic symptoms could be taken over and 'used' by hysteria, meant that patients whose symptoms had already been diagnosed as having a physical cause could, either simultaneously or subsequently, be treated for hysteria *without* needing first to determine which diagnosis was correct. Conversely if a symptom which had been treated as hysterical was subsequently rediagnosed by another physician as the sign of an organic disease, this second diagnosis could be accepted without there being any need to question the correctness of the first one.

It might seem that, at least in this case, Freud, by introducing these various modifications into his theories, was deliberately and dishonestly taking steps to avoid refutation. Once again, however, to take this view would be to misrepresent Freud's own attitude. For Freud's own motive, it would seem, was not the negative one of avoiding refutation; it was the positive one of preserving a theory which he believed had immense therapeutic value. From his perspective the various objections which orthodox physicians might make to his diagnoses of 'hysteria' were flimsy and insubstantial. Such objections could only be advanced by the neurologically untutored, who remained unaware of the scientific progress which had been made by Charcot and the extraordinary therapeutic discovery which had been made by Breuer. By modifying his theory to incorporate the supposed counter-instances, Freud was not trying deviously to avoid refutation. He was attempting with the utmost sincerity to demonstrate that the facts which others insisted on construing as genuine counter-instances were nothing of the kind. The degree of 'unsinkability' which Freud conferred upon his own theories in this manner is perhaps best judged by considering the case of M–1, which has already been cited. In this case, as we have seen, even the death of one of Freud's patients from a tumour which gave rise to pains which he had judged 'hysterical' is not treated as a counter-instance of any kind. Unable to tolerate disconfirmation because he could not live without the sense of fulfilment which his theories brought him, Freud, it would seem, had created a theory which had risen above the very possibility of refutation.

It must be said, however, that although Freud may have devised his scientific procedures in an attempt to protect the supposedly immense therapeutic benefits of psychoanalysis, one of the problems which he repeatedly faced was the difficulty of obtaining any persuasive evidence of these benefits. This was just as much the case in his own treatment of Frau Emmy as it had been in Breuer's treatment of Anna O.

The true measure of Freud's therapeutic success in his own first attempt at psychoanalysis is perhaps best conveyed by the footnote which he himself appended to his case history in 1924. In this note he recounts how, some years after he had last seen Frau Emmy, he met a prominent physician from her part of the country:

> I asked him if he was acquainted with the lady and knew anything of her condition. Yes, he said, he knew her, and had himself given her hypnotic treatment. She had gone through the same performance with him – and with many other doctors – as she had with me. Her condition had become very bad; she had rewarded his hypnotic treatment of her by making a remarkable recovery, but had then suddenly quarrelled with him, left him, and once more set her illness going to its full extent. It was a genuine instance of 'the compulsion to repeat'.[24]

It is both instructive and poignant to compare these words, with their implicit assessment of Frau Emmy as a malicious 'hysteric' who deliberately contrives to 'set her illness going' when she pleases, to the words which Freud had written in his original case history nearly thirty years previously:

> Frau Emmy von N. gave us an example of how hysteria is compatible with an unblemished character and a well-governed mode of life. The woman we came to know was an admirable one. The moral seriousness with which she viewed her duties, her intelligence and energy, which were no less than a man's, and her high degree of education and love of truth impressed us greatly; while her benevolent care for the welfare of all her dependents, her humility of mind and the refinement of her manners revealed her qualities as a true lady as well.[25]

Reading these two different descriptions of the same woman it is difficult to avoid coming to the conclusion that Freud continued to wrestle with the demon of diagnostic doubt for many years after he first pronounced Frau Emmy to be suffering from 'hysteria'. So long as she could still be regarded as the first promising prototype for Freud's own application of the cathartic procedure, she was praised and flattered. But when it becomes clear from her subsequent condition that she might prove to be an embarrassing and all too easily identifiable monument to one of Freud's most significant therapeutic failures, Freud suddenly reverts to the traditional negative and misogynistic view of the hysterical woman, as if in an attempt to vindicate his own original diagnosis and to punish his patient for having refused to get better.

Thirty years on it would seem that Freud was still troubled by the case. Given his medical training, his undoubted skill as a diagnostician and his own familiarity with the organic aetiologies of many neurological diseases, it is entirely conceivable that he was still afflicted by doubt as to the correctness of his diagnosis. If so, then it would seem that this doubt became not a hypothesis to be explored but a demon to be exorcised, a demon easily confused with Frau Emmy herself. Freud's last reference to his first psychoanalytic patient, which he included in his 1924 note, has a certain poignancy. 'It was not for another quarter of a century,' he writes, 'that I once more had news of Frau Emmy.' On this occasion the patient's elder daughter had approached Freud for a report on her mother's mental condition on the strength of his former treatment of her:

> She was intending to take legal proceedings against her mother, whom she represented as a cruel and ruthless tyrant. It seems that she had

broken off relations with both her children and refused to assist them in their financial difficulties. The daughter who wrote to me had obtained a doctor's degree and was married.[26]

In this tragic and seemingly cruel valediction, the woman whose intelligence and energy Freud had chauvinistically rated as 'no less than a man's' and whose 'benevolent care for the welfare of all her dependents' he had praised, is described by her daughter as a 'ruthless tyrant' and Freud, noting the daughter's doctor's degree and married status, appears to accept the judgement.

In fact Freud's words were a valediction in more senses than one, for he ventured to publish his footnote only on his patient's death in 1924. We know this because scholars have established the real identity of 'Frau Emmy' as Fanny Moser, who was the widow of an industrialist and one of the wealthiest women in Europe. When Freud replied to Frau Emmy's daughter in 1918 he declined to side with her against her mother and extolled her noble character. As soon as she died, however, his attitude appears to have changed dramatically and his footnote suggests that he has taken the side of the daughter. Freud's inconsistency in this regard seems not to have been widely noticed.[27]

There are, of course, many different circumstances which might have led the mother to quarrel with her daughter. One possibility is that Frau Emmy had been driven to distraction by physicians who refused to believe in the reality of her illness, and who offered instead ineffective remedies for an emotional disorder from which she did not suffer. This possibility is one which Freud, for all his supposed fearlessness in the face of truth, appears unable to contemplate.

SIX

More Medical Mistakes

ALTHOUGH THE THEORY which is presented in *Studies on Hysteria* was worked out in relation to a large number of patients whom Freud had treated during the previous seven or eight years, it contained only five full case histories. Breuer's account of the treatment of Anna O. is followed by four case histories written by Freud. In at least three cases Freud may have been prompted to select his patients by the contribution which their treatment made to the technique of psychoanalysis. Emmy von N. was not only the first patient Freud treated with Breuer's method, she was also, in a sense, the originator of the technique of free-association. For when Freud bombarded her with questions about the origins of her various symptoms, she insisted on exploring her own memories in her own way. Freud concluded that listening to his patients probing their own memories could be a much better way of exploring their past than hypnosis.

During his treatment of Lucy R., an English governess who suffered from strange olfactory hallucinations, Freud tried to apply this lesson and also developed what he called his 'pressure technique'. It would appear that he first used this 'technique' when he was treating the rheumatic pains suffered by the woman he calls Elisabeth von R. Finding that it was impossible to hypnotise her, Freud borrowed from Bernheim the idea of applying pressure to his patient's head with his hands, instructing her to report faithfully 'whatever appeared before her inner eye or passed through her memory at the moment of pressure'. Freud rapidly developed such faith in the effectiveness of this method that he came to regard it as infallible, maintaining that if no images or memories were produced by the first application of pressure, repeated pressure would invariably be effective.[1]

The two cases in which Freud originally worked out this method have played a crucial role in the legend of psychoanalysis, and, as we shall see, they both possess a particular interest for those who seek to unravel the legend. In order to make our survey of Freud's case histories complete, however, some account should be given of Freud's brief encounter with the patient he discusses in his third case history – a girl he refers to as Katharina.

Freud's story of Katharina is one of the most simple and attractive of all his case histories. It is also the most unusual since Katharina was not one of Freud's paying patients, but the daughter of an inn-keeper who approached him while he was on holiday in the Alps in 1893. Having deduced that Freud was a doctor from his signature in the visitors' book, Katharina consults him while he is gazing at the mountain scenery:

> 'The truth is, sir, my nerves are bad. I went to see a doctor in L– about them and he gave me something for them; but I'm not well yet.'
>
> So there I was with the neuroses once again – for nothing else could very well be the matter with this strong, well-built girl with her unhappy look.

Having ruled out any physical ailment on the grounds of her robust appearance Freud elicits a description of Katharina's symptoms and learns that she suffers from periodic fits:

> 'It comes over me all at once. First of all it's like something pressing on my eyes. My head gets so heavy, there's a dreadful buzzing, and I feel so giddy that I almost fall over. Then there's something crushing my chest so that I can't get my breath.'
>
> 'And you don't notice anything in your throat?'
>
> 'My throat's squeezed together as though I were going to choke.'
>
> 'Does anything else happen in your head?'
>
> 'Yes, there's a hammering, enough to burst it.'

Katharina goes on to describe how these attacks are accompanied by anxiety and by a recurrent hallucination in which she sees 'an awful face that looks at me in a dreadful way'. She tells Freud that these attacks began two years ago but that she has no idea where they came from.

Freud identifies Katharina's fits as 'anxiety attacks' and assumes that they are hysterical manifestations of an emotional trauma. Having come to the conclusion that he can scarcely hypnotise Katharina on the top of a mountain, he decides to try 'a lucky guess' which he makes on the basis of his view that, in the case of girls, anxiety is frequently a consequence of the horror by which a virginal mind is overcome when it is faced for the first time with the world of sexuality . . . So I said: 'If you don't know, I'll tell you how *I* think you got your attacks. At that time, two years ago, you must have seen or heard something that very much embarrassed you, and that you'd much rather not have seen.'[2]

Katharina immediately tells the story of how, two years ago when she was sixteen, she had chanced to observe her father, making love to a young servant-girl in his room.* She then goes on to recall an earlier occasion on which her father had made sexual advances to her which she had repulsed. Although she had at first had no recollection of the origin of her fits she now accepts Freud's suggestion that they were precipitated by the scene with the servant-girl. According to Freud's account, she even claims to remember experiencing some of the characteristic symptoms of her fits immediately after observing the scene.

While there is no reason to doubt Katharina's story of her father's attempt to seduce her, or her subsequent discovery of his affair with the servant-girl, there is every reason to doubt Freud's dogmatic insistence that she was suffering from 'hysteria'. The most straightforward objection is that, without having made any clinical examination, or seen the girl during one of her fits, Freud was simply not in a position to make any diagnosis. In fact a number of the symptoms she describes would be compatible with temporal lobe epilepsy which, as we have seen, was consistently misdiagnosed as hysteria throughout the nineteenth century. Mild temporal lobe seizures do not involve loss of consciousness and the symptoms reported by those who suffer them sometimes include recurrent hallucinations involving a 'spectral face'. Katharina's symptoms might also suggest panic attacks brought on by hyper-ventilation and there are a number of other possibilities which any responsible physician would wish to eliminate before suggesting a purely psychological cause.[3]

Freud recognises that Katharina's attack is preceded by an 'aura'. But following faithfully in the footsteps of Charcot, he declines to consider the possibility that her symptoms might have an organic basis and insists instead on an elaborate psychological aetiology. That a chance meeting on a mountain-top should have subsequently been presented as a serious medical case history speaks eloquently of his

---

* In Freud's case history Katharina talks about her 'uncle'. In a footnote added in 1924 Freud revealed that the 'uncle' was in reality the girl's father.

hubris and self-regard. That Freud's diagnosis should continue to be treated with respect by some supporters of psychoanalysis even today is perhaps best understood as an indication of the profound mistrust which many supporters of psychoanalysis have developed for conventional medicine and conventional methods of clinical investigation.

Largely as a result of this legacy of mistrust hundreds, if not thousands of patients suffering from temporal lobe epilepsy continued to be misdiagnosed even after this syndrome had been identified. That this kind of misdiagnosis was still being made in the 1970s becomes clear in Karen Armstrong's remarkable autobiographical work, *Beginning the World*. In this book the author describes how, after suffering from mysterious fits, she was referred by her doctor to a psychiatrist. During three years of psychotherapy she frequently described her fits in detail without it once being suggested that she had an EEG. Only when she eventually experienced a *grand mal* fit and was referred through the casualty department of a hospital to a neurologist were her fits recognised for what they were – classic symptoms of temporal lobe epilepsy.[4]

Another patient of Freud's whose symptoms strongly suggest an organic aetiology was the woman whom Freud called Miss Lucy R., who was referred to Freud after she had developed recurrent olfactory hallucinations centring on the smell of burnt pudding. Although Freud treated these hallucinations as hysterical symptoms, it is significant that Lucy R. had developed them only after having been treated for some time for a chronic nasal infection which was associated with caries of the ethmoid bone – the structure between the nose and the skull. She subsequently lost her sense of smell entirely and it was at this point that her hallucinations began.[5]

In the latter part of the nineteenth century it is understandable that, even though Lucy R.'s illness began with symptoms which had an unmistakable organic basis, Freud should turn to a psychogenic hypothesis in order to explain the onset of hallucinations. Since Freud's time, however, it has become clear that hallucinations are very often the product of *organic* factors rather than psychological ones. This applies just as much to smells as it does to any other form of hallucination. By the end of the nineteenth century John Hughlings Jackson, the British neurologist whose pioneering work on epilepsy paved the way for the eventual recognition of temporal lobe epilepsy, had already come to the conclusion that 'a sudden and temporary stench in the

nose with transient unconsciousness' was an epileptic event. His conclusion has been confirmed by modern neurologists. Henri Gastaut,
for example, describes olfactory seizures as consisting in 'a sensation
of an odour which the patient usually considers neutral or disagreeable
– e.g., the smell of gasoline, of gas, sulphur, formalin, bad eggs, faeces,
etc.' Doris Trauner, who observes that there are almost as many types
of complex partial seizures as there are patients with epilepsy, comes
even closer to describing Lucy R.'s main symptom when she writes
that 'Some patients complain of intense olfactory hallucinations that
in most cases are unpleasant (e.g., a smell of rotten eggs or burnt
toast).'[6] Whether Lucy R.'s hallucinations were associated with epilepsy is not entirely clear since Freud's descriptions of her symptoms
are inconsistent. At first he describes the patient as being 'almost continuously pursued by one or two subjective olfactory sensations'. But
he then goes on to talk of 'recurrent hallucinations', which he describes
as 'equivalents of a hysterical *attack*'.[7] If Lucy R.'s hallucinations were
indeed recurrent rather than constant, it is possible that they too were
manifestations of temporal lobe epilepsy.[8] Whether or not Lucy R.'s
hallucinations were, strictly speaking, epileptic in character, it seems
virtually certain that they were related to the patient's nasal infection,
and that their explanation was to be found in neurology rather than
psychology. Perhaps the most plausible diagnosis was that she was
suffering from parosmia occasioned by damage to one of the olfactory
nerves.

Characteristically, however, Freud does not allow for the many gaps
in medical knowledge which then existed. Instead he makes an *a priori*
assumption that Lucy R. is suffering from hysteria and embarks upon
his usual quest for the trauma which supposedly precipitated her condition. By way of an extraordinarily elaborate chain of causality, he
eventually traces the smell of burnt pudding to her disappointment at
being rebuffed by the employer with whom she had fallen in love.

The case of Katharina and the case of Lucy R. are relatively straightforward, since in each case Freud treats his patients' main symptoms
as *purely* psychogenic. In the case of M–l, however, who died of her
undiagnosed tumour, we have seen that Freud sometimes treated real,
organically based symptoms as though they could be taken over or
'used' by hysteria. As I have already suggested, this was not simply a *post
hoc* addition to Freud's theory, developed in order to meet a particularly
embarrassing circumstance, but was part of the theory from the very

beginning, making its appearance originally in the case of Emmy von N. In Freud's case history of Fräulein Elisabeth von R. it is developed further, and in this relatively complex case many of the most remarkable features of Freud's theory of hysteria are displayed. Because of this it is worth looking at in some detail.

Freud describes Elisabeth von R. as 'a young lady who had been suffering for more than two years from pains in her legs and who had difficulty in walking'. She walked with the upper part of her body bent forwards but she did not use a stick and her gait was 'by no means strikingly bad'.[9] The sceptical reader who seeks to counter Freud's diagnosis of hysteria with the objection that Elisabeth von R.'s pains could well have an organic cause finds that this objection is easily absorbed. For Freud himself writes that Elisabeth von R.'s pains were 'rheumatic in origin', and that subsequently they became 'a mnemic symbol of her painful psychical excitations'.[10]

He then suggests a whole series of factors which have supposedly led to this psychical 'appropriation' of Elisabeth von R.'s organic symptom. The precipitating cause, Freud argues, was her disappointment in love; during a period when she had been nursing her sick father, she had been attracted to a young man but had been forced to choose between erotic satisfaction and daughterly duty. It was because she had repressed her own erotic impulses that her organic illness had been perpetuated and exacerbated. Since it is not self-evident why repressed love should manifest itself through rheumatic pain, Freud offers a number of reasons why this particular 'path of conversion' had been followed. These include the fact that the patient's father used to rest his leg on her thigh while she was changing his bandage, and the fact that she had been either *walking, lying down* or *standing* at certain emotionally significant moments in her life. 'For instance,' Freud writes, 'she was *standing* by a door when her father was brought home with his heart-attack.'[11] The reason that these emotional traumas had expressed themselves through the rheumatic pains which she was already suffering from can, to use Freud's own remarkable words, 'scarcely be looked for elsewhere than in the circumstance that walking, standing, and lying are functions and states of those parts of her body which in her case comprised the painful zones, namely, her legs'. At first Freud's explanation seems to imply that any emotionally significant events which happened while Elisabeth von R. was not walking, lying or standing should be discounted as factors in her illness. But Freud promptly goes on to discuss another scene which took place when she was *sitting*. Since he is evidently prepared to interpret any bodily posture as a 'function' of the legs, Freud's entire explanation turns out, in this instance at least, to be not only unpersuasive, but empty.[12]

It is perhaps because he senses this that Freud goes on to furnish even more explanations. He observes that, because of her particular emotional circumstances, Elisabeth von R. frequently complained that 'standing alone' was difficult and that she felt unable 'to take a single step forward'. Because of her use of these figures of speech Freud writes that he 'was forced' to conclude that his patient had sought 'a symbolic expression of her painful thoughts and that she had found it in the intensification of her sufferings'. He describes his view 'that the somatic symptoms of hysteria can be brought about by symbolisation of this kind' as a 'fact' but suggests that in this particular case it only played a subsidiary role.[13]

But although Freud has by now launched an entire armada of aetiologies into the sea of speculation with which he has surrounded his patient's symptoms, he finds himself obliged to confess that her illness has remained unconquered. At this point he introduces a modification to the 'pressure technique' which he had adopted from Bernheim. As we have seen, Freud believed that by pressing with his hands on his patients' forehead and commanding them to remember, it was possible to release memories of traumatic events which would otherwise remain hidden in the unconscious. He notices, however, that Elisabeth von R. sometimes appears to be suppressing the ideas or memories which come into her mind. He describes such reticence as 'concealment' and decides to take stern measures against it:

> I no longer accepted her declaration that nothing had occurred to her, but assured her that something *must* have occurred to her. Perhaps, I said, she had not been sufficiently attentive, in which case I would be glad to repeat my pressure. Or perhaps she thought that her idea was not the right one. This, I told her, was not her affair; she was under an obligation to remain completely objective and say what had come into her head, whether it was appropriate or not. Finally I declared that I knew very well that something *had* occurred to her and that she was concealing it from me; but she would never be free of her pains so long as she concealed anything. By thus insisting I brought it about that from that time forward my pressure on her head never failed in its effect.[14]

In the final phase of her therapy Elisabeth von R. thus finds herself treated not only as a patient but also as a kind of suspect who is obstinately concealing the traumatic scene which Freud 'needs' in order to complete his analysis. Freud himself writes that he 'had formed a particular suspicion':

> I did not venture yet, however, to adopt it as the basis of my further action. But a chance occurrence decided the matter. One day while I was working with the patient, I heard a man's footsteps in the next room and a pleasant voice which seemed to be asking some question. My patient thereupon got up and asked that we might break off for the day: she had heard her brother-in-law arrive and inquire for her. Up to that point she had been free from pain, but after the interruption her facial expression and gait betrayed the sudden emergence of severe pains. My suspicion was strengthened by this and I determined to precipitate the decisive explanation.[15]

As is hinted in this passage, Freud had come to the conclusion, in advance of any revelation provided by his patient, that she had fallen in love with her brother-in-law and that the primary cause of her illness should be traced to the inadmissible feelings this love had aroused in her. The fact that her pains reappeared with the arrival of her brother-in-law may well seem to point in this direction and certainly seems to be the decisive factor so far as Freud himself is concerned. Yet if we read Freud's account carefully it becomes clear that there is another possible explanation for the reappearance of Elisabeth von R.'s pains. This explanation is so simple and so obvious that to Freud, with his permanent interest in hidden motives and buried meanings, and his temporary thraldom to the tyrant suspicion, it has clearly become completely invisible. What he fails to draw attention to is that, as his own account intimates, Elisabeth von R.'s immediate reaction to the sound of her brother-in-law's voice was to stand up and move around the consulting-room. While it is conceivable that the sudden re-emergence of her pain had some deep psychological cause, it seems a great deal more likely that it was the result of her change of posture and her sudden movement.

Without pausing to consider this possibility Freud plunges into the final phase of his analysis. Rather than allowing his patient to guide him through her memories it would seem that he guides her, observing that while 'she seemed not to notice the end to which she was steering', it had 'become clear to me long since what all this was about'. He gradually elicits from her the story of how she and her mother had journeyed to see her sister after she had been taken ill, and had arrived to find her already dead. According to Freud's account, Elisabeth von R. was unable at this point to refrain from thinking about her brother-in-law:

> At that moment of dreadful certainty that her beloved sister was dead ... another thought had shot through Elisabeth's mind, and now forced itself irresistibly upon her once more, like a flash of lightning in the dark: 'Now he is free again and I can be his wife.'[16]

Freud presents Elisabeth's hidden thought as though she herself has discovered it lurking in her unconscious and has spontaneously produced it at the revelatory moment of the analysis. Most commentators have therefore assumed that this is indeed what took place. Yet if we read Freud's other contributions to *Studies on Hysteria* it becomes clear that matters are by no means as straightforward. In his essay on 'The Psychotherapy of Hysteria', which is included in the volume, Freud writes that, in the final stages of the therapy, 'it is of use if we can guess the ways in which things are connected up and tell the patient before we have uncovered it.' He goes on to claim that, since the truth will always out, there is no risk of the therapist introducing false trails. 'We need not be afraid, therefore,' Freud concludes, 'of telling the patient what we think his next connection of thought is going to be. It will do no harm.'[17] Since the words which are attributed to Elisabeth bear the stamp of Freud's own thinking, it seems possible that they express not so much her confession of her thoughts as Freud's construction of them. It is certainly conceivable that Freud, in his role as the suspicious investigator, determined to extract the truth which he believed his patient was concealing, had, as it were, written a 'confession' which he had then persuaded his patient to 'sign'.

This hypothesis would certainly be consistent with what happens next. For when Freud puts the situation 'drily' before his patient with the words, 'So, for a long time you had been in love with your brother-in-law', he reports that she rejected this explanation, saying that 'it was not true' and that Freud 'had talked her into it'.[18] Disregarding her repeated objections, however, Freud clings to his view that Elisabeth von R.'s rheumatic pains are the product of unrequited love, and in the final stages of the case seeks to 'get rid of the excitation which had been piling up for so long by "abreacting" it'.[19] At this point in the analysis Elisabeth von R.'s supposed hysterical symptom should, according to the theory promulgated by Breuer and Freud, have disappeared 'permanently and immediately'. Freud, however, is obliged to admit that, although he brought his patient's treatment to an end on the assumption that she was cured, her symptoms subsequently recurred. Months later he heard from a colleague that his patient had recovered, 'though she still suffered occasionally from slight pains'. Freud eventually manages to obtain an invitation to a private ball she was attending. He reports that he was able to observe his former patient 'whirl past in a lively dance' and adds that she subsequently married 'someone unknown to me'. Although at least six months must have passed between the end of Freud's course of treatment and the final (equivocal) evidence of her recovery, Freud does not hesitate to claim the 'cure' as his own achievement. This view was certainly not shared by his patient. Years later, talking to her daughter, she described Freud as 'just a young, bearded nerve specialist they sent me to'. He had tried 'to persuade me that I was in love with my brother-in-law, but that wasn't really so'.[20]

Freud's case history of Elisabeth von R. provides an intriguing insight into the early stages of the therapeutic method which would eventually develop into psychoanalysis. In the first place, in a manner with which we should by now be familiar, Freud declines to accept a straightforward diagnosis of simple rheumatism, and at the same time seems scarcely to consider the possibility his patient's symptoms might have some other quite genuine pathology. It might well be argued, of course, that the patient *was* suffering from rheumatism, but that such a diagnosis scarcely explains the seriousness of her disability. In this respect, however, it is interesting to observe that Freud passes over another possible explanation of Elisabeth von R.'s condition. For almost every physician has at some point encountered patients who, while they are demonstrably suffering from a physical ailment, appear to be experiencing a degree of pain or incapacity which is scarcely commensurate with their real illness: unconsciously, semi-consciously or even quite consciously they have dramatised or exaggerated their physical ailment either because of the anxiety which it has aroused or because of the emotional benefits which can accrue from playing the role of the invalid.

Although this latter explanation calls for little more than ordinary psychological insight, and although many observers mistakenly associate such psychologically perceptive attitudes with classical psychoanalysis, it must be stressed that Freud does not consider it. In the first place at least, it is not the *psychological* elaboration of a real illness which interests him, but its *physiological* elaboration. Since this point is so frequently misunderstood it should be laboured. For if we are to have any insight into Freud's approach to his patients it is essential to grasp that, like Charcot before him, he believed that hysteria was a discrete disease entity, one of whose characteristics was that it could actually imitate other diseases. He also believed, as has already been noted, in the existence of a neurophysiological mechanism whereby the nervous energy created by emotional traumas could be transformed into physical symptoms.

It is Freud's unshakeable conviction in the reality of this entirely speculative neurophysiological mechanism which leads him to put forward a series of arguments which supposedly show how Elisabeth von R.'s emotional traumas were converted into rheumatic pains in her legs. As we have seen, these arguments are based on a variety of observations, such as the patient's posture at certain emotionally significant moments, the place where her father used to rest his foot, and her use of certain figures of speech involving the feet or the legs. In all these arguments it seems quite clear that Freud is simply clutching at whatever straws are to hand and plaiting them into spurious aetiologies.

One of the factors which made Freud's speculative aetiologies seem more reasonable to some of his contemporaries than they may now seem to us was the influence of a particular kind of *physiological* associationism on nineteenth-century Viennese psychiatry. In 1865 Freud's teacher Meynert had published a paper in which he proposed that an association was actually a physiological linkage between different cells of the brain in which associated ideas were stored.[21] Many of Meynert's ideas about the physiological, cortical basis of psychological associations were highly plausible, and some remain so even today. This should not stop us from recognising, however, that Freud's attempts to use Meynert's theories in order to solve the problem of 'hysterical' symptoms led him into an entirely speculative realm. In this realm he was free to develop his own concept of a pathogenic memory structure purely on the basis of hunches, whims and the kind of neurological guesswork on which he increasingly came to rely. Freud's account of the case of Elisabeth von R. shows this tendency clearly. Perhaps the most interesting and most characteristic feature of Freud's arguments is the manner in which he assumes that since *he* is able to perceive or construct a link between two discrete phenomena, then this link has some kind of operative reality: Freud's own internal and idiosyncratic logic is treated as though it were a real, external chain of causality. The most charitable observation we can make about this kind of reasoning is that it is neither odd nor abnormal. For it is exactly the kind of reasoning habitually encountered in necromancy, astrology, phrenology and many other forms of investigation with which psychoanalysis is not normally associated.

It must immediately be said that the reasoning by which Freud eventually 'resolves' the case of Elisabeth von R. is both more interesting and, initially at least, a great deal more persuasive. It is certainly possible that a shy young woman who has been disappointed in love might feel some romantic attraction towards her widowed brother-in-law. It is also conceivable, though rather less probable, that this romantic attraction might have developed before her sister's death. If this were the case then her reaction to the news of her sister's death would have been marked by ambivalence and her ostensible sadness might have hidden an inner gladness. Freud was particularly interested in such ambivalent reactions to death and would eventually write one of the most interesting of all his papers on this subject – 'Mourning and Melancholia' (1917).

The problem with his use of this idea in his treatment of Elisabeth von R. is perhaps best defined in some of his own words which appear in the same case history. 'I have not always been a psychotherapist,' he writes. 'Like other neuropathologists, I was trained to employ local diagnoses and electro-prognosis, and it still strikes me as strange that the case histories I write should read like short-stories and that, as one might say, they lack the serious stamp of science.'[22] These words, which read almost like an oblique confession, point to the central difficulty which is raised by the final part of Freud's analysis. For, as we have seen, Freud himself boldly intimates at one stage of his case history that he had divined the ending of Elisabeth von R.'s tale before she did. When this admission is placed alongside his equally frank description of how he is in the habit of 'guessing the ways in which things are connected up' and telling his patient in advance, it is difficult not to come to the conclusion that Freud has indeed abandoned the role of the scientist for that of a novelist. Instead of patiently establishing what actually happened, he has used his own considerable artistic talent to imagine a dénouement for the case which is both psychologically interesting and plausible. Having done this he has constructed a number of links between this dénouement and Elisabeth von R.'s supposed hysterical symptoms and has then proceeded to treat this constructed romance as though it were real. In other words, even though the last phase of the analysis seems to bear the mark of more sophisticated thinking than the earlier phases, the underlying nature of Freud's reasoning is no different. Here, as previously, Freud ends by mistaking his own speculative constructions for the empirical reality he is attempting to explicate. Having placed himself in the position of the omniscient god who 'knows' what happened in Elisabeth von R.'s mind, he is even able to argue with her when she denies it.

It must immediately be conceded that this account of the workings of Freud's mind is itself a speculative construction, even though it is based on a great deal more empirical evidence than may be found in Freud's case histories. Since speculative constructions *do* sometimes correspond to reality we cannot rule out the possibility that Freud did uncover emotional states and desires in Elisabeth von R. of which she remained unaware. It may also be that her desires were frustrated. But even if Freud was right about this, there is still no evidence for his assumption that these particular instances of frustration and denial were the cause of his patient's illness. A more realistic approach to such matters has been suggested by Slater. 'Unfortunately,' he writes, 'we have to recognise that trouble, discord, anxiety and frustration are so prevalent at all stages of life that their mere occurrence near to the time of onset of an illness does not mean very much.'[23]

SEVEN

Mysterious Mechanisms

GIVEN THE UNPERSUASIVE NATURE of so many of the case histories which are presented in *Studies on Hysteria*, one cannot but wonder how it was that Freud, who was both an experienced medical researcher and a trained scientist, could believe in a therapeutic method which, quite apart from its medical implausibility, frequently and demonstrably failed to work.

One answer which can be given to this question is to suggest that, just as many people sustain their belief in the efficacy of religious rituals by their faith in the existence of unseen powers and invisible beings, Freud defended his own therapeutic rituals by surrounding them with similar metaphysical beliefs. By far the most important of the invisible entities he came to believe in at this time was the neurophysiological mechanism which he thought underlay hysteria.

If this mechanism is not usually recognised for the spiritualist construct it is, this is largely because of the solidly physicalist language in which Freud describes it. For Freud was convinced that the 'mind' could and should be described as though it were a piece of physical apparatus. The model which he favoured was one which showed it as a complex system of 'forces' and 'energies' which could be charged and discharged, invested and displaced like the current in a complicated piece of electrical apparatus. As Frank Sulloway has observed, one of the clearest statements of the psychophysicalist presuppositions of both Freud and Breuer is to be found in Freud's conclusion to his 1894 paper, 'The Neuro-Psychoses of Defence':

> I should like, finally, to dwell for a moment on the working hypothesis which I have made use of in this exposition of the neuroses of defence. I refer to the concept that in mental functions something is to be distinguished – a quota of affect or a sum of excitation – which possesses all the characteristics of a quantity (though we have no means of measuring

it), which is capable of increase, diminution, displacement and discharge, and which is spread over the memory-traces of ideas somewhat as an electric charge is spread over the surface of a body.

This hypothesis, which, incidentally, already underlies our theory of 'abreaction' in our 'Preliminary Communication' (1893), can be applied in the same sense as physicists apply the hypothesis of a flow of electric fluid. It is provisionally justified by its utility in co-ordinating and explaining a great variety of psychical states.[1]

One of the most useful applications of Freud's 'electrical' model of the human mind was, as is implicit here, to explain the way in which 'hysterical' symptoms could be both formed and cured.

According to any modern understanding of physiology or neurology there is no mechanism whereby the emotions aroused by a traumatic experience could *themselves* be converted into a physical symptom – such as a paralysed limb for example. Freud, however, assumed the existence of just such a direct link and did not hesitate to construct a series of completely speculative mechanisms which supplied exactly the physiological base his theory required at any particular point in its development.

In their *Studies on Hysteria,* and in a series of other writings, Freud and Breuer put forward a number of different hypothetical mechanisms by which hysterical symptoms were supposedly produced. Their central proposition was that every mental trauma, like any other emotional 'event', gave rise to a certain 'quantity' of emotional excitation. An emotional event would lead to a sudden rise in the overall 'sum' of excitation inside the organism. So long as the organism remained healthy it would automatically tend to 'discharge' this excess of emotion by 'disposing associatively' of it 'or by discharging it by an appropriate motor reaction'. In some cases, however, emotional excitations were not disposed of or discharged in the normal way. In these cases the 'sum' of the excitations would be converted by being forced into 'the wrong channel'. Instead of a psychological cause provoking a psychological effect, the nervous energy aroused would be forced into the physical innervation of the body and would then cause bodily symptoms. These bodily symptoms could then only be undone by reversing the process of conversion so that the emotional energy which had become 'trapped' in a particular part of the body would flow back and be released in the normal way. It was this process which Breuer and Freud described as 'abreaction'.[2]

Breuer and Freud went on to outline three different mechanisms which might be responsible for producing what they termed 'strangulations of affect'. The first of these, which seems to have been derived from Charcot's theory of traumatic hysteria, assigned a crucial role to ideas which were encountered by a patient during involuntary or self-induced 'hypnoid states' similar to those produced by periods of 'absence' or by hypnosis itself. The second was based on instances when a strong emotion was felt but denied immediate expression, and the third postulated a process of psychic defence which sought to suppress from consciousness ideas which, because of their strong emotional or sexual content, were intolerable to what Freud, like Charcot before him, referred to as 'the ego'.[3]

Freud gradually left behind the first hypothesis relating to 'hypnoid states' and concentrated more and more on the phenomena which he termed 'defence' and 'repression'. In the view which he expounded in 1894, the process of repression began with a defensive 'act of will' on the part of traumatised individuals in which they attempted to forget thoughts which had large quotas of affect associated with them and which were incompatible with their egos. The unintended consequence of this act of repression was that the emotional charge was detached from the original traumatic idea and channelled into bodily processes, thereby producing such physical symptoms as paralyses or contractures. A 'powerful idea' could be turned into a 'weak one' by robbing it of its affect, and forcing this affect into the wrong channel:

> The conversion may be either total or partial. It proceeds along the line of the motor or sensory innervation which is related – whether intimately or more loosely – to the traumatic experience. By this means the ego succeeds in freeing itself from the contradiction; but instead it has burdened itself with a mnemic symbol which finds a lodgement in consciousness, like a sort of parasite, either in the form of an unresolvable motor innervation or as a constantly recurring hallucinatory sensation, and which persists until a conversion in the opposite direction takes place.[4]

This idea appears to have been arrived at by marrying together Meynert's physiological associationism with some ideas about discharging affects which had been put forward by John Hughlings Jackson.[5] As happens frequently in his theoretical writings, the solidly physicalist language which Freud uses helps to build the illusion that we are reading the words of a cautious empirical scientist. For Freud writes as though he is describing a process which has been discovered and carefully mapped in the laboratory. Yet if we read his words more critically we will see that his ostensibly exact scientific prose is actually being used to accommodate a great deal of inexactitude.

One of the most crucial questions raised by Freud's whole remarkable hypothesis is what determines the kind of physical symptom which is supposedly produced by a particular emotional trauma. In the passage quoted above, this question is answered only in the most general terms; we are told simply that the conversion 'proceeds along the *line of the motor or sensory innervation which is related – whether intimately or more loosely – to the traumatic experience*'. The only way of finding out what this extremely vague formulation means in practice is to turn back to Freud's own case histories. In these, as we have already seen, there is virtually no limitation on the kind of associations which Freud is prepared to accept as neurophysiological causes. In the case of Elisabeth von R. 'the line of the motor or sensory innervation' along which her emotional trauma is conducted is supposedly determined, as I have noted above, by a bewildering variety of factors, including a clutch of metaphors concerned with independence or 'standing on one's own feet'. According to Freud it is such factors as these, which are indeed but 'loosely' related to the traumatic experience, that channel excitatory energy along specific nervous pathways with the result that a case of unrequited love leads to rheumatic pains in the legs. If we look at Freud's other cases, we find that the causal factors he proposes are no more persuasive. In the case of Lucy R., for example, the 'trauma' she suffers consists, improbably, in receiving a letter from her mother which, according to Freud, prompts the thought that she must leave her employer with whom she has fallen in love. At the time this letter arrives, the children Lucy R. is looking after become so excited that they forget about a pudding they are cooking and allow it to burn. According to Freud this chance occurrence, combined with the fact that she is at the time suffering from a heavy cold, is sufficient to determine the kind of physical symptom which is produced. For the excitatory energy resulting from the 'trauma' is immediately forced into the somatic innervation associated with the nose. It is in this way that Lucy R.'s unrequited love is converted not, as in the case of Elisabeth von R., into rheumatic pain in her legs, but into a strange and persistent smell in her nostrils.

In view of the perfectly reasonable explanations which can be offered of the symptoms which Freud insisted on treating as 'hysterical', it would seem that we have no alternative but to dismiss his elaborate neuropathological mechanisms as a product of the same highly creative imagination whose workings were examined in the last chapter. If we are finally to lay this particular psychoanalytic ghost, we must go even further than this and insist that the 'quantities' of affect to which Freud refers, the 'quotas' and 'sums' of excitation, along with all the various processes of 'increase', 'diminution', 'displacement' and 'discharge' are no more real than the 'channels' by which Freud imagines that all these complex messages are telegraphed around the mind. The whole construct is a huge and elaborate fiction which Freud has conjured into existence not on the basis of any empirical evidence but in order to surround with abstruse theological complexity a series of therapeutic rituals which need to be defended in this manner for the simple reason that, as we have already seen, they are almost completely ineffective.

Freud himself appears to have been unable to interrogate his own fiction sceptically. Once again we find him treating his own idiosyncratic logic as though it were a real, external chain of causality. For although at first he explicitly presents the supposed neuropsychological mechanism as a speculative construction, before very long it is evident that he has come to regard it as a real entity, in terms of which alone the internal workings of the mind can be explained. Indeed, instead of resting content with the relatively simple model which he devised to explain the electrical circuitry of hysteria, Freud progressively subjected this model to a wholly fantastic elaboration.

The first signs of what was eventually to be a major theoretical eruption in Freud's development, became visible just a month after he had completed the last chapter he was writing for *Studies on Hysteria*. It was at this point that he began to construct what James Strachey has called an 'extraordinarily ingenious working model of the mind as a piece of neurological machinery'.[6] Over the next few months, Freud's *Project for a Scientific Psychology* became his consuming passion, his 'tyrant' as he put it. 'I am so deep in the Psychology for Neurologists,' he wrote in a letter to Wilhelm Fliess in April 1895, 'that it quite consumes me, until I have to break off out of sheer exhaustion. I have never been so intensely preoccupied by anything. And will anything come of it? I hope so, but the going is hard and slow.'[7] In October, in a torrent of inspiration, Freud filled two notebooks consisting of one hundred manuscript sheets with his speculative system. Some days after he had sent these notebooks to his friend Fliess he wrote to express the state of intellectual exultation which he had now reached:

> Now listen to this. During an industrious night last week, when I was suffering from that degree of pain which brings about the optimal conditions for my mental activities, the barriers suddenly lifted, the veils dropped, and everything became transparent – from the details of the neuroses to the determinants of consciousness. Everything seemed to fall into place, the cogs meshed, I had the impression that the thing now really was a machine that would shortly function on its own. The three systems of n[eurones]; the free and bound states of Qn [quantity]; the primary and secondary processes; the main tendency and the compromise tendency of the nervous system; the two biological rules of attention and defence; the characteristics of quality, reality and thought; the state of the psychosexual group; the sexual determination of repression; finally the factors determining consciousness as a function of perception – all that was correct and still is today! Naturally I can scarcely manage to contain my delight![8]

Freud's imagery here suggests that his intellectual delight has an almost religious intensity. As the barriers lift and the veils are dropped it is as though he feels that he has been vouchsafed a revelation or a mystical vision of a secret reality which is concealed from all others. We are reminded, perhaps, of Descartes' dream in which the supposed divine rationality of the universe was suddenly revealed to him.

Freud's joy was short-lived, however. By the end of November he was writing to Fliess in a very different tone: 'I cannot understand the state of mind in which I hatched the psychology; I cannot conceive how I could have inflicted it on you . . . to me it appears to have been a kind of madness.'[9]

It is perhaps not surprising that Freud's *Project for a Scientific Psychology* should have ended by producing such disillusion. For although Freud described his model of mind in remorselessly scientific language, it remained no less speculative in its nature than any of his other metapsychological structures. It was a kind of conceptual version of an ultra-modern Heath Robinson machine constructed out of an extraordinary range of terminological hardware, borrowed from physics, neurology, cerebral physiology and psychology. Central to the workings of this machine was a hypothetical substance which Freud dubbed Q. This was the 'quantity' or 'energy' whose flow through the system was supposedly governed by the laws of motion. The system itself was constructed out of 'material particles' which Freud labels 'neurones'. In order to make the system work Freud decided that three different kinds of neurone were necessary and he designated these by different letters of the Greek alphabet. The 'phi' neurones received excitation from outside the body, but did not retain it; the 'psi' neurones were either excited by the 'phi' neurones or by internal stimuli such as appetite and instinct. They were ruled by the 'principle of constancy', retained stimulation and were responsible for memory. Finally, the 'omega' neurones were stimulated either by the 'phi' neurones or by the body. They differed from the other two in that they transformed quantity into quality and provided the basis of perception. The three different kinds of neurone were all assigned certain neurophysiological qualities, such as permeability and impermeability. For example, 'psi' neurones were initially impermeable at their 'contact barriers' but became increasingly permeable with the passage of Q or 'psychical quantity'. It was by ringing the changes on this extraordinary system of particles, substances and relationships that Freud sought to explain the inner mental workings which lay behind such varied psychological phenomena as wishing, hallucinatory states, judgement, defence, cognition, expecting, remembering, observing, the psychopathology of hysteria, sleep and dreaming.[10]

Yet although Freud, after a period of regarding his *Project* as a kind of epiphany or revelation, does seem to have overcome his initial infatuation with it, it would be wrong to suggest that he ever came to realise the full extent of the intellectual folly he had created. For, as a number of scholars have pointed out, many of the concepts which originally surfaced in the *Project* would reappear in Freud's subsequent writings. Richard Wollheim, for example, suggests that the theory of mind that Freud put forward in the *Scientific Project* had 'a powerful and probably incalculable influence over his whole thinking' and that 'most of his greatest work was achieved in its shadow'.[11] Frank Sulloway, in his *Freud: Biologist of the Mind*, does not go quite this far, but he does treat the *Project* with the utmost seriousness and assigns to it a crucial role in the development of psychoanalysis.[12]

Some of the reasons why Freud remained in thrall to the bizarre kind of reasoning which is found in the *Project* become clear in Sulloway's own book. For although Sulloway rarely offers any direct criticism of Freud's theoretical formulations, his book does perform an immensely valuable service by showing the extent to which Freud's entire theoretical enterprise was shaped by contemporary scientific developments.

What becomes clear from the work of Sulloway, Ellenberger and other scholars is that, although Freud's speculative mechanical model of the mind was probably more intricate, more extreme and more improbable than that of any other contemporary neurologist or psychologist, comparable models were produced during the nineteenth century and were regarded, in some circles at least, as a form of entirely legitimate science. The immediate inspiration for the *Project* was probably provided by Freud's former teacher, Sigmund Exner, who in 1894 published a description of a psychomechanical model of mind with many of the features which would eventually appear in Freud's sketch. This was not the only link between Freud's enterprise and the work of contemporary scientists. For, as both Sulloway and Ellenberger point out, many of the psychophysical theories which underpin Freud's thinking both in the *Project* and elsewhere are derived directly from the work of Gustav Fechner. It was Fechner who introduced into psychology the principle of the conservation of energy, and it was this principle which, in Freud's hands, was eventually to become one of the fundamental principles of psychoanalysis. Freud also took from Fechner the basic concept of mental energy, the 'topographical' concept of mind, the principle of pleasure–unpleasure and the principle of repetition. As Henri Ellenberger writes: 'A large part of the theoretical framework of psychoanalysis would hardly have come into being without the speculations of the man whom Freud called the great Fechner.'[13]

It is at this point, however, that the accounts given by Ellenberger and Sulloway diverge in a highly significant manner. For although Frank Sulloway carefully locates Freud's theories in their immediate scientific context, he omits to recognise that this particular context itself needs to be contextualised if we are to appreciate its real significance. Sulloway introduces Fechner into his narrative in terms which might well create the impression that he was an entirely orthodox 'modern' scientist. Yet this is very far from being the case. It is only if we consider Fechner's contribution to psychology in relation to his entire intellectual career that Freud's *real* intellectual genealogy begins to emerge.[14]

It is certainly true that Gustav Fechner was, in one respect, a conventional scientist. After studying medicine at Leipzig he became interested in theoretical physics and in 1833, at the age of thirty-two, he was appointed to the post of Professor of Physics at Leipzig University. Yet Fechner's career as a theoretical physicist was but a pale shadow of his other career – as what might best be termed a 'spiritual scientist'.

One of Fechner's early works, published under the pseudonym of Dr Mises, was entitled *Comparative Anatomy of the Angels*. In this book, in the words of Henri Ellenberger:

> Fechner followed the curve of the evolution of the animal kingdom, from the amoeba to man, and then, by extrapolation, attempted to construct the ideal form of a still higher being, an angel. He concluded that such beings must be spheric, must perceive universal gravitation in the same way as humans perceive light, and communicate with each other by means of a language of luminous signs, much as humans converse with each other by means of an acoustic language.[15]

Some time after he became Professor of Physics at Leipzig, Fechner fell into a deep depression. As he recovered he began to experience feelings of grandeur and eventually became convinced that he had been chosen by God and was now able to solve all the world's riddles. This feeling of divine election led in turn to a conviction that he had discovered a universal law which applied to the whole of the spiritual world in the same way that Newton's law of gravity applied to the physical world. Fechner called this 'the principle of pleasure'. Eventually, having written a number of mystical works on the psychology of plants and on a theory of the earth as a living being, he became preoccupied with the relationship between the physical and the spiritual worlds. He tirelessly sought after the mathematical formula in terms of which he could express this relationship and eventually drew up something which he called the psychophysical law. He now devised a series of experiments to test the truth of this formula and published his findings in the two volumes of his *Psychophysics* which appeared in 1860.

Gustav Fechner, then – 'the great Fechner', as Freud called him – although he is introduced by Frank Sulloway as though he were a cautious scientist working within a positivist tradition, was in fact nothing of the kind. For while he had started off as a conventional physicist, despising the spiritualistic beliefs which were fundamental to the nineteenth-century tradition of *Naturphilosophie*, Fechner eventually became an adherent of the philosophy of nature himself.

In following this pattern of intellectual development Fechner was by no means unique. For one of the most interesting facets of nineteenth-century intellectual history was the extraordinary difficulty which many scientists found when it came to the task of renouncing theistic explanations of the universe which invoked terms such as 'spirit' or 'soul'.

One of the basic tenets of the philosophy of nature which had grown up out of German Romanticism was that 'nature' and 'spirit' were an indissoluble unity. According to this doctrine the whole of the organic and visible world was a manifestation of the 'world soul', which itself gave rise not only to nature but to consciousness in man. It was therefore a fundamental tenet of the philosophy of nature that natural phenomena cannot be understood through mechanical and physical concepts alone, but that the ultimate task of the scientist was to elucidate the *spiritual* laws by which all nature was governed.

This view of the relationship between matter and spirit applied not only to the study of nature, but also to medicine. In Romantic medicine there was no absolute dichotomy between spirit and body or mind and body. As in traditional physiology, mind and body were linked by channels, which were called nerves. The animal spirits which conveyed sense and motion to the body were the 'handmaidens of the soul'.

The terms of this essentially theistic view of nature were challenged in a particularly uncompromising way by the materialist and positivist philosophies which gained power in Europe after the middle of the nineteenth century with the rise of a new class of professional scientists. Extreme proponents of such views sought to cleanse science of every trace of religion and metaphysics, so that at times they even denied the reality of anything which could not be reduced to physical or mechanical categories.

This rigorous intellectual policing, however, had quite unforeseen consequences. For the theistic, 'spiritualist' views of nature which had grown up in the nineteenth century were not simply products of some superficial Romanticism which could be swept away. They were rooted in the Judaeo-Christian tradition itself. Whether or not Marx was right in describing religion as the opium of the people, it seems quite clear that theistic views of nature had been the principal intellectual narcotic for generations of European intellectuals. When extreme positivists sought to suppress this narcotic, a significant number of intellectuals, while publicly renouncing metaphysics, began to smuggle theistic views back across the frontiers of science, and secrete them in their theories in a disguised form.

Instead of abandoning the ancient occult fictions of 'soul' and 'spirit' which had constantly been invoked in order to explain the inexplicable, these nineteenth-century scientists systematically translated them into positivistic language, using concepts and terminology drawn from the physical sciences. In this way they constructed fictional entities which were no less occult than their precursors but which, since they were described in the language of science, were often treated as though they were science.

Among the many academic disciplines which succumbed to this particular form of disguised, pseudo-scientific spiritualism was psychology. Here Fechner himself was the prime culprit, elaborating an extraordinarily complex theory of psychological energetics which had no more scientific value than his musings on the morphology of angels, but which, because it constantly drew on the conceptual apparatus of contemporary physics, was regarded in many quarters with high scientific seriousness. The developments in the discipline of psychology for which Fechner was responsible were paralleled by a similar proliferation of spiritualistic pseudo-science among both physiologists and neurologists. For, throughout the nineteenth century, empirical investigations into the anatomy of the brain and the nervous system co-existed with a completely non-scientific tradition in which scientists followed the example of the philosophers of nature they outwardly spurned, and created vast speculative structures. In the latter part of the century this style of speculation was even given a name and described as *Hirnmythologie* or 'brain mythology'. Very often this essentially theological mode of thinking was followed by the same people who were simultaneously engaged in the empirical study of brain anatomy. Among Freud's own teachers, Brücke, Meynert and Exner all promoted a positivistic and strictly scientific approach to the study of neuroanatomy. But alongside their legitimate scientific researches they all engaged in the contemporary fashion for brain mythology, producing, under the influence of Fechner's energetics, vast speculative structures scarcely less extensive and bizarre than the psychomechanical model elaborated by Freud.[16]

This was the tradition which provided Freud's immediate inspiration. It was because the tradition was so well established and had achieved such a degree of academic respectability that the scientifically spurious nature of Freud's own mysterious brain mechanisms tended to be invisible to his contemporaries. This has in turn made it more difficult for historians of psychoanalysis to view Freud's speculations in a realistic critical perspective. Even Henri Ellenberger, although he clearly recognises that Freud's *Project* belongs to the tradition of brain mythology, and that this whole tradition was 'nothing but the late resurgence of the philosophy of nature', seems unable to face up to the full implications of Freud's intellectual genealogy.[17]

Yet what becomes abundantly clear if we study this genealogy dispassionately is that Freud, the proudly atheistic scientist and the sceptical foe of the 'illusions' fostered by religion, was himself in thrall to a particularly subtle form of theistic fantasy. It was this crypto-theological view which sustained his belief that he could find the key which would unlock the mysteries of human nature by studying the mechanism of the 'spirit' or 'soul' which supposedly controlled human behaviour.

In elaborating this view Freud unwittingly revived some of the most superstitious forms of physiological speculation which went back well beyond Romantic nature philosophy to the ancients. In its simplest form the most influential pre-scientific physiology had been based on a very specific theory of nervous function. This postulated the existence of 'animal spirits' who were the messengers and handmaidens of the soul 'travelling back and forth in either direction through nerves believed hollow, taking motion and sensation to whatever parts they visited'. The ancient theory further maintained that, as they travelled through the nerves in order to do the soul's bidding, the animal spirits could find their path blocked by a particular kind of 'morbific humour' such as 'cold phlegm'. When this happened they would be forced into the 'wrong channel' and might end by giving rise to a bodily symptom.

In the century following the Enlightenment the original terms of this ancient and superstitious physiology gradually disappeared. But the physiological fantasy which the ancients had created survived. What happened in effect was that key terms such as 'animal spirits', which too easily disclosed their theistic origins, were translated into modern-sounding 'scientific' concepts – in this case 'nervous energy' or 'nervous force'. These were then discussed by having recourse to metaphors drawn from electricity or hydraulics so that, almost imperceptibly, the ancient fantasy was reconstructed in terminology appropriate to positivist science. It was this mechanistic reworking of ancient physiology which Freud inherited from his teachers and adapted to provide an explanation of 'hysterical conversion' – which was itself but an updated version of the similar notion of conversion which was incorporated into the older physiology. It was the same updated fantasy which he then subjected to an extraordinary process of elaboration whereby it became the model of mind described in such meticulous detail in the *Project*.[18]

The fact that many of Freud's doctrines about the nature of the mind were drawn from contemporary neurology and biology does not render them any more acceptable. For in a detailed examination of Freud's main assumptions Robert Holt shows how they have been contradicted point for point by the findings of modern neurology. 'Freud,' he concludes, 'was wrong, as his teachers had been before him . . .'

> The nervous system is not passive, does not take in and conduct out again the energies of the environment, and shows no tendency to 'divest itself of' its own impulses. The principle of constancy is quite without any biological basis. The notion of homeostasis, which is more a point of view than a working concept in physiology today, is only a vague analogy and cannot be used to prop up this hoary anachronism.

Holt, like a number of other scholars, suggests that the errors of the *Project*, far from being left behind when Freud abandoned his essay, were carried over into his later theorising and writes that *'many of the obscurities, fallacies, and internal contradictions of psychoanalytic theory are . . . direct derivatives of its neurological inheritance.'*[19]

If we replace Holt's own relatively modern perspective by the longer historical view I have outlined, we are led to the conclusion that, although the vocabulary in which the *Project* is written is modern and scientific, the habit of mind which it embodies is ancient and pre-scientific. Freud's speculations, indeed, have no more empirical validity than the ancient humoral theory they displaced, and his own elaborately constructed network of neurones and contact-barriers is nothing more than a work of ingenious fiction. Psychoanalysis and humoral theory perform similar intellectual functions. For in both cases an entirely fictional model of nervous function is used to surround with a theoretical smoke-screen a series of physiological fallacies, diagnostic errors and medical mistakes. The only major difference between the two versions of pseudo-science is that Freud's is still taken seriously by at least some psychiatrists today.

The hidden continuity between Freud's ultra modern neuroanatomical fiction and the ancient anatomical fallacies it displaced is one of the most remarkable aspects of medical history. But perhaps even more significant is the more personal link between Gustav Fechner and the most famous of all the intellectuals he influenced. For although Freud is normally portrayed as one of the children of the Enlightenment, strictly raised in a severely scientific and rationalistic intellectual regime, the link with Fechner shows a quite different set of influences at work. As we have seen, 'the great Fechner' was a conventional scientist only in appearance. Beneath his modern scientific persona he preserved intact some of the most crucial characteristics of the Judaeo-Christian religious culture which was his inheritance. He was at once a religious mystic and a messiah who believed he had been chosen by God to be vouchsafed a vision of an ultimate reality which had been withheld from others. In this respect, as in many others, Freud was indeed his natural intellectual heir. For Freud did not leave behind those profoundly messianic traits I have already discussed in relation to his earlier career. The closer he came to finalising the theoretical propositions out of which psychoanalysis was wrought, the more completely he adopted the role of the messianic prophet.

Freud's theory of sexuality, which was to be the doctrinal rock on which his own church was founded, certainly bears all the marks of his messianic and profoundly mystical personality. It is to his 'discovery' of this remarkable sexual theory that we must now turn.

EIGHT

Sex, Masturbation and Neurasthenia

WHEN, IN OCTOBER 1895, Freud had sent to his friend Wilhelm Fliess the two notebooks containing his *Project for a Scientific Psychology*, he enclosed a covering letter drawing attention to the crucial role which he had assigned to sexuality. 'Just think,' he said, 'among other things I am on the scent of the following strict precondition for hysteria, namely, that a primary sexual experience (before puberty), accompanied by revulsion and fright, must have taken place; for obsessional neurosis, that it must have happened, accompanied by *pleasure*.'[1] In these words we may see the beginnings of what was eventually to become Freud's 'seduction theory' in which he would put forward the idea that all his hysterical patients had been sexually seduced as children. It should be noted, however, that there were other compelling reasons why Freud 'needed' sexuality to be a key element in his explanatory model of the mind. In the first place his whole model, as we have seen, depended on a theory of mental 'energetics'. As such it could not work at all without a constantly renewable source of energy. Breuer had already written in *Studies on Hysteria* that 'the sexual instinct is undoubtedly the most powerful source of persisting accretions of excitation (and consequently of neuroses)'.[2] Freud now incorporated this view into his *Project* and, by doing so, he effectively supplied the 'fuel' on which his mechanical model of mind could run.

Another of the reasons why Freud needed sexuality to play a role in his model of mind was that, for all his flights into psychology and metaphysics, he remained, both by training and by aspiration, a physiologist. As such he never gave up seeking to ground his psychological theories in biology. The crucial role he assigned to sexuality enabled him to claim that all his speculations rested on a firm 'organic foundation'. This point is brought home in a comment Freud made in 1908 in a letter about Jung's chief, Bleuler: 'I am rather annoyed with Bleuler,' he wrote, 'for his willingness to accept a psychology without sexuality, which leaves everything hanging in mid-air. In the sexual processes we have the indispensable 'organic foundation' without which a medical man can only feel ill at ease in the life of the psyche.'[3]

Throughout the rest of his intellectual development Freud remained a biological fundamentalist in that his commitment to the concept of sexual energy and to the pathogenic centrality of sexuality never wavered. Given this fact, one of the most surprising features of his intellectual biography is just how long it was before he developed any marked theoretical interest in sexuality.

If we survey the work of Freud's earlier intellectual heroes from Brücke to Charcot, there is little sign of the subject which would later preoccupy him. Nor is there any indication in Freud's biography that his attitude towards sex was anything other than conventional until relatively late in his life. But it would nevertheless be wrong to date the beginning of his theoretical interest in sexuality to the writing of the *Project*. The glimmerings of Freud's later sexual theories are, as we have already seen, already present in some of the cases of hysteria discussed in the *Studies*. And Freud's own account of the first clues he was given as to the supposed pathogenic significance of sexuality goes back even further. He recalled that early in 1886 he was present at one of Charcot's evening receptions when he happened to hear 'the great teacher' arguing that a disturbed young woman owed her nervous problems to her husband's inadequate sexual performance:

> For Charcot suddenly broke out with great animation: '*Mais dans des cas pareils c'est toujours la chose génitale, toujours, toujours, toujours*' [But in cases like this it's always the genital thing – always, always, always]: and he crossed his arms over his stomach, hugging himself and jumping up and down on his toes several times in his own characteristically lively way. I know that for a moment I was almost paralysed with amazement and said to myself: 'Well, but if he knows that, why does he never say so?'[4]

Freud went on to recall how Breuer had once hinted that nervous disorders always involve *secrets d'alcove* – secrets of the bedchamber. He then reported a statement made by the physician Chrobak, who remarked that the only hope of curing one patient lay in prescribing regular doses of a normal penis:

Penis normalis
dosim
repetatur![5]

It has been objected that Freud's own explanation of the origins of his emphasis on sex is hardly sufficient. None of the three examples which Freud gives, writes Ronald Clark, 'testifies to more than the effects of frustrated sexual satisfaction, a point that is unlikely to have escaped his notice by the time he had reached his thirties'. The facts suggest, Clark continues, that Freud was driven to his conclusion about the importance of sexuality 'by a multitude of small details noted in his patients'.[6] Ronald Clark's alternative explanation certainly conforms more closely to the legendary view of Freud as the cautious and observant scientist. It must be said, however, that Freud's own version of the story is much more plausible. For, as we have seen, Freud was given not only to speculative flights of ideas, but he was also, at times, almost cravenly dependent on the authority of others. The notion that he should pursue the role of sexuality in the aetiology of the neuroses only after this idea had first been legitimated by two of his greatest intellectual heroes – Charcot and Breuer – seems entirely reasonable.

What is perhaps just as important about Freud's story is the insight it gives into the climate of opinion in which Freud would eventually seek to propagate his sexual theories. For the clutch of stories which Freud presents, including the unpleasantly chauvinistic remark of Chrobak, indicates that crude theories of sexual aetiology, while they were very far from being medically respectable, had the status of locker-room orthodoxies in at least some medical circles. Such notions derived ultimately from the traditional view of hysteria as having sexual origins. The very fact that this view had survived in this way meant that if any theorist were to translate such outdated lore into modern medical terminology, he could rely on a significant number of physicians being receptive to it. Freud, as a perceptive observer of therapeutic trends, can scarcely have failed to register this possibility.

The first glimmerings of Freud's sexual theories appeared in an article about hysteria which he wrote in 1888 for a medical encyclopaedia. Although he suggested that sexual factors were sometimes allotted too much significance in accounting for hysteria, he nevertheless expressed the view that 'conditions related functionally to sexual life play a great part in the aetiology of hysteria (as of all neuroses) and they do so on account of the high psychical significance of this function especially in the female sex.'[7] Although this view was developed further in relation to the patients which were described in *Studies on Hysteria*, it was in relation to another category of patients that he began to conceive of sexuality as the essential or sole cause of a particular condition. Freud announced what he evidently considered to be a major theoretical breakthrough to his friend Wilhelm Fliess in a letter sent in February 1893. He prefaced his communication with a note advising Fliess to 'keep the manuscript away from your young wife'. Freud's subject in the clandestine essay he sent to his friend was the condition of 'neurasthenia'.

At the time Freud wrote, 'neurasthenia' was often considered to be one of the two main neuroses, the other being 'hysteria'. Whereas the former was thought to be predominantly a male condition, the latter was usually, though not always, associated with women. These two categories had evolved more as the result of changes in medical fashion than out of any advance in scientific knowledge. In the eighteenth century the two most fashionable neuroses had been the *vapeurs* of society women and 'hypochondriasis', which was usually suffered by men. By the middle of the nineteenth century these once fashionable labels had almost disappeared but they were replaced by others. In 1831 an ostensibly new condition appeared under the name of the 'wear and tear syndrome'. The English physician James Johnson described this as a disease which was peculiar to the English. It supposedly resulted from physical and mental overexertion and the stress attendant on life in a newly industrialised society. The remedy he prescribed was relaxation and travel abroad.

In 1869 the American neurologist George Beard described a similar condition to which he gave the name of 'neurasthenia' – a term indicating weakness of the nerves which was already current, but which had not usually been treated as a disease in itself. The basic symptoms of 'neurasthenia', according to Beard, were physical and mental exhaustion; other indications included loss of appetite, weakness of the back and spine, sleeplessness, sick headaches, fugitive neuralgic pains 'and other analogous symptoms'.[8] At first Beard maintained that 'neurasthenia' was caused by de-phosphorisation of the nervous system and recommended the use of chemical tonics. Subsequently, however, he redefined it as an essentially American neurosis caused by the climate, the intensive economic conditions and religious freedom; liberty was seen as 'a cause of nervousness'. He predicted that 'neurasthenia' would spread abroad if European life were to be Americanised.

Beard periodically revised not only the aetiology of this putative disease but also its symptoms. By 1881 the number of symptoms had grown enormously, so much so that even to list them in the Contents section of his book *American Nervousness* took up more than a page.

The symptoms now included noises in the ear, atonic voice, deficient mental control, bad dreams, nervous dyspepsia, heaviness of the loin and limb, flushing and fidgetiness, palpitations, spinal irritation, uterine irritability, impotence, hopelessness and fears such as claustrophobia, agoraphobia and fear of contamination.[9] In his new explanation of the supposed disease, Beard placed great emphasis on the overexpenditure of the 'vital force' or nerve force. He assumed that there was a balance of nervous energy which was proper to each individual, and that this balance might become overdrawn because of the pace of modern American life. Any form of excess in life, whether it be too much work, too much anxiety, or too much sexual activity might dangerously deplete the vital forces. Like so many other contemporary neurologists Beard could not resist the temptation to use a model drawn from electricity. 'Men, like batteries,' he wrote, 'need a reserve force, and men, like batteries, need to be measured by the amount of the reserve, and not what they are compelled to spend in ordinary daily life.'[10]

Although the medically spurious nature of Beard's formulations will be readily apparent to most modern observers, Beard's new diagnostic category proved immensely popular not only with many patients but also with a number of his fellow physicians. It did so primarily because it was formulated at a time when very considerable confusion still reigned around a whole host of organic conditions which had not yet been adequately described or delimited and an equally large number of psychological or behavioural syndromes which were similarly unmapped. The term 'neurasthenia' thus came, even more than 'hysteria' – whose symptoms remained relatively specific – to function as a catch-all diagnosis which offered both physicians and patients a way of escaping from feelings of therapeutic helplessness. The new label, with its implicit claim to scientific precision, could be applied to a number of organic conditions which had either not been identified at all, or for which adequate diagnostic tests had not been developed, including glandular fever, tuberculosis, lead poisoning, some cardiac conditions, tinnitus, Addison's disease and various endocrinal disorders. At the same time it could be used to give a false physical aetiology to a number of psychological conditions, such as anorexia nervosa, agoraphobia, and various anxiety-states. It functioned both to protect physicians from having to admit the depths of their ignorance and to prevent patients from losing faith in the medical profession altogether.[11]

Some of Beard's medical contemporaries were astute enough to recognise the emptiness of his new diagnostic category almost immediately. The distinguished neuroanatomist Spitzka, for example, expressed the opinion that *American Nervousness* was 'not worth the ink with which it is printed, much less the paper on which this was done'.[12] Such criticisms, however, were insufficient to quell the enormous interest created by Beard's work. By the mid 1880s the medical literature devoted to neurasthenia already comprised several hundred books and papers, a number of which appeared in Germany. In the view of one historian, the 'decisive period in the evolution of neurasthenia' was ushered in by Charcot, who 'legitimized neurasthenia as a major neurosis, comparable only to hysteria'.[13]

Charcot's endorsement of the diagnosis was, it would seem, sufficient to dispel any scepticism on Freud's part, and by 1887 he was already referring to neurasthenia as 'the commonest of all the diseases in our society'.[14] He was particularly taken by the idea that neurasthenia might sometimes have a sexual aetiology. This notion had its origins in Beard's own writings. In his book *Sexual Neurasthenia*, Beard sketches various relationships which supposedly exist between 'excessively frequent' seminal emissions and the symptoms of neurasthenia. When Freud eventually took up the problem in earnest in the early 1890s he was characteristically ambitious in his approach. The notion that sexuality might *sometimes* be a factor seems not to have appealed to him. For Freud was rarely attracted by piecemeal solutions. Indeed one of the characteristics of his intellectual style was 'the longing to be able to open all secrets with a single key'.[15] In this particular case it would seem that Freud was also profoundly influenced by his admiration for the germ theory of disease which had been put forward by Koch and Pasteur. What this theory proposed, in effect, was that all genuine diseases had a single cause and that one of the purposes of medical research was to discover the micro-organism or other agent which was responsible for specific diseases.[16]

In keeping with this strictly medical approach, the theoretical 'innovation' which Freud communicated to Fliess in his letter of 1893 consisted in the suggestion that sexual factors were not simply one among many possible causes of neurasthenia, but that they were *the sole cause*: 'It may be taken as a recognised fact,' he wrote, 'that neurasthenia is a frequent consequence of an abnormal sexual life. The assertion, however, which I wish to make and test by observations, is that neurasthenia actually can *only* be a sexual neurosis.'[17] Freud then went on to expound his belief that certain forms of abnormal sexual activity resulted in the production of what he called sexual 'noxae', which caused a kind of neurological poisoning. The chief agent of such sexual poisoning was, in Freud's considered view, masturbation. He expressed this opinion to Fliess in the following remarkable words:

> *Neurasthenia* in males is acquired at the age of puberty and becomes manifest when the man is in his twenties. Its source is masturbation, the frequency of which runs completely parallel with the frequency of male neurasthenia. One can observe in the circle of one's acquaintances that (at least in urban populations) those individuals who have been seduced by women at an early age have escaped neurasthenia. When this noxa has operated long and intensely, it turns the person concerned into a sexual neurasthenic, whose potency, too, has been impaired; the intensity of the cause is paralleled by a lifelong persistence of the condition. Further evidence of the causal connection lies in the fact that a sexual neurasthenic is always a general neurasthenic at the same time.[18]

Masturbation, according to Freud's newly formulated theory, was the first of the 'sexual noxae' which were liable to lead to neurasthenia. The second noxa, which supposedly afflicted men at a later stage in their life, was *onanismus conjugalis*, which Freud defined as 'incomplete intercourse in order to prevent conception' and in which he included coitus interruptus, extravaginal intercourse, and intercourse in which a condom was used. A healthy man, Freud believed, could tolerate such practices for quite a long time. But eventually they would take their toll even on such an individual. 'His only advantage over the masturbator,' Freud wrote, 'is the privilege of a longer latency.'

Freud almost immediately added a refinement to this argument, proposing that a certain group of symptoms which he had initially associated with neurasthenia should be seen as marking an independent clinical entity. When patients reported themselves to be suffering from general irritability, or anxious expectation associated with trembling, sweating, vomiting or diarrhoea, they were to be diagnosed as suffering from 'anxiety neurosis', a condition supposedly associated specifically with coitus interruptus. Both neurasthenia and anxiety neurosis were eventually categorised as 'actual neuroses', a term which conveyed Freud's belief that they were caused by sexual problems in the present, rather than by repressed sexual traumas in the patient's past.[19]

Freud did not only take a strong therapeutic line on the harmful effects of masturbation and coitus interruptus but he also constructed elaborate theoretical models which attempted to explain the mechanics of the toxicological processes they supposedly gave rise to. In these models Freud postulated, in his customary manner, a whole series of entirely imaginary pathways, diversions, blockages and holes through which sexual excitation supposedly travelled around the body. 'Here, then,' he writes in a draft which he sent to Fliess, 'there is a similarity to neurasthenia. In neurasthenia a quite similar impoverishment takes place, owing to the excitation running out, as it were, through a hole. But in that case what is pumped empty is s. S. [somatic sexual excitation]; in melancholia the hole is in the psychic sphere.'[20]

Like almost all the other bizarre features of Freud's thought, these theories about masturbation and neurasthenia were not simply a momentary aberration in Freud's thinking but a crucial link in the chain of logic which led eventually to the creation of his mature psychoanalytic theories. Indeed Freud would frequently reiterate his belief in the pathogenic nature of masturbation during the first two decades of the twentieth century. The belief had important implications for Freud's therapeutic practice. For as a matter of course he now questioned his patients on whether they had masturbated as children, whether they still masturbated, what mode of sexual intercourse they engaged in and whether they used any contraceptive methods. Far from driving patients away, Freud found, initially at least, that many patients responded positively to being questioned about such intimate matters. 'Things have become more lively,' he wrote to Fliess in October 1893. 'The sexual business attracts people who are all stunned and then go away won over after having exclaimed, "No one has ever asked me about that before!" '[21]

From a scientific point of view all Freud's theories about the sexual aetiology of neurasthenia were, it need scarcely be said, completely spurious. Not only were the poisonous effects which Freud attributed to masturbation and coitus interruptus entirely imaginary, but the syndrome of neurasthenia itself was the product of medical fantasy and ignorance. By far the most intriguing aspect of Freud's idiosyncratic theories about neurasthenia, however, is their historical genealogy. For the opinion that masturbation, and all other forms of non-procreative sexual activity, were harmful and wrong clearly has its origins not in nineteenth-century medicine at all but in Christian theology.

The traditional Christian doctrine which maintained the sinfulness of non-procreative sexual acts had a number of sources. Among these was the New Testament, with its combined stress on the institutional goodness of marriage, the sacredness of sexual intercourse, the sin-fulness of the 'flesh' and the superiority of virginity. The specific doc-trine of marital intercourse expounded by the Christian fathers, however, owes quite as much to Stoicism as it does to the Scriptures. The Stoics sought to control bodily desire by reason. While they did not condemn marriage, passion in marriage was regarded as suspect. The rational basis of marriage, they held, was to be found in the part it played in the propagation of the race. The purpose of sexual activity was thus held to reside purely in its biological function. On this view any form of sexual activity which was engaged in purely for pleasure was an unnatural act. Masturbation, coitus interruptus, and any sexual act which obstructed conception were automatically seen as unnatural and immoderately sensual. 'All love of another's wife is shameful,' wrote Seneca; 'so too is too much love of your own. A wise man ought to love his wife with judgment, not affection. Let him control his impulses and not be borne headlong into copulation. Nothing is fouler than to love a wife like an adulteress . . . Let [men] show themselves to their wives not as lovers but as husbands.'[22]

The Stoic distinction between natural and unnatural sexual acts was taken over by the early Christian Church and became the basis of its moral teaching on marriage. From the very beginnings of the Church masturbation was defined as a sin, and an Irish penitential of about AD 575 laid down a two-year penance for its practice by monks. The view that both masturbation and coitus interruptus were sinful acts became one of the central tenets of the Church's teaching on sexuality; in the Roman Catholic Church it has remained so until this day. The fact that a very similar view was adopted by a nineteenth-century Jewish neurologist in Vienna might well, because of the wide cultural gap separating the two contexts, be dismissed as a coincidence. To draw this conclusion, however, would be to fail to recognise the complex threads of cultural continuity which joined the medieval Church to nineteenth-century medicine in general and to nineteenth-century sex-ology in particular.

Freud's contemporary, the British sexual researcher Havelock Ellis, was himself aware of the essentially Christian roots of modern sexual research. In the General Preface (1897) to his *Studies in the Psychology of Sex* Ellis wrote that one of his aims was to sweep away the 'rigid secrecy' which had come to surround sexual behaviour in order to replace it by what he called 'a sane and natural reticence'. He went on to observe:

This secrecy has not always been maintained. When the Catholic Church was at the summit of its power and influence it fully realised the magnitude of sexual problems and took an active and inquiring interest in all the details of normal and abnormal sexuality. Even to the present time there are certain phenomena of the sexual life which have scarcely been accurately described except in ancient theological treatises. As the type of such treatises I will mention the great tome of Sanchez, *De Matrimonio*. Here you will find the whole sexual life of men and women analysed in its relationships to sin. Everything is set forth as clearly and as concisely as it can be . . . in the coldest scientific language; the right course of action is pointed out for all cases that may occur, and we are told what is lawful, what a venial sin, what a mortal sin . . . We need today the same spirit and temper applied from a different standpoint. These things concern everyone; the study of these things concerns the physiologist, the psychologist, the moralist.[23]

Ellis's account of the roots of modern sexual research is in many respects historically perceptive. But what it fails to stress sufficiently is the intrinsically repressive and censorious character of the kind of sexual science which was brought into being by the Roman Catholic Church.

In the centuries after the Reformation the traditional concern of the Christian Church with the details of human sexual behaviour gradually disappeared as more and more rigid forms of puritanism were adopted both by Protestant churches and, under the influence of the Counter Reformation, by the Roman Catholic Church. But at the same time both the Church's authority to deal with sexual questions and its repressive moral assumptions began to be transferred to the medical sciences. Significantly enough, the first medical treatise which dealt in detail with the supposedly harmful effects of masturbation was written by an anonymous clergyman, who published *Onania, or the Heinous Sin of Self-pollution* in about 1710. 'If we turn our eyes on licentious Masturbators,' wrote one of the authorities he cited, 'we shall find them with meagre Jaws, and pale Looks, with feeble hams and legs without Calves, their generative faculties weakn'd if not destroyed in the Prime of their Years; a jest to others and a torment to themselves.'[24]

The purpose of the author of *Onania* was to promote a patent medicine designed to cure the various ailments supposedly caused by masturbation. His approach, however, was rapidly taken up by the highly respected physician and hygienist Tissot, who was also the Pope's adviser on the control of epidemics. Tissot now sought to use a whole variety of medical diagnoses as a way of rationalising in scientific terms the traditional Catholic doctrine on masturbation. His own book on this subject, *Onanism: a Treatise on the Disorders Produced by Masturbation*, was published in Lausanne in 1758 and widely translated. In it Tissot proposed his own theory of sexual energetics in which he maintained that all sexual activity was dangerous because it produced a rush of blood to the brain, thereby starving the nerves and making insanity more likely. Solitary orgasm, according to Tissot, was especially dangerous and gave rise to a wide variety of symptoms, including perpetual exhaustion, melancholy, fits, blindness, catalepsy, impotence, indigestion, idiocy and paralysis.

By the beginning of the nineteenth century Tissot's success in translating some of the most repressive sexual doctrines of Christianity into pseudo-psychiatric terms bore fruit with the hypothesis of masturbational insanity. In 1812, in the first American textbook of psychiatry, Benjamin Rush included among the effects of masturbation 'seminal weakness, impotence, dysury, tabes dorsalis, pulmonary consumption ... epilepsy hypochondriasis, loss of memory, manalgia, fatuity and death'. By 1816 it was possible for Esquirol, a highly regarded French authority, to write that masturbation 'is recognised in all countries as a common cause of insanity'. The notion of masturbational insanity reached England in about 1829, and in 1852 it was held that 'the habit of solitary vice' gave rise to hysteria, asthma, melancholia, mania, suicide, dementia and general paralysis of the insane.[25]

Ultimately the whole tendency of nineteenth-century psychiatrists to treat masturbation as a significant factor in the aetiology of mental illness derived from what might be termed the 'sexualism' of the Christian Church. For during the eighteenth and nineteenth centuries it became increasingly common for Christians to rationalise their traditional attitudes towards sexuality in medical terms. During the same period the authority which Christianity had once had to legitimate investigations into sexual behaviour gradually passed to medicine and the natural sciences and from the nineteenth century onwards, 'objective' science increasingly took over a role which had once belonged almost exclusively to religion – that of mounting culturally respectable investigations into the realm of the obscene.

It was this kind of 'medicalised Christianity' which formed one of the most important parts of the intellectual inheritance of all nineteenth-century psychiatrists. Freud was no exception and what is interesting is that, at a time when some medically oriented investigators were beginning to free themselves from this oppressive tradition, Freud

seems unconsciously to have found within it an answer to his own
need to defer to authority and to established cultural traditions. Freud
himself represented his entire theory of neurasthenia, including his
hypotheses about sexual noxae and the harmful effects of masturbation
and coitus interruptus, as a revolutionary breakthrough which pushed
back the frontiers of medical science. Yet to any observer versed in
cultural and medical history it should have been clear that, beneath
their superficial medical terminology, Freud's ideas were deeply
traditional.

The extraordinary lengths to which Freud took his new theory are
perhaps best illustrated by considering some of the case histories he
wrote at the time:

No. 3

Dr Z., a physician, age 34. Has suffered for many years from organic
sensitivity of the eyes: phosphenes [flashes], dazzle, scotoma and the
rest. This has increased enormously, to the point of preventing his
working, in the last four months (since the time of his marriage).

Background: A masturbator since the age of 14, apparently continued
up to recent years, Did not deflower his wife, potency much reduced . . .

No. 4

Mr D., nephew of Mrs A., who died a hysteric. A highly neurotic family.
Age 28. Has suffered for some weeks from lassitude, intracranial pressure, shaky knees, reduced potency, premature ejaculation, the beginnings of perversion: very young girls excite him more than mature ones.

Alleges that his potency has always been capricious; admits masturbation, but not too prolonged; has a period of abstinence behind him
now. Before that, anxiety states in the evening.

Has he made a full confession?[26]

Given the cultural genealogy of Freud's theories as I have outlined it
above, it is perhaps scarcely surprising that some of his case histories
at this time read as though they might be extracts from an eighteenth-
century manual of moral improvement, or even from the diary of a
confessor.

Far from being an odd or aberrant episode in his intellectual
biography, Freud's theoretical solution to the non-existent problem
of neurasthenia provided a pattern on which a number of his most
important intellectual 'discoveries' were subsequently based. One of
these was the revised theory of hysteria which he developed after the

publication of *Studies on Hysteria* in 1895. This theory, which is generally known as the 'seduction theory', and which assumed that hysteria was the product of sexual abuse suffered during infancy, has been the subject of much controversy in recent years. There is perhaps no part of Freud's theoretical enterprise which has been more widely misunderstood and misrepresented. As we shall see, however, it would be quite wrong to blame either Freud's followers or his latter-day opponents for originating this distortion. For the first person to misrepresent the seduction theory was none other than Freud himself.

NINE

The Seduction Theory

WHEN FREUD FIRST ENCOUNTERED the idea that 'hysteria' should be regarded as a psychogenic affliction, one which could be precipitated by *ideas*, there was no suggestion that these ideas might have an exclusively sexual content. For, while Charcot's theory of hysteria did not eschew sexual factors, it tended to look for causes among ordinary traumatic experiences such as those involving falls, accidents or physical injuries. In Freud and Breuer's Preliminary Communication, 'On the Psychical Mechanism of Hysterical Phenomena' (1893), Charcot's approach to hysteria was scarcely challenged. For at this time Freud and Breuer regarded hysteria as an affliction which could be precipitated by any psychical trauma. 'Any experience which calls up distressing affects,' they wrote, '– such as those of fright, anxiety or physical pain – may operate as a trauma of this kind.'[1]

Gradually, however, sexual factors came to loom larger and larger in the new theory. There is one very straightforward explanation which can be offered for this development, an explanation so strikingly simple that few seem to have considered it seriously. For Freud and Breuer persuaded themselves at a very early stage of their investigations that the causes of hysteria would be found primarily among those thoughts and memories which their patients did not or could not normally retrieve. This assumption was derived directly from the work of Charcot, for it was he who had suggested that a key role was played in hysterical phenomena by an idea or series of ideas which had become psychically isolated from normal waking consciousness. Charcot himself was not particularly concerned to establish the exact nature of these ideas. In order to develop their own notion of cathartic therapy, however, Breuer and Freud found it necessary to delve into their patients' past experiences in order to identify the particular factors which had supposedly given rise to hysteria. They did this at first by using hypnosis and then by using the technique of free-association developed by Freud. Since they deliberately set out to find aspects of their patients' mental life which were hidden, these premises led almost inevitably, in view of the degree of fear and reticence which surrounds sexuality in almost every human society, to the conclusion that sexual factors were among the prime causes of hysteria.

Breuer and Freud differed in the way they treated this conclusion. In his theoretical discussion of hysteria, Breuer expressed the view that symptoms arose when a particular traumatic idea was 'fended off and therefore repressed from consciousness'. 'The most numerous and important of the ideas that are fended off and converted,' he continued, 'have a sexual content.' He then embarks on an extended discussion of sexual factors, in the course of which he suggests that 'the great majority of severe neuroses in women have their origin in the marriage bed.' Breuer, however, does not imply that all hysteria is sexual. 'Alongside sexual hysteria,' he writes, 'we must at this point recall hysteria due to fright – traumatic hysteria proper – which constitutes one of the best known and recognised forms of hysteria.'[2] Although in theory Freud himself never completely ruled out the possibility of hysteria being precipitated by non-sexual traumas, in practice he gradually succumbed to his obsessive need to 'open all secrets with a single key'. Just as, in the case of 'neurasthenia', he had replaced the existing mixed theory of causation, in which masturbation was regarded as one cause among many, with a pure theory in which sexual 'noxae' were seen as the exclusive cause, so he now set out to reduce all cases of 'hysteria' to a single, sexual explanation. Freud's insistence on this view was one of the factors which eventually led to his split with Breuer. 'Freud,' Breuer would write in 1907, 'is a man given to absolute and exclusive formulations: this is a psychical need which, in my opinion, leads to excessive generalisation.'[3]

What is perhaps most interesting about this development in Freud's thinking is the fact that it led him to modify his own therapeutic technique in such a way that the kind of evidence he required could scarcely fail to emerge. We have already seen how, having come to the conclusion that one of his patients had related a story untruthfully in order to avoid an 'erotic factor', Freud decided that he would 'regard as incomplete any story that brought about no improvement'.[4] If, while being treated with Freud's 'pressure technique', patients protested that they were not keeping back anything Freud would, as a matter of principle, refuse to accept their assurances: 'We must not believe what they say, we must always assume, and tell them too, that they have kept something back because they thought it unimportant or found it distressing. We must insist on this, we must repeat the pressure and represent ourselves as infallible, till at least we are really told something.'[5] Whether Freud was prepared to accept that a patient's confession really was 'something' depended ultimately on whether it fitted with his own theoretical preconceptions. Thus, when one of Freud's patients traces her anxiety attacks to the time when she had applied iodine to a swollen thyroid gland, Freud is unimpressed. 'I naturally rejected this derivation,' he writes, 'and tried to find another instead of it *which would harmonize better with my views on the aetiology of the neuroses*' (italics added). Where patients did not of their own accord provide material which could be construed in sexual terms, Freud did not hesitate to point them in the 'right' direction. Indeed he candidly confesses at one point that he would often lead his patients' attention to 'repressed sexual ideas *in spite of all their protestations*' (italics added).[6]

In some respects Freud's obsessive need to elicit sexual confessions from his patients underscores the parallel which has sometimes been drawn between psychoanalysis and the Christian confessional – a parallel which will be examined in more detail later (see below, Chapter 16). But although Freud frequently played the part of confessor, there are times when his attitude towards his patients is so overbearing and aggressive that another parallel is almost inescapable. For he sometimes sounds less like a priest and more like a prosecutor, an inquisitor or a policeman. Lest this comparison should seem a harsh one it seems necessary to point out that it has been made before – not simply by Freud's critics but by commentators who are sympathetic to psychoanalysis, or even partisans in the cause. Frank Sulloway, writing at a time when his attitude towards Freud was much more positive than it is now, observes how 'Freud as psychoanalyst ... became Freud the prosecuting attorney within his own clinical court of psychoanalytic law.'[7] The journalist Janet Malcolm, who has been one of the most influential advocates of psychoanalysis in recent years, makes a similar point in even more telling terms. In her book *Psychoanalysis: The Impossible Profession* she discusses the case of Dora, the good-looking and intelligent eighteen-year-old whom Freud treated for hysteria around the year

1900.* Following the eccentric belief of his friend Fliess that masturbation gave rise to enuresis, Freud forced Dora to confess that she
had been a late bed-wetter. He also claimed that her catarrh signified
that she was a masturbator, as did her stomach troubles. In one of
the most bizarre of all his interpretations Freud even suggested that
Dora's nervous cough was the result of a suppressed fantasy of
fellatio. As Janet Malcolm observes, all these interpretations are
presented to a young, vulnerable teenager who has trustingly related
to Freud a story of exploitation and betrayal by the adults around
her.

> But instead of giving her the fatherly concern and compassion that she
> expected . . . Freud treated Dora as a deadly adversary. He sparred with
> her, laid traps for her, pushed her into corners, bombarded her with
> interpretations, gave no quarter, was as unspeakable, in his way, as any
> of the people in her sinister family circle, went too far, and finally drove
> her away.[8]

In the course of discussing the case history of another psychoanalyst,
Malcolm presses her critique even further. For she had found this case
history 'baffling, irritating, boring, insulting to women, and self-
damning':

> In its unrelenting pursuit of sexual matter and meaning, it brought to
> mind the Dora case, in which Freud often conducted himself more like
> a police inspector interrogating a suspect than like a doctor helping a
> patient. 'Aha!' Freud would say to poor Dora, an attractive and intelli-

---

* Although Freud set out to cure Dora of 'hysteria' it may be confidently presumed that
she was not suffering from this non-existent disease any more than Freud's other celebrated
early patients. In his excellent article 'Was Dora "Ill"?' Anthony Stadlen notes that one of
Dora's childhood ailments was appendicitis, which had been diagnosed by at least two
doctors. This had been accompanied by a dragging of her right foot. Freud, however, denied
that Dora had ever had appendicitis and declared that both her presumed appendicitis and
the problem with her foot were 'hysterical'. Stadlen cites two distinguished surgeons in
support of the view that Dora's dragging foot could have been caused by *pelvic* appendicitis.
One of these surgeons points out that 'pain in the right leg is even used as a *diagnostic test*
(the psoas spasm) for pelvic appendicitis.' Stadlen writes that 'These prosaic possibilities
were ignored by Freud . . . [His] diagnosis that these ailments were "hysterical" ignored
the most obvious and probable explanations.' To be fair to Freud the diagnosis of *pelvic*
appendicitis was probably neither obvious nor probable at the end of the nineteenth century.
Freud seems once again to have been resorting to the medical fiction of 'hysteria' in order
to cover gaps in medical knowledge, just as he did with Dora's later symptoms. See Anthony
Stadlen, 'Was Dora "Ill"?' in Laurence Spurling (ed.), *Sigmund Freud: Critical Assessments*,
Routledge and Kegan Paul, 1989, vol. 2, pp. 196–203.

gent eighteen-year-old girl suffering from a nervous cough, migraine, and a kind of general youthful malaise. 'Aha! I know about you. I know your dirty little secrets. Admit that you were secretly attracted to Herr K. Admit that you masturbated when you were five. Look at what you're doing now as you lie there playing with your reticule – opening it, putting a finger into it, shutting it again!'[9]

The idea of Freud as a police inspector is far removed from the image which tends to be projected onto the founder of psychoanalysis by most of his followers. But Janet Malcolm's characterisation is a telling one. For in his relations to Dora, and indeed in a very significant number of other cases, Freud's attitude *is* strikingly similar to that of a policeman. Not only does he frequently treat his patients as though they are deliberately and maliciously attempting to conceal the true facts from him, but on a significant number of occasions he appears to decide in advance that his patient is guilty of a particular action, thought or desire, and then to interpret replies to his intensive questioning in such a way that his suspicion is substantiated. Freud's tendency to use his particular hermeneutic strategies in order to 'plant' evidence on his patients emerges clearly in his treatment of Dora. Having decided in advance that his patient is suffering from the effects of masturbation, he uses his own misconceptions about the biology of masturbation in order to construe her catarrh as circumstantial evidence of her guilt. When he puts pressure on Dora to solve the enigma of her illness 'by confessing that she had masturbated, probably in childhood', Dora is unable to comply, saying only that she can remember no such thing. A few days later, however, Freud notices that she is fidgeting with her reticule and immediately construes this as a 'step towards the confession':

> Dora's reticule, which came apart at the top in the usual way, was nothing but a representation of the genitals, and her playing with it, her opening it and putting her finger in it, was an entirely unembarrassed yet unmistakable pantomimic announcement of what she would like to do with them – namely, to masturbate.[10]

Perhaps the most significant feature of Freud's procedure is that, although his conclusion that Dora had masturbated is based purely on his own medical misconceptions and on an entirely speculative and somewhat prurient interpretation of a very common action, he now proceeds to talk about 'the occurrence of masturbation in Dora's case' as something which has been 'verified'.[11] While on some occasions, as was noted in the last chapter, Freud effectively writes confessions on behalf of his patients and then prevails on them to sign them, the case of Dora shows that on other occasions he was quite prepared both to write *and* sign confessions on behalf of his patient. This tendency, which undoubtedly grew not out of any essential dishonesty, but out of Freud's burning zeal both to substantiate his own theories and to effect a cure, is crucial to the understanding of psychoanalysis as a whole. Above all it suggests that we should treat with extreme scepticism any data which Freud puts forward about the inner biography of his patients and allow for the possibility that what he presents as verified facts may be no more than his own speculative, and theoretically wishful guesses.

Some understanding of Freud's tendency to play the part of an over-zealous policeman, determined to secure a conviction, is necessary if we are to unravel the next most significant development in Freud's sexual theories – the formulation and subsequent repudiation of the seduction theory. As we have seen, this theory was first hinted at in the note which Freud enclosed when he sent the draft of his *Project* to Fliess on 8 October 1895. A week later Freud wrote to Fliess again. What he had initially presented as a hunch or a vague suspicion had by this time been transformed into a 'secret', which Freud now imparted to his friend as a fact:

> Have I revealed the great clinical secret to you, either orally or in writing? Hysteria is the consequence of a presexual *sexual shock*. Obsessional neurosis is the consequence of a presexual *sexual pleasure*, which is later transformed into [self-]*reproach*. 'Presexual' means actually before puberty, before the release of sexual substances; the relevant events become effective only as memories.[12]

The exact process of reasoning which led Freud to this conclusion is not clear. What is clear is that a number of his trains of thought at that time converged at a point not very far removed from it. Most important of all was Charcot's original contention that hysteria had its origin in a *trauma*. When this was combined with Freud's growing theoretical fascination with bio-energetic speculations about sexuality and the sexual character of the confessions he coaxed or constructed from his patients' associations, specifically *sexual* traumas almost inevitably came under consideration as possible causes of hysteria. Since the occurrence of childhood seduction was a well-documented fact, featuring, for example, in the work of Krafft-Ebing, it would have been surprising if Freud had not expanded Charcot's theory of the traumatic aetiology of hysteria in order to include sexual traumas of this kind. It was characteristic of Freud's intellectual style, however, that instead of treating seduction as one factor among many, he almost immediately submitted himself completely to the tyranny of his latest idea, proclaiming that he had discovered in seduction the *sole* cause not only of hysteria but also of obsessive neurosis and paranoia.

Freud's tendency to engage in single-factor analyses of any specific phenomenon he was studying was clearly an essential part of his scientific temperament; it was a kind of aetiological monotheism. This tendency was strongly reinforced by his medical training. In part this was because of his respect for the germ theory of Koch and Pasteur which, as we have already seen, influenced his search for the sexual noxae which supposedly caused neurasthenia. But no less important in the evolution of psychoanalysis were the kind of diagnostic habits which Freud had developed as a neuropathologist, in which he had become accustomed to tracing complex neurological deficits to their source in a specific lesion in the brain. The practice of looking for a single pathological lesion is one which he appears to have transferred from neurology to psychiatry and to the study of 'neurasthenia' and 'hysteria', which he evidently continued to regard as diseases in the narrowest medical sense of the word.

In the case of hysteria, as before in the case of neurasthenia, Freud eventually came to believe that he had discovered the equivalent of the single pathogen or lesion which was responsible for causing the disease. Given the nature of Freud's conclusion, and given the widespread and apparently reasonable assumption that Freud's theories had at least some foundation in fact, it has been quite widely assumed that Freud formulated his new theory on the basis of memories of childhood seduction which were furnished by his patients. This certainly is how Jeffrey Masson construes Freud's theory in his book *The Assault on Truth*:

> Freud's female patients had the courage to face what had happened to them in childhood – often this included violent scenes of rape by a father – and to communicate their traumas to Freud, no doubt hesitating to believe their own memories and reluctant to remember the deep

shame and hurt they had felt. Freud listened and understood and gave them permission to remember and speak of these terrible events.[13]

This account of Freud's theories, which clearly implies that his patients spontaneously produced memories of childhood seduction, has been widely accepted. A small number of scholars, however, including Frank Cioffi, E. M. Thornton and subsequently Han Israëls and Morton Schatzman, have pointed out that Freud's own original account of his therapeutic methods suggests that the reality was very different. For one of the essential articles in Freud's doctrine of seduction maintained that episodes of childhood seduction would have a pathological effect *only* if the supposed victim had no conscious recollection of the episode. The purpose of Freud's therapeutic sessions was not to listen to recollections which patients freely offered, but to encourage them to discover or construct scenes of which they had *no* recollection. This is made quite clear in Freud's paper 'The Aetiology of Hysteria':

> Before they come for analysis the patients know nothing about these scenes. They are indignant as a rule if we warn them that such scenes are going to emerge. Only the strongest compulsion of the treatment can induce them to embark on a reproduction of them. While they are recalling these infantile experiences to consciousness, they suffer under the most violent sensations, of which they are ashamed and which they try to conceal; and even after they have gone through them once more in such a convincing manner, they still attempt to withhold belief from them, by emphasising the fact that, unlike what happens in the case of other forgotten material, they have no feeling of remembering the scenes.[14]

It might well seem that we should not discount the possibility that the initial inspiration for this view actually came from the memories of one or more of his patients. Yet if we are to take Freud at his word, it is precisely this possibility which we must discount since his patients, by definition, have no such memories until they have submitted to what Freud himself calls 'the strongest compulsion of the treatment'.

In this case, as in others, it would seem that Freud has formulated a theory deductively, without the benefit of any evidence at all, and has later confirmed his hunch – to his own satisfaction – by assembling evidence from his patients' associations. In this connection it is perhaps significant that one of Freud's problems at this time concerned the inappropriateness of some of the sexual frights which he initially considered as possible causes for hysteria. In 'The Aetiology of Hysteria' he gives examples of experiences which were sexual, which occurred at puberty, and which *seemed* to be 'the ultimate traumatic experiences' yet which were sometimes 'astonishingly trivial'.

> In one of my women patients, it turned out that her neurosis was based on the experience of a boy of her acquaintance stroking her hand tenderly and, at another time, pressing his knee against her dress as they sat side by side at table, while his expression let her see that he was doing something forbidden. For another young lady, simply hearing a riddle which suggested an obscene answer had been enough to provoke the first anxiety attack and with it to start the illness.[15]

Rather than confer on these 'trifling events' the status of traumas Freud decided to adopt a procedure which he had already used with other patients. 'If the first-discovered scene is unsatisfactory, we tell our patient that this experience explains nothing, but that behind it there must be hidden a more significant, earlier experience ... A continuation of the analysis then leads in every instance to the reproduction of new scenes of the character we expect.'[16] What Freud discloses in these words, with remarkable frankness, is a therapeutic procedure which was, in effect, self-confirming. For by his own admission he approached his patients not with an open mind but with a firm preconception as to the kind of memory he was seeking. As soon as Freud began to adopt the view that hysteria was due to seduction, it was almost inevitable that each case he treated would end by yielding 'evidence' for his hypothesis. If, as is entirely conceivable, the patient recalled a real instance of sexual seduction *spontaneously*, Freud was obliged by his theories actually to discount such an episode as a pathological factor. Instead of attending to any real sexual traumas which had been recalled, Freud would require his patients to produce memories relating to an earlier and earlier stage of their lives. According to Freud's own implicit therapeutic rules the analysis would not be completed until such a scene had either been uncovered or 'constructed' by the therapist on the basis of the patients' associations. Lest patients themselves should be in any doubt as to what kind of memories or associations they were supposed to produce, it was evidently Freud's normal practice to tell them. For, as we have seen, he writes that 'they are indignant as a rule if we warn them that such scenes are going to emerge. Only the strongest compulsion of the treatment can induce them to embark on the reproduction of them.'[17]

Given this approach it is scarcely surprising that Freud again and again claimed to have 'discovered' scenes of sexual seduction belonging not primarily to that period of late childhood or early puberty which his patients might be expected to remember, but to 'the earliest years of childhood' and to a period which his patients had forgotten. Indeed Freud himself observed that his patients consistently attempted to withhold belief from these supposed infantile experiences. With characteristic confidence Freud interpreted his patients' inability to remember these scenes of seduction as a proof of their reality, and claimed that since he had uncovered scenes of sexual seduction in all of the eighteen cases of hysteria he had treated in this way his theory could be regarded as proved. In view of Freud's approach it is perhaps not surprising that even some psychoanalytically oriented critics have reached the conclusion that, once he had formulated his theory, Freud engaged in an 'aggressive pursuit of evidence to substantiate it' and that 'once generalised, the hypothesis was essentially forced on fresh case materials although it did not fit at least some patients...' Observers unfettered by any affiliation to Freud or psychoanalysis might well be inclined to take this argument further. For in view of the fact that Freud's deduction that his patients had suffered infantile sexual traumas was based entirely on his own speculations about the aetiology of a disease whose very existence has never been demonstrated, there is some reason to suppose that Freud's hypothesis did not fit even a single patient. Once again, in his role as therapeutic 'policeman', Freud showed himself quite unable, at this stage at least, to tolerate the possibility that the 'guilt' of his patients lay in his theoretical preconceptions and not in their inner biographies.[18]

At the same time Freud showed great ingenuity in constructing an escape route from the theoretical impasse into which his seduction hypothesis was in danger of leading him. For the most obvious objection to the new development of his theory was that, by pushing the supposed traumatic origin of hysteria further and further back into the earliest years of childhood, it ruled out a sexual cause. At this stage Freud himself certainly remained a firm believer in the view that sexuality emerged only at puberty and that the earliest years of childhood belonged to a 'presexual' stage of development. He had dissolved the contradiction before it even arose, however, by improvising another piece of theoretical fiction. In his theory of 'deferred action' he boldly maintained that, although most traumatic experiences had an effect on the nervous system immediately, sexual seductions during childhood had no immediate repercussions because of the absence of the sexual instinct in childhood. Such traumas, however, were stored away in the memory as 'mnemic psychical traces', eventually to be activated by the physiological events of puberty. 'Thanks to the change due to puberty,' he wrote, 'the memory will display a power which was completely lacking from the event itself. *The memory will operate as though it were a contemporary event*. What happens is, as it were, *a posthumous action by a sexual trauma*' (italics added).[19]

Freud's seduction theory did not belong simply to a passing phase in his intellectual development, for he spent almost two years under its spell, reconstructing episodes in his patients' lives which he construed as confirming it, and seeking to win over his medical colleagues. He expended all this energy for the very simple reason that, as once before in the case of his 'discovery' of the therapeutic effects of cocaine, he persuaded himself that he had at last been vouchsafed the world-redeeming revelation which he sought. In 'The Aetiology of Hysteria' he gave a public estimate of the importance of his new theory, actually claiming to have discovered 'the source of the Nile' in the field of neuropathology.[20] In private he saw it as bringing the fulfilment of the dreams of fame he had entertained almost constantly for the previous ten years: 'The expectation of eternal fame was so beautiful,' he wrote, 'as was that of certain wealth, complete independence, travels, and lifting the children above the severe worries that robbed me of my youth.'[21]

If such sentiments are already familiar to us from earlier episodes in Freud's biography, there is at least one other element in the story which suggests the recurrence of an old pattern. We have already seen how Freud's immense psychological need for medical fame repeatedly led him to view his own therapeutic results through the lens of his theoretical ecstasy. In almost all the cases which he reported in *Studies on Hysteria* he claimed at least some degree of therapeutic credit even though there was no evidence that he had effected any cure. In the case of Anna O. he encouraged Breuer to make such a claim while knowing full well that no such cure had taken place. In the case of Fleischl-Marxow, as we have seen, he engaged in an astonishing rush to publication in order to claim a cure which he anticipated but which he was never in fact to achieve. In formulating his seduction theory it would seem that Freud succumbed to a similar temptation. In his 1896 paper he sought to counter objections to his theory with the following words:

Only the most laborious and detailed investigations have converted me, and that slowly enough, to the view I hold today. If you submit my assertion that the aetiology of hysteria lies in sexual life to the strictest examination, you will find that it is supported by the fact that in some eighteen cases of hysteria, I have been able to discover this connection in every single symptom, and, where circumstances allowed, to confirm it by therapeutic success.[22]

Here Freud has characteristic recourse to what might be called the 'rhetoric of empiricism' without offering any evidence that any real empirical investigations have actually been undertaken. He thus represents as 'laborious and detailed investigations' the idiosyncratic methods he has himself invented for uncovering putative psychic conflict. Having invited his audience to submit his assertion about the aetiology of hysteria to the strictest examination, he denies them the opportunity to do this by withholding all clinical details of his patients. He then deftly substitutes for his original invitation a request that they should submit to his authority, and his unsupported claim that in eighteen cases he has been able to discover a connection with a sexual trauma. The implication of these words is that he had completely analysed all eighteen cases. Yet if we read Freud's words carefully we will see that their relatively clear implicit meaning is at odds with their rather more obscure explicit sense. For Freud claims only that *he* has been able to discover a sexual connection in their symptoms – an achievement which, given his hermeneutic ingenuity, is scarcely impressive. It should also be noted that Freud nowhere claims to have cured a *patient*. The therapeutic claim he makes is severely qualified, and it is applied to symptoms only. What this suggests is that Freud, as he habitually did, may have been taking credit for the disappearance of individual symptoms without claiming to have removed the illness to which they supposedly belonged.

Freud's ambiguity on this issue appears to be studied and deliberate. In view of this it is interesting that he goes on to discuss the possibility that his nineteenth and twentieth cases might run counter to his theory. Freud writes that he does not share this expectation and adds that he is 'prepared to let my belief run ahead of the evidential force of the observations I have made so far'.[23] Once again it is possible to read these words as an oblique confession to a scientific misdemeanour rather larger that that which Freud explicitly acknowledges. Just how far he had allowed belief to run ahead of evidence became clear only with the publication of Freud's letters to Fliess. For what these letters revealed was that Freud had not actually completed the analysis of *any* of the eighteen cases whose satisfactory outcome he had implicitly, though ambiguously, claimed. The first person to point this out was E. M. Thornton. More recently Han Israëls and Morton Schatzman, following Thornton's example, have trawled through Freud's correspondence with Fliess and discovered even more instances in which this curious fact is acknowledged. The first instance is found in a letter which Freud wrote on 4 May 1896, two weeks *after* he had read a version of his paper 'The Aetiology of Hysteria' to the Vienna Neurological Society. In this letter, however, he complained that he was getting no new cases for treatment and noted that 'not one of the old ones is finished yet.' In July 1896, a month after the published version of his paper had appeared, he wrote to Fliess: 'I am frantically trying to "finish" several people.' In December he renewed his lament that 'so far not a single case is finished; I feel I am missing an essential piece somewhere. As long as no case has been clarified and seen through to the end, I do not feel sure and I cannot be content.' In January of 1897 he wrote to Fliess proposing that they should meet at Easter. 'Perhaps by then,' he added, 'I shall have carried one case to completion.' In February he was still desperately hoping to finish by Easter: 'By then perhaps, one case will be entirely finished. Until this has been accomplished, there really can be no certainty.' By March, he was no nearer to his goal: 'I have not yet finished a single case,' he confessed.[24] In citing these various instances, Han Israëls and Morton Schatzman draw the conclusion that, in his 'Aetiology of Hysteria' paper, Freud had announced a result as having been reached which he hoped to reach soon:

> In 1896 Freud firmly believed in the truth of the seduction theory, so firmly that he was sure of soon reaching the results that the theory predicted, and thus believed it was safe and legitimate to announce these results. This means that after publishing his seduction theory he must have felt strong pressure to reach these results.[25]

Yet as the correspondence with Fliess shows, Freud's hopes that he might complete even one of the eighteen cases he claimed (although only thirteen are cited in the correspondence) were repeatedly dashed. In the letter which he wrote to Fliess on 3 January 1897 Freud gives an example of the quite extraordinary interpretative lengths to which he was prepared to go in order find the evidence which he still needed.

He describes one woman patient who had a speech impediment and who was also suffering from eczema around her mouth and from lesions in the corner of the mouth. Having noted that these lesions were caused by saliva accumulating during the night, Freud remarks that 'Once before I traced back entirely analogous observations to sucking on the penis.' He then claims that the woman's speech inhibition first appeared at the age of twelve when 'with a *full* mouth, she was fleeing from a woman teacher'. Noting that her father 'has a similarly explosive speech, as though his mouth were full', Freud suddenly interrupts his letter to utter an exclamation of scientific delight:

Habemus papam!

In a passage which does much to illuminate the manner in which the 'confessions' made by Freud's patients emerged, Freud goes on to recount how he presents his patient with the conclusion he has by now evidently reached – that both her cracked mouth and her speech impediment are hysterical symptoms and that they were caused by her father forcing her to suck his penis when she was a young child. In this case Freud's reconstruction is resisted after the young woman has relayed her physician's completely speculative allegation to the father who had supposedly seduced her:

> When I thrust the explanation at her, she was at first won over; then she committed the folly of questioning the old man himself, who at the very first intimation exclaimed indignantly, 'Are you implying that I was the one?' and swore a holy oath as to his innocence.
> She is now in the throes of the most vehement resistance, claims to believe him, but attests to her identification with him by having become dishonest and swearing false oaths. I have threatened to send her away and in the process convinced myself that she has already gained a good deal of certainty which she is reluctant to acknowledge.[26]

This extraordinary passage not only illustrates the dogmatic recklessness with which Freud attempted to force his own aetiological fantasies onto his patients but also points to the increasing stress he was now laying on the pathogenic role supposedly played by sexual perversions. This was in part, it would seem, because Freud was aware that, when real instances of sexual abuse had been reported by physicians, a specific role was frequently played by sexual acts involving the mouth and the anus. But Freud was also influenced by the much more general theories

which he had by now began to develop about the existence of 'erotogenic zones' specifically centred on the mouth and the anus. A number
of his letters at this time reveal the extent of this preoccupation. In a
letter written on 17 December 1896, Freud attempts to explain why
one of his male 'hysterics' has an aversion to shaving and drinking
beer. He claims that he has been able to 'elucidate' this 'by a scene in
which a nurse sits down *podice nudo* [with bare buttocks] in a shallow
shaving bowl filled with beer in order to let herself be licked . . .'[27]
Although the fact that Freud refers to 'a scene' may suggest that he is
relating an incident which his patient has recalled, Freud's theoretical
presuppositions about the impossibility of such direct memories suggest that the bizarre episode which he relates to Fliess is, once again,
one that he has arbitrarily reconstructed in his normal manner.

In another letter to Fliess written a month later, he seeks evidence
for his new hypothesis that epilepsy was caused by a sexual trauma
suffered before the age of one and a half years. He claimed that he
had already traced an attack that 'merely resembled epilepsy' to an act
of anilingus performed by the patient's nurse when he was two. Now
he wrote to Fliess asking if he could supply him with a case of childhood
convulsions which he could trace back to sexual abuse 'specifically to
lictus [licking] or finger in the anus'.[28] In yet another letter written
only the day before, he had already made a specific link between oral
and anal symptoms when he described how one of his patients had
attacks of dipsomania which, according to Freud, regularly started
'either with diarrhoea or with a cold and hoarseness (the oral sexual
system!)'. He immediately goes on to suggest that these symptoms
actually arise because the patient in question is reproducing his own
passive experiences of oral and anal sexual abuse.[29]

All these speculations about various forms of oral and anal abuse
which Freud believed his patients had suffered were relayed to Fliess
during the period when Freud was anxiously trying to finish at least
one of the eighteen cases whose completion he had already implicitly
claimed. Given the highly specific nature of the infantile scenes which
Freud had constructed, and which he was now attempting to force
upon his patients, it is perhaps not surprising that he repeatedly failed
in this attempt. This failure was rendered even more decisive by the
fact that Freud's speculative theory-building increasingly led him to
accuse the father of his patients of having perpetrated sexual abuse,
something which had formed no part of the original theory. It would
appear from the case cited above that Freud repeatedly made such

accusations without any evidence at all in response to his own theoretical doctrines. Where such accusations did find their way back to the fathers in question there is no reason to suppose that their reaction would be any different from that of the man whom Freud had implicated, solely on the basis of his daughter's eczema and her speech impediment, in an act of incestuous fellatio. Quite apart from their complete therapeutic ineffectiveness, Freud's methods were for this reason also legally perilous and could only prove in the long term professionally disastrous. It should therefore be scarcely surprising that, in spite of the huge psychological investment he had made in his seduction theory, Freud eventually came to the conclusion that he must abandon it.*

The claim made by Jeffrey Masson that Freud abandoned his seduction theory because he could not face up to the uncomfortable truths which it contains is a highly plausible one. As such it has been accepted by many who are unfamiliar with Freud's early investigations and with his general intellectual style. Yet placed against what Freud actually wrote, both in his papers on hysteria and in his letters to Fliess, Masson's claim cannot be sustained. Freud was never driven to abandon a crucial set of truths for the simple reason that he had never assembled such a set in the first place. The memories of scenes of childhood seduction were not real memories at all. They were, as a matter of theoretical necessity, constructed, suggested or forced on patients by Freud himself. In short there *were* no truths for Freud to abandon.

One of the reasons that this realisation was not made long before it was pointed out by Cioffi, by Thornton and, even more clearly, by Schatzman and Israëls, is that Freud himself subsequently attempted to cover over the traces of the manner in which he actually formulated his theory. In his *Autobiographical Study* of 1925, Freud looked back on the episode and represented himself as a naive researcher who had believed what he called the 'stories' of his patients. Interestingly he does momentarily concede that he might have been responsible for planting these stories in his patients' minds: 'I was at last obliged to recognise,' he wrote much later, 'that these scenes of seduction had never taken place, and that they were only fantasies which my patients had made up or *which I myself had perhaps forced on them . . .*' (my italics). But he then immediately goes on to discount this possibility:

* For a discussion of Freud's motives, see below, Chapter 11.

'I do not believe even now that I forced the seduction fantasies on my patients, that I "suggested" them.'[30] Later still, in the account of the episode which he gave in 1933, even this gesture towards the truth disappears, and he simply represents himself as the victim of untrue stories told to him by his patients:

> You will recall an interesting episode in the history of analytic research which caused me many distressing hours. In the period in which the main interest was directed to discovering infantile sexual traumas, almost all my women patients told me that they had been seduced by their father. I was driven to recognise in the end that these reports were untrue and so came to understand that hysterical symptoms are derived from fantasies and not from real occurrences.[31]

Freud's motives for distorting history in this way may not be immediately clear. But, as Morton Schatzman has pointed out, the distortion was necessary if Freud was to protect his later theoretical constructs against criticism.[32] For he had arrived at his theory of the Oedipus complex not by considering direct evidence but by making inferences in therapy sessions and by reconstructing episodes in his patients' psychic life. His mature psychoanalytic method thus depended on exactly the same method of inference and reconstruction which had led him initially to the false conclusion that all his patients had suffered seduction. Since an accurate account of the seduction theory episode would have clearly demonstrated the unreliability of the very technique of reconstruction on which the entire psychoanalytic method still rested, Freud was almost obliged to invent the fiction that his patients had told him about the seductions rather than admit that they too were the product of a process of therapeutic reconstruction.

Freud's fictional version of events has been accepted unquestioningly by countless Freud scholars, including Jeffrey Masson. The interesting conclusion which Masson derives from his distorted account of Freud's abandonment of the seduction theory is that

> by shifting the emphasis from an actual world of sadness, misery, and cruelty to an internal stage on which actors performed invented dramas for an invisible audience of their own creation, Freud began a trend away from the real world that, it seems to me, is at the root of the present-day sterility of psychoanalysis and psychiatry throughout the world.[33]

This view can be set alongside some words of Ferenczi which Masson himself quotes in a later book:

> I think that in the beginning Freud really believed in analysis; he followed Breuer enthusiastically, involved himself passionately and selflessly in the therapy of neurotics (lying on the floor for hours, if necessary, next to a patient in the throes of a hysterical crisis). However, certain experiences must have first alarmed him and then left him disillusioned more or less the way Breuer was when his patient [Anna O.] suffered a relapse and he found himself faced, as before an abyss, with the counter-transference. In Freud's case the equivalent was the discovery of the mendacity of hysterical women. Since the time of this discovery, Freud no longer likes sick people. He rediscovered his love for his orderly, cultivated superego ... Since he suffered this shock, this disappointment, Freud speaks much less about traumas, and the constitution begins to play the major role. This involves, obviously, a degree of fatalism. After a wave of enthusiasm for the psychological, Freud has returned to biology; he considers the psychological to be nothing more than the superstructure over the biological and for him the latter is far more real. He is still attached to analysis intellectually, but not emotionally.[34]

Even though they are based on Freud's distorted account of the seduction theory, which Ferenczi embroiders by actually attributing mendacity to his patients, the assessments which are offered by Masson and Ferenczi contain a considerable element of truth. For it is undeniably the case that Freud's repudiation of his seduction theory has repeatedly led to real instances of sexual abuse being overlooked or denied by psychoanalysts intent on treating memories as fantasies. It would, nevertheless, be wrong to accept the views of Masson and Ferenczi in their entirety. For in both cases they tend to idealise and sentimentalise Freud's attitude towards his patients during the time that he still adhered to the seduction theory. It is certainly true that his early theories of hysteria, by virtue of the fact that they compelled him to seek out 'traumatic' experiences, led him to concern himself closely with the biographies of his patients. Yet it would be a mistake to see in this any real sympathetic identification with his patients' feelings or any real engagement with what Masson calls 'the actual world of sadness, misery, and cruelty'. For to Freud, patients' traumas were first and foremost *medical* events. His prime interest was not in their emotional complexities, but in their supposed role in an internal, invisible pathological process which allegedly led to the production of a set of physical symptoms. It was his compulsive belief in this entirely imaginary physiological process which led him to construct sexual traumas even where none had taken place, just as it would eventually lead him to ignore them where they had taken place.[35]

What happened when Freud repudiated his seduction theory, then, was not that he abandoned the real world of human emotions for an invisible world of internal biological processes. For he had been preoccupied with just such an internal world ever since he began his speculations on the aetiology of hysteria. What happened was that this invisible world was at last almost completely freed from the constraints of empirical reality. Freud, whose essentially religious frame of mind had always led him to prefer speculating about the invisible to observing the visible, finally abandoned an aetiological theory which, because it was rooted in the real world of human behaviour, was susceptible to refutation. The theory he would eventually put in the place of his seduction hypothesis was ostensibly derived from the realm of biological science. Yet, instead of moving away from the wildly speculative brain-mythology of his early work towards scientific thoroughness, Freud now elaborated further the cryptic theology which had already begun to play an important role in his thinking. The main vehicle for this elaboration was his theory of infantile sexuality. It is to the development of this theory, and the role played in it by Freud's extraordinary friendship with the Berlin physician Wilhelm Fliess, that we must now turn.

TEN

Freud, Fliess and the Theory of Infantile Sexuality

FREUD ANNOUNCED THAT he had abandoned his seduction theory in a letter he wrote to Fliess on 21 September 1897. He had originally written to Fliess to impart to him the 'secret' of his discovery. Now, some eighteen months later, he wrote to him again in order to reveal another 'secret':

> And now I want to confide in you immediately the great secret that has been slowly dawning on me in the last few months. I no longer believe in my *neurotica* [theory of the neuroses]. This is probably not intelligible without an explanation; after all you yourself found credible what I was able to tell you. So I will begin historically [and tell you] where the reasons for disbelief came from. The continual disappointment of my efforts to bring a single analysis to a real conclusion; the running away of people who for a period of time had been most gripped [by analysis]; the absence of the complete success on which I had counted; the possibility of explaining to myself the partial successes in other ways, in the usual fashion . . .[1]

Freud was certainly not exaggerating when he described this piece of information as a 'secret'. For it was not until 1905 that he could bring himself to admit in public that some parts of his seduction theory were in need of revision. And it was only in 1914 that he began to acknowledge in public that his theory, which he had once described as the equivalent of the discovery of the source of the Nile, had been mistaken.[2] It seems clear that Freud's main motive for remaining silent was to preserve his reputation. For to have retracted so swiftly a theory he had advocated with such supreme self-assurance would have done little to enhance his standing among his medical colleagues in Vienna. It is perhaps significant that he did not publicly call his original theory into question until he had formulated an alternative. For his change of direction was eventually announced in the context of the theoretical statement which would serve as the cornerstone of mature psychoanalytic theory – his *Three Essays on the Theory of Sexuality*, which appeared in 1905.

What might be described as the 'official' view of this phase in Freud's intellectual development maintains that the seduction theory broke down under its own inherent improbability, that Freud stoically resigned himself to the theoretical vacuum which resulted, and that he then set about slowly filling this vacuum by carrying through to its completion the most heroic of all his projects – his own self-analysis through which he gradually discovered the importance of infantile sexuality. The great advantage of this view is that it sustains the image of Freud as an intrepid and conscientious scientist, one who was willing to sacrifice a much-loved hypothesis out of respect for the evidence provided by the real world, and who then constructed a new theory on the basis of patient observation of his own psychic life.

There can be no doubt that this official view contains an element of truth. For it is clear that Freud *was* troubled by an apparent misfit between his theory and the evidence needed to support it. In his letter to Fliess he returns to the theme which, as we have seen, had preoccupied him for many months and laments once again his inability to bring 'a single analysis to a real conclusion', adding the telling admission that a number of his patients has shown a tendency to 'run away'. It is interesting that, among other factors which persuaded him to doubt his seduction theory, Freud went on to include the fact that it led him in each case to accuse the father of sexual perversion. This would have implicated his own father, and he was unable to accept this. But, as I have already suggested, it would be quite wrong to see these sources of doubt as indicating an increasingly scrupulous relationship between Freud's theories and the real world. For he ultimately sought to vindicate his scepticism by reference to his own speculative theories about the nature of the unconscious. Accordingly he invoked what he called 'the certain insight' that there were no indications of reality in the unconscious, 'so that one cannot distinguish between truth and fiction that has been cathected with affect'.[3] Freud had decided, in other words, that the inner workings of the unconscious were ultimately more important than events in the real world and that, when it came to constructing psychological theories, the latter should sometimes be disregarded in favour of the former.

Far from indicating that his abandonment of the seduction hypothesis left him with a theoretical vacuum, Freud's comments suggest that he was operating very much on the basis of a theoretical plenum. The more closely we examine the way in which his ideas subsequently developed, the clearer it becomes that this was indeed the case. Instead of his self-analysis leading the way to a new theoretical orientation, it was Freud's compulsive elaboration of speculative theories which guided his self-analysis and shaped the 'discoveries' he made through it at almost every point.[4] The most important of all these discoveries would be the theory of infantile sexuality. The 'official' version of Freud's intellectual biography represents this as a major theoretical advance. From the point of view of the development and prosperity of the psychoanalytic movement it most certainly was just that. For the theory of infantile sexuality was much more attractive than the seduction hypothesis both to potential disciples and to potential patients. It also appeared to have a much greater explanatory capacity. One commentator, Walter Kendrick, has even made the interesting suggestion that Freud's motive for abandoning the seduction theory was not cowardice, but a desire to escape from its relative narrowness:

> If neurosis were caused exclusively by violation of children, psychoanalysis would have become merely a specialised form of therapy. Freud was too ambitious for that; he wanted to account for the whole of human culture, all the way back to the caves, and he never could have done that with a technique tailored to a minority. Ambition, then, rather than cowardice, was his motive . . .[5]

Whether or not we accept Kendrick's suggestion it is certainly true that Freud's later theories – and the theory of infantile sexuality in particular – were constructed on an altogether more sublime and world-encompassing scale than either his seduction theory or his earlier hypotheses about neurasthenia and hysteria. This does not mean that the new theory necessarily had any greater validity than the one which Freud silently discarded in 1897. There are other possible explanations for its success. In order to discover what these might be we need to examine the origins of the theory. We cannot do this without considering the way in which Freud's relationships with his intellectual supporters were beginning to change.

There can be no doubt at all that one of the most significant developments in this respect was the rapid cooling which took place in

Freud's friendship with Josef Breuer. For gradually, as Freud became more and more rash in his speculations about exclusive sexual aetiologies, his more cautious colleague had begun to express reservations. By 1894, even before the publication of *Studies in Hysteria*, their scientific collaboration had effectively come to an end and, from this time onwards, Freud evidently grew increasingly frustrated at Breuer's scepticism. Although the criticisms Breuer levelled at Freud were entirely reasonable, focusing as they did on his zeal to reduce all mental illness to a single sexual formula, Freud seems to have regarded these criticisms as a betrayal. His relationship to Breuer eventually broke down completely in an atmosphere of bitterness and hostility.

By the end of 1896 Freud had not only cut himself off from the most steadfast of all his professional supporters, he had also, by his uncompromising evangelism in the cause of his seduction theory, caused a number of his other colleagues to distance themselves from him. These included such influential figures as Richard von Krafft-Ebing, who had publicly described the seduction theory as 'a fairy tale'.[6] Looking back on this period of his life in 1914, Freud referred to it as his 'splendid isolation'.[7] 'At that time,' he would later write to Ferenczi of the year 1896, 'I had reached the peak of loneliness, had lost all my old friends and hadn't acquired any new ones; no one paid any attention to me . . .'[8] Freud's memories of this period of intellectual loneliness are poignant. But his characterisation of this time in his life is also profoundly misleading. For although he had indeed cut himself off from almost all those who had once supported him, the severing of these ties had not led to complete isolation at all. On the contrary it would seem that the deep feelings of insecurity aroused by the *possibility* of loneliness had thrown Freud headlong into the closest and most remarkable of all his intellectual relationships – his friendship with the physician Wilhelm Fliess.

Wilhelm Fliess was a nose and throat specialist who practised in Berlin. In the autumn of 1887 he had travelled to Vienna in order to undertake postgraduate studies and, at the suggestion of Josef Breuer, he attended some of Freud's lectures on neurology. Freud conceived an immediate regard for the Berlin physician and entered into a correspondence with him. The two physicians had a great deal in common. Both were Jewish, both were involved in medical research of an unusual kind and both were given to flights of theoretical speculation. Not only this but both had recently visited Paris to study under Charcot.

If their relationship did not immediately become an intimate one it was largely because at this point Freud's abiding need for a mentor and intellectual companion was still being met by Josef Breuer. But as Breuer began to draw back from Freud and what he saw as his tendency to 'excessive generalisation', Freud gradually transferred his affection, his respect and his intellectual regard to Fliess. By 1892 he was addressing Fliess in his letters not with the formal *Sie* but with the intimate *du*. Between 1895 and 1900, when their relationship was at its closest, Freud wrote to Fliess on average once every ten days and they frequently exchanged manuscripts and papers.[9]

Perhaps the most remarkable feature of this correspondence is that Freud would later attempt to suppress both sides of it and was very nearly successful in doing so. What happened was that at some point after Fliess's death in 1928, his widow sold Freud's letters to a bookseller in Berlin. She did so on the clear understanding that they were never to be sold to Freud himself, having apparently come to the conclusion that if he should ever get his hands on them he would not hesitate to destroy them. After Hitler came to power in Germany the letters were smuggled out of the country to Paris, where they were sold to one of Freud's most devoted disciples, Marie Bonaparte. On 30 December 1936 she wrote to Freud to let him know that she had purchased the letters. This news caused Freud considerable disquiet and he immediately replied in the following terms:

> The matter of the correspondence with Fliess has affected me deeply. After his death his widow asked that I return his letters. I agreed unconditionally, but was unable to find them. I do not know to this day whether I destroyed them, or only hid them ingeniously . . . Our correspondence was the most intimate you can imagine. It would have been highly embarrassing to have it fall into the hands of strangers. It is therefore an extraordinary labour of love that you have got hold of [the letters] and removed them from danger. I only regret the expense you have incurred. May I offer to share half the cost with you? After all I would have had to acquire the letters myself if the man had approached me directly. I do not want any of them to become known to so-called posterity . . .[10]

Marie Bonaparte, however, had acquired the letters on the strict understanding that she should not sell them, either directly or indirectly, to the Freud family. She was also personally opposed to their suppression or destruction. 'Perhaps you yourself . . . do not perceive your full greatness,' she wrote to Freud. 'You belong to the history of thought like Plato, should we say, or Goethe.' She had not yet read all the letters herself, but she did not wish to see any part of the history of psychoanalysis suppressed simply because of a few personal remarks the letters might contain. 'I love you . . . and revere you,' she continued, 'and that is why I have written to you in this manner.' Freud, however, was tenacious, renewing his pleas to his disciple on the grounds that even the factual letters to Fliess were personal since they indicated 'all the hunches and false paths connected with the birth of analysis'.[11]

Later, in Vienna, Freud told Marie Bonaparte that he wanted the letters to be burnt. She, however, remained steadfast in her determination to preserve them, convinced, as any faithful disciple would be, that they could contain nothing which would in any way damage Freud's reputation. Having initially deposited the letters in Vienna at the Rothschild Bank, she subsequently rescued them from under the eyes of the Gestapo, saved them once more from the German armies during the invasion of Paris, and eventually had them wrapped in waterproof material, tied to buoyancy bags and conveyed by ship across the mine-filled English Channel to London. They arrived safely some three years after Freud's death in 1939.

The letters were transcribed and Freud's daughter Anna, together with her fellow analysts Ernst Kris and Marie Bonaparte herself, now attempted to effect a compromise between the legitimate interest of scholars and Freud's determination to suppress the correspondence. They made a selection of the letters which was published in German in 1950 and in English in 1954 under the title *The Origins of Psychoanalysis*. The complete correspondence, including a large number of letters which had not been published, was then zealously guarded by Anna Freud, who allowed only a few scholars, including Ernest Jones and Max Schur, to see them. In 1970 Anna Freud donated the entire correspondence to the Library of Congress on condition that it was not to be seen again until the year 2000. Subsequently she relaxed these conditions slightly and eventually gave permission for the full correspondence to be published under the editorship of Jeffrey Masson. This edition eventually appeared in 1985.

The extraordinary saga of chance, danger and attempts at suppression which is attached to the correspondence has always given it an added fascination. The most interesting question of all is why Freud himself was so anxious to have the letters destroyed. The most plausible answer is that his letters to Fliess effectively destroy one of the most impressive elements of the complex legend in which Freud had shrouded both his own personality and the origins of psychoanalysis. For while Freud had spun an entire mythology around what he called his period of 'splendid isolation', portraying himself as the rugged and lonely explorer, an omnipotent father-figure who commanded respect by his own intellectual self-reliance, his letters to Fliess tell a quite different story. They show a man who, rather than inspiring awe in others, appears both fallible and credulous. For Freud frequently adopts towards Fliess an attitude of reverence and submission, and looks to his younger colleague at almost every stage for guidance, advice and scientific enlightenment.

Freud's attitude towards Fliess was all the more significant in view of the ideas which the Berlin physician was committed to. For although Fliess began his medical career as an orthodox nose and throat specialist, he soon stepped into a self-created labyrinth of medical error and misdiagnosis which led him to formulate some of the most remarkable theories in the whole of nineteenth-century medicine.

The entrance to this labyrinth was formed by Fliess's belief that he had discovered a new form of nervous disease – the nasal reflex neurosis. The main symptoms of this syndrome, he held, were headaches, migraines, cardiac and respiratory irregularities, vertigo, various neuralgic pains in the stomach, arms and shoulders and difficulties in menstruation and pregnancy. In 1893, in a monograph announcing the discovery of this new syndrome, Fliess claimed that he had found 130 cases among his own patients. In all these cases, he maintained, the various symptoms had their origin in the nose which, if examined carefully, would usually reveal swelling of the mucosa. One of the distinctive features of the syndrome was that the symptoms could be temporarily diminished by anaesthetising the inside of the nose with a local application of cocaine. In extreme cases, however, surgical intervention was necessary in order to remove the turbinate bone.

In Fliess's view the key to the understanding of the new syndrome was provided by its treatment. For since symptoms which were remote from the nose, such as migraines or pains in the chest, could be relieved by a purely local application of cocaine to the nose, Fliess concluded that there was a hidden link between the nose and various other parts of the body – including, in the case of menstrual problems, the genitals. Ever since the revolutionary description in 1875 by Erb and Westphal of the tendon reflexes there had been an upsurge of scientific interest in the subject of reflexes and Fliess was quick to follow medical fashion by postulating a complex theory of reflex action between the nose and other organs.

The most perceptive commentary on this aspect of Fliess's thinking has once again been offered by E. M. Thornton. What she points out is that the entire elaborate architecture of Fliess's theory was founded on a simple medical error. Fliess had failed to ascertain the precise mode of action of cocaine. When he applied it to the mucous membrane of the nose he believed this was the equivalent of applying it to any other part of the body, where it functioned as a purely local anaesthetic. He did not understand that by applying it to the nose he was in fact ensuring its speedy absorption into the bloodstream, where it acted directly on the brain. The fact that cocaine applied to the nose helped to relieve migraines or painful menstruation did not indicate that there was any reflex mechanism operating at all. 'The effects Fliess deemed local and reflex,' writes Thornton, 'were actually the direct effects of cocaine on the brain.'[12] The nature of Fliess's mistake can perhaps best be conveyed if we consider the hypothetical case of a doctor unversed in elementary pharmacology who discovers that he can relieve the pain of a rheumatic knee by getting his patient to swallow an aspirin. If he reasoned that this indicated the existence of a 'stomach reflex neurosis' and of a direct reflex link between the walls of the stomach and the knee, he would be making exactly the same kind of error as Fliess.

For Fliess, however, the idea of the nasal reflex neurosis was only the first stage of a much more elaborate theory. Having observed the effect of cocaine applied to the nose on menstrual pain in women, he concluded that there was a special link between the nose and the genitals. He went on to postulate the existence of 'genital spots' on the inside of the nose and held that these spots were not only associated with neuroses but also influenced the menstrual cycle of women. Fliess's theories about genital spots were used to show that many complaints had a sexual aetiology – a view which he applied to men as well as women. Like Freud he saw masturbation as one of the most common causes of a variety of complaints, all linked to the nose by way of 'genital spots'. 'I will only mention a recent case,' he wrote, 'in which, in a typical neurasthenic episode associated with ophthalmic migraine caused by onanistic abuse [masturbation], the nasal mucous membranes were very much swollen.'[13]

These views were developed further in Fliess's monograph of 1897,

The Relations between the Nose and the Female Sexual Organs from the Biological Aspect. Having traced the assumed relationship between the nose and a whole cluster of supposedly neurotic symptoms, Fliess went on to develop his theory of menstruation. He eventually concluded that the two periods of 28 and 23 days, which he derived from the menstrual cycle, contained within them a key by which the mysteries of the entire realm of biology might be unlocked. For in Fliess's view the periods of 23 and 28 days determined all the stages in the growth of human beings, including their date of birth, the dates of their illnesses and the date of their death. These periods were also common 'to the animal kingdom and probably to the whole organic world'. Indeed, through them organic life could be related to the motions of the stars, for 'the wonderful exactitude with which the period of 23 or 28 whole days is maintained allows one to presume a profound relationship between astronomical conditions and the creation of organisms.'[14]

Fliess thus postulated a kind of universal mathematical pattern which could be found underlying not only the individual lives of all men and women but the entire structure of the cosmos. By trying to unravel this mathematical pattern Fliess was attempting to give to the discipline of biology the same kind of mathematical basis which Newton had already given to physics. One of the ways in which he sought to prove the truth of his theories was by taking crucial dates in the lives of individuals and then showing that they were all related one to another. This he did by performing various arithmetical calculations using not only the figures 23 and 28 themselves but also their sum (51) and their difference (5). He eventually came to accord equal significance to the squares and cubes of these numbers, to their product and to other arithmetical transformations of them.

Although the phenomenon of biological periodicity is a real one, the most level-headed assessment of Fliess's achievement is perhaps that made by Martin Gardner, who has pointed out that Fliess's 'Teutonic crackpottery' depended on analysing all his data in terms of the general formula $x \cdot 23 \pm y \cdot 28$. Gardner observes that any two positive integers which, like 23 and 28, have no common denominator, can be used in this general formula to produce any positive number which is desired. Since Fliess's formula contained every possible answer, no problem of periodicity could, *a priori*, avoid falling victim to its explanatory power.[15]

If Fliess's theories were remarkable in themselves, Freud's reaction to them was even more so. So committed did he feel to them that he was unable to tolerate any criticism of his friend, however soundly it might be based. When Fliess's book, *The Relationship between the Nose and the Female Sexual Organs*, was published in 1897 it was reviewed in the *Wiener klinische Rundschau* by Dr Benjamin Ry. The review was severely critical:

> After one has laboriously worked one's way through this work, which in view of its meagre content is quite voluminous, one retains in memory only a single positive assertion – that it is possible to remove labour pains by the cocainisation of certain parts of the nasal mucosa. The reviewer, having made inquiries at obstetrical clinics, learned that experiments in respect thereof – which at the time were also widely discussed in the daily press – did not lead to positive results; therewith any need to deal further with this point of Fliess's work is obviated. The rest of what the book contains has nothing to do with medicine or natural science. For if one nowadays seeks to render the kind of mystical nonsense that aspires to intellectual wealth capable of discussion, the attempt founders on the realisation that it is not the business of science to embark on a critique of the fantasy creations of every author, for such idle disquisitions can be neither refuted or confirmed.

After going on to relate how Fliess asserts the existence of a periodic relationship between the development of the tonsils and the eye muscles, which enables diseased tonsils to render children cross-eyed, Ry exclaims: 'This is indeed disgusting gobbledygook! No wonder that in not a few places the reader of this book has the impression that the author is making fun of him.'[16]

Far from allowing this review to modify his estimate of his friend's theories, Freud immediately sent a copy of the review to Fliess, describing it as an example of 'that type of impertinence which is characteristic of absolute ignorance'. In a gesture of support he resigned from the editorial board of the journal which had published it. Three years later, in 1901, Freud was still expressing the view that Fliess's book contained 'a fundamental biological discovery'.[17] As these words suggest, Freud found it impossible to regard Fliess's ideas with anything other than credulity. He frequently talked about the nasal reflex syndrome as though it were an established fact and, when he himself suffered from migraine, he adopted Fliess's solution of applying cocaine to the nose. In the words of his physician, Max Schur, 'he was prone to relate his headaches to the nose, with the result that he had not only made frequent local applications of cocaine, but also permitted Fliess to perform several cauterisations and perhaps some surgery of the turbinate bone . . .'[18] It seems quite conceivable in view of this information that Freud had decided not simply that he was himself suffering from the nasal reflex syndrome but that, as Fliess's theories maintained, the ultimate cause of his migraines was masturbation. Freud, indeed, may even have been the selfsame patient described by Fliess in the passage quoted above – the victim of ophthalmic migraines caused by 'onanistic abuse'.

Whether or not Freud asked Fliess to treat him for the presumed effects of his own masturbation it is quite clear that he *did* prevail on his friend to treat some of his patients who were supposedly suffering from the effects of masturbation. The most remarkable instance was the case of Emma Eckstein, whose treatment was described in a letter which was deliberately suppressed in the original edition of Freud's letters to Fliess. In 1895, after having apparently identified Eckstein as a victim of the nasal reflex neurosis brought on by masturbation, Freud summoned Fliess to Vienna and asked him to perform the ultimate surgical intervention which he advocated – removal of the turbinate bone in Emma Eckstein's nose. Fliess was an inexperienced surgeon and this operation was apparently one of his first ventures into major surgery. He soon returned to Berlin but his patient did not make a good recovery, suffering from a purulent secretion, massive haemorrhaging and considerable pain. Freud called in a surgeon to insert a drainage tube, but when the bleeding continued together with a fetid odour, he was forced to summon another surgeon, his friend Ignaz Rosanes. In the letter to Fliess which was originally suppressed Freud describes what happened next:

> Rosanes cleaned the area surrounding the opening, removed some sticky blood clots, and suddenly pulled at something like a thread, [and] kept on pulling. Before either of us had time to think, at least half a meter of gauze had been removed from the cavity. The next moment came a flood of blood. The patient turned white, her eyes bulged, and she had no pulse.[19]

After the cavity had been packed the bleeding stopped and Emma Eckstein made a partial recovery. But she continued to have severe haemorrhages. Instead of facing up to the fact that he had damaged his patient's health and almost caused her death through an entirely unnecessary operation, Freud tried to exculpate both himself and Fliess by arguing that her haemorrhaging was actually hysterical, and was motivated by an unconscious wish to 'entice' Freud to her bedside.[20] Instead of revising his estimate of Fliess in the light of this experience, Freud elevated him even higher in his regard, describing him as a true healer, 'the type of man into whose hands one confidently puts one's life and that of one's family'.[21]

What was perhaps even more remarkable was that Freud's regard for Fliess extended to his numerological speculations. For, far from being sceptical in the face of Fliess's attempt to construct a mathematical biology, Freud was deeply impressed by it. He once called Fliess 'the Kepler of biology' and he wrote to him in ecstatic terms about the way in which 'the enigmas of the world and of life were beginning to yield an answer' as a result of his mathematical approach.[22]

Freud's extraordinary credulity in the face of Fliess's work and the reverence with which he regarded it has never been satisfactorily explained. In 1979 Frank Sulloway devoted a section of his book *Freud: Biologist of the Mind* to a discussion of Fliess's mathematical ideas and attempted to restore to these ideas some semblance of scientific respectability. By carefully locating Fliess's theories in what he calls their 'historical biomedical context' Sulloway certainly establishes that some of the biological theories advanced by nineteenth-century thinkers were almost as speculative and scientifically irresponsible as Fliess's own. He also points out what should be self-evident – that the phenomenon of biological periodicity has always been and will always be a genuine scientific problem.[23] Sulloway's book will always remain one of the most significant and valuable contributions to Freud scholarship. But his view of Fliess fails to persuade. The commonness of delusional beliefs has never provided grounds for regarding those who entertain them as reasonable. At the same time the genuineness of a scientific problem does not confer equal legitimacy on all possible solutions to it; the fact that geologists may frequently research into the composition of moon-rock does not render any more plausible the proposition that the moon is made of blue cheese. Moreover, as Ry's trenchant review of Fliess's monograph should demonstrate, Fliess's scientific waywardness is not something which has become visible only in the latter part of the twentieth century. It was quite apparent to the more sceptical of his contemporaries.

A much more interesting attempt to explain away Freud's embarrassing intellectual dependence on Fliess's theories was made long ago by Ernest Jones in his biography of Freud. Jones suggests that the relationship with Fliess was essential to Freud's intellectual development. Freud needed this relationship because, after spending many years successfully internalising the discipline of science, he had at last reached a point where he could safely liberate his speculative side; Fliess was the catalyst who enabled him to do this.[24]

Ernest Jones's account of the Freud–Fliess relationship has the merit of being a form of psychological explanation, and it is perhaps partly for this reason that it has been widely accepted within the psychoanalytic movement. It should be reasonably clear, however, that Jones's version of Freud's intellectual biography itself belongs to the realm of legend rather than fact. Jones himself evidently genuinely believed that Freud's regard for Fliess could only be explained as an aberration.[25] Yet this view had come about because Jones, like countless commentators on psychoanalysis both before and since, had failed to probe Freud's ready acceptance of the teachings of his earlier mentors – especially Charcot and Breuer. Like many intensely religious personalities, Freud could sometimes be tough-minded and sceptical towards the belief-systems of others. But as we have seen in relation not only to Charcot and Breuer, but also in his early papers on cocaine, such scepticism was by no means a constant feature of Freud's character. For Freud never ceased to be driven by his own huge and messianic ambitions. If any scientific or medical doctrine seemed to promise a way of realising these ambitions, his habit was to fall passionately and uncritically in love with that doctrine – to the exclusion of all scepticism and all intellectual moderation.

One of the most striking features of Freud's correspondence with Fliess is the emotional intensity of the relationship it reveals. On one occasion Freud wrote that he was 'looking forward to our congress as to a slaking of hunger and thirst'. On another occasion he 'panted' for the time when they would again exchange ideas, and afterwards wrote that he was 'in a state of continuous euphoria and working like a youth'. His attitude towards Fliess's ideas is often one not simply of intellectual admiration but of religious awe, and that kind of deferential reverence which a disciple shows towards the teachings of his master. Once Freud wrote that he had set his hopes on Fliess solving a particular problem 'as on the Messiah'.[26]

The religious intensity of Freud's relationship to Fliess can be understood only if we can imaginatively grasp Freud's personal predicament and appreciate its growing seriousness during the period of his friendship with Fliess. For Freud evidently remained deeply marked by his family's conditional worship of him and by his parents' urgent expectations of his future greatness. In the early stages of his medical career it would seem that he remained reasonably confident that he could realise his dreams of glory without ever leaving the relatively safe field of neuropathology. In this field he had actually achieved considerable distinction. Looking back on his early career in 1925 he conveys some idea of the reputation which he had developed:

> In the course of the following years, while I continued to work as a junior physician, I published a number of clinical observations upon organic diseases of the nervous system. I gradually became familiar with the ground; I was able to localise the site of a lesion in the medulla oblongata so accurately that the pathological anatomist had no further information to add; I was the first person in Vienna to send a case for autopsy with a diagnosis of polyneuritis acuta. The fame of my diagnoses and their post-mortem confirmation brought me an influx of American physicians, to whom I lectured upon the patients in my department in a sort of pidgin-English.[27]

Although Freud's contributions to neurology were scarcely revolutionary, they were to be of lasting importance and they undoubtedly testified to a rare anatomical skill. There seems every reason to suppose that these scientific achievements also had a significant psychological effect on Freud himself. When Robert Bunsen discovered spectral analysis we are told that it changed both his vision of the world and his entire personality; from then on 'he bore himself as a king travelling incognito.'[28] The phrase is one which seems strikingly applicable to Freud at this particular juncture of his career and it may well be that Freud's success as a research neurologist was one of the factors which had helped to confirm the sense of inner election which had been created during his childhood. Yet if this was so, Freud's moderate professional success would only have served to underline the huge disjunction between this feeling of inner election and the recognition he had actually achieved. For Freud could clearly never remain content to travel incognito. His existential predicament could only be solved if he could persuade others to recognise his kingship. Throughout the decade leading up to the formulation of the seduction theory he had alternated between the conviction that he had made a world-shaking discovery himself, a conviction which he first succumbed to during the cocaine episode, and the belief that he had been granted equally significant revelations by others – notably by Charcot in relation to hysteria and by Breuer in relation to Anna O. Even at the age of forty, when his relationship with Fliess was at its most intense, Freud still had not found the theoretical assurance he needed in order to realise his messianic identity.

At this period in his life Freud, then, was in the position of the prophet who knows he has been chosen but who has begun to despair of ever receiving the revelation for which he waits. His own seduction theory promised, initially at least, a way out of his dilemma. But the icy reception of Freud's paper by his colleagues and his subsequent failure to achieve the results he had anticipated (and, indeed, implicitly announced) can only have heightened his sense of uncertainty. Even before this new setback, it would seem that he had sought relief from his anxiety and his deep sense of failure by projecting his own messianic identity onto Fliess. It was for this reason that he set his hopes on Fliess 'as on the Messiah' and repeatedly credited him with having produced an intellectual system which would elucidate the world. His intense admiration for Fliess derived from the fact that his compulsive messianic need for a revelation overbalanced his capacities for sceptically interrogating any revelation under whose spell he had fallen. He repeatedly urged Fliess to enlarge the scope of his theories and, in one of the most significant letters he ever wrote, he looked forward with mystical ecstasy to a meeting at which Fliess would impart to him a new aspect of his doctrine: 'At Aussee I know a wonderful wood full of ferns and mushrooms, where you shall reveal to me the secrets of the world of lower animals and the world of children.'[29]

It is at this point that another crucial element in the intellectual relationship between Freud and Fliess enters our story. For when Freud spoke of 'the secrets of the world of lower animals and the world of children' he was referring to Fliess's application of contemporary Darwinian biology to child-psychology – to Fliess's theory of infantile sexuality. Of all the dimensions of the Freud–Fliess relationship which have been systematically suppressed by the psychoanalytic movement itself, there can be no doubt that Fliess's influence on Freud's theory of infantile sexuality is the most important. For until the appearance of Frank Sulloway's intellectual biography of Freud in 1979, the entire secondary literature on Freud contained no reference to this aspect of the Freud–Fliess relationship.[30] Under Freud's own oblique direction the history of psychoanalysis had been rewritten in order to exclude one of its most decisive episodes. What is perhaps even more significant is that Sulloway himself originally repaired the historical record only on the assumption that Fliess's ideas on infantile sexuality made him a genuine scientific pioneer. It seems reasonably clear, however, that Fliess's sexual theories were no more scientifically fruitful than his mathematical biology.

This was partly because Fliess's interest in sexuality was intimately related to his 'nasal reflex neurosis' and was informed by the same kind of medical fallacies. But an even more important role in Fliess's thinking was played by the ideas of Ernst Haeckel, the most influential of all Darwin's followers in Germany. For, at almost every stage of its development, Freud's theory of infantile sexuality was linked to and dependent on Ernst Haeckel's 'biogenetic law'. As both Frank Sulloway and Stephen Jay Gould have helped to show, this 'biogenetic law' is one of the least recognised but most important influences on countless aspects of our modern intellectual culture. For not only did it provide the biological basis for the theory of infantile sexuality which Freud adopted from Fliess, but it also provided the assumptions on which a whole range of modern intellectual theories are based, including Piaget's theories of child-development, Rudolf Steiner's educational theories and Dr Benjamin Spock's approach to child-rearing.[31]

Haeckel's 'fundamental biogenetic law' was in fact a speculative deduction made primarily from observations of the way in which mammalian embryos develop. Haeckel noted that human embryos pass at first through a fish-like stage when they have gills and a tail and then through stages where they resemble other more complex mammals until they eventually assume a recognisably human form. From these observations of the development of the foetus – which have become a part of our own scientific 'common sense' – Haeckel derived the principle that 'the embryonic development is an epitome – a condensed and abbreviated recapitulation – of the historical development of the species.'[32]

The observations on which this principle was based were sound enough. But what was not scientifically sound was the manner in which Haeckel translated a number of straightforward observations into a universal scientific law on the basis of which he proceeded to make a series of far-reaching generalisations.

Haeckel, however, was not simply a biologist in the sense that we would use that word today. For he saw himself – and was seen by many German intellectuals and artists in the latter part of the nineteenth century and the early part of the twentieth century – as the founder of a new 'scientific religion'. He called his philosophy 'monism' and saw himself as the leader of a movement of aggressive rationalism which would eventually rid Germany of the last traces of superstitious religion and replace Christianity as Germany's national ideology with a 'religion' which glorified modern science. In this respect it must be suggested that Haeckel's most significant intellectual heir was not Freud, nor even Thomas Mann, but a thinker whose ideas have often been misrepresented as muddled and of little intellectual import – Adolf Hitler. For as Daniel Gasman has shown, in a book which should be much more widely known than it is, Hitler's entire philosophy of history, as expressed in *Mein Kampf* and elsewhere, was profoundly influenced by Haeckel's evolutionary theorising.[33]

There can be little doubt that Haeckel's militant and religiously anti-religious sensibility affected his own application of 'the fundamental biogenetic law'. For he was not prepared to rest content with a principle which applied only to the physical development of babies in the womb. Paradoxically his 'monistic' creed, like Christianity, assumed the reality of the 'soul' which it sought to account for in evolutionary terms. In Haeckel's view the soul was a universal characteristic of animal organisms whose evolution could be traced from the 'simple cell-soul' of protozoa to the complex soul of human beings. Haeckel also believed, however, that the consciousness or soul of an organism depended for its development on external stimuli in a way that the body did not. For this reason he maintained that while the body recapitulated the entire history of evolution in the womb, where it visibly developed from a unicellular organism to a fully formed human being, the soul did not develop at the same rate. Instead, during the whole time that the foetus is developing in the womb, the soul remains 'in a state of embryonic slumber, a state of repose which Preyer has justly compared to the hibernation of animals'.[34]

The implication of this view was that the newly born baby possessed, within a completely evolved human body, a human soul which was only partly evolved. The young child would then recapitulate at the level of consciousness or mental life the same stages of evolutionary development which had already been recapitulated at the level of physical development inside the womb.

It was with the help of such speculations that Haeckel extended the principle of recapitulation beyond its embryological application into an all-encompassing law of human development – 'the fundamental biogenetic law', which maintained that the development of human beings not simply in the womb, but from the stage of the fertilised egg to adulthood, consists in the recapitulation of the entire history of the species. In the last two decades of the nineteenth century this biogenetic law gained wide acceptance and, as a mark of its respectability, one might cite the use made of it by Darwin's friend and colleague George Romanes. In his studies *Mental Evolution in Animals* (1883) and *Mental Evolution in Man* (1888) Romanes sought to establish the truth of evolution by pointing to resemblances between the psychological development of children and the mental capacities of animals. According to a chart reproduced in both books, the human infant at birth had reached a psychological stage corresponding to the mental consciousness of the sea-urchin. Subsequently babies recapitulated the psychological development of insects and spiders, which they did by the time they were ten weeks. The mental life of babies then gradually progressed through the eras of fish, reptiles and birds until, at about the age of twelve months, children reached the stage of psychological development achieved by monkeys and elephants. At the age of fifteen months they reached the intellectual stage of apes and dogs and began to develop, in addition to powers of abstract reasoning, what Romanes described as 'indefinite morality'.[35]

Although Freud's most important encounter with Haeckel's ideas was probably through Fliess, he was also directly acquainted both with Haeckel's own ideas and with those of other evolutionary thinkers. He read and extensively annotated Romanes's *Mental Evolution in Man* and was therefore aware of the biogenetic psychology implicit in it, according to which the mental development of children lagged behind their physical development and 'caught up' only by means of a rapid recapitulation of archaic animal phases of consciousness during the early years of childhood.[36] Indeed, so much was the biogenetic view of child-psychology a part of the intellectual environment of both Freud and Fliess that it would seem they treated it as axiomatic, assuming its general truth as a matter of course. Fliess appears to have been the pioneer in developing a concept of infantile sexuality which was based on biogenetic precepts, and his early writings are remarkable in that they disclose an interest in both oral and anal manifestations of sexuality, topics which would be crucial in mature psychoanalytic theory. When, in 1896, Freud used some of Fliess's hints in order to formulate a genetic theory of sexual perversion, it was thus almost inevitable that he should do so in biogenetic terms. His initial suggestion, made in a letter to Fliess, explained the scatological and fetishistic character of many human sexual 'perversions' by deriving them from a stage of pre-human animal development when, because of the dominance of the sense of smell, 'hair, faeces, and the whole surface of the body – and blood as well – have a sexually exciting effect.'[37] Implicit in this view was the assumption that the acquisition of disgust by infants was brought about by a recapitulation of that phase in animal development when the sense of smell lost its dominance. Freud linked this idea to the view that the child also recapitulated phases in pre-human development in which animals had been influenced sexually by factors associated with the mouth and the anus. The child would thus experience briefly those particular animal appetites and drives which humans had 'evolved beyond'. Normally these would be left behind as the child's animal consciousness caught up with its human frame. Where this did not happen, however, the result would be perversion. It was this biogenetic view which Freud expressed in a letter written to Fliess on 14 November 1897. Although this letter was written some six weeks after he had told Fliess of his disenchantment with his seduction theory, it would be wrong to see the new theoretical construct as emerging suddenly in order to replace the old. For Freud makes it clear in his letter that he had been working at his new idea for some time – 'it had repeatedly shown itself and withdrawn again.' What he now describes is his 'synthesis' to date:

> A few weeks ago I mentioned that I wanted to get behind [the phenomenon of] repression to the essential that lies behind it, and that is what I am writing to you about now.
>
> I have often suspected that something organic played a part in repression; I have told you before that it is a question of the attitude adopted to former sexual zones, and I added that I had been pleased to come across the same idea in Moll. Privately I would not concede priority in the idea to anyone; in my case the suggestion was linked to the changed part played by the sensations of smell: upright carriage was adopted, the nose was raised from the ground, and at the same time a number of what had formerly been interesting sensations connected with the earth became repellent – by a process of which I am still ignorant. ('He turns up his nose' = 'he regards himself as something particularly noble.') Now, the zones which no longer produce a release of sexuality in normal and mature human beings must be the regions of the anus and of the mouth and throat ... In animals these sexual zones retain their power ... where they do so in human beings the result is perversion. We must assume that in infancy sexual release is not so much localised as it becomes later, so that zones which are later

abandoned (and possibly the whole surface of the body) stimulate to some extent the production of something analogous to the later release of sexuality.[38]

In these words we can see clearly an early outline of the theory of infantile sexuality. Although Freud appears to have adopted this theory initially in order to solve the problem of repression, it simultaneously held out the promise of a solution to the problem which Freud was left with as a result of the collapse of the seduction theory. As Malcolm Macmillan has put it: 'There was, if I can so put it, a bonus: the areas of the body once able to release sexuality – the anus and the mouth and the throat – were precisely the areas that seemed to have been involved in the childhood seduction "experiences".'[39]

Freud did not immediately see how neatly his new formulation would allow him to find a way out of the theoretical maze in which he had by now managed to lose himself. But in 1899 he began to realise that if he postulated the existence of a sexual impulse in earliest childhood which took an *auto-erotic* form and which could generate sexual sensations in the anus and the mouth, many of his theoretical problems could be solved. Above all the various perverse sexual scenes which he had constructed, and which he had previously explained by postulating real seductions, could now be explained in a different way. These scenes derived not from real seductions but from fantasies which belonged to a later period and had been projected back into the earliest years of childhood and experienced in terms of infantile sexual impulses.[40]

The ideas which he had gleaned from Fliess thus enabled Freud to solve some of his old theoretical problems at the same time that they opened up entirely new vistas. As Sulloway has pointed out, the eventual sequence of oral, anal and genital stages of sexuality which Freud postulated in the mature version of his sexual theory corresponded precisely to the conventional evolutionary account of the development of sexual anatomy in non-human animals. For according to the argument of another German evolutionary thinker, Wilhelm Bölsche, the line of evolutionary development was one in which simple organisms used the mouth as a reproductive organism, sexual reproduction being originally 'a sort of higher eating'.[41] In more complex organisms such oral reproduction was displaced by the cloacal intercourse practised by reptiles and birds and described by Bölsche as 'anus pressed against anus'.[42] This form of copulation was in turn displaced among crocodiles and saurians by the penis and vagina. If a general notion of recapitulation was applied to these aspects of the evolutionary process then it could be argued that the human child would, in the first years of its life, recapitulate this phylogenetic sexual inheritance according to a genetically predetermined sequence. Each stage of 'perverse' and implicitly animal sexuality, would eventually succumb to automatic *organic* repression. The child would gradually progress from having the 'sexual consciousness' of a simple animal to having that of a reptile. These oral and anal stages of sexuality would then be left behind as the child achieved the sexual consciousness of the crocodile, and thereafter gradually became fully human.

Freud did not, of course, express his theory of infantile sexuality in these precise terms. But it was this view which he eventually adopted, together with its biogenetic rationale. In his *Introductory Lectures on Psychoanalysis*, he referred to Bölsche's work, reminding his audience that, just as the libido developed through certain stages in humans, so 'in one class of animals, the genital apparatus is brought into the closest relation to the mouth, while in another it cannot be distinguished from the excretory apparatus, and in yet others it is linked to the motor organs.'[43] In his essay on infantile sexuality he was even more explicit about the biogenetic dimensions of his argument. One of the most common formulations of Haeckel's biogenetic law was that ontogeny (the development of the individual organism) recapitulates phylogeny (the evolutionary history of the species). It is this formulation which Freud has in mind in the following passage:

> The order in which the various instinctual impulses come into activity seems to be phylogenetically determined; so, too, does the length of time during which they are able to manifest themselves before they succumb to the effects of some freshly emerging instinctual impulse or to some typical repression. Variations, however, seem to occur both in temporal sequence and in duration, and these variations must exercise a determining influence upon the final result.[44]

A failure on the part of any individual to progress normally through this sequence of development might result in sexual 'perversion' or neurosis. In order to expound this part of his argument, Freud made use of the existing biological concepts of fixation and regression, or reversion. Sexual 'perversions' were in all cases seen as having a phylogenetic base. 'Perverted' sexual behaviour was seen as deriving from a primitive stage of animal sexuality which had, as it were, erupted into life in the consciousness of a particular individual. 'Among animals,' wrote Freud, in one of the most bizarre of his many *ex cathedra* pronouncements, 'one can find, so to speak in petrified form, every species of perversion of the [human] sexual organisation.'[45]

While Freud saw the child's environment and traumatic events or 'accidents' as playing a role in bringing about 'perversions', such external factors could not on their own influence the development of the individual's sexual identity; they needed to work on a point of constitutional weakness. In order to account for neurotic disturbances Freud thus came to rely on a makeshift version of the evolutionary concept of variation, holding that the biological programme which determined the unfolding of the sexual instinct might vary from individual to individual and that this would predispose some individuals to pathological disturbances in their sexual identity.[46] They would then become fixated at stages of 'sexual consciousness' which belonged phylogenetically to reptiles, crocodiles or other forms of primitive animal life, and this fixation would manifest itself in forms of sexual behaviour which Freud sometimes described as 'archaic'.[47]

Perhaps the most important element in Freud's entire argument was his assumption that repression was primarily an organic, phylogenetically determined process. This belief in the automatic nature of repression would eventually be modified with the introduction of the concept of the 'superego'. But it would never be discarded entirely (see Chapter 13). Freud certainly conceded that education played a role in the development of disgust, shame and morality. But once again he seems to have used a biological model in assessing this role, conceiving of shame and repression primarily as instincts which, like many reflex actions of animals, needed to be triggered by an external stimulus before they became part of the animal's behavioural repertoire:

> It is during the period of total or only partial latency that are built up the mental forces which are later to impede the course of the sexual instinct and, like dams, restrict its flow – disgust, feelings of shame and the claims of aesthetic and moral ideals. One gets an impression from civilised children that the construction of these dams is a product of education, and no doubt education has much to do with it. But in reality this development is organically determined and fixed by heredity, and it can occasionally occur without any help at all from education. Education will not be trespassing beyond its appropriate domain if it limits

itself to following the lines which have already been laid down organically and to impressing them somewhat more clearly and deeply.[48]

Elsewhere Freud reinforced the same point by referring to disgust,
shame and morality as 'historical precipitates of the external inhibitions
to which the sexual instinct has been subjected during the psychogenesis of the human race'. He went on to suggest that in the development
of individuals 'they [shame and disgust] arise at the appropriate
moment, as though spontaneously, when upbringing and external
influence give the signal.'[49]

Frank Sulloway, the only scholar who has considered the role of
biogenetic hypotheses in Freud's thought in any depth, has given the
impression that Freud's theory of psychosexual development was a
relatively straightforward deduction which followed from applying
Haeckel's biogenetic law to the evolutionary evidence. If, however,
we bear in mind the distinction which Haeckel made between the
inter-uterine development of the foetus and the post-natal development of the soul, it would appear that Freud's phylogenetically inspired
account of childhood is based at best on an expedient adaptation of
the biogenetic law. For since the transition from oral to cloacal sexuality, and thence to genital, was evidently a morphological process
involving *anatomical* evolution, then it should presumably have been
recapitulated not in the early years of the child's development, but
inside the womb. It would in any case clearly belong to a phase of
development much earlier than the changes which Freud associated
with the adoption of the erect posture. Yet Freud's theory conflates,
in a somewhat blurred manner, the relinquishing of cloacal sexuality
by saurians with the hypothetical repression of coprophilia by proto-
hominids. Not content with deriving shame and disgust and the human
impulse towards purity from these two different phylogenetic scenarios, Freud also added a third, by making use of the Lamarckian
assumption to the effect that morality was a cumulative genetic inheritance and that taboos and repressions acquired by one generation were
organically transmitted to the next. As well as being applied to all
manner of general restraints, this Lamarckian notion of inheritance
was also used to account for specific prohibitions such as the incest
taboo, with Freud writing, for instance, that children 'are compelled
to recapitulate from the history of mankind the repression of an incestuous object-choice'.[50]

All in all it is difficult to avoid the impression that Freud used biogenetic notions not as a source of scientific hypotheses but as a kind of folklore which he could draw on to help him construct the plot of the reasonably good scientific story he had to be able to tell in order to confer legitimacy on psychoanalysis. Into this plot he would then weave the 'characters' which, since they were drawn from the realm of observable phenomena, made his stories seem more realistic and plausible. If the behaviour of some of the characters did not seem exactly to fit the demands of the plot then this did not pose an insurmountable difficulty, since Freud was occasionally prepared to waive his otherwise stern demands for consistency. At the same time he was evidently willing to tolerate a considerable degree of chronological dissonance. Ultimately it mattered little whether the repression of coprophilia derived from the saurians, from proto-hominids or from the taboos of primitive cultures, for the general impression that these impulses belonged to some dark and undiscovered past was created in all cases. Similarly, although there was no evidence to suggest that either reptiles or birds indulged in sadistic intercourse or used scatological rituals in order to bring each other to orgasm, this did not stop Freud from associating them with humans who did, or from writing of 'anal-erotism' that 'the predominance in it of sadism and the cloacal part played by the anal zone give it a quite peculiarly archaic colouring.'[51]

The fundamental role played in Freud's theory of sexuality by extrapolations from contemporary biological theory has frequently been denied by Freud's followers. As Sulloway has pointed out, this process was in some respects initiated by Freud himself. For although Freud never made any attempt to conceal his biogenetic determinism, and makes this explicit throughout his work, he did deny that his theories had been *derived* from biological hypotheses. In the preface to the third edition of *Three Essays on the Theory of Sexuality* he thus wrote that: 'Ontogenesis may be regarded as a recapitulation of phylogenesis, in so far as the latter has not been modified by more recent experience.' But having pointed out that his work was compatible with contemporary biogenetic theories, he then went on to write:

I must, however, emphasise that the present work is characterised not only by being completely based on psychoanalytic research, but also by being deliberately independent of the findings of biology. I have carefully avoided introducing any preconceptions, whether derived from general sexual biology or from that of particular animal species, into this study . . .[52]

Such denials as these have been taken at face value by large numbers of psychoanalysts, with the result that the intellectual origins of psycho-analysis have been effectively obscured. It is Sulloway's dramatic but, I think, irrefutable contention that:

> The expedient denial and refashioning of history has been an indispens-able part of the psychoanalytic revolution. Perhaps more remarkable still is the degree to which the whole process of historical censorship, distortion, embellishment, and propaganda has been effected with the co-operation of psychoanalysts who would instantly proclaim such phenomena as 'neurotic' if they spotted them in anyone else.[53]

So effective has this mythologising away of history been, it would appear that many of the most distinguished theoreticians of psychoan-alysis remained until relatively recently genuinely ignorant of the his-torical development of some of its most crucial doctrines, a position which perhaps has a parallel only in the case of some modern Christian theologians. One of the most remarkable instances is provided by Erik Erikson in his book *Childhood and Society*. During the course of his discussion of the theory of infantile sexuality, Erikson suggests that in order to understand it we should have recourse to an analogy: 'Embryology now understands *epigenetic* development, the step-by-step growth of the foetal organs. I think that the Freudian laws of psycho-sexual development can best be understood through an analogy with physiological development *in utero*.'[54] As we have seen, the recapitu-lation theory which underlies the theory of infantile sexuality was itself derived from observation of physiological development *in utero*. Unless Erikson is being deliberately disingenuous in the presentation of his ideas, we are here confronted with a remarkable instance of a distin-guished psychoanalytic theorist accidentally reconstructing one of the intellectual origins of psychoanalysis under the impression that he is offering merely an illuminating analogy.

It must be said, however, that Freud himself remained true to the biological inspiration which lay behind psychoanalytic theory through-out his life. Sometimes he even seemed to discount the secondary role which psychoanalysis continued to ascribe to environmental factors. 'Constitution is everything,' he remarked to Ludwig Binswanger on the occasion of his eightieth birthday.[55] A small but significant minority of Freud's admirers have actually gone against the larger trend and pointed to the biological basis of Freudian theory as one of its most important assets. Alex Comfort, for example, describes Freud as 'profoundly hard-centred by inclination – one of the hardest ever'. He goes on to suggest that this is why 'he appeals more to biologists than his successors.'[56] A similar point is made by Philip Rieff in his *Freud: The Mind of the Moralist*:

> No doubt many of Freud's personal biases are frozen into his instinct theory ... But his instinctualism is chiefly what gives an admirable sharpness to his estimate of human nature, and makes it more valuable as a defense of the individual than the critique of his position ... carried out by such neo-Freudians as Karen Horney and Erich Fromm ... The liberal revisers of Freud, in their efforts to avoid the pessimistic implications of his genetic reasoning, tend to let the idea of the individual be absorbed into the social, or at best to permit it a vague and harried existence. Freud himself – through his mythology of the instincts – kept some part of character safe from society, restoring to the idea of human nature a hard core, not easily warped or reshaped by social experience.[57]

As Rieff suggests, however, there are many modern versions of psychoanalysis in which the biological origins of Freud's theory of infantile sexuality have been either obscured or entirely suppressed. Some of the resulting confusion was cleared up by Sulloway in 1979, and his book remains the only study which has considered the influence of Haeckel on Freud's thought in any detail. As a commentator who is apparently sympathetic to sociobiological approaches to human nature, however, Sulloway is not a disinterested observer, and the account he gives of Haeckel's theories is sometimes over-sympathetic. His general estimate of the influence of Darwinian ideas on Freud is an extremely positive one. '[P]erhaps nowhere,' he writes, 'was the impact of Darwin, direct and indirect, more exemplary or fruitful outside of biology proper than within Freudian psychoanalysis.'[58] Only when we recognise the wildly speculative nature of Haeckel's reasoning about child psychology does the full significance of Freud's dependence on this particular brand of Darwinism become clear. For the unretouched version of Haeckel's 'biogenetic law' which I have tried to present here is so strange that, if there were not so many other examples of Freud's credulity, it would be difficult to believe that so influential a thinker ever seriously entertained such a hypothesis, let alone based his entire intellectual system upon it.

In view of the shakiness of the foundations on which the whole edifice of psychoanalytic theory is constructed it is perhaps not surprising that the psychoanalytic movement has tended to obscure the exact outline of these foundations and has sometimes even denied their existence. Instead of admitting that his theories were actually *inspired* by contemporary biological theories, Freud himself – without, perhaps, consciously intending to deceive – made use of an ingenious intellectual stratagem: after first using biogenetic logic in private in order to create his theoretical 'treasure' and bury it, he subsequently used the methods of psychoanalysis in order to ceremoniously dig it up and present it in public.

By systematically suppressing the biological origins of his theories, Freud was able to claim to have mined out independently, using the perilous and heroic methods of psychoanalysis, the most humanly significant aspect of the same 'truth' which other investigators had already located using the ostensibly safer methods of biology. What Freud never calculated upon was that the ideas which he had stolen from evolutionary biology as theoretical gold, and buried in his own psychoanalytic garden, would disintegrate in the course of time into the mere ash of speculation. Yet this was what happened when Haeckel's biogenetic law was discredited or repudiated by professional biologists. Many of Freud's followers reacted to this intellectual impasse by rejecting or trying to ignore the biological foundations of the theory while attempting to maintain the psychological structure which had been constructed on them. Freud's own reaction was more stubborn and showed a kind of grim realism. When Ernest Jones once tried to dissuade him from publicly supporting a Lamarckian theory of evolution, Freud obstinately persisted, claiming that the neo-Darwinian biologists were 'all wrong'.[59] In view of the way in which Lamarckian theory is blent together with the biogenetic law in the theory of infantile sexuality, Freud was maintaining the only possible intellectual course. For to accept that the neo-Darwinian biologists were right would entail the much more painful recognition that psychoanalysis was wrong.

ELEVEN

Exploring the Unconscious: Self-Analysis and Oedipus

ALTHOUGH SOME OF the key features of Freud's theory of infantile sexuality are apparent in the letters to Fliess written during the years 1896 and 1897, it took Freud a long time to develop the theory fully and it was not until 1905 that he actually published it. But from about 1897 onwards this incomplete theory of infantile sexuality, together with the biogenetic law from which it derived, were major factors shaping almost all his theoretical speculations and psychoanalytic investigations.

The thread of continuity which joins Freud's relationship with Fliess to his mature theorising has been obscured by psychoanalytic legend. The chief author of this particular legend, after Freud himself, was Ernest Jones. For in his biography Jones portrays Freud's intellectual infatuation with Fliess almost as a period of bewitchment – a period from which Freud eventually escaped in order to rejoin the realm of empirical science and rationality from which he had briefly strayed. That Freud should have subordinated his judgements and opinions to those of Fliess for so long was, in the view of Jones, unusual. 'But,' he wrote, carefully building a rhetorical crescendo, 'for that man [Freud] to free himself by following a path hitherto untrodden by any human being, by the heroic task of exploring his own unconscious mind: that is extraordinary in the highest degree.'[1]

According to Jones it was in the summer of 1897 that 'the spell began to break'. Only then, he implies, did Freud find the inner strength he needed to embark on the heroic feat of self-analysis. 'It is hard for us nowadays,' writes Jones of Freud's self-analysis, 'to imagine how momentous this achievement was, that difficulty being the fate of most pioneering exploits. Yet the uniqueness of the feat remains. Once done it is done for ever. For no one again can be the first to explore those depths.'[2] The impression we are left with is that Freud descended into the labyrinth of the Unconscious like a hero of old and emerged fearless and free, having slain the Minotaur of Fliess's occult influence with the sword of reason. This particular myth, however, stands reality on its head. For when Freud disappeared into the depths of the labyrinth, far from escaping the influence of Fliess, he was following in his foot-steps. The path which Fliess had already taken determined, in part at least, the nature of the 'discoveries' which Freud made. It also meant that the further Freud progressed the more lost he became in a maze of para-scientific Fliessian logic which was increasingly cut off from the real world – a maze from which he was never, in the end, able to escape.

It is only if we adopt this perspective, I believe, that we can under-stand the role which was played by Freud's self-analysis in the develop-ment of psychoanalysis. It is certainly not true to suggest, as psychoanalytic legend constantly does, that it was the self-analysis which led to the discovery of a hidden world of infantile sexuality. For, as Frank Sulloway has written, 'it is clear that [Freud] was already looking for evidence of childhood sexual activity in his own childhood . . . when he finally undertook this self-analysis.'[3]

One of the main purposes of Freud's self-analysis was to develop further the hypothesis which was playing a larger and larger role in Freud's thinking, and which would eventually accommodate almost the whole of psychoanalysis. This hypothesis, which Freud initially took over from Charcot and which he developed in his *Project for a Scientific Psychology*, held that there was a previously undiscovered region of the mind which, because of the crucial role it supposedly played in generating particular kinds of illness, was a legitimate subject for medical research. The mental region in question was, of course, the Unconscious.

There can be little doubt that postulating the existence of an uncon-scious mind was one of the most successful and plausible of all Freud's strategies. Not only has the hypothesis of an Unconscious been almost universally accepted within the psychoanalytic movement, but it has also appealed to some of Freud's critics. It is interesting, for example, that the philosopher Ernest Gellner, who has written so sceptically and well about psychoanalysis, singles out the thesis of the Unconscious as one aspect of psychoanalytic theory which he believes to be true.[4] The reasons why the notion of the Unconscious has found such favour are not difficult to establish. For even the most casual acquaintance with human behaviour suggests that human beings are frequently unaware of their motives, that they habitually hide feelings, emotions and desires, and that they tend to be driven by impulses or needs which rationalistic estimates of human nature usually fail to recognise. Since we deceive ourselves so frequently about our own motives, and since it is undeniably true that we tend not to be fully conscious of our motives most of the time, it is entirely reasonable to point out that human behaviour is profoundly influenced by forces or factors of which we are not conscious.

The originator of *this* idea, however, was most certainly not Freud. For the notion that some aspects of the self are sometimes hidden from ordinary consciousness is as old, almost, as human consciousness itself. Versions of the idea were put forward by Plotinus in the third century, by St Augustine in the fourth, and by countless other thinkers in practically every century since.[5] When Pascal wrote that 'the heart has its reasons which reason knows not', he was making the point succinctly, while Shakespeare frequently alluded in his poetry to the unknown and at times apparently unknowable depths of the self:

> My affection hath an unknown bottom, like the bay of Portugal.
> (*As You Like It*, IV, i, 212)

> My mind is troubled, like a fountain stirr'd;
> And I myself see not the bottom of it.
> (*Troilus and Cressida*, III, iii, 311).

'Our clear concepts,' wrote Leibniz in the seventeenth century, 'are but islands which rise above the oceans of obscure ones.' A very similar image was developed, probably quite independently, by the nineteenth-century Scottish art critic, E. S. Dallas:

> Outside consciousness there rolls a vast tide of life which is perhaps more important to us than the little isle of our thoughts which lies within our ken ... Each is necessary to the other ... Between our unconscious and our conscious existence there is a free and a constant, but unobserved traffic for ever carried on.[6]

What Dallas points out here, and what many others had pointed out before him, is that the capacity for conscious awareness to which we tend to attribute such huge powers is in some respects a very narrow ability with a relatively small focus. At any one time most individuals tend to be *unconscious* of most of their experience, desires, feelings and memories, as they concentrate on whichever physical or mental task they have in hand. The self, together with its memories and experiences, may in this respect be compared to a many-roomed mansion with only one occupant; most of the rooms will remain unentered and unobserved for most of the time. Not only this but some parts of the imagination are, because of the power of taboo, more shrouded in darkness than others; there are forbidden rooms in the self which, like the chamber in Bluebeard's castle, are opened only rarely and perhaps only furtively in the dark secrecy of the individual consciousness.

This understanding of the self as a complex and by no means entirely rational entity, in which certain appetites, impulses and inclinations are subject to taboo, or are represented as impure and unclean, has a very wide currency indeed. For something like it can be found in countless different historical periods in a wide variety of different cultures, both Western and non-Western. Indeed, so ordinary is the model and so pervasive, that we sometimes do not recognise its existence any more than we are given to noticing the air that we breathe. We maintain it, for the most part, intuitively rather than formally, and because it is felt in its strongest form by those who are most imaginatively fluent, it is probably recognised more readily by children and by the untutored than it is by philosophers and psychologists.

Yet although the model is held in its strongest and fullest version informally, a recognisable adaptation of it could for centuries be found expressed in Judaeo-Christian dualism, with its vision of human beings riven by a conflict between the flesh and the spirit, between good and evil. It was only when this traditional picture of the human self was gradually destroyed by the rise of Protestant rationalism in general, and scientific rationalism in particular, that modern 'psychologically empty' models of the human self were adopted on a significant scale. For, as Enlightenment rationalism and materialism gradually gained intellectual ascendancy during the eighteenth and nineteenth centuries, views of the self began to emerge which, either implicitly or explicitly, denied the reality of almost all aspects of human nature which could be deemed 'irrational'.

One cultural reaction to the triumph of Enlightenment rationalism came in the form of Romanticism – and perhaps above all in the rise of the Gothic novel with its stress on all those irrational, dark or demonic aspects of human nature which rationalism had implicitly repudiated. Unfortified by any form of science, however, Gothic

Romanticism posed no real threat to the hegemony of rationalism. An alternative response was to encase romantic rebellion within the rhetoric of rationalism and to present it as though it were itself a contribution to the scientific study of human nature. It was this kind of cultural impulse which, in the decades immediately preceding the emergence of psychoanalysis, led to the gradual adoption by philosophers and psychologists of the word 'unconscious' as a kind of technical term.

By the time Freud started formulating the principles of psychoanalysis during the closing years of the nineteenth century both the general notion of there being aspects of the self of which we are not conscious, and the specific term 'unconscious' were well established. In developing the idea of unconscious mental processes he was therefore following a cultural trend rather than starting one.

Largely because Freud's concept of the unconscious appeared to embrace many of those irrational or demonic aspects of human nature which had been implicitly repudiated by Protestant rationalism it possessed very considerable psychological resonance. If Freud had himself grasped the nature of his achievement it might well have been genuinely illuminating. But the founder of psychoanalysis had little or no understanding of the huge cultural and historical forces of which his own outlook was a product. Instead of recognising the traditional basis of his psychology, he genuinely believed he was making a new scientific discovery. It was partly in order to preserve this precious illusion that he did almost exactly what he had done in the case of his concept of catharsis: he reintroduced an ancient intuitive view only after he had first both medicalised and technicalised it.

What was novel in Freud's theories was that, instead of simply accepting the ancient intuitive insight that some aspects of the self were less accessible to the conscious mind than others, he put forward the idea that there was a mental entity whose specific function was to harbour our hidden thoughts, memories and impulses. He called this hypothetical entity 'the Unconscious' and treated it as an autonomous region of the mind 'with its own wishful impulses, its own mode of expression and its peculiar mental mechanisms which are not in force elsewhere'.[7] He simultaneously claimed that certain mental states became unconscious because they were 'repressed', that these repressed mental states might have pathological consequences and that the resulting illness could be cured by making conscious what had been unconscious. Freud further believed that in psychoanalysis he had discovered the one and only method by which this previously unknown region could be observed.

Given Freud's belief that psychoanalysis was, in the first place, a contribution to medical science, his understanding of the Unconscious as a repository of potentially pathogenic forces was extremely important. Since this understanding was based on the chain of mistaken medical reasoning about hysteria which we have already examined, it may be safely suggested that, in this respect at least, Freud's theory of the Unconscious was misleading. But this theory, while constantly sustained by its ostensible correspondence to traditional psychological insights, was also misleading in other respects.

The first point which needs to be made in relation to Freud's various claims is that the rational consciousness which we tend to take for granted is by no means the natural, 'biological' entity which Freud implies. For the kind of mental concentration which is the necessary precondition of our ability to perform complex mental tasks – such as working out a mathematical problem or learning a foreign language – is one which often has to be actively taught to children. By repeatedly being set a whole variety of different tasks, children are taught the general lesson that developing their attention-span and their ability to concentrate *against the grain of their own interests* is virtuous, and that lapses of attention are undesirable and even shameful. This lesson is taught from such an early age and inculcated so deeply that we rarely recognise the extent to which people spend their childhood acquiring what are, in effect, techniques of imaginative self-discipline. For it is only by learning to control a whole variety of interests, appetites, fantasies, desires and temptations and to banish these temporarily from our awareness that it is possible to develop the intelligent, clear and rational frame of mind which is idealised within our culture.

The fact that we frequently hide or control certain desires, inclinations and appetites, and have developed a work ethic which idealises such self-control, should not, however, lead us to conclude that all those aspects of the self which are subject to this kind of restraint are banished from consciousness altogether. One of the appetites which children learn to control at a relatively early age is that of hunger. In very young infants the capacity to deny, suppress or temporarily frustrate hunger seems to be scarcely present at all. As a result young children appear to be unable to defend themselves against the periodic invasion of their consciousness by feelings of hunger, which tend to be disruptive of all other behaviour. Gradually, however, children learn that the instant satisfaction of hunger is neither practicable nor socially desirable, and they tend to be strongly rewarded if they resist such feelings. Yet the observation that most children quickly learn to deny feelings of hunger and to postpone gratification is unlikely to lead us to conclude that these feelings are entirely repressed or cast into some dark region of the mind from which they cannot be retrieved by human consciousness. For although the capacity to repress feelings and appetites may be biologically necessary to the survival of the human species, the capacity to reverse such repression is, self-evidently, an even greater biological necessity.

What is true of the realm of food and hunger applies with even greater force to the realm of sexuality. Partly because they are even more disruptive both of the demands of work and of the bonds of the family, sexual impulses are subject, in almost all human cultures, to even more severe taboos than hunger. But although these taboos have the effect of making it psychologically easier for individuals to banish sexual thoughts from their minds in certain contexts, it would once again be a great mistake to treat such repression as a permanent feature of human consciousness. The very fact that sexual behaviour has not died out altogether is evidence to the contrary. For sexual intercourse among humans is not a reflex act powered purely by biological instincts of which we remain unconscious. It is a pre-eminently *conscious* form of behaviour, in which the ability to use the sexual imagination and to fantasise consciously about sexual activity appears to be a precondition of full orgasmic potency.

Freud himself did not deny the possibility of mental traffic between the conscious and the unconscious mind, and even gave the name 'preconscious' to describe a vestibule which supposedly existed between the two areas of the mind. In general, however, the theory of 'repression' which he worked out inclined him to regard certain impulses as belonging almost exclusively to the unconscious mind and as gaining access to the conscious mind only after they had been rendered cryptic by the process of censorship.

This does not mean that Freud regarded the act of repression itself as an entirely unconscious process. His early theory saw the repression of traumatic memories as originating in an 'act of will', in which individuals deliberately set out to drive certain thoughts out of their minds. But although he saw some repression as being consciously *instigated*, he did not believe that repression remained under conscious control. In his view a person who has supposedly suffered a pathogenic trauma could not generally recall it without psychoanalytic assistance. For according to Freud, 'The idea in question was forced out of consciousness and out of memory. The psychical trace of it was apparently lost to view. Nevertheless that trace must be there.' The task of the psychoanalyst was to encourage patients to retrieve or reconstruct 'memories' which they had supposedly repressed by focusing on their putative psychical 'traces'.[8]

Far from modifying this early theory of repression in order to recognise the subtlety, depth and relative efficiency of human memory and human consciousness, Freud's later theories continued to stress *unconscious* processes of repression. In particular he laid increasing emphasis on the manner in which sexual and instinctual impulses were supposedly subjected to automatic biological repression in the course of individual development.

Freud's belief that repression was sustained by biological forces, or by a quantity of psychical energy, stopped him from recognising the extent to which individuals differ greatly in the degree to which they have internalised cultural taboos, and that some individuals, who are temperamentally given to defying taboos, have a much greater capacity to explore the obscene levels of their own imagination than others.

For one of the most striking aspects of the sexual imagination is the degree to which its susceptibility to restraint differs from one individual to another. The extraordinary ferocity of the taboos which can be levelled against sexual behaviour in our culture certainly does have the effect of banishing the most obscene levels of the human imagination from most public contexts. Nor is the effect of such taboos limited to the public sphere. For it is clear that some people are so stricken by the fear and anxiety with which they have been taught to regard sexuality that they find immense difficulty in 'connecting' themselves with their own sexual impulses or in allowing these into consciousness at all without acute feelings of guilt. Other individuals, however, although they may themselves have been subjected to a great deal of anti-sexual propaganda, and although this may be effective at the level of public behaviour, have relatively little difficulty in exploring in the privacy of their own consciousness even the most extreme and obscene levels of the imagination. Indeed, there exists in our own culture, and has always existed in most other cultures, an entire sub-culture of pornographic or erotic literature and art, *one* of whose cultural functions appears to be that of unfreezing the sexual imagination and thus enabling people to explore – in the secrecy of the individual imagination – the entire realm of the obscene.

Freud, who was himself very much a prisoner of the respectability he believed he had transcended, was curiously reluctant to acknowledge such variations in people's ability to make their sexual imagination conscious. His theoretical preconceptions reinforced this reluctance. For his belief that the Unconscious was a discrete area of the mind to which the techniques of psychoanalysis could alone give access led inevitably to the conclusion that the sexual imagination of individuals was hidden from the ordinary observer and that neither introspection, nor analysis of the behaviour of human beings could, in itself, lead to any ultimate psychological truth. For in psychoanalysis human behaviour and human consciousness are treated as intrinsically misleading phenomena which are supposedly devoid of meaning until they have been illuminated by insights drawn from a secret inner realm – which is dominated by sexuality and which is supposedly accessible and intelligible only to those trained in psychoanalysis.

The plausibility of this view of human nature derives in part from the fact that, even though our deepest sexual and emotional impulses may, contrary to Freudian assumptions, frequently be *accessible* to the conscious mind, this does not mean that we automatically understand them or accord them their full significance in the formal or informal theories we hold about human nature. One reason for this is that, while it is relatively easy to slip free of the constraints of respectability in the privacy of the individual consciousness, the realm of public discourse to which our theories of human nature generally belong usually falls victim to these constraints. The duality of our private and public lives in this respect was well characterised by Thomas Hobbes, writing in *Leviathan* more than two centuries before Freud:

> The secret thoughts of a man run over all things, holy, profane, clean, obscene, grave and light, without shame or blame; which verbal discourse cannot do, farther than the judgment shall approve of the time, place, and persons. An anatomist, or a physician, may speak or write his judgment of unclean things; because it is not to please or profit: but for another man to write his extravagant, and pleasant fancies of the same, is as if a man, from being tumbled into the dirt, should come and present himself before good company. And it is the want of discretion that makes the difference.[9]

It is not only respectability, however, which contributes to our riven consciousness. For the attitude which Hobbes points to has been powerfully inscribed in our intellectual tradition, and rationalistic hostility to the entire realm of emotional and sexual behaviour pervades both our formal and our informal theorising about human nature. As a result we have immense difficulty in formulating satisfactory explanations of our own behaviour.

The difficulty we have in formulating *satisfactory* explanations of our behaviour, however, does not stop us clinging anxiously to unsatisfactory ones. Frequently indeed we are unaware of our true motives not because the evidence for these is locked up in some hidden mental region but because we have followed the extremely common pattern of formulating an incorrect theory about our own behaviour which, by carefully selecting some evidence, has made other equally accessible evidence seem obscure.

It is the fact that we so frequently deceive ourselves about our own motives in this way, and that most people show a marked tendency to minimise the role played in their own lives by powerful emotions and 'obscene' sexual impulses, which makes psychoanalysis both so plausible and so attractive. One of the central objections to Freud's methodology, however, is that by positing the existence of an Unconscious he effectively deepens the very mysteries which he claims to unravel. For the Unconscious is not simply an occult entity for whose real existence there is no palpable evidence. It is an illusion produced by language – a kind of intellectual hallucination.

Of course there are occasions when it is tempting to claim that a person has an 'unconscious memory' of a particular incident or that somebody feels 'unconscious rage' towards another person. Yet although the terms 'unconscious memory' and 'unconscious rage' may seem expressive and useful, we should recognise that they are semantically treacherous. A memory is something you have remembered and it defies logic to characterise as a memory something whose salient characteristic is that it has actually been forgotten. A similar objection applies to the term 'unconscious rage' since to use this term is to apply a word denoting the uninhibited expression of anger to a situation defined by the fact that no anger has been expressed.

In order to extricate ourselves from these treacherous semantic sands we need to consider the conditions under which our imperfect use of language would still communicate effectively. If we use the misleading term 'unconscious rage' then its meaning will remain reasonably clear so long as it is understood to refer to the emotional state of a person who has undergone an experience of the kind which might normally be expected to elicit an angry response but which in this case did not. The crucial point here is that an expression which appears to refer to invisible mental events, or to an invisible mental state, is meaningful only so long as we recognise that it is actually part of a statement about human behaviour. The great danger in using such mentalistic language is that the more we use it, the more we habituate ourselves to the deformation of logic which it embodies, and the more likely we are to treat expressions such as 'unconscious rage' and 'unconscious memory' as though they referred to real entities located mysteriously in a hypothetical region of the self.

It was into the quicksands of just such an assumption that Freud progressively betrayed himself by his own use of such language and by his tendency to technicalise expressions which, left in the realm of the colloquial, would be unlikely to wreak conceptual havoc. Not only did he assume that there was a real invisible entity called the Unconscious, but he further assumed that, if intrepid explorers could penetrate into the interior of this uncharted land, they would discover the various strangulated and suppressed motives and desires which had been banished from the conscious mind, freely disporting themselves in an entirely unstrangulated and unsuppressed manner. Just as Charcot had done before him, Freud found that by postulating the existence of this sunken continent he was able to solve a number of his theoretical problems at a stroke. At the same time the concept of the Unconscious provided an ideal research agenda for the nascent science of psychoanalysis. For he now went on to claim that in psychoanalysis in general, and in the technique of free-association in particular, he had discovered a unique method whereby the newly discovered continent could actually be observed and mapped. The purpose of his self-analysis was to carry out such mapping while at the same time seeking to resolve some of his own neurotic traits. Not the least important aspect of it was that he conducted it primarily by an analysis of his own dreams.

Freud's interest in dreams pre-dated the creation of psychoanalysis but he began to integrate it with his work as a neurologist during the time he was collaborating with Breuer on the problem of hysteria. He discovered that when he asked his patients to free-associate they would frequently relate dreams or allude to them. As a result Freud began to see dreams as having a special relationship to the Unconscious and affording a kind of privileged access to it. By analysing his own dreams he believed that he was not simply investigating his own unconscious but that he was actually making discoveries which, in some cases at least might be universally valid.

The great advantage of this intellectual strategy was that through it Freud had stumbled upon a way of providing his own hypotheses and theoretical speculations with a pseudo-empirical basis. For by assuming the existence of a previously unobserved entity and by claiming that he was in possession of the only investigative instrument through which this entity could be explored, Freud placed himself in a position where he could himself supply evidence to 'substantiate' practically any theory he chose to formulate. The intellectual consequences which flowed from this arrangement are perhaps best understood if we note the resemblance between the orthodox empirical scientist and the honest entrepreneur. Whenever an orthodox scientist constructs a theoretical explanation of some aspect of the natural world, he is, we might say, seeking to fund a new venture by writing out a theoretical cheque. This cheque is likely to be honoured by his bank only if the entrepreneur has deposited sufficient evidence in his account. If he overdraws on his account the bank will, as a publicly regulated body, be forced to intervene, the cheque will bounce and the scientist's theoretical venture will fail through lack of funds. Freud's achievement was to find a way around the regulatory mechanisms of normal empirical science. The way in which he did this was, in effect, to set up his own private bank. What this meant was that, however large were the sums for which he wrote out his theoretical cheques, his bank would always ensure that the funds of evidence needed to honour these cheques were available – if necessary by printing its own currency. Since Freud could transfer evidence into his account at will the only constraint on his theoretical adventurousness was the scepticism of the public. So long as his own private bank went through the outward motions of respectable scientific banking, confidence in the currency it issued would be maintained and its counterfeit nature would not be universally suspected. While Freud was, in reality, running up a huge evidential overdraft he could appear in public as a man of vast scientific wealth and substance. Most importantly of all, the complexity and ingenuity of these banking arrangements meant that Freud, whose gullibility in such matters we have already witnessed, was actually able to persuade himself of his ultimate scientific solvency. As a result of this genuine act of self-deception he was ideally placed to persuade others as well.

The full intricacy and the ultimate fragility of the vast intellectual empire which Freud constructed in this way would only begin to become apparent with the publication of his *Three Essays* in 1905. But the insecure foundations of this empire were laid as soon as Freud moved from the unexceptionable observation that people's emotional reactions to traumatic events were sometimes repressed to the unwarrantable assumption that an entity called the Unconscious exists and can be exclusively observed by the methods of psychoanalysis. For the first role Freud called upon his newly postulated Unconscious to play was that of providing evidence to support the theories of infantile sexuality which he had begun to formulate during the period of his correspondence with Fliess. Like Fliess he assumed that certain biologically innate sexual impulses were destined by the biogenetic law to be repressed from consciousness as being incompatible with the sexual organisation of adults. Reasoning that these would be relegated to the Unconscious, he set out to discover them.

One of the most important of the developments which now took place was Freud's formulation of the Oedipus complex. Although this development was first reported in public in *The Interpretation of Dreams*, it originally came about, like much else in that book, as a result of Freud's efforts in self-analysis in the autumn of 1897. It has generally been presented as a 'discovery' which Freud made spontaneously while sifting through the dreams and childhood memories which furnished him with the materials for this analysis. Ernest Jones introduces it as the breakthrough which allowed Freud to escape from the tyranny of his seduction theory and the suspicions he had been forced to focus on his own father. 'He had now recognised,' writes Jones, 'that his father was innocent, and that he had projected onto him ideas of his own. Memories had come back of sexual wishes about his mother on the occasion of seeing her naked ... He had discovered in himself the passion for his mother and jealousy of his father; he felt sure that this was a general human characteristic ...'[10]

If we place Jones's account of the discovery of the Oedipus complex alongside Freud's own words, however, we find that Freud's version is significantly different. Freud writes that, between the age of two and two and a half, 'my libido towards *matrem* was awakened, namely on the occasion of a journey with her from Leipzig to Vienna, during which we must have spent the night together and there must have been an opportunity of seeing her *nudam* (you inferred the consequences of this for your son long ago as a remark revealed to me) . . .'[11] From this passage it is reasonably clear that when Jones wrote that 'memories had come back of sexual wishes about his mother on the occasion of seeing her naked', he was engaged in the characteristic psychoanalytic activity of 'empiricising' something which was not actually part of Freud's experience at all. For Freud, it would seem, had remembered neither seeing his mother naked nor being sexually aroused. He had remembered only a long train journey from whose duration he *deduced* that he might have seen his mother undressing. His further deduction that he was sexually aroused by this hypothetical sight is based, as he himself indicates, on something which Fliess had already told him. He is referring, in fact, to Fliess's report that his son Robert had an erection at a similar age – supposedly as a result of seeing his mother naked.[12]

Less than two weeks after he had confided this artificially reconstructed memory to his friend Fliess, Freud used it as the basis for a universal law which he first formulated in another letter to Fliess. 'Being totally honest with oneself,' he writes, 'is a good exercise. A single idea of general value dawned on me. I have found in my own case too [the phenomenon of] being in love with my mother and jealous of my father, and I now consider it a universal event in early childhood.' Freud went on to refer to 'the gripping power' of *Oedipus Rex*, suggesting that the drama drew its potency from the fact that it seized on a compulsion which everyone recognises. 'Everyone in the audience was once a budding Oedipus in fantasy and each recoils in horror from the dream fulfilment here transplanted into reality . . .'[13]

According to Freud's subsequent formulation, the impulse which lies at the heart of the Oedipus complex emerges gradually during the phallic phase of sexual development:

When a boy (from the age of two or three) has entered the phallic phase of his libidinal development, is feeling pleasurable sensations in his sexual organ and has learnt to procure these at will by manual stimulation, he becomes his mother's lover. He wishes to possess her physically in such ways as he has divined from his observations and intuitions about sexual life, and he tries to seduce her by showing her the male organ which he is proud to own. In a word his early awakened masculinity seeks to take his father's place with her . . . His father now becomes a rival who stands in his way and whom he would like to get rid of.[14]

According to Freud the boy's sexual interest in his mother will eventually be met with the threat of castration. In the face of this horrifying threat, the boy abandons his sexual designs upon his mother, identifies with the father, and eventually seeks sexual satisfaction from other women.

There can be little doubt that the idea of the Oedipus complex, particularly when delivered from Freud's own improbably circumstantial and concrete account, was one of the most interesting of all Freud's psychological formulations. The idea has a resonance which has certainly been taken by some to indicate that it contains a genuine psychological insight.

One of the reasons Freud's formulation of the Oedipus complex has been so widely accepted is that it appears to encompass many aspects of the most intense of all human relationships, one which is fraught with complexity and a great deal of emotional ambivalence. At the same time Freud's idea boldly breaks the taboo which led some Victorians to deny the significance of the mother–son relationship altogether. Not only does it postulate that this supposedly non-sexual relationship possesses a sexual dimension, but it also seems to offer an explanation of the ambivalence of the relationship by suggesting that this initial sexual relationship will inevitably be overlaid by repression and denial. Yet, as in the case of the Unconscious, Freud's formulation of the Oedipus complex has a resonance and an intuitive appeal which, if we examine it sceptically, bears very little relation to its actual explanatory power.

For in formulating the Oedipus complex, as in every other aspect of his theorising, Freud continued to rely on the quasi-mechanical schema of biological development which he had worked out in the course of his correspondence with Fliess. What this meant is that, although Freud himself seems to have sensed the resonance of his concept, the concept itself was narrow and in many respects anti-psychological. Because of his own fixed views about the relationship of sexual instincts to biology, he saw the son's supposed sexual attraction to his mother not as a part of a complex emotional relationship developed as a result of nurture, but as a merely instinctual impulse – a developmental phase through which all human males automatically passed, in almost exactly the same way that they would later pass through puberty.

The resonance of the idea remained, and Freud himself played upon this resonance when he presented it in public. But ultimately his formulation excluded and implicitly denied the levels of emotional complexity it evoked. It is undeniably true that the relationship between parents and their children is often, in strict biological terms, potentially a sexual relationship. It is also clear that in all human cultures there are powerful taboos against incest. These taboos, however, are directed primarily not against young children but against their parents. It would, indeed, seem reasonable to suggest that the sexual identity and sexual feelings both of the mother and the father – or more precisely the powerful cultural need to control, negate or suppress these feelings – will play a significant role in shaping their relationship to their children. By focusing instead on entirely hypothetical sexual impulses felt by very young *children* towards their parents, Freud was effectively inverting this pattern. This distortion was pointed out long ago by the American anthropologist George Devereux, when he suggested that psychoanalysis tendentiously ignored what he called the *Laius complex*. He assumes that this failure to deal with the role of the parents

> is rooted in the adult's deep-seated need to place all responsibility for the Oedipus complex upon the child, and to ignore, whenever possible, certain parental attitudes which actually stimulate the infant's Oedipal tendencies. This deliberate scotoma is probably rooted in the authoritarian atmosphere characteristic of nineteenth-century family life . . .[15]

Devereux's criticism is a relatively conservative one since he evidently accepts that Freud's formulation contains a fundamental truth, and refers to 'the infant's Oedipal tendencies' as though to an established biological fact. There is no evidence at all, however, to suggest that a boy's sexual feelings towards his mother, in so far as such feelings are not suppressed or redirected by the power of taboo, are at their strongest or most significant between the ages of three and five. Nor is there any evidence to suggest that sexual feelings at this age take the form of a desire for coitus. What is perhaps even more important is that the whole idea of separating out a purely biological dimension of the mother–son relationship seems misconceived. The very strength of the incest-taboo and the religious fierceness with which it is upheld in every human culture, not excluding our own, means that it affects practically all child-rearing behaviour. In particular the taboo has a powerful influence on the manner in which parents may legitimately express affection towards their children. It thus tends to shape and render psychologically complex almost every aspect of the ostensibly non-sexual or counter-sexual relationship which parents establish with their children. Any empirically based psychological theory would, of necessity, depend on close observation and analysis of the immensely complex pattern of child-rearing behaviour which results. Such a study would include a detailed survey of parents' own conscious attitudes, beliefs, fantasies and anxieties about their relationship to their children.

By far the most extraordinary feature of Freud's own theories is their almost complete disregard for any such empirical factors. Because so much subsequent research into the child–parent relationship has been projected back onto the figure of Freud, this aspect of his work is frequently obscured. Yet, as Morton Schatzman has pointed out, even in the case of Little Hans, when Freud was supposedly conducting an analysis of a child, the manner in which Hans was treated by his parents was almost systematically ignored.[16]

It was partly because Freud, through his theory of the Unconscious, had created his own limitless fund of pseudo-empirical evidence that he was able to construct a theory like that of the Oedipus complex, which, for all its resonance and its superficial congruence with one or two of the observed facts of human behaviour, actually runs counter to the mass of evidence which is available.

Some psychoanalysts have themselves commented on the deficiencies of the Oedipus complex. One of the most interesting comments was made by Erich Fromm when he saw in Freud's formulation a rationalistic attempt to avoid facing up to the emotional intensity of his relationship to his own mother:

> This intense attachment of Freud to his mother, most of which he concealed from others, and probably from himself, is of the greatest importance not only for the understanding of Freud's character, but also for the appreciation of one of his fundamental discoveries, that of the Oedipus complex. Freud explained the attachment to the mother – quite rationalistically – as being based on the sexual attraction of the little boy to the woman with whom he is most intimate. But, considering the intensity of his attachment to his own mother, and the fact that he tended to repress it, it is understandable that he interpreted one of the most powerful strivings in man, the craving for the care, protection and all-enveloping love and affirmation of Mother, as the more limited wish of the little boy to satisfy his instinctual needs through Mother. He discovered one of the most fundamental strivings in man, the wish to remain attached to Mother, and that is to the womb, to nature, to

pre-individualistic, pre-conscious existence – and at the same time he negated this very discovery by restricting it to the small sector of instinctual desires. His own attachment to Mother was the basis of his discovery and his resistance to seeing his attachment was the basis for the limitation and distortion of this very discovery.[17]

In this passage Fromm certainly points to the way in which Freud has substituted a narrow concept for a complex psychological reality. Yet it is by no means clear that Fromm's own view of the psychological reality in question is any more satisfactory. His bland references to 'Mother' – as though mothers were the incarnation of some impersonal life-force – and his willingness to analyse the mother–son relationship in terms of vague abstractions suggest that his own thinking about it has been shaped by the limitations of the very theory he criticises.

Yet in spite of the many objections which it is possible to level against Freud's theory of the Oedipus complex, some of which were actually made by contemporary critics, Freud was unmoved. Although the claims he made for the theory were initially modest, they progressively became more and more grandiose so that towards the latter part of his career he wrote, with a fervour and self-belief which were truly messianic, that 'if psychoanalysis could boast of no other achievement than the discovery of the repressed Oedipus complex, that alone would give it a claim to be included among the precious new acquisitions of mankind.'[18]

Freud's deluded confidence in the explanatory power of the Oedipus complex was constantly sustained by his central fiction of the Unconscious. But this fiction was in turn intimately dependent on the theory of dreams which Freud worked out during the closing years of the nineteenth century. The dream theory was one of the most important parts of the intellectual banking system which Freud had devised in order to create the illusion of intellectual solvency. No external audit of the psychoanalytic movement would be complete without a close examination of the kind of intellectual transaction on which this theory rested.

TWELVE

Dreams and Symptoms

ONE OF THE REASONS Freud invested the Oedipus complex with such significance was that in it he believed he had discovered a formula through which he could unite the realm of psychopathology with his growing interest in the creation of a general psychological theory. In its role as a 'pathogen' the complex eventually came virtually to take over the place in Freud's theory of neurosis which had originally been occupied by traumatic experiences in general and sexual traumas in particular. By regarding his new formulation in this way Freud was belatedly able to represent the collapse of his seduction theory not as a failure but as one more step along the path which led to yet another of those putatively great discoveries which he regularly believed he had made. For he eventually realised that he could present the seduction scenes which he had fancifully reconstructed (and which at first scarcely involved fathers at all) as the unrecognised precipitates of incestuous fantasising on the part of his patients. It was this legendary and truth-defying view which he put forward in 1925 in his 'Autobiographical Study'.

> It could not be disputed that I had arrived at these scenes by a technical method which I considered correct, and their subject-matter was unquestionably related to the symptoms from which my investigation had started. When I had pulled myself together, I was able to draw the right conclusions from my discovery: namely that the neurotic symptoms were not related directly to actual events but to wishful fantasies, and that as far as the neurosis was concerned psychical reality was of more importance than material reality. I do not believe even now that I forced the seduction fantasies on my patients, that I 'suggested' them. I had in fact stumbled for the first time upon the *Oedipus complex*, which was later to assume such an overwhelming importance, but which I did not recognise as yet in its disguise of fantasy.[1]

259

The crucial pathogenic role which was supposedly played by the Oedipus complex in neurotic illnesses was one which Freud repeatedly stressed. 'The Oedipus complex,' he wrote, 'may justly be regarded as the nucleus of the neuroses.'[2] At the same time, however, he saw the task of growing through and dealing with this complex as a normal feature of both psychological and biological development. The formulation thus belonged to the universalising tendency through which Freud was now beginning to link his original purely medical orientation to an increasingly ambitious attempt to construct a general theory of psychological development.

It was, it would seem, a similar impulse which lay behind his interest in the phenomenon of dreaming. For this too appeared to offer a means of linking the realm of psychopathology to normal psychology. Freud's first published reference to dreams occurs in one of the many notes which he appended to his translation of Charcot's *Leçons du Mardi*. Here he compared dreams to hysterical deliria, and saw both as elaborations of thoughts which had been inhibited, broken off or rejected by the normal waking consciousness. A letter which he wrote to Fliess in September 1895 indicates that by then he had already formulated the main principle which was to lie behind the argument he expounded in *The Interpretation of Dreams*. For he claimed that a recent dream had 'yielded the funniest confirmation of the conception that dreams are motivated by wish-fulfilment'.[3] It was this idea which he now proceeded to work out in great detail over the next few years.

Freud's interest in interpreting dreams was certainly not unprecedented. Indeed so many investigators had come before him that he felt obliged to preface his *Interpretation of Dreams* with a long survey of 'The Scientific Literature dealing with the Problems of Dreams'. Some of those who had made a study of dreams had put forward theories which bore a resemblance to the ideas which Freud eventually endorsed. Von Schubert, for example, in his *The Symbolism of Dreams*, had suggested that some dreams could only be understood as forms of wish-fulfilment. What was dramatic and potentially revolutionary about Freud's approach to dreams was that he sought to explain *all* dreams by a single formula.

In this respect Freud was submitting once again to what was perhaps the single most characteristic impulse in his scientific imagination – 'the longing to be able to open all secrets with a single key'.[4] If one source of this impulse was, as I have suggested, the germ theory of Pasteur and Koch, another was Freud's scientific education in the school of Helmholtz. For here he would have imbibed the principle of 'algorithmic compression' which, while it is scarcely appropriate to the biological sciences and still less to psychology, has always underpinned Newtonian and post-Newtonian physics. The principle held, in effect, that truly scientific explanations were inherently simple and that it was in the very nature of science to reduce complex phenomena to simple formulae – the classical example of an algorithm being $E = mc^2$. We have already seen how Freud's simplifying impulse led him first to assert that all 'actual neuroses' had a sexual cause and how he subsequently went further to claim that all hysterical illnesses had sexual origins. It was after he had made this latter theoretical leap that Breuer had characterised Freud as a man 'given to absolute and exclusive formulations' and saw him as driven by a 'psychical need' for 'excessive generalisation'. Now Freud's compulsion to submit complex phenomena to the tyranny of a single simple idea manifested itself again in his theory of dreaming. For with extraordinary audacity he put forward the idea not simply that *some* dreams were disguised wishfulfilments but that they *all* were. Not satisfied with this general claim Freud went further to assert quite specifically that dreams did not only represent current wishes, but that they were also invariably disguised expressions of infantile desires which had been repressed and stored in the Unconscious. 'Our theory of dreams,' he wrote, 'regards wishes originating in infancy as the indispensable motive force for the formation of dreams.'[5] If these infantile wishes – which were predominantly sexual in character – were expressed in an undisguised form, they would disturb the dreamer's sleep. Consequently they were censored and disguised and only allowed into consciousness in a cryptic form. The psychoanalyst's job was to strip dream-symbols of their disguise and thus to recover the pristine wishes and desires which they concealed.

Had Freud been content to apply this hypothesis only to its original object, his theory of dreams would have remained little more than an interesting offshoot of the psychoanalytic enterprise. Yet so enraptured did Freud become with his theory and so readily was he drawn to large explanatory schemes that he soon began to apply the theory of wish-fulfilment, which he had originally worked out in relation to the dreams of the healthy, to the symptoms of the unhealthy.

In his original aetiology of hysteria, as we have seen, Freud explained the origin of the physical symptoms suffered by his patients by postulating a complex physiological process whereby traumatic stress was subjected to a process of 'conversion'. The relationship between trauma and symptom was, on this view, an arbitrary one. Gradually, however, Freud began to develop the idea that symptoms might have some kind of intrinsic meaning so that, if they were interrogated in the right way, they would themselves proclaim their neurotic origin. As Malcolm Macmillan has noted, the first intimation of this new understanding of symptoms is contained in a letter which Freud wrote to Fliess in May 1896. Symptoms are not yet seen as representing wishes. But they are viewed as 'compromise formations' which reflect a conflict between uninhibited mental processes and the inhibitory force of thought.[6] On 17 December 1896 he gave his first example of a symptom which supposedly represented such a compromise. The symptom in question was 'anxiety about throwing oneself out of a window'. Freud suggested that this 'symptom' concealed an unconscious fantasy of 'going to the window to beckon a man to come up, as prostitutes do'. According to Freud, who was by now rarely able to resist his aetiological *idée fixe*, this idea would lead to a release of sexual pleasure. This pleasure would then be repudiated and anxiety would be the result. In the same letter Freud goes on to give another example of his new approach to symptoms. Although, characteristically, he produces no evidence to back up his claim, he writes that he had now 'actually confirmed' a conjecture he had entertained for some time about the mechanism of agoraphobia in women: 'No doubt you will guess it if you think of "public" women. It is the repression of the inter.tion to take the first man one meets in the street: envy of prostitution and identification.'[7] This attitude towards symptoms, in which they were regarded as a form of hieroglyph, bearing in themselves the imprint of the trauma or the desire in which they originated, appears again in a letter which Freud wrote in January 1897. It is here that Freud traces back a speech impediment associated with a full mouth to a putative act of fellatio committed on the patient by her father (see above, Chapter 9). By the end of May 1897 Freud explicitly formulated the idea that a symptom was the result of a libidinal impulse which had given rise to a subsequent wish for that impulse to be punished. 'Symptoms, like dreams,' he wrote to Fliess, 'are *the fulfilment of a wish*.'[8]

Freud's new explanation of symptoms seems to have disappeared temporarily with the collapse of the seduction theory. In 1899, however, he reintroduced it in his letters quite explicitly and described it as the 'key which opens many doors':

I want to reveal to you only that the dream schema is capable of the most general application, that the key to hysteria as well really lies in dreams ... Not only dreams are wish fulfilments, so are hysterical attacks. This is true of hysterical symptoms, but probably applies to every product of neurosis ... A symptom arises where the repressed and the repressing thought can come together in the fulfilment of a wish. The symptom is the wish fulfilment of the repressing thought, for example, in the form of a punishment.[9]

It is almost exactly the same account of symptom formation which Freud reproduces in *The Interpretation of Dreams*, in which he puts forward the supreme justification for devoting so much attention to the phenomenon of dreaming:

If such a thing as a system *Ucs.* [i.e. the Unconscious] exists ... dreams cannot be its only manifestation; every dream may be a wish-fulfilment, but apart from dreams there must be other forms of abnormal wish-fulfilments. And it is a fact that the theory governing all psychoneurotic symptoms culminates in a single proposition which asserts that *they too are to be regarded as fulfilments of unconscious wishes.* Our explanation makes the dream only the first member of a class which is of the greatest significance to psychiatrists and an understanding of which implies the solution of the purely psychological side of the problem of psychiatry.

The other members of this class of wish-fulfilments – hysterical symptoms, for instance – possess one essential characteristic, however, which I cannot discover in dreams. I have learnt from the researches which I have mentioned so often in the course of this work that in order to bring about the formation of a hysterical symptom *both* currents of our mind must converge ... The determinant which does not arise from the *Ucs.* is invariably, so far as I know, a train of thought reacting against the unconscious wish – a self-punishment, for instance. I can therefore make the quite general assertion that *a hysterical symptom develops only where the fulfilments of two opposing wishes, arising each from a different psychical system, are able to converge in a single expression.*[10]

Freud goes on to give the example of one of his women patients who suffered from persistent vomiting. Ruling out, as he habitually did, the numerous organic diagnoses which might have been made, Freud claimed that the woman's vomiting was the fulfilment of an unconscious fantasy dating from her puberty – 'of a wish that she might be continuously pregnant and have innumerable children, with a further wish, added later, that she might have them by as many men as possible.' According to Freud a powerful defensive impulse had sprung up in reaction to this wish. But in view of the fact that the woman 'might lose her figure and good looks as a result of vomiting, and so might cease to be attractive to anyone' the symptom was acceptable to this punitive impulse as well. Since it was acceptable to 'both sides' the symptom could become a reality.[11]

It was partly because of the crucial role which was played by Freud's theory of dreams in generating his psychiatric theories of symptom-formation and partly because of its supposed role in mapping the psychology of non-neurotic individuals that Freud made his celebrated pronouncement that '*The interpretation of dreams is the royal road to a knowledge of the unconscious activities of the mind.*'[12] It is because of the crucial role played by *The Interpretation of Dreams* in the entire architecture of psychoanalysis that the central thesis of the book and the quality of the arguments which Freud brought forward in order to elucidate both individual dreams and dream-symbols need to be briefly considered.

To claim that some dreams are wish-fulfilments would be merely a truism. For in some cases dreams transparently possess just such a character. To claim that every single dream was *clearly* of this nature would be to occupy a position it would be impossible to defend. But to claim, as Freud did, that all dreams were *disguised* wish-fulfilments was at least strategically feasible. For if the psychoanalyst himself made up the rules for decoding dreams, these could be formulated in such a way that dreams would always yield the desired conclusion even when their surface content suggested a quite different meaning. This was the strategy that Freud consciously, or unconsciously, adopted. If the strategy already seems familiar it may well be because of its close resemblance to Fliess's use of arithmetic.

While Fliess used a series of arithmetical transformations to change his key numbers 23 and 28 into any number he needed in order to prove the correctness of the formula, Freud juggled with symbols in a similar way so that even the most apparently frustrating, tragic or pessimistic dreams could be interpreted as secretly fulfilling some wish or desire of the dreamer. The English psychiatrist W. H. R. Rivers pointed to one of the most remarkable features of Freud's hermeneutic strategies early on in the development of the psychoanalytic movement. Although Rivers was sympathetic to Freud's enterprise, he drew attention to the fact that one of Freud's rules was that only the analyst, studying the dream as a whole, was in a position to decide whether a particular symbol in a dream should be interpreted in one way or its opposite. 'Such a method,' wrote Rivers, 'would reduce any other science to an absurdity, and doubts must be raised whether psychology can have methods of its own which would make it necessary to separate it from all other science and put it in a distinct category.'[13]

The force of this objection is best recognised by studying some of the ways Freud managed to argue even the most seemingly unruly dreams into conformity with his narrow principle. Most glaring of all are the examples in which entire dreams are, as it were, picked up bodily and turned upon their heads. At one point in *The Interpretation of Dreams* Freud cites the case of a young woman who was violently averse to the idea of spending her summer holidays near her mother-in-law and who had recently successfully avoided this possibility by booking rooms for herself in a distant resort. Soon after Freud had explained to her that dreams were invariably fulfilments of wishes she reported a dream in which she found herself travelling down with her mother-in-law to the place where they were going to spend their holiday together. 'Was not this,' writes Freud, 'the sharpest possible contradiction of my theory that in dreams wishes are fulfilled?' Unruffled by his own self-interrogation, however, Freud immediately goes on to perform a feat of interpretation which is majestic in its sheer audacity. 'No doubt;' he writes, 'and it was only necessary to follow the dream's logical consequence in order to arrive at its interpretation. The dream showed that I was wrong. *Thus it was her wish that I might be wrong, and her dream showed that wish fulfilled*' (Freud's italics).[14]

The extraordinary hermeneutic strategy which Freud resorts to here is not an isolated instance, for he brings forward a whole clutch of dreams which appear to confute his theory, but which he analyses in exactly the same way. He even brings forward the case of a friend who had been at school with him. Soon after hearing Freud give a lecture in which he put forward his belief that all dreams are wish-fulfilments, this friend – a barrister – dreamt that he had lost all his cases. When he confronts Freud with this dream Freud takes comfort in the thought that he had always been ahead of his friend at school: 'Considering that for eight whole years I sat on the front bench as top of the class while he drifted about somewhere in the middle, he can hardly fail to nourish a wish, left over from his school days, that some day or other *I* may come a complete cropper.'[15] Freud thus attributes a desire for vengeance to his friend, and construes his dream as the fulfilment of this desire.

The notion that many of his patients were perverse and obstinate, harbouring a secret desire to prove him wrong, provided an excellent way of dealing with a great deal of recalcitrant material. But it could scarcely be invoked in those cases where dreams had been dreamt without prior knowledge of Freud's theories. Perhaps for this reason Freud added a paragraph to the 1909 edition of *The Interpretation of Dreams* in which he identified another motive for what he termed 'counter-wish' dreams. This second motive was 'so obvious that it is easy to overlook it, as I did myself for some considerable time'. There is, Freud continues, a group of people who can be described as 'mental masochists'. 'It will at once be seen that people of this kind can have counter-wish dreams and unpleasurable dreams which are nonetheless wish-fulfilments since they satisfy their masochistic inclinations.'[16]

By defending his theory with this two-pronged account of 'counter-wish dreams' Freud could guarantee the integrity of his ideas against practically every form of attack. Indeed, by virtue of the extraordinary audacity with which he treated his critics, every dream which was offered as a counter-instance to his theories could immediately be recruited to the cause and presented as though it were yet another confirmation of Freud's essential rightness. It was not always necessary, however, to invert entire dreams. Sometimes the same effect could be obtained by taking a single element from a dream and construing it in the opposite sense from that which was most obvious. In a paragraph which he added to his book in 1914, for example, Freud cited the case of a physician who had dreamt that he had seen on his left index finger 'the first indication ['*Primäraffekt*'] of syphilis'. Freud's comment on this dream is that, if we only take the trouble to analyse it, it becomes clear that *Primäraffekt* is the equivalent to a *prima affectio* or a first love.[17] Once it has been subjected to this linguistic transformation it becomes clear that the ugly syphilitic ulcer is not what it appears to be at all, and that an ostensibly anxious dream about venereal disease is actually a wish-fulfilling dream about the joys of young love. One of the most obvious objections to this particular analysis is that people tend to dream in images and only subsequently translate these into words. This being so it would be almost impossible to claim with certainty that the word *Primäraffekt* was a part of the original dream. Even if it were, there is no reason at all to identify this German word with a relatively unusual expression in Latin – *prima affectio*. Freud's elaborate and implausible interpretation, far from bearing out his theory that all dreams are examples of wish-fulfilment, merely demonstrates that scientific theories which are unsupported by empirical evidence are themselves liable to become vehicles for wish-fulfilment.

This was certainly not the only case in which a single element in a dream was inverted in order that the meaning of the dream could be brought into conformity with Freud's theory. Freud routinely invoked the principle of 'reversal', as when he argued that a dream in which a sword was *taken out* of its scabbard symbolised the penis *entering* the vagina, or when he wrote, yet more improbably, that 'Tables, tables laid for a meal and boards also stand for women – no doubt by antithesis, since the contours of their bodies are eliminated in the symbols.'[18]

A much more elaborate example of Freud's interpretative strategies is provided by the case he reports in which an intelligent and cultivated young woman

> dreamt she was going to the market with her cook ... After she had asked the butcher for something he said to her 'That's not obtainable any longer,' and offered her something else, adding 'this is good too.' She rejected it and went on to the woman who sells vegetables, who tried to get her to buy a peculiar vegetable that was tied up in bundles but was of a black colour. She said: 'I don't recognise that; I won't take it.'

Freud explains that the dream had originated from the woman's experience the previous day when she had gone to the market too late and got nothing. 'The situation,' he writes, 'seemed to shape itself into the phrase "Die Fleischbank war schon geschloßen" [the meat-shop was closed].' This in itself might seem a curious way of glossing a dream in which the butcher's shop was clearly open. But Freud offers this odd summary for a particular reason. Feigning surprise at the phrase he has deliberately and ingeniously interpolated into the woman's dream, he continues his speculative analysis: 'I pulled myself up: was not that, *or rather its opposite*, a vulgar description of a certain sort of slovenliness in a man's dress.' Freud is referring to the Viennese slang expression '*Du hast deine Fleischbank offen*', which means 'your flies are undone'. He concedes that the woman did not use the expression (or its opposite) herself but suggests that she may have deliberately avoided doing so. He then goes on to offer a sexual explanation of her dream which is in harmony with this hypothesis. Without any pretence at argument he introduces a rule according to which 'anything in a dream which has the character of direct speech' is held to derive from 'something actually spoken in waking life'. He then goes on to speculate as to why the butcher had used the words 'it's no longer obtainable'. Although the phrase in question is an extremely common one which might well have been spoken to the woman in any number of contexts, Freud confidently asserts that she has used it because he had recently told her that the earliest experiences of childhood were 'not obtainable any longer'. He concludes that *he* is the butcher. He then inquires as to the origin of her remark 'I don't recognise that; I won't take it.' The phrase 'I don't recognise that' is even more common than the previous one, but Freud does not hesitate to trace it back to something the woman had said the day before during a dispute with her cook. On that occasion she had supposedly gone on to say: 'Behave yourself properly!' Seeing in this phrase, which did not occur in the dream at all, a possible allusion to improper, sexual behaviour, Freud immediately brings into operation another arbitrary rule of interpretation and concludes that 'at this point there had clearly been a displacement . . . those would have been the appropriate words to use if someone had ventured to make improper suggestions and had forgotten "to close his meat-shop".'

Having successfully smuggled two sexual, or semi-sexual allusions into the dream from outside, Freud now suggests that the incident with the vegetable-seller is a further indication that his interpretation is correct. Although the clearest information we are given about the vegetables was that the dreamer did not recognise them, Freud, noting that they were tied in bundles, suggests that they were asparagus. 'No knowledgeable person of either sex,' he writes, 'will ask for an interpretation of asparagus.' The inconvenient fact that the vegetables were black is no bar to Freud's interpretative ingenuity. The vegetable, he declares, is not asparagus *tout simple* but 'a dream-combination of asparagus and black (Spanish) radishes'. This whimsical solution to an interpretative impasse is immediately rendered yet more whimsical when Freud suggests that '*Schwarzer Rettig*' (black radish) can be construed as an entirely different phrase which it happens to sound similar to – '*Schwarzer, rett' dich!*' ('Blacky! Be off!') Although these words, which, once again, have been smuggled into a dream in which they play no part, might be construed in many different ways, Freud apparently sees them as a reprimand issued to a Negro and, in a piece of *fin-de-siècle* racialism, assumes that what is in question can only be a rebuff to a sexual advance. 'It too,' he writes, 'seems to hint at the same sexual topic which we suspected at the very beginning.' The odd fact that Freud has treated asparagus at a purely visual, symbolic level, while Spanish radishes are allowed to exist only at the level of tortured wordplay, is overlooked. So too is the consideration that, however phallic a single shoot of asparagus may be, the same can scarcely be said of a 'dream-combination' of bundled asparagus and radishes. Freud, indeed, seems to have an almost infinite capacity for tolerating such inconsistencies so long as they lead eventually to a confirmation of his own preconceptions. The only conceivable reason that intellectuals have taken seriously his broken logic, his snatched solutions, his constant intellectual self-deception, and the crossword-puzzle cleverness which he repeatedly offers in place of real psychological insight, is that he almost invariably uses such modes of argument to scratch at the spot of sex. The imaginative stimulation which results is, it must be suggested, an extremely effective distraction from the poverty of the intellectual operations which lie behind it. In this particular case Freud uses his elaborate interpretation in order to suggest that his patient was actually engaging unconsciously in sexual fantasies which had him as their object. Or rather, to use Freud's own slightly more modest formulation: 'The dream concealed a phantasy of my behaving in an improper and sexually provocative manner, and of the patient putting up a defence against my conduct.'[19]

Although Freud himself objected to those critics who accused him of interpreting dreams in exclusively sexual terms, pointing out that some psychoanalytic explanations refer to non-sexual wishes, *The Interpretation of Dreams* focuses so often on sexual interpretations that his protests seem disingenuous. In 1911 Freud even added a note in which he referred to a psychologist who had taken issue with what he saw as the tendency of psychoanalysts to exaggerate the hidden sexual significance of dreams. This psychologist had objected that his own commonest dream was of going upstairs and had suggested that there could not possibly be anything sexual about *that*. Freud seems to have treated this criticism as a challenge:

> We were put on the alert by this objection, and began to turn our attention to the appearance of steps, staircases and ladders in dreams, and were soon in a position to show that staircases (and analogous things) were unquestionably symbols of copulation. It is hard not to discover the basis of the comparison: we come to the top in a series of rhythmical movements and with increasing breathlessness, and then, with a few rapid leaps, we can get to the bottom again. Thus the rhythmical pattern of copulation is reproduced in going upstairs.[20]

One of the interesting features of this passage is its pseudo-empiricism and the manner in which Freud manages to suggest, by the use of such phrases as 'we were soon in a position to show' and 'unquestionably', that his conclusion was the result of a careful scientific investigation. It is quite evident, however, that, like so many of Freud's theories, it was no more than a piece of armchair speculation. What is characteristic is the manner in which Freud singles out a minimal number of relatively insignificant similarities between copulation and going upstairs and then uses these in order to proclaim a symbolic equation between the two acts. Logically his observation is not dissimilar from the proposition that, since alligators and elephants both have four legs, alligators are actually elephants. The fact that Freud's argument could be applied to practically any form of rhythmical muscular exercise from sawing down a tree, to running for a tram, from rowing a boat to polishing a floor, is silently ignored.

When Freud goes on to argue that women's hats 'can very often be interpreted with certainty as a genital organ (usually a man's)', that the same is true of overcoats and ties, and that not only tools and weapons but all forms of luggage and some kinds of relatives (particularly sons, daughters and sisters) frequently symbolise genitals, as do eyes, noses, ears and mouths, it is difficult not to suspect a kinship between Freud's hermeneutics and Fliess's arithmetic.

Perhaps the most remarkable feature of Freud's approach to dreams is that, in his anxiety to uncover hidden levels of meaning buried in the depths of the 'unconscious', he persistently failed to recognise sexual and erotic fantasies which sometimes lay upon the surface, open for all to see. The point was made by Wittgenstein, when he observed that 'Freud very commonly gives what we might call a sexual interpretation. But it is interesting that among all the reports of dreams that he gives, there is not a single example of a straightforward sexual dream. Yet these are as common as rain.'[21] An even more straightforward, yet no less telling objection to Freud's theory of dreams was made by George Orwell in a diary entry towards the end of his life. After offering a conventional Freudian interpretation of his 'ever recurrent fishing-dream', he pauses to interrogate his own Freudian approach: 'But why do sex-impulses which I am not frightened of thinking about when I am awake have to be dressed up as something different when I am asleep? And then again, what is the point of the disguise if, in practice, it is always penetrable?'[22] Orwell's objection was by no means unprecedented. When *The Interpretation of Dreams* first appeared in 1899 the Viennese philosopher Heinrich Gomperz offered himself to Freud as a 'victim' on whom he might test his dream theories. After several months the exercise was abandoned: 'The experiment proved a complete failure. All the "dreadful" things which he suggested I might have concealed from myself and "suppressed" I could honestly assure him had always been clearly and consciously present in my mind.'[23]

The objection which was made independently both by Gomperz and by Orwell goes to the heart of Freud's entire theory of dreams. For the most questionable part of his doctrine is his apparent inability to recognise the extent to which the conscious waking mind of most ordinary people engages in sexual imaginings of the kind Freud is able to find only, or primarily, in what he sees as the hidden world of dreams.

Freud, it would seem, had made the most elementary of all the mistakes it is possible to make about the role played by sex in the life of the mind. He had mistaken the conscious censorship which most people exercise over the extent to which they express their most intimate sexual fantasies in public, for an entirely unconscious mechanism which is part of every human being's biological inheritance. He had, in short, taken the veil of respectability which people conventionally draw over their more obscene thoughts to be the reality of their sexual consciousness.

Freud's view of mental life has almost always been represented as striking a blow for liberation. Yet although Freud advocated a rather dry form of 'enlightened' openness about sexual matters, his theories implicitly accepted that a degree of sexual primness was a necessary consequence of the biological development of the individual. This view was well suited to an intellectual culture in which puritanism ruled so firmly that the whole realm of sexual fantasy was one whose existence was scarcely recognised. Freud's own view was that well-adjusted individuals never indulged in day-dreams. What he clearly never suspected was that his preoccupation with investing ostensibly unerotic dreams with explicitly erotic meanings, and of interpreting his patients' symptoms in a similar manner, was his own way of indulging indirectly, under the cover of medical hermeneutics, the kind of sexual fantasies which others, who were less intellectually austere, regularly indulged openly – or, at least, at a fully conscious level of the mind. The improbability that the unconscious mind should spend its time obtaining obliquely and cryptically the wish-fulfilments which the conscious mind is sometimes perfectly capable of obtaining directly, was something which never seems to have struck Freud.

When, in his case history of the attractive eighteen-year-old girl Dora, he responds to a dream in which she smelt smoke by pointing out that he is himself a heavy smoker, and goes on to interpret the dream as a cryptic allusion to her desire to be kissed by him; when he goes on to assure her that in opening, fingering and fidgeting with her reticule she is making an 'unmistakable pantomimic announcement' of what 'she would like to do with her genitals'; and when he further attempts to persuade her that the tickling in her throat which gives rise to her nervous cough is an allusion to the stimulus that would be experienced during the act of fellatio, it would seem only reasonable to conclude that his hermeneutics amount to an attempt to sexualise in the imagination a relationship which medical ethics forced him to regard as asexual. Freud, in this respect, was merely taking one stage further the approach which we have already seen in his interpretation of the dream about the market-place: he was using the interpretative strategies he had developed in order to fantasise that one of his patients was fantasising about him. Freud himself, however, was conspicuously lacking in such 'Freudian' insight into his own techniques. Instead of facing up to the fact that his interest in his patients was at least partly erotic, personal and spontaneously human, Freud anxiously and repeatedly denied that his therapeutic relationships afforded him any gratification. While he made it clear that he did not hesitate to discuss sexual matters openly and frankly with young women such as Dora, he insisted that this was for the purest of scientific motives, adding, with that self-deceiving naivety which frequently characterises his attempts at self-analysis, that 'it would be the mark of a singular and perverse prurience to suppose that conversations of this kind are a good means of exciting or gratifying sexual desires.'[24] The assumption which is made here – that the dreams of his patients which do not refer to sexual behaviour are sexually gratifying, whereas the explicitly sexual conversations he has with them are not – is one that recurs throughout his work.

So arbitrary and self-confirming is the method of interpretation which Freud applies to dreams that his arguments would scarcely merit either examination or refutation were it not for the central role which they played both in the development of his mature psychoanalytic theory and, by extension, in the entire evolution of modern psychiatry. For, as has already been noted, Freud's theory of dreams was simultaneously a theory of symptoms. As such his approach to dreams determined the manner in which he constructed the psychiatric aetiologies of his patients' 'illnesses'. It also provided him with a crucial strategic resource through which he was able to introduce psychoanalysis to groups of people who were not nerve-specialists or psychiatrists and who were therefore not familiar with the kind of problems presented by 'neurotic' patients. For while by no means everyone has suffered from neurotic symptoms, everybody has had dreams, just as everybody has made the kind of errors or slips of the tongue which were another focus for Freud's hermeneutics at this time. It was no doubt for this reason that, when Freud eventually came to give courses on psychoanalysis to general audiences, he tended to hold back discussion of neurotic patients until relatively late, and introduced his techniques and his theories by way of extensive discussions of errors, slips of the tongue and dreams. In his *Introductory Lectures on Psychoanalysis* (1915–17), for example, Freud devoted the first fifteen lectures to these subjects.

Only in his sixteenth lecture did he introduce his first case history. The case in question was evidently chosen because it provided a reasonably succinct example of the relationship which supposedly existed between dreams and symptoms. It concerned a 'well-preserved' woman of fifty-three whom Freud had been asked to treat by her son-in-law. She had been happily married for thirty years and could not praise her husband's affectionate solicitude highly enough. But the previous year she had received an anonymous letter accusing her husband of conducting a love affair with a young girl. The woman was sure she knew who the sender of the letter was and was entirely convinced that it was the result of a malicious fabrication. Yet in spite of this conviction she found herself devastated by the letter. Her entire happiness was destroyed, and she only had to meet the young woman who had been named in the letter for her to experience a fresh attack of distrust, pain and jealousy.

Although the woman had broken off her consultations with Freud after only two sessions, Freud does not treat her evident lack of enthusiasm for psychoanalysis as reflecting on his methods. Instead he interprets it as a sign of resistance and dread about what the analysis might reveal. Undeterred by his patient's flight Freud goes on to offer a confident analysis of her 'illness' based on a few remarks which she had 'let fall' before her departure. Discounting, without any evidence, the possibility that the woman's husband might well have been engaged in an affair, Freud concludes that her reaction is entirely irrational. Assuming that she is suffering from an 'illness' which he identifies as 'delusions of jealousy', he proceeds to offer an analysis of what he construes as the 'symptom' of this illness. He suggests, without offering any evidence for his conjecture, that the woman was herself secretly in love with a young man – with the very son-in-law who had brought her to Freud in the first place. In order to find relief from this 'monstrous and impossible' emotion (of which she was not herself aware), she had displaced her passion onto her husband:

> If not only were she, the old woman, in love with a young man, but if also her old husband were having a love affair with a young girl, then her conscience would be relieved of the weight of her unfaithfulness. The phantasy of her husband's unfaithfulness thus acted as a cooling compress on her burning wound. Her own love had not become conscious to her, but its mirror-reflection, which brought her such an advantage, now became conscious as an obsession and delusion. No arguments against it could, of course, have any effect, for they were only directed against the mirror image and not against the original which gave the other its strength and which lay hidden, inviolable in the unconscious.[25]

It should immediately be said that in this passage we encounter Freud at his most eloquent, his most persuasive and his most interesting. For it would seem reasonable to suggest that human emotions and human relationships are sometimes *at least* as complex and as fraught with ambiguity and hidden layers of significance as Freud here implies. If we set Freud's analysis alongside that of a psychiatrist who discounts the woman's feelings of jealousy as irrational and meaningless and who pronounces her to be suffering from a hereditary defect, then it must be said that Freud's account is a great deal more attractive. It is perhaps for this reason that he introduces it only after having set up a straw-psychiatrist who offers the very account of the woman's jealousy that I have given here. Yet the fact that Freud's explanation of the woman's feelings may be more complex and more interesting than that of the mythical psychiatrist does not mean that it is either correct, or even psychologically astute. The first objection to Freud's analysis is that it is purely speculative. Freud assumes that the woman has conceived a passionate love for her son-in-law on the basis of no evidence whatsoever. She might equally well have fallen in love with her gardener – or indeed with her maid. Here Freud, while taking considerable imaginative liberty in one respect, is being characteristically unimaginative in another. It seems equally likely that she has not conceived any passionate sexual affection for any of her current acquaintances and that envy rather than displacement might be one of the motives for her jealousy. The simple fact is that neither we nor Freud are in a position to know. The proposition which we might very reasonably reject, however, is Freud's curious claim that the woman was 'intensely in love' with her son-in-law even though 'she herself knew nothing, or perhaps only a very little, of this love.'[26] For what Freud ignores is that the state of being in love is generally accepted as being one of almost complete mental abandonment to a complex of powerful emotions. Moreover it is the act of abandoning control to such feelings which, in the case of those who are married, is generally held to constitute unfaithfulness. It is certainly true that some moral teachers in the Judaeo-Christian tradition, notably Jesus, have held that even those who stop short of the deed of adultery may, and indeed should, be convicted of unfaithfulness if they have thought or fantasised about it. What is remarkable about Freud's analysis is that, in constructing his psychological theories at least, he appears to have taken such Judaeo-Christian rigour one stage further. For under the moral regime of psychoanalysis, it would seem, even those who keep themselves spotless in both word *and* thought may still find themselves seeking deliverance from what Freud describes as 'the burden of unfaithfulness'.

Freud's analysis of his patient's 'symptom', although it may seem urbane, sophisticated and plausible, turns out on inspection to be fraught with a quite extraordinary moral severity at the same time that it seems to express a deep confusion both about the legitimacy of adulterous passion, and about the psychology of transgression and guilt. All in all it is difficult to resist the conclusion that Freud's 'solution' to this psychological conundrum does more to express his own deep confusion about his feelings for his sister-in-law, with whom he may or may not have had an adulterous sexual liaison, than it does to clarify the predicament of the woman who, probably wisely, chose to abandon her therapist after only two sessions of treatment.[27]

What is perhaps even more important to the argument here is that the analysis which Freud proposes is prompted not by any external evidence – for there is none – but by his theoretical presuppositions as to the nature of symptoms. Once Freud has decided that the woman's feelings of jealousy can be correctly construed as the 'symptom' of an 'illness' his psychoanalytical precepts leave him with no alternative but to construct a scenario in which the woman punishes herself for indulging in a wishful fantasy. The resulting fiction may not fit the facts. But it does fit the theory. This in the end is what appears to be decisive for Freud.

When Freud goes on to consider the case of a young woman who has developed a ritual in which she removes all watches and clocks from her bedroom before going to sleep on the grounds that she does not wish to be disturbed by noise, he does not hesitate to interpret this 'symptom' along similar lines. 'Our patient gradually came to learn,' writes Freud (who, as we have seen, was never a gentle or passive teacher), 'that it was as symbols of the female genitals that clocks were banished from her equipment for the night.' Freud goes on to develop this argument quite solemnly:

> Clocks and watches – though elsewhere we have found other symbolic interpretations for them[28] – have arrived at a genital role owing to their relation to periodic processes and equal intervals of time. A woman may boast that her menstruation behaves with the regularity of clockwork. Our patient's anxiety, however, was directed in particular against being disturbed in her sleep by the ticking of a clock. The ticking of a clock may be compared with the knocking or throbbing in the clitoris during sexual excitement.

Freud, whose testimony in such matters is, as we have seen, open to doubt, claims that his patient 'had in fact been repeatedly woken from her sleep by this sensation which had now become distressing to her'.[29] Although he does not make the point explicitly it seems clear that he is once again employing his dream theory of symptoms, and that he construed his patient's desire to remove clocks from her bedroom as a self-punishment for her unconscious wish for sexual stimulation.

While there is no evidence whatsoever to support Freud's claim that clocks symbolise the female genitals, and while his account of ticking is little more than a piece of psychoanalytical whimsy, it does seem reasonably clear that Freud in this case, as previously in the case of Dora, is using hermeneutics as a way of engaging in a form of sexual fantasy which involves his patient. It does not require much imagination to understand how difficult it must have been for Freud's patients to dismiss such interpretations or for the subsequent auditors at his lectures to raise objections to them in public.

The very fact that Freud was able to present his clinical romances as 'case histories' and to offer his intellectually contrived sexual acrostics as a scientific contribution both to the interpretation of dreams and the understanding of symptoms, illustrates the extent to which psychoanalysis was protected rather than hindered by the forces of taboo. For the taboo on the realm of the obscene did not only engender the obscurity which made incorrect or pseudo-scientific explanations of sexual behaviour acceptable; it also encouraged the insecurity and confusion which surround most people's normal sexual identity. As a result many refrained from levelling against psychoanalysis the obvious charge of vicarious sexual indulgence lest they should themselves be accused of prurience – an accusation which, as we have seen, Freud himself did not hesitate to make. At the same time the forces of taboo helped to keep many practising psychoanalysts – most significantly Freud himself – in a genuine and profound ignorance of their own motivation.

Freud's theory of dreams, like his theory of the Oedipus complex, did have a real psychological resonance. But in both cases it would be misleading to accept the conventional view according to which his theories were the product of a heroic process of self-analysis through which Freud finally liberated himself from Fliess. For these new Freudian modes of explanation were, in so many respects, but subtle reworkings, or oblique imitations, of the style of explanation Fliess had pioneered. If we now consider the theory of infantile sexuality which Freud eventually presented in his *Three Essays* we will find that the further he progressed towards his mature theory the more pronounced this resemblance became.

THIRTEEN

Developing the Doctrine

ALTHOUGH *THE INTERPRETATION OF DREAMS* was published in November 1899 it was dated 1900, as though to coincide with the beginning of a new era. Freud himself certainly looked upon the book as his most important publication to date and, just as he had once hoped that his paper on cocaine would bring him the world-redeeming status he had always coveted, so he now looked to his dream book to do the same. Yet although it was treated by some reviewers with respect, the general reaction was both critical and highly sceptical. By March 1900 Freud was contemplating ruefully the fact that his huge ambitions had been thwarted once again. 'After last summer's exhilaration,' he wrote to Fliess in March 1900, 'when in feverish activity I completed the dream book, fool that I am, I was once again intoxicated with the hope that a step toward freedom and prosperity had been taken. The reception of the book and the ensuing silence have again destroyed any budding relationship with my environment.'[1] Freud's immediate reaction was to take refuge in his daily therapeutic work and escape for the rest of his day into the various hobbies he industriously pursued. He tried to avoid thinking about his theoretical problems: 'I give myself over to my fantasies, play chess, read English novels; everything serious is banished. For two months I have not written a single line of what I have learned or surmised. As soon as I am free of my trade, I live like a pleasure-seeking philistine.'[2]

Freud, however, seems to have been marked so deeply by his ambitions that he was psychologically incapable of putting his career to one side. Before long he resumed his writings and in the summer of 1901 he published in a medical journal a two-part paper on which he later based his *The Psychopathology of Everyday Life* – a work in which the kind of crossword-puzzle hermeneutics found in *The Interpretation of Dreams* was applied to lapses of memory and slips of the tongue in an attempt to show that these were always unconsciously motivated.[3] There was never any question, however, even in Freud's own mind, that these new speculations about the Unconscious would bring him the fame and fortune which his earlier work had failed to deliver. Freud therefore began to consider an alternative route to distinction – one which until now his own scruples had ruled out.

Until this point in his career he had clung obstinately, and with considerable integrity, to the view that the authority and academic advancement which he sought should be gained purely by his own intellectual qualities and by the recognition he believed they would eventually bring. This, however, had simply not happened. In 1901, at the age of forty-five, Freud remained in the relatively humble position of *Privatdozent* – the academic position which he had now occupied for sixteen years. For several years, beginning in 1897, his name had gone forward to the Ministry of Education along with other nominations for the position of Associate Professor. Freud's nomination was not accepted, however. The standard explanation of his failure to gain academic advancement invokes a combination of anti-semitism and resistance to his daring investigations into sexuality. Yet it is by no means clear that either of these factors was decisive. It has been pointed out by assiduous Freud scholars that seven of the ten candidates who were nominated for professorships along with Freud in 1897 appear to have been Jewish. In 1900 all these nominees were belatedly accepted, while Freud alone was rejected.[4] Nor does it seem likely that Freud's interest in sexuality was in itself grounds for the rejection. Similar interests in yet more disturbing aspects of sexual behaviour had not barred Freud's colleague Krafft-Ebing from promotion. Since Freud's former teacher, Sigmund Exner, suggested to him in 1902 that 'personal influences' were working against him at the Ministry of Education, the most likely explanation is that somebody in a position of power opposed Freud's candidacy because of their doubts about the value of his work. Something like this explanation has been tentatively put forward by Frank Sulloway. 'That Freud's controversial views on sexual etiology,' he writes, 'added to his prior reputation as a fanatic who had defended dubious causes like Charcot and cocaine, might have annoyed someone with influence at the ministry is certainly not implausible.' It is interesting that Sulloway immediately seeks to balance this view by pointing out that Freud's scientific sponsors 'unswervingly supported Freud's candidacy'. To back up this observation he quotes the remarks made by Krafft-Ebing in a report to the Ministry of Education which was also signed by Nothnagel and four other professors:

> The novelty of [Freud's] researches and the difficulty of their verification allow no hasty judgment at the present time concerning their import. It is possible that Freud overrates these [findings] and generalises his discoveries too far. In any event his researches in this field are evidence of unusual talent and the ability to direct scientific investigations into new pathways.

Sulloway himself describes these words as 'charitable'.[5] A more reasonable description might be 'cautious'. For Krafft-Ebing couches his remarks in just the kind of terms one would expect from someone who had publicly described Freud's unretracted seduction theory as 'a scientific fairy-tale'. His words are sufficiently kind to meet the obligations of friendship and loyalty to a colleague. But they carefully leave open the possibility that the objections which had been made to his theories might be well founded. In view of this it seems entirely plausible that Freud's failure to gain academic preferment was due not to the prejudices which are traditionally cited, but to straightforward reservations about the scientific value of his work.

Whether or not this was the case, Freud himself eventually came to the conclusion that he would have to put his scruples on one side and use the influence of friends and supporters to gain the position which had otherwise eluded him: 'I could see that waiting for recognition might take up a good portion of my life and that in the meantime none of my fellow men would bother about me . . . So I made up my mind to break with strict virtue and take appropriate steps, as other humans do.'[6]

What actually happened is that he persuaded two of his well-connected women patients to intercede with the Minister of Education on his behalf. One of these 'bribed' the Minister by donating a painting to a public gallery and Freud's elevation duly followed. Although such strategies were far from unusual in Vienna at the time, Freud was sufficiently ashamed of the action he had taken to feel obliged to confess it to Fliess while simultaneously asking him to keep to himself the contents of the letter in which he did so.[7]

Viewed from the perspective of the international eminence he subsequently acquired, Freud's elevation to a Viennese professorship in 1902 seems scarcely significant. Yet to Freud at the time, the title was immensely important. 'One must look somewhere for one's salvation,' he wrote, 'and I chose the title as my saviour.'[8] Although Freud knew perfectly well that his title had been procured by patronage he seems to have regarded it as an official seal of approval for psychoanalysis, an attitude which is reflected in the account he gave of the response to the news:

> Public acclaim was immense. Congratulations and flowers are already pouring in, as though the role of sexuality has suddenly been officially recognised by His Majesty, the significance of the dream certified by the Council of Ministers, and the necessity of a psychoanalytic therapy of hysteria carried by a two-thirds majority in Parliament.[9]

Freud felt not only that psychoanalysis itself had suddenly acquired prestige but he also sensed a change in public attitudes towards him. In his most difficult years he had felt that everyone regarded his ideas as odious. As he later put it, people treated him like a freshly painted wall; they never dared touch him. After news of his promotion began to spread in Vienna, all this seemed to change:

> I have obviously become reputable again; my most reluctant admirers greet me in the street from afar . . .
> I have learned that the old world is ruled by authority, as the new is by the dollar. I have made my first bow to authority and so may hope to be rewarded. If the effect on wider circles is as great as it is on the closer ones, I may be hopeful with good reason.[10]

Freud, however, was far too shrewd to rely merely on his hopes. In many respects authority did indeed resemble the dollar and, as if following the logic of his own parallel, Freud now embarked on an industrious and careful programme to invest his newly acquired capital. Already, in his position as *Privatdozent*, he had been able to lecture regularly on his own chosen subjects. Now he continued this lecturing in the knowledge that his enhanced status would lend much greater weight to his views, and protect him, to some extent at least, against the ridicule he had frequently suffered.

One of the consequences of Freud's new confidence was that he now felt able to develop and publish some of the ideas which underpinned psychoanalysis, and which he had first conceived during his friendship with Fliess. For the first time, the theory of infantile sexuality was worked out in a coherent form and expounded in public in *Three Essays on the Theory of Sexuality*, which was published in 1905. In view of the crucial role which they played in the development of the psychoanalytic movement it seems particularly important to examine the principal arguments which were advanced in *Three Essays*, and to submit them thoroughly to the kind of scepticism which Freud himself frequently advocated, but which he rarely practised.

One of the most striking features of Freud's book is that although the ideas Freud eventually puts forward in it are extravagant and speculative, its style is a triumph of measured reasonableness and seeming restraint. The book was evidently designed as a vehicle for the ontogenetic and phylogenetic accounts of sexual development which Freud had begun to work out during his correspondence with Fliess. But by way of preparing the ground for what was to come Freud set out in his first essay to offer a survey of what are termed 'sexual aberrations'. To many of Freud's lay readers in the first decade of the twentieth century this in itself would have seemed daring and revolutionary. That it was not quite so revolutionary as it might appear was acknowledged by Freud himself in a footnote. For, as he points out, he was far from being the first to write about sexual 'perversions'. The information contained in his essay was, as he writes, 'derived from the well-known writings of Krafft-Ebing, Moll, Moebius, Havelock Ellis' and a number of others.[11]

Some of the information which Freud collated was undoubtedly of genuine scientific interest. Indeed in some respects the essay is a constructive and potentially useful one, since it clearly identifies certain aspects of sexual behaviour as problematic and as standing in need of systematic investigation – and explanation. Freud directs attention to the prevalence of homosexual behaviour, both among men and among women, to fetishistic behaviour, including foot-fetishism and hair-fetishism, to sadistic and masochistic sexual practices and to a variety of other 'perversions'. In pointing out the deficiencies of existing explanations – such as the notion that homosexuality can be accounted for by invoking 'degeneracy' – Freud is frequently acute and just. Not only this, but he also writes of the so-called sexual perversions in a manner which, while never approaching the almost rapturous enthusiasm of a Havelock Ellis, was considerably more humane than that of many contemporary physicians. He still retained the term 'perversion', but he did so in way which did not stigmatise those who practised 'perversions' to the extent that had been customary in nineteenth-century medical literature. At times, indeed, he draws back from using the term at all. During a discussion of oral-genital contact, for example, he writes that 'those who condemn [these] practices (which have no doubt been common among mankind from primaeval times) as being perversions, are giving way to an unmistakable feeling of *disgust*, which protects them from accepting sexual aims of the kind.'[12]

Such remarks as these, the like of which can be found elsewhere in Freud's writings, are not only psychologically acute, but have a genuinely liberating quality. They illustrate the extent to which Freud was motivated in part by a desire to remove the veil of secrecy from sexual behaviour and to lift the burden of guilt from those who had previously felt constrained by it. This aspect of Freud's work is extremely important and needs to be fully acknowledged if we are to understand the appeal which his writings had – and still have – to many readers. But the undoubted genuineness of Freud's moral mission seems sometimes to have obscured from his followers, and from Freud himself, the intellectual spuriousness of his theoretical work. In the first essay it is notable that what begins as an even-handed account of abnormal sexual behaviour gradually assumes a tendentious character, as Freud stacks the evidence in such a way that it will support the biogenetically inspired account of sexual development which is due to be presented in the second essay. For although Freud briefly surveys a great variety of sexual behaviour, he maintains a predominantly physiological perspective throughout. This means that, unlike his contemporary Havelock Ellis, he shows no interest in subjective accounts of unusual sexual behaviour by those who engage in it. For this reason he tends to ignore the dimension of sexual fantasy – and with it a great deal of the psychological complexity by which all sexual behaviour is surrounded. Instead he returns at several points in his essay to the question of which parts of the human body – apart from the genitals – are stimulated during sexual activity. Having devoted separate paragraphs to 'Sexual Use of the Mucous Membrane of the Lips and Mouth' and 'Sexual Use of the Anal Orifice', he goes on to suggest that 'these anatomical extensions' inform us that there is a factor at work in human sexuality 'which is strange to popular knowledge':

> Certain regions of the body, such as the mucous membrane of the mouth and anus, which are constantly appearing in these practices, seem, as it were, to be claiming that they should themselves be regarded and treated as genitals. We shall learn later that this claim is justified by the history

of the development of the sexual instinct and that it is fulfilled in the symptomatology of certain pathological states.[13]

Freud goes on in his second essay to put forward the theory of infantile sexuality, whose origins in the work of Haeckel and the speculations of Fliess we have already examined. According to this theory in its developed form, human sexual desire is compounded of a number of 'component instincts' which, in normal development, are eventually organised under the primacy of the genitals. Before this final mature stage is reached, however, all individuals pass through stages of development in which first the mouth and then the anus assume primacy and are the main focus of sexual desire. Psychoneurosis and hysteria, according to Freud's new formulation, resulted from a failure to follow the normal course of development as a result of which individuals became 'fixated' at an earlier stage.

The difficulty posed by this theory is not – or at least should not be – deciding whether it is a scientifically useful hypothesis. For if, as I have already argued, the entire theory of infantile sexuality was derived directly, with the help of the highly unreliable Fliess, from biologistic theories which have long been known to be false, then it is the theory's survival and its relative longevity which require explanation. It would, of course, be far from true to suggest that the theory has survived intact. Nevertheless it has retained a recognisable outline even beneath the innovations introduced by such different theorists as Melanie Klein, Erik Erikson, Erich Fromm and Norman O. Brown.

Perhaps the most important factor in the success which the theory has enjoyed is the fact that Freud's ingenious account of the course of sexual development provides at least the *appearance* of an explanation for the extraordinarily wide range of oral, excremental and sadistic behaviour which undeniably tends to be associated with sexual practices and sexual fantasies.

Yet it does so only by virtue of a mode of argument which is Fliessian both in some of its fundamental assumptions and in its manipulation of concepts. This begins to become clear as soon as we start to consider the evolutionary logic which underlies Freud's theory of infantile sexuality. One of the observations on which Freud based this theory was that the stimulation of the mouth or the anus can, like the stimulation of the genitals, give rise to feelings of physical pleasure. This observation is evidently sound. The first deformation of evolutionary logic in Freud's argument occurs, however, when, directly following Fliess, he assumes that the pleasure in question is in some way intrinsically sexual. To make this assumption is to fail to ask the much more fundamental question, which is not why sucking or defaecation should lead to pleasure but why copulation should. The answer, though an evolutionary truism, is one that clearly needs to be stated. As a general rule organisms react with pleasure to those non-reflex actions and functions which promote their survival and with pain to those stimuli which threaten their survival. The beating of the heart or the working of the kidneys are not attended by pleasure for more or less the same reason that the turning of a clock's wheels one against another brings with it no ecstasy of friction. Sexual activity, however, is not something which happens when the clock of our body chimes. Among humans, indeed, it is almost entirely independent of any organically fixed pattern. If it were not rewarded by pleasure there would be no likelihood that our remote hominid ancestors – who were, we may presume, more impulsive than us – would have engaged in it at all. The same is also true of many other functions of the body, including eating, drinking, urination, defaecation and, in women, breast-feeding. In all these cases there is a general pattern of physiological tension followed by pleasurable stimulation leading to relief from tension. To suggest, however, that sucking results in sexual pleasure is no more sensible than to suggest that copulation results in eating-pleasure. If I use two-thirds of my carrot to reward my carthorse and give the other third to my sheepdog I will not presume that the wagging of the latter's tail signifies equine satisfaction. It is certainly true that in the human organism, as in all organisms, there is an intimate connection between different bodily functions. Oxytocin, for instance, which is sometimes called 'the happiness hormone', is released both during orgasm and during breast-feeding. Breast-feeding can thus induce feelings of physical pleasure in women just as all forms of tactile stimulation, including that of the mouth and the anus, can intensify the pleasure experienced during intercourse. But this does not establish the intrinsically sexual character of pleasure; it simply indicates that the body-functions or organs in question are linked to the same pleasure-giving physiological mechanism. This indeed is what we would expect, for natural selection operates according to the strictest of budgets. Having equipped organisms with an eternal carrot and a serviceable stick, there is no reason why it should give them an apple and allow them to brandish a whip as well.

Freud, however, insists on using the notion of pleasure as though it were inherently sexual. More importantly still, the whole theory of infantile sexuality is given over to establishing as normal a sequence of development in which 'libido' is gradually withdrawn from other bodily functions and 'organised' under the primacy of the genitals. Having thus carefully steered his disciples past the rock of evolutionary logic and onto the sands of Fliessian subjectivity, Freud proceeds to build upon those sands a veritable cathedral of theory.

Once again it cannot be denied that Freud's theory is ingenious in the extreme and that it provides an initially plausible explanation of many aspects of sexual behaviour. This applies in particular to behaviour involving the mouth and the anus, whose indisputable susceptibility to stimulation appears to lend weight to the Freudian hypothesis. Yet such susceptibility is also possessed by other parts of the body – the nipples and the ear-lobes, for instance. The sensitivity of any part of the body to pleasurable stimulation can scarcely be used in itself to demonstrate the truth of an entire theory of development. As for the various attempts which have been made to explain particular kinds of 'perverse' sexual behaviour by invoking the notion of instinct components, they too must be met with scepticism.

The real status of the psychoanalytic 'explanations' which are offered by the theory of infantile sexuality is perhaps best illustrated if, in addition to the three stages of sexual development described by Freud – oral, anal and phallic – we postulate the existence of two further stages of sexual development which intervene between the anal and the phallic stages and relate to the erotogenic significance of the hands and the feet. These new stages of psychosexual development would be known as the pedal stage and the manual stage. Their initial explanatory function would be to focus on aspects of the Oedipal tie between the mother and child which are often neglected. Thus the pleasure displayed by the child in response to having its feet tickled by its mother would be seen as an overt manifestation of pedal-erotism, later destined to be displaced by the manual-erotism of that compulsive hand-holding so frequently indulged by mothers and children in our culture. This revised account of psychosexual development would, in addition to explaining the pre-eminence of manual fondling during sexual foreplay, also explain such perverse sexual practices as foot-fetishism and digital stimulation of the anus during love-making, the former deriving from a fixation at the pedal level of development, the latter showing a mixture of anal-erotic and manual-erotic instinct components. It would also illuminate the role played by the hand in auto-erotic practices and would thus extend Freud's own observation, made initially, as we have seen, in relation to the mouth and the anus, that 'certain regions of the body . . . seem, as it were, to be claiming that they should themselves be regarded and treated as genitals.'

The concept of the manual stage would be particularly important in therapeutic practice, helping to draw attention to the aetiology of the 'manual character'. This character-type is found in two basic forms, both showing infantile traits. In the manual-erotic personality we find a series of interrelated character-traits in which an excessive generosity or *open-handedness*, sometimes amounting to fecklessness, is found in association with compulsive, dependent or *'clinging'* behaviour, together with an over-readiness to submit to authority. In the manual-sadistic personality this character syndrome is found in an inverted form as a consequence of reaction-formations; hence meanness – *tight-fistedness* – will be found in association with officiousness – the desire to *manipulate* others. Finally, as a result of this new development in the theory of infantile sexuality, light could be thrown on some collective archaic rituals which have survived in our own culture. Both football and rugby would be seen as polymorphously perverse – or, to use Stekel's term, panerotic rituals. Football, focusing as it does on the gratification of pedal and aggressive instinct components, represents an archaic regression to that stage in the phylogenetic development of the primal horde in which taboos on pedal-erotism had not been internalised. Rugby, while preserving this archaic pedal character, evidently belongs to a later and higher stage of phylogenetic development where manual-erotism also plays a part. Superimposed on these phases of development, and for ever threatening to subordinate the infantile pleasures to its own primacy, is a later genital organisation which inevitably brings with it Oedipal conflicts. It is this new element of Oedipal conflict which is responsible for the introduction of a ball into what were, phylogenetically, originally primitive contact-games similar to those described by Malinowski in his Trobriand monograph. The ball is to be regarded as a penis, detached in fantasy as a result of castration anxiety. As is implicit in this symbolism the goal is the mother's vagina. Repeated entry into this goal secures the vanquishing of the opposing team – here symbolically playing the part of the father.

The problem with Freud's fiction of oral and anal erotism is that it has in practice functioned as just the kind of infinitely elastic catch-all hypothesis which is exemplified by my own fiction of pedal and manual erotism. Although his scheme of development originally played only a modest role, he gradually enlarged it in a series of papers on character-development, until eventually practically any behaviour involving the mouth, the anus or excrement could be located within it, where, after the incantation of formulae such as 'fixation', 'regression', 'sublimation' or 'reaction-formation' it became, in a sense, self-explanatory. The more bizarre, obscene or arousing any piece of behaviour was, the more speedily would it be consigned to this process of theoretical digestion, with the advantage that psychoanalysis could, while laying claim to a fearless emancipation of the intellect, effectively short-circuit the discussion of disturbing or embarrassing aspects of human behaviour by providing a pseudo-explanation of them instead of a real one.

The infinitely flexible nature of psychoanalytic explanations might well be compared to the flexible nature of an explanatory procedure which was both historically and personally close to psychoanalysis – that devised by Wilhelm Fliess.

The specifically Fliessian character of Freud's explanatory hypotheses is perhaps best conveyed in the most important statement which Freud ever made about the way in which infantile 'instinct-components' supposedly determine the personalities of adult 'neurotics'. This statement will be found in Freud's paper of 1908, 'Character and Anal Erotism':

> We ... can lay down a formula for the way in which character in its final shape is formed out of the constituent instincts: the permanent character traits *are either unchanged prolongations of the original instincts, or sublimations of those instincts, or reaction formations against them* [italics added].[14]

If we consider this 'formula' sceptically in relation to the kind of arithmetical strategies which were employed by Fliess it is difficult to escape the conclusion that, in the way he manipulated such concepts as 'anal-erotism' and 'oral-erotism', Freud succeeded in translating Fliess's numerological mysticism into a more subtle, and ultimately more plausible conceptual mysticism. For Freud could not only combine his original concepts together into such amalgams as oral-anal, or anal-sadistic, but he could also subject them to quasi-arithmetical transformations and inversions by using such conceptual 'operators' as 'reaction-formation', 'sublimation' and 'fixation'. Just as Fliess's periodic values of 28 and 23 led an extraordinary double life, concealing behind their outward mathematical sobriety a bewildering polyvalence and promiscuity of application, so Freud's ostensibly stable concepts led a similar double life and it was this which gave them the catch-all qualities which I have tried to illustrate in my own contribution to psychoanalytic theory.

Freud, no less than Fliess, tended to become trapped within the logic of his own theory. If we attempt to reconstruct Freud's processes of thought in relation to one particular problem we may perhaps see how his inability to interrogate his theories sceptically and his determination not to break the thread of his logic often led him deeper and deeper into intellectual mazes from which he could emerge only by inventing evidence which did not exist.

At one point in his researches Freud made the empirical observation that children often believe that babies are born through the anus. In one of his attempts to interpret this common children's theory in his paper 'On Transformations of Instinct as Exemplified in Anal Erotism' (1917), Freud took as his starting-point the assumption that children made an 'imaginative equation' between babies and faeces. Freud, however, believed that he had already discovered an *organic* equation between the *penis* and faeces, since both these 'solid bodies' stimulated an organ lined with mucous membrane: 'The faecal mass, or as one patient called it, the faecal "stick", represents as it were the first penis, and the stimulated mucous membrane of the rectum represents that of the vagina.' Disregarding the fact that, according to his own logic, both the mother's nipple and the child's thumb had a prior claim to be regarded as 'the first penis', Freud now set out to combine children's theories of anal birth with his own 'organic analogy'.[15] The result was a theory of correspondences, according to which the concepts *faeces*, *baby* and *penis* were treated by the Unconscious 'as if they were equivalent and could replace one another freely'.[16]

The theory of correspondences was apparently originally worked out in the course of Freud's analysis of the Wolf Man, and then elevated to the status of a general theory. In the analysis of the Wolf Man one of the functions of the theory was to 'prove' that the interest which boys showed in babies was really a disguised interest in excrement, and therefore anal-erotic in origin. This in turn raised the question of how the theory might be used to illuminate the development of women. Its most obvious implication was that women's desire for babies itself had an anal-erotic dimension, and it was this general view which Freud expounded in his 1917 essay. But if babies were to be equated not only with faeces but also with penises, then there was a far more specific and striking theoretical implication. For Freud had already observed that little girls did not have penises and had suggested that they were envious of men who did. If babies were really penises then it would become clear why some women wanted them so much. It would also explain why some women did not appear to suffer from penis-envy. In such cases it could simply be claimed that the wish for a penis 'is replaced by a wish for a baby'. Freud was unable to resist this line of reasoning and developed the argument at some length. 'It looks,' he wrote, 'as if such women had understood (although this could not possibly have acted as a motive) that nature has given babies to women as a substitute for the penis that has been denied to them.'[17]

It would appear, however, that in the course of developing this argument, Freud never ceased to be aware that his theory of correspondences had been constructed out of two quite different forms of evidence. For whereas the equation of baby and faeces was derived primarily from children's theories of anal birth, the equation of penis and faeces was based on the 'organic analogy' which he had himself constructed. In order to repair this methodological fracture Freud was obliged to find an organic basis for the 'psychological' equation between baby and faeces. His problem was, in a sense, an arithmetical one, since it could only be solved by finding 'the lowest common organic factor' of the three terms, baby, faeces and penis. The curious answer which Freud found to this curious question rested on the observation that babies when they were being born were rather like penises, in that both of them stimulated the walls of the vagina. It was with this spurious but undeniably logical thread that Freud stitched together the three components of his theory into a single extended 'organic analogy'. 'Faeces, penis and baby,' Freud solemnly wrote, 'are all three solid bodies; they all three, by forcible entry or expulsion, stimulate a membranous passage . . .'[18]

Having invented an imaginary organic basis for the equation between faeces and baby, Freud could now argue backwards to the original empirical evidence and claim that, through their theories of anal birth, children had, in effect, discovered the 'organic analogy' between babies and faeces, and translated it into psychological terms. At this point, however, the logic of Freud's theory demanded that a further extension should be made to it. For if children had translated the organic analogy between babies and faeces into psychological terms, it would follow that the original organic analogy between penis and faeces should also be translated into psychological terms. Driven on by the logic of one element in his theory, Freud found himself trapped by another. For unfortunately he had already come to the conclusion the children were generally unaware of the role played by the penis in sexual intercourse. In order to preserve the symmetry of his theory Freud therefore found himself in need of a way of demonstrating the reality of a hypothetical association in the minds of children which, according to his theories, should not be present at all. Since no authentic children's theory was to hand Freud solved the problem by inventing a theory of his own and then attributing it to children. He maintained that when boys discover that women have no penis they conclude 'that the penis must be a detachable part of the body, something analogous to faeces, the first piece of bodily substance the child has to part with.'[19] By constructing this fiction Freud was able to claim that his own fanciful organic analogy between penis and faeces was indeed translated by children into psychological terms. 'It is interesting to note,' wrote Freud, in the tone not of an author admiring the effect of his own fiction but of a physical scientist dispassionately observing phenomena over which he has no control, 'that after so many detours an organic correspondence reappears in the psychical sphere as an unconscious identity.'[20]

After initially setting out to find the physiological 'cause' of a real psychological 'effect' – children's theories of anal birth – Freud was thus driven to invent an imaginary psychological 'effect' to explain the existence of an equally imaginary physiological 'cause' – his own 'organic analogy' between penis and faeces. It was only in this way that Freud could emerge from his intellectual maze with the logic of his theory unbroken.

The entire theory of correspondences, including Freud's pronouncements on mothers, is but a small part of Freud's concept of 'anal erotism', a concept which he compulsively extended until practically any form of human behaviour could be 'explained' by it. It is only by observing closely the way in which such key Freudian concepts behave in practice that is possible to appreciate the bizarre and truly Fliessian nature of the double life which they lead. For these concepts are themselves polymorphous, changing shape, mutating, inverting themselves and dissolving their hard outlines in a manner which would have delighted Ovid and perplexed Mendel. Such conceptual instability is determined, as I have tried to show, not by Freud's lack of respect for systematic thought, but by his anxiety to preserve the logic of an initially simple theoretical structure *against* all empirical evidence. It is in order to preserve the outward rigour and simplicity of his system that Freud is obliged to allow each of his key-concepts to become infinitely flexible and amorphous. Exactly the same analysis might also be made of the mathematical theories of Wilhelm Fliess. For what gave Fliess's theories their profoundly unscientific nature was his willingness to allow a reverence for systematic logic, and his own compulsive need for a world-revealing vision, to override all empirical considerations and destroy all conceptual restraints. Instead of the shape of his theories being determined by the world, the shape of the world was determined by his theories.

It was the same reverence for theory, combined with an anxious impulse to avoid internal inconsistencies and contradictions, which would lead Freud to introduce significant revisions into his theory of personality in the two decades which followed the formulation of his theory of infantile sexuality. There can be little doubt that the most important of these came in 1923 when, in *The Ego and the Id*, Freud introduced his tripartite division of the mind into id, ego and superego. The considerations which lay behind this theoretical innovation have been explored by a number of scholars, with the most exhaustive account being that offered by Malcolm Macmillan. But the complex web of metapsychology which Freud wove around these entirely hypothetical entities should not be allowed to obscure the fact that their undoubted appeal arose directly from their resemblance to concepts which were already well established. Allen Esterson makes this point well:

> [Freud] observes that the ego's 'three tyrannical masters are the external world, the super-ego and the id', but since this is saying little more than that man's consciousness is governed by his environment, his conscience, and his innate instincts, it is hardly a great revelation.[21]

Freud himself was obliged to recognise the objection which was most commonly made against his ego-psychology – that it 'comes down to nothing more than taking commonly used abstractions literally, and in a crude sense, and transforming them from concepts to things'.[22] The objection was one which he was ultimately unable to meet.

It is certainly true that Freud, through the concept of the superego, was able to offer what was, ostensibly, a more psychological account of repression. But he did not abandon his large phylogenetic scenarios, or his tendency to engage in unsubstantiated biological speculation. For the concept of the superego allowed him to introduce the notion of 'secondary repression' while still retaining his belief in primal, biological repression. In his view the conscience and the other moral values contained within the superego were originally 'acquired phylogenetically out of the father-complex'. Since this would have meant that only men would develop moral values in the first place, Freud did not hesitate to postulate that these values were subsequently transmitted 'by cross-inheritance' to women.[23]

In spite of the great importance which Freud eventually ascribed to the superego and to 'secondary repression', he continued to view primal, biological repression as the key to psychopathology. In 1926 he even went out of his way in order to emphasise that secondary repressions always 'presuppose the operation of earlier, *primal repressions* ... There is a danger of overestimating the part played in repression by the superego'. In this respect Malcolm Macmillan is right to stress that, contrary to prevailing misconceptions, 'the further one goes in the development of Freud's theory, the larger is the importance of innate, hereditary factors, and the smaller the role of the environment.'[24]

In working out the superstructure of the personality theory which he eventually built on the foundations of his theory of sexuality, Freud thus continued to use many of the most significant features of Fliess's explanatory style, and continued to allow his theories to shape the world. In a discussion of Freud's ego-psychology and what he calls Freud's 'newly formulated entities' – ego, superego and id – Allen Esterson makes a similar point:

> Not only are they speculations of a kind not amenable to empirical validation, their functions are so imprecisely delineated that they can be employed in almost arbitrary fashion to provide support for virtually any theoretical formulation. Their advantage from Freud's point of view is the versatility of the functions they may perform and the explanations they may furnish, separately or in concert. McDougall summed up the fault in this kind of theorising when he observed that 'if we allowed ourselves the laxity of reasoning which is habitual to Freud and many of his disciples, and if we possessed his fertile ingenuity, there would be literally no limits to the possibilities of application of his principles.'[25]

Just as Fliess's constant use of mathematics helped to invest his biological theories with the aura of scientific authority, so Freud's compulsive use of biological and technical terminology tacitly proclaimed a similar ethos. Just as Fliess had sought to embrace the universe within his theories, so Freud constantly sought to encapsulate within his theories the entire history of organic evolution. The world-revealing elasticity of the system which he created can best be seen in those arguments about evolutionary recapitulation which are fundamental to his theories and which he derived from the biogenetic hypotheses of Fliess, Haeckel and Bölsche. For by applying these theories it was possible not only to explain the 'laws' of the unconscious, but also to relate the sexual anatomy of prehistoric birds to the obstinacy of two-year-old children and the organic evolution of crocodiles to the meanness of Viennese aristocrats.

The elastic qualities of psychoanalytic interpretation have, of course, been noted before. In 1913 Knight Dunlap wryly observed, with particular reference to Freud's theory of dreams, that 'there is absolutely nothing in the universe which may not readily be made into a sexual symbol':

> All natural and artificial objects can be turned into Freudian symbols. We may explain, by Freudian principles, why trees have their roots in the ground; why we write with pens; why we put a quart of wine in a bottle instead of hanging it on hooks like a ham; and so on.[26]

Knight Dunlap's words have been cited by Frank Cioffi. Although Cioffi himself does not discuss the methods of Fliess or Freud's relationship to him, his characterisation of Freud's interpretative style brings out very well the Fliessian qualities of psychoanalytic explanation – which are as evident in his individual case histories as they are in his more purely theoretical works:

> Examination of Freud's interpretations will show that he typically proceeds by beginning with whatever content his theoretical preconceptions compel him to maintain underlies the symptoms and then, by working back and forth between it and the explanandum, constructing persuasive but spurious links between them. It is this which enables him to find allusions to the father's coital breathing in attacks of dyspnoea, fellatio in a *tussis nervosa*, defloration in migraine, orgasm in an hysterical loss of consciousness, birth pangs in appendicitis, pregnancy wishes in hysterical vomiting, pregnancy fears in anorexia, an accouchement in a suicidal leap, castration fears in an obsessive preoccupation with hat

tipping, masturbation in the practice of squeezing blackheads, the anal theory of birth in an hysterical constipation, parturition in a falling cart-horse, nocturnal emissions in bed-wetting, unwed motherhood in a limp, guilt over the practice of seducing pubescent girls in the compulsion to sterilise banknotes before passing them on, etc.[27]

Although Freud's fluency in the art of mystical exegesis helps to create the illusion of explanatory power on which the success of psychoanalysis partly depends, it would be wrong to suggest that the illusion has no other source. The acceptability of incorrect scientific theories depends not only on the internal coherence, elegance or plausibility of the explanations which they offer, but also on the obscurity, inaccessibility, indeterminacy or partial invisibility of the phenomena they purport to explain. The main reason that the phlogiston theory was accepted for so long by eighteenth-century chemists was that combustion then consisted in the invisible absorption of an undiscovered substance. It was only after the discovery of oxygen, and after the adoption of new experimental techniques which involved the retention of the gaseous products of reactions and a greater use of the chemical balance, that the necessary observations were made and the phlogiston theory was replaced by an account which recognised that oxygen was necessary to combustion and was absorbed by substances during combustion.

There can be little doubt that the resilience and success of psychoanalytic explanations owes much to similar qualities of invisibility and inaccessibility possessed by the phenomena on which it focuses. For although the sexual behaviour of men and women may now have been documented in considerable detail, the most threatening, arousing or obscene aspects of sexual behaviour are almost inevitably subject to denial at some level of the mind, with the result that their reality is rarely if ever fully acknowledged by theorists. Freud himself insisted time and time again that unconscious resistance had prevented wider acceptance of psychoanalytic theory. The reality, it must be suggested, is very different. For it is partly because of the widespread resistance to the most disturbing details of human sexual behaviour and the consequent reluctance of doctors, therapists and theorists to re-examine the entire realm of sexual behaviour, that Freud's Fliessian science, which repeatedly offers pseudo-explanations of sexual behaviour rather than real explanations, has survived, and indeed flourished.

II

THE CHURCH AND THE PSYCHOANALYTIC GOSPEL

FOURTEEN

'Freud, who was my Christ!'

IN 1899, WHEN FREUD had published *The Interpretation of Dreams*, he was virtually unknown outside a small circle of Viennese medical practitioners. By 1905, after three years as a professor and with the appearance of *Three Essays on the Theory of Sexuality*, the situation was already beginning to change. Gradually medical practitioners, sexologists and psychiatrists in a number of different countries began to take note of his work. In 1908 Freud arranged the first International Psychoanalytic Congress, which took place in Salzburg. A total of forty-two men attended, and although more than half of these were from Austria the number included delegates from Switzerland, Germany, Hungary, Britain and the United States. By 1920, when the Sixth International Psychoanalytic Congress took place at The Hague, the portentous title which Freud had conferred on these gatherings twelve years previously no longer seemed excessive. For the psychoanalytic movement had by that time become the truly international and cosmopolitan organisation it has remained ever since.

It is sometimes imagined, by those who are unfamiliar with the history of psychoanalysis, that the movement grew up spontaneously in response to Freud's writings and to the success of his therapeutic methods. It is true that Freud's writings did carry his views far afield. But it would be quite wrong to imagine that Freud himself remained a passive spectator who merely watched his movement grow. We have already seen the extent to which Freud's entire intellectual development, from his early papers on cocaine onwards, was shaped by his messianic character. Now, as he took the steps which would eventually lead to the creation of the psychoanalytic movement, this aspect of his intellectual biography became more prominent.

Freud's academic elevation, taken together with his success in attracting a small circle of devoted followers, seems to have strengthened his long-held belief that he had made a potentially world-redeeming discovery, and that he was in possession of truths which, as a matter of duty, he should now assiduously propagate. When, in 1906, he received a letter from his first Swiss correspondent, Max Eitingon, who wrote to say that his superiors 'Prof Bleuler and Dr Jung' had called Freud's work to his attention, Freud was quick to express his delight at seeing a young man attracted, as he put it, 'by the truth content of our teachings'.[1] 'We possess the truth,' he wrote to Ferenczi in 1913; 'I am as sure of it as fifteen years ago.'[2]

To suggest that his mission now took on an increasingly religious character is not to venture an insight which is in any respect new. For even the most orthodox and respectful commentators on psychoanalysis have been obliged to register the change which now came over Freud. Ronald Clark, one of Freud's more recent biographers, who is in no sense hostile to psychoanalysis, characterises the change well. As psychoanalysis began to attract attention, he writes:

> Freud's belief that he had discovered the subterranean motives of conduct was subsumed into a fervour compounded of dedication and an almost divine mission in life. From the Jewish doctor convinced that he had found the key to human behaviour, the decent man anxious to ameliorate some of the miseries of the world, there emerged the leader determined to guide the human race towards the promised land.[3]

Ronald Clark's language, which might seem excessive if applied to any other modern thinker, is entirely appropriate to the case of Freud. What it suggests once again is that Freud's achievement cannot be understood if we treat him simply as a scientist, a psychologist or even as the creator of a biological pseudo-science; it can be understood, finally, only if we regard him in the way in which, deep within his own heart, he saw himself – as a messiah and as the founder of a new religion.

Freud's new religion was, in very many respects, but a reformulation of a very old religion. It is this old religion which still stands in the way of a real understanding of its latter-day transformations. For because of our residual respect for the Christian tradition and for a faith whose major prophet was traditionally viewed in supernatural terms, we are not used to thinking naturalistically about messianic personalities. As a consequence of this the *psychology* of messiahdom has rarely, if ever, been considered in any depth. Of those who have touched upon the subject, one of the most interesting commentators is Frank Manuel, to whose study of Newton's religious development I have already referred. Newton, as we have seen, himself had messianic inclinations which were, if anything, even stronger than those of Freud. Yet, in spite of the strength of these inclinations and the manner in which they shaped Newton's development from boyhood onwards, it would probably be wrong to suggest that Newton was ever possessed by messianic *convictions*. Indeed it is Frank Manuel who suggests otherwise when he writes that it is the fate of the messiah to believe passionately that he has been chosen and yet still inwardly to doubt:

> To believe that one had penetrated the ultimate secrets of God's uni-
> verse and to doubt it, to be the Messiah and to wonder about one's
> anointedness, is the fate of prophets. Newton's conviction that he was
> a chosen one of God, miraculously preserved, was accompanied by the
> terror that he would be found unworthy and would provoke the wrath
> of God the Father.[4]

No words could summarise more succinctly the profound conflicts which cannot but rage within the messianic soul. Throughout history those possessed by messianic fantasies have betrayed in their outward behaviour the pattern of doubting conviction which Frank Manuel describes. Again and again, as if in the quest for some outward and public confirmation of their own most passionate and secret beliefs, they have 'dared God' openly to reveal his will, and they have done so by engaging in prophecy or by leading their followers into political predicaments, rebellions or wars, from which no merely human resources could ever be expected to deliver them.[5] Classically, however, the messiah's quest for some external confirmation of his own secret identity has also manifested itself in a more common form – in the desire to attract followers, and having done so, to make huge demands of loyalty, as if to test the obedience of his disciples, and to prove his own supernatural ascendancy by the quality and completeness of the submission he can command.

This pattern can certainly be discerned in the portrait of Jesus drawn in the Bible. For, read sceptically, the gospels portray Jesus not as a messiah confident of his calling, but as a self-doubting prophet whose tendency to submit to others is almost as great as his impulse to lead. He is first introduced not as a religious leader at all, but as a follower of another itinerant preacher, John the Baptist, whom he apparently regarded as divinely inspired. In Jesus's initial submission to John the

Baptist it is not difficult to see the characteristic insecurity of the messianic personality who, doubting his own divine calling, feels compelled to project his sense of election onto others. Only gradually does he assume for himself the role of the messianic prophet, and, as if to reassure himself that this role is indeed his, his entire life becomes a quest for followers who are prepared to swear obedience to him and publicly bear witness to their love for his person.

If we place this classic messianic pattern alongside the behaviour of a much later prophetic personality, Isaac Newton, there are some interesting divergences. Newton in one sense was a traditional messianic figure who seems to have experienced an acute sense of divine election and who manifested this sense of his own specialness partly through his interest in the prophetic books of the Bible.[6] Yet it could scarcely be claimed that Newton showed any marked tendency to seek out disciples or that he demanded unswerving obedience from a group of followers. He certainly seems to have believed that he had been called by God to provide a unique insight into the mysteries of the universe, and the divine mind itself. As Frank Manuel suggests, it is improbable indeed that such huge aspirations would not be surrounded by a considerable degree of self-doubt. Yet Newton's methods of stilling these doubts were significantly different and more modern than those of earlier 'prophets'. Traditional apocalyptists and students of prophecy had made elaborate use of numerology and arithmetic in an attempt to calculate the future course of history and accurately predict the Second Coming. Newton, however, while himself a compulsive student of such prophecies, developed alongside this religious arithmetic of the unseen a more profound mathematics of the seen – a calculus of nature whose predictions, theories and laws could be verified by meticulous observation and experiment. Ultimately he did not need to create a band of disciples around him in order to reassure himself about his own perspicacity. Convinced that Nature was both the creation and the reflection of the omnipotent mind of God, he was able to test out his own natural theology and the sense he had of his own prophetic mission against the reality of the world as it was experienced through the senses. Scientific empiricism had come of age. Although it grew directly out of Christian theology, its reliance on observation and experiment had created an epistemology which could, in theory at least, confute its own theistic premises.

When, in the middle of the nineteenth century, Charles Darwin formulated the theory of natural selection, the Christian science of

Newton and his successors was finally replaced by a thoroughgoing secular empiricism. It is not difficult, however, to discover behind Darwin's apparent scientific assurance the same pattern of doubting conviction which can be discerned in the behaviour of earlier prophetic figures. Even as he sent off copies of *The Origin of Species*, after twenty years of hesitating on the brink of publishing his theory, he was racked by doubts. The doubts are painfully expressed in the notes which accompanied the complimentary copies he sent to his friends and colleagues. 'I may . . . be egregiously wrong,' he wrote to Jenyns. And to the Oxford geologist John Phillips he predicted 'You will fulminate anathemas.' Even more revealing is the note he sent to the palaeontologist Hugh Falconer, which hints, perhaps, at the depth of his own secret messianic identity: 'Lord how savage you will be,' he wrote, '. . . how you will long to crucify me alive.'[7] As such comments imply, Darwin was deeply concerned about how his colleagues would react to his book, craving acceptance and fearing that he might 'have devoted [his] life to a fantasy'. He himself admitted that he was 'foolishly anxious' about how Charles Lyell would receive his book.[8] But although Darwin accepted supporters gratefully, he did little actively to seek them out, still less to organise them into a movement. He stilled his own doubts primarily by the care with which he thought through his arguments and tested them against an extraordinary wealth of evidence culled from years of patient observation and experiment. By the time he put forward his theory Darwin had become, as he put it, 'a complete millionaire in odd and curious little facts'. 'I am like Croesus,' he said on another occasion, 'overwhelmed with my riches in facts.'[9]

It must be said that Darwin's respect for evidence and sound argument was not a feature of his writings on human nature and human society and that these assumed a reckless and wholly unscientific character as a result. But so long as he focused his attention on the world of animals and plants he showed himself a scientist of unparalleled sensitivity, imagination and theoretical acuteness. His painful uncertainty about the rightness of his theories became the very engine of his science, impelling him to seek out ever more profound matches between theory and empirical fact until his own objections and those of others collapsed under the massive weight of evidence and argument which was heaped upon them. Although others, including Thomas Huxley, proselytised the creed of evolution with near-religious fervour, Darwin himself did not need to. He sought security in science, and found it ultimately in the integrity of his own empirical methodology.

To turn from the examples of Newton and Darwin to that of Freud is in one sense to travel backwards in history rather than forwards. For while the effort Freud devoted to elaborating his theories is clear enough, there were other respects in which he resembled the traditional prophet more closely than he did the modern scientist – not least in his reliance on the numerological mysticism of Wilhelm Fliess. As a trained scientist thoroughly schooled in nineteenth-century empiricism, Freud himself could not but be obliquely aware of the deficiency of his own theories. Ultimately, as he must have known, there was no method of testing out these theories or of assessing their worth which was not predicated upon the assumption of his own genius. Whereas Darwin's theories, built patiently, carefully and lovingly on an accumulated bedrock of evidence, were a source of existential security, Freud's theories were like an immense, flawed structure suspended over an abyss. Unconsciously, in order to protect this precarious structure against the scepticism of his critics, Freud began to fortify the psychoanalytic movement with his own messianic personality.

In this respect, Freud's activities as a lecturer were particularly important to the nascent psychoanalytic movement. For he was a talented public speaker with very considerable gifts of exposition and an unusual ability to present his own highly speculative theories in a manner which made them seem reasonable and restrained. Wearing the mantle of academic authority easily, he had clearly developed a style which conveyed not simply his own ideas but also his own very considerable charisma and personal magnetism, qualities which he now exploited with increasing confidence and effectiveness.

Even before his academic elevation Freud had occasionally attracted disciples. In 1900, for example, after the publication of *The Interpretation of Dreams*, he had been contacted by a young Viennese physician, Wilhelm Stekel, who had hailed his book as one which inaugurated 'a new science of dream interpretation'. Stekel rapidly became one of Freud's most devoted followers and in the autumn of 1902 his suggestion that Freud should start a discussion group devoted to exploring his ideas was eagerly accepted. Freud asked two Viennese physicians who had been attending his lectures to join the group. He also invited Alfred Adler, a doctor who had recently become interested in the study of mental disorders. The result was the first meeting of what became known as the Wednesday Psychological Society, which would eventually be transformed in 1908 into the Vienna Psychoanalytic Society. According to Stekel's recollections, the early meetings of the Wednesday group proved inspirational. 'There was complete harmony among the five, no dissonances; we were like pioneers in a newly discovered land, and Freud was the leader. A spark seemed to jump from one mind to another, and every evening was like a revelation.'[10]

Freud in this respect continued to follow a messianic pattern of development. Like countless other messianic figures, having waited unsuccessfully for the world at large to recognise his unique value and the significance of the truths he believed he had uncovered, he now set about building a small select group of followers who would supply him with the adulation he craved and which he genuinely believed he merited. For several years this role had been played, in part, by Fliess. But Freud's relationship to Fliess had been complex and he frequently tended, as we have seen, to project onto him his own messianic identity. After his academic elevation, by which he set so much store, Freud was at last beginning to claim that identity as his own. He began deliberately to seek out the kind of intelligent, imaginative but also deeply insecure intellectuals who he felt were worthy of his attention and who he intuitively felt would submit to his leadership. Finding such suitable disciples became one of the most important of his preoccupations during the early years of the century. Significantly, he even recalled the words which Jesus had used to his disciples in order to describe the task of evangelism, referring to himself as a 'fisher of men'.[11]

That the first meetings of the Wednesday group had something of a religious character is perhaps indicated already by Stekel's description. Alongside this we may place the confession which he made elsewhere in his autobiography: 'I was the apostle of Freud who was my Christ!'[12] The picture of the Wednesday group as a kind of religious sect with Freud as the leader is lent further support by Max Graf, who was eventually driven out of the circle by what he saw as Freud's dogmatism:

> The gatherings followed a definite ritual. First, one of the members would present a paper. Then, black coffee and cakes were served; cigars and cigarettes were on the table and were consumed in great quantities. After a social quarter of an hour the discussion would begin. The last and the decisive word was always spoken by Freud himself. There was the atmosphere of the foundation of a religion in that room. Freud himself was its new prophet who made the heretofore prevailing methods of psychological investigation appear superficial. Freud's pupils – all inspired and convinced – were his apostles . . . However, after the

first dreamy period and the unquestioning faith of the first group of apostles, the time came when the church was founded. Freud began to organise the church with great energy. He was serious and strict in the demands he made of his pupils; he permitted no deviations from his orthodox teaching.[13]

It is a measure of Freud's powers of persuasion that Graf himself, even though he left the group, remained convinced that Freud's strategy was justifiable in pragmatic terms since his doctrines had to be preserved against 'hesitations and weakening'. The more sceptical and, I believe, the more truthful view is that Freud's dogmatism and his need to proselytise reflected not the assurance of a true discoverer, but the anxiety of an intellectual adventurer whose outer confidence was but a mask for a profound sense of intellectual insecurity. Freud, on this view, felt himself inwardly driven to disguise the deficiency of his theories by veiling himself in the charisma of the prophet. He then went on to represent, both to himself and to others, the fundamentally religious dependence of his followers as objective intellectual assent to psychoanalysis.

The Wednesday Society, having started as a circle of five men who gathered around Freud, quickly grew until there were more than twenty members. In 1905 a young, shy intellectual named Otto Rank joined the circle. Other recruits included Hans Sachs, a lawyer, and Sandor Ferenczi, a Budapest physician who had been trained as a neurologist, and who had begun to experiment with psychoanalysis after reading some of Freud's works. To the casual observer there was nothing in the constitution of the society which suggested that it was anything other than a debating chamber for psychological ideas. Freud himself frequently reiterated his commitment to open discussion and would listen to all the contributions which were made with scrupulous attention. Yet at the same time, although the Wednesday Society encouraged informality at many levels, there was never any question of intellectual egalitarianism. Freud remained decisively in the position of leader, arbiter and judge of his pupils and their work. When dissension began to break out in the group in 1907, Freud took the extraordinary measure of disbanding the entire group. During September he sent members a circular letter announcing that he wished to dissolve his 'little Society' and immediately afterwards call it to life again as the Vienna Psychoanalytic Society. He suggested that any members who did not feel as enthusiastic about the discussions as they had in the past might now take the opportunity to resign. The intention behind Freud's action was apparently to eliminate any potential dissidents and to compel those who wished to continue to reaffirm their loyalty to him. He was, in effect, asking them to make their marriage vows over again.

Although he maintained cordial relationships with his followers, he rarely permitted intimacies of any kind and held himself aloof even from those he had known for a long time. When Hans Sachs met him in London shortly before Freud's death he recorded that his mentor remained just as remote as when he had first met him in Vienna thirty years previously.[14] The emotional distance which Freud preserved between himself and almost all his followers was crucial to his style of leadership. Just as such remoteness led Freud's patients to redouble their efforts to secure emotional recognition from their analyst, so Freud's followers were forced into a similar position. The more he played the part of an inscrutable god, the more they felt the need to compete for some sign of his favour. Hans Sachs is one of many commentators who has pointed to the role which was played in the early psychoanalytic movement by 'the rivalry for Freud's acclaim and approbation'.[15] When the emotional intimacy which Freud's disciples sought was not forthcoming they often adopted the characteristic attitude of the disciple, treating Freud with reverence and awe and sometimes openly identifying with him. Fritz Wittels recalls that the small group of Freud's earliest followers who attended Freud's Saturday evening lectures at the University of Vienna used to accompany Freud 'in triumph' as he left the lecture theatre, deliberately making themselves as conspicuous as possible.[16] They knew Freud's works by heart – even the footnotes, according to Wittels.

Paul Roazen quotes one of Mahatma Gandhi's followers in order to illustrate the dedication that disciples can develop for their master: 'I am not going to Gandhiji with the ambition of achieving success. I want to live like his shadow . . .' Roazen comments that 'many of Freud's followers had exactly this feeling towards the master'.[17] The dedication which Freud's disciples showed to their leader was evident not only in the religious enthusiasm with which they evangelised his cause, but also in some of the smaller details of their own behaviour. Many of Freud's closest followers took to smoking cigars like him. According to Paul Roazen some of them even acquired Freud's neurotic traits; Sachs became obsessional about railway trains in exactly the same way as Freud. Another well-known follower, Theodor Reik, 'always sought to imitate Freud – in his smoking, in his style of writing, and even in the way he talked. Once in America he grew a beard like Freud's.'[18] Many commentators on psychoanalysis will insist that the 'pure' theoretical issues raised by psychoanalysis can be entirely separated from such 'personal' details as these or from the manner in which Freud behaved towards his disciples. Richard Wollheim, for instance, has adopted this attitude towards Paul Roazen's *Freud and His Followers*, in which the above details are recorded. He describes Roazen's book as 'a prime example' of 'the denigratory school' and writes that it contains 'a battery of miscellaneous and uncoordinated criticism ... much of it aimed at a target that conflates the thought and the man'.[19] Yet the craven dependence which many of Freud's followers showed towards his ideas cannot ultimately be treated separately from the dependence they showed towards him as a person. In scientific terms the reasons for adopting his theories were, as I have tried to show, no better than the reasons which might be given for imitating his way of talking or taking over his neurotic habits. In both cases we are confronted not by a reasoned decision but by an act of irrational submission to the power of Freud's personality and to the capacity he had for projecting himself, both in his life and his writings, as a prophet, sage, healer, and even redeemer.

The resemblances of the psychoanalytic movement to an organised religion have frequently been noted both by the movement's opponents and by its adherents. As Frank Sulloway has written: 'Few theories in science have spawned a following that can compare with the psychoanalytic movement in its cultlike manifestations, in its militancy, and in the aura of a religion that has permeated it.'[20] Sulloway points out that the psychoanalytic movement's sect-like characteristics were many and various. He cites the sociologist George Weisz to the effect that the most prominent of these characteristics

> were the group's elitism and sense of exclusiveness, combined with an extreme mistrust of and hostility toward the outside world; an eschatological vision of reality which made adherence to the group an experience approaching religious conversion; and, more important, an exaggerated reverence for the founder which transcended the normal bounds of scientific authoritarianism ...[21]

Weisz goes on to point out that one of the factors which encourages movements to adopt such cult-like characteristics is the nature of the doctrine which they promulgate; doctrines which seek to answer fundamental questions about life and death are more likely to be embraced with sectarian fervour than those which treat less universal issues. This contention in itself seems reasonable enough. But it is scarcely sufficient to explain the quite remarkable success which psychoanalysis has enjoyed among twentieth-century intellectuals. There have, after all, been many attempts to answer fundamental questions about life and death which have never shown any signs of developing into coherent and historically influential movements. Many of the theories of Fliess were, as we have seen, concerned with just such large issues. But only those ideas which Freud took over from him have survived. Most of Fliess's vast theoretical edifice, especially his numerological approach to periodicity, has disappeared from history with scarcely a trace.

What does seem clear is that the doctrine which did more than any other to give the psychoanalytic movement its distinctive identity was Freud's theory of infantile sexuality, as expounded in his *Three Essays on the Theory of Sexuality*. Of this small book one of Freud's most approving biographers, Peter Gay, has written that Freud 'used it as a kind of touchstone, separating those who truly accepted his libido theory from those who were unwilling to grant sexuality the prominent place he himself assigned to it, or who had found it prudent to retreat from his scandalous ideas'.[22] Gay's observation is entirely accurate. Perhaps even more revealing are the comments of some of Freud's contemporaries. In 1924 Fritz Wittels wrote:

> He watches over this theory jealously, will not tolerate the smallest deviation from it, and fences it round with a palisade. It was on account of differences concerning this theory that breaches occurred between Freud and three of the most noted among his scientific collaborators: Jung, Adler and Stekel.[23]

The sacredness of the libido theory is borne out by Jung's recollections:

> There was no mistaking the fact that Freud was emotionally involved in his sexual theory to an extraordinary degree. When he spoke of it his tone became urgent, almost anxious, and all signs of his normally critical, sceptical manner vanished. A strange, deeply moved expression came over his face, the cause of which I was at a loss to understand . . .
> I can still recall vividly how Freud said to me, 'My dear Jung, promise me never to abandon the sexual theory. That is the most essential thing

of all. You see, we must make a dogma of it, an unshakeable bulwark.'
He said that to me with great emotion, in the tone of a father saying,
'And promise me one thing, my dear son: that you will go to church
every Sunday.'[24]

The theory of infantile sexuality was in effect adopted as the creed of
the Freudian church. Those who embraced it were accepted. Those
who did not were rejected. Thus when Max Graf looked back on the
expulsion of Adler he saw his refusal to accept the libido theory as a
heresy punished by excommunication: 'Freud – as the head of a church
– banished Adler; he ejected him from the official church. Within the
space of a few years I lived through the whole development of a church
history . . .'[25]

Freud's theory of infantile sexuality was entirely based on false science
and was elaborated by spurious logic. Yet in spite of its deficiencies,
it has not simply survived, but has served as the theoretical cornerstone
of the entire psychoanalytic movement. The question which inevitably
arises is how such a flimsy and ill-conceived theory ever came to occupy
a position of such prominence, and why it succeeded in attracting
successive generations of followers – some of them possessed of
unusual creative and intellectual gifts.

One partial answer to this question is that it was intrinsically a
much more attractive theory than Freud's earlier sexual hypothesis.
For Freud's seduction theory suffered from the fact that it was, from
a professional point of view, almost completely self-defeating. Not
only did it set itself against sexual orthodoxies in a way that repelled
rather than attracted disciples, but, as we have seen, it also meant that
any father prepared to pay for his daughter to be given therapy by
Freud might very well be paying in order to be incriminated as a sexual
pervert. Freud's theory of infantile sexuality suffered from neither of
these drawbacks. For although its involvement with sexuality still
deterred some potential disciples, it did not run counter either to
biological orthodoxies or, perhaps more importantly still, to the dominating sexual ideology of Judaeo-Christian culture.

At the broadest and most general level, Freud's nineteenth-century
biologism drew its scientific authority from Darwin's theory of natural
selection. But it was by no means a purely scientific phenomenon. For
one of the major cultural functions of Darwin's evolutionary theory had
been that of legitimating the nineteenth-century doctrine of inevitable

progress, and making this doctrine seem as though it were merely an expression of natural laws. Although it is widely held that 'Social Darwinism' was based on a corrupted version of Darwin's theories, almost all the doctrines associated with it can be traced back to Darwin himself. It is quite true that Charles Darwin once wrote, in the form of a reminder to himself, 'Never use the words higher and lower.' Yet, after he had written these words, Darwin himself admitted that he was in a 'muddle' about teleology and he repeatedly failed to heed his own most subversive principle. Instead he consistently portrayed evolution as a competitive struggle for ascendancy and he himself wrote in the closing pages of *The Descent of Man*, to cite but one example, of how 'man' had 'risen, though not through his own exertions, to the very summit of the organic scale' and also spoke of the possibility of 'a still *higher* destiny in the future'.[26]

That the fundamental idea which lay behind all nineteenth-century theories of evolutionary progress was a moral and religious one is perhaps indicated most clearly in some words written by Havelock Ellis: 'It has been well said that purity – which in the last analysis is physical clearness – is the final result after which Nature is ever striving.'[27] It was this crypto-theological notion of evolution as an ever-upward progress away from earlier forms of animal life and towards spiritual and social perfection which came to be inseparable from the way Darwinian biology was received and interpreted.

Freud frequently expressed scepticism about the more facile manifestations of this conception of biological progress. Yet for all the pessimism with which he tempered his own philosophy, he never succeeded in escaping from the *Zeitgeist* of evolutionary progressivism. At the very heart of all his theorising about sexual development and human history is a passionate, culturally orthodox belief, derived ultimately from Judaeo-Christian apocalyptic, that human beings are fulfilling their historic destiny by progressively leaving behind their animal origins and developing a more rational and sublimated consciousness. To put the matter in traditional religious terms, Freud saw human history as a difficult upward progress from the realm of the flesh towards the realm of the spirit. While not sharing the optimism of those rationalists who held that future progress towards an even higher spiritual level was inevitable, his hierarchy of values never ceased to be shaped by the traditional view. He once told a patient that 'the moral self was the conscious, the evil self was the unconscious.'[28] In describing the underlying aspiration of psychoanalytic treatment, he wrote the following words which have been quoted already in the Introduction:

> [We] liberate sexuality through our treatment, not in order that man may from now on be dominated by sexuality, but in order to make a suppression possible – a rejection of the instincts under the guidance of a higher agency . . . We try to replace the pathological process with rejection.[29]

As these words themselves suggest, there is a constant tension in Freud's writings between the desire to explore the animal origins of human beings, together with their instinctual heritage, and the impulse to transcend this animality. But there is never ultimately any question that the path of transcendence – or 'sublimation' – represents the ideal. 'We have no other means of controlling our instinctual nature but our intelligence,' he wrote, '. . . the psychological ideal [is] . . . the primacy of the intelligence.'[30]

There can be little doubt that this consonance between the ethos of psychoanalysis and that of Judaeo-Christian orthodoxy was partly responsible for the initial success of psychoanalysis, and that it helps to explain why Freud's followers sometimes behaved more like the members of a church than an association of scientists. The survival of the psychoanalytic movement and its continuing strength today, however, seems to require a more specific explanation than can be supplied by vague comparisons between the ethos of psychoanalysis and that of the Judaeo-Christian tradition.

One way of approaching this problem is to consider the manner in which Freud's own attitude towards the ideas of health and illness changed and developed during the twenty years which elapsed between his visit to Charcot in Paris and the publication of his theory of sexuality. At the outset Freud was concerned almost exclusively with patients who, since they presented eminently physical symptoms, would have been deemed 'ill' by most physicians. By the time he published his sexual theory, however, many of his patients were not 'ill' in the traditional sense of that word. For increasingly Freud began to concern himself not with people suffering from physical symptoms, but with individuals who were clearly experiencing acute emotional distress – such as the woman afflicted by jealousy or the young woman with the obsessional bed-time rituals whose cases were discussed earlier (see above, Chapter 12).

From the fact that Freud progressed in this manner away from illnesses characterised by physical symptoms towards the analysis of people's emotional difficulties, we might well conclude that he eventually succeeded in freeing himself from his narrow medical orientation towards 'illness', and replacing this attitude with a completely psychological viewpoint which was entirely independent both of biology and of medicine. This point of view is advanced frequently not only by the advocates of psychoanalysis but also by many ostensibly independent onlookers. Yet to accept this view – with its implicit disjunction between Freud's early and later work – would be to paint an entirely false picture of how psychoanalysis actually developed.

For, from the time of his collaboration with Breuer onwards, Freud never ceased to regard himself, and to seek to be regarded by others, as a healer. It is quite true that, like many messianic personalities before him, he was not prepared to allow himself to be constrained by the apparent limitations of this role. But it was not by turning away from those who were ill towards those who were healthy that he sought to escape these. It was by enlarging the notion of disease and applying it to those who, in reality, were not ill at all.[31]

Freud's success in progressively universalising the concept of illness was almost entirely due, in the first place, to his unsceptical embrace of Charcot's theories. For once he had accepted the basic medical misconception propagated by Charcot – that *real* physical symptoms such as paralyses or contractures could be *directly* caused by ideas or emotions concealed in some unconscious area of the mind – then it seemed to follow that any form of abnormal behaviour which appeared to have emotional conflict as its cause was *ipso facto* a form of illness. When Freud originally accepted Charcot's confabulated solution to the problem of hysteria, his notion of a pathogenic unconscious, capable of generating disease, applied only to a small number of patients. The scope of Freud's seduction theory was similarly limited. Yet by the time Freud had elaborated his doctrine of the Unconscious with the help of ideas drawn from Breuer and Fliess, and developed fully his theory of infantile sexuality, his concept of illness seemed to apply to almost everybody. For everybody, if not actually ill, was now deemed to carry within them the pathogenic impulses which might engender 'neurotic illness' at almost any juncture in their lives.

The course taken by Freud in starting as a healer who at first dispenses supposedly miraculous cures to a small number of sick people, and then subsequently universalises the concept of illness so that all individuals might be deemed to be in need of a physician, should be familiar to us. For a similar pattern of development is implicit in the doctrines of Jesus and the subsequent development of the Christian Church. The general pattern is noted by David Bakan in his study of the influence of Jewish mysticism on Freud's thought:

> That psychoanalysis should have grown up in the context of the healing of the sick who were incurable by orthodox medical means accords with the Messianic quality of the psychoanalytic movement. For Messianism characteristically proves itself first by miraculously healing the sick. Thereafter it reaches out to large-scale social reform. So Freud's psycho-analysis reached out from the healing of individuals to the healing of society.[32]

Freud himself is clearly unaware of the depth of his own submerged religious traditionalism when, in a significant passage, he introduces psychoanalysis as one of the great blows inflicted on 'the naive self love of man'. The previous blow, he says, had come from Darwin, who had proved 'man's . . . ineradicable animal nature'.[33] This passage, in which Freud is clearly referring to his theory of the Unconscious, is frequently quoted by commentators on psychoanalysis. But its full significance is not always appreciated. For what Freud ignores, and what we tend not to notice, is that his words belong not to the realm of objective science, but to the realm of ethics. More importantly still, the moral aim which Freud implicitly professes is precisely the same as that of St Augustine, when he elaborated the doctrine which was to lie at the heart of Christian orthodoxy until at least the beginning of the eighteenth century – the doctrine of Original Sin. The very essence of that doctrine was to be found in the attack it made on spiritual pride – or what Freud called 'the naive self love of man'. The way in which it made this attack was by offering a theory of human nature according to which men and women, rather than being in con-trol of their own lives, were doomed to remain the prey of a seething and unclean mass of impulses and desires which had become, through Adam's fall, an ineradicable part of their nature. Individuals might seek to control these impulses through the use of reason, but they could never hope to escape from them within their earthly lives. The religious importance of this doctrine was that through it, and it alone, could the need for Christian redemption be established. For one of the essential points of the doctrine was that it universalised the concept of illness. By postulating that all human beings were afflicted by sickness of the soul it suggested that all equally stood in need of a physician. In the words of Pascal, the traditional Christian faith rested on two things, 'the corruption of nature and redemption by Jesus Christ'.[34]

The doctrine of Original Sin reigned for centuries as perhaps the most important psychological theory of Christian Europe. Its immense historical significance and its deep psychological appeal is an essential part of the heritage of modern intellectual culture. Yet one of the eventual outcomes of the rational spirit of the Reformation, and of the Counter-Reformation in the Roman Catholic Church, was that the doctrine tended increasingly to be repudiated by theologians and intellectuals. Quoting Pascal's words, and referring mainly to Protestant England, T. O. Wedel has written that 'half at least of Pascal's formula is seldom spoken of after 1700.'[35]

Yet although the doctrine of Original Sin has tended to be progressively weakened by the central tradition of Protestant rationalism, one of the main projects of religious traditionalists has always been to restore the doctrine to a position of theological centrality. If we wish to place the psychoanalytic movement in perspective, and understand the religious psychology which underpins both its cult-like features and the messianic role adopted by its founder, one way of doing so is to consider it in relation to earlier, more overtly religious movements which have taken a particular interest in the doctrine of Original Sin.

One of the most significant of all such movements in England was the Methodist Church founded by John Wesley. Wesley's longest written work was actually entitled *The Doctrine of Original Sin* (1757). In this work, after surveying the host of optimistic views of nature and human nature which prevailed in the middle of the eighteenth century, Wesley inveighed against the arrogance of 'the present generation of Christians':

> How many laboured panegyrics do we now read and hear on the dignity of human nature! . . . I cannot see that we have much need of Christianity. Nay, not any at all; for 'they that are whole have no need of a physician' . . . Nor can Christian philosophy, whatever be thought of the pagan, be more properly defined than in Plato's words: 'the only true method of healing a distempered soul.' But what need of this if we are in perfect health?[36]

It would be difficult to find a clearer example of the tendency of Christianity to universalise the concept of illness. One of the aims of Wesley's movement, indeed, was to re-establish the 'reality' of the

Christian's distempered soul. It did this by vitalising all the anxieties about irrational and sexual impulses which Christians had traditionally been encouraged to feel but which had been, as it were, disconnected from the consciousness of mainstream Protestant rationalism. Wesley and his followers believed that it was necessary to bring these buried anxieties back into the Christian consciousness, for it was only by doing this that they could establish people's need for the religious therapy which they offered.

Wesley was by no means alone in seeking to revive the traditional doctrine of Original Sin. The work which he referred to most frequently in his own disquisition on the doctrine was none other than Jonathan Swift's *Gulliver's Travels*. For, as one or two largely forgotten literary critics have recognised, Swift's scatological satire was, no less than Wesley's religious propaganda, directed against the spiritual pride and naive self-love of 'man', which he felt was expressed by the rationalist optimism which surrounded him.[37] In place of the view of human beings which saw them existing in harmonious, rational integration, Swift reasserted the traditional Christian view according to which they were profoundly divided between their rational souls and their carnal bodies. We can only understand Swift's satirical intentions if we recognise that the excrement-loving Yahoos which Gulliver encounters in his Fourth Voyage are to be seen as an imaginative representation of this sinful carnal body. 'Unregenerate man' is in this way presented by Swift in very much the same way as he had been by St Paul, St Augustine and countless other exponents of the traditional doctrine of Original Sin – as a 'lump of deformity and diseases both in body and mind, smitten with pride'.[38]

Deane Swift, the biographer of his cousin Jonathan, recognised this in a way that modern literary critics have generally failed to do when he defended *Gulliver's Travels* against the attacks of Anglican rationalists. In describing the Yahoos, Swift was, wrote his cousin, fulfilling his duties as 'a preacher of righteousness' and 'a watchman of the Christian faith':

> And shall we condemn a preacher of righteousness, for exposing under the character of a nasty, unteachable *Yahoo* the deformity, the blackness, the filthiness, and corruption of those hellish abominable vices, which inflame the wrath of God against the children of disobedience.[39]

We should recall here that the Yahoo vices by which the 'children of disobedience' are seen as 'inflaming the wrath of God' are, in Swift's imaginative restatement of the doctrine of Original Sin, the same vices against which Christian moralists had always warned. For the Yahoos are portrayed not only as excrementally unclean, but as driven by uncontrollable sexual and sadistic impulses and as possessed by an animal lust for financial gain. The implicit moral of Swift's religious satire is that Gulliver can be saved from his own destructive and naive self-love only by accepting the hideousness of his animality and the depth of his carnal sinfulness. For it is only when he has first done this that he will be made aware of his own deep need for the redemption offered through Christianity.

The relevance of these largely forgotten aspects of religious history to the creation of psychoanalysis and its twentieth-century reception should not be difficult to divine. For in the intellectual environment of nineteenth-century Vienna Freud found himself in a cultural predicament which was in many respects similar to that experienced by Jonathan Swift in the eighteenth century. With certain significant exceptions the intellectual climate was one of assured rational optimism. Many of the most influential rationalist thinkers seemed determined to forget that men and women had ever possessed such things as bodies and all those animal impulses and appetites with which bodies are associated. These, together with all forms of sexual behaviour, were often treated as the animal residue of a nature which could eventually be refined, by the power of science, into pure rationality.

Freud believed that the strategy which he chose in order to resist this intellectual trend was a scientific one. It was, as we have seen, within the framework of biological assumptions which had been created by Darwin and Haeckel that he constructed his theory of infantile sexuality, in which he proclaimed the discovery of such component-instincts as 'oral-erotism' and 'anal-erotism'. While many of Freud's contemporaries were outraged by his views, the success which psychoanalysis ultimately enjoyed itself indicates that there were other reactions. In 1917 the Harvard biologist William Morton Wheeler spoke for many when he contrasted the theories of psychoanalysis with other more rationalistic psychologies:

> After perusing during the past twenty years a small library of rose-water psychologies of the academic type and noticing how their authors ignore or merely hint at the existence of such stupendous and fundamental biological phenomena as those of hunger, sex, or fear, I should not

disagree with, let us say, an imaginary critic recently arrived from Mars, who should express the opinion that many of these works read as if they had been composed by beings that had been born and bred in a belfry, castrated in early infancy and fed continually for fifty years through a tube with a stream of liquid nutriment of constant chemical composition . . .

Now I believe that the psychoanalysts are getting down to brass tacks . . . They have had the courage to dig up the subconscious, that hotbed of all the egotism, greed, lust, pugnacity, cowardice, sloth, hate and envy which every single one of us carries about as his inheritance from the animal world.[40]

Wheeler's caricature of contemporary rationalistic psychology expresses an entirely reasonable criticism. But he fails to recognise the true character of Freud's instinctualism. In this respect the most revealing part of his statement is his conclusion. For what is presented as a plea for biological realism is couched in the language of traditional Christian morality. Indeed, while ostensibly discussing the biological basis of human nature, Wheeler comes very close to presenting a list of the seven deadly sins.

The confusion which is apparent in Wheeler's language accurately mirrors that which lies at the heart of psychoanalysis. For, as should by now be clear, Freud's 'scientific' enterprise followed almost exactly the same pattern as many earlier attempts to revive the doctrine of Original Sin. Freud, no less than Swift or Wesley, offered a view of the personality which saw human nature as radically divided against itself. The animal impulses and appetites which he located in the self were characterised in predominantly negative terms. The most obscene levels of the sexual imagination were not, according to Freud, to be affirmed or incorporated into the whole identity and liberated as part of the riches of the self. Rather they were to be intellectually acknowledged and then controlled and sublimated through the power of reason.

Freud himself was not averse to using the traditional rhetoric of Judaeo-Christian moralism in order to express this aspect of his vision. Although his attitude towards sexual 'perversion' was benign in comparison to that of the most repressive Victorian commentators, he continued to employ the concept and sometimes came close to endorsing conventional views, as when he compared 'perverts' to 'the grotesque monsters painted by Breughel for the temptation of St Anthony', and characterised their sexual practices as 'abominable'.[41]

He used similar demonological imagery to describe the wishes behind dreams. These were, he once wrote, the 'manifestations of an unbridled and ruthless egotism . . . These censored wishes appear to rise up out of a positive Hell . . .'[42] Elsewhere Freud sometimes actually employs the term 'evil' in order to describe the Unconscious. As we have already seen, he refers at one point to the contrast between the moral self and the 'evil' self – equating the latter with the Unconscious.[43] In *A Short Account of Psychoanalysis* he writes that the 'impulses . . . subjected to repression are those of selfishness and cruelty, which can be summed up in general as evil, but above all sexual wishful impulses, often of the crudest and most forbidden kind.'[44] In a discussion of group psychology, he suggests that the individual tends to lose his repressions when he becomes part of the mass: 'The apparently new characteristics he then displays are in fact the manifestations of this unconscious, *in which all that is evil in the human mind is contained as a predisposition*' (italics added). That Freud sees it as desirable to suppress and control this 'evil' part of the mind is made quite clear: 'Our mind . . .' he writes, 'is no peacefully self-contained unity. It is rather to be compared with a modern State in which a mob, eager for enjoyment and destruction, has to be held down forcibly by a prudent superior class.'[45]

Freud genuinely believed that, by invoking evolutionary biology in the manner that he did, he was using science to sweep away superstition and introduce a new view of human nature. His real achievement in creating psychoanalysis, however, was to hide superstition beneath the rhetoric of reason in order to reintroduce a very old view of human nature. By portraying the unconscious or the 'id' as a seething mass of unclean impulses, and seeing men and women as driven by dark sexual and sadistic impulses and a secret love of excrement which was associated with a compulsion to hoard money, Freud in effect recreated Swift's Christian vision of 'unregenerate man' as a Yahoo. By casting his intense moral vision in an ostensibly technical form he effectively reinvented, for a modern scientific age, the traditional Christian doctrine of Original Sin.

FIFTEEN

Freud, Satan and the Serpent

THE VIEW THAT THERE are significant similarities between psychoanalysis and the Christian doctrine of Original Sin is not a new one. In an interesting essay published in the collection *Psychoanalysis Observed*, John Wren-Lewis has considered Freud's contention that psychoanalysis represents the third and final stage of a scientific revolution against the 'naive self-love' of human beings. He points out that Freud's view is a 'complete misrepresentation' of the effects of the scientific revolution and goes on to suggest that his words betray 'a wish to be morally censorious about humanity, a desire to make people feel small, exactly parallel to the traditional theological castigation of man for sinful pride'. More recently Ernest Gellner has drawn a direct parallel between Christian doctrine and psychoanalysis. One of the purposes of the doctrine of Original Sin, he observes, is to ensure that no one may shelter behind a consciousness of virtue:

> It is a spiritual equivalent of universal peasant indebtedness. Such universal and *starting-point* moral indebtedness makes certain that no one can even begin life with a clear ledger. Everyone then has ever-renewable and self-perpetuating debts to pay right from the very start, and must work arduously to pay them off, if he is to be granted even the hope of salvation. *The Unconscious is a new version of Original Sin.*[1]

In 1948 R. S. Lee, in his book *Freud and Christianity*, actually attempted to enlist psychoanalytic theories in defence of Christianity, seeing Freud's ideas as offering a scientific explanation of the doctrine of Original Sin:

> Here too is found the explanation of Original Sin ... It is not our concern to discuss the theological conception here, but psychoanalysis has thrown considerable light on what underlies the conception, The sense of sin comes, we have seen, from the personalisation of the Super-

ego at the resolution of the Oedipus Complex, by which the wish to destroy the father and possess the mother are mastered in the developing infant. If these wishes had not existed there would have been no need to form the Super-ego and so develop a moral conscience. Thus the precondition of getting a knowledge of good and evil at all is that we have sinned psychologically. A sense of guilt is inherent in our make-up. The original sin is the complex of wishes in the Oedipus Complex which we develop before we have a moral sense, but which remain, in varying degrees of fixation after we have developed that moral sense in dealing with them as dangerous wishes.[2]

Writing in 1960, David McClelland, a Quaker descended from radical Protestants, who was also a Harvard psychologist, suggested that Freud's attitude towards human sinfulness is one of the reasons 'why psychoanalysis has had such a great appeal to American intellectuals':

> Its insistence on the evil in man's nature, and in particular on the sexual root of that evil, suited the New England temperament well which had been shaped by a similar Puritan emphasis. In fact, to hear Anna Freud speak of the criminal tendencies of the one and two-year-old is to be reminded inevitably of Calvinistic sermons on infant damnation.[3]

Similar observations have been made by a number of different commentators. Yet although some observers have had no difficulty in spotting the *external* resemblance between psychoanalysis and the doctrine of Original Sin, the deeper significance of this resemblance has proved more elusive.

One reason for the failure to investigate the parallel has been the assumption that the superficial similarities conceal deeper and more significant differences. It is often assumed, for example, that whereas exponents of the traditional Christian doctrine of Original Sin have been deliberately setting out to create anxiety, and exacerbate feelings of guilt, Freud had discovered a way in which these feelings could be alleviated. To see the problem in this way, however, is to fail to understand the extent to which Freud, far from subverting Judaeo-Christian doctrines, merely adopted a modernised version of the sexual realism which was itself an integral part of traditional teachings. For Freud was by no means the first Judaeo-Christian thinker to take the view that 'we ought not to exalt ourselves so high as completely to neglect what was originally animal in our Nature.'[4] This view of human nature, which is above all a commentary on human *pride*, is Augustinian rather than Darwinian. As we have seen, it was just such a view which lay at the heart of the traditional doctrine of Original Sin. Nor should we see Freud's claim that some sexual impulses 'have a right to direct satisfaction' as in any way standing outside the traditional Judaeo-Christian view.[5] For mainstream Christian doctrine has always seen sexual impulses as being a part of human nature and – outside the priesthood at least – as having a right to direct expression; this view, indeed, is even more strong in Freud's own Jewish tradition than it is in Christianity. It was only the gradual rise of some of the extreme forms of religious and scientific rationalism encouraged by the Reformation, and the cultural dominance which such rationalism achieved in the eighteenth and nineteenth centuries, which had begun seriously to challenge this view. It was against this kind of rationalist extremism, and not against more traditional manifestations of Judaeo-Christian ideology, that Freud attempted to rebel.

The fact that his rebellion resembles, in some respects at least, that undertaken by Jonathan Swift in the eighteenth century may appear to vindicate psychoanalysis. There can, I believe, be no doubt that Swift was in some respects an acute and interesting psychologist – much more acute and interesting, perhaps, than Freud himself. It would nevertheless be quite wrong to suggest that Swift ever managed to subvert, or even to see clearly, the rationalistic orthodoxies he sought to criticise. In *Gulliver's Travels* his implicit moral had been clear: that only if people acknowledged the reality of their own sinful 'Yahoo' natures would they cease to project their corrupt nature onto others; by this means, and this means alone could human destructiveness be controlled and subdued.[6] The psychological truth which Swift cannot bring himself to confront, however, is that to expect people wholly to accept their sensuality *and* simultaneously to define that sensuality as sinful, is to make an impossible demand on the human personality. It is rather like expecting a poor man to accept a debt on the assumption that it will increase his solvency. For the very concept of sin implies an idealisation of some elements of the identity and a rejection of others. To portray human carnality in the form of a loathsome, sadistic, compulsively acquisitive, excrement-loving Yahoo, and *simultaneously* to demand that this carnality should be fully accepted as a part of the human identity is not, finally, to triumph over rationalist optimism; it is to concede defeat to it. For what we cannot but observe is that, although Swift saw himself as battling against the rationalist spirit of the Enlightenment, one of the basic assumptions of Swiftian psychology is itself rooted in a form of Enlightenment optimism. Swift assumes that a full acknowledgement of the 'sinful' elements of the identity can be made *in spite* of the emotional factors which militate against this; he implicitly assumes that this can be done through the power of human reason. Swift's works contain their own refutation of this view. His satire, for all the psychological insights it contains, is frequently both corrosive and bitter. His opposition to rationalism becomes at times an uncontrolled rage. In this raging hatred we cannot but see a form of that very projection against which he implicitly warns.

The possibility which Swift could not entertain was that the ills which he divined in eighteenth-century rationalism derived not from a rejection of Christianity but from a profound internalisation of its doctrines. For the contemporary trend towards the denial of the doctrine of Original Sin, which disturbed both Swift and Wesley so deeply, was in one sense a direct psychological consequence of the 'success' of that very doctrine. It suggested that, among some deeply ascetic intellectuals, a sense of the loathsomeness of the human body and its appetites had become so acute that the only psychologically viable reaction was to 'disconnect' the body altogether and take refuge in dreams of the rational, scientific or military domination of nature. It is ironic that, in satirising these dreams of power, Swift consistently offers as an 'objective' religious truth the very degrading self-image which is their psychological source.

The confusion which we find at the heart of Swift's psychology is not essentially different from that which is also present in psychoanalysis. For Freud, no less than Swift, assumes that it is possible for us to reconcile ourselves, through the power of human reason, to a self-image which is, in emotional terms, abhorrent and degrading. Just as the impossible nature of such a demand is reflected in Swift's corrosive satire, which is frequently directed *against* his own implicit universalism, so Freud's universalism frequently founders on the same kind of anxieties. The most valuable aspect of psychoanalysis is to be found in the way that it, like traditional expositions of the doctrine of Original Sin, forces back into our consciousness elements of our identity which we would prefer to conceal, and in this way points to a human predicament which is universal. Freud himself could on occasions be remarkably tolerant and generous, even in relation to homosexuality, which he found personally distasteful. In a letter which he wrote to the mother of a homosexual, Freud offered reassurance:

Homosexuality is assuredly no advantage, but it is nothing to be ashamed of, no vice, no degradation; it cannot be classified as an illness; we consider it to be a variation of the sexual function, produced by a certain arrest of sexual development. Many highly respected individuals of ancient and modern times have been homosexuals, several of the greatest among them (Plato, Michelangelo, Leonardo da Vinci, etc.). It is a great injustice to persecute homosexuality as a crime – and a cruelty, too.[7]

The generosity and the considerable moral courage which Freud shows here were very real features of his character. He always refused to submit to bullying by those whom he saw as self-righteous moralists and many of his patients undoubtedly benefited from his relatively liberal stance on matters of sexual morality. But, like countless more traditional prophetic figures, Freud's capacity for emotional generosity was enclosed within a harshly demanding moral vision of his own. As a result, the positive universalism which is discernible in psychoanalysis is again and again overpowered by its tendency to reject or implicitly condemn aspects of human sexuality – or indeed whole categories of men and women.

According to traditional Christian doctrines (which have been widely repudiated by modern theologians), those who refuse to accept the cleansing baptism of Christ are liable to eternal damnation and are frequently seen by Christians of an apocalyptic turn of mind as 'children of the Devil' or followers of Satan. Psychoanalysis, it need scarcely be said, possesses no article of doctrine which corresponds to the Last Judgement. Nevertheless Freud himself frequently endorsed just the kind of sheep-and-goats habit of mind which underlies Judaeo-Christian eschatology. He tended to divide human beings into those he considered susceptible to psychoanalytic therapy and those who were not – who were in effect 'beyond redemption'. The people who could be helped by psychoanalysis were seen as morally significant – worthy of keeping company with Freud himself. Most people, however, did not belong to this category of psychoanalytic worthiness and were regarded quite differently. Writing about another homosexual, Freud said that 'in the most unfavourable cases, one ships such people . . . across the ocean with some money, let's say to South America, and there let them seek and find their destiny.'[8] At another point, in a letter to Lou Andreas-Salomé, Freud even made the explicit confession that one of his own worst qualities was 'a certain indifference to the world . . . In the depths of my heart I can't help being convinced that my dear fellow men, with a few exceptions, are worthless.'[9] In a letter to his friend and follower, the Protestant minister Oskar Pfister, he amplified this view:

> I do not break my head very much about good and evil, but I have found little that is 'good' about human beings on the whole. In my experience most of them are trash, no matter whether they publicly subscribe to this or that ethical doctrine or none at all . . . If we are to talk of ethics, I subscribe to a high ideal from which most of the human beings I have come across depart most lamentably.[10]

Much earlier in his career Freud made clear that his sympathy for patients, never conspicuously strong, was restricted to a very narrow range. 'I cannot imagine bringing myself,' he wrote, 'to delve into the psychical mechanism of a hysteria in anyone who struck me as low-minded and repellent, and who, on closer acquaintance, would not be capable of arousing human sympathy . . .'[11]

If such passages as these point towards the existence of an implicit Freudian demonology, this impression is reinforced elsewhere in Freud's writings where, again and again, we may discern a tendency to project what Freud would regard as negative human characteristics onto specific categories of people. Freud's moralism is frequently disguised by his habit of translating moral categories into clinical labels – rather in the same way that he objectified his distaste for homosexuality by characterising it as a developmental anomaly. But once we recognise that Freud's clinical labels – such as 'anal-erotic' – tend to have a hidden moral content, the pattern of psychoanalytic demonology begins to become clear.

In Christian demonology the devil has traditionally been portrayed as a bestial creature who is lecherous, sadistic, and a lover of excrement. Medieval tradition associated Jews with the devil and the Christian stereotype of the Jew corresponded closely to the portrayal of the devil, who was also seen as a kind of pedantic infernal treasurer, hoarding in the infernal regions stockpiles of gold.[12] If we regard psychoanalysis as a disguised continuation of our religious tradition, we will not be surprised to find that a configuration of diabolic character-traits is used to define the concept of the 'anal character'. Freud represents the 'anal character' by the image of a man who, like the devil, is given to hoarding, sadism and pedantry, and who, like the devil, is a secret lover of excrement. We will also not be surprised to find that the concept of the 'anal character' has frequently been used by psychoanalysts to launch bitter attacks against individuals, or against entire cultures. There is, admittedly, a difference between an intolerant Christian calling Hindus 'heathen savages in bondage to Satan' and a psychoanalyst finding the anal-erotism of the Hindus confirmed by their concern with ritual impurity, their irritability, hypochondria, miserliness, pettiness, proneness to bore and obstinacy, and writing that 'the anal erotism of the Hindu produces a congeries of character traits which are the very antithesis to those of Europeans, especially the English.' This was the position adopted by Owen Berkley-Hill in the *International Journal of Psychoanalysis* in 1921.[13] There is, admittedly, a difference between calling Jonathan Swift a 'diabolical monster' and claiming, as one psychoanalyst has done, that 'Swift was a neurotic who exhibited psychosexual infantilism, with a particular showing of coprophilia, associated with misogyny, misanthropy, mysophilia and mysophobia.' This is what Ben Karpman wrote in the *Psychoanalytic Review* in 1942.[14] There is, admittedly, a difference between calling Hitler 'an agent of Satan' and arguing that he embodied an extreme type of the anal-hoarding character, and that he displayed all the characteristics of 'a withdrawn, extremely narcissistic, unrelated, undisciplined, sado-masochistic, and necrophilous person'. This is what Erich Fromm argued in 1977, in his book *The Anatomy of Human Destructiveness*.[15] There are, admittedly, differences. But those differences are largely matters of terminology. Today we are more likely to accept the kind of 'scientific' language used by Erich Fromm than we are to give serious attention to talk about angels and demons. Yet the concerns remain recognisably the same. When Fromm seeks to persuade us that Hitler was a pure 'necrophile', whereas Albert Einstein, Albert Schweitzer and Pope John XXIII were pure 'biophiles', he talks in the language of modern scientific neologism. Yet his naive desire to divide the world into good and evil evidently springs directly from Judaeo-Christian apocalyptic. In this respect Fromm is only grotesquely exaggerating a tendency which is fundamental to classical psychoanalysis and which was originated by Freud himself – the psychoanalytic habit of inventing or exaggerating differences between human beings – differences between 'moderns' and 'savages', between the mature personality and the 'neurotic', between men and women.

Throughout all the centuries of Christian history there has functioned what the French historian Léon Poliakov has called 'that terrible mechanism of projection that consists in attributing to the loathed people of God one's own blasphemous desires and unconscious corruption.'[16] The millennial movements of the Middle Ages, the Great European Witchhunt, modern anti-semitism and Stalin's purges have all alike been marked by collective fantasies in which groups identifying themselves as the 'pure' have sought to annihilate entire classes of human beings imagined as 'evil' or 'unclean'.[17] Yet if we turn to psychoanalysis in order to gain insight into the fundamental process of demonological projection which has scarred the face of Christian history, what we find is nothing other than a less destructive version of the same process. Psychoanalysis does not only project men's feelings of inadequacy onto women, and the anxieties and obscene impulses of the normal personality onto 'neurotics', it also, perhaps most significantly of all, projects adult impulses and desires onto children.

According to Freud's theory of infantile sexuality and the associated concepts of fixation and regression, all of the darker and most destructive aspects of adult human behaviour originate in the earliest stages of the child's natural development and represent eruptions of childhood energies and instincts into adult life. This attitude to childhood is perhaps encapsulated most clearly in a passage in Freud's *Introductory Lectures* where he actually uses the term 'evil' in order to characterise the mental life of children. As soon as we recognise that '*what is unconscious in mental life is also what is infantile,*' Freud writes, 'the strange impression of there being so much evil in people begins to diminish':

> This frightful evil is simply the initial, primitive, infantile part of mental life, which we can find in actual operation in children, but which, in part, we overlook in them on account of their small size, and which in part we do not take seriously since we do not expect any high ethical standard from children.[18]

By such arguments as this an abstract ideal is created in which the 'normal', 'well-adjusted' or 'healthy' adult is portrayed as relatively free of conflict, tension, anxiety, inner rage and violence. In contrast the unregenerate child is portrayed, either implicitly or explicitly, as seething inwardly with sexual perversion and sadistic rage. To use Erik Erikson's approving description, Freud's theories present a view of the 'infantile organism' as 'a powerhouse of sexual and aggressive energies'.[19]

The process of projection by which all manner of 'badness' is attributed to children is fundamental not only to Freud's own theories, but to almost all later adaptations of them. The emphasis which Melanie

Klein places on the supposed existence of an intense and violent fantasy-life during the child's first years makes Kleinian theory into one of the clearest expressions of this tendency. Klein has no hesitation in attributing to normal children desires to lacerate the mother's breasts or body and to suck or bite off the father's penis. Klein maintains that in all normal children 'urethral and anal sadism' are added to aggressive biting in order to produce what she calls 'the stage of maximum sadism':

> Every other vehicle of sadistic attack that the child employs, such as anal sadism and muscular sadism is, in the first instance, levelled against its mother's frustrating breast, but it is soon directed to the inside of her body, which thus becomes the target of every highly intensified instrument of sadism. In early analysis these anal-sadistic, destructive desires of the small child constantly alternate with desires to destroy its mother's body by devouring it and wetting it, but their original aim of eating up and destroying her breast is always discernible in them.[20]

What we cannot but observe here is that, while the fantasies which Klein describes are not suggested by any aspect of the behaviour of one-year-old children, or ever divined by ordinary mothers, these fantasies do correspond, in every single respect, to the sexual fantasies of adults. Fantasies in which the bodies of women are compulsively defiled or become 'the target of every highly intensified instrument of sadism' are, indeed, frequently expressed both in medieval demonology and visions of hell and in modern pornography. If we accept psychoanalytic theory we will seek to explain away this coincidence by adopting the view that the sadistic and scatological fantasies of adults are not the products of any process of cultural conditioning, but are a direct expression of infantile impulses which some may succeed in sublimating or repressing but which others do not. We will thus find ourselves arguing that de Sade systematically subjected women to torture, degradation and defilement in his literary fantasies not because he was a fully grown, cruel man (who had probably been abused by adults when he was young) but because he had never ceased to be a child. The alternative to this view is to conclude that in Klein's description of 'the stage of maximum sadism', as in much psychoanalytic writing, the observer's own distinctively adult fantasies and anxieties have been attributed to the children who are being analysed. Dreams of destruction, of sadistic cruelty or of 'perverted' sexual behaviour, which adults find difficult to acknowledge as their own, can in this way be imaginatively disowned but still indulged and expressed under the guise of an 'analysis' of children's 'inner mental life'. Children thus come to be treated in the same way that Jews have historically been treated by Christians, or, indeed, in the same way that women are often treated by men. Recreated in the imagination as stereotypes, or as creatures of fantasy, they have projected onto them all those elements of our own identity which cultural propriety forbids us to express in a direct form.

Examples of this attitude towards children in twentieth-century writing might be drawn from practically any field of knowledge. One particularly instructive instance is provided by an analysis of Hitler's character offered by a distinguished German historian:

> The dominant trait in Hitler's personality was infantilism. It explains the most prominent as well as the strangest of his characteristics and actions. The frequently awesome consistency of his thoughts and behaviour must be seen in conjunction with the stupendous force of his rage, which reduced field marshals to trembling nonentities. If at the age of fifty he built the Danube bridge in Linz down to the last detail exactly as he had designed it at the age of fifteen before the eyes of his astonished boyhood friend, this was not a mark of consistency in a mature man, one who has learned and pondered, criticized and been criticized, but the stubbornness of the child who is aware of nothing except himself and his mental image and to whom time means nothing because childishness has not been broken and forced into the sober give-and-take of the adult world. Hitler's rage was the uncontrollable fury of the child who bangs the chair because the chair refuses to do as it is told; his dreaded harshness, which nonchalantly sent millions of people to their death, was much closer to the rambling imaginings of a boy than to the iron grasp of a man . . .[21]

This passage is taken from Ernst Nolte's *Three Faces of Fascism*. It tells us very little about Hitler, but a great deal about the irrationality of our own theories of childhood. Nolte's words imply that normal children are stubborn, awesomely consistent, filled with inner rage, driven naturally to dominate others, ruthlessly narcissistic and capable of fantasies resembling those which drove Hitler to send millions of people to their death. The other violent feelings which appear in the passage are offered as ideals of the way in which children should be treated. Childishness is something, we are told, which should be '*broken* and *forced* into the sober give-and-take of the adult world'.

This attitude towards childhood flies in the face of our own experience and any intuitive assessment of the mental life and character of small children. Yet the very fact that a historian can offer such an analysis of Hitler's character without apology or explanation shows that the attitude must be very close to being one of the 'official doctrines' of our own culture. What is fascinating about this particular example is that, from the passage itself and its context, it is all but impossible to determine whether Nolte's view of childhood has been derived directly from psychoanalysis or not. The use of the term 'infantilism' suggests that there may indeed be a psychoanalytic influence at work, and Nolte's implied theory of childhood development is very close indeed to the theory of childhood espoused by Freud. But the general style of Nolte's remarks seems to owe almost as much to homespun, culturally traditional views of childhood as it does to psychoanalysis.

The fact that it is so difficult to locate Nolte's analysis accurately is itself instructive. There can be no doubt that, in its modern intellectualised form, this attitude towards children derives directly from Freud's theories. But one of the reasons that this part of Freudian theory has met with such wide acceptance is that it too, like so many other aspects of psychoanalytic theory, secretes within it a form of Judaeo-Christian traditionalism. Freud himself, as we have seen, frequently lapses into traditional rhetoric, as when he uses the term 'evil' in order to characterise the mental life of children. But, working as he did in an intellectual environment which had been radically purified of religious traditionalism, Freud was evidently quite unable to understand the cultural significance of his own rhetoric. Freud thus repeatedly propagated the myth that until his own 'discoveries' it had been almost universally assumed that childhood was a time of innocence. This may have been true of his own immediate intellectual environment. But it is the very essence of the doctrine of Original Sin that children do not come into the world and then learn how to sin, but come into the world bringing their sinful sensuality with them. Freud's attitude to childhood, far from being so new that nobody had thought of it, was in fact so old that many had succeeded in forgetting it. In the Middle Ages it was believed that the newly born child was not only polluted by contact with the impure body of its mother – one of Eve's daughters – but was actually possessed by the Devil. It was for this reason that the traditional ritual of infant baptism included the ceremony of exorcism.[22] This attitude towards the supposed evil propensities of young children has become deeply internalised into our cultural consciousness, and the pious portrayal of children as 'little angels' tends merely to be the sentimental expression of the fear that children may in reality be but 'little demons'. This fear has shaped many of our culture's attitudes towards child-rearing, and, whenever the fear has been dimmed by the waning vitality of the doctrine of Original Sin, there have always been Christians who have sought to revive it. Writing in 1621, the Puritans Robert Cleaver and John Dod must be seen not as putting forward a new view of childhood but as reaffirming an old one:

> The young child which lieth in the cradle is both wayward and full of affections; and though his body be but small, yet he hath a great heart, and is altogether inclined to evil ... If this sparkle be suffered to increase, it will rage over and burn down the whole house. For we are changed and become good not by birth but by education ... Therefore parents must be wary and circumspect ... they must correct and sharply reprove their children for saying or doing ill ...[23]

In view of the fearsome and wholly unrealistic view of childhood which inevitably results from the traditional Christian doctrine, it is scarcely surprising that there should be a constant tendency on the part of parents to reject the orthodox view by superimposing on it the alternative fantasy of the child's innocence. Thus, nearly two hundred years after Cleaver and Dod gave their advice to Puritan parents, the Evangelical Hannah More found it necessary to remind parents of old truths that were in danger of being forgotten, writing that it is a 'fundamental error to consider children as innocent beings, whose little weaknesses may perhaps want some correction, rather than as beings who bring into the world a corrupt nature and evil dispositions, which it should be the great end of education to rectify.'[24] Freud's own attitude towards childhood can only be assessed in the light of these historically orthodox views.

So close are Freud's views to traditional doctrines that it is tempting to suggest that he has done nothing more than disguise an ancient doctrine in modern technical terms. But if we inspect his theories more closely it should become clear that there is a significant difference. This can be seen if we consider a passage from *The Interpretation of Dreams* in which Freud discusses his view of childhood:

> It is easy to see that the character of even a good child is not what we should wish to find it in an adult. Children are completely egoistic; they feel their needs intensely and strive ruthlessly to satisfy them ... But

we do not on that account call a child 'bad', we call him 'naughty'; he is no more answerable for his evil deeds in our judgment than in the eyes of the law. And it is right that this should be so; for we may expect that, before the end of the period which we count as childhood, altruistic impulses and morality will awaken in the little egoist and . . . a secondary ego will overlay and inhibit the primary one . . . If this morality fails to develop, we like to talk of 'degeneracy', though what in fact faces us is an inhibition of development.[25]

The crucial point about Freud's view of evil is that he sees it not as a permanent, inescapable condition of human beings, but as a developmental stage which all healthy individuals are biologically destined to leave behind them as they grow to maturity. By taking this view, Freud is able to preserve many of the traditional features of the doctrine of Original Sin while at the same time implicitly (and sometimes explicitly opposing some of the more repressive child-rearing strategies which had grown from it. What most historians of psychoanalysis have not recognised is that the 'permissiveness' of psychoanalysis grows almost inevitably from its biological premises. For since Freud believed that repression was primarily a biological phenomenon and that civilisation itself was passed on largely by inheritance, it followed that excessive parental intervention in children's natural development was not necessary. 'Sinfulness' was no longer seen as something which needed to be disciplined, or beaten out of children; most individuals would leave their 'evil' selves behind naturally and those who did not could be helped through their inhibited development by psychoanalysis.

Without consciously designing his theories to meet a historical need, Freud had in effect created a body of psychological doctrine which, although it was completely spurious from a scientific point of view, was ideally suited to twentieth-century Judaeo-Christian cultures. For, to societies which were beginning to lose touch with their traditional orthodoxies, Freud's ideas offered an all but traditional theory of evil which, unlike the older versions of the theory, was completely compatible with the doctrines of individual freedom which had grown up out of the Enlightenment and out of nineteenth-century European Romanticism.

Thus, beneath Freud's own schismatic and revolutionary presentation of his ideas, a deep cultural continuity was preserved. This combination of scientific modernism with religious traditionalism was deeply appealing and there can be little doubt that it was Freud's skill in updating the doctrine of Original Sin, rather than the explanatory value of his theory of childhood development, that helped to give the psychoanalytic account of childhood the wide cultural currency it has today.

SIXTEEN

Priests, Penitents and Patients

ON 6 MAY 1906 FREUD WAS FIFTY. As we have already seen, he had already begun to establish a reputation both in Vienna and beyond. In order to celebrate his birthday, a small circle of his admirers presented him with a medallion designed by a well-known Viennese sculptor. On one side this bore a portrait of Freud in profile. On the other side was a Greek design showing Oedipus giving his answer to the question posed by the Sphinx. The Greek inscription was a line taken from Sophocles' *Oedipus Tyrannus*: 'He solved the riddle of the Sphinx and was a man most mighty.'

In his biography of Freud, Ernest Jones records a curious incident which took place at the presentation of this medal. 'When Freud read the inscription he became pale and agitated and in a strangled voice demanded to know who had thought of it. He behaved as if he had encountered a *revenant*, and so he had.'[1] After Paul Federn made it clear that he had chosen the inscription, Freud revealed that while he was a student at the University of Vienna he used to stroll around the court surveying the busts of former professors, and indulging in the fantasy that when his bust eventually appeared there, it would be inscribed with the very same words which Federn had chosen for the medallion.

Federn's choice of inscription was presumably a coincidence. But it is the kind of coincidence which would probably never have happened were it not for the fact that Freud had by now reached a point in his career where his own fantasies of greatness were becoming increasingly apparent to others. By 1906 the fundamental elements of psychoanalytic doctrine were certainly already in place. Both the theory of dreams and the theory of infantile sexuality were complete and Freud had also published not only a book on jokes but also his book about errors, *The Psychopathology of Everyday Life*. In the years to come Freud would introduce significant modifications to these theories. He would, for example, replace his concept of the conscious and the unconscious mind with the tripartite scheme of ego, superego and id. He would also extend his conception of the libido and introduce the notion of a death instinct. But these were elaborations of the doctrinal position which he had already formulated, rather than essentially new developments. The major task which now faced him was not that of creating new theories but that of ensuring that the doctrines he had already formulated would be preserved and disseminated.

In this regard Freud evidently did not feel he could rely on his immediate followers in Vienna, for in his eyes their quality left a great deal to be desired. In a sense the main function of these followers, so far as Freud was concerned, was to create around him an aura of importance sufficiently strong to attract disciples from further afield. In 1907, Karl Abraham came from his studies in Switzerland to attend one of Freud's Wednesday meetings for the first time. He described his reactions to his friend Eitingon:

> I am not too thrilled by the Viennese adherents. I was at the Wednesday session. *He* is all too far ahead of the others. Sadger is like a Talmud disciple; he interprets and observes every rule of the Master with ortho- dox Jewish severity. Among the physicians Dr Federn made the best impression on me. Stekel is superficial, Adler one-sided, Wittels too much the phrase-monger, the others insignificant. The young Rank seems very intelligent, Dr Graf just as much . . .[2]

Ernest Jones was another visitor from abroad who was attracted by Freud's growing reputation but who remained unimpressed by his Viennese followers. In his view they 'seemed an unworthy accompani- ment to Freud's genius, but in the Vienna of those days, so full of prejudice against him, it was hard to secure a pupil with a reputation to lose, so he had to take what he could get.'[3]

Yet in spite of such reservations on the part of some, Freud's circle continued to grow. Soon after the Swiss contingent – including Jung and Abraham – had begun to arrive in 1907, Freud was visited by others who would eventually play a crucial part in the movement, including Ferenczi from Budapest, Jones from Britain and the Ameri- can A. A. Brill, who was to become Freud's first translator.

In recording these early stages in the development of the psychoana- lytic movement, Peter Gay offers one explanation as to why some of the early meetings of Freud's followers generated so much acrimony and resentment. 'After all,' he writes, 'none of the men who in those heroic, exploratory years tactlessly and confidently invaded the most intimate sanctuaries of others, and their own, had been analyzed.'[4] In this passing observation Gay identifies one of the crucial organisational reforms which Freud would soon begin to introduce. For, after the first completely informal years, it soon became obligatory for all who joined the new movement to undergo a 'training analysis' either administered by Freud himself or by one of his close followers. Interestingly, Freud himself felt that training analyses could 'not be conducted exactly like therapeutic analyses'.[5] He softened his requirements for remoteness and neutrality on the part of the analyst and felt that his analytic students were entitled to social ties with him which would otherwise have been strictly outlawed.[6] It is perhaps because their experience of analysis was untypical in these respects that few of Freud's earliest followers appear to have understood the full significance of yet another of the remarkable resemblances between psychoanalysis and organised religion. For it was part of Freud's peculiar genius that, in addition to translating an ancient doctrine of sin into modern biologistic terms, he also found a place within his system for one of the most powerful and binding of all religious institutions – the institution of confession. The aspect of religious ritual which had been renounced by Protestantism as a superstition was thus restored by Freud in the name of science.

On a number of occasions in his work Freud himself openly acknowledged the parallel between the ritual of confession and the particular kind of 'talking-cure' offered by psychoanalysis. 'One works to the best of one's power,' he writes in *Studies on Hysteria*, 'as an elucidator (where ignorance gives rise to fear), as a teacher, as the representative of a freer or superior view of the world, *as a father confessor, who gives absolution, as it were, by a continuance of his sympathy and respect after the confession has been made*' (italics added).[7] Given Freud's frankness on this issue it is not surprising that the resemblances between Freud's modern confessional ritual and its ancient counterpart have frequently been noted in passing by commentators on psychoanalysis. The resemblances are plentiful enough. In the thirteenth century, to take but one example, Cardinal Hostiensis produced a confessional manual under the title 'What Questions Can or Should Be Asked by One Hearing Confessions'. This focused on what was considered the gravest sin – 'the sin against nature'. The confessor was instructed to explain this sin to the penitent by saying: 'You have sinned against nature when you have known a woman other than as nature demands.' The confessor was not to reveal the different ways in which a sexual act might be against nature but he was permitted to interrogate the penitent cautiously in the following terms: '"You know well the way which is natural. Did a pollution ever happen to you otherwise?" If he says, "No," ask nothing further. If he says, "Yes," you may ask, "Sleeping or waking?" . . . If he says, "Waking," you may ask, "With a woman?" . . . If he says, "With a woman," you may ask, "Outside the vessel or within it, and how?"'[8]

In this way priests deliberately set out to elicit from their penitents confessions to 'perverted' sexual acts, to masturbation and coitus interruptus. Some of the inquiries traditionally made by confessors about their penitents' sexual sins were, in short, designed to elicit almost exactly the same admissions which, from about 1893 onwards, Sigmund Freud would seek from those of his patients he believed might be suffering from neurasthenia. More generally, the essence of both confessional rituals is to be found in their intimate and secret nature. In the traditional Roman Catholic confessional reticence was ruled out on principle, for it was considered a mortal sin for anyone, whether man or woman, to conceal anything in the confessional out of shame. In psychoanalysis, similarly, the patient is called on to 'tell with perfect candour everything that he knows and that occurs to him, and not to be deterred from that intention even if some things are disagreeable to say'.[9] Or as Freud put it elsewhere:

> The talk of which psychoanalytic treatment consists brooks no listener . . . For this concerns what is most intimate in [the patient's] mental life, everything that, as a socially independent person, he must conceal from other people, and, beyond that, everything that, as a homogeneous personality, he will not admit to himself.[10]

These apparent congruences between Christian and Freudian therapeutic rituals can easily be dismissed as merely superficial. Yet if we consider the two rituals in more detail, the resemblances go much deeper.

The reluctance to explore these similarities has undoubtedly been reinforced by the deep hostility which exists towards the traditional Catholic ritual of confession in almost all Protestant and secularised cultures. The ferocity with which reformers have sometimes attacked the whole notion of a confessional ritual is perhaps best illustrated in François Rabelais' *Gargantua and Pantagruel*. Rabelais' attitude towards the unreformed Roman Catholic Church has deep affinities with that of Erasmus – with whom he corresponded – and of Martin Luther. What has not always been sufficiently recognised is that many of Rabelais' most bawdy passages are the vehicle of a deep Christian seriousness. Through his characteristic use of a cryptic form of obscenity, it is Rabelais who best expresses the attitude towards the institution of confession which lay at the heart of the Catholic movement to reform it, and which was eventually to be associated with its abolition by the Protestant Church.

In a parable in *Gargantua and Pantagruel*, Rabelais represents 'Man' as a lion and the priests of the unreformed Catholic Church as a fox – the traditional symbol of hypocrisy. One day the poor lion was walking in the forest reciting his private devotions when a charcoal-burner, who had climbed a tree in order to cut wood, threw down his axe at the lion and severely wounded him in the leg. The lion ran limping all over the forest until he met a carpenter, who kindly looked at his wound, cleansed it as best he could, and then told him that he must wipe it well and keep it clean while he went off to find some herbs to heal it. One day, not long after this, the lion was walking in the forest when a woman, seeing it approaching, tumbled over backwards in such a way that the wind blew her dress and petticoat over her shoulders. 'At this sight the lion ran up out of pity to see if she had done herself any harm; and when he looked at her what-d'ye-call-it, he said, "Oh, my poor woman, who gave you that wound?"' The lion then called 'brother fox', showed him the woman's vagina, and asked him to keep this 'wound' clean:

> Look brother, look, my friend! Someone has given this old woman a dreadful wound here, between the legs. There's a manifest cleavage in the flesh ... It must have been a hatchet blow and I suspect that it is an old wound. You must keep the flies off it, so wipe it well, I beg of you, inside and out. You have a good long tail; wipe it, my friend, wipe it, I implore you, and in the meantime I'll go and find some moss to put in it. For so we ought to succour and help one another. Wipe it hard, like this, my friend. Wipe it well. For this wound ought to be wiped often. Otherwise the creature will be uncomfortable. Now wipe it well, my little fellow, wipe away! God has provided you with a tail, a long one and correspondingly thick. Wipe hard and don't get tired. A good wiper who wipes continuously, and keeps wiping with his wiper will never be visited by flies. Wipe away, my dear fellow. Wipe, my little darling, I won't be away a moment.[11]

In Rabelais' obscene Christian parable, the charcoal-burner is the Devil and the wound which he inflicts on the lion – 'Man' – is the wound of Original Sin, whose reality Rabelais, like Swift and Wesley, never for a moment doubted. The carpenter is Jesus who, through his baptism, cleansed his followers of sin, and promised to come again so that they might finally be redeemed. Rabelais, however, takes the traditional Reforming view by suggesting that the ideals of Christianity have been corrupted by men. What he is suggesting is that, by identifying the wound of Original Sin with sexual appetites – and above all with the sexual appetites of women – and then appointing priests to cleanse that wound through regular and intimate confessions, the Church was encouraging its priests to indulge in vicarious sexual fantasy; by regularly wiping the wound of sex, priests were in effect stimulating both themselves and their penitents to fantastic excesses.

Many of the charges which Rabelais implicitly made in his parable can easily be substantiated by a study of Church history. For one of the roles of the Catholic confessor from the late Middle Ages onwards was not simply to receive confessions which were freely and directly made, but to encourage penitents to search the very depths of their souls for 'sins' which they had forgotten or omitted to confess. In order to facilitate what was, in effect, a systematic dredging of the penitents' consciences, confessors often minutely questioned them, reminding them of every possible form of sin and placing particular emphasis on sexual sins. They would often discuss in detail sexual perversions and enumerate to penitents different techniques of masturbation in order to elicit specific confessions. Writing at the beginning of the eleventh century, Bishop Burchard of Worms gave examples of the kind of questions which he believed it was permissible for confessors to put to women:

> Have you done what certain women are wont to do, contriving a certain engine or mechanical device in the form of the male sexual organ, the dimensions being calculated to give you pleasure, and binding it to your own or another woman's pudenda, and have you thus committed fornication with other evilly disposed women or they, using the same or some other apparatus with yourself?

The confessor would then go on to ask his next question: 'Have you done what certain women are wont to do, sitting on the aforesaid instrument or some other device of similar construction, and thus committing fornication upon yourself in solitude?'[12]

In asking such questions, medieval confessors were unconsciously – or indeed sometimes quite deliberately – stimulating the sexual imagination of their penitents, and one of the recurrent problems of Church discipline was that women often accepted the sexual invitations which priests gave them in the secrecy of the confessional, or alternatively became the victims of aggressive sexual advances and even rape.

Because of such abuses the ritual was continually reformed throughout the Middle Ages and confessors were encouraged to avoid overexplicit questioning. In the late twelfth-century *Penitential* of Bartholomew of Exeter, the confessor is told to begin, 'Dearly beloved, perhaps all the things you have done do not now come to mind, and so I will question you.' The penitent was then to be interrogated about the seven deadly sins but there were no specific questions on sexual sins, the priest being warned to ask simply, 'Brother, recall if you have committed some sin some time which was against nature or otherwise very abominable.' Such sins were not to be specifically named by the priest, 'for we have heard of both men and women by the express naming of crimes unknown to them falling into sins they had not known'.[13]

A similar reticence was recommended by many other medieval authorities, but it is clear that such advice was not always heeded. For even after the medieval movement towards reform, the charge of sexual licentiousness was repeatedly made against priestly confessors. The problem was even conceded by Pusey when he revived the practice of secret confession among Ritualistic clergymen of the Church of England in 1838. 'You may,' he warns them in his confessional manual, 'pervert the sacrament into a subtle means of feeding evil passion and sin in your own mind.'[14]

Rabelais' implicit analysis of confession was, then, based upon a very real abuse of the ritual and his attitude towards confession was very similar to that which was later to be adopted by mainstream Protestantism. To this day one of the main objections which fundamentalist Protestants make against the institution of auricular confession is that it pollutes the minds of priests and fills the minds of women with lewd thoughts they might not otherwise have had.

Yet if we are to understand the significance of the similarities between the traditional Christian confessional and the confessional of psychoanalysis, we must recognise that neither Rabelais' parable nor mainstream Protestant doctrine presents an adequate analysis of the ritual they oppose. Rabelais' own contribution, indeed, is little more than a skilful piece of propaganda in which an extremely complex and psychologically interesting ritual is reductively caricatured by exaggerating one of its features. The most interesting response to such propaganda is perhaps that of Helen Waddell who, in a discussion of Rabelais and some of his Reforming contemporaries, wrote that 'no one who hasn't read them knows what cesspools the Reformation stirred – and emptied – on its opponents' heads.'[15]

The first point which needs to be made in any more balanced analysis is that confessional rituals satisfy – or appear to satisfy – a profound psychological need. The urge to confess may not always be overpowering. For relatively minor confessions may be made simply in order to remove a feeling of cognitive dissonance, or because openness feels better and is less complicated than concealment. But in other more extreme cases the impulse to confess can be extraordinarily powerful. In the novels of Nathaniel Hawthorne who, along with Dickens and Dostoevsky, is one of the greatest anatomists of guilt, the extremity of the need to confess is a recurrent theme. In *The Marble Faun*, when the central character Hilda finally makes her confession, Hawthorne describes her sense of relief as unspeakable, as the satisfaction of a great need of the heart, the passing away of a torture. She cries out about her previous state of unconfessed guilt: 'I could not bear it. It seemed as if I had made the awful guilt my own by keeping it hidden in my heart. I grew a fearful thing to myself. I was going mad.'[16] In *The Scarlet Letter*, the Reverend Arthur Dimmesdale is kept by his own timidity from confessing to his adultery with Hester Prynne, who has borne his child. Dimmesdale becomes deeply depressed and finds himself yearning for the time when he can confess: 'Of penance I have had enough! Of penitence there has been none . . . Had I one friend – or were it worst enemy! – to whom, when sickened with the praises of all other men, I could daily betake myself, and be known as the vilest of sinners . . .' His wish is granted when he makes public confession on the pillory which had been the scene of Hester's shame, and dies in her arms. He dies, according to Hawthorne, as one who in the crisis of acutest pain has won a victory.[17]

What Hawthorne implicitly recognises in his novels is the desperation of the need which people sometimes feel for their 'evil' selves – or their 'badness' – to be acknowledged by others. Among individuals seeking psychotherapy it is quite common to find people who, if they ever lose their sense of being bad or dirty, begin to develop feelings of unreality. One of the most perceptive of Freud's followers, the

American psychoanalyst Lawrence Kubie, cites a case which illustrates this predicament well:

> She said of herself 'All social presence, clothes and politeness, kindness to others, that is all unreal – a mere imitation.' She identified herself completely with the contents of her body. 'I am my own body and the only reality of that is its products, my bowels and my urine.' At times this was associated with an explosive, expulsive protest, to let nothing remain but the faeces, underlying which there was a deep unconscious fantasy of world-destruction. But at the same time she was caught in a difficult therapeutic impasse. She could not tolerate her sense of dirtiness because it shamed her, made her afraid of people, made her asocial and in every way cost her all confidence and joy in living. On the other hand she could not let herself feel clean because that meant an explosion of terrifying feelings of unreality.[18]

Although the extremity of this predicament is unusual, the underlying pattern is extremely common. The roots of this divided sense of identity are deep and complex, but one crucial aspect of the problem was put succinctly by another woman, who was once diagnosed as schizophrenic, and whose case has been discussed by R. D. Laing. This woman expresses her yearning to reintegrate dissociated elements of her personality. In the first place she indulges a utopian dream:

> Everyone should be able to look back in their memory and be sure that he [sic] had a mother who loved him; even his piss and shit. He should be sure that his mother loved him for just being himself; not for what he could do. Otherwise he feels he has no right to exist. He feels he should never have been born.

At another point the same woman subtly analyses her own masochistic impulses. To her therapist she says: 'I kept asking you to beat me because I was sure you could never like my bottom but, if you could beat it, at least you would be accepting it in a sort of way. Then I could accept it and make it part of me. I wouldn't have to fight to cut it off.'[19]

These words throw a great deal of light not only on the role of masochistic fantasies and practices in sexual relationships, but also on the impulse to confess. For what they suggest once again is the acuteness of the need which is felt by many people to secure some acknowledgement for a part of the self which is normally kept secret and rejected as unclean. So extreme is this need in some cases that even negative sanctions against the 'sinful' self are construed as a form of acknowledgement, as we can see clearly both in this case, and in the case of the adulterous Dimmesdale, for whom death is liberation because it brings with it the chance to confess.

The power of the compulsion to confess is almost always proportionate to the degree of anxiety with which individuals have initially felt impelled to conceal certain actions, impulses or desires. Such concealment tends in itself to be motivated by fears that if the person in question should actually reveal their adulterous liaison, their obscene fantasies, their violent impulses or their deepest sexual obsession they will forfeit the love and respect of their family, their friends, and even their most intimate partners. Yet the strategy of concealment tends to bring with it both guilt about the deceit which is being practised and acute feelings of unworthiness or unreality as people try to 'disconnect' themselves from their own deepest feelings. Paradoxically, the very strategy which has been adopted in order to combat fears about losing the love and respect of others can end by multiplying these fears, as people feel that the esteem in which they are held by those around them is based on a pretence, that their 'real' self is essentially worthless and unlovable and that in any case by concealing this self they have effectively cut themselves off from the very possibility of love.

The experience of living permanently over an abyss of rejection can become so intolerable that it drives people compulsively to find a way out of the complex of concealment which has become their taskmaster. On the one hand they are impelled by a desperate need to recapture a sense of psychological wholeness or integration, and on the other hand they are driven by a desire to prove that they are not ultimately unlovable, but that they can reveal their 'sinful' self, if not with impunity, then at least without suffering ultimate rejection. In his book *Why Men Confess*, O. John Rogge offers a succinct summary of the motives which lie behind the compulsion to confess: 'Those who confess are trying to obtain or regain love and ward off feared retaliation. They are in effect saying: forgive me and love me again; punish me, beat me, but love me again.'[20] Making an explicit confession is certainly not the only strategy which people resort to in order to escape this dilemma. In one sense adultery is itself a confessional relationship in which the adulterous partners confer absolution on one another for their own 'sinfulness'.[21] Perhaps even more clearly, the compulsion with which some men are drawn to prostitutes has a psychological and not merely a physiological basis, with men frequently seeking acknowledgement of fantasies and obsessions which are normally kept secret.

In originally placing a confessional ritual at the centre of its sacramental structure in the early Middle Ages there can be little doubt that the Roman Catholic Church added immeasurably to its power as an organisation. This was partly because it was able to offer to its adherents a powerful source of psychological consolation. Yet this positive aspect of the ritual of confession went hand in hand with a more repressive function. Both positive and negative aspects of the ritual can perhaps be seen most clearly if we consider the unreformed version of the medieval confessional against which Rabelais and others campaigned. For the intimate sexual questioning of penitents had a psychological function which is very similar to that of the traditional scatological rhetoric of Original Sin. In a characteristic example of such rhetoric, John Donne, preaching one of his Lincoln's Inn sermons, reminded his listeners that 'Between that excremental jelly that thy body is made of at first, and that jelly which thy body dissolves to at last; there is not so noisome, so putrid a thing in nature.'[22] Often the traditional rhetoric of Original Sin enumerated the specific lusts and desires which were supposedly contained within the 'excremental jelly' of the body, and Christians were explicitly reminded that their bodies were a seething repository of lascivious desires, unclean impulses, fornication and adultery. One of the sources of the psychological power of this rhetoric is that it actually offers a form of oblique reassurance to people who feel guilty by implicitly recognising the reality of their own obscene imaginations. Without necessarily being aware of what is happening, 'sinners' will in this way be drawn into a kind of psychological intimacy with the preacher because of his own apparent familiarity with their secret thoughts. They simultaneously learn, however, that this intimacy cannot be consummated since the very aspect of their identity which the preacher seems to have recognised and vitalised through his rhetoric is the one he most wishes to negate. The pattern which we encounter is thus one not of direct endorsement of those parts of the identity which have been touched into life, but of 'affirmation-in-negation'.

In some respects this ambivalent reaction is itself a source of solace. Yet it by no means brings complete relief from anxiety. For what people who make an intimate 'unclean' confession unconsciously seek is not the imposition of a penance, or even absolution. What they desire most of all is a reassurance that the elements of their identity they have repudiated as unclean belong to their full and undivided being; that they are part not of any realm of disease or sin, but of the riches of the human imagination. It is just this kind of reassurance, however, that Christian priests have always been doctrinally unable to give – and this was as true in the Middle Ages as it is today. They are obliged by orthodoxy to withhold all such positive responses and, by giving penance, to prescribe what is in effect a voluntary punishment. The incentive to undergo this punishment – an incentive whose immense psychological power should not be underestimated – is provided by the promise that those who repent will still receive the love of Christ. It is, in effect, by accepting that an aspect of their self *is* unclean and sinful that penitents can assure themselves that they will not be ultimately rejected.

There can be no doubt that the most psychologically precarious aspect of the Catholic ritual of confession is to be found in the relationship which inevitably comes into being, at some level at least, between the penitent and the priest. The great danger from the point of view of the Church was not simply that this relationship might fall victim to lust but, perhaps more seriously still, that it might fall victim to love. In other words that the reassurance sought by penitents might be provided by the priest not in the doctrinally correct form but in a form shaped by natural human warmth and spontaneous sympathy. If the priest were to react in this human way, there was a very distinct possibility that penitents who came to seek the reassurance that they were not unworthy and unlovable might look for this reassurance in the wrong place. They might, in short, end by falling in love with their confessor.

So ready are we today, in our Protestant, post-Protestant or secularised puritanism, to condemn the lustfulness of medieval Roman Catholic priests that their capacity to love tends to be ignored. Yet it is priestly love which probably poses an even deeper threat to the sacrament of confession than priestly lust.

Freud himself does not seem to have grasped this point. But he was certainly aware of the way in which the medieval Catholic confessional had ended in open sensuality and scandal. He also appears to have understood that his own analytic technique was susceptible to the same fate and that the scandal which might result from this would be difficult, if not impossible, for the psychoanalytic movement to withstand. It was partly in response to such fears that he constrained the analytic relationship by an etiquette of formality, impersonality and distance, an etiquette which was justified in the name of scientific 'objectivity'. Although analysts were indeed to discuss sexual topics with their clients, they were to do so in a manner which was, to use Freud's own words, 'dry and direct'. They were to repress any sign of spontaneity and conceal their own personality and opinions. Any comments which the psychoanalyst made were to be delivered flatly, without any display of emotion, without conveying either approval or disapproval. Ideally, during the analytic session, they would sit in a position where they were actually invisible to the person who was disclosing the most intimate secrets of his or her life to them. 'The doctor,' wrote Freud, 'should be opaque to his patients and, like a mirror, should show them nothing but what is shown to him.' He also suggested that 'emotional coldness in the analyst . . . creates the most advantageous conditions for both sides.'[23]

It need scarcely be said that Freud's own stern code of therapeutic conduct has not always been followed by all psychoanalysts. Many have strayed from Freud's ideal without intending to. Others have deliberately rebelled against the classical form of analysis, rejecting Freud's aspiration towards objectivity as misguided. In some cases at least the practice of psychoanalysis has been considerably enriched by such dissidence. Yet Freud's ideals are still revered by a number of psychoanalysts and they remain both influential and historically revealing. What is perhaps most significant is that, if we read between the lines of Freud's own account of what happens during the process of psychoanalysis, there are a number of respects in which the emotional dynamics of his therapy follow the same pattern which we have already observed in more traditional confessional rituals.

In the early stages of treatment, encouraged by the intimate secrecy of the analytic session, by the explicit licence which is given to them by the psychoanalyst, and by the unconsciously suggestive nature of his 'interpretations', patients will almost inevitably feel that elements of their identity which are normally denied are now being offered recognition. They, no less than the traditional penitent, will be drawn into psychological intimacy with the analyst and, in an attempt to imaginatively consummate this intimacy, they will feel compelled to confess, through the technique of free-association, some of the deepest secrets of their sexual, emotional and imaginative lives.

Freud himself presented this confessional aspect of psychoanalytic therapy in objective terms. What was happening in his view was not an emotional transaction but a clinical investigation in which the patient was giving the analyst the opportunity to examine potentially pathogenic material. Indeed, Freud compared the role of the analyst with that of the surgeon:

> I cannot advise my colleagues too urgently to model themselves during psychoanalytic treatment on the surgeon, who puts aside all his feelings, even his human sympathy, and concentrates his mental forces on the single aim of performing the operation as skilfully as possible.[24]

It might well be that digging out episodes and memories which had supposedly been repressed would sometimes prove painful and would give rise to conflicting feelings. But in Freud's view the emotional turbulence would be confined to the patient, and the intimacy, intensity or obscenity of what they revealed would not significantly affect their relationship to the analyst.

What is most striking about this particular judgement is its psychological naivety. Freud seems not to recognise that by commanding his patients to reveal aspects of their lives and of their feelings which they would normally keep secret, he was placing them in a position of extreme emotional vulnerability. In normal human relationships such revelations tend to be reserved only for those who are emotionally close and intimately trusted. Alternatively they are actually made by would-be lovers as part of an implicit invitation to become intimate. The natural reaction of anyone who makes such revelations during the course of psychotherapy is to expect the analyst to reciprocate their own feelings of intimacy, for it is only in this way that they will be reassured that the 'unclean' elements of their identity which they have revealed in analysis will not cause them to suffer rejection. When such reciprocation is withheld, as it was of necessity – and quite properly – by all orthodox psychoanalysts, it should not be surprising if patients express their deep longing for such intimacy: that they should, in effect, fall in love with their analyst. Nor, when analysts refuse to offer the kind of reassurance which patients feel compelled to seek, should it be at all surprising if patients express the anger and hostility which is aroused by such rejection.

Freud himself, however, remained so much in thrall to his speculative theories that he did not understand this. For although he observed what he called the 'strange phenomenon' that the patient 'directs towards the physician a degree of affectionate feeling (mingled, often enough, with hostility)', he claimed that this 'was based on no real relation between them'. The entire course taken by psychoanalysis was, in his view, unpredictable:

> It was perhaps the greatest of the analyst's surprises to find that the emotional relation which the patient adopts towards him is of a quite peculiar nature ... For this emotional relation is, to put it plainly, in the nature of falling in love. Strange, is it not? Especially when you take into account that the analyst does nothing to provoke it but on the contrary rather keeps at a distance from the patient ... and surrounds himself with some degree of reserve ... This love is of a positively compulsive kind ... In the analytic situation it makes its appearance with complete regularity without there being any rational explanation for it.[25]

Although psychoanalytic patients, no less than traditional penitents, naturally seek reassurance, the psychoanalyst is in no position to provide this. For many of the secrets which have been revealed to him are defined by psychoanalytic doctrine as belonging to 'infantile' or 'neurotic' dimensions of the human personality. For him to endorse or affirm these levels of the personality would be the equivalent of a Christian priest affirming the richness and vitality of sin. And just as the Christian priest is constrained not only by doctrine, but by his own anxiety, so the orthodox psychoanalyst is likely to find that his therapeutic hands are bound by anxiety. In order to reassure himself that he has not provoked either the love or the hostility which the patient now shows towards him, he is likely to redouble his etiquette of distance and formality. To do otherwise would be to betray himself into the very kind of emotional or sexual intimacy with his patient which, as a human being he may well desire, but which as an analyst he has been taught to shun.

At this stage of the treatment the psychoanalyst will almost inevitably find himself projecting his own feelings of guilt onto his patient. This process of projection has, indeed, been legitimated and institutionalised in the psychoanalytic movement through the doctrine of 'transference'. For although patients' craving for psychological intimacy with the therapist is an entirely natural reaction to the situation in which they have been placed, and is in fact a sign of their emotional vitality, it is interpreted in psychoanalytic doctrine as a confirmation of their emotional 'illness'. While to the outside observer one of the most striking features of the analytic relationship is the analyst's own deep emotional insecurity, the doctrine of transference inverts this view and sees the patient's need for intimacy and reassurance as pathological in its nature, deriving from unsatisfactory relationships with his or her parents. According to the theory of transference, conflicts which have arisen from these relationships are unconsciously transferred to the patient's relationship with the analyst, who will now interpret any signs of anger against, or dependence on, him as symptomatic of a deep-seated disturbance in his patient's personality. As Freud himself puts it: 'our work has had the result of driving out one form of illness with another.'[26]

Patients thus find themselves placed in a position which is analogous to that of the traditional penitent. For the very imaginative vitality and emotional spontaneity which they have been able to recreate in the intimacy of the confessional is now construed as a confirmation of psychoanalytic doctrine, and as evidence of their own neurosis. But there is a significant difference between the traditional relationship between priest and penitent and the modern relationship between analyst and patient. For whereas the priest is licensed to express his disapproval of the penitent's sins by prescribing a form of penance, the analyst is obliged by doctrine to preserve an attitude of dispassionate detachment and emotional neutrality. In psychoanalytic theory this attitude is justified by reference to the ideal of scientific 'objectivity' or 'detachment'.

Perhaps the most interesting perspective on the way in which the analyst is expected to conduct himself during treatment is provided, however, in a paper by Ernest Jones:

> He makes himself as inaccessible as possible and surrounds his personality with a cloud of mystery . . . the broad tendency of aloofness displays itself by the desires, on the physical side of being inaccessible, on the mental side of being mysterious. The person aims at wrapping himself in an impenetrable cloud of mystery and privacy. Even the most trivial pieces of information about himself, those which an ordinary man sees no point in keeping to himself, are invested with a sense of high importance, and are parted with only under some pressure. Such a man is very loth to let his age be known . . . let alone to talk about his private affairs . . . The veil of mystery and obscurity which he casts over himself is naturally extended to cover all those pertaining to him. Thus he never spontaneously refers to his family, speaking of them reluctantly when any inquiries are made about them, and the same applies to any affairs in which he may have become involved.[27]

These words describe almost exactly the way in which the orthodox psychoanalyst behaves towards his patients. What is significant is that they occur not in an essay on analytic technique but in a discussion of a syndrome of emotionally insecure behaviour to which Jones gives the appropriate name 'the God complex'. This cannot be seen as a coincidence. What it suggests is that Freud, in aspiring towards an ideal of total 'scientific' objectivity, and attempting to defend his confessional technique against the attacks he knew would be made on it, had unconsciously succeeded in recreating, as the ideal medium for analytic therapy, not so much the relationship which traditionally existed between priest and penitent, but the very penitential relationship which is idealised by the Protestant conscience – a direct, unmediated relationship between the believer and a remote, inscrutable, invisible, and often silent God.

Whereas the Roman Catholic penitent is to some extent protected against his or her fantasies of divine punishment and self-recrimination by the mediation of the priest, the Protestant 'sinner' has traditionally been condemned to feeling exposed, naked, unclean and alone beneath the pure eye of God, forced, because of the absence of any limited form of penance imposed by the priest, to imagine God's wrath in the limitless perspective of eternity. It is only if we can imaginatively grasp the significance of the inscrutable and God-like persona which the orthodox psychoanalyst adopts during analytic sessions that we can understand that psychoanalytic patients will almost inevitably feel a similar sense of helpless vulnerability in relation to the remote and mysterious personality of the analyst. Displaying their natural emotional vitality, they may well react to the studied aloofness of their analyst with hostility and anger. Psychoanalysts, however, secure in the belief that they have displayed no part of their personality, and not recognising that their personality is expressed through the very therapeutic technique they have chosen to adopt, will interpret these signs of spontaneity and vitality not as justifiable reactions to their own emotional coldness, but as symptoms of pathological disturbance. Through their own doctrinal security, conferred upon them by their membership of the psychoanalytic 'church' and by the creed of 'transference', they will probably succeed in convincing their patients of their psychological 'immaturity'.

Unable to break off their analysis at this point – because to do so would be to leave the psychoanalyst in possession of some of the most intimate elements of their identity without knowing his judgement upon them – most patients will now seek desperately some sign of approval from the remote and God-like figure who has induced them to expose to him the 'sinful' obscenity of their own imaginations. Even if it is only by reacting to inflections of the analyst's voice which it is impossible for him to suppress, they will soon find that it is not by expressing their newly found emotional vitality that they will earn approval, but by bridling it. Finding that the psychoanalyst will not descend from that heaven of dispassionate neutrality in which he has taken up a position, the most insecure and suggestible patients will inevitably find themselves adopting his inscrutable and self-controlled personality as the model according to which they attempt to reconstruct their own identity. Yearning for intimacy with the analyst who – by virtue of having looked into the most secret and unclean depths of their hearts and souls – has become their God, they will conclude that such intimacy will be possible only if they imaginatively disown the very elements of their identity which compel them to seek it. Like the traditional Christian they will now pursue the fantasy of a sublime and spiritualised version of the rich psychological intimacy which they unconsciously desire. In order to achieve this intimacy they will find that they are forced to purify themselves by consciously condemning all those elements of their identity which were liberated and affirmed in the initial confessional stage of the analysis. This indeed is the explicit goal of psychoanalytic treatment according to Freud's own writings:

> What, then, becomes of the unconscious wishes which have been set free by psychoanalysis? Along what paths do we succeed in making them harmless to the subject's life. There are several such paths. The most frequent outcome is that, while the work is actually going on, these wishes are destroyed by the rational mental activity of the better impulses which are opposed to them. *Repression* is replaced by a *condemning judgement* carried out along the best lines. That is possible because what we have to get rid of is to a great extent only the consequences arising from earlier stages of the ego's development.[28]

However, although Freud recognised this as the outcome of psychoanalysis, he believed that the process whereby an unconscious *repression* is replaced by a conscious *condemning judgement* was psychologically inevitable. What he did not recognise is that this condemning judgement springs not from the biological structure of the psyche, but from the traditional Judaeo-Christian morality which is deeply internalised into psychoanalytic doctrine. In the analytic session itself this condemning judgement is expressed in one of the most powerful of all forms by the psychoanalyst. It is expressed in a way which is likely to be invisible to the patient since it is conveyed not through any word or action, but rather through inaction and silence. It is expressed finally through an aggressive and insecure withholding of the very kind of reassurance which patients naturally seek, and which they might well expect to find. For by his very silence, or by his dispassionate neutrality, the orthodox psychoanalyst powerfully negates all those aspects of his patient's imagination which were liberated in the initial, confessional stage of the analysis.

Although Freud himself saw psychoanalytic therapy as bringing relief from anxiety, this cannot, by the very nature of the psychoanalytic ethic, be its real psychological outcome. For no form of therapy which allows elements of the human imagination into consciousness only on condition that they are subsequently 'condemned' by the conscious mind, can bring relief from anxiety. The effect of psychoanalytic treatment is not so much to undo the knot of anxiety completely, but, having undone it and liberated something of the vitality of the imagination, to do it up again in a different way. This therapeutic process may certainly bring some degree of psychological relief, just as the parallel Christian ritual may do. But ultimately the effect of analytic therapy can only be to maintain, rather than dissolve, guilt. Just as the Roman Catholic ritual of confession has always functioned to lock penitents into psychological dependence on the institutions of the Church by constantly vitalising feelings of guilt, so analytic therapy has tended to function in the same way. Just as the ideal of Christianity is one of interminable confession, so the ideal of psychoanalysis is, to use Freud's own words, one of 'interminable analysis'.

Fortunately for those who undergo psychotherapy, by no means all modern forms of therapy are modelled on psychoanalysis, and even those that are have often deliberately softened Freud's own stress on rigour and neutrality. This, however, can bring new dangers, with some psychotherapists falling headlong into the emotional turbulence of patients they are supposed to be helping. While there can be no doubt that skilled, sympathetic and emotionally secure therapists can sometimes bring great benefit to those whom they counsel, any psychotherapeutic relationship remains fraught with emotional hazard. In this respect Freud's own almost complete failure to understand the emotional dynamics of the psychoanalytic relationship should stand as an example and a warning both to psychotherapists and their clients. That Freud himself should be given credit for psychotherapists who do treat their clients with the kind of sympathy, insight and understanding which was exiled from classical psychoanalysis, would be unjust and misleading indeed.

The account which I have offered of the dynamics of psychoanalysis was originally drafted some ten years ago, and I have reproduced it here without significant alterations. One of the most interesting developments in psychoanalytic history which has taken place in the meantime has been the publication of the suppressed 'secret diary' of Sandor Ferenczi, perhaps the most important and the most original of all Freud's early followers. This diary, which covers the year 1932, was originally published in a French translation in 1985. It contains much orthodox matter. But, as Jeffrey Masson pointed out in his book *Against Therapy*, it also contains some criticisms of psychoanalysis which are so remarkable and so heretical that they virtually ensured that the diary would remain unpublished for fifty years. It is interesting that there are some striking resemblances between Ferenczi's criticisms of orthodox therapy and the analysis which I have presented here. In his entry for 13 August 1932, for example, Ferenczi recorded the complaints which one of his own patients had made against psychoanalysis, and focused in particular on her charge that psychoanalysts took advantage of 'transference':

> *Index of the Sins of Psychoanalysis* (Reproaches made by a woman patient): Psychoanalysis entices patients into 'transference'. Naturally the patient interprets the [imagined] deep understanding of the analyst, his great interest in the fine details of the story of her life and her emotions, as a sign of deep personal interest, even tenderness. Since most patients have been emotionally shipwrecked, and will cling to any straw, they become blind and deaf to signs that could show them how little *personal* interest analysts have in their patients.[29]

Commenting on these words Masson notes the way in which 'the analyst ignores the request for understanding (that is, validation) on the part of the patient and, instead, responds with needs of his own (for example, validation of psychoanalytic theory . . .)'[30] He goes on to quote an even more extreme criticism which Ferenczi makes:

> Analysis is an easy opportunity to carry out unconscious, purely selfish, unscrupulous, immoral, even criminal acts and a chance to act out such behaviour guiltlessly (without feeling guilt), for example, a feeling of

power over the numbers of helplessly worshipful patients, who admire the analyst unreservedly; a feeling of sadistic pleasure in their suffering and their helplessness; no concern for how long the analysis lasts, in fact the tendency to prolong it for purely financial reasons; in this way, if the analyst wishes, the patient is made into a lifelong taxpayer. As a result of infantile experiences similar to this it becomes impossible for patients to detach themselves from the analysis even after long and unsuccessful work ... just as it is impossible for a child to run away from home, because, left on its own, it would feel helpless.[31]

What is perhaps most interesting about this passage is the language which Ferenczi uses in order to describe the one-sided relationship which develops between the orthodox analyst and his patient. The psychoanalyst, he suggests, develops feelings of power over his 'helplessly worshipful patients' and even takes a 'sadistic pleasure' in their helplessness. The implication is that he behaves with god-like hauteur. This view is made explicit by Ferenczi in a passage in which he records, with remarkable candour, his disillusion with the therapist by whom he had himself been analysed:

> Why should the patient place himself blindly in the hands of the doctor? Isn't it possible, indeed probable, that a doctor who has not been well analysed (after all, who is well analysed?) will not cure the patient but will rather use her or him to play out his own neurotic or psychotic needs? As proof and justification of this suspicion, I remember certain statements Freud made to me. Obviously he was relying on my discretion. He said that patients are only riffraff. The only thing patients were good for is to help the analyst make a living and to provide material for theory. It is clear we cannot help them. This is therapeutic nihilism. Nevertheless we entice patients by concealing these doubts and by arousing their hopes of being cured ... A further proof is [Freud's] dislike ... of psychotics and perverts, in fact, his dislike of everything that he considers 'too abnormal' ... Further, his method of treatment as well as his theories result from an ever greater interest in order, and the substitution of a better superego for a weaker one. In a word he is becoming a pedagogue ... *He looms like a god above his poor patient, who has been degraded to the status of a child. We claim that the transference comes from the patient, unaware of the fact that the greater part of what one calls the transference is artificially provoked by this very behaviour* [italics added].[32]

This view of Freud playing the role of a god not simply to his followers, but to his patients as well, and by so doing provoking the very 'transference' he held up as the product of, and the evidence for, the patient's neurosis, is extremely close to the view which I have outlined here. It should immediately be said that some of Ferenczi's other remarks make it quite clear that his overall view of psychoanalysis is different from the one I have presented here. But, in the passages I have quoted, he does supply some fascinating circumstantial evidence from inside the psychoanalytic movement which significantly strengthens the case I have made against it from the outside.

In placing what was, in effect, a confessional ritual at the very heart of the psychoanalytic movement, it seems clear that Freud was not, as he himself believed, engaging in a form of scientific innovation. Rather he was unconsciously institutionalising his own profound religious traditionalism at the same time that he was creating for himself a ritual stage on which he could play out his own 'God complex' in relation to patients he regarded as inferior and in need of redemption. Just as, through his theory of infantile sexuality, he had revived in a disguised technical form the ancient doctrine of Original Sin, so he also brought back to life, under a clinical disguise, the most important ecclesiastical ritual which had traditionally helped to sustain that doctrine, and to create psychological dependency among those who unburdened themselves in the secrecy of the confessional.

SEVENTEEN

Critics and Dissidents

THE VIEW THAT THE RITUAL of confession was the means by which the medieval Roman Catholic Church attained its vast power and spread its influence through Europe probably rests on an exaggeration. But it would be no exaggeration to suggest that the fifty-five-minute psychoanalytic sessions which Freud initially instituted in order to treat his patients rapidly became the bedrock on which he built his entire psychoanalytic church. For what was conceived as a method of curing illness soon began to be used as an initiation ritual, an induction course and a ceremony of ordination for Freud's most intimate followers, who would in their turn become 'fishers of men', spreading the psychoanalytic gospel both by word and by therapeutic deed.

In the early days of the psychoanalytic movement Freud's 'training analyses' were sometimes surprisingly informal. When Max Eitingon came to Vienna in 1907, attracted, as he put it, by the 'astonishing range' of Freud's conception of hysteria, Freud took him for walks though the streets and parks of Vienna, analysing him as they went. 'Such,' Ernest Jones would later write, 'was the first training analysis.'[1] Thirteen years later there were still no formal qualifications for aspiring psychoanalysts. But the training analysis entailed a much more serious commitment. In a speech given to the British Psycho-Analytical Society in 1963, James Strachey described how he became accepted as a psychoanalyst in the early 1920s. He could offer, he recalled,

> the barest of BA degrees, no medical qualifications, no knowledge of the physical sciences, no experience of anything except third-rate journalism. The only thing in my favour was that at the age of thirty I wrote a letter out of the blue to Freud, asking if he would take me on as a student.
>
> For some reason, he replied, almost by return of post, that he would, and I spent a couple of years in Vienna ... I got back to London in the summer of 1922. And in October, without any further ado, I was

356

elected an associate member of the Society. I can only suppose that Ernest Jones had received instruction from an even higher authority, and that he had passed them on to the unfortunate Council. A year later I was made a full member. So there I was, launched on the treatment of patients, with no experience, with no supervision, with nothing to help me but some two years of analysis with Freud.[2]

What Strachey's words help to demonstrate is that at the heart of the entire psychoanalytic movement there lies much more than a body of theory and doctrine which had to be mastered. For even more important than this was a personal relationship with Freud. Ordination into the psychoanalytic church could originally be performed only by Freud himself or by another analyst who had been ordained by Freud previously. The particular kind of relationship which Freud expected prospective analysts to develop with him was implicit in his doctrine of transference. It becomes startlingly explicit in what Janet Malcolm has described as 'an incredible moment' in the training analysis undertaken by the poet H. D. (Hilda Doolittle) with Freud in 1933–4:

> In response to something which the forty-seven-year-old poet said ... the seventy-seven-year-old psychoanalyst furiously pounded the back of the couch on which she was lying and said, 'The trouble is, I am an old man – *you do not think it worth your while to love me.*' This caused H. D. to sit bolt upright on the couch in astonishment, one part of her thinking that this might be some device of Freud's to speed the flow of association, and another part of her feeling upset and appalled: 'He was a terribly frightening old man, too old and too detached, too wise and too famous altogether, to beat that way with his fist, like a child hammering a porridge-spoon on the table.'[3]

Freud's intense psychological need for the love bestowed upon him by his disciples is something we have already noted. So long as he felt that this love was being given, that his ascendancy was being duly acknowledged and his doctrines accepted, he was capable of reciprocating. For there can be no question but that Freud bestowed on his followers both love – of a rather distant kind – and loyalty. He was even able to accept a certain degree of open debate and criticism. But once he felt that his own position was being undermined in any way his entire approach changed. His manner of dealing with critics who disturbed him is illustrated by a dispute he had with Albert Moll in 1908. Moll was not one of Freud's immediate followers, but, as a highly respected sexologist, he had followed the development of psychoanalysis closely and even employed its methods himself. In his book *The Sexual Life of the Child*, however, he made a number of sharp but carefully reasoned criticisms of psychoanalysis. While acknowledging that children did have sexual experiences he rejected Freud's account of sexual development. He went on to argue that the cures which Freud claimed as his own might equally well have been produced by suggestion. He also believed that Freud's failure to investigate the sexual life of children directly, and his reliance instead on the suggestive questioning of adults was the cause of Freud's extreme views about the role of sexual factors in neurosis. 'The impression produced in my mind,' he wrote,

> is that the theory of Freud and his followers suffices to account for the clinical histories, not that the clinical histories suffice to prove the truth of the theory. Freud endeavours to establish his theory by the aid of psycho-analysis. But this involves so many arbitrary interpretations, that it is impossible to speak of proof in any strict sense of the term.[4]

Coming from a critic who spoke with as much authority as Moll this was a damaging charge indeed. Freud's first reaction was to complain that 'several passages in *The Sexual Life of Children* really merit the charge of libel.' Subsequently he launched a personal attack on Moll in front of his followers at the Vienna Psychoanalytic Society: 'Moll's character is only too well known . . . He is a petty, malicious, narrow-minded individual. He never expresses a firm opinion . . .'[5]

After Moll had visited Freud at home and suggested that he should learn to accept justified criticism, Freud gave an account of the visit to Jung. He claimed that he had caused Moll to 'take flight' but confessed that he was not fully satisfied as he watched him go. 'He had stunk up the room like the devil himself,' wrote Freud 'and partly for lack of practice and partly because he was my guest I hadn't lambasted him enough. Now of course we can expect all sorts of dirty tricks from him.'[6]

Freud's manner of dealing with Moll through personal insult and demonological abuse set the pattern for future disputes with his more intimate followers. The first of the numerous splits which took place in the early years of the psychoanalytic movement was with Alfred Adler. Although Adler was no more careful a thinker than Freud, he was attracted to originality in very much the same way and soon began to develop his own version of psychoanalysis, which stressed power rather than sexuality. At first the differences did not seem too acute. Thus, in 1910, when the Viennese Society was formally constituted as a member of Freud's recently founded 'International Psycho-analytical Association', Adler was appointed as President. Yet the very organisational change which had brought about his elevation would, in a sense, also lead to his eventual expulsion from the movement. For although the new International Association had an impressively impersonal name, its constitution laid down that its purpose was 'The cultivation and promotion of the psychoanalytic science inaugurated by Freud . . .' What this meant, in effect, was that the organisation was specifically dedicated to preserving Freud's own doctrines, and that serious deviations from these would not ultimately be tolerated.

It soon became apparent that Adler was claiming the kind of intellectual authority which Freud wished to reserve for himself. After a period of initial tolerance, Freud decided to counter-attack. He explained his feeling in a letter to Oskar Pfister, the Swiss Protestant pastor who had allied himself to the psychoanalytic movement:

> [Adler's theories are] departing too far from the right path and it [is] time to make a stand against them. He forgets the saying of the apostle Paul, the exact words of which you know better than I: 'And I know that ye have not love in you.' He has created for himself a world system without love, and I am in the process of carrying out on him the revenge of the offended goddess Libido. I have always made it my principle to be tolerant and not to exercise authority, but in practice it does not always work.[7]

During a meeting of the Viennese Society in which Adler had been expounding his theories, Freud took the opportunity to reply critically in what Fritz Wittels characterised as an attempt to 'annihilate his adversary'. Freud's closest supporters then took their cue from their leader and, as Wittels puts it, 'made a mass attack on Adler, an attack almost unexampled for its ferocity even in the fiercely contested field of psychoanalytical controversy'.[8] In attacking Adler as he did, Freud was deliberately forcing the issue. Late in February 1911 he achieved one of his aims when Adler resigned his position of President of the Viennese Society. Wilhelm Stekel, a friend and supporter of Adler, resigned the office of Vice-President at the same time. By June Freud had pushed Adler into resigning from the society altogether. In August 1911 Freud explained to Ernest Jones that the dispute with Adler had been inevitable and that he had deliberately 'ripened the crisis'. The intensity of Freud's anger with Adler can be judged by the manner in which he characterised the crisis. 'It is the revolt of an abnormal individual, driven mad by ambition,' he wrote to Jones, 'his influence on others depending on his strong terrorism and *Sadismus*.'[9] Not content with a partial victory, Freud rejoined battle when the Society reconvened in the autumn of 1911. He announced that Adler had resigned along with three of his followers and that they had formed a new Adlerian group. Fearing that this group might now begin to undermine his own Society from the outside, Freud announced that membership of it was incompatible with continued allegiance to psychoanalysis. He demanded that all those present should choose between the two groups and let him know of their decision within a week. Once again Freud set a test of loyalty in order to rid his own group of potential dissidents. As a result six members resigned from the society. The reasons for their action are not entirely clear. Peter Gay has described the six as 'Adler partisans'.[10] Hans Sachs, however, was of the opinion that most of those who resigned did not share Adler's views; 'their decision was influenced by their belief that the whole proceeding violated the "freedom of science".'[11]

Freud now congratulated himself on the success of his strategy. 'Rather tired after battle and victory,' he wrote to Jung, 'I hereby inform you that yesterday I forced the whole Adler gang (six of them) to resign from the Society. I was harsh, but I don't think unfair.' Even after his victory, however, Freud's hostility towards Adler continued unremittingly. In 1914 he wrote to Lou Andreas-Salomé of the 'specific venomousness' of Adler, whom he went on to describe as a 'loathsome individual'. Later still a comment made in a letter to Stefan Zweig revealed just how deeply Freud had internalised the Christian culture which surrounded him, including its anti-semitism. For when Adler died suddenly during a scientific congress in Aberdeen, Freud wrote: 'For a Jew boy out of a Viennese suburb, death in Aberdeen is an unheard-of career in itself and a proof of how far he had got on. The world really rewarded him richly for his services in having contradicted psychoanalysis.'[12]

Even with the ejection of Adler, Freud could not rest easy. For although the ranks of his Society had been purged, dissidence still threatened to break out. Freud was particularly uneasy about Wilhelm Stekel who, in spite of his sympathy for Adler, had not offered his resignation. Stekel's approach to scientific methodology and the use of evidence was, if anything, even more erratic than Freud's. It therefore seems possible that Freud's hostility to him stemmed from an oblique insight into the defectiveness of his own methodology; that in the mirror of Stekel he saw and chastised his own shortcomings. Freud's anger certainly reached entirely irrational proportions on several occasions. Having begun by characterising him as 'fundamentally decent', he subsequently altered his judgement, speaking of Stekel's 'moronic petty jealousies'. He also described him as a 'liar', an 'uneducable individual' and a 'swine'; 'that pig, Stekel', he wrote contemptuously in a letter to Ernest Jones.[13] As well as abusing Stekel as loathsome and unclean, Freud seems to have felt inwardly compelled to portray him as tiny and insignificant. He once described him as being 'the size of a pea'. On another occasion Freud reacted harshly to Stekel's half-modest boast that a dwarf on the shoulders of a giant could sometimes see further than the giant himself. 'That may be true,' Freud commented bitterly, 'but a louse on the head of an astronomer can see nothing at all.'[14]

The final break with Stekel came when Freud had attempted to ensure that another of his followers, Victor Tausk, should supervise the book reviews in the *Zentralblatt* journal, of which Stekel was a founder and co-editor. Stekel was not prepared to concede editorial power in this way and refused. Although he continued in his editorial role, Stekel eventually resigned from the Viennese Society. Interestingly, Freud went on to misrepresent the nature of the final dispute to at least one of his followers when he wrote to Karl Abraham in Berlin. 'The occasion for the split was not a scientific one,' wrote Freud, 'but presumption on his part against another member of the Society *whom he wished to exclude from the reviews in "his paper"*, which I could not permit' (italics added).[15] By representing Stekel's defence of his editorial independence as an attempt at censorship, Freud was being less than straightforward. Stekel's real offence, there can be no doubt, was not against Tausk but against Freud, and it was for disputing his authority that he was punished. As in almost all his other broken friendships, from Breuer and Fliess onwards, Freud rationalised the breakdown in a relationship by offering a hostile analysis of the character of the friend who had become an enemy. According to what he wrote in 1924, Stekel was suffering from 'moral insanity'. When Stekel attempted to repair their broken relationship, Freud was unable to refrain from making a direct attack on him. 'It was exclusively your personal qualities,' he wrote, 'which made collaboration with you impossible for my friends and myself.'[16]

The bitterness with which Freud attacked his more independent-minded followers, effectively excommunicating them for daring to disagree with his doctrines, only lends weight to the comparison of psychoanalysis with a religious cult. Freud himself constantly strengthened the parallel by his own informal pronouncements. When Ludwig Binswanger questioned Freud as to why it was his oldest and most talented disciples who had broken with him, citing as examples Jung and Adler, Freud replied, 'Precisely because they, too, wanted to be Popes.'[17] In 1924 Freud employed the religious metaphor again when he wrote of Jung and Adler as 'the two heretics'.[18] In using these terms he was unknowingly endorsing the analysis which would eventually be made by Max Graf:

> Freud . . . insisted . . . that if one followed Adler and dropped the sexual basis of psychic life, one was no more a Freudian. In short, Freud, as head of the church, banished Adler; he ejected him from the official church. Within the space of a few years I lived through the whole development of church history; from the first sermons to a small group of apostles, to the strife between Arius and Athanasius . . .'[19]

Freud's followers, particularly Ernest Jones, always denied that parallels with religions offered any real insight into the nature of the psychoanalytic movement. In 1988 another partisan biographer, Peter Gay, reiterated this view when he called such parallels 'facile and unfortunate'.[20] Yet the only plausible argument for rejecting such parallels would take a quite different form. It would involve recognising that talk of *resemblances* between psychoanalysis and religion misses the point. For psychoanalysis, it would seem, is quintessentially a religion and should be treated as such. The doctrinal relationship between psychoanalysis and the Judaeo-Christian tradition has already been discussed. The behaviour associated with psychoanalytic heresy-hunts suggests that there is an even deeper congruence between the emotional dynamics of the early Freudian movement and those of more traditional messianic cults.

In order to understand this aspect of psychoanalytic history it is essential to unravel the complex relationship between love, power and submission which underlies messianic movements in the Judaeo-Christian tradition. Although a materialistic analysis of such movements might suggest that what is in question is a straightforward relationship between an authoritarian leader and a group of essentially submissive disciples, the situation is in reality a great deal more complex. For, as a matter of orthodoxy, the submission which the messiah demands from his followers exactly parallels his own submission to the God he believes has chosen him (or alternatively to the divine laws he believes he has discovered). At a conscious level the messiah seeks out followers not because of a simple desire to lead, but because he has come to regard himself as the perfect follower; because he believes he has a duty to lead others to the truth which has been revealed to him. Were he to neglect this duty he would be rewarded not with the divine love which he craves but with divine wrath and ultimate rejection. It is in order to avoid this fate that the messiah characteristically proselytises his faith with such energy. He undertakes his mission, in other words, for no other reason than to escape rejection and to gain unending love.

Ultimately, however, since the God he worships is purely imaginary, there is no way in which he can be reassured about his own sense of election. It is for this reason, as I have already suggested, that he is thrown into a relationship of such profound emotional dependence on his followers. For their esteem for him, and their willingness to accept his word as law, become his sole means of reassuring himself that he is indeed in possession of the Truth. The earthly love of his followers thus becomes the base but necessary token of the love of God. And because he is himself gripped by a fantasy of intimacy, or even identification, with the God he worships, the messiah veils his own personality in legend and mystery and demands that he should himself be treated almost as a divinity by those who follow him. The psychological urgency of this demand grows directly out of a feeling that if he cannot prove himself in this way, his own essential worthlessness will be detected. Indeed his very anxiety to identify with the fantasised omnipotence of God is itself a reflection of a sense of inner humiliation. It is because of the acuteness with which the messianic personality experiences his own secret identity as tiny, unclean and insignificant that he is attracted so strongly by the alternative fantasy of a vast, pure and supremely valuable god. It is because he fears that he will be rejected as a worm that he craves so compulsively, and with such compensatory zeal, to be recognised and loved as a messiah.

Perhaps the most remarkable aspect of messianic cults and the key to understanding their emotional dynamics is the fact that the pattern of doubting conviction which can be discerned in the behaviour of messiahs is almost exactly duplicated in the behaviour of those who follow them. In the end, indeed, both messiahs and their disciples are motivated by the same complex of anxieties which has already been discussed in relation to the ritual of confession; both fear rejection because of the uncleanness of their 'secret' self and, in order to allay their fears, both seek confirmation of their own value. Whereas the messiah turns to a remote and imaginary God, his followers anxiously compete with one another for his recognition. Their ultimate fantasy is that he will acknowledge them as 'special' and confer some token of his love upon them. Their ultimate fear is that they will prove unworthy of his love and be spurned and rejected by him.

Messianic cults are in this way bound together on the one hand by love and on the other hand by the fear of rejection. While these bonds can be immensely powerful, there is one respect in which such cults are inherently unstable. For while the messiah's fantasy-identification with God can never be consummated in reality, the disciple's parallel identification with his leader can easily lead to disputes about authority and, ultimately, about the very role of messiah. The psychological impact of such challenges can only be appreciated if we can grasp the precariousness of the messianic identity. So long as he enjoys the complete loyalty and obedience of his followers the messianic leader will find it relatively easy to sustain a self-image which stresses his own superiority, his own chosenness and his own sense of being in possession of an essential truth. Yet if any of his followers – or indeed any critic from outside the group – should begin to contest his teachings in a way that undermines his authority, he tends to experience this as an attack on the very foundations of his identity. For what such criticism brings with it is the possibility that the messiah's carefully constructed persona of mysterious authority will be shattered, leaving him with his alternative persona of the unclean rejected 'worm'. The most likely consequence is that the messiah will violently assert his own authority over the group, and do so by attributing his own sense of inner uncleanness (and his own violence) to the dissident. Critics and dissidents are thus likely to find themselves anathematised as satanic beings and to have all manner of corruption and viciousness projected onto them.

Such furious acts of projection bring immense relief to the messianic personality. In the first place they provide a means of unloading feelings of aggression and inner unworthiness. For by defining others as vicious and unclean the messiah is able in effect to empty his own corruption onto their heads, thus reassuring himself about his own righteousness. In the second place the strategy of pouring 'holy abuse' on anyone who dares to criticise orthodoxy is a way of pre-emptively bullying any other followers who might in future stray from orthodoxy. The messianic personality thus tends to use the tactic of excommunication in very much the same way as the tyrant uses execution. By making an example of any outright dissident, he effectively creates an atmosphere of emotional terror which will serve to intimidate his other followers. By putting on a show of violent strength he also reassures those disciples who are anxious to be led that their posture of individual submission will ultimately lead to the group becoming stronger.

What is remarkable about Freud's leadership of the psychoanalytic movement is that although he quite clearly did not believe in any kind of supernatural creator, he adopted almost without exception the traditional strategies of those who did. In effect he treated his own theories as if they were part of a personal revelation granted to him by God, and demanded that others should accord to them the reverence which the sacred word usually commands. Those who criticised his theories, whether from inside or outside the psychoanalytic movement, were ruthlessly attacked. At times Freud used conventional religious imagery, as when he complained to Jung that Moll 'had stunk up the place like the devil'. He also used psychologically revealing imagery, as when he denounced Stekel as a 'louse' and compared him to a pea. More commonly still, psychoanalysis itself was used as a weapon and was deployed against the supposed character-defects of those who opposed it. Thus Stekel was denounced not only for his supposed 'terrorism and *Sadismus*' but also, more sweepingly still, for 'moral insanity'. Diagnosis became a substitute for demonology. Since, as we have already seen, many of Freud's diagnostic categories were themselves little more than disguised forms of demonology, this strategy was itself extremely close to the traditional one.

There are many other respects in which the psychoanalytic movement's 'secret' identity as a messianic cult was made manifest. That Freud's followers anxiously sought out recognition and signs of esteem from him should already be apparent. That they actually sought love, or compared their relationship to Freud to being in love, was occasionally made explicit. Theodor Reik, for example, who would eventually embark on an informal programme of *imitatio Christi* in relation to his secular messiah (see above, Chapter 14), has spoken of his feelings just before he met Freud. As he climbed up the stairs at 19 Berggasse, he has recalled, 'I felt like a young girl going on a date, my heart was beating so fast.'[21] 'Everybody around Freud,' wrote Helene Deutsch, one of his closest followers, 'wanted to be loved by him . . .'[22] Years after their first meeting the pastor Oskar Pfister told Freud of his 'vehement hunger for love' and went on to say that 'without analysis I should have broken down long since.'[23] Interestingly, Pfister appears intuitively to have grasped the psychoanalytic movement's intimate relationship to the Judaeo-Christian tradition. In his view Freud's teachings were directly related to those of Jesus and their deep content belied the lack of belief which they proclaimed: 'For whoever lives for the Truth lives in God,' wrote Pfister in a letter to Freud, 'and whoever fights in order to liberate love is, according to John's gospel, in the bosom of God . . . A better Christian than you, there never was.'[24]

The attitude of love and reverence with which Freud's followers regarded him went hand in hand with an almost complete submission to his will. 'All,' writes Helene Deutsch, '. . . created the same atmosphere about the master, an atmosphere of absolute and infallible authority on his part.'[25] That Freud's followers feared rejection and excommunication just as much as the members of more conventional messianic cults seems clear. Indeed the point has been made quite specifically by Paul Roazen in an attempt to explain why the early members of the psychoanalytic church, for all their obvious intelligence, remained so docile:

> For one thing, their intense dedication to psychoanalysis was reinforced by their fear of excommunication. Freud needed to dominate and be master, and his pupils were afraid of being excluded from his community . . .
>   The anxiety 'of being isolated and of becoming an outcast through having thoughts and feelings which nobody would share' might be enough to induce conformism. At any given period orthodox pupils would check to see whether members of the circle were unobtrusively slipping into the mistakes of earlier outcasts. To be so stigmatised was to run the risk of getting lost, being dropped from the movement and thereby forfeiting a place in history (and this risk was real, for once out of the movement a heretic's work no longer was cited).[26]

What such views suggest, and what is amply confirmed by the testimony of those who were close to him at this time, is that Freud's religion of love – like the three great monotheistic faiths of Judaism, Christianity and Islam – was also a religion of fear and even, at a certain extreme, of hate. Hans Sachs, looking back at Freud's campaign to drive Adler out of the movement, saw his behaviour as an almost virtuoso display of controlled hatred: 'In the execution of this duty he was untiring and unbending, hard and sharp like steel, a "good hater" close to the limit of vindictiveness.'[27] Freud's extraordinary capacities as a leader were due to the fact that he combined in his own person great charisma and an unusual capacity for what might be termed self-interested love, with a ruthless will to dominate others in the cause of what he believed to be the truth. As a young man he had himself submitted almost totally to a series of harsh and demanding authority-figures – Exner, Brücke, Meynert and, above all, Charcot. Now his own experience of discipleship became the key with which he locked others into the same pattern of submission and oblique humiliation. That he grasped at a conscious level at least some of the authoritarian principles of leadership which his practice embodied is suggested by a passage which occurs in *Group Psychology and the Analysis of the Ego*. 'A group is an obedient herd,' writes Freud, 'which could never live without a master.'

> It has such a thirst for obedience that it submits instinctively to anyone who appoints himself its master. Although in this way the needs of a group carry it half-way to meet the leader, yet he too must fit in with it in his personal qualities. He must himself be held in fascination by a strong faith (in an idea) in order to awaken the group's faith; he must possess a strong and imposing will, which the group, which has no will of its own, can accept from him.[28]

Freud possessed all the attributes which he saw in the ideal leader and with very few exceptions he succeeded in imposing his will on his followers in the manner he describes. It was in the end, however, these exceptions, and the manner in which Freud dealt with them, which revealed most about Freud's own psychology and the dynamics of the movement which he founded. If this is evident in the cases of Adler and Stekel, it is even more clearly so in the case of the follower whom Freud once called his 'beloved son' and to whom he once believed he would bequeath the leadership of his movement. It is to the conflict between Freud and the most significant of all the psychoanalytic heretics, Carl Gustav Jung, that we must now turn.

EIGHTEEN

Jung: Crown Prince and Beloved Son

CARL JUNG FIRST ENCOUNTERED the work of Freud when he read *The Interpretation of Dreams* soon after its publication in 1900. At this time Jung, a twenty-five-year-old Swiss doctor, had just been appointed as a physician to the Burghölzli psychiatric hospital in Zurich. It would appear that the hospital's director, Eugen Bleuler, had tentatively recommended Freud's book to his young assistant, and that Jung had been duly impressed by it. Gradually psychoanalysis was introduced into the treatment of psychiatric patients at Burghölzli. In 1906 Jung sent Freud a copy of a book he had written about word-association tests (deriving originally from Galton), and Freud replied expressing both his gratitude that Jung had endorsed some of his ideas and his willingness to accept correction.

Later that same year Jung came to Freud's defence when a German professor of psychiatry, Gustav Aschaffenburg, attacked Freud's case history of Dora at a congress of psychiatrists and neurologists at Baden-Baden. Jung answered the attack in a paper entitled 'Freud's Theory of Hysteria: A Reply to Aschaffenburg'. Significantly, however, Jung's paper contained some reservations. 'When I first read Freud's writings,' he said, 'it was the same with me as with everybody else: I could only strew the pages with question marks.'[1] He then put forward the view that Freud's theory of hysteria was a provisional one, since Freud 'has not examined all the hysterias there are'. Jung pointed out not only that there might be some forms of hysteria which Freud had never observed, he even went on to suggest that Freud's material might, as a result of his theoretical constructs, have become 'somewhat one-sided' and that not all cases of hysteria had sexual roots.[2] At this point Jung had not yet met Freud. The link between Zurich and Vienna was not established on any personal level until January 1907, when Freud was visited by one of Jung's younger colleagues, Max Eitingon. The next month Jung himself arrived, together with his wife and a pupil, Ludwig Binswanger. Jung was deeply impressed by Freud, describing him as 'the first man of real importance I had encountered'. He recalled that they 'met at one o'clock in the afternoon and talked virtually without a pause for thirteen hours'.[3]

Freud was, if anything, even more impressed by Jung and there were a number of extraneous factors which predisposed him to favour the young psychiatrist. Perhaps the most important of these was Freud's anxiety that his own followers in Vienna were not really worthy of him and could not be relied on to gain for psychoanalysis the international recognition which Freud craved. At the same time that he doubted the quality of some of his Viennese followers, Freud remained deeply anxious about his own status in the eyes of the medical establishment. Ever since his early disastrous papers on cocaine there had been no shortage of reasons for the medical profession in general, and Austro-German psychiatrists and neurologists in particular, to treat Freud and his ideas with caution. In consequence Freud, notwithstanding his professorship, still felt that he was an outsider with no real access to the corridors of medical power. The fact that he should be visited by Jung, who by this time was second in the Burghölzli hierarchy and therefore in the very forefront of academic psychiatry in Europe, meant that he was as close as he had ever been to receiving academic recognition. What was no less important to Freud was that this recognition should appear to be coming from outside the predominantly Jewish circle of his closest followers. For Freud was acutely conscious of the strength of anti-semitism both in Europe and America. Dreaming as he did of a universalist future for his ideas, he was sensitive to the manner in which his own Jewishness and that of many of his closest followers might be a handicap to psychoanalysis. It would scarcely be an exaggeration to say that, in Jung, Freud glimpsed the possibility of a Gentile alter-ego who could help to redeem psychoanalysis from its own Jewish origins and spread it throughout the non-Jewish world. 'I nearly said,' Freud once wrote to Abraham, 'that it was only by his [Jung's] appearance on the scene that psychoanalysis escaped the danger of becoming a Jewish national affair.'[4]

The grounds for Jung's intense reaction to Freud would appear to have been more intimate. During most of his career as a psychotherapist Jung rarely revealed directly the depth and urgency of his own religious needs. But towards the end of his life he was less circumspect. In 1952 he spoke of his relationship to God to a young clergyman: 'I find that all my thoughts circle around God like the planets around the sun, and are as irresistibly attracted by Him. I would feel it to be the greatest sin if I were to oppose any resistance to this force.'[5] In *Memories, Dreams, Reflections*, the autobiographical volume which appeared towards the end of his life, Jung revealed almost for the first time the depth of the religious turbulence he suffered during adolescence. In particular he relates the part played in his development by obscene or scatological dreams which he felt were blasphemous, but which at the same time he believed were part of a personal revelation made to him by God. In one of these dreams he saw what he later decided was a giant phallus which was in some way identified with Jesus. In a vision which he had when he was twelve years old he thought he saw God enthroned above the shining roof of a new cathedral. After agonising whether to let a thought which he felt was sinful into consciousness, he decided 'that God Himself was arranging a decisive test for me, and that everything depended on my understanding him correctly.'

> I gathered all my courage, as though I were about to leap forthwith into hell-fire, and let the thought come. I saw before me the cathedral, the blue sky. God sits on his golden throne, high above the world – and from under the throne an enormous turd falls upon the sparkling new roof, shatters it, and breaks the walls of the cathedral asunder.

As a direct result of his visions Jung tells us that, in private at least, he felt that grace had come upon him and he experienced 'an unutterable bliss such as I had never known'. At the same time, however, he knew that what he took to be his own experience of God was deeply heretical and that he could not communicate it to anyone else. 'I had experienced a dark and terrible secret. It overshadowed my whole life, and I became deeply pensive.'[6]

In one respect the religious visions which Jung had experienced by the age of twelve led to a deep feeling of spiritual superiority. He recounts how he was 'seized with almost vehement pity' for his father, a Protestant pastor, whose sense of God he felt was deficient. In another respect, however, Jung's shameful religious visions heightened his isolation. 'The experience,' he writes, 'also had the effect of increasing my sense of inferiority. I am a devil or a swine, I thought; I am infinitely depraved.' Jung's inner conflicts thus followed the classic messianic pattern. Above all he was trapped by the feeling that he had enjoyed intimacy with God in a way he could not communicate to others:

With [this] experience . . . I at last had something tangible that was part of the great secret – as if I had always talked of stones falling from heaven and now had one in my pocket. But actually, it was a shaming experience. I had fallen into something bad, something evil and sinister, though at the same time it was a kind of distinction. Sometimes I had an overwhelming urge to speak, not about that, but only to hint that there were some curious things about me which no one knew of. I wanted to find out whether other people had undergone similar experiences. I never succeeded in discovering so much as a trace of them in others. *As a result I had the feeling that I was either outlawed or elect, accursed or blessed* . . . [italics added]

My entire youth can be understood in terms of this secret. It induced in me an almost unendurable loneliness. My one great achievement during those years was that I resisted the temptation to talk about it with anyone.

As an adolescent Jung found some consolation in the New Testament, and above all in the stress which it placed on Jesus's ministry to those who were considered unclean and sinful. He recalls that he read 'with a certain satisfaction about the Pharisee and the publican, and that reprobates are the chosen ones'.[7] But he found conventional Christianity stale and empty and throughout his adolescence he remained, in a sense, the sole member of a church of which he was the founder. It seems reasonably clear that these early religious experiences played a significant role in his decision to join the psychoanalytic movement. Not long after his first meeting with Freud, indeed, Jung admitted to him that, 'My old religiosity had secretly found in you a compensating factor . . .'[8] In the light of this admission it might be suggested that Jung was drawn to psychoanalysis for the very reasons which have already been given to explain the appeal of Freud's confessional ritual. For Jung quite clearly suffered acute anxiety because he felt that his 'real' identity was secret, shameful and unclean, and that it could not be acknowledged in public without attracting the suspicion of madness, heresy, or both. In psychoanalysis it would seem that he found an oblique but significant acknowledgement of this part of his identity. And in Freud himself he felt that he had discovered an original thinker whose heresies were on the same scale as his own. 'I would never have sided with you in the first place,' he wrote to Freud in 1912, 'had not heresy run in my blood.'[9]

The relationship which eventually developed between Freud and Jung certainly had great emotional power and complexity and both parties repeatedly had recourse to religious metaphors in order to explain it. According to Ernest Jones, Jung's enthusiasm for Freud at this time was beyond question. 'His encounter with Freud he regarded as the high point of his life, and a couple of months after first meeting him he told him that whoever had acquired a knowledge of psychoanalysis had eaten of the tree of Paradise and attained vision.' Significantly, however, it was Freud who took most of the initiatives in this relationship. Almost as soon as he met Jung he began to think of him as his successor. He called him his 'son and heir', writing that 'when the Empire I founded is orphaned, no one but Jung must inherit the whole thing.'[10] According to this secular model Freud regarded Jung quite openly as his 'crown prince'. Yet behind the secular view was a stronger religious vision. Thus at one point Freud referred to the occasion 'when I formally adopted you as my eldest son and anointed you – *in partibus infidelium* [in the lands of the unbelievers] – as my successor and crown prince.' At about the same time Freud identified himself, as he was to do throughout the latter part of his life, with Moses: 'If I am Moses,' he wrote to Jung in 1909, 'then you are Joshua, and will take possession of the promised land of psychiatry, which I shall only be able to glimpse from afar.'[11]

In spite of the fact that he repeatedly referred to Jung as his 'heir', Freud was not prepared to wait until his own death before handing over leadership of the psychoanalytic movement. In 1910, at an International Congress in Nuremberg, he delegated to Ferenczi the task of announcing his plan to form an international psychoanalytical association which was to have Jung as its permanent President. Under Freud's proposal Jung would be given extraordinary powers, which would include the appointment and deposition of analysts and the right to vet their writings before they were published. The proposal, which left Freud's Viennese followers feeling insulted and rejected, led to uproar, and the Viennese came close to outright rebellion. Freud attempted to persuade them to accept his plan in an impassioned speech:

> Most of you are Jews, and therefore you are incompetent to win friends for the new teaching. Jews must be content with the modest role of preparing the ground. It is absolutely essential that I should form ties in the world of general science. I am getting on in years and am weary of being perpetually attacked. We are all in danger ... They won't even leave me a coat to my back. The Swiss will save us – will save me, and all of you as well.[12]

Eventually a compromise was effected in which Jung was appointed to the presidency for a period of two years only, without the powers of censorship which Freud had initially demanded.

The episode was a curious one. Nor was it the only occasion on which Freud had attempted to relinquish the leadership of the movement he had founded. According to Hans Sachs,

> It was Freud's enduring wish to be relieved from wearing the insignia of power. He went out of his way in his search for the right man to whom he could entrust the leadership of the psychoanalytic movement; when he thought he had found him he tried to invest the man of his choice – Adler, Jung, Rank – with full authority.[13]

In attempting to justify his choice of Jung, Freud himself once explained 'I wished . . . to withdraw into the background both myself and the city where psychoanalysis first saw the light.'[14]

There was an interesting precedent for such apparent shyness about the role of leader. It was, of course, in relation to Fliess. For it was during this friendship, the most passionate of all his intellectual 'affairs', that Freud repeatedly submitted to Fliess in the manner of a disciple. On one occasion, as we have seen, Freud wrote that he was looking forward to Fliess solving a particular problem 'as to the Messiah'. On another occasion he adopted a tone of almost masochistic humility:

> Your kind should not die out, my dear friend; the rest of us need people like you too much. How much I owe you: solace, understanding, stimulation in my loneliness, meaning to my life that I gained through you, and finally even health that no one else could have given back to me. It is primarily through your example that intellectually I gained the strength to trust my judgment . . . For all that, accept my humble thanks! I know that you do not need me as much as I need you, but I also know that I have a secure place in your affection . . .
>
> Your letters, as again the last one, contain a wealth of scientific insights and intuitions, to which I unfortunately can say no more than that they grip and overpower me.[15]

In both cases we may sense Freud's deep insecurity and his anxiety to avoid taking full responsibility for his own theories. Yet there is a crucial difference. For whereas, in the earlier case, Freud seemed to want to disappear into the background *beneath* Fliess, in the later case he sought to disappear *above* Jung – in such a way as to retain ultimate control over the movement which he had founded.

The difference in Freud's attitude which this implies is perhaps conveyed best if we consider a passing remark in Fritz Wittels's memoir of him. According to Wittels: 'Freud's face beamed whenever he spoke of Jung. "This is my beloved son in whom I am well pleased."'[16] The words which are quoted here are, of course, taken from the gospels. However extraordinary it may seem in relation to a movement which was not only Jewish but also rationalistic and atheistic, they are the words supposedly spoken by God at the time that Jesus was baptised by John (Matthew 3:17). In any other context it would be tempting to dismiss such a quotation as being without real significance. Yet in the context of Freud's profoundly religious imagination it is difficult to do this. What the quotation seems to imply is that, in fantasy, Freud identified not simply with Moses or with other prophetic or messianic characters, but with God. That such a fantasy-identification is not so unusual as might be supposed is suggested by Ernest Jones in his paper on the God complex which has already been referred to. Jones introduces this paper by noting that the tendency to identify the self with the 'loved object' occurs in almost every form of affection and is certainly often found in the attitudes of sons towards their fathers. Having noted that almost every son imitates his father, pretends to himself that he is the father, and to some extent actually models himself on him, he concludes that 'It is therefore only natural that a similar attitude may develop in regard to the more perfect Heavenly Father, and in a sense this is directly inculcated in the religious teaching that one should strive to become as like the divine model as possible . . .'[17] Jones goes on to suggest that the fantasy in which people identify their personality with that of God 'is not at all rare' and that 'it possibly occurs here and there in all men.' What is striking about his paper is that, as Paul Roazen has observed, many of the tendencies which Jones associated with the 'God complex' corresponded to those which, elsewhere, he also attributed to Freud.[18] Parts of his paper, indeed, might even be read as an oblique and unintended criticism of the very man he publicly venerated and defended:

> The tendency to aloofness also manifests itself on the purely mental side quite directly. Such men are both unsociable and unsocial, in the wider sense. Any influence they exert is done so quite indirectly, by means of stimulating more active admirers. Their ideal is to be 'the man

behind the throne', directing affairs from above while being invisible to the crowd. To follow, to participate, or even to lead, in a general movement, is repugnant to them, and they use every effort to maintain a policy of magnificent isolation ...

More often a higher form of sublimation occurs, and this typically takes the form of *interest in psychology*. If the person in question is endowed with a natural intuition for divining the minds of others, is a judge of human nature, he will make use of this in his profession whatever it may be; if he is not so endowed he tends to become a professional psychologist or psychiatrist ... He takes a particular interest in any methods that promise a 'short-cut' to the knowledge of other people's minds ... The more unusual the method the more it attracts him, giving him a feeling of possessing a key that is accessible only to the elect ...

One of the most distressing character-traits of the type under consideration is the attitude of disinclination towards the acceptance of new knowledge. This follows quite logically from the idea of omniscience, for anyone who already knows everything naturally cannot be taught anything new; still less can he admit that he has ever made a mistake in his knowledge ... In the first place men with this type of character talk even more than other men about their capacity to assimilate new ideas ... But when put to the test of being confronted with a new idea which doesn't proceed from themselves, they offer an uncompromising resistance to it ...

The subject of religion is usually one of the greatest interest to such men ... As a rule they are atheists, and naturally so because they cannot suffer the existence of any other God ...[19]

In their original context many of the observations quoted above are carefully qualified so that they could not be construed as a criticism of Freud himself or of psychoanalysis. But it seems likely that Jones had Freud in mind in at least some parts of his paper. It is certainly worthy of note that he goes out of his way to stress that the God complex is not always negative and that, if 'guided and controlled by valuable higher factors, it may give us a man who is truly god-like in his grandeur and sublimity.' He also gives an account of a variation of the God complex which reads very much like a retrospective judgement on the character of Jung – a judgement made many years after both Jones and Freud had accused Jung of anti-semitism and Freud had given his final verdict that Jung was 'incapable either of accepting or of exercising authority'. Jones introduces this account by suggesting that the most important variation of the God complex is that which depends on the idea of the Son of God or of Christ:

This gives a special stamp to the type in question, which must shortly be indicated. The three chief characteristics are: revolution against the father, saving fantasies, and masochism, or in other words, an Oedipus situation in which the hero-son is a suffering saviour . . . There is thus constantly present an intolerance of authority of any kind, and any person invested with [authority] . . . may be viewed in the light of this complex so that the figure is artificially distorted into the *imago* of the wicked father. With this Christ type there invariably goes an anti-semitic tendency, the two religions being contrasted and the old Hebraic Jehovah being replaced by the young Christ.[20]

If these words are indeed an allusion to Jung then it is clear that the account they give of his conflict with Freud is biased in favour of the latter. But the general implication that, behind the greatest schism in the psychoanalytic movement, there is a religious drama in which Freud attempts to play the role of the divine father, seems broadly true. Jung, who was smitten by God at an early age, was certainly smitten by Freud in a manner which was almost as dramatic. He himself confessed to Freud that his 'veneration' of him had 'something of the character of a "religious" crush', and wrote that Freud was 'a human hero and higher god'.[21] From the very beginning he evidently had great difficulty disentangling the emotional aspects of their relationship from the intellectual.

Even before he met Freud, Jung had developed a philosophy of his own which meant that his attitude towards psychoanalysis was, as we have already seen, far from being uncritical. At first, however, it would seem that this critical side of Jung was all but overpowered by the sheer force of Freud's personality. In one of the letters Jung wrote soon after their first meeting he expressed considerable uncertainty about Freud's 'broadened conception of sexuality'. But in the same letter he went on to write: 'I am no longer plagued by doubts as to the rightness of your theory. The last shreds were dispelled by my stay in Vienna, which for me was an event of the first importance.'[22] Not long afterwards Jung wrote again and used the vocabulary of religion in order to reassure Freud that he accepted his full authority:

I have the feeling of having made considerable progress since I got to know you personally; it seems to me that one can never quite understand you and your science unless one knows you in the flesh. Where so much still remains dark to us outsiders only faith can help; but the best and most effective faith is knowledge of your personality.[23]

The extent to which Jung became locked into Freud's own messianic outlook is perhaps indicated best by his enthusiasm to share Freud's private demonology. In a letter written in May 1910, Freud relates to his 'son' how he had been visited at his apartment by Hofrat Friedländer, one of the sharpest critics of psychoanalysis. After alleging that he gave his name incorrectly as 'Schottländer' in order to gain entrance, Freud refers to him as 'the demon' and writes that, when he sought to rebut one of his criticisms, 'Beelzebub pulled in his horns, emitted his well known stench, and went on denouncing.' Freud goes on to recount how he attacked his visitor with 'a series of insulting remarks . . . I told him that he knew nothing of the analytic technique . . . that he was essentially a brute, a retarded guttersnipe (this in more polite language to be sure)'. Jung's reply is remarkable, in that far from objecting to the excesses of Freud's language, he multiplies them:

> I was amazed by your news. The adventure with Schottländer is marvellous; of course the slimy bastard was lying. I hope you roasted, flayed and impaled the fellow with such genial ferocity that he got a lasting taste for once of the effectiveness of PsA [psychoanalysis]. I subscribe to your final judgment with all my heart. Such is the nature of these beasts. Since I could read the filth in him from his face I would have loved to take him by the scruff of his neck. I hope to God you told him all the truths so plainly that even his hen's brain could absorb them. Now we shall see what his next coup will be. Had I been in your shoes I would have softened up his guttersnipe complex with a sound Swiss thrashing.[24]

Jung's vision here, like that of Freud, is characteristic of the apocalyptic religious thinker who sees himself and his followers as islands of purity surrounded by a sea of corruption and filth. Jung would later write with seeming objectivity about how Freud described psychoanalysis as a wall of truth 'against the black tide of mud'.[25] It is clear, however, that in the early years of their relationship he shared just such a view. So long as he was able to convince himself that he and Freud had formed their relationship in order to protect and further a 'holy' scientific truth, his scepticism was held in check.

The turning-point came in 1909 during the trip which they made together to the United States, where they had been invited to speak on the occasion of the twentieth anniversary of Clark University. During their seven-week trip they fell into the habit of analysing one another's dreams. It was at this point that something happened which, as Jung put it, 'proved to be a severe blow to the whole relationship'.[26] Freud had some dreams which troubled him a great deal and which, in Jung's view, referred to his supposed sexual affair with his wife's younger sister, Minna:

> Freud had no idea that I knew about the triangle and his intimate relationship to his sister-in-law. And so, when Freud told me the dream in which his wife and her sister played important parts, I asked Freud to tell me some of his personal associations with the dream. He looked at me with bitterness and said, 'I could tell you more but I cannot risk my authority.'[27]

In the version of this story which appears in *Memories, Dreams, Reflections*, Jung writes that from the very moment that Freud attempted to make his authority more important than the pursuit of psychological truth, 'he lost it altogether. That sentence ['I cannot risk my authority'] burned itself into my memory; and in it the end of our relationship was already foreshadowed.'[28]

How accurately this recollection captures the exact turning-point in the relationship will never be known. There were certainly other factors which weakened the relationship, including Jung's insistence on feeling slighted when Freud visited Switzerland without meeting him in 1912. What does seem clear is that Jung eventually lost faith in the man whom he had begun by worshipping as a god. Freed from his former attitude of religious awe, he began to express some of the reservations and doubts which he had felt about Freud's theories from the beginning. While he did not immediately seek to break with Freud, and indeed appears to have valued his position within the psychoanalytic movement, he increasingly strayed from orthodoxy into independent formulations of his own.

This became particularly apparent in 1912, when Jung returned to America on his own in order to deliver a series of lectures at Fordham University in New York. The purpose of these lectures was to expound the basic principles of psychoanalysis and a great deal of what Jung had to say was not original. Yet on a number of crucial issues Jung was careful to overlay Freud's teachings with qualifications of his own. He rejected the view that obtaining pleasure was the same thing as sexuality and dissociated himself from what he called 'the boundless extension of the concept of sexuality' in psychoanalysis. As well as repudiating Freud's account of infantile sexuality, he also translated

Freud's Oedipus complex into his own much milder terms. Having correctly explained that Freud took 'the tendency towards incest to be an absolutely concrete sexual wish', Jung went on to suggest that Freud was inclined 'to reduce practically the whole psychology of the neuroses ... to this one complex'. Jung felt that if the Oedipus complex were regarded merely as 'a formula for childish desires in regard to the parents and for the conflict which these desires evoke' then 'the matter might seem more acceptable.'[29]

In expressing these views Jung knew very well that he was transgressing the holiest of all psychoanalytic taboos. For by this time he had already had the conversation in which Freud insisted that his sexual theory should be treated as 'a dogma ... an unshakable bulwark' (see above, Chapter 14). Jung later expressed the view that the rigidity with which Freud upheld the sexual theory was a substitute for the rigidity of the God he no longer worshipped:

> In place of the jealous God whom he had lost he had substituted another compelling image, that of sexuality. It was no less insistent, exacting, domineering, threatening and morally ambivalent than the original one ... The advantage of the transformation for Freud was, apparently, that he was able to regard the new numinous principle as scientifically irreproachable and free from all religious taint.[30]

Whether we regard Freud as having made a deity of his theory, or of himself, ultimately makes little difference. The crucial development was that Jung, having initially bowed submissively in the direction of psychoanalysis, and having treated its founder with veneration, increasingly began to claim for himself the authority he had at first been prepared to locate elsewhere.

Freud's response to Jung's waywardness was characteristic; as in the case of Adler and Stekel and many others, he used his own theories as a defensive weapon, imputing to Jung an unresolved father complex. In December 1911 Freud had already written to Jung that 'the trouble with you younger men seems to be a lack of understanding in dealing with your father complexes.'[31] Freud returned to this theme on a number of occasions and it seems likely that he tacitly (or even actively) encouraged his followers to meet Jung's increasingly independent pronouncements with similar psychoanalytic rebukes. Instead of allowing himself to be cowed by such tactics Jung came near to open rebellion when he objected to the tendency of psychoanalysts to

misuse psychoanalysis for the purpose of devaluing others . . . by insin-
uations about complexes . . . A particularly preposterous bit of nonsense
now going the rounds is that my libido theory is the product of anal
erotism . . . Anything which might make them think is written off as a
complex. This protective function of PsA [psychoanalysis] badly needs
unmasking.[32]

At this point Jung's criticism of Freud was oblique and he carefully
avoided any more personal confrontation by criticising other analysts
rather than Freud himself. But after Freud had irritated him by treating
a slip of the pen in one of his letters as a symptomatic action, Jung
wrote a letter of defiance:

> May I say a few words to you in earnest? I admit the ambivalence of my
> feelings towards you, but am inclined to take an honest and absolutely
> straightforward view of the situation . . . I would . . . point out that
> your technique of treating your pupils like patients is a *blunder*. In that
> way you produce either slavish sons or impudent puppies (Adler – Stekel
> and the whole insolent gang now throwing their weight around in
> Vienna). I am objective enough to see through your little trick. You go
> around sniffing out all the symptomatic actions in your vicinity thus
> reducing everyone to the level of sons and daughters who blushingly
> admit the existence of their faults. Meantime you remain on top as the
> father, sitting pretty. For sheer obsequiousness nobody dares pluck the
> prophet by the beard and inquire for once what you would say to a
> patient with a tendency to analyse the analyst instead of himself. You
> would certainly ask him: 'Who's got the neurosis?'
>
> You see, my dear Professor, so long as you hand out this stuff, I
> don't give a damn for my symptomatic actions; they shrink to nothing
> compared to the formidable beam in my brother Freud's eye. I am not
> in the least neurotic – touch wood! I have submitted *lege artis et tout
> humblement* to analysis and am much the better for it. You know, of
> course, how far a patient gets with self-analysis; *not* out of his neurosis
> – just like you. If ever you should rid yourself entirely to your complexes
> and stopped playing the father to your sons, and instead of aiming
> continually at their weak spots, took a good look at your own for a
> change, then I will mend my ways and at one stroke uproot the vice of
> being in two minds about you. Do you *love neurotics* enough to be always
> at one with yourself? But perhaps you *hate* neurotics. In that case how
> can you expect your efforts to treat your patients leniently and lovingly
> *not* to be accompanied by somewhat mixed feeling? Adler and Stekel
> were taken in by your little tricks and reacted with childish insolence.
> I shall continue to stand by you publicly while maintaining my own
> views, but privately shall start telling you in my letters what I really
> think of you. I consider this procedure only decent.

No doubt you will be outraged by this peculiar token of friendship, but it may do you good all the same.[33]

Jung's tone bears the impress of continued psychological subservience to the man he is attacking; his manner is impudent and rebellious rather than calm and assured. Yet the criticisms which he now levelled at his master contained an uncomfortably large amount of truth. Freud was particularly stung by Jung's suggestion that his self-analysis had been ineffective. His immediate reaction was to seek reassurance from more docile followers. On 26 December he wrote a letter to Ernest Jones in which he described Jung as 'crazy' and 'out of his wits'.[34] On the same day Ferenczi, who had already heard of Jung's attack and who at this point remained completely under Freud's spell, wrote to Freud telling him that he was the only psychoanalyst who had no need of analysis and reassuring him fawningly that 'you were right in everything.'[35] Early in January 1913 Freud wrote back to Jung suggesting that by shouting about his normality 'while behaving abnormally' he was giving grounds for the suspicion that he lacked insight into his 'illness'. He went on to suggest that personal relations between them should cease.[36] Freud thus effectively confirmed Jung's own analysis of his methods of leadership; for daring to question Freud's authority Jung was, in effect, dismissed as being mentally ill. The diagnosis was subsequently confirmed by Jones, who expressed his feeling that Jung 'does not react like a normal man and that he is mentally deranged to a serious extent'.[37]

Merely ending his friendship, however, did not bring a solution to Freud's problem. For having carefully groomed Jung as his crown prince, and placed him in a position of power within the psychoanalytic movement, Freud was faced with the very real prospect that he might seize the throne. The task now was to win back the International Psychoanalytic Association from Jung's presidency and the main psychoanalytic journal, the *Jahrbuch für psychoanalytische und psychopathologische Forschungen*, from his editorship. There followed a concerted campaign against Jung which one commentator, François Roustang, has characterised as 'an assassination plot' designed to eliminate a 'traitor'.[38] In view of the fact that Jung could still count on the votes of the Zurich contingent there was no prospect of ousting him from the presidency at the Munich Congress, which was held in 1913. But Karl Abraham suggested that Freud's supporters should prevail upon their societies to express their disapproval for Jung through block abstentions. As a result of this pressure, twenty-two of the fifty-two participants abstained. At the same time the members of Freud's inner circle all gave papers which contained criticisms of Jung.[39]

The first fruit of this campaign came in October 1913 when Jung resigned as editor of the *Jahrbuch*. But he remained in place as President of the International Association. Freud, Ferenczi and Rank took the view that they should break away from the International Psychoanalytic Association and form a new group but this plan was abandoned when Jones suggested they would then be perceived as the outsiders by Jung's supporters in America. Freud then decided that the future might be secured through a polemical attack on Jung presented under the title 'On the History of the Psychoanalytic Movement'. As he worked furiously on this project, he referred to it as his 'bomb'.[40] At the same time Abraham was composing a critique of Jung's work which Freud praised as though it were a honed dagger: 'excellent, cold steel, clean, clear and sharp'.[41] The atmosphere of almost murderous hatred with which Jung was now pursued was captured well by Freud in a letter to Abraham in March 1914. 'I enclose Jones's letter,' he wrote. 'It is quite remarkable how each one of us in turn is seized with the impulse to kill, so that the others have to restrain him. I suspect Jones himself will produce the next plan.'[42]

On 20 April Jung, who was undoubtedly aware of the hostility towards him, and who may already have learnt of the imminent publication of Freud's polemic, resigned from the presidency. For the time being he remained a member of the Association. But in July 1914, some three weeks after Freud's 'bomb' was finally detonated, Jung resigned his membership. A few days later the entire Zurich group voted to follow his example. In a letter to Abraham, Freud characteristically took the opportunity to use his betrayal by Jung, and the hatred it had aroused, as a way of playing on the feelings of those disciples who had remained:

> So we are at last rid of them, the brutal sanctimonious Jung and his disciples. I must now thank you for the vast amount of trouble, the exceptional clear-sightedness, with which you supported me and our common cause. All my life I have been looking for friends who would not exploit and then betray me, and now, not far from its natural end, I hope I have found them.[43]

The story of Jung's departure from the psychoanalytic movement has been told many times, usually from the point of view of one of the two main protagonists. To some followers of Freud, Jung remains the incarnation of psychoanalytic perfidy. At the height of the conflict with him intellectual distaste for his views was converted into something approaching physical revulsion and he and his followers were hunted down with an attitude which is almost reminiscent of that shown by Stalin towards Trotsky. Much of the bitterness survived long afterwards. In 1975 Paul Roazen accurately observed that, of all possible accusations, 'Jungian' is still probably the most devastating among Freud's intellectual descendants. 'Every subculture has its villains,' he wrote, 'and Jung is a particularly odious figure, partly because Freud had placed such high hopes on him.'[44]

When he is portrayed in the most unsympathetic light by Freudians, Jung emerges as a kind of inverted Judas figure, who first seeks to further the wholly scientific mission of his master but who then betrays him and succumbs to religion and mysticism. Whereas Freud is depicted as a hard-headed realist who fearlessly confronts the most unpalatable aspects of the human psyche, flinching in the face neither of violence nor of sexuality, Jung is dismissed as a muddled sage who, spurning the hard disciplines of rationalism, spent his life trying to construct a personal form of psychotherapeutic mysticism whose avowed aim was to replace the religious beliefs which he had lost as a child. He is charged, as Victor White has put it, 'with abandoning the physician's coat for the professor's gown, and the professor's gown for the clergyman's surplice, if not the robes of the magician, the prophet, the mystagogue'.[45]

If Jung is seen by his opponents as destructively regressive, psychoanalysis is sometimes seen by those of a Jungian persuasion as a way of reducing the richness and complexity of the human soul to mere animality or mechanism. Freud's determination to reject religion not simply as superstition but as neurosis is seen as symptomatic of the pride of materialism. Psychoanalysis, on this view, sets out to reduce to base instincts the parts of human behaviour it claims to understand and to dismiss as irrelevant the spiritual and religious needs it does not.

Both these caricatures contain an element of truth. For it is beyond question that there were significant differences between the ideas of the two men. Whereas Freud was constantly mistrustful of the Unconscious, seeing it as a residue of childhood which should be repressed and sublimated, Jung saw in the non-rational elements of human experience a source of dark fertility and potential healing. He refused to follow Freud in dismissing ritual and mysticism as neurosis and he did not always share his therapeutic interest in the past. Whereas Freud was interested in the acorn – in the supposed infantile origins of a neurosis – Jung became more and more interested in the oak. To a much greater degree than Freud he began to focus on present conflicts and on the future – on the 'life-task' which remained to be accomplished.[46]

The differences between the Freudian and the Jungian positions are real. Yet the partisans of either side who place a massive stress on these differences end by obscuring more than they reveal. For these differences are ultimately significant only if they are viewed in the perspective of the underlying similarities. It was certainly not a fundamental difference in temperament which brought Freud and Jung together in the first place, and which led them to engage in a correspondence in which they wrote to each other every few days over a period of seven years. At the very heart of the relationship lay a profound feeling of mutual affinity, in which each man came very close to identifying with the other and in which each treated the other as a kind of intellectual *alter ego*. In some respects this passionate feeling of mutual identification rested, as in the case of more conventional love affairs, on an illusion. Yet an illusion so mighty needed some solid foundations and it is clear that there were deep psychological similarities between the two men. By far the most important of these was the way in which both had, as a result of parental influence and childhood experience, developed a profoundly messianic personality. In both cases, moreover, a fundamentally religious temperament was cut off from the living religious tradition out of which it had grown and cast instead into an intellectual environment of rationalistic positivism which was ostensibly hostile to all forms of religious belief.

Stranded on the shores of the fast-receding sea of faith, Freud and Jung found themselves, like a host of their contemporaries – from Edward Carpenter and D. H. Lawrence to Karl Marx and Vladimir Ilich Lenin – under a profound psychological compulsion to immerse themselves once more in belief. Whereas Carpenter and Lawrence sought to construct personal creeds by way of a fierce and sometimes extremely radical critique of modern science, the visions eventually developed by Freud and Jung were presented as part of the advance of science, and in this respect had something in common with the scientific socialism of Marx and Lenin.

Neither Freud at his most prophetic nor Jung at his most mystical ever gave up the belief that they were essentially scientists, and that they worked in the same intellectual tradition which had brought about modern advances in physics, chemistry and biology. It was because of their determination to cast an essentially religious vision in the mould of modern science that both were forced to loosen standards of scientific rigour, evidence and consistency to a degree almost unprecedented in Western intellectual history. We have already seen how Freud's deep psychological need for a revelation, and for an intimate relationship with a man he considered as a visionary and a seer, led him to embrace uncritically Fliess's essay in numerological astrology. It must be suggested that very similar psychological pressures led Jung to lay aside his initial sceptical reaction to *The Interpretation of Dreams*, and to embrace the cause of psychoanalysis with a fervour which he later found deeply embarrassing. In many respects, indeed, the correspondence between Jung and Freud, and the very course of their relationship, recapitulates Freud's earlier infatuations and dependencies.

Readers who are unfamiliar with Freud's intellectual biography might well be surprised to read the following passage in a letter which was sent to him on 12 June 1911, by the man who was his closest collaborator and to whose care he had entrusted the fate of his entire movement:

> My evenings are taken up very largely with astrology. I made horoscopic calculations in order to find a clue to the core of psychological truth. Some remarkable things have turned up which will certainly appear incredible to you. In the case of one lady, the calculation of the position of the stars at her nativity produced a quite definite character picture, with several biographical details which did not pertain to her but to her mother – and the characteristics fitted the mother to a T. The lady suffers from an extraordinary mother complex. I dare say that we shall one day discover in astrology a good deal of knowledge which has been intuitively projected into the heavens. For instance, it appears that the signs of the zodiac are character pictures, in other words libido symbols which depict the typical qualities of the libido at a given moment . . .

The same readers might be even more surprised by the way in which Jung's letter was received by Freud. For although Freud had initially reacted sceptically to Jung's interest in the occult, he had eventually come to regard this aspect of his work with almost exactly the same credulity he once bestowed on the ideas of Fliess. 'In matters of occultism,' he replies, 'I have grown humble since the great lesson Ferenczi's experiences gave me. I promise to believe anything that can be made to look reasonable.'[47] Freud's words, 'I promise to believe anything that can be made to look reasonable', might well be used to summarise the intellectual ethos of psychoanalysis itself. For his most enduring achievement was, as has already been argued, to take a fundamentally superstitious and irrational view of the world, deriving directly from the Judaeo-Christian tradition, and re-present it in the vocabulary of modern science. As a result of the extraordinary skill with which he did this, psychoanalysis has continued to offer to intellectuals what it also gave to its founder – a means of using science (or rather the rhetoric of science) in order to fortify traditional religious doctrines against the scepticism of science.

Jung himself was evidently powerfully attracted by just this feature of Freud's thought. It would be wrong to suggest, however, that this was merely a passing phase in his development. For just as Freud, when he eventually broke with Fliess, transferred his credulity to his own theories, so Jung, when he parted company from Freud, employed a scientific style very similar to that he had admired in his mentor in order to construct his own visionary system. The extraordinarily complicated Jungian theories of animus and anima, of archetype and association, were elaborated with just as much *élan* and adventurousness as had been shown by Freud, and with just as little regard for ordinary scientific criteria of evidence, argument and consistency. Just as Freud, through his theory of the unconscious, created a bank of pseudo-empirical evidence on which he was able to draw at will in order to 'prove' practically any theoretical construct he cared to present, so Jung, by taking over and modifying this same concept, was able to furnish 'evidence' for any precept put forward in the name of 'analytical psychology'.

Both psychoanalysis and analytical psychology, then, functioned ultimately as ways of restoring to their founders, and to their founders' followers, elements of a religious faith which they had lost. For all the similarities, however, there is one crucial respect – over and above those already mentioned – in which Jung's psychological system differs from Freud's. For whereas Freud developed psychoanalysis in passionate opposition to all superstitious modes of thought, and genuinely believed that the most 'valuable' human beings had, like himself, evolved to a stage of rationality where they had no use for religious modes of thought, Jung took a different view. Instead of dismissing religion as part of the problem, he saw it as a potential solution and as a source of healing. 'During the past thirty years,' he wrote in 1932,

> people from all the civilised countries of the earth have consulted me ... Among my patients in the second half of life – that is to say, over thirty-five – there has not been one whose problem in the last resort was not that of finding a religious outlook on life. It is safe to say that every one of them fell ill because he had lost that which the living religions of every age have given to their followers, and none of them has been really healed who did not regain this religious outlook.[48]

The claims which Jung made for this kind of religiously based therapy are as open to question as the claims made for the effectiveness of psychoanalytic therapy. But Jung's words clearly imply a much greater insight into his own religious identity than was ever shown by Freud. Jung's understanding of his relationship to religious tradition is frequently expressed elsewhere in his writings, and he is particularly interesting when he points to the pervasive influence of Christianity on Western intellectual culture:

> We always think that Christianity consists in a particular confession of faith, and in belonging to a Church. No, Christianity is our world. Everything we think is the fruit of the Middle Ages and indeed of the Christian Middle Ages. Our whole science, everything that passes through our head, has inevitably gone through this history. It lives in us and has left its stamp upon us for all time and will always form a vital layer of our psyche, just like the phylogenetic traces in our body. The whole character of our mentality, the way we look at things, is also the result of the Christian Middle Ages; whether we know it or not is quite immaterial. The age of rational enlightenment has eradicated nothing. Even our method of rational enlightenment is Christian. The Christian *Weltanschauung* is therefore a psychological fact that does not allow of any further rationalisation; it is something that has happened, that is present. We are inevitably stamped as Christians, but we are also stamped by what existed before Christianity.[49]

So close does this appear to be to the assumptions which inform the critique of psychoanalysis which I have presented in earlier chapters, that the two points of view might well be taken to be identical. One of the many reasons that this is not so is that Jung, as is usually the case, rests his analysis on the same kind of phylogenetic argument and psycho-Lamarckism we encounter in the work of Freud. He assumes, in other words, that acquired cultural attitudes can be transmitted by inheritance and that this phylogenetic mechanism is the main agency of the cultural continuity which he points to.

Beneath this biologically untenable argument, however, it seems clear that Jung does possess a real insight both into his own religious identity and into the religious nature of the needs he is seeking to meet through his psychological researches. And it is perhaps Jung himself who, in a series of reflections on the problem of self-realisation, captures most clearly the reasons why Freud parted from him in such exasperation and in an atmosphere of so much hatred and animosity:

> Our unwillingness to see our own faults and our projection of them onto others is the source of most quarrels, and the strongest guarantee that injustice, animosity, and persecution will not easily die out.

> A man's hatred is always concentrated on the thing that makes him conscious of his bad qualities.

> When we allow ourselves to be irritated out of our wits by something, let us not suppose that the cause of our irritation lies simply and solely outside us, in the irritating thing or person. In that way we simply endow them with the power to put us into the state of irritation ... We then turn around and unhesitatingly condemn the object of offence, while all the time we are raging against an unconscious part of ourselves which is projected into the exasperating object.

> A man who is unconscious of himself acts in a blind, instinctive way, and is in addition fooled by all the illusions that arise when he sees everything that he is not conscious of in himself coming to meet him from outside as projections upon his neighbour.

> Projections change the world into the replica of one's own unknown face.[50]

So long as Jung displayed his religiosity by worshipping Freud as a god, Freud saw his attitude as embodying the purest form of scientific rationality. But as soon as Jung started to show his independent interest in other religious systems, and to acknowledge openly his own profoundly religious nature, Freud's attitude changed dramatically. In the mirror of Jung's ideas, Freud glimpsed, almost for the first time, the mysticism, the religiosity and the pseudo-scientific nature of his own world-redeeming system. Unable to confront, or even to recognise, his own unknown face, he turned upon Jung, as he had turned upon

Fliess, with hatred and contempt. Indeed, it was soon after Jung had written his fateful letter in December 1912 that Freud began to talk of the need 'to make a sharp division between us and all Aryan religiosity'.[51] Thereafter his constant complaint against Jung was that he was preaching 'a new message of salvation' and that he had created 'a new religio-ethical system' which rested on 'speculation' rather than on scientific 'observation'.[52]*

At the root of the conflict between Freud and Jung we may thus discern Freud's flight from his own religiosity. The more he denied the reality of his religious personality, and the more he tried to represent his own crypto-theological system as a purely scientific construct, the more discomfited he was to see his most prominent disciple openly displaying the very religiosity he was suppressing. Ultimately, as his contemptuous reference to *Aryan* religiosity implies, Freud turned upon Jung the mirror-image of the anti-semitism which Jung had undoubtedly shown towards him, and recoiled from him in almost physical disgust.

---

* Only as this book went to press was I able to consult Richard Noll's fascinating new study of Jung's religious identity, *The Jung Cult: Origins of a Charismatic Movement*, Princeton University Press, 1994. Noll's work contains a wealth of detailed evidence which is directly relevant to the argument which I have put forward in this chapter.

NINETEEN

The Secret Committee: From Formation to Failure

JUNG'S QUARREL WITH FREUD was the most serious of all the disputes which took place in the psychoanalytic movement in Freud's lifetime. For both men it was a disturbing experience. According to Anna Freud it was the only occasion on which she remembers her father being depressed. For Jung it would seem that the split was even more traumatic, leading to a spell of psychiatric treatment.[1] Yet it was not only the two main protagonists who were affected. The quarrel threatened the entire psychoanalytic movement and for almost all Freud's closest followers the effect was deeply unsettling, not least because it exposed the perilous insecurity of Freud's own position.

It was in response to the anxieties thus aroused that Ernest Jones wrote to Freud in July 1912 in order to put forward a proposal. Calculating, perhaps, that he was unworthy to play the coveted role of Freud's son, Jones suggested that the future of the movement should be safeguarded in a different way. Having expressed anxiety about Jung, whose behaviour he regarded as 'altogether inexplicable', he proposed that a secret committee should be formed in order to protect Freud and his doctrines. One of the implicit aims of this committee would be to monitor Jung as well as any future dissidents. Freud, as we have seen, was obsessively concerned with maintaining the orthodoxies which he had created. In terms which came close to implying his own divinity he once wrote of psychoanalysis that he was 'uneasy about what the human rabble would make out of it when I was no longer alive'.[2] Jones was thus caressing, as he no doubt realised, the most sensitive and vulnerable part of his master's identity. It was therefore not surprising when Freud responded by embracing the idea wholeheartedly:

What took hold of my imagination immediately was your idea of a secret council composed of the best and most trustworthy among our men to take care of the further development of and defend the cause against personalities and accidents when I am no more . . . I daresay it would make living and dying easier for me if I knew of such an association existing to watch over my creation.[3]

Anxious to take full credit for a suggestion which had evidently met with his master's approval, Jones replied to Freud by stressing that 'The idea of a united small body, designed like the Paladins of Charlemagne, to guard the kingdom and policy of their master, was the product of my own romanticism.' He went on to reiterate that the committee he envisaged would be both unofficial and secret, but that it would keep 'in the closest possible touch with you for the purposes both of criticism and instruction'.[4] The Committee was duly formed after Freud had proposed as members Jones, Ferenczi, Otto Rank, Hans Sachs and Karl Abraham. In May 1913 the entire Committee met for the first time and, after a discussion of Jung's wayward views, the meeting became an informal ritual as Freud presented each of the members with an antique Greek intaglio which was to be mounted in a gold ring and worn as a secret badge of office.

For the next ten years the members of the Committee acted as an invisible steering-group whose task was to oversee the development of the psychoanalytic movement and maintain the purity of Freud's doctrines. In the secret meeting which they held in The Hague in 1920 after the Sixth Congress of the International Psychoanalytic Association, Freud proposed that they should engage in a regular correspondence, circulating weekly letters to one another in which they would co-ordinate activities in Vienna, London, Berlin and Budapest. Abraham then suggested that the Committee members should address one another with the familiar *du* since they were all 'brothers', and an extraordinary secret correspondence was continued on this basis for three years until the frequency of the circular letters was reduced from weekly to monthly.

In Freud's imagination it would seem that the main function of the Committee was to take over from Jung the task of ensuring that psychoanalysis would continue after his death. He had replaced his 'son and heir' with a band of brothers who had solemnly undertaken to perpetuate his teachings. 'I bask in satisfaction and I am easy at heart to see my frail child of much care, the labour of my life, protected and in safekeeping for the future,' wrote Freud in 1918.[5] Yet this fantasy of a secure future for his 'frail child' was as far removed from reality in the case of the Secret Committee as it had been in the case of Jung. What had happened in the earlier relationship was that Freud had, as a result of his own deeply insecure need for adulation, inadvertently given confidence to a potential rival by treating him as special and elevating him above his other disciples. By doing this he strengthened Jung's own fantasies of chosenness and reinforced in him the very messianic tendencies which would eventually lead him to compete with his master. A similar pattern of conflict soon began to emerge in Freud's relationship to his Committee. For although the declared purpose of Freud's followers in forming the Committee had been that of offering protection to their master, the move clearly served another purpose – that of conferring rank, status and influence on those who were elected to join it. It was almost inevitable that some of Freud's new adopted sons would, like Jung before them, use the power and self-confidence which they gained through membership of the Committee in order to contest the very doctrines they had vowed to perpetuate.

This was to happen most clearly in the case of Otto Rank. Rank was a Viennese Jew whose father had deserted him when he was an adolescent, causing him to break off his formal education and work in order to support his mother. Rank continued to read widely, however, and, after discussing the works of Freud with his family physician Alfred Adler, found himself being introduced to his intellectual hero. He came to Freud in 1906 at the age of twenty-two, bringing with him an essay entitled 'The Artist'. Freud was so impressed that he persuaded Rank to complete his education to university level; Rank eventually gained a doctorate from the University of Vienna in 1912. Meanwhile Freud found in him 'a loyal helper and co-worker' and he rapidly became, in the words of Anaïs Nin, Freud's 'research worker, his proof-reader, his adopted son'.[6]

Living as he did in Vienna and enjoying regular contact with Freud, Rank rapidly became one of his favourites. After the break with Jung this position was consolidated, and when Rank married in 1918 he and his wife became almost a part of the Freud family, entertaining for Freud in his own house and being treated as though they were his own children. But at the same time that Rank was enjoying the favour of his adopted father, he began to develop theories which, in stark contrast to Freud's focus on the child's relationship with its father, focused on the mother. Even more specifically, he began to work out a theory according to which the whole of mental development was to be explained by reference to the psychological trauma which all children supposedly experienced during the act of birth.

Freud's own reaction to Rank's book was surprising. For, initially at least, he seems to have welcomed it. In 1923, after reading the manuscript, he even wrote to Rank saying that he would gladly accept the book's dedication to him. Later he hovered between praising *The Trauma of Birth* and reserving judgement on it. The reaction of some of the other members of the Secret Committee was much harsher, however. Accurately perceiving that Rank's book contained an implicit refutation of some of the basic tenets of Freud's own thought, both Abraham and Jones expressed their opposition to it. Jones in particular saw the issue as one in which faith in the theory was being brought into conflict with faith in the leader. It was this point of view which he expressed in a letter to Abraham in April 1924:

> It would be a strange irony if we lost some of Prof's [Freud's] intimate friendship through too great loyalty to his work, but it may possibly prove to be so. We may possibly have to choose between Psa and personal considerations, in which case you may be sure that I for one shall have no doubt.

Jones went on to suggest that Freud was avoiding a confrontation with Rank because, old and ill as he was, 'he can hardly face the possibility of having once more to go through the Jung situation and this time much nearer home, with someone who perhaps means more to him than his own sons.'[7]

The problem posed by Rank's new-found intellectual independence was greatly intensified by the envy of Jones and Abraham as they wrestled with him for the role of favourite. Freud himself was eventually forced by the zeal of his most orthodox disciples to take a stand against Rank. The dispute which followed was bitter and complex and contained many elements also present in the earlier conflict with Jung. In one letter to Rank, for example, Freud levelled against him the old accusation of mental illness, suggesting that the entire quarrel had come about because of Rank's neurosis and the fact that he had not himself been analysed.[8] The first victim of the power-struggle which now took place among Freud's closest followers was the Secret Committee itself, which had become a conflict-ridden formality, and which

Freud dissolved in April 1924. The Committee would be brought back to life later in the year. For the time being however, Freud's energies were engaged elsewhere. During July 1924 his relationship with Rank, who was by then practising in America, became increasingly difficult, with Freud alternating between attempts at tolerance and anger at Rank's stubbornness.

As before in the case of Jung it seemed that a final break was inevitable. But in September 1924 Rank returned to Europe. At this point Freud dictated to Ferenczi a letter for him to send to Rank in which, after being particularly severe, he stressed that Freud was still willing to forgive him. There then ensued a series of disputes between Rank and the Viennese analysts which included a long and difficult meeting with Freud. At the end of November Rank left Vienna for Paris, but then immediately returned to Vienna in a state of deep depression. He then suddenly appeared before Freud, as the latter put it, 'completely contrite, in order to confess'. He saw Freud for long, supposedly therapeutic sessions and sent out a letter of penance to all the members of the Committee in which he begged forgiveness for his insulting behaviour to his teacher in the past, pleading that he had succumbed to a neurosis brought on by 'the trauma occasioned by the dangerous illness of the Professor':

> From analytical interviews with the Professor, in which I could explain in detail the reactions based on affective attitudes, I gain the hope that I was successful in clarifying ... the personal relationship, since the Professor found my explanations satisfactory and has forgiven me personally ... I confidently hope, therefore, to be able to make good again as much as possible.
>
> But before this can happen I would like to ask every single one of you to understand my affective utterances against him as stemming from this state of mind and to forgive them as reactions not to be taken personally. May I also stress the mitigating circumstance that I have never carried these utterances beyond our most intimate circle, so that they appeared only in the circular letters and sessions of the committee and finally in two letters which I wrote the Professor from America in the summer. Before all I feel in duty bound to give satisfaction to Abraham, whose critical remarks I have obviously used as a stimulus to stronger reactions and against whose role as accuser with the Professor I reacted so violently because of my brother complex. I can only hope, dear Abraham, that my painfully won insight into this situation and my most sincere regret will allow you to forgive and forget the insult to you arising from this state of mind.[9]

Rank went on to offer similar craven apologies to Jones, Sachs, Ferenczi and Eitingon and ended his letter by expressing the hope that they might soon work together again.

Commenting on this letter, Phyllis Grosskurth observes that 'Freud seems to have acted as the Grand Inquisitor, and Rank's grovelling "confession" could have served as a model for the Russian show trials of the 1930s.'[10] The comparison is an apt one in many respects. But the more straightforward parallel is with the kind of confession or act of penance religious believers often make to the God they worship in order to secure forgiveness of their sins. For Rank, as for Jung, it would seem that, in a number of significant respects, Freud *was* God, and that the possibility of losing the love of this God had given rise to an emotional upheaval in him on a scale so fearsome that he was eventually driven to make a confession of his 'sins'.

The reconciliation which his letter helped to bring about proved short-lived. After returning to America in 1925, Rank took up his old heretical position once again and compounded the offence which this gave to Freud and the guardians of psychoanalytic orthodoxy by introducing the concept of short courses of psychoanalytic treatment. In January 1927, for example, Ferenczi reported to Freud from America that Rank had been boasting of his ability to 'cure' homosexuality in six weeks.[11] For such intellectual and therapeutic recidivism, Rank was effectively cast out of the psychoanalytic movement and this expulsion was ratified formally in 1930 when his honorary membership of the American Psychoanalytic Association was taken away.

The apostasy of Rank was disastrous for the Secret Committee, which Ernest Jones had managed to re-establish at the end of 1924. But it was not the end of the troubled story of Freud's 'paladins'. Throughout his disputes with Jung and with Rank, Freud had repeatedly sought comfort from Ferenczi, whom he often treated as an alternative favourite. Ferenczi, however, appears to have been caught in the same kind of emotional trap into which Freud almost always seemed to lure his closest disciples. For when Ferenczi treated Freud with the kind of filial devotion which his overbearing personality seemed to demand, Freud responded by instructing him not to idolise him and warning him that he was 'no Psa superman'.[12] During the lifetime of the Secret Committee Ferenczi was almost constantly striving to escape from his emotional dependence on Freud. 'It is susceptible of no doubt that I too,' he wrote to Freud in 1922, 'could not resist the temptation to "make you a present" of the whole measure of overtender and oversensitive emotions appropriate to my physical father. The stage in which I now seem to find myself is a – badly delayed – weaning and the attempt to submit to my destiny.'[13]

As had happened in the case of Adler, Jung and Rank before, however, Ferenczi's struggle to assert his independence would eventually lead to a full-scale rebellion against his master. The central point of dispute in this case was not theory but therapeutic technique. Disregarding the taboos and prohibitions with which Freud had surrounded the analytic ritual, Ferenczi began to develop what he called 'active therapy' and 'mutual analysis', which involved bestowing affection on patients and introducing an element of mutuality into the relationship, so that intimate disclosures were made not only by the patient but also by the analyst. When Ferenczi disclosed to Freud that his therapeutic practice sometimes involved kissing his patients as a token of his affection, and allowing them to kiss him, Freud could no longer contain himself. Having initially instructed Ferenczi to assert his independence, he now chastised him for the manner in which he did so. 'The need for defiant self-assertion . . .' he wrote, 'is more powerful in you than you recognise.'[14]

In January 1932 Ferenczi began to keep the 'clinical diary' from which a number of passages have already been quoted. The pages of this diary are interspersed with penetrating passages about psychoanalytic objectivity and critical observations on Freud's personality. Freud, Ferenczi had eventually concluded, could not truly love even his own disciples. 'He loves nobody,' he wrote, 'only himself and his work.'[15] But the clinical diary also contained, alongside some of Ferenczi's more mystical and utopian speculations, a great deal of material on the sexual abuse of children. This was because, as Ferenczi struggled to assert his own independent therapeutic vision, he gradually began to embrace almost exactly the same idea which Freud had put forward in his 'seduction theory' of 1896, and which he had later comprehensively repudiated. Ferenczi, in short, adopted the view that the source of neurosis lay in sexual seductions suffered by children and began to use this aetiological theory to drive out every other account of neurosis. In every case which he discussed in his clinical diary, for instance, Ferenczi traced the patient's neurosis back to traumas occasioned by sexual abuse suffered during childhood.[16]

There seems some reason to suppose that Ferenczi's putative insight was in reality no more securely based than Freud's original seduction theory. In the case of one patient, for instance, who had asked why she could not remember having been raped, but dreamed of it incessantly, Ferenczi wrote that he knew from other analyses 'that a part of our being can "die" and while the remaining part of the self may survive the trauma, it awakens with a gap in its memory.'[17] What these words clearly suggest is that, in some cases at least, Ferenczi's patients were not presenting their own memories any more than Freud's had been in 1896, and that Ferenczi's conviction that they had suffered sexual abuse was based, like Freud's, on his own theoretically wishful reconstructions.

Whatever its empirical status may have been, however, Ferenczi expounded his new seduction theory in a paper called 'Confusion of Tongues between Adults and the Child', which he planned to deliver at the Wiesbaden Congress of 1932. The paper began by launching an attack on the hypocrisy of psychoanalysts who dissembled feelings of concern towards their patient when in reality they often felt hostility. 'The analytic situation,' he wrote, 'with its reserve and coldness, professional hypocrisy and dislike of the patient that it masks, which the patient could feel in his bones, was essentially no different from what had led to the illness in his childhood.' He went on to observe that 'patients do not react to theatrical phrases expressing compassion, but only to genuine sympathy.'[18] By rejecting the false objectivity which Freud had counselled, and replacing it with genuine sympathy and human warmth, Ferenczi believed that it was possible to establish an atmosphere of trust in which the patient's real feelings and real traumas could be explored without them being dismissed as fantasies. Psychoanalysts for the first time, he implied, could begin truly to *listen* to what their patients were saying.

Ferenczi's paper was a curious mixture in which real psychological insight and sensitivity were blended with the tendency to overgeneralise which had always characterised Freud's own thought. When Freud first heard of the paper, however, his initial reaction was to attempt to suppress it. 'He must not be allowed to give the paper,' he wrote to Eitingon. 'Either another one or none.' After Ferenczi had insisted on reading the paper aloud to his master, Freud came to the conclusion that to attempt to prevent him from delivering the paper would merely cause further problems. But at the same time he tried to persuade Ferenczi to refrain from publishing it and sent a telegram to Eitingon in which he described it as 'stupid'.[19]

Freud, who was too ill to attend the conference, parted from Ferenczi coldly. At the conference itself Eitingon, with the support of other analysts, tried to forbid Ferenczi's paper. Jones, however, insisted that there would be less scandal if Ferenczi were allowed to go ahead. This was what happened with the result that, in public at least, the psychoanalytic movement was able to preserve a façade of intellectual tolerance. In private, however, Ferenczi was ostracised. As in previous psychoanalytic disputes, diagnosis was used as a substitute for demonology and the real illness from which he was suffering, one of whose symptoms was acute anaemia, was held to be but the physical substratum of a severe psychological disturbance. Ferenczi, it was maintained, by Jones and Freud in particular, had been suffering from 'paranoia', 'delusions', 'regression', 'mental disturbance' and 'repressed sadism' coupled with 'ideas of persecution'. When Ferenczi died on 24 May 1933, with the dispute still unresolved, his death was treated as the final confirmation of such diagnoses. Jones's account of Ferenczi's fatal illness is instructive in this respect:

> The mental disturbance had been making rapid progress in the last few months ... Then there were the delusions about Freud's supposed hostility. Towards the end came violent paranoia and even homicidal outbursts, which were followed by a sudden death on May 24. That was the tragic end of a brilliant, lovable and distinguished personality, someone who had for a quarter of a century been Freud's closest friend. The lurking demons within, against whom Ferenczi had for years struggled with great distress and much success, conquered him at the end, and we learnt from this painful experience once more how terrible their power can be. [20]

What is most interesting about this account is the manner in which Ferenczi is imaginatively split by Jones into two entirely distinct characters. On the one hand there is a lovable, almost saintly figure, who was one of Freud's most faithful and obedient followers. On the other hand there is a sick and deranged man who actually ventured to criticise Freud and psychoanalysis. Jones evidently cannot bring himself to contemplate the possibility that Ferenczi's dissidence might have been a product of his sanity. In most contexts the description which he goes on to elaborate of Ferenczi's struggle against 'the lurking demons within' would be seen as a colourful way of expressing an essentially rational appraisal of Ferenczi's behaviour. Yet there is no evidence to substantiate the charges of mental illness which were preferred against Ferenczi. The psychoanalyst Michael Balint, who was close to him during the last days of his illness, has written that he 'never found him deluded, paranoid or homicidal. On the contrary, though he was physically incapacitated by his ataxia, mentally most of the time he was quite fresh . . .'[21] In the light of this testimony, it is difficult to avoid the impression that Jones's talk of lurking demons is precisely what it appears to be – another example of psychoanalytic demonology. Ultimately Ferenczi – like Adler and Jung before him – was driven out into the darkness in the same spirit as heretics and blasphemers have been driven out of churches through the centuries. For daring to quarrel with orthodox doctrine, and for questioning the views of Freud, Ferenczi was treated as though he were possessed by the devil, while his often astute criticisms were dismissed out of hand as the products of disease and mental disturbance.

Several years before Ferenczi's death the Secret Committee had been effectively disbanded. At a meeting of the Committee held at the Innsbruck Congress of 1927 it was decided that, since the psychoanalytic movement had grown strong enough internationally, there was no longer any need for it to be directed secretly. The Committee would in future be made up of the officers of the International Psychoanalytical Association – Eitingon, Ferenczi, Jones, the Dutch psychoanalyst van Ophuijsen and Freud's daughter Anna.

During the lifetime of the Secret Committee psychoanalysis had remained a surprisingly uniform body of theory largely because Freud valued the purity of his doctrines more highly than the unity of his movement and was always prepared to precipitate schisms and disputes if he felt that the essential tenets of psychoanalysis were under threat. So severely did Freud and his Committee rule over the intellectual kingdom he had created that Fritz Wittels, who temporarily deserted Freud at the time of Adler's expulsion, was led to observe in 1924 that 'He has become a despot who will not tolerate the slightest deviation from his doctrine; holds councils behind closed doors; and tries to ensure, by a sort of pragmatic sanction, that the body of psychoanalytic teaching shall remain an indivisible whole.'[22] So skilfully did Freud create a series of ostensibly democratic structures that he successfully mystified his own role. Ultimately this proved a more effective way of dominating the movement he had created. As Thomas Szasz has written:

Overt tyranny can be appraised for what it is, and there are many ways of resisting it. Freud's leadership, however, was deceitful. He created a pseudo-democratic, pseudo-scientific atmosphere, but was careful to retain for himself the power to decide all important issues ... Freud's essential concept of leadership seemed to be to bestow tokens of power on his competitors, only to discredit them if they dared to use it.[23]

If psychoanalysis had indeed been the empirical scientific discipline which it was sometimes presented as by its protagonists, the disappearance of the Secret Committee and its inquisitorial vigilance could only have benefited the cause. Yet one of the reasons why the Committee had been necessary in the first place was that Freud had effectively created a body of theory in which the normal constraints of empirical science had been entirely dissolved. Ultimately the criteria of psychoanalytic 'truth' were entirely subjective. The great danger attendant on the collapse of the Secret Committee was that Freud's own personal definition of truth would be overthrown and replaced by other equally subjective visions shaped by cultural and intellectual fashion or by the charismatic qualities of their originators.

This is exactly what happened to the psychoanalytic movement in the second half of the twentieth century. While some psychoanalysts remained faithful to Freud's original teachings and preserved the sacred terminology of psychoanalysis almost intact, others began the process of doctrinal revision which is characteristic of newly founded religious movements. In this respect the example of Otto Rank, and the stress he placed on the role of the mother, was in some respects a portent of what was to come. Rank's rebellion showed up a particular area of weakness in Freud's entire theoretical edifice. For to a quite extraordinary degree Freud had managed to construct a theory of human development which focused upon the father, and which paid relatively little attention to the role of the mother and to women's sexuality.

It was in this particular area that the theoretical structure of psychoanalysis which Freud bequeathed to his followers seemed to invite, almost to compel, revision. The revisions which were made to the psychoanalytic picture of women during the fifty years following the collapse of the Secret Committee were very often made by women. It would be quite wrong, however, to conclude that the women who contributed to psychoanalytic theory during this period were necessarily helping to free the theory from its patriarchal origins.

This is particularly so in the case of the woman whom Freud himself had come to regard as his natural successor – his own daughter Anna.

Freud's relationship with Anna was one of the most important intellectual alliances in the entire history of the psychoanalytic movement – just as important, in its own way, as his relationship with Jung. Yet although this fact has been recognised for some time within the psychoanalytic movement (or some parts of it at least), the story of Freud's relationship with his daughter is very far from being generally known and its significance has yet to be fully appreciated. In order that we may bring Freud's own intellectual biography to a conclusion, it is this story which must now be told.

TWENTY

Anna Freud: Daughter and Disciple

ANNA FREUD WAS BORN on 3 December 1895 to a mother who had already given birth to five children in eight years. Unable or unwilling either to breast-feed her newest baby or to engage a wet-nurse, Martha Freud fed her with a baby formula and subsequently employed a Catholic nursemaid to look after her. Years later Anna Freud herself maintained that if any effective means of contraception had been available to her parents, she would not have been born at all.[1] Yet Freud's youngest and least wanted child would eventually become not only his constant companion and his nurse throughout his long last illness, but also his most devoted intellectual ally. When he died in London in 1939 it was to her that he entrusted his own 'frail child' – to use the term which he had applied, on at least one occasion, to the psychoanalytic movement. Anna Freud guarded her charge with all the jealousy and all the fierceness of a mother protecting her own child. For carrying out her filial duty with such devotion and for her own contributions to psychoanalytic theory, she was rewarded with the lasting esteem of many of her colleagues, particularly in America. When, in 1971, a survey was conducted among American psychiatrists and psychoanalysts, in order to establish who they regarded as their most outstanding colleagues, both psychiatrists and psychoanalysts mentioned Anna Freud more often than anyone else.[2]

Behind Anna Freud's transformation from unwanted child to indispensable helpmate and intellectual ally there lay what was perhaps the greatest love affair in the entire history of the psychoanalytic movement. It was a love affair conducted by a father – Freud – with his own daughter, and it was conducted, in part at least, through the medium of psychoanalysis. Yet psychoanalytic theory is conspicuously inadequate when it comes to the problem of understanding this relationship. Freud himself appears to have been the first victim of this inadequacy. For, by allowing his own theories to guide his conduct, he entered deeper and deeper into exactly the kind of fierce and exclusive relationship with his daughter from which, consciously at least, he was seeking to release her.

Although the roots of Freud's deep attraction to, and deep affection for, his youngest daughter go back a long way, Anna did not begin life as his favourite child. This position seems to have been held by Sophie, who had been born two and a half years earlier and who would eventually die in the great influenza epidemic of 1920. Anna envied the close relationship Sophie enjoyed with their mother. She also envied Sophie on account of her beauty and her name, which she considered lovely and sophisticated in contrast to her own. Anna's feeling on the one hand that she was excluded from her mother's affections, and on the other hand that she was frequently left out by her older brothers and sisters, led her early into a sense of emotional isolation. Her most promising means of escape was by way of her relationship with her father, and there seems little doubt that he responded to the emotional needs of his youngest daughter. One of the most important memories of her early childhood concerned a particular summer holiday when she was eight or nine. At one point during this holiday, the 'others' all went off in a boat, leaving Anna alone either because the boat was too full or because she was too small. On this occasion she did not complain, however, and her father, who was watching the scene, praised her and comforted her. 'That made me so happy,' recalled Anna much later, 'that nothing else mattered.'[3]

Freud was particularly attracted by the cheekiness which his youngest daughter sometimes showed. He referred to her affectionately as 'Black Devil'. 'Little Anna,' he wrote, 'is positively beautified by naughtiness.'[4] Anna was clearly gratified by his attention. But at the same time she evidently noted the extent to which her father was absorbed in a world which she perceived as serious and worthy. It did not take her long to recognise intuitively that, although as a child she might endear herself to her father through her 'naughtiness', as an adult she would have to pass much sterner tests if his affection for her was to endure. Given his extraordinary asceticism, the only safe way to her father's heart was through his work and through his involvement with psychoanalysis.

The rapidity with which Anna Freud learnt this lesson was not recognised for a long time by scholars of the psychoanalytic movement. In 1975 Paul Roazen made the seemingly bold claim that, although not a member, Anna Freud 'attended meetings of the Vienna Society

at least as early as November 1918'.[5] Only with the publication of
Elisabeth Young-Bruehl's biography, in 1988, did it become clear that
Anna Freud first attended the meetings of the Vienna Psychoanalytic
Society not in 1918 but in 1909. For it was then, at the age of thirteen
or fourteen, that she had been introduced to psychoanalysis as a science. She retained a vivid memory of an occasion when her father
took her for an after-dinner walk. As they walked past some particularly
beautiful Viennese homes he related to her what was, in effect, a
parable of psychoanalysis: 'You see these houses with their lovely
facades? Things are not necessarily so lovely behind the facades. And
so it is with human beings too.' At about the same time she was
introduced to the Wednesday-evening meetings of the Vienna Society,
where she was allowed 'to sit on a little library ladder in the corner
and listen to her father and his colleagues discussing one another's
presentations'. So fascinated was she by what she understood of psychoanalysis that she begged unsuccessfully to be allowed to accompany
her father, Jung and Ferenczi on their 1909 visit to America.[6]

Excluded by her youth from the most serious parts of her father's
life, Anna increasingly took refuge in a world of intense fantasy and
day-dreaming. She was particularly drawn to tales which recounted
heroic deeds and one of her favourite poems was Heine's 'Grenadiere'.
The poem tells the story of two French soldiers who, after being
captured in Russia during Napoleon's campaign, trudge back home
through Germany only to discover that their Emperor has been captured. One of the soldiers, when begged by his friend to consider his
wife and his children, dismisses them in favour of what he sees as a
much greater duty. In lines which had a particular appeal for the young
Anna Freud, he pledges renewed allegiance to his Emperor:

> What matters wife? What matters child?
> With far greater cares I'm shaken.
> Let them go beg with hunger wild.
> My Emperor, my Emperor is taken!

Knowing that he is near to death, the soldier asks his friend to take
his body back to France so that he may be buried in French soil, with
his musket in his hand and his sabre strapped around his body. Then,
he says, he will wait until the Emperor who has been taken returns in
triumph, at which point he will rise up from his grave in order to
defend him:

Then I will lie and listen and wait,
A sentinel down in the grass there,
Till I hear the roar of the guns and the great
Thunder of hooves as they pass there.

The Emperor will come and the columns will wave,
The swords will be flashing and rending,
And I will rise full-armed from the grave,
My Emperor, my Emperor defending![7]

Heine's poem, and the particular place it occupied in Anna Freud's childhood fantasies, have been noted by both her main biographers. Yet the full significance of the poem in terms of cultural history has not been recognised. For the fantasy of a mighty Emperor long thought to be dead, who would return in wrath to defeat his enemies, was not invented by Heine. A similar fantasy had been current in Europe since the third century, and the legend of the Emperor of the Last Days had, ever since that time, been woven into the apocalyptic fantasies which had fascinated generations of believers. In the original legend the Emperor was imagined either as a harbinger of the second coming of Christ or as a warrior-saviour who would himself usher in an age of endless bliss.[8] Heine's poem about an Emperor who returns and brings about the resurrection of his dead followers is, in effect, a secularised version of Judaeo-Christian apocalyptic. For Anna Freud it would seem that this emperor-fantasy became a kind of personal childhood religion. Elisabeth Young-Bruehl confirms this view, writing that when, much later in her life, Anna Freud told a friend about her youthful 'emperor-faith', she seemed scarcely to believe that anyone could ever have been a doubter: 'As a child I thought why was everyone surprised when he came? Of course, he had to come.'[9]

The obvious parallel between the Emperor in Heine's poem and Freud has been drawn on a number of occasions. What should also be noted, however, is that Heine's poem is not only a disguised apocalyptic dream. It is also a dream of redemption or of recognition. For the implicit fantasy offered by the poem is that a mere grenadier, obscure and completely undistinguished, will eventually, because of the diligence and dedication with which he serves a remote emperor, be recognised and rewarded. For performing his duty with such devotion he will be lifted up and cherished by the Emperor as one of the immortals. It was just such a fantasy, it would seem, which animated the young Anna Freud, and which she would spend her life living out in relation to the remote figure of her father, for whose affection and intimate regard she would undertake almost any task and undergo almost any hardship. Just as Freud, trapped by the conditional love of his own parents, had found himself under a psychological compulsion to achieve recognition by the world, so his youngest daughter was now driven by the same kind of conditional love to achieve the recognition which she felt he alone was in a position to bestow.

Anna Freud's predicament was that the very Emperor whom she worshipped and whose undivided attention and affection she craved, was all the time surrounded by other, older admirers whose claims on his attention were treated more seriously than hers. In many respects Anna's life became, from early adolescence onwards, an almost constant battle against those she perceived as rivals for her father's affection – especially her mother, her aunt Minna and her sister Sophie. When her brothers Ernst and Oliver spent part of the summer of 1910 in Holland alone with their father, Anna was consumed by envy. 'I, too, would very much like to travel alone with you,' she wrote, 'just as Ernst and Oli are doing now.' Once again she sought to come closer to her father through his work, this time by borrowing and reading a copy of his *Delusions and Dreams in Jensen's Gradiva*. Around the same time, perhaps sensing her father's own insecurity and his own deep need for love and affection, she began to go against her emotionally undemonstrative upbringing and to sign off her letters with hugs and kisses, begging her father to write more often and telling him how much she missed having him call her 'Black Devil'.[10]

It would seem that one of the reasons that Anna Freud lavished so much affection on her father and eagerly encouraged him to reciprocate her regard was that, by the age of sixteen, she had already become something of a lonely and abstracted child, cut off from many potential friends by her deep seriousness and her interest in the intellectual world of adults in general and her father in particular. Yet Anna's earnestness and her seemingly academic nature were at odds with the educational provisions her parents had made for her. Like her sisters, and in contrast to her brothers, she had not had a *Gymnasium* education but had been sent to the less academic *Lyceum* or high school. She completed her schooling here in 1912 at the relatively early age of sixteen without having resolved the question of her future.

Although Anna Freud had by now raised the possibility of becoming a teacher, the plan made by her family was that she should set off at the end of the summer of 1912 on a miniature Grand Tour of Sicily and

Italy. This tour was to last eight months and Anna was to be accompanied by Minna, her aunt. Just at this time, however, her sister Sophie became engaged to be married and her aunt's services were required to run the Freud household in Vienna while Martha helped the engaged couple to set up an apartment in Hamburg. Since her Grand Tour was no longer possible it was decided that Anna should spend the winter holidaying in Merano, before finally deciding on her future.

In December, about a month before Sophie's wedding was due to take place, Anna learned from her father that she was expected to stay on in Italy and miss the wedding:

My dear little Anna,

I hear you are already worrying again about your immediate future. So it seems that putting on 3¼ pounds still hasn't changed you much. I now want to set your mind at rest by reminding you that the original plan was to send you to Italy for eight months in the hope that you would return straight and plump and at the same time quite worldly and sensible. Actually we hadn't dared to hope that a few weeks in Merano would achieve this transformation, and so had already prepared ourselves at your departure for not seeing you at the wedding or so soon afterwards in Vienna. I think you must now slowly accustom yourself to this terrible prospect. The ceremony can be performed quite well without you, for that matter also without guests, parties, etc., which you don't care for anyhow. Your plans for school can easily wait until you have learned to take your duties less seriously. They won't run away from you. It can only do you good to be a little happy-go-lucky and enjoy having such lovely sun in the middle of winter.

So now, if you are reassured that your stay in Merano won't be interrupted in the immediate future, I can tell you that we all enjoy your letters very much but that we also won't be worried if you feel too lazy to write every day. The time of toil and trouble will come for you too but you are still quite young.[11]

The real reason why Anna Freud was effectively banished from her sister's wedding has never been clear. What is implicit in her father's letter, however, is that she has been sent away in an attempt to improve her health – both psychological and physical. The anxiety about her weight suggests that she may well have been anorexic, and her father's evident concern about her earnestness and the excessive demands she was making on herself would be consonant with this view. Freud may well have been following the strategy originated by Charcot for dealing with anorexia. The essential element in this treatment was, it will be recalled, that the patient should be removed from the direct influence of her family.

The goal of Freud's therapy for Anna was apparently to rescue her from a path of excessive sublimation and make her 'feminine', 'normal' and, perhaps above all, marriageable. It would seem that in Freud's view this would involve Anna coming to terms with her own sexuality and her own sexual impulses. This much is certainly hinted in a letter which Freud sent to his daughter soon after Sophie's wedding:

> You will have understood from the books you have read that you were so overzealous, restless and unsatisfied because you have run away like a child from many things of which a grown up girl would not be afraid. We will notice a change when you no longer withdraw from the pleasures of your age but gladly enjoy what other girls enjoy. One hardly has energy for serious interests if one is too zealous, too sensitive, and remains removed from one's own life and nature; then one finds oneself troubled in the very things one wishes to take up.[12]

For Anna, however, the greatest benefit of her trip was that it enabled her to spend some time alone with her father. For in March of 1913 she met him in Bolzano, from where she travelled with him to Venice. They returned to Vienna after a trip lasting a week, with Anna having been briefly what she aspired to become permanently – her father's closest and most trusted companion.

While on the one hand her father sought to release her from this fate, his own behaviour sometimes rendered it more likely. When, in 1914, Anna Freud undertook a trip to England, her father intimated to her in a letter that he considered Ernest Jones to have predatory sexual designs upon her, and made it quite clear that he considered any romance between them would be inappropriate. As if to explain his jealous regard for his daughter, Freud himself confessed to some of his colleagues that Anna had become his Cordelia. In his essay on 'The Theme of the Three Caskets' he discusses the relationship between Lear and Cordelia and writes that 'the doomed man is not willing to renounce the love of women; he insists on hearing how much he is loved . . . But it is in vain that an old man yearns for the love of woman as he had it first from his mother.'[13]

Freud's action in allowing his daughter to travel on her own to England, while simultaneously binding her body in a fine thread of parental anxiety and prohibitions, was deeply ambivalent. So too was his behaviour when it came to making arrangements for Anna to undergo psychoanalysis. This development came about because, although she went ahead with her plans to become a teacher in an elementary school, and was evidently extremely successful in the early stages of this career, she continued her interest in psychoanalysis. Though her father discouraged her from becoming a doctor, he acquiesced in her plan to become a lay psychoanalyst. Since the Budapest Congress of 1918 had ruled that undergoing a personal analysis should be a condition of becoming an analyst, it now became a necessity for Anna Freud to be analysed herself. By far the most remarkable feature of the analysis which now took place was that it was conducted by her father.

The fact that Freud analysed his own daughter, while it was known by a handful of Freud's early followers, rapidly became one of the many aspects of the history of psychoanalysis which was subjected to repression. As Phyllis Grosskurth observes, 'Many Freudians have clearly experienced grave embarrassment over the revelation that Freud analysed Anna. It is seldom discussed, and some people wish the information had never seen the light of day.'[14] The significance of Freud's choice of himself as Anna's analyst is sometimes minimised through the suggestion that he had committed merely a technical infraction which raised problems about 'transference'. Another plea which is sometimes entered on Freud's behalf invokes the case of Piaget, who based much of his work on observations of his own children. Yet Freud's analysis of his daughter raises quite different issues precisely because of the emotionally intimate nature of psychoanalysis.

Freud himself, as we have seen, had always insisted that psychoanalysis could only work by seeking to uncover all those emotions, impulses and desires which were normally regarded as private. He was particularly insistent on pursuing sexual interpretations of his patients' dreams and symptoms even – or perhaps especially – when this gave rise to resistance. Freud evidently did not make any exception when it came to analysing his own daughter. This is indicated by his paper 'A Child is Being Beaten' (1919), in which he discusses masochistic masturbatory fantasies and where, as has now been recognised, he includes the case of Anna among his examples. It is further confirmed by the paper which Anna herself read to the Vienna Psychoanalytic Society in 1922. This paper, entitled 'Beating Fantasies and Daydreams' was, in effect, her application for membership of the Society. In it she described only one patient – a young girl whose case is reconstructed to the age of fifteen. Anna Freud noted that the patient in question had been the subject of 'a rather thoroughgoing analysis' but she did not identify the analyst. In the latter part of her life, in order to protect herself and, perhaps more importantly, her father, she frequently sought to give the impression that the girl who formed the subject of her paper had been one of her own patients. In fact, however, the case which she presented was not one which she had conducted at all. It was one in which she was the patient and her father the unidentified analyst.[15]

The possibility that Anna Freud might herself be the patient described in her first psychoanalytic paper was discussed by Uwe Henrik Peters in his biography, which was published in Germany in 1979 and in America in 1985. Yet he rejects the suggestion, writing that 'it is hardly probable that Anna Freud would have described her own life so unreservedly.'[16] Only with the publication of Elisabeth Young-Bruehl's biography – excellent in so many ways – was the story behind the writing of Anna Freud's paper given general currency. Young-Bruehl's psychoanalytically orthodox account, however, scarcely begins to engage with the problems which are raised by the paper.

In the paper Anna Freud gives an account of a girl who had the kind of fantasies described in Freud's paper 'A Child is Being Beaten'. According to her the first fantasies featuring a child being beaten appeared before the girl entered school, between her fifth and sixth years. The beating fantasy supposedly derived from an earlier incestuous fantasy involving her father. Each of the beating scenes ended by arousing the girl to masturbation. The beating fantasies continued to be indulged by the girl until they were replaced, between the age of eight and ten, by what she called her 'nice stories'. These 'nice stories' seemed to the girl to have no connection with the earlier fantasies. They generally portrayed a weak young man who had done something wrong and who was threatened with punishment by a stronger older man. Finally, however, the man was pardoned in a scene of reconciliation.

Although the girl could initially see no connection between these 'nice stories' and the earlier beating fantasies, we are told that she came, as a result of her psychoanalysis, to understand that both types of fantasy shared the same structure. We are further told that sometimes the nice stories failed to drive the old fantasies away:

> During difficult periods, i.e., at times of increased external demands or
> diminished internal capabilities, the nice stories no longer succeeded in

fulfilling their task. And then it frequently happened that at the conclusion and climax of a fantasized beautiful scene the pleasurable and pleasing love scene was suddenly replaced by the old beating situation together with the sexual gratification associated with it, which then led to a full discharge of the accumulated excitement. But such incidents were quickly forgotten, excluded from memory, and consequently treated as though they had never happened.[17]

The picture which emerges from Anna Freud's paper, one which is presented by her authorised biographer as an accurate reflection of her own inner life, is of a young adolescent girl who occasionally relapses into masturbation after failing in her attempts to fully repress masochistic sexual fantasies involving her father which go back to early childhood.[18]

Although the provenance of this particular psychoanalytic case history is bizarre, students of psychoanalytic history have tended, naturally enough, to accept Freud's portrait of his daughter as authoritative. The fact that it is the daughter herself who communicates the portrait has seemed to place its authenticity beyond question. Yet if we consider the matter with the scepticism which ought properly to be induced by any case history which has its origin in Freud's own clinical practice, doubts almost inevitably arise.

The first observation which should be made is that the case history of Freud's daughter is by no means the first in which a central role is played by masturbation supposedly engaged in by a young woman. In his analysis of Dora, as we have seen, Freud confidently constructs what he supposes to be the fact of her childhood masturbation from her own innocent report that she once suffered from catarrh. In that case he maintains that his entirely speculative reconstruction has been verified and even goes on to construct a scenario which led to Dora giving up masturbation, after having overheard the sound of her parents engaging in sexual intercourse. This entirely hypothetical event, Freud speculates, may 'very easily have made the child's sexuality veer round and have replaced her inclination to masturbation by an inclination to anxiety'.[19]

Behind Freud's anxiety to believe that his female patients were engaging in secret masturbation we may discern one of the most common of imaginative inhibitions – the difficulty which many men have in persuading themselves of the reality of women's sexual identities. Because of this difficulty the fantasy that all woman are *covertly* sexual, and that they engage in secret masturbation, tends to appeal strongly to the male imagination. Sometimes this fantasy corresponds to a reality. For many women eventually learn to enjoy masturbation, and some masturbate successfully and in secret throughout their childhood. It remains the case, however, that taboos against masturbation in general, and female masturbation in particular, are exceptionally severe. Because of this many women relinquish genital play early in childhood and either never masturbate at all, or learn to do so only in late adolescence or early adulthood. Nancy Friday has offered an illuminating picture of a very common kind of childhood experience in which masturbation plays no part:

> No one I knew admitted to masturbation or discussed it . . . Nor do I remember any punishment or words spoken against masturbation. Giving up the right to touch myself was a sacrifice made as unquestioningly as I'm sure my mother had made it with her mother . . .
>
> As leader of my group, the intrepid one who would take any dare, I climbed the highest walls, rode on the back of Charleston's horse-drawn ice waggons, explored the abandoned, shuttered house across the street, even stole from Belk's apartment store.
>
> Since I broke all these other rules in what I now understand was my youthful determination to learn bravery, to never be anxious and frightened as I perceived my mother to be, why didn't I explore and master my own body? . . .
>
> My answer would be that I had already made a bargain with my mother. Made it so long ago and at a time when I was most vulnerable – probably the first year of life – that it had been carved into my very soul – much as a deep cut in a young tree is incised forever . . .
>
> At some point very early in my life I had unconsciously promised my mother never to masturbate if she would love me in the way I always wanted her to love me. How did I grasp the seriousness of what it meant to her, this business of touching myself? Was it the pained look on her face, the grimace, the turning away, the sharp intake of breath that I would come to associate with her anxiety? I easily gave it up. After all I was dependent on her for everything, for life itself.
>
> The fact that she never held to her side of the bargain, never loved me in the way I wanted her to, didn't mean I broke my end of the deal; children have a self-protective way of blaming themselves for mother's failures and inadequacies. Clearly the fault lay in me, and if I'd been a better child she would have loved me more.[20]

Nancy Friday's characteristically perceptive account of her own childhood helps to place the problems raised by Freud's account of his daughter in a broader perspective. For although we have no means of knowing to what extent Anna Freud may have internalised taboos against masturbation at a similarly early age, the deep asceticism of her character, and her evident difficulty in coming to terms with her own sexuality, suggests that this possibility should at least be considered.

With this possibility we are bound also to consider whether Freud on this occasion was not once again indulging in his habit of presenting his own theoretically wishful reconstructions of episodes in his patient's past as real events. One passage which has already been quoted does suggest that something like this may have happened in at least one part of Anna Freud's analysis. For when the twenty-six-year-old would-be psychoanalyst describes the kind of daydreams she indulged in as a fifteen-year-old girl, she concludes her description of how these daydreams were broken into by 'the old beating situation together with the sexual gratification associated with it' with the following words: *'But such incidents were quickly forgotten, excluded from memory, and consequently treated as though they had never happened'* (italics added). The question which must be asked is how, if these incidents were indeed excluded from memory, had it been possible for Anna Freud to recall them? The obvious answer, given Freud's characteristic method of working, is that they were not recalled. They were reconstructed by the psychoanalyst in the normal way by interpreting the patient's dreams, slips, symptoms and free-associations.

Whether the obvious answer is in this particular instance also the correct one is impossible to say with certainty. But we cannot rule out the possibility that, while Anna Freud's 'nice stories' and adolescent daydreams were evidently real, the entire masturbatory prehistory which Freud created for them was a speculative construction, corresponding either imperfectly or not at all to his daughter's actual childhood imaginings. In her original paper Anna Freud herself indicates that the memories the 'patient' supposedly had of the beating fantasies were very far from clear. 'It is to be supposed,' she writes, 'that when enacted before the imagination of the girl the various scenes were very vivid; the record, however, given of them during analysis was anything but circumstantial and illuminating.' These words tend to muffle meaning rather than communicate. But at a later point in Anna Freud's original paper, the point is amplified:

> Even during analysis, as was mentioned before, the girl never gave any detailed account of any individual scene of beating. Owing to her shame

and resistance all she could ever be induced to give were short and covert allusions *which left to the analyst the task of completing and reconstructing a picture of the original situation.** [italics added] She behaved quite differently with the 'nice stories'. As soon as her first resistance to free talking had been overcome, she volunteered vivid and circumstantial descriptions of her various daydreams.[21]

What this passage suggests is that while the daydreams could be recalled quite easily, Anna Freud herself was unable to recall her earlier fantasies in any detail, and was actually uncertain of their content. The fact that she eventually came to accept what she herself acknowledges to be the analyst's reconstruction of her fantasies may seem to confirm the accuracy of his reconstruction. Familiarity with Freud's own therapeutic technique, however, would tend to weaken this argument. For, as should by now be clear, Freud sometimes showed extraordinary determination in his attempts to persuade his patients of the reasonable nature of his reconstructions. It is quite true that his patients were sometimes successful in resisting some of his more improbable interpretations. But this was partly because they were able to do what Dora eventually and very sensibly did. They were able to run away. This option was scarcely open to Freud's own daughter. Brought up to believe that her father was a scientist of genius who had invented a technique for revealing hidden parts of the mind, Anna Freud was simply not equipped for scepticism. If her father maintained that as a young girl she had indulged in masochistic masturbatory fantasies whose unconscious prototype had him as their object, then memory alone, treacherous as it sometimes is, could provide her with no grounds for rejecting this suggestion. At the same time her own idealisation of her father, and her acute psychological need for his continuing love and affection, provided powerful motives for accepting it.

The question which is raised here cannot be resolved definitively because of the fragmentary nature of the evidence. At the very least,

---

* In construing Anna Freud's words, we should bear in mind the technical meaning of the term 'resistance'. Charles Rycroft, in his *A Critical Dictionary of Psychoanalysis*, defines resistance as 'the opposition encountered during treatment to the process of making UNCONSCIOUS processes CONSCIOUS. Patients are said to be in a state of resistance if they oppose the analyst's INTERPRETATIONS and to have strong or weak resistances according as to whether they find it easy or difficult to allow their analyst to understand them' (Penguin, pp. 142–3).

The larger issue raised here concerns the entire relationship of psychoanalysis to the contemporary recovered memory movement. For a discussion of this issue see the Afterword, 'Freud's False Memories'.

however, we can say that there is a strong possibility that the masturbatory scenes which Anna Freud thought she remembered were the precipitates not of true recollections of her childhood but of 'false memories' which had been artificially reconstructed by her therapist – who in this case was also her father.

What is perhaps even more important than whether the fantasies Freud attributes to his daughter were real or imaginary is the fact that he deemed it appropriate to discuss such questions with his daughter at all. Freud's own conscious motives for conducting the analysis of his daughter in the way that he did seem reasonably clear. For he evidently believed, and had good grounds for believing, that his daughter was excessively devoted to him and that what he sometimes referred to as her 'father-complex' was making it difficult for her to form any normal sexual relationship with a man. It was a theme to which he frequently returned. In 1921 he wrote to Max Eitingon and, after expressing his gladness at seeing Anna in such good spirits, added his wish that 'she would soon find some reason to exchange her attachment to her old father for some more lasting one.'[22] In 1924 he wrote to Lou Andreas-Salomé: 'The child gives me enough worries: how she will bear the lonely life [after Freud's death], and whether I can drive her libido from the hiding-place into which it has crawled.' A year later he returned to the same problem: 'I am afraid that her suppressed genitality may some day play her a mean trick. I cannot free her from me, and nobody is helping me with it.'[23]

According to Freud's own theories his analysis of his daughter was an attempt to resolve her problems with her sexuality. For it was evidently Freud's analytic opinion that his daughter's problem was associated with a failure to follow the normal path of female sexual development. His own theories insisted that full 'genitality' could be achieved by women only when they had left behind the supposedly 'masculine' phase of clitoral sexuality, and the auto-erotic activities associated with it, and progressed to full vaginal sexuality. Psychoanalytic theory suggested that Anna had become fixated at an essentially infantile stage, and that she had simultaneously identified with the father who had supposedly been the object of her first sexual desires. By using a process of analytic reconstruction in order to bring his daughter's putative unconscious conflicts into consciousness, Freud apparently believed that he might free her from her developmental fixation and enable her suppressed and essentially 'feminine' genitality to emerge.

Since the distinction between 'phallic' and 'genital' sexuality in women does not correspond to any real developmental process, and, like the entire theory of infantile sexuality, is nothing other than a product of Freud's theoretical imagination, it should not be surprising that Freud completely failed to achieve the goal which he set himself when he embarked on his daughter's analysis. What *is* surprising, even in relation to the view of Freud which I have presented in earlier chapters, is his evident failure to understand the human implications of his own decision to take his daughter into analysis. For what he seems not to have grasped is that, in the daily psychoanalytic sessions he held with his daughter, he was steadily intensifying and deepening the very psychological predicament he was consciously seeking to resolve.

So profound was Freud's belief that psychoanalysis was a scientific technique which could be employed objectively in order to achieve medical ends, and so lacking was he in ordinary psychological insight, he appears not to have recognised that in discussing with his twenty-six-year-old daughter her supposed masturbatory fantasies, and her putative sexual fixation on him, he was entering a psychological mine-field. Apart from anything else, by showing such an interest in his daughter's sexual imagination, he was clearly transgressing a powerful taboo – and doing so in a manner which evidently gratified his own sexual curiosity. Most people possessed of any degree of ordinary psychological insight would tend intuitively to judge such behaviour as misguided. In the particular circumstances which confront us here, however, it is perhaps worth considering, with rather more care than we generally take, exactly why we might come to such a judgement.

The conventional explanation might very well be that, by behaving in the manner that he did, Freud was sexualising a relationship which, for the psychological well-being of his daughter, should have been kept entirely asexual. There may be a sense in which this is true. But there is also, I believe, an important sense in which it actually inverts the truth. For, in some respects at least, the relationship between father and daughter will always tend to have a sexual dimension. One of the functions of the unwritten rules which govern such relationships is not to suppress this sexual dimension entirely but to allow it to exist, and even flourish, in an area of psychological safety. In a close relationship which is well bounded by such unwritten rules, both father and daughter may, to a certain extent, feel able to express towards one another warm affection, which is quite possibly tinged by sexual attraction, and which can be expressed physically without the danger that the relationship will ever become fully sexual. Written or unwritten rules in this area, as in many other areas of human behaviour, actually serve to safeguard a degree of *relative* freedom. When such rules are broken, as they evidently were in Freud's analysis of his daughter, the possibility of absolute transgression – of incest – is imaginatively opened up. Because incest is deeply threatening to most people, one of the psychological dangers of such licence is that both father and daughter, unprotected by explicit or implicit rules, will be thrown back onto the resources of the conscience. They may then feel forced to submit to the exacting and cruel demands which the conscience has a tendency to make. Unprotected by an external framework of rules, father and daughter may find themselves obsessively creating an internal framework of inhibition. In doing this there is a great danger that they may empty their relationship of the last traces of emotional warmth and physical affection in an anxious attempt to reassure themselves about their essential virtuousness. In this manner what may appear to be a dangerous attempt to sexualise a relationship, may lead to a cold and conscience-stricken *desexualisation* of the very bond which was once most warm and affectionate.

In the particular case of Freud and his youngest daughter the destructive elements of the therapeutic bond which he formed with her can only have been exacerbated by the one-sided nature of the analytic relationship. By making intimate confessions to her father Anna Freud was, psychologically speaking, allowing the deepest springs of her vitality to be wholly possessed by him. At this very obvious level she was becoming *more* intimate with her father, not less so. At the same time, she was almost inevitably made to feel guilty about the supposedly 'infantile' character of her own sexual life and in particular by her father's insistence on discussing the real or imaginary masturbatory fantasies which play such a negative role in the analytic picture he drew of her. It was this negative picture which, in deference to the massive authority of the father, she willingly accepted.

Formally, Freud seemed always to hold to his view that the complexity of his relationship to Anna had come about because of what he termed her 'father-complex' and the suppression of her 'genitality'. He would perhaps have come nearer to the truth had he recognised that, partly in response to her own emotional distress and vulnerability at feeling herself excluded from her mother's affection, *he* had fallen in love with *her*. The most tragic aspect of their relationship was that what had begun, almost, as an irresponsible and carefree 'affair', in which the anarchic impulses in Freud's soul were attracted by his daughter's 'naughtiness' or 'badness', was gradually transmuted by seriousness until the girl whom Freud had known affectionately as 'Schwarzer Teufel' – 'Black Devil' – was almost completely effaced by a dedicated young woman, given excessively to what she herself called 'altruistic surrender'. Increasingly, a relationship which had been founded on affection and respect was gradually emptied of its emotional freshness as Anna became more and more an intellectual colleague, a secretary, a manager and a nurse to her increasingly famous father. Driven by his own deep emotional need for followers, Freud was unable to resist, finally, demanding of his daughter the kind of single-minded devotion he asked of all his disciples. She in turn, because of the very acuteness of her own need for affection, did not have the emotional strength to resist those demands.

After Anna Freud was accepted as a member of the Vienna Psychoanalytical Society on the basis of her paper about beating fantasies, she gradually developed an extremely full and outwardly successful career as a psychoanalyst. During the early years of her psychoanalytic practice, which she conducted from a consulting room next to her father's, she treated some adult patients. But, influenced in part by her experience as a teacher, she gravitated more and more towards the analysis of children. In one of her earliest psychoanalytic papers, which she first presented at a session of the Vienna Society in March 1923, she gave an interesting and in some respects revealing example of her own interpretative style in relating an incident in the life of a young boy. According to the boy's mother the incident occurred at a time when she and her children were living in a house with a courtyard in which there was a deep well. She had repeatedly warned all the children not to play near this well and had vividly described the dangers of falling in. One day she was standing near the well with one of her children, a boy of two and a quarter years, when a full bucket which had just been drawn broke from its chain and crashed down to the bottom of the well. The boy was obviously deeply impressed and spoke of the bucket as if it was a naughty child: 'Bucket was naughty; bucket fell into the well.' He then began to imagine that he was the child who had fallen in. A little later, after they had gone inside and his mother started to take off his coat he began to scream. He cried out that his arm hurt and that he had 'broken it to bits' when he fell into the well. He now kept his arm rigidly bent and was so adamant about the reality of his injury that his mother eventually called the doctor. The doctor humoured the child by prescribing poultices. The boy still screamed when anyone touched his arm but, when he woke from his afternoon nap, his mother decided to distract him. She and a friend then played with him for so long, and in such a diverting way, that he gradually joined in. Finally, while playing at being a bird and flying, he had stretched, turned and dropped both arms. Nothing more was heard of his injured arm.

In venturing to interpret this episode Anna Freud writes that a large part of what she calls 'the mechanism of symptom formation' is plainly evident: 'Probably the little boy had often wished to disobey his mother and go near the tempting well. On the basis of this wish feelings of guilt arose, which enabled him to put himself in the place of the bucket and to transfer to himself what he imagined to be the bucket's punishment.' Although this simple explanation might seem sufficient, Anna Freud cannot resist supplementing it with what she calls 'a further stage in the mechanism':

> We are probably justified in supposing that the feelings of guilt, which related to playing by the well, were reinforced by other, more serious feelings arising from the actual, and not merely fantasied, transgression of a prohibition; I refer to the prohibition of masturbation. If this were so, what the child saw happen at the well – the breaking away of the bucket from the chain and its fall into the depths of the water – must have signified to him a symbolic execution of the threat of castration; the loss of a guilty and highly prized bodily organ – first of all the penis itself, and then, by a process of displacement, the arm and the hand which had shared the forbidden activity.
>
> From this point of view the child's symptom had a double meaning. The stiffness and immobility of his arm would represent the influence of moral tendencies, since these symptoms would constitute a direct punishment for masturbation and a renunciation of the habit. The way in which he held his arm tightly pressed to his body and anxiously shielded it from every interference from outside would represent a defence against the instinctual wish and a precautionary measure against the castration which he feared.
>
> Of course, from a distance and without any possibility of testing one's supposition, it is impossible to decide how far the explanation I have suggested is really correct.[24]

This particular contribution to psychoanalysis is revealing, for in many ways it serves to encapsulate Anna Freud's character as a theorist.

In the first place it clearly shows her readiness – indeed her eagerness – to emulate her father's interpretative style. The distinctive features of this style emerge in this example with particular clarity because of the contrast with the young boy's own imaginative activity. For if we read Anna Freud's account with care, one of the things which becomes clear is the extraordinary level of logical consistency and coherence at which the boy's imagination evidently worked. What he in effect does is to apply a kind of grammatical logic to 'parse' the situation imaginatively. It is this logic which leads him to identify himself with the bucket and it is the same deductive process which leads to the conclusion that, if he is the bucket, he must have been injured by the fall. The pain which he claims to feel is, as it were, supplied imaginatively purely in order to maintain the coherence and internal consistency of the fantasy, and exactly the same can be said about the manner in which he treats his 'injured' arm. Since the imaginative logic which governs the boy's actions can be plainly discerned by attending to the 'surface' of his behaviour and relating it to its context, no further level of analysis seems necessary – other than Anna Freud's initial perceptive remarks.

The specifically psychoanalytic account which she goes on to offer is, in this respect, entirely gratuitous. The theme of masturbation is introduced not because of any external evidence but because of an internal theoretical need. Once it has been thus arbitrarily introduced it determines the manner in which the entire scene is interpreted. The bucket now becomes, improbably, a symbol of the boy's penis. This interpretation would be slightly less implausible than it is if it was maintained consistently. But while the imaginative logic of the two-and-a-quarter-year-old boy is strikingly coherent, the same cannot be said of the logic of the analytic account which we are offered. For no sooner has the boy been symbolically castrated than his penis is mysteriously restored to him, and identified conveniently 'by displacement' with the arm and the hand which had supposedly manipulated it. The boy is now said to be carefully protecting his arm against the very castration which he has supposedly already suffered in his imagination. The inconsistency is significant. Whereas, by reconstructing the boy's imaginative logic from a careful consideration of his behaviour, we are able to offer a perfectly adequate explanation of this behaviour, we cannot use the gratuitous psychoanalytic account given by Anna Freud for the same purpose. For, far from explaining the boy's behaviour, it actually renders it problematic.

The explanatory weakness of Anna Freud's account is characteristic and it clearly derives directly from the example of her father, whose theoretical pronouncements she was no more able to interrogate sceptically than he was himself. Yet it would be wrong to ignore the curious and somewhat plaintive paragraph with which she ends her paper. For her implicit concession that her psychoanalytic account is a speculative one which ought to be tested against reality indicates a willingness to make theoretical compromises which is not accidental. Anna Freud's residual impulse towards empiricism and her distrust of academicism seems to have gone hand in hand with her practical orientation and her involvement, as a teacher, with some of the day-to-day realities of childhood. This empirical impulse would always remain relatively weak, but it would nevertheless play a significant role in her development as a psychoanalyst.

This development was closely connected, as had been the case with Freud himself, with a small number of key patients whose case histories would figure prominently in Anna Freud's subsequent writings. In November 1924 she began treating Minna, the fifteen-year-old daughter of Eva Rosenfeld, a woman with whom she later became friendly. In the spring of 1925 she interviewed another woman, Dorothy Burlingham, with a view to taking her ten-year-old son Bob into analysis. Bob was later to appear in Anna Freud's *Introduction to the Technique of Child Analysis* as 'the boy who could never tell the truth and wanted to give up this habit'. Emotionally troubled, asthmatic and given to compulsive stealing and lying, he had been brought to Vienna by his mother, who had heard of Anna Freud's work with children and was seeking help.

When she eventually came to write about her analysis of Bob Burlingham, Anna Freud gave clear evidence of how strong her theoretical impulse was and how far she had wandered into the labyrinth of psychoanalytic doctrine:

> We have to free a part of this boy's masculine aggressiveness and his object love for his mother from repression and from the overlay by the present passive-feminine character and mother-identification. The conflict involved is an inner one . . . The father has been internalised, the superego has become the representative of his powers, and the fear of him is felt by the boy as castration anxiety. At every step which the analysis takes on the path toward making conscious the repressed oedipal tendencies, it encounters outbreaks of this castration anxiety as an obstacle. Only the laborious historico-analytic dissolution of this superego permits the work of liberation to progress.[25]

It remains quite clear, however, that the relationship which she formed with her patient was by no means merely theoretical. Recognising that children did not enter psychoanalysis of their own accord, but that they were usually sent by their parents, Anna Freud took the view that children needed to be eased into analysis by establishing some form of friendly or co-operative relationship with them. Although Bob Burlingham started off with an intense feeling of hostility towards her, she was able to overcome this by becoming involved in his interests – from his passion for stamp-collecting to his keenness on pirate adventures. She became the diplomatic go-between who helped to repair his relationships with his family, returning money he had stolen, confessing to various misdemeanours on his behalf and protecting him from punishment.

In the analysis proper, however, she would interpret the children's dreams in the manner of an adult analyst and would also analyse their daydreams and their drawings, returning frequently in her interpretations to the themes of her own analysis and to the notions of Oedipal conflict and masturbation guilt. At one point Mabbie, Bob Burlingham's sister, entered into analysis herself and recounted a dream in which she had helped Bob to light the gas water-heater. When it exploded she had been punished by being held in the fire by her nanny. Anna Freud interpreted the dream as one which had arisen out of guilt over masturbation.

In her pursuit of this kind of *idée fixe*, and in many other respects, Anna Freud's clinical practice followed the pattern that had been established by her father in relation to adults. But in seeking to win her patients' affection before she started to analyse them, she was in some respects departing significantly from the clinical and objective austerity of his technique. Her experience as a teacher, and the fact she was working with children and adolescents who had not necessarily internalised social taboos, led her also to adopt at times an explicitly pastoral or educational role similar to that of the parent. In her view the child analyst had to play a dual role:

He has to analyse and educate, that is to say, in the same breath he must allow and forbid, loosen and bind again. If the analyst does not succeed in this, analysis may become the child's charter for all the ill conduct prohibited by society. But if the analyst succeeds, he undoes a piece of wrong education and abnormal development, and so procures for the child, and whoever controls his destiny, another opportunity to improve matters.[26]

Anna Freud's desire to reshape the behaviour and even the character of the children she was analysing led her to an involvement with all those aspects of the child's environment which seemed to have an influence on the child's behaviour – above all with the child's family. This in turn has frequently led to the accusation that she deserted psychoanalysis for pedagogy or that she neglected internal psychic reality in favour of the mundane world of human relationships. In some respects the accusation is well founded. But it is an accusation which reflects more on psychoanalysis than it does on Anna Freud. Perhaps a more realistic assessment of her work would suggest that while she was constantly tempted away from the sphere of analysis as it had been defined by Freud, the pull of analytic theory was too great for her. This, together with her continuing awe for her massively idealised image of her father, meant that she was ultimately unable to strike out in the new theoretical direction which alone could have given coherence to her work. Indeed she eventually came to withdraw her early technical recommendation that child analysis required a period of non-analytic preparation in which the patient's trust was won. She also considerably modified her early stress on the need for the analyst to perform a pedagogic function.

Anna Freud's theoretical dependence on her father was bound up with her personal dependence on him. In 1923, after living at home for the first twenty-seven years of her life, she clearly thought very seriously about applying for membership of the Berlin Psychoanalytic Society and moving her practice there. It was just at this critical time, however, that her father, who had never been able to reconcile himself to the possibility of losing her, began to suffer from a painfully swollen palate. The diagnosis of cancer was eventually made and he underwent the first of a long series of operations on his jaw. Freud's illness now became the decisive factor which enabled them both to surrender to their emotional need for one another. 'You are right,' Anna wrote to Lou Andreas-Salomé. 'I would not leave him now under any circumstances.'[27] She unhesitatingly added the demanding role of nurse to the many secretarial and organisational roles she already undertook for her father, and jealously guarded this new role against the rival claims of her mother and of Minna, her aunt.

Although Freud's illness made his tie with his daughter closer, it did not give her emotional security. She was constantly aware of the many women who had claims on her father's attention and was particularly jealous of those whom he took into analysis. Many years later, when Ernest Jones was writing his biography of her father, she confessed to this kind of jealousy freely. 'I wondered a bit about your mentioning Mrs [Joan] Riviere ... [among] the women in his life,' she wrote. 'She must have played a part since I remembered being jealous of her (a sure sign!)'[28] Anna Freud's response to such jealousy was similar to that of many women whose self-esteem has been rendered precarious or non-existent by the patriarchal values which surround them. She constantly sought to empty herself of what she felt to be her badness, and to engage more and more in what she herself termed 'altruistic surrender' – as if she might earn the esteem of others only by extinguishing her own personality and desires. Yet giving up her own desires and seeking to fulfil them vicariously through others only intensified her feelings of emotional emptiness. In this she resembled the hollow figure described by Rilke in a poem, '*Der Dichter*', which was one of her favourites:

> *Ich habe keine Geliebte, kein Haus,*
> *keine Stelle auf der ich lebe.*
> *Alle Dinge an die ich mich gebe,*
> *werden reich und geben mich aus.*

> I have no home, no loved one waiting at the door.
> There is no place in which I feel I live.
> All those things to which I fondly give
> Myself grow rich. But I grow poor.[29]

She herself would eventually offer a revealing analysis of her predicament in the book she published in 1936, *The Ego and the Mechanisms of Defence*. In that book, as Elisabeth Young-Bruehl has noted, the central example of 'altruistic surrender' is 'a governess' who is clearly a disguised version of Anna Freud herself. This woman, we are told,

> displaced her ambitious fantasies onto her men friends and her libidinal wishes onto her women friends. The former succeeded to her affection for her father and her big brother, both of whom had been the object of her penis envy, while the latter represented the sister upon whom, at a rather later period of childhood, the envy was displaced in the form of envy of her beauty. The patient felt that the fact she was a girl prevented her from achieving her ambitions and, at the same time, that she was not even a pretty enough girl to be really attractive to men. In

her disappointment with herself she displaced her wishes onto objects who she felt were better qualified to fulfil them.[30]

Anna Freud's biographer, however, does not recognise the full significance of these words. For what is perhaps most interesting about them is that they constitute a striking instance of the very pattern of behaviour which Anna Freud is seeking to anatomise. For her words make one of her own psychological insights – about the tendency of those afflicted by feelings of unworthiness to lead their lives through others – subservient to her father's theories about penis envy and object-choice. Unable to claim her psychological perceptiveness as her own, Anna Freud cannot use it in order to unpick the false logic of psychoanalysis. Instead she actually presents her genuine insight as though it has been generated by that logic and is entirely compatible with it. In this respect Rilke's lines, 'All those things to which I fondly give/Myself grow rich. But I grow poor', might well be applied to Anna Freud's entire relationship to the theoretical system which had been created by her father.

Anna Freud's painful lack of self-esteem, coupled with her immensely strong and complex relationship with her father, seemed to make it all but impossible for her to form any deep relationship with a man. Indeed it would seem that she tended to construe any emotional yearning she felt as a temptation to infidelity. In February 1926, a few months after she had taken Bob Burlingham and his sister Mabbie into analysis, she confessed to Max Eitingon that thoughts of these children filled her mind, 'thoughts which go along with my work but do not have a proper place in it'. What she recognised was that her interest in the children went beyond her purely therapeutic role:

> I think sometimes that I want not only to make them healthy but also, at the same time, to have them, or at least have something of them, for myself. Temporarily, of course, this desire is useful for my work, but sometime or other it really will disturb them, and so, on the whole, I really cannot call my need other than 'stupid' . . . Curiously enough, though, I am very much ashamed of all these things, especially in front of Papa, and therefore I tell him nothing about it. This is only a small illustration, but actually I have this dependency, this wanting-to-have-something [Etwas-Haben-Wollen] – even leaving my profession aside – in every nook and cranny of my life.

What perhaps made Anna feel most guilty of all is that her *Etwas-Haben-Wollen*, her 'wanting-to-have-something', extended beyond the children to their mother – 'Towards the mother of the children it is not very different with me.'[31] A little later, in July 1926, she took Max Eitingon further into her confidence. 'Being together with Mrs Burlingham is a great joy for me,' she wrote, 'and I am very happy that you also have such a good first impression of her.'[32]

From this point onwards Dorothy Burlingham, while never taking over the place of Anna's father, gradually became Anna's most trusted friend and her almost constant companion. What gave their relationship its emotional strength was not only their shared concern with Dorothy's children, all four of whom were soon being analysed by Anna, but certain striking similarities in their background. Dorothy, like Anna, was a youngest child, and she too had constantly felt left out by her elder brothers and sisters. Her relationship with her own rich, eccentric and somewhat tyrannical father had always been tense and her problems had been compounded by a difficult marriage to her emotionally unstable husband, Robert, who would eventually commit suicide. She had come to Vienna to escape from life with her husband and to find an emotional haven. The Freud family would eventually provide this haven. Not only did she eventually buy a house with Anna Freud and become her partner in her therapeutic and educational enterprises, but she also went into analysis with her father. 'Our symbiosis with an American family (husbandless),' wrote Freud in 1929, 'whose children my daughter is bringing up analytically with a firm hand, is growing continually stronger . . .'[33]

After her relationship with her father and with the psychoanalytic movement which he founded, Anna Freud's friendship with Dorothy Burlingham was the most important bond in her life. Given the role played by sexuality in psychoanalysis it is perhaps not surprising that, both inside and outside the psychoanalytic movement, it has frequently been suggested that the relationship was 'really' a sexual one. Yet the suggestion that Dorothy and Anna consummated a sexual relationship covertly seems curiously unimaginative. Above all it underestimates the extraordinary austerity and asceticism of the relationship which Anna Freud had formed with her father. There is, ultimately, no good reason to dispute the poignant and, in a sense, tragic conclusion of Anna Freud's authorised biographer that she did not, in the 1920s or afterwards, have a sexual relationship either with Dorothy Burlingham or with anyone else: 'She remained a "vestal" – to use the apt word

Marie Bonaparte later chose to signal both Anna Freud's virginity and her role as the chief keeper of her father's person and his science, psychoanalysis.'[34]

As her father's cancer gradually progressed, necessitating sixteen operations in as many years, the need to provide for the future of psychoanalysis became more acute. At first Anna's battles in this regard were fought out in Vienna, where the birth of psychoanalysis had preceded her own birth by a matter of months. But on 12 March 1938 Hitler occupied Vienna and the full and vicious force of Austrian anti-semitism, long nurtured by the Christian churches but simultaneously restrained by Christian civility, was suddenly unleashed. Public acts of brutality against Jews became routine and a climate of terror was rapidly established. On 16 March the Austrian essayist and cabaret performer Egon Friedell, seeing storm troopers climbing up the stairs to his apartment, jumped from a window to his death. His suicide was the first of many, and during the spring some five hundred Viennese Jews killed themselves in order to avoid interrogation and torture.[35] On 15 March, the day after Hitler's arrival in Vienna, Freud's apartment was invaded by brown-shirted fascists. They held Martin Freud prisoner all day, but eventually departed taking only money after Freud, now aged eighty-one, entered the room with 'blazing eyes that any Old Testament prophet might have envied'.[36]

Freud's friends had for some time been attempting to persuade him to leave Austria. This would almost certainly have been impossible but for Freud's international reputation and the fact that those who now sought to help him were powerfully connected. Ernest Jones, who visited Freud on 16 March, was on good terms with Sir Samuel Hoare, the British Home Secretary. Princess Marie Bonaparte had considerable influence in French government circles and William Bullitt, who had collaborated with Freud on a book about Woodrow Wilson and was now the American Ambassador to France, brought Freud's plight directly to the attention of President Franklin Roosevelt. As a result of a series of high-level interventions the matter of obtaining exit visas for Freud and his family was eventually taken up with Himmler and the necessary documents were obtained. Freud himself had at first opposed the plan, but after a long argument he had eventually been won over by Ernest Jones.[37]

Freud still remained reluctant. On 22 March, however, the same day that Himmler was approached about Freud's exit visa, the apartment at

Berggasse was visited by the Gestapo and Anna Freud was taken away for questioning in an open car surrounded by four heavily armed SS men.

Without Freud's knowledge Anna and her brother Martin, anticipating interrogation, had secretly obtained a supply of the drug Veronal from Freud's family physician. If necessary they had decided that they would choose suicide in preference to torture. It turned out that the Gestapo were trying to track down a group of suspected Jewish terrorists. When she was questioned about the organisation she belonged to, Anna Freud gave her captors a description of the activities of the International Psychoanalytic Association. By seven o'clock in the evening she had returned home.

Freud's biographers have tended to portray him as preserving at least a degree of stoicism and self-control on this occasion. It is perhaps to his credit that this was not really so. 'I'll never forget,' wrote Dorothy Burlingham to Anna, in 1939, 'the time you were . . . with the Gestapo and he was so dreadfully worried – the only time I ever saw him like that – I realised then fully what you meant to him.' When Anna Freud eventually returned that evening, her father, who was normally so restrained, broke down in tears and declared that he wanted them all to flee Vienna at once.[38]

It was not until 4 June, more than two long months later, that Freud, accompanied by his wife and by Anna, boarded the train to Paris on the journey which would take them to England. After crossing the Channel by the night boat, they arrived at Victoria Station on the morning of 6 June. Freud had come to England, he said, 'to die in freedom'.[39]

During the last year of his life Freud continued to write, completing his *Moses and Monotheism* and beginning work on his *Outline of Psychoanalysis*. He also continued to see patients. In September 1938 his writing was interrupted when his cancer became active once again. His old surgeon was eventually summoned from Vienna and Freud underwent what was to be the last operation he had to remove cancerous tissue from his jaw. On 27 September he moved into the house which had been prepared for him at 20 Maresfield Gardens in Hampstead, north London. Here, surrounded by his antiquities, his books and the other possessions which had been rescued from Vienna, he lived out the last year of his life nursed by Martha, Minna, and above all by Anna.

Here, as had been the case ever since his arrival in England, a seemingly unending procession of visitors came to pay court to him. In January 1939 his English publishers, Leonard and Virginia Woolf, who ran the Hogarth Press, were invited to take tea with him. Leonard Woolf would later recall his impression that he had met a great man. He felt, he wrote in his autobiography,

> no call to praise the famous men whom I have known. Nearly all famous men are disappointing or bores, or both. Freud was neither; he had an aura, not of fame, but of greatness . . . There was something about him as of a half extinct volcano, something sombre, repressed, reserved. He gave me the feeling which only a very few people whom I have met gave me, a feeling of great gentleness, but behind the gentleness, great strength.[40]

A month later, after Freud had suffered renewed pains, a biopsy showed that his cancer was spreading again. This time it was so far back in his mouth that it was impossible to operate. Freud bore the last phase of his illness with iron determination not to lose control of his bodily and mental functions, and to retain his dignity. He continued to read, to see patients and to follow the reception of his newly published *Moses and Monotheism*. Only on 1 August 1939, in a gesture of finality, did he formally bring his medical practice to a close and give himself almost completely into the care of Anna, who nursed him in his final days with heroic dedication.

At the beginning of September Freud was still alert enough to follow the outbreak of war, but his cancer was growing worse. The ulcerated tissue in his mouth gave off such a fetid smell that his faithful chow shrank back from its master and could not be persuaded to come near him. As his pain intensified Anna nursed him around the clock. On one occasion, when she had left the room for a moment, he took the opportunity to confide in Max Schur, his physician. 'Fate has been good to me, that it should still have granted me the relationship to such a woman,' he said, '– I mean Anna of course.' Schur recalls that Freud's comment was utterly tender, even though he never normally showed his affection for his daughter.[41]

On 21 September Freud, racked by pain, reached out from his bed and took his physician's hand. He reminded him that he had agreed, when the time came, that he would not let him suffer. 'Now it is nothing but torture,' he said, 'and makes no sense.' He continued to hold Schur's hand, and then said: '*Sagen Sie es der Anna*' ('Tell Anna about this'). Anna was reluctant but she eventually agreed. Schur now injected Freud with a dose of morphine somewhat greater than was required for a sedative, and Freud fell into a calm sleep. Schur repeated the injection the next day. Freud went into a coma and died early in the morning of 23 September 1939. Many years later Anna Freud, who had kept the vigil by his bedside, wrote to a friend whose father was dying: 'I believe that there is nothing worse than to see the people nearest to one lose the very qualities for which one loves them. I was spared that with my father, who was himself to the last minute.'[42]

Freud had spent some fifteen months in England after his flight from Vienna and from Hitler. For much of this time he was in pain. But there had also been moments of elation. On 28 June 1938 his lifelong dream of fame was consummated in a particularly significant way. Three secretaries from the Royal Society had come to visit him, bringing 'the sacred book of the Society' for his signature. 'They left a facsimile of the book with me,' wrote Freud to Arnold Zweig, 'and if you were with me I could show you the signatures from I. Newton to Charles Darwin. Good company!' Freud's belief that he was a great scientist had always been sustained by this kind of recognition. He evidently felt particularly honoured that the Royal Society had broken its rules in order to bring their Charter Book to him. They had only done this once before, for the King of England.[43]

Freud, who had recreated the kingdom of his childhood by fashioning the psychoanalytic movement, thus found in his old age that he himself was being treated like royalty. When he died, the kingdom which he had created lived on after him and it was clear that he regarded Anna as his natural and rightful heir. She, who, as a child, had dreamed of guarding the empire of a departed emperor, implicitly accepted her own succession.

Some time after her father's death, she took his *Lodenmantel* – the green Austrian overcoat which he had worn – and, after carefully cleaning it and repairing it, hung it in the wardrobe in her own bedroom. There it would remain, unused, almost until she died. But for as long as she lived she would continue to wear the mantle of her father's authority, endeavouring as she did so to guard the kingdom which was her inheritance. It was therefore not surprising that, during the latter part of her career, her central ideas remained subordinated to those of her father – sometimes to a quite painful degree. But it would be wrong and personally unjust, both to Freud and to his daughter, to suggest that her own individuality was entirely destroyed by her love affair with him. Some aspects of their analytically mediated romance were indeed negative and destructive. But within the hard and sometimes brittle shell of her psychoanalytic orthodoxy Anna Freud preserved an element of originality – a fragment, perhaps, of the imaginative dissidence, the *Unartigkeit*, which had originally inspired her father to christen her his 'Black Devil'. Partly because she was a woman, and partly because her dual career, first as a teacher and then as a child analyst, gave her far more opportunities for observing human behaviour than had ever been available to her father, the contributions which she made to psychoanalysis were sometimes both interesting and original. Yet the very fact that she was a woman, suffering from those acute feelings of unworthiness which are frequently inflicted upon women in our intellectual culture, made it difficult for her to develop her ideas. Her rebelliousness did not in the end have sufficient force to enable her to question the particular authority which had both smothered and claimed her originality – the authority of her father.

Instead of rebelling, Anna Freud, whose tenacity and capacity for controlled aggression were sometimes awesome, would spend a great deal of the latter part of her career fighting a battle in defence of her father and her father's kingdom. On the one hand she would defend this kingdom against those she regarded as theoretical interlopers – above all her great rival Melanie Klein, who had attempted to revise Freud's theory of the Oedipus complex by ascribing to young children an even greater innate perversity, and an even more voracious sexual fantasy-life than he had dared to postulate. On the other hand she would fight a rearguard action against all those critics, biographers and would-be biographers who, in her view, were seeking to mount unjust attacks on her father's reputation.

On both these fronts, however, Anna Freud found herself in the position of a believer who is obliged to moderate the fierceness with which she defends her faith out of her very respect for the figure whom she venerates. This can be seen most clearly, perhaps, in one of the areas where Melanie Klein was most vulnerable to criticism – her manner of interpreting children's play. In Klein's view the play of young children was, in certain cases at least, the exact equivalent of free-association in adults. She therefore took the view that, particularly when there was any sign of anxiety or guilt (of which she was to be the judge), no element in children's play was arbitrary and every element was determined by the child's unconscious fantasies. Given Klein's theoretical beliefs this meant, in effect, that the play of young children tended to be interpreted as a continuous sexual soliloquy, in which children ceaselessly imagined how they might fellate or castrate their fathers, defile or attack their mother's breast, or, even more frequently, imagine (or recall) their parents engaging in coitus. Anna Freud's objection to this approach was straightforward:

> If the child overturns a lamppost or a toy figure, she [Melanie Klein] interprets this action, e.g. as an aggressive impulse against the father; a deliberate collision between two cars as evidence of the child having observed sexual intercourse between the parents . . . [But] the child who upsets a toy lamppost may have witnessed some such incident in the street the day before; the car collision may be reproducing a similar happening.[44]

This criticism might well seem both sound and reasonable. It should also be immediately clear, however, why Anna Freud was unable to push her criticism home. For the simple fact was that Melanie Klein's intellectual methods, her reckless disregard for empirical restraints and her theoretically wishful interpretations were all derived from a single example – that of Freud himself.

A similar problem confronted Anna Freud in a quite different area of her dispute with Melanie Klein. For Klein had frequently criticised her rival for her belief that it was necessary to establish a personal relationship with children who were being analysed. Yet Melanie Klein herself had based her earliest case histories on analyses she had conducted of her own children – whose identities she had then deliberately disguised in a manner which reflected ill on her integrity as a scientist.[45] Once again, however, Melanie Klein had merely followed the example of Freud himself, and it would seem that Anna Freud was bound to silence on this front lest the secret of her own analysis should be made public by Klein and her supporters.

It is both ironic and in some respects poignant that Anna Freud's battle to preserve her father's authority should ultimately have been defeated by the only force in her life which was greater than her will to win this battle – her own respect for this authority, and her own desire to preserve her father's image not only against damaging false-hoods, but also against the truth. When Paul Roazen eventually revealed the story of her analysis by her father in his study of Victor Tausk in 1969, and followed this book with his 1975 volume, *Freud and His Followers*, Anna Freud reacted by attempting to guard Freud's papers more closely and, in some cases, to preserve them entirely from the prying eyes of scholars and biographers. As a result of this policy some letters and documents held in the Library of Congress would eventually be placed under an embargo for periods extending as far ahead as the twenty-second century.

The policy of locking away Freud's letters and papers proved both short-sighted and self-defeating, for it served only to heighten fascination with the figure of Freud and to convince those who had doubted it that the psychoanalytic establishment had something significant to hide.

Yet in one respect the policy adopted by the Sigmund Freud Archives may have contributed, almost accidentally, to preserving the Freud legend for a little longer than might otherwise have been the case. For the zealous restrictions placed on some documents tended to encourage a view which was consonant with the entire ethos of psychoanalysis – that the ultimate secrets of Freud's life were in some way hidden and inaccessible to ordinary observation. The reality was very different. Many of the most revealing and damaging facts about Freud and the intellectual methods of psychoanalysis have been in the public domain already for up to a century. These facts are contained in Freud's own published psychoanalytic papers and in the mass of historical and biographical material which has already accumulated around him. The Freud-myth has been sustained in the very midst of the facts which ought to undermine it, not by embargoes or restrictions, but by something much more potent – by the power of faith and legend and by the deep need of countless twentieth-century intellectuals for a system of over-arching certainties and doctrines which could replace the religious beliefs of the common culture they had lost.

Few of Freud's followers can have felt the need to preserve the myth of the greatness of the founder of psychoanalysis more acutely than his own daughter. The tragedy of the final years of her life was that much of her time was spent fending off the approaches of scholars whose determination to sift through every literary remain left by her father seemed to her both an act of desecration and a violation of her own privacy. The only consolation brought by her final illness – which was ushered in by a stroke which she suffered on 1 March 1982 – was that she no longer had to deal with the scholars who had begun to take away her peace of mind. 'Now I can hide behind my illness quite legitimately,' she wrote.[46]

Anna Freud died early in the morning of 9 October 1982. In the last months of her life she had hidden herself increasingly not only in her illness but also in the warm and immensely reassuring folds of her father's legend. In this respect, as in many others, some of Anna Freud's most private moments resonated with a larger public significance, and at times she seemed to personify an entire intellectual culture. During her long hospital stay her friend and colleague Manna Friedmann had frequently pushed her in her wheelchair to the nearby paths of Hampstead Heath, to the pond where they could feed the ducks and watch the children sailing their toy boats.[47] One afternoon, as her biographer Elisabeth Young-Bruehl recounts, Anna Freud sensed that the summer weather was turning cooler. Struggling to speak, she asked Manna Friedmann to call in at 20 Maresfield Gardens on her way to the hospital and to bring, from the wardrobe in her bedroom, her father's *Lodenmantel*. When they went to the park the next day, Manna Friedmann stood to one side and watched as the diminutive figure of Anna Freud, now as small as a schoolgirl, sat wrapped inside her father's big wool coat.

III

PSYCHOANALYSIS,
SCIENCE
AND THE FUTURE

TWENTY-ONE

Psychoanalysis, Science and Human Nature

'THE OPINION IS GAINING GROUND,' Peter Medawar has written, 'that doctrinaire psychoanalytic theory is the most stupendous intellectual confidence trick of the twentieth century: and a terminal product as well – something akin to a dinosaur or a zeppelin in the history of ideas, a vast structure of radically unsound design and with no posterity.'[1] These words express what is perhaps the most dismissive and contemptuous verdict on psychoanalysis which has ever been passed. It is the kind of verdict towards which the view of Freud I have offered here might seem logically to lead. But although Medawar's conclusion that psychoanalytic theory is a 'structure of radically unsound design' is eminently reasonable, I believe it would be wrong to accept his judgement in its entirety.

In the first place psychoanalysis cannot fairly be described as a 'confidence trick'. For this description quite clearly implies a conscious and deliberate attempt to deceive. Although the image of Freud as an arch-deceiver has been favoured by some recent critics of psychoanalysis, it seems to misrepresent both Freud's own character and that of his followers. For, whatever his moral failings and his sometimes less than scrupulous attitude towards the truth, Freud sought to persuade others to accept psychoanalysis for no other reason than that he believed in it himself. Psychoanalytic theory is no more a confidence trick than Christianity, Islam, Judaism or any other system of religious belief.

What may seem more plausible is Medawar's claim that psychoanalysis should be seen as a 'terminal product . . . with no posterity'. In one respect at least, this charge seems just. So far as Freud himself is concerned, the evidence which I have presented must, I believe, lead to an overwhelmingly negative estimate of his actual scientific achieve-

437

ment. Freud made no substantial intellectual discoveries. He was the creator of a complex pseudo-science which should be recognised as one of the great follies of Western civilisation. In creating his particular pseudo-science, Freud developed an autocratic, anti-empirical intellectual style which has contributed immeasurably to the intellectual ills of our own era. His original theoretical system, his habits of thought and his entire attitude to scientific research are so far removed from any responsible method of inquiry that no intellectual approach basing itself upon these is likely to endure. Still less is it likely to solve the enigma of human nature which Freud himself believed he had within his grasp.

Yet, having said all this, we are still not in a position to endorse Medawar's prediction that psychoanalysis is likely to have no posterity. Indeed to underwrite this view would be to take a very considerable risk. We have only to consult the history of science to recognise that false theories can sometimes play a key role in scientific progress and that failure to recognise this may actually impede such progress.

One of the most significant examples offered by the history of science concerns the role played by astrology. For although the intellectual foundations of astrology were originally entirely without substance, a few empirically minded and sceptical astrologers always recognised that their system was in need both of verification and refinement. Towards the end of the seventeenth century the astrologer John Goad kept a thirty-year record of the observations he had made of the supposed influence of the planets on weather and epidemics. In the course of his investigations he noted, probably for the first time in human history, the seasonal variation in suicide rates. He thus observed a real sociological phenomenon for which there is still no entirely satisfactory explanation.[2]

The failure of some conventional scientists to recognise that astrologers were not immune to making real discoveries played an extremely significant role in the history of science at the beginning of the seventeenth century. Because Copernicus was an astrologer, his conjecture that the tides were influenced by the moon was scornfully rejected by Galileo, who persisted in his erroneous view that tides were caused by the earth moving around the sun.[3]

Astrology is by no means the only false theory which has helped to generate real discoveries. We should perhaps recall that the phlogiston theory played a quite crucial role in the development of modern chemistry. This theory maintained that in the process of combustion, phlogiston, a hypothetical element, was separated out from every combustible material. Although the theory was incorrect it was not scientifically barren. For it was by analysing carefully the mistaken observations on which this theory was based that later scientists were led eventually to the discovery of oxygen. It was Lavoisier's oxygen theory of combustion which eventually led to a reformulation of chemistry so vast that it is usually known as 'the chemical revolution'.[4]

It is because scientific discoveries are sometimes the product of a process of fruitful error that we would do well to draw back from Medawar's confident assertion that psychoanalysis is a 'terminal idea . . . with no posterity'. This does not mean that we should credit Freud with insights which he did not have or that we should attribute to him an intellectual subversiveness which was never realised in his theories. For as I have tried to show in this book, many of Freud's ostensible victories over the repressive forces of the Judaeo-Christian tradition were hollow or illusory. But one of the greatest mistakes we can make in assessing any messianic movement is that of automatically convicting its members of the follies and failings of their leader. It is part of the very nature of messianic prophets that they tend to overvalue their own putative insights, theories and beliefs, while simultaneously undervaluing the insights and wisdom of others. If we make use of a critique of Freud's own theories in order to ridicule or dismiss the work of all those who have ever invoked Freud's name, we merely end by perpetuating the tyrannical self-estimate of the prophet we purport to criticise.

The fact that almost all psychoanalysts have hugely overvalued Freud's theories, and that some, such as Melanie Klein and Jacques Lacan, have sunk even deeper into epistemological quicksands than Freud himself, does not mean that we can safely reject the work of every psychoanalyst as being without value.[5] For to do this would be to risk making exactly the kind of mistake that Galileo made when he rejected the Copernican theory of lunar tides. Scientific ideas should be judged not by their intellectual provenance but by their explanatory power. As I have already argued in the Introduction, a small but significant number of those who have worked within the psychoanalytic tradition have left it much richer than they found it and have added appreciably to the sum of our psychological knowledge.

Peter Medawar's assessment of psychoanalysis does not recognise this. The danger of such sweeping and contemptuous judgements is that they play into the hands of those who are hostile to all forms of deep psychological explanation and who seek to discredit or discount not simply psychoanalysis, but all forms of psychotherapy. It is because Peter Medawar's verdict on psychoanalysis might be construed as underwriting such an attitude that I have taken issue with it here at such length. For Medawar's view seems all too like that of the scientist who, because he is dissatisfied with the phlogiston theory, decides to deny the reality of the phenomenon of combustion. The task of the scientist is not to deride or destroy unsatisfactory scientific theories, but to analyse carefully why these theories do not work and then to replace them by theories which do.

To say this is not to deny the value of purely negative critiques of psychoanalysis. It is merely to emphasise that no critique of an inadequate scientific theory, including the one I have offered here, can ever be regarded as a complete refutation of that theory. In practice science proceeds not by dismantling old hypotheses and then erecting new ones in their place, but by using new hypotheses to *displace* old ones. This much should be apparent from even a cursory acquaintance with the history of science. The point has been underlined, however, by Thomas Kuhn in his discussion of theories which achieve paradigmatic status:

> Once it has achieved the status of a paradigm, a scientific theory is declared invalid only if an alternate candidate is available to take its place. No process yet disclosed by the historical study of scientific development at all resembles the methodological stereotype of falsification by direct comparison with nature. That remark does not mean that scientists do not reject scientific theories, or that experience and experiment are not essential to the process in which they do so. But it does mean – what will ultimately be a central point – that the act of judgment which leads scientists to reject a previously accepted theory is always based on more than a comparison of that theory with the world. The decision to reject one paradigm is always simultaneously the decision to accept another, and the judgment leading to that decision involves the comparison of both paradigms with nature *and* with each other.[6]

The proposition that psychoanalysis is a theory of human nature that can be refuted only by putting in its place a better theory may seem straightforward. Western intellectual history, however, suggests that this proposition is fraught with difficulties. There is clearly a very significant difference between theories of combustion and theories of human nature. During the history of modern science the need for a theory of combustion, and the intellectual legitimacy of attempting to construct such a theory, have never been at issue. Yet throughout the same period the very possibility of constructing a theory of human nature has frequently been either dismissed or surrounded with intellectual taboos. It is partly because of the depth of our cultural and intellectual confusion about this issue that psychoanalysis, itself a product of the same confusion, has survived as long as it has. If we wish to understand why scepticism about Freudian theory has not triumphed sooner, we need to examine some of the reasons why our intellectual culture is itself so sceptical about the kind of large-scale theories which alone might serve to displace psychoanalysis.

There are a number of apparently different grounds on which such scepticism is based. Perhaps the most common argument derives from the traditional view of science which sees it as being concerned above all to illuminate the structure of matter or of non-human nature. According to this view science is simply not the kind of enterprise which can be legitimately focused on the problem of human nature. One of the most recent and influential statements of this position has been made by Peter Medawar himself. In his essay *The Limits of Science* Medawar sets forward his own view that the greatest glory of science is that 'there is no limit upon the power of science to answer questions of the kind science *can* answer.' But he simultaneously advances the view that there are a number of crucial questions which science is unable to answer and which 'no conceivable advance of science would empower it to answer.' These questions are characterised by Medawar as the 'childlike elementary questions having to do with first and last things – questions such as "How did everything begin?" "What are we all here for?" "What is the point of living?"' He goes on to suggest that, while science should concern itself with answering material questions, it is right and proper that, when it comes to 'the ultimate questions' we should seek 'transcendent' answers which 'belong to the domains of myth, metaphysics, imaginative literature or religion'. While making it clear that he does not himself believe in God – something which he regrets – Medawar openly suggests that, in the case of the great mysteries of human existence, 'religious explanations are by far the best' even though accepting this entails what he calls 'a momentary abdication of the rule of reason'. In his view the acceptability of transcendent answers is ultimately to be measured not by their explanatory power but 'by the degree to which they bring peace of mind'.[7]

Medawar's agnostic willingness to lean on the hypothesis of God is interesting and, in one respect at least, refreshingly honest. For the position which he states quite openly is very often held covertly or surreptitiously by rationalist thinkers. It is the position which might be called 'reversible rationalism', in which a scientific attitude towards nature co-exists with a transcendental, or superstitious, attitude towards human nature.

The reason Medawar is able to put forward this apparently self-contradictory view with scarcely a note of apology or explanation is that 'reversible rationalism' is deeply rooted in our intellectual culture, and might indeed be characterised as one of its central orthodoxies. For when the creators of modern science laid the foundations of physics in the seventeenth century the rational empiricism which underlay their approach to the realm of matter was itself derived from creationist doctrines. Descartes, Galileo, Newton and Robert Boyle, to name but four representative figures, all believed that they had triumphantly succeeded through their science in bearing witness to the majesty and rationality of God. But although they believed that the mystery of the rational design of *matter* and of the physical universe was theirs to unlock, they sometimes openly recognised that the ultimate mysteries of human nature were known to God alone and would be revealed only when the apocalyptic moment finally came. The orthodox position of reversible rationalism, which was held in its most extreme form by Descartes, was implicitly maintained by the Christian instigators of the scientific revolution. It was challenged but never entirely dislodged by the most extreme forms of Enlightenment rationalism, and has repeatedly been reasserted in modern times. One of the most interesting twentieth-century instances is that provided by Alfred Wallace, who formulated a theory of natural selection at the same time as Darwin. Wallace eventually took the view that, while the theory could account for evolution in general, it could not be invoked to explain the human mind, whose mysteries compelled one to postulate the existence of God – or of a world spirit working above and beyond the material world.[8]

Medawar's seemingly contemptuous dismissal of psychoanalysis is evidently conditioned, in part at least, by his own allegiance to the orthodox position, and his belief that any theory which seeks to address the deepest problems of human existence is treading beyond the proper sphere of science and trespassing upon the preserve of religion or myth. What is odd about his position is not that it should be held at all, but that such an explicitly God-centred view should be seriously entertained by a thinker who simultaneously disavows belief in the God his philosophical position compels him to postulate.

It is partly in order to avoid this kind of logical muddle that another version of 'reversible rationalism' has gradually emerged among liberal intellectuals during the second half of the twentieth century in the philosophy of 'pluralism'. Like the traditional version it implicitly accepts the legitimacy of scientific theories about the realm of matter. But whereas the traditional view renounces only scientific or materialist theories of human nature, and upholds theological ones, the modern liberal humanist adaptation of it implicitly renounces all theories of human nature whether of a transcendent or non-transcendent kind. The theism of the traditional position is thus replaced by scepticism about the very possibility of putting forward any acceptable account of human nature.

The factor which has shaped this distinctively modern form of scepticism, with its particular distrust of any form of messianic politics, is nothing other than the course of modern European history. The crucial moment which liberal pluralism simultaneously celebrates and recoils from is the rise of Enlightenment rationalism in eighteenth-century France. For although the most influential proponent of modern liberal pluralism, Isaiah Berlin, is sometimes mistakenly seen as an opponent of rationalism, he has described himself as 'a liberal rationalist' and is fundamentally sympathetic to the values of the Enlightenment. In his orthodox rationalist view Diderot, Helvétius, Holbach, Condorcet, and above all Voltaire, were the great liberators of European humanity. 'They liberated people from horrors, obscurantism, fanaticism, monstrous views. They were against cruelty, they were against oppression, they fought the good fight against superstition and ignorance and against a great many things which ruined people's lives. So I am on their side.' At the same time that he endorses the values of the Enlightenment, however, Berlin is painfully aware that the very form of rationalism which set out to deliver Europe from tyranny was itself potentially tyrannical. What he implicitly recognises is that the attempt to overthrow the traditional attitude of 'reversible rationalism' and to make human nature itself into the object of rigorous, coldly rational scientific analysis, contained the seeds of moral disaster on an unimaginable scale. For until the rise of scientific atheism in eighteenth-century France human beings had effectively been protected against the cruel astringency of Christian rationalism by nothing other than Christianity itself and its belief in the distinctive reality of the human soul. With the rise of atheistical rationalism, human nature was stripped of its divinity and began to be regarded by the most thorough-going rationalists as a suitable object for exactly the same kind of abstractionist analysis that had hitherto been applied only to dead matter. The search began for the laws of human nature – the rigid invariant laws which, if only human beings could be brought into conformity with them, would usher in the perfect society where all would live in peace, brotherhood and equality. Again and again in his essays Berlin points to the dangers of this approach. One of his axiomatic beliefs, which is also found in many forms of modern liberal pluralism, is succinctly expressed in a passage in his essay on Moses Hess:

> A sense of symmetry and regularity, and a gift for rigorous deduction, that are prerequisites of aptitude for some natural sciences, will, in the field of social organisation, unless they are modified by a great deal of sensibility, understanding and humanity, inevitably lead to appalling bullying on one side and untold suffering on the other.[9]

The tragic truth contained within these words was demonstrated again and again in the great human 'experiments' which were carried out in the name of a rational scientific view of human nature in modern Europe. Two of these experiments were particularly significant. In the French Revolution, in the revolution of 1848 and once again in the Russian Revolution of 1917, a rigid, scientific, utopian quest for social perfection, launched amidst dreams of ultimate harmony, ended on both occasions in blood, terror and tyrannical repression.

It would be difficult to overstate the influence exercised by these tragic excursions into revolutionary faith, culminating as they did in the Terror of Lenin and the Great Terror of Stalin, on the manner in which twentieth-century intellectuals have perceived and assessed modern attempts to formulate theories of human nature. For obvious reasons it has been those intellectuals who belong to the same generation as Isaiah Berlin who have been most deeply and most traumatically affected. For many years, until the advent of structuralism, post-structuralism and other linguistically based philosophies, the dominant ethos in a number of British and American universities was that of pluralism – a pluralism whose character was deeply marked by the writings of Berlin himself and his intellectual contemporaries. The doctrine of pluralism rests on one central negative premise, namely that 'there is no single answer'. The enemies of the pluralist are, in the words of Isaiah Berlin, the 'terrible simplifiers'. They are the 'great despotic organisers', 'single-minded monists, ruthless fanatics, men possessed by an all embracing vision'. The pluralist rejects such single-mindedness in favour of wide intellectual tolerance and a belief that intellectual diversity is intrinsically valuable. In this defence of diversity what is held to be at stake is political freedom, for 'dogmatists who claim to know the certain answer will become tyrants'. The equation at its simplest is thus one between intellectual system-building and totalitarianism. The ultimate dread is not of any merely theoretical dogmatism but of the terrible practical dogmatism of Hitler and Stalin.[10]

In an extremely significant intellectual genealogy, it would seem that this dread has been passed down directly by thinkers such as Isaiah Berlin to some of the recent advocates of postmodernism. Gilbert Adair, for example, has put forward the view that 'every "ism", as the world has learnt to its cost, eventually degenerates into a terrorism.' Detecting a new estrangement from Freud, he sees this 'as only part of a growing antipathy to all totalising doctrines, all grand master-texts. (Totalising sounds too much to our 20th century ears like totalitarian and master-text has a slightly queasy echo of master race.)' Adair goes on to suggest that 'postmodernism is less a genuine doctrine than a ruefully ironic recognition that the doctrinal era has passed. The postmodernist thinker is one who accepts, as perhaps Marx and Freud could not, that his ideas are of a basically *interim* nature, destined, often much sooner than expected, to be rendered obsolete.'[11]

In assessing such scepticism about large-scale theories of human nature, we should recognise that the dangers against which pluralists warn are real. It must indeed be suggested that intellectual totalitarianism is not simply an aberration from our central intellectual tradition but a pattern which recurs with such regularity that it appears to be a normal phenomenon rather than an abnormal one – one which is perhaps endemic in any culture which has been shaped by monotheism. From Aquinas to Marx, from Plato to Lévi-Strauss, our intellectual culture has again and again demonstrated a seeming predilection for global, theory-centred doctrines of human nature in which empirical evidence has been either ignored or eclipsed. Lest there should be any doubt about the continuing appeal of such over-arching doctrines, the example of psychoanalysis itself should be sufficient to dispel such doubt.

The problem both with the traditional kind of 'reversible rational-ism' preached by Medawar, and with pluralist adaptations of this pos-ition, is not that the dangers against which they warn are illusory. The real problem is that while the liberal pluralist position involves an ideological elision, the traditional position, as put forward by Medawar, is a cultural anachronism.

One version of the liberal position which bears directly on psychoan-alysis, while simultaneously illustrating the ideological elision of which I speak, has been put forward by Frederick Crews in his volume of essays, *Skeptical Engagements*. Astute, pungent, and often extremely perceptive, Crews's essays are examples of modern rational empiricism at its most brilliant. His trenchant analyses of structuralist and post-structuralist trends and his many attacks on psychoanalysis are charged with the kind of energy which can only be sustained by a direct current of genuine insights. But, like many liberal intellectuals, Crews is at his most effective when he is disengaging himself from established beliefs, and he shows little enthusiasm for the project of replacing such beliefs with any new, systematic theory of human nature.

In this respect it is significant that, in the introduction to *Skeptical Engagements*, Crews implicitly defines both Marxism and psychoanaly-sis as intellectual drugs, and implicitly holds out as an ideal the intellec-tual who has conquered 'the fear of facing the world without an intellectual narcotic ready at hand'.

> My equipment for understanding the power of that fear was acquired the hard way, through trying to work myself free of a seductive dogma that had promised quick, deep knowledge. For a decade or so I was convinced that psychoanalysis, with its distrust of appearances and its stoic willingness to face the unspeakable, was a useful adjunct to my skeptical principles. Only in halting stages did I come to reverse that opinion and acknowledge that Freudianism is a faith like any other . . . This experience of conversion followed by self-deprogramming explains why psychoanalysis occupies a central place in *Skeptical Engagements* . . . Freudianism has become for me the paradigmatic example of a doctrine that compels irrational loyalty.[12]

The implication of these words is that Crews holds no faith, that he has passed entirely beyond the need for doctrines which compel irrational loyalty, and that he has triumphed over the most characteristic need of intellectuals – the need for certainty. Given Crews's tone, at once reasonable and rigorous, there would seem to be no grounds for doubting his own scepticism.

Yet if we are to meet Crews's robust scepticism with scepticism of our own, it is precisely this kind of doubt which we must entertain. For the belief that we have freed ourselves from irrational faiths is, historically, one of the most dangerous of all beliefs. It is, indeed, just this belief which lies at the heart of Marxism and psychoanalysis themselves. What Marxism and psychoanalysis both illustrate is not that revolutionary ideologies are dangerous. What they illustrate is that orthodoxies are dangerous – particularly in the hands of those who believe they have transcended them. One of my main purposes in writing this book has been to explore this predicament. What I have tried to show is how powerful the creationist assumptions of Judaeo-Christian irrationalism are and how deeply we have internalised them.

It is because, as a culture, we have theorised about our own nature more extensively, more deeply and more pervasively than we usually admit to ourselves, and because our theories have achieved the invisibility of orthodoxy, that the sceptical withdrawal from ideology which is preached by many liberal intellectuals should itself be treated with scepticism. For what it means, in effect, is that most disavowals of belief are, in reality, nothing other than tacit proclamations of faith.

This view might well be applied to the position adopted by Frederick Crews. It is interesting in this respect that, by the end of the very introduction in which he implicitly renounces all forms of irrational faith, he makes it clear that his own position assumes the presence rather than the absence of belief, and that it rests, if not on any certainty, at least upon a degree of 'assurance'. 'My own starting point,' he writes, 'is an acknowledgement that we do, by now, know a great many things with enough assurance to profit from their consequences.'[13] The claim is a moderate one indeed, and, given its non-specific nature, difficult to challenge. In the context of this discussion, however, it should be clear that the great danger of taking such a position, particularly when it is combined, as it is by Crews, with a seemingly uncritical celebration of 'empiricism' and 'common sense', is that the apparently inert white powder of the particular kind of empiricism and common sense which is favoured might turn out, in reality, to be nothing other than the pure opium of orthodoxy.

It might seem that by saying this – and in particular by expressing scepticism about the tradition of scientific empiricism to which modern liberal humanists frequently appeal – I am implicitly rejecting both science and empiricism. I should therefore emphasise that I am not doing anything of the kind. As should be clear from the criticisms which have been made of Freud throughout this book, I believe that an empirical approach is a prerequisite of genuine science and, indeed, that empiricism is perhaps the most valuable element in the entire intellectual tradition of the West. Nevertheless I am suggesting that, if scepticism is to serve us well, we must be consistent about the manner in which we apply it, and we must interrogate our own tradition of scientific empiricism just as carefully and just as critically as we do the more obvious vehicles of ideology or cultural orthodoxy. Above all we must be wary of the possibility that the irrational faith we believe we have renounced might be secreted in the very mode of knowledge which claims to have passed beyond religious unreason.

For just as there can be no genuine theoretical science without empiricism, so there can be no empiricism which is independent of theoretical assumptions or presuppositions. Although we sometimes see Western science as being founded on empiricism pure and simple, such a view seriously misrepresents intellectual history. For the most powerful intellectual ideology in Western culture from the time of Plato to the time of Descartes and beyond is almost entirely independent of empirical attitudes, and in some cases actively hostile to them. It is this ideology – the ideology of rationalism – which has dominated our intellectual culture for more than two millennia and continues to shape and determine the particular kind of 'empiricism' which is associated with the research we deem scientific.

For modern science is not simply a neutral, value-free technique for assembling knowledge which can be treated as historically and ideologically innocent. While science is by no means monolithic, there are many who would suggest that its dominating ethos remains actively hostile to any theory of human nature which seeks to accommodate the full emotional depth and complexity of the human personality. 'Scientific objectivity,' Ted Hughes has written,

> has its own morality . . . and this is the prevailing morality of our time. It is a morality utterly devoid of any awareness of the requirements of the inner world. It is contemptuous of the 'human element'. This is its purity and its strength. The prevailing philosophies of our time subscribe to this contempt with a nearly religious fanaticism, just as science itself does.[14]

The words of Ted Hughes, with their stress on the 'puritanism' of science, might well serve to remind us of one of the many aspects of our cultural history which we now have difficulty in acknowledging. For, as the tradition of 'reversible rationalism' itself illustrates, the commonly held view that science grew up in opposition to religion is a myth.

The tradition of scientific research goes back to the Greeks and beyond. But what we now know as modern science was born in the sixteenth and seventeenth centuries in Europe. What took place at this time was a scientific revolution. Twentieth-century physicists such as Planck, Einstein and Bohr have modified the course of this revolution but they have not undone it or made Newtonian science obsolete. As historians of science have recognised, however, 'the classical-modern science built up from Copernicus to Newton made most of ancient and medieval science null and void.'[15] In historical reality as opposed to cultural myth this revolution was carried through almost exclusively by zealous Christians who were seeking not to escape their faith but to confirm and magnify it. As a few historians and sociologists have long recognised there was a particularly close association between Puritanism and the emergence of the modern scientific method. The Puritan idealisation of reason, which was itself a secularised transformation of the form of rational asceticism worked out during the Middle Ages in the great monasteries of the West, depended crucially on an act of renunciation. It depended above all on the Puritan view that it is not simply pleasure or sexual temptation which may distract the mind of the Christian from God but ordinary human affections. The duty of the Puritan was to control such affections rigorously and never to allow them to usurp the controlling power of the rational soul. To be ensnared in the world of human relationships was itself to succumb to the realm of the flesh, which was imagined as unclean. To rise above this world, and to be able to hold in spiritual contempt the emotions engendered by it, was the only route to redemption.[16]

Both our contemporary intellectual culture, and our political culture, remain deeply marked by the legacy of seventeenth-century Puritan rationalism. For the invisible ethical medium of all modern Western capitalist societies is a profound ideological hostility towards all those who proclaim the value of community, of co-operation or of intimate human relationships as opposed to economic individualism. The abstractionist, impersonal ethos of science is, as Ted Hughes suggests, one of the chief vehicles of this ideology.

It is because of the enduring association between the ethos of science and puritanical rationalism that we would do well to be wary of cultural critics who appeal unscepetically to the tradition of scientific empiricism as a remedy for our contemporary intellectual ills. Many intellectuals are sympathetic to the psychoanalytic tradition precisely because they distrust the rationalistic epistemology of orthodox science. They regard this epistemology as being intrinsically hostile to affectivity and therefore inimical to any recognition of the complexity of human behaviour and human motives. Nor should we assume that this kind of distrust is felt only by those who are not scientists themselves. In this respect we should recognise that the traditional version of 'reversible rationalism' expounded by the scientist Peter Medawar is very close to the critique of science offered recently by the non-scientist Bryan Appleyard. For both these very different thinkers implicitly see science as hostile to the human soul and seek to confine it to the realm of matter.[17] Very frequently those who dismiss such caution out of hand do so because they do not understand the intellectual power of science and are consequently less concerned to guard against its abuse. It is perhaps significant that one of the most powerful critiques of the false science associated with post-structuralist literary criticism has been made not by a literary critic but by a professor of medicine, Raymond Tallis. And it is in a book written jointly by two professors of mathematics, Philip J. Davis and Reuben Hersh, that we may find some of the most perceptive, imaginative and morally alert discussions of the dangers of mathematics. In an essay entitled 'Loss of Meaning through Intellectual Processes: Mathematical Abstraction', they offer a warning which should be widely heeded:

> Whenever anyone writes down an equation that explicitly or implicitly alludes to an individual or a group of individuals, whether this be in economics, sociology, psychology, medicine, politics, demography, or military affairs, the possibility of dehumanisation exists. Whenever we use computerisation to proceed from formulas and algorithms to policy and to actions affecting humans, we stand open to good and to evil on a massive scale. *What is not often pointed out is that this dehumanisation is intrinsic to the fundamental intellectual processes that are inherent in mathematics.*[18]

Historically speaking, awareness by scientists of the dangers which mathematical and scientific abstractions can pose to human beings and to human societies is not unusual and it is partly because of this that the traditional version of 'reversible rationalism' outlined by Medawar still has considerable cultural currency.

To express this kind of caution about science and the dangers of rationalism is to come very close in some respects to the position of Isaiah Berlin. Yet if we are to place his particular version of pluralism in perspective it is essential to recognise that Berlin himself was never able to step outside the magic circle of that rationalism whose destructive spell he attempted to anatomise. His critique of rationalism is offered, as we have seen, not as a way of challenging the values of the Enlightenment but as a kind of apologia for its excesses. It is as though Berlin believes that if repeated warnings are given about how sharp, how dangerous and how murderous the sword of rationalism has proved to be during the last two centuries, then the great rationalist enterprise may after all be redeemed from its bloody and tyrannical past and set upon a more constructive course in the future. Once again we are brought face to face with the ideological elision which lies at the heart of modern liberal pluralism. For just as Frederick Crews tacitly endorses both the values and the ethos of modern science, so Isaiah Berlin underwrites the very ideology which he so sceptically and so brilliantly interrogates. The liberal pluralism he has so influentially expounded, which sets its face with such determination against every kind of all-embracing ideology, proves, if we only pause to inspect it closely, to be conceived as a kind of distraught defence of one of the largest and most all-embracing ideologies in the whole of human history – Enlightenment rationalism itself.

To make this recognition should not prevent us from simultaneously recognising the immensely valuable contribution which both Crews and Berlin, in their very different ways, have made to the critical evaluation of modern ideologies. We should also recognise, I believe, that Frederick Crews's assumption that human nature can and should be treated as a proper subject for scientific investigation is more in tune with the contemporary *Zeitgeist* than either the traditional doctrine of 'reversible rationalism' or Berlin's particular version of pluralism. For the belief that science has a proper sphere within which alone it may legitimately work, and that this sphere *excludes* human nature, is a cultural anachronism. This argument is anachronistic for the very simple reason that it is based on an assumption about the nature of modern science which, while it was originally sound, and while it held good (against considerable opposition) throughout the seventeenth and eighteenth centuries, collapsed in the middle of the nineteenth century with the publication of Darwin's *The Origin of Species*. Until that time the notion that science did have limits, and that the great questions of human existence would always be excluded from its realm of jurisdiction, remained both coherent and plausible even though it was opposed by some Enlightenment rationalists. Only with the publication of Darwin's theory of human origins were the foundations of the traditional argument finally destroyed by science itself. Nor were some of Darwin's own followers unaware of the long-term implications of his work. Reviewing *The Origin of Species* in 1860, in terms which we might well consider ominously and revealingly militant, T. H. Huxley hailed it as a 'Whitworth gun in the armoury of liberalism' and looked forward to 'the domination of Science' over 'regions of thought into which she has, as yet, hardly penetrated'.[19] It should be noted that two of Darwin's greatest admirers, Karl Marx and Sigmund Freud, were among the many nineteenth-century thinkers who sought to carry forward the revolution which Huxley both prophesied and proselytised.

The momentous nature of the Darwinian revolution and the unprecedented scale of the intellectual upheaval which it brought about can perhaps best be judged by the evident difficulty which many Western intellectuals have had in reconciling themselves to the fact that it has taken place at all. The predicament of many liberal intellectuals in this respect is analogous to that of a hypothetical group of Russian aristocrats who, even in the latter part of the twentieth century, cannot bring themselves to believe in the reality of the 1917 Revolution and insist on constructing their world-view on the assumption that the Tsar is still in power. The anachronistic assumption that science has *agreed* limits, and that the ultimate questions of human existence lie beyond these limits, signifies the persistence of an illusion which is just as far removed from historical reality. It is especially fascinating that Peter Medawar, himself a distinguished biologist, should have resisted the implications of the Darwinian biological revolution so steadfastly. In his *The Limits of Science* Medawar writes of what he calls 'the ultimate questions' of human existence that 'whatever else may be in dispute, *it would be universally agreed* that it is not to science that we should look for answers' (italics added).[20] We should recall that the three examples of 'ultimate questions' given by Medawar are: 'How did everything begin?', 'What are we all here for?', and 'What is the point of living?' 'These,' writes Medawar, 'are the questions that children ask.'[21] For confirmation that the 'universal agreement' spoken of by Medawar is an illusion, we have only to consult the work of one of the most prominent, lucid and influential exponents of Darwinian theory among modern biologists, Richard Dawkins. The first chapter of his *The Selfish Gene* (which appeared six years before Medawar's essay) bears the title 'Why are people?' The chapter begins with the following paragraph:

> Intelligent life on a planet comes of age when it first works out the reason for its own existence. If superior creatures from space ever visit earth, the first question they will ask, in order to assess the level of our civilisation, is: 'Have they discovered evolution yet?' Living organisms had existed on earth, without ever knowing why, for over three thousand million years before the truth finally dawned on one of them. His name was Charles Darwin. To be fair, others had had inklings of the truth, but it was Darwin who first put together a coherent and tenable account of why we exist. *Darwin made it possible for us to give a sensible answer to the curious child whose question heads this chapter. We no longer have to resort to superstition when faced with the deep problems: Is there a meaning to life? What are we for? What is man?* After posing the last of these questions, the eminent zoologist G. C. Simpson put it thus: 'The point I want to make now is that all attempts to answer that question before 1859 are worthless and that we will be better off if we ignore them completely' [italics added].[22]

Dawkins goes on to make a very similar point to the one I have already made, observing that although the theory of evolution is about as much open to doubt as the theory that the earth goes round the sun, 'the full implications of Darwin's revolution have yet to be widely realized ... Philosophy and the subjects known as "humanities" are still taught almost as if Darwin had never lived.'[23]

It is not only modern biology which has crossed the traditional frontiers of science. In his *A Brief History of Time* Stephen Hawking has offered cosmological physics as a way of answering the 'ultimate questions'. He suggests that, once a complete cosmological description of the universe has been made,

> we shall all – philosophers, scientists and just ordinary people – be able to take part in the discussion of the question *why is it that we and the universe exist.* If we find the answer to that, it would be the ultimate triumph of human reason – for then we would know *the mind of God* [italics added].[24]

A quite different scientific approach to the problem of human nature, one which many observers see as far more significant than Hawking's cosmological approach, has been put forward by the biologist and neuroscientist Gerald Edelman. Edelman has attempted to formulate a general developmental theory of neural organisation and consciousness which is compatible with Darwinian biology. His theory is based on the assumption that the development of the human brain and its capacity to change its biochemical properties as a result of experience can be understood as an example of natural selection. Edelman's 'neural Darwinism' postulates that pre-existing groups of neurons and their synaptic connections are subject to continuous selection in response to environmental challenges or restraints. Although this theory remains controversial, it has been described by Oliver Sacks as 'the first truly global theory of mind and consciousness, the first biological theory of individuality and autonomy'.[25]

It is because the construction of a coherent theory of human nature has already been widely recognised as the single most important project of contemporary biological science, and because just such a project has long been implicit in the Darwinian theory of evolution, that the liberal humanist aversion to grand theories of human nature lacks a coherent rationale. In a pre-Darwinian age it would be entirely reasonable to counter the claims of psychoanalysis purely with scepticism and to place the burden of refutation on negative critiques of the kind which Frederick Crews, Frank Cioffi, Malcolm Macmillan, Allen Esterson, Robert Wilcocks and others have already offered and which I have attempted to develop here. In our own post-Darwinian era, however, the crucial question must ultimately be not whether psychoanalysis is an inadequate theory of human nature but whether it is possible to offer an alternative which does possess genuine explanatory power.

It is quite true that there are a number of seemingly powerful arguments against the construction of any such large-scale theory. But the fact that there are also many cogent objections to participating in civil government is not in itself a conclusive argument for anarchism. The danger which faces those who renounce *political* power for idealistic, pacifistic or politically moderate motives is that they jeopardise the very values they seek to preserve by placing all power in the hands of their ideological opponents. Liberal intellectuals who, out of their own moderation, distrust large theories of human nature because of their historical association with extremism, face a very similar danger. For by renouncing the *intellectual* power of theory they too jeopardise the values they seek to protect and play into the hands of the very forces they seek to oppose.

What we should recognise, I believe, is that the project of constructing a general theory of human nature – a theory which, unlike those of Marx or Freud, does have a genuinely empirical foundation – is not one which belongs purely to some speculative future. It is a project which is already under way, and which has in fact been in progress ever since the publication of *The Origin of Species*. Because of the enduring power of the orthodox position which I have called 'reversible rationalism', many liberal humanists will continue to distrust this project. I believe that they are right to do so. For our scientific tradition, as it is presently constituted, does tend to be corrosive of human aspirations and of human complexity. But it is precisely because scepticism (including scepticism about science) is necessary to the construction of adequate theories that a policy of participation is more appropriate than a policy of non-participation. For those whose distrust of theory is so great as to lead them to repudiate it altogether need have no doubt that the very large-scale theories they are averse to will be constructed without them. In all probability they will be constructed by thinkers who do not distrust theories sufficiently to make good ones, and who may be entirely without the kind of scepticism and sensitivity which are appropriate to any theory which seeks to construe human behaviour, human feelings and human motives.

To suppose that we might sustain an adequate and complex vision of human nature without resorting to theories at all would be both to ignore the pervasiveness of the creationist theory of human nature we have internalised and to underestimate tragically the value which the currency of 'theory' now possesses in our science-dominated culture. In this culture any position which is not defended by a coherent theory is, by definition, a vulnerable position – it is a position which has, in effect, already been abandoned by those who nominally occupy it.

It is for this reason, I believe, that no negative critique of psychoanalysis, however powerful, can ever constitute an adequate refutation of the theories which Freud put forward. For in scientific reality bad theories can only be driven out by better theories. What we need to recognise is that the science of matter is by no means the whole of science, and that it is, perhaps, the least important part of it. For any human culture which devotes a large proportion of its intellectual and economic resources to the investigation of the 'laws' of matter, while all the time allowing the 'laws' of human nature to remain veiled in mystery, is a culture which, by definition, operates in ignorance of its own motives. The more confidently such a culture characterises itself as rational or scientific, the more it confirms its own deep irrationality.

A culture which operates in ignorance of its own motives and which simultaneously regards itself as rational and scientific runs the risk of committing itself irrevocably to social and economic policies which, because they disregard the constraints of human nature, will end by exacerbating the very problems they are intended to solve. It is for this reason that the task of formulating a better theory of human nature than that propounded by Freud – one which, unlike psychoanalysis, *is* consonant with Darwinian biology – is so important.

What the work of some modern Darwinian theorists suggests is that the construction of such a theory is not an optional item on some future intellectual programme. It is an essential item on an intellectual programme which is already in existence and which has already been advanced in a number of significant directions.

TWENTY-TWO

The Ghost in the Psychoanalytic Machine

IT MIGHT WELL BE THOUGHT THAT, if the task of constructing an empirically based theory of human nature is one which must be undertaken within the framework of Darwinian biology, then such a theory is primarily the concern of biologists and evolutionary scientists. On this view those who are not biological scientists can do little more than wait for those who are to refine and develop the ideas which they have already begun to formulate. This position certainly seems to have some currency among those who work in the humanities. Long used to deferring to scientists, it would seem that some thinkers, even if they do accept the legitimacy of global theories of human nature, are quite prepared to leave the task of serious theory-building to others.

If this point of view were to be widely adopted, however, it would have a particularly odd consequence. For it might mean that the construction of a theory of human nature would be left primarily to those trained in the *natural* sciences – which have traditionally excluded human beings from their field of study – while those professionally engaged in what are sometimes called 'the human sciences' would make no contribution to it.

This odd situation seems undesirable for a number of reasons. Perhaps the most important of these is that, historically speaking, the contributions which Darwinian science have made to our conception of human nature have left a great deal to be desired. For although Darwin's theory provides a solution to the problem of species and an account of the development of organic forms, the many attempts which have been made to apply it to human behaviour are by no means always persuasive. While incidental insights are plentiful, Darwinian theory cannot yet offer any adequate or *comprehensive* explanation of the development of human culture or the complexity of human behaviour.

The limitations of the theory of natural selection in this respect were not always recognised by Darwin himself and they have certainly not always been recognised since. These limitations have frequently led to the formulation of extreme hereditarian theories of human behaviour such as the 'hard-core' model of human nature which was put forward by the biologist C. D. Darlington:

> Owing to inborn characters we live in different worlds even though we live side by side. We see the world through different eyes, even the part of it we see in common . . . The materials of heredity contained in the chromosomes are the solid stuff which ultimately determines the course of history.[1]

In recent years a number of influential sociobiologists have attempted to explain human behaviour in terms of similarly narrow hereditarian categories. In doing so they have contrived – as scientists frequently do – to disregard what some would see as one of the most important of all scientific principles. For instead of sceptically testing out their theories against the hardest and most refractory forms of evidence, some biologically orientated thinkers have sought out just those aspects of human behaviour which can be fitted most easily into crude forms of genetic determinism. Sociobiologists frequently observe that primates copulate; they do not frequently observe that some primates publish poetry, that other primates worship the Virgin Mary, and that others still are professional philosophers. It is just such facts as these, however, which remain anomalous and unaccounted for in neo-Darwinian biology. If we wish tacitly to maintain a theistic view of the world, this will not, of course, disturb us. But if we wish to use the theory of natural selection in order to illuminate human nature, then it is just these mysteries which must be turned into problems.*

The science of genetics *is* important and Alex Comfort is undoubtedly correct when, writing as a biologist, he reminds us that 'if we reject Mendel as bourgeois, we find that we have no beef.'[2] But what we must always bear in mind is that Mendel's theories were designed to explain how the peas in his monastery garden reproduced their species, and not why the monks in the chapel within had renounced the opportunity to reproduce theirs. The fact that neither our ascetic and religious behaviour nor our complex non-reproductive sexual behaviour can be explained by the existing theory of natural

---

* For a fuller discussion of these issues see note 1, pp. 610–3.

selection appears to indicate that some crucial element is missing from that theory. The ultimate aim of any empirical study of human nature must be to supply that momentously important missing element. It must thus set out to complete the enterprise which Darwin started by adding to his theory of the evolution of organic forms a theory which is capable of accounting for the complexity of the human imagination, the development of human culture, and the course of human history.

In this respect one of the most interesting contributions to a Darwinian theory of human nature to have emerged from within the discipline of biology itself is that made by Gerald Edelman. Behind Edelman's work on the extraordinary complexity and biological plasticity of the human brain there lies a very large theoretical aspiration. For he himself sets out to go beyond the hard-centred hereditarianism of some neo-Darwinian theory in order to complete Darwin's intellectual project. 'I have written this book,' Edelman writes in the preface to *Bright Air, Brilliant Fire,*

> because I think its subject is the most important one imaginable. We are at the beginning of the neuroscientific revolution. At its end we shall know how the mind works, what governs our nature, and how we know the world. Indeed, what is now going on in neuroscience may be looked at as a prelude to the largest possible scientific revolution, one with inevitable and important social consequences.[3]

Edelman explicitly recognises that his own theory has limitations and implicitly acknowledges that his scientific approach, which draws primarily upon the tradition of the natural sciences, leaves many aspects of human behaviour out of account. Yet even given these qualifications, the aspirations which lie behind his theory are huge and they promise – or threaten – an intellectual revolution which would transform the entire way in which we study and reflect upon our own nature.

Thinkers of a liberal humanist or pluralist disposition are likely to react to this prospect with alarm, and will point, as they habitually do, to the dangers posed by the kind of overarching theory Edelman seeks to construct. It would, I believe, be wrong to discount such warnings entirely. For Edelman's project is only likely to succeed if it incorporates the lessons which can be learned from earlier failures. The fact that the most general exposition of his ideas is dedicated not only to Darwin but also to Freud may itself raise at least a flicker of doubt in this respect. Any such doubt is not likely to be dispelled by Edelman's discussion of psychoanalysis, which includes the claim that '[Freud's] basic theses about the action of the unconscious were essentially correct'.[4] But what is perhaps even more important is that, although Edelman is a physiologist whose work is entirely concerned with the human body, and above all with the most complex part of the human body – the brain – he presents his own work as a study of the human 'mind'. Not only this but he frequently refers to the 'mind' as though it were a real entity which can be illuminated by biological research. As we have seen, the goal of the neuroscientific revolution which Edelman has announced is not to understand human nature. It is to 'know how the mind works . . .'

It is just here, I believe, that we need to question Edelman's project most carefully. It might well be thought that the project of constructing a genuinely biological theory of human nature which goes beyond psychoanalysis is one which is entirely dependent on the kind of neuroscientific and biological expertise which a scientist like Edelman is uniquely well qualified to provide. There is perhaps a sense in which this is true. But I believe it would also be true to see the success of such a project as being dependent not simply on *overcoming* intellectual difficulties but on recognising that many of the difficulties with which theorists traditionally grapple are in fact illusions of their own creation. The main task, it might be said, is not to tie new and ever more complex intellectual knots, but to untie old ones which need never have been tied in the first place.

There can be little doubt that of all the ancient and unnecessary intellectual knots which have prevented us from unravelling the strands of our own nature, the most important is the dispute as to whether theories of human nature should be based on a study of the observable behaviour of men and women or on a study of the workings of the human 'mind'. In this connection we must recall that Freud himself did not set out to provide a theory of human behaviour. As the word 'psychoanalysis' itself suggests, he set out to provide a theory of 'mind' and a very large part of his writings is given over to an attempt to construct a model of the internal structure and 'mechanism' of 'mind'.

The problem of 'mind' and 'behaviour' has not only occupied psychoanalytic theorists, but it has also perplexed philosophers, academic psychologists and anthropologists alike. The anthropologist Lévi-Strauss has assumed the problem solved and has put forward what is, in effect, an entire theory of human nature which is based solely on hypotheses about the internal structure of the 'mind'. The philosopher

Gilbert Ryle has argued that the very concept of 'mind' is a philosophical illusion hailing chiefly from Descartes and sustained by logical errors and 'category mistakes' which have become habitual.[5] More recently cognitive psychologists have found in the computer an ostensibly mind-like machine which they have frequently treated not simply as a metaphor but as a model for the human mind.[6] More recently still the philosopher Colin McGinn has argued that the very nature of the human mind precludes us from finding a solution to the mind–body problem.[7]

The difficulty which has come to surround the problem of 'mind' and 'behaviour' is, I believe, largely illusory. But because that difficulty now looms so large over any attempt to construct a theory of human nature we can scarcely proceed as though its shadow did not exist, for to do this would merely give rise to even greater intellectual confusion.

Much of the intellectual confusion which already surrounds this issue derives directly from that universal modern predicament to which I have already referred – our culturally orthodox lack of familiarity with the orthodoxies of our own culture. For the view that the secrets of human nature can be unlocked only by a theory of mind is, although commonly held by secular philosophers and psychologists, essentially a Christian idea. This idea has its most significant source in the ancient Christian-Platonic belief that human beings are made up of two separate entities: an animal body which was created by God, and a mind, spirit or soul which was given by God uniquely to Man.

It was on this ancient theological doctrine that the discipline of psychology was first constituted. For psychology was originally itself a branch of Christian theology, the word having been created in the fifteenth century by theologians who were engaged in the study of the human soul.[8] In the eighteenth century the word began to be applied to more 'scientific' forms of analysis, and at the end of the nineteenth century it was adapted by Freud and applied to his own methods of analysis and treatment. By this time the theological origins of psychology had been all but forgotten. But the theological and moral assumptions which had always been associated with it had survived almost intact and continued invisibly to determine the way in which both Freud and many other psychologists approached the problem of human nature. If we are to appreciate the immense significance of the invisible moral theology which still underlies the thought of many of the most influential secular thinkers in the twentieth century, then we must first reconstruct that theology in its original form.

The most influential Christian psychologists never needed to accord themselves that name, for there is a sense in which Christianity is itself a psychological theory. This theory was first formulated by Jesus and Paul, and it was developed over the centuries by monks, bishops, theologians and Christian scholars, who sometimes found in the philosophy of Plato an ideal vehicle for their own distinctive theology. Right at the very heart of Christian psychology there lies the issue of the relationship between the flesh and the spirit – between the animal body of men and women and their supposedly immortal and non-animal soul. In view of the nature of Christian doctrine, this relationship could not be seen as anything other than a profoundly moral one. In one succinct formulation of Christian orthodoxy the function of the 'mind' or 'soul' was to act as 'God's viceroy' in man. By disciplining and subjugating the unruly desires and appetites of the flesh, it would, in an ideal world, force man to behave in a way that constantly reflected his inward spiritual nature. Reason would play its proper role of chastising concupiscence, and by chastising it, would make men and women chaste. In reality, however, such an ideal subordination of the carnal body of human beings to their divine soul was by no means always realised. For, through Adam's fall, sin had entered into the world, and men and women's fleshly appetites were now in a constant state of rebellion against the pure spirit which had originally been designed to rule over them at all times.

This did not mean, however, that the unique spiritual essence of human beings had been destroyed. For the fact that men and women might at times behave like animals, and copulate with every evidence of animal lust and enjoyment, was not to be taken to indicate that they actually were animals. It was, rather, a sign that they had allowed their 'real' spiritual nature to be overcome by their carnality and had thus failed to reflect their inward essence in their outward bodily behaviour. In this respect at least the behaviour of men and women might very well be an extremely unreliable guide to their true nature, and might, indeed, bear no relationship to it at all. For this reason, although human behaviour was always a matter of concern to the Christian moralist, it was never a stumbling-block for the Christian theologian. For whenever the unruly, violent or lustful behaviour of men and women seemed to offer evidence that their 'real' nature was not reasonable, spiritual and chaste, the theologian could deal with this evidence by the simple expedient of disregarding it – or, to be more precise, by invoking the myth of the Fall in order to explain it away. Whatever men and women might do, or whatever they might say that they felt, desired or lusted after, these actions and utterances could never be taken as a reliable guide to their 'true' nature. For although the purity of the soul might be defiled by lustful and concupiscent behaviour, it always remained susceptible to cleansing, and could never be destroyed except by God himself.

It would be wrong to suggest, however, that this faith in the reality of men and women's spiritual soul ever led Christian psychologists to entirely disregard the evidence which was offered to them by human behaviour. For just as it was possible for the rebellious forces of the body to overthrow the authority of the divine reason which had been ordained to rule within human beings, so it was also possible for men and women to use their rational souls in order to chastise concupiscence and thus subdue and control their fleshly appetites. The Christian had, indeed, been enjoined by Paul to 'put to death' these fleshly appetites and to live the life of the pure spirit. When Christians sought to obey this injunction and led lives which were reasonable and chaste in all outward respects, then the evidence of their behaviour, far from being disregarded, was treated in an entirely different way by theologians, and was immediately construed as an outward sign of their inward reality and of man's 'true' spiritual nature.

It was, however, this inward spiritual reality, and not any behavioural manifestation of it, which always remained the real focus of Christian psychology. For since all men and women were deemed to be subject to Original Sin, no form of human behaviour, however apparently sinless, could ever quite convey the true reality of the spirit. Spotless behaviour might well be a reliable indicator of the general nature of that reality, but it was not the pure spirit itself. For the spirit was an immaterial entity, imperceptible to mere bodily senses. In view of this its real nature could be approached most closely only by the rational soul itself, meditating in silence upon its own attributes and defining these in purely abstract and rational ways, undefiled by the corruptions of the flesh.

It was this view of human beings' God-given and rational soul which would eventually lead, in the fifteenth century, to the creation of psychology as a specific area of theological inquiry. More importantly still, however, it was this view which was preserved almost intact when, some two hundred years later, the modern discipline of psychology began to emerge. At this stage in its development psychology was seen as the scientific counterpart of Newtonian physics, and it is crucial to recognise that the fundamental assumptions of both these disciplines were still quite explicitly grounded in Christian theology. Just as Newton had seen himself as exploring the manifestations of God's rationality in the physical world, so psychologists saw themselves as students of the same divine rationality as it was manifested in the postulated 'non-physical' world of the mind. In the words of Gilbert Ryle:

> It was supposed that . . . as Newtonian scientists studied the phenomena of the one field, so there ought to be scientists studying the phenomena of the other field. 'Psychology' was supposed to be the one empirical study of 'mental phenomena'. Moreover, as Newtonian scientists found and examined their data in visual, auditory and tactual perception, so psychologists would find and examine their counterpart data by counterpart non-visual, non-auditory, non-tactual perception.[9]

Strictly speaking, as Ryle's words imply, the original programme of psychology granted to psychologists no licence to investigate those aspects of human behaviour which are accessible to the ordinary observer. Secular psychologists, like the most rigorous kind of Christian psychologists, were expected to concern themselves solely with the immaterial 'reality' of the mind itself.

In practice, however, secular psychologists are no more likely than theologians to keep their speculations unsullied by the evidence of their senses. For, as Ryle remarks, 'a researcher's day cannot be satisfactorily occupied in observing nonentities and describing the mythical.'[10] The official strict programme of psychology was never abandoned completely, but it did undergo a series of expedient adaptations. In making these adaptations secular psychologists unconsciously followed the patterns of thought which had been established by their theological predecessors and which had been deeply internalised into their own intellectual outlook. Just as Christian theologians had concluded that certain kinds of 'pure' behaviour were related more closely to the inner essence of the soul than other kinds of behaviour, so psychologists came to the conclusion that certain kinds of human behaviour betrayed the structure of internal mental phenomena more directly than others. Since such capacities as memory, intelligence, learning and perception all seem to be possessed of the necessary ghostly characteristics – they do not immediately betray their unclean physicality or the marks of their animal origins – eighteenth- and nineteenth-century psychologists singled out these as legitimate areas of study. In this way rationalist psychology redefined some aspects of human behaviour as 'mental' in order that it might facilitate its own researches. But the orthodox pre-Darwinian psychologist would no more have dreamed of using the observable sexual behaviour of men and women as a key to the reality of 'mind' than would an orthodox theologian have regarded fornication or adultery as forms of 'spiritual behaviour' or as evidence of the real nature of the human soul. Secular psychologists thus tacitly preserved the Christian-Platonic view of the soul's 'complete incontamination', and continued to regard the larger part of human behaviour, particularly that which could be deemed emotional, sensual or immoral, as being entirely irrelevant to their own concerns.

This tacit definition of the 'mind' or 'soul' as an area of purity and abstract rationality was challenged by some philosophers, and it would eventually be challenged in a particularly interesting way by Freud. Partly because of his Darwinian orientation, Freud's concept of mind was significantly less chaste than any which can be found in the mainstream of rationalist psychology. We have already encountered William Wheeler's view that the theories of orthodox psychologists at the turn of the nineteenth century 'read as if they had been composed by beings that had been born and bred in a belfry, castrated in early infancy, and fed continually for fifty years through a tube with a stream of liquid nutriment of constant chemical composition.'[11] When it is contrasted with the kind of orthodox theories Wheeler refers to, Freud's 'sexualisation' of the concept of mind does indeed seem radical and revolutionary. Yet, as we have seen, Freud did not repudiate many of the central doctrines which had always been associated with the traditional theological concept of mind. Rather he took over this traditional concept and attempted, as it were, to extend it downwards. He continued to regard rational consciousness as the distinctive quality of human beings and, following the psychobiologism of Ernst Haeckel, tended to regard sexual and sadistic impulses not as an intrinsic part of the 'conscious soul' but as a residue of man's animal past which had now been relegated to the 'Unconscious'. In this way Freud preserved the moral dualism of the Judaeo-Christian tradition, but now located that dualism within the mind itself. Whereas theologians had traditionally seen human beings as riven by a conflict between their invisible rational soul and their all too visible sexual desires and sinful behaviour, Freud's attempt to extend the concept of mind compelled him to see sexuality itself as a mental phenomenon. He went on to apply systematically to the entire realm of visible sexual behaviour the same principles of interpretation which Judaeo-Christian psychology and theology had developed in order to safeguard the belief in an invisible rational soul. Just as they had disregarded the evidence of observable human behaviour, and seen it as an entirely unreliable indicator of internal mental phenomena, so Freud, inheriting this profoundly sceptical attitude, set out to study not the whole range of sexual behaviour or the sexual fantasies in which men and women consciously engage, but the invisible mental events which allegedly lie behind such behaviour. Just as theologians had traditionally seen the 'spiritual behaviour' of virtuous men and women as but an imperfect and often misleading extrusion of the internal reality of the pure spirit, so Freud saw the sensual behaviour of men and women as an imperfect and often misleading extrusion of that internal psychical reality which he believed ultimately to be the sole legitimate object of scientific psychology.

The immediate result of Freud's attempt to extend the traditional concept of mind was thus not to render a larger area of human behaviour susceptible to scientific observation but to effectively remove the 'flesh' from the realm of the visible and redefine it as belonging to the realm of the invisible. Throughout his theoretical writings Freud maintains this attitude of modified theological traditionalism and sees himself not as a scientific investigator of human behaviour, but as a student of the human soul – *die Seele*. He repeatedly refers to this 'soul' as though it were a corporeal body extended in space and, as we have seen, a large part of his work is given over to an attempt to lay hold of this ghostly body and to describe its anatomy, its ghostly digestive system and its intimate internal functions by using models drawn from electricity, hydraulic systems and other complex physical phenomena. This can be seen both in the fabulous mechanical excesses of the early *Project* and in his later work where he postulates the existence of a 'psychical apparatus' – a mind or soul which inhabits and in some mysterious way pilots the body. Throughout his writings Freud continues to describe, anatomise, particularise, and occasionally anticipate Lacan by presenting diagrams of the internal shape and dynamics of the mind. It was in the course of his pursuit of these speculative studies of the human soul that Freud convinced himself of the reality not only of such well-known concepts of mental geography as the ego, the superego and the id but also of numerous abstruse mental processes which he then named: cathexis, decathection, counter-cathexis, object-choice, condensation, displacement, imago, object-representation, constancy-principle, fusion, defusion, anaclitic model, mnemic residue.

All these and many other terms were invented or adopted by Freud (or his translators) not to describe any observable entities or behaviour, but to postulate the existence of the spiritual entities and mental processes which he 'needed' in order to construct his theory of mind.

In his selection of problems Freud never ceased to be influenced by his theory of mind. A very significant portion of his work was given over to the study of dreams, jokes, errors and slips of the tongue – all areas of human behaviour which might be held to afford the investigator some kind of privileged access to invisible 'mental phenomena'. His therapeutic interests were presented as part of the same programme. Freud believed that the minds of his patients had, in effect, been turned inside out as a consequence of their 'neurosis':

> If we throw a crystal to the floor, it breaks; but not into haphazard pieces. It comes apart along the line of its cleavage into fragments whose boundaries, though they were invisible, were predetermined by the crystal's structure. Mental patients are split and broken structures of the same kind . . . They have turned away from external reality, but for that very reason they know more about internal, psychical reality and can reveal a number of things to us that would otherwise be inaccessible to us.[12]

Even though Freud's biologically based concept of mind extended the range of behaviour which could be considered psychologically significant, this behaviour was held to be relevant only because it could be regarded as a luminous extrusion of 'internal psychical reality' – a representative of the spirit-world of the mind which had inadvertently become incarnate in a bit of physical behaviour. The kinds of behaviour to which psychoanalysis does attribute significance in this way are frequently odd, obscure or abnormal. What ordinary men and women do, what they believe, and what they say that they feel – which is to say the larger part of human behaviour and human history – is treated as though it constituted suspect evidence, or as though it belonged merely to some external, mechanical realm which bears no direct relationship to 'mental phenomena' and can therefore hold no interest for the psychologist. It is for these complex traditional reasons that the psychoanalytic movement has very often disregarded the very research into human behaviour which it has helped to inspire. At the same time psychoanalysts, in their doctrinally inspired search for hidden or cryptic manifestations of the 'unconscious mind', have frequently failed to study with sufficient attention the complexities of ordinary human consciousness.

In all these respects orthodox psychoanalytic theorists are in very much the same position as those spiritualists or theists whose psychological assumptions Freud inherited. Secure in their faith in an invisible psychical reality, they have very little motivation to consider the merely visible, particularly when this is a source of counter-instances to their own theories. Psychoanalysts normally defend this position by maintaining that through 'clinical experience' they have privileged access to this invisible reality. For, as Charles Rycroft writes, the data of psychoanalysis 'are derived not from the direct observation of human behaviour, but from the analyst's experience of a particular kind of therapeutic relationship invented by Freud'.[13]

It must be recognised that the therapeutic relationship which Freud invented was itself designed according to a model suggested by his theory of mind. In constructing this abstruse theological theory Freud never ceased to be influenced by the central tradition of Judaeo-Christian psychology, and never succeeded in emancipating himself from the contempt in which this tradition held the evidence offered by human behaviour. For this reason Freud, in his attempt to construct a theoretical model of human nature, was very often in the position of the astronomer who is so engrossed in making mathematical calculations in his notebook that he considers his observatory a distraction and his telescope an impediment to science.

When, more than half a century before the psychoanalytic movement was born, Darwin had set out to solve the problem of species, he had never ceased to be acutely aware of the theological origins of the disciplines of geology and biology in which he worked. Although he never succeeded in throwing off this religious inheritance entirely, and eventually capitulated to a secularised form of Christian teleology, Darwin always endeavoured to divest his chosen disciplines of the abstruse theological complexities which had grown up around them, and to study anew that evidence which he could see with his own eyes and touch with his own hands. Later, when he attempted to account for his success in formulating the theory of natural selection, Darwin said simply that he 'saw what the clever men had missed'. At the end of the nineteenth century Freud attempted to bring about a similar revolution in the discipline of psychology. Freud, however, was unaware of the theological origins of his own discipline. Rather than divesting that discipline of its needless theological complexities, he saw it as his duty to multiply those complexities. His theory failed because, too often, in his anxiety to construct an abstract and intellectually complex theory of mind, he missed what simple men could see.

Freud's theories provide one very significant example of the manner in which ancient theological attitudes towards the problem of 'mind' and 'behaviour' continue invisibly to determine the shape of modern theories of human nature. It is important to recognise, however, that whereas Freud challenged the traditional view of mind as an area of purity and abstract rationality, the mainstream of our rationalist intellectual culture has preserved the orthodox Judaeo-Christian view in an almost intact form. There is no clearer example of the direct continuity between traditional theological rationalism and modern secular rationalism than that provided by the emergence in the latter part of the twentieth century of structuralism and post-structuralism. Since the structuralist movement and its more recent derivatives have made a very significant contribution to shaping the intellectual environment in which any new theory of human nature must be worked out, the traditionalism which underlies its supposed 'postmodernism' needs to be borne in mind.

The very fact that structuralist theories succeeded in attracting such a large number of adherents throughout the Western world during the 1960s and the 1970s would in itself seem to indicate a certain compatibility between structuralist doctrines and older and more revered elements in our cultural tradition. Observers of the structuralist movement, indeed, like observers of the psychoanalytic movement, have sometimes noted a powerful religious element in the way the structuralist 'faith' has been spread by its advocates. This religious dimension of the structuralist movement was certainly visible in the group which formed itself round Jacques Lacan. At his most extreme Lacan projected himself not simply as a messiah but as an inscrutable god. The young psychoanalysts who were his students frequently referred to him as 'God the Father', and one of his former patients, Danièle Arnoux, has even recounted how she sought out Lacan rather than enter into analysis with one of his followers on the grounds that 'it was better to deal with God than his saints'.[14] It is not only in relation to Lacan that such cryptic religious traditionalism may be discerned. For the case of Claude Lévi-Strauss, who is generally agreed to be the 'purest' of all structuralist thinkers, provides an even more interesting example.

The anthropologist Adam Kuper has described how, during the 1960s, several leading British anthropologists succeeded in 'converting' some of their most promising students to the new structuralist doctrines. He adds that their success

> was facilitated by the almost religious enthusiasm of some of the proponents of Lévi-Strauss's ideas. 'Structuralism' came to have something of the momentum of a millennial movement and some of its adherents felt that they formed a secret society of the seeing in a world of the blind. Conversion was not just a matter of accepting a new paradigm. It was, almost, a question of salvation.[15]

The significance of such religious fervour can be appreciated only if we examine Lévi-Strauss's own ideology. For at the very heart of Lévi-Strauss's intellectual system there lies a belief which is so unimpeachably orthodox that it has often entirely escaped observation. He maintains, with no less rigour than the strictest kind of theologian, that human beings are made up of two separate entities, whose theological origins he minimally disguises by describing them as 'the organism' and 'the intellect'. In his view the sole business both of the psychologist and the anthropologist is to investigate the operations of the 'intellect', for it is by this means alone that the distinctive essence of human nature – '*l'esprit humain*' – can be uncovered. Throughout his work, Lévi-Strauss implicitly characterises this 'human spirit' in the same way that theologians have traditionally characterised man's God-given soul – it is orderly, chaste and rational, and apparently undefiled by any form of emotion or desire. Indeed Lévi-Strauss makes it quite clear that the study of human emotions is irrelevant to anthropology as he conceives it:

> As affectivity is the most obscure side of man, there has been the constant temptation to resort to it, forgetting that what is refractory to explanation is *ipso facto* unsuitable for use in explanation . . .
> Actually, impulses and emotions explain nothing: they are always results, either of the power of the body or the impotence of the mind. In both cases they are consequences, never causes. The latter can be sought only in the organism, which is the exclusive concern of biology, or in the intellect, which is the sole way offered to psychology, and to anthropology as well.[16]

It should be said that Lévi-Strauss's scepticism about explanations which invoke affectivity as a causal factor is, in one respect, entirely legitimate. To claim that people resort to redemptive rituals because they afford relief from guilt is not to offer an explanation; it is simply to beg the question as to what the nature of guilt is, and why particular rituals offer relief from it. But what is distinctive about Lévi-Strauss's position is that his methodology makes it impossible to ask such questions. For, as can be seen from the passage quoted above, he proceeds from the truistic observation that human emotions are difficult to explain to the arbitrary conclusion that anthropologists should disregard emotional factors. Instead the human animal is divided into the fictions of 'intellect' and 'organism', the intellect being held to exist in some obscure and mystical way outside the organism. Our emotions are, apparently, neither part of the organism nor of the intellect. They appear to exist in some undefined limbo where no human science may legitimately address its attentions.

The ontology presented here bears no relationship to any possible post-Darwinian view of the human organism. The main difference between Lévi-Strauss's view of the 'human spirit' and traditional theological views is that, whereas theologians tended to regard the human soul as being composed of a kind of immaterial essence of rationality and goodness, Lévi-Strauss attributes to it the very characteristics of order, regularity and pattern which are found in mathematics, and sees it as being composed of unconscious mental 'structures'. As Edmund Leach puts it in his study of Lévi-Strauss, the object of analysis 'is conceived as a kind of algebraic matrix of possible permutations and combinations'.[17] Like his theological predecessors Lévi-Strauss sees the distinctive reality of 'man' as residing entirely within this invisible spiritual entity. Like them he is thus compelled to adopt an extremely radical attitude towards the evidence which is provided by human behaviour. For, since the days when the fundamental tenets of Judaeo-Christian psychology were first formulated, men and women have not, by and large, become any less unruly, any less violent or any less lustful, and their behaviour still seems to provide evidence that their 'real' nature is far from being chaste, rational and orderly. Lévi-Strauss deals with this evidence by adopting the simple theological expedient we have already encountered – he disregards it. Because Lévi-Strauss is a rational intellectual living in the middle of the twentieth century he does not, of course, appeal to the doctrine of Original Sin in order to justify this ancient strategy. But it is precisely because he is a rational intellectual living in the middle of the twentieth century that he does not need to. For both that doctrine and the Judaeo-Christian psychology which is associated with it have now become so deeply internalised into our habits of thought that they have come to form a kind of invisible intellectual environment from which secular thinkers may draw assumptions without ever recognising that they have done so and without it ever being noticed by their readers.

Lévi-Strauss's greatest difficulty is thus not in persuading his readers to disregard the evidence of human behaviour, but in finding evidence to support his own theory of the particular character of the human soul. In past centuries traditional Christian missionary-anthropologists who took to journeying among savage and barbarous peoples in remote corners of the earth often experienced similar difficulties in verifying their theories. For although there was, among the lewd and obscene rituals of primitive tribes, much evidence to be had for the truth of the doctrine of Original Sin, there was very little of that chaste and rational behaviour which might be expected from those in possession of God-given souls. Such difficulties were not insuperable, however. For if these missionaries examined the taboos of primitive cultures closely enough, they would invariably discover some faint glimmerings of moral awareness, some sign that the immortal soul had not been entirely lost. Kneeling down beside these glimmerings of God, they would at once begin to fan them into the true flames of the spirit. Before very long the natives in question would be persuaded to desist from their barbarous rituals, fornicate less frequently or less openly, and begin to exhibit more and more of that kind of virtuous behaviour which alone offers confirmation of the tenets of Christian psychology.

Lévi-Strauss's difficulties, it must be conceded, are far more acute than those of the traditional Christian missionary. For whereas Christian theology has always characterised the human soul as both wholly *good* and wholly rational, Lévi-Strauss, in an unconscious attempt to disguise from himself the moral nature of his own theology, has found the essence of the human soul to reside purely in its rationality. Since he believes that this rationality takes a specific logical and algebraic form, this means that no ordinary behaviour, however good it may be, can satisfy his need for evidence. What his theories demand from the members of primitive cultures is evidence not so much of good morality as of good mathematics. For if the 'human spirit' is indeed logical and algebraic in its essence, then it follows that even primitive cultures will provide some evidence of this. Expectations which are too reasonable, however, are very often thwarted. While it is moderately easy to find evidence of algebraic skill and absorption in abstract intellectual problems in the classrooms of the Sorbonne, the same task becomes a great deal more difficult when it is pursued in the jungles of South America.

Historically speaking, however, poverty of evidence has never been an obstacle to faith. Lévi-Strauss's solution to an apparently intractable theological problem is to claim that the abstract logical skills of the members of primitive cultures have been secreted all the time in their myths and marriage customs without either them, or any other anthropologist, ever having been aware of this fact. Using his own Freud-like powers of rational exegesis and abstract ingenuity, Lévi-Strauss proceeds to analyse these myths and marriage customs in such a way that the evidence which is required by his hypothesis emerges from them. His approach to myth derives directly from the kind of linguistic analysis pioneered by Jakobson. Just as structural linguistics treats phonemes as though they were the smallest components of an autonomous entity called 'language', so Lévi-Strauss breaks down myths into something which he calls at one point 'mythemes', which are held to be the smallest components of *'l'esprit humain'*. As structural linguistics disregards the affective and semantic content of language, so Lévi-Strauss disregards entirely the affective content of myths, together with their surface meaning. Following Jakobson he maintains that myths are made up of elements which are related by a process of abstract binary logic, opposing pairs of concepts such as culture and nature, the raw and the cooked, the fresh and the rotten, honey and ashes.

It is in this manner that the 'human spirit' is shown to be no less pure, rational and logically astringent in primitive cultures than it is in modern post-Cartesian cultures. It is by assuming the existence of an invisible spiritual entity which is separate from the human organism, and attributing to it the characteristics of order, regularity and systematic logic, that Lévi-Strauss quietly, and with very little fuss, undertakes a massive repudiation of what the non-specialist might regard as the historically constituted subject-matter of anthropology. For anthropology, as Lévi-Strauss conceives it, is not a study of human societies in all their historical, economic, religious and political dimensions. Still less is it a study of human behaviour or of the relationships which exist between parents and children, women and men, leaders and led. Anthropology is seen rather as consisting solely in the study of unconscious processes of logic which are both hypothetical and invisible. It is thus converted into a branch of speculative psychology. Any myths or customs which anthropologists have traditionally had difficulty in explaining are immediately assumed by Lévi-Strauss to be vehicles for invisible mental structures, and as such worthy of 'structural analysis'. Any aspect of human behaviour which cannot be so redeemed by intellectuality is cast by Lévi-Strauss into the category of the 'organism', or regarded as emotional and therefore of no interest to the student of the intellect. The consciously held beliefs of men and women, their emotions, their everyday conduct, their habits of work, the wars that they fight, their family life and their attitudes to children, may be matters of concern to the biologist, the historian, the economist or the novelist. But they cannot – or should not – be the concern of the anthropologist who, in Lévi-Strauss's view, is nothing other than the scientist of the human soul.

The concealed religious traditionalism of Lévi-Strauss's attitude towards human behaviour has generally escaped observation by his colleagues. One exception is the American anthropologist Stanley Diamond. As Diamond writes: 'Lévi-Strauss emerges as a type of religious and philosophical thinker, a theologian in spite of himself, who cannot accept an apocalyptic notion of God and thus adopts an anthropological stance in order to ground his arguments in "reality".'[18]

Lévi-Strauss's intellectual vision, indeed, merely intensifies, and attempts to modernise, what have always been the central tenets of Judaeo-Christian rationalism. Just as Paul, one of the most fiercely ascetic of Christian psychologists, came to perceive his own renunciation of the flesh as the very core of selfhood, and could experience other men and women as 'real' only to the extent that he could see them as purely spiritual, so Lévi-Strauss, in offering his own apocalyptic vision under the guise of a theoretical apprehension of social reality, effectively purges human beings of all trace of carnality. Falling victim to the most subtle form of cultural chauvinism, the most refined form of racialism, he proclaims the humanity of the 'savage' only after he has delivered him from his body, his emotions and his customary behaviour. He embraces the savage only after he has recreated him in his own image – the wholly rational, bodiless image of the twentieth-century intellectual.

In Christian psychology, as I have tried to show, a moral theory of how men and women ought to behave became the basis of a theological theory of how men and women had actually been created. This theory maintained that human beings contained within them a pure and rational spiritual entity which was the very essence of their nature. The underlying moral theology of Christianity has been preserved in a tacit form both by structural anthropology and, in a more complex and subtle form, by psychoanalysis. For both these theories are premised upon the notion that the human animal can be divided into rational and non-rational parts. Both assume the superiority of the supposed rational portion of the human being, and both see its function being to control, suppress or subjugate a non-rational part of the self, which is deemed to be inferior and animal.

It is certainly true that the ethos of psychoanalysis is significantly different from that of structural anthropology. The crucial difference between the two philosophies is that, while structuralism tends to maintain the ancient dualism of mind and body, and to see emotions and physical impulses as residing in some way outside the mind, psychoanalysis, as we have already seen, extends the concept of mind 'downwards' and characterises one particular region of the mind as being rich with impulses, emotions and appetites. Yet it would be wrong to conclude that psychoanalysis offers a theory of human nature of a fundamentally different kind from that found in the work of Lévi-Strauss. For both theories are mentalistic philosophies which reject the evidence of human behaviour. Both are dualistic and postulate a basic antinomy between entities which resemble the 'flesh' and the 'spirit'. In this way the underlying moral theology of the Judaeo-Christian tradition has been tacitly preserved. Neither structural anthropology nor psychoanalysis can, for this reason, be seen as original or autonomous psychological theories. Rather they must be regarded as adaptations of traditional Judaeo-Christian psychology. Although the different claims about human nature put forward by Freud and Lévi-Strauss clearly conflict, the dispute between them is not substantially different from the dispute between Christian rationalists and Christian traditionalists in the eighteenth century (see above, Chapter 14).

It is because our traditional doctrine of 'mind' is itself the vehicle of a particular theory of human nature that any attempt to complete Darwin's project by applying the theory of natural selection to human nature must, if it is not to be ensnared by orthodoxy, begin by repudiating that doctrine. If Gerald Edelman's work develops in this direction, and joins a neuroscientific account of the brain's functioning to a theory of human behaviour, it may very well make an enduring contribution to the study of human nature. So long as it continues to be a theory of mind, a theory which respectfully seeks to incorporate the findings of Freud into its own outlook, its large ambitions will not be realised, even though Edelman's contribution to our understanding of the brain will remain – and will remain significant.

TWENTY-THREE

The Behaviour of the Body

ONE OF THE MANY PARADOXES which lies behind Freud's achieve-ment is that it was only through his membership of the 'church' of rationalism that he was able to find the intellectual security he needed in order to launch an attack on some of the most repressive doctrines of that church. For this reason Freud's vision, no less than Lévi-Strauss's, remains deeply marked by a form of rationalist apocalypticism. His central and anxious mission was not to liberate the sensual body but to redeem it. Although he radically extended the scope of psychology in order to deal with phenomena which had often been excluded from it, he did this not so much by sexualising the realm of the intellectual as by intellectualising the realm of the sexual. In Freud's compulsive use of technical terminology, in his religious commitment to the doc-trine of mind, and in the abstruse theological complexity of his 'metap-sychology', we are confronted not by a truly scientific enterprise, but by a more traditional project which is also found in the works of such thinkers as Norman O. Brown, Herbert Marcuse, Jacques Lacan and Roland Barthes – a doomed and tragic attempt to reconstruct at the level of the intellect a sensual identity which has been crucified at the level of the spontaneous and vital body. Once again the pattern is characteristic of apocalyptic thought, in which the body is redeemed only after it has first been purified.

The disguised apocalypticism and transcendentalism which is a feature of all mentalist philosophies is the first and most important reason why the attitude towards human behaviour which is contained in the doctrine of mind must be rejected in any genuinely scientific attempt to formulate a neo-Darwinian theory of human nature. For mentalist philosophies are essentially negative in their approach to visible evidence. The strict para-Newtonian psychologist must, as we have seen, concern himself solely with the non-physical events which are alleged to lie behind human conduct. If there did indeed exist some autonomous non-physical realm, possessed of its own structure, processes and laws, then this programme might be eminently reasonable. But if no such realm exists, and if, as any naturalistic view of the universe would suggest, the key to human nature may be discovered only by the patient observation and interpretation of human behaviour in all its complexity – and by studying the human body, especially the functioning of the human brain – then the programme is both superfluous and misleading. Indeed, any psychologist who adhered rigidly to the para-Newtonian programme might well be compared to the spy who, having intercepted a coded message on his radio, decides he may find out the meaning of that message only by switching the radio off and speculating on the inner essence of its transistors. The fact that the spy might describe his speculations as government secrets and the para-Newtonian psychologist might describe his as psychology should not dissuade us from cataloguing both as ghost-stories, since the events they describe belong evidently to the realm of the occult.

In their enterprising desire to steal the riches of human nature from 'inside' the mind, both Freud and Lévi-Strauss have failed to notice that the said riches, far from being locked up in some psychical treasury, have lain all the time on the outside, open to observation and free for the taking. For as Gilbert Ryle has argued, the association of 'mental phenomena' with some non-physical, exclusively inward reality rests on a category mistake. The overt behaviour of human beings is not a clue to the working of minds. According to Ryle's argument, it *is* those workings:

> Abandonment of the two-worlds legend involves the abandonment of the idea that there is a locked door and a still to be discovered key. Those human actions and reactions, those spoken and unspoken utterances, those tones of voice, facial expressions and gestures, which have always been the data of all other students of men, have, after all, been the right and only manifestations to study. They and they alone have merited, but fortunately not received, the grandiose title 'mental phenomena'.[1]

Abandonment of the two-worlds legend means, strictly speaking, the end of the discipline of psychology. For once psychologists give up the idea that there exists some occult psychical reality which it is their special duty to study, then their field is no longer 'mind', or those aspects of human behaviour which are ghostly or 'mind-like' enough to be considered non-physical, but the whole range of human behaviour and human history.

The theoretical enterprise which would result would in no way resemble that proposed by the narrow evangelists of behaviourism. For a diminished and mechanistic view of human nature such as behaviourists espouse will result only if we adopt a diminished and mechanistic definition of human behaviour. The expression of religious ecstasy, the accumulation of capital, the writing of *King Lear*, the witch-trials of the seventeenth century, the telling of an obscene joke and the conduct of a love affair are all examples of human behaviour and there is no reason why they should not be treated as such.

One common objection to behaviourism is that, in its most extreme form, it tries to tell people that they do not have any thoughts or feelings which they keep to themselves and do not exhibit in any way.[2] Such an approach is indeed objectionable for it seeks tacitly – or sometimes quite loudly – to deny the importance of what we normally refer to as our 'inner life'. The position adopted by such behaviourists is untenable since there are many sensations and feelings which are ultimately private and which, while they are palpably real to those who have them, can never be experienced by others. The particular sensation of happiness or strangeness or *déjà vu*, or even simply of hotness, which I have when I go to a certain corner of the South of France is my own and can never be either experienced by, or transferred to, anyone else. The same can be said of practically any human sensation, from the pain of being scorched to the pleasure of being caressed, or the complex fulfilment which is afforded by religious worship. To deny that such sensations or feelings are real is to deny what all those who are not philosophers know to be true.

The attitude towards human nature which I am advocating here, however, is not a form of behaviourism and it makes no such denial.[3] For there is no reason to dispute the commonly held view that human beings have an 'inner life' and that this inner life is made up of feelings, sensations, memories, beliefs and convictions which can have great complexity and enormous power. Our sense of self tends to be intimately connected with this inner life, which we experience as something which is both deeply personal and private. As Thomas Traherne put it:

> A secret self I had enclosed within
> That was not bounded with my clothes or skin.[4]

Traherne's words communicate extremely well the idea we have of the self as an intimate area which is ultimately hidden from other people. At the same time, however, his words also exemplify one of the most interesting and significant capacities of human beings – the ability we generally possess (and which we exercise with varying degrees of willingness and success) to express our 'inmost' feelings in terms which are comprehensible to others and thereby make public the very areas of the self which we sometimes experience as intimately private.

One of the reasons that we are able to do this is that what we habitually refer to as our 'inner life' is not always as exclusively inward as we sometimes tend to assume. A feeling of grief would generally be seen as something belonging to our inner life. Yet in most cultures, and even in many parts of our own, grief can be a very public emotion, powerfully expressed in tears and outward displays of sorrow. By shedding tears we do not, of course, transfer our own inner sensation of sorrow to other people. But we do communicate feelings very effectively. At a much more complex and sophisticated level poets, playwrights and novelists are often judged according to their success in dealing with the 'inner lives' of their characters, or indeed in expressing their own most intimate feelings. The novel has been interestingly described as an 'anti-solipsistic device' and this formula might very well be applied to any form of verbal expression which successfully conveys complex and powerful feelings. For one of the satisfactions afforded by literature is to be found in the way it allows readers to recognise as a part of common humanity feelings which they had previously regarded as individual or private.

Thus, although we habitually categorise emotions as belonging to our 'inner' life, it would be more accurate to recognise that they are constantly being translated from the private to the public sphere and that in many respects they belong to the latter just as much as they do to the former. Acute observers of human nature intuitively rely upon this fact, and when we praise writers for their insight into the 'depths' of other people's characters what we are often responding to is their ability to record and intelligently construe the intricate 'surface' of other people's behaviour. As Henry James once remarked, 'What is character but the determination of incident? What is incident but the illustration of character?'[5]

Though novelists may sometimes appear to be particularly gifted students of human nature, the capacity to 'read' other people's feelings is not a special or unusual capacity. It is characteristic of the human species and is probably one of the most biologically useful of all the intellectual abilities which we have developed over the millennia of our evolution. The psychologist Nicholas Humphrey has even argued that the human intellect has not evolved in order to allow us to indulge reflexively in its own abstract pleasures, or to allow us to solve practical problems of an economical or technical nature. Over and against these conventional explanations, Humphrey suggests that the complexity of the human intellect is directly related to the complexity of human social structures. It is his suggestion that we, in common with all primates, have evolved our imaginative intellect – which includes all those 'emotional' capacities we tend to abstract from our intellectual powers and label as 'sympathy', 'insight', 'reason' and 'feeling' – primarily in order to enable us to predict and respond to the enormously complex behaviour of other organisms and of our own social group. Our intellect enables us to assess personal, social and political strategies, to shape or modify the behaviour of others, and to order our social affairs in such a way that we may continue to reproduce our own species successfully.

Although it is far from clear that this is the *primary* function of the human intellect, as Humphrey suggests, it does seem reasonable to claim that one of the main functions of the intellect is to enable us to be our own intuitive and practical social psychologists.[6] When people say, as they frequently do, 'I know exactly how you feel,' they are making use of this evolutionary capacity. At the same time they are putting into practice intuitively the same kind of bodily epistemology which the Rylean position implies. For the conviction of one person that they understand the feelings of another is certainly not based on the belief that they have been granted special access to the invisible mental events which supposedly lie behind these feelings. It is invariably based on close attention to other people's behaviour – or, to use Gilbert Ryle's terms, to 'those human actions and reactions, those spoken and unspoken utterances, those tones of voice, facial expressions and gestures' which philosophers and psychologists frequently ignore, but 'which have always been the data of all other students of men'.

Part of the Rylean position can be clarified further if we take the example provided by human thought. Practically everyone would accept that if a person is thinking he is engaging in something which would normally, and quite properly, be described as 'mental activity'. Since a great deal of the activity we tend to describe as 'thinking' is conducted privately, in a kind of silent, internal monologue, we frequently characterise thought itself as a process which is in some way intrinsically private and silent. And having characterised it in this way we tend to construct a figurative realm in which it supposedly takes place, which we refer to as 'the mind'. We underline this sense of privacy when we maintain, as we frequently do, that we cannot see into another person's mind any more than we can read their thoughts. Yet while it is quite possible to think privately in internal soliloquy it is equally possible to think out loud in perfectly audible soliloquy. But thinking out loud is presumably a form of mental activity in just the same way as thinking silently is. And if it is true that I am engaging in mental activity when I think out loud in audible soliloquy, then it must also be true that I am engaging in mental activity when I think out loud in other contexts – when I am conversing or debating or negotiating or agreeing or disagreeing with other people, for example – or when (as now) I am writing a book which other people can read. The more sceptically we review our own 'mental activity', indeed, the more we are driven to recognise that something we habitually characterise as private and unobservable is in fact very often public and accessible.

If we take an evolutionary perspective on the development of language this should not be in any way surprising. For it seems reasonable to suppose that language, which is now the primary medium for human 'mental activity', evolved as a method of communication and not, in the first place at least, as a device for private cogitation. Speaking to ourselves is a relatively late and sophisticated accomplishment. Yet so powerful is the dogma of the ghost in the machine and the 'private-theatre' concept of mind, that most people forget this most of the time. As Ryle observes, they 'even come to suppose that there is a special mystery about how we publish our thoughts instead of realising that we employ a special artifice to keep them to ourselves'.[7]

By pointing out that a great deal of our 'mental activity' is not private and unobservable, as the official Cartesian doctrine maintains, what Ryle is trying to stress is that the principal theatre of the mind is not the private one of our dreams and imaginings, however important this may be; it is the public theatre of our actions and utterances. It is none other than the world of human relationships and human history, and it is by studying this public world that the mystery of human mental activity – which we misleadingly call the human 'mind' – may best be understood.

In his rebuttal of mentalist philosophies Ryle is thus deliberately endorsing the kind of epistemology which we all use every day in our relations with others. The fact that we may base theories of human nature on the evidence provided by human behaviour does not in itself, of course, guarantee the scientific value of these theories. But what Ryle's argument does imply is that any theories of human nature which repudiate the evidence of behaviour and refer solely or primarily to invisible mental events will never in themselves be able to unlock the most significant mysteries of human nature.

One of the questions that remains is why Ryle's arguments, which are put forward in *The Concept of Mind* in such depth, and with such lucidity and vigour, have failed to bring about the revolution in human knowledge they might reasonably have been expected to.

One answer is that Ryle's objection to mentalist philosophies is not adequate in itself. For, although his argument effectively dissolves the largest and philosophically most weighty part of the mind–body problem, a significant residue remains. This is the problem posed by the 'subjective' aspect of our own experience – our sensations, our memories, our consciousness, our sense of self. One of the most interesting questions is whether this residue is indeed the trace – or perhaps even the essence – of 'mind'. Ryle has argued cogently and interestingly that it is not.[8] But a very significant number of contemporary philosophers, neuroscientists and psychologists have taken the opposing view. Indeed, far from disappearing from the scene, as one might expect in the post-Rylean era, the philosophy of mind appears, in the eyes of some observers at least, to have usurped the throne so recently occupied by the philosophy of language and to have been installed, as Simon Blackburn has put it, as the 'Queen of the philosophical sciences'.[9]

The focus of much of this recent work has been the problem of consciousness. This problem has been formulated in a variety of different ways. In a much-quoted passage from a much-cited paper, the philosopher Colin McGinn put the matter like this:

> We know that brains are the *de facto* causal basis of consciousness, but we have, it seems, no understanding whatever of how this can be so . . . Somehow, we feel, the water of the physical brain is turned into the wine of consciousness, but we draw a total blank on the nature of this conversion. Neural transmissions just seem like the wrong kind of materials with which to bring consciousness into the world, but it appears that in some way they perform this mysterious feat. The

mind–body problem is the problem of understanding how the miracle is wrought . . .[10]

As has already been noted, McGinn goes on to argue that the very nature of our minds precludes us from finding a solution to this problem. His philosophical pessimism on this issue, however, has not been universally accepted and attempts to solve the mind–body problem have continued. One of the most interesting of these is Nicholas Humphrey's *A History of the Mind*.[11] This luminously argued book is, in effect, an answer to McGinn's paper. When it appeared in 1992, Humphrey's argument was roundly and predictably rejected by McGinn, who made a number of detailed criticisms of it.[12] But one reviewer in particular managed to convey both something of the flavour of Humphrey's book and its unusual nature. Describing the book as a 'persuasive tour-de-force', Julian Dibbell wrote that

> Humphrey unfolds this story so suspensefully it would be like telling the end of a mystery novel to outline his hypothesis in any detail. But it doesn't ruin any surprises to note that his basic premise – that consciousness emerged from the wriggling of primordial skin – brings a pungent whiff of the carnal into cognitive science's often creepily body-hating atmosphere.[13]

Although Humphrey himself offers his book as an attempt to solve the entire mind–body problem, this is misleading. For what he actually does, as Julian Dibbell implies, is to use the theory of natural selection to suggest that the problem of consciousness is not fundamentally a problem which belongs to the philosophy of *mind*, but to the evolutionary biology of the *body*. The problem of 'mind' is, in effect, an illusion produced by our failure to understand the evolutionary history and the neurophysiological complexity of the human organism.

If I am right in characterising Humphrey's achievement in this way, then he has effectively dissolved the final residue of dualism even though a number of the details of his hypothesis remain highly speculative, and open to the kind of objections which McGinn has made against them. For, by showing that any account of the origin of consciousness must address itself to the evolutionary development not of the mind nor even of the brain, but of the entire body and all its sensory apparatus, Humphrey implicitly demonstrates that the pursuit of consciousness as an aspect of some non-physical, non-bodily 'mind' is a chimaera.

Some of the reasons for saying this will emerge most clearly if we consider Colin McGinn's confident claim that 'We know that brains are the *de facto* causal basis of consciousness.' The most obvious objection to this claim, as we know from the pickled remains of Lenin, Einstein and Jeremy Bentham, is that the human brain, once unhitched from the body of whose complex nervous and sensory system it is a part, is neither intelligent nor, indeed, conscious. This objection is by no means as trivial as it might appear to be. For, anatomically speaking, the brain reflects the structure of the body and is in one sense an image of the body – a neural chart onto which every part of the body is intricately mapped in a form which is then projected back onto the periphery of the body with its richly innervated organs, musculature and skin.[14] The brain and the rest of the body form a complex, functionally indivisible unity, and just as it would be wrong to attribute the faculty of sight exclusively either to the eye or the brain, so it is fundamentally misleading to characterise the brain as the causal basis of consciousness. To do this is to commit a category error of the kind made by the visitor to the House of Commons who, after seeing a number of Members of Parliament in session, reports that he has seen a democracy; or the visitor to King's Cross Station, or Clapham Junction, who claims he has seen Britain's railway system. Human beings are intelligent not because they are piloted by a non-physical entity called the mind or soul, nor even because they are controlled by a physical entity called the brain, but because of the extraordinary neurophysiological complexity of their entire bodies. It is certainly true the brain is an extremely important part of the human organism, structurally more complex than any other part, or indeed than any object in the known universe. But in so far as it is logically correct at all to characterise our brains as 'intelligent' we should also speak of ourselves as having intelligent eyes, intelligent ears, intelligent noses, intelligent tongues, and, in comparison with those of other species, and judging by the richness of their innervation, exceptionally intelligent hands. In the end, however, none of these descriptions can be justified biologically. For the human organism is an indivisible unity. Both consciousness and intelligence are properties, ultimately, not of the brain or of any organ or set of organs, but of both acting together. We are intelligent because we have intelligent bodies. We are conscious not because we have minds, but because consciousness is one of the properties of the particular kind of intelligent body we have evolved during the course of evolutionary history.

This way of dissolving the mind–body problem has been implicit in the theory of natural selection ever since it was first formulated. In view of this it would be only reasonable to inquire why it has not found more favour among Darwinian thinkers, and why we had to wait for considerably more than a century from the time that *The Origin of Species* was published until the first coherent Darwinian dissolution of the mind–body problem was offered by Nicholas Humphrey. We might further inquire why one of the foremost Darwinian thinkers of our day, Gerald Edelman, frequently refers to the 'mind' as though it were a biological entity – or as though the Cartesian ghost in the machine, which supposedly acts as the invisible pilot of the body, were real after all.

To the extent that Edelman's work actually focuses on the structure and function of the human brain, his use of mental concepts may be regarded, in part at least, as merely residual. But his habit of using the essentially Cartesian, or pre-Darwinian, terminology of 'mind' to expound an explicitly post-Darwinian theory of the function of the brain is fraught with philosophical hazard. It provides an excellent example of how difficult we find it to come to terms with the notion that we are *all body*, and how ready even Darwinian thinkers are to smuggle a form of mind–body dualism back into their theorising by resorting to what might be called 'brain–body' dualism. So familiar has the concept of mind become that we regard it as a 'fact' of human existence and treat it and other mentalistic concepts as though they were raw empirical data, or 'common sense', while simultaneously allowing them to eclipse much of the real data of human behaviour. We even construct our own identity in terms drawn from a dualistic, essentially theological theory of the human organism and it is this, more than anything else, which makes it so difficult for us to think clearly and objectively about human nature. We find it psychologically difficult to think fluently or coherently in any other terms. For while we may, with relative ease, free ourselves from ancient and fallacious theoretical perceptions of the material universe – for these scarcely affect our own identity – it is much more difficult to free ourselves from fallacious theories about our own nature. For these theories are frequently not only invisible but *constitutive* of our very identity.

If orthodox dualism accurately reflected our nature and we thought with our minds – abstract non-physical thinking-systems which, because they are the very essence of rationality, can be infinitely and effortlessly reconfigured so that they correspond at all times with reality – we would, in theory at least, find it relatively easy to abandon our old pre-Darwinian theories about human nature and formulate a new theory. But one of the most significant of all the discoveries made by modern biologists researching into human learning effectively confirms the position which I have argued here – that we think with our bodies.

Perhaps the clearest account of the research which makes it possible to formulate such a conclusion has been given by the biologist and neuroscientist Steven Rose. Much of Rose's own work over the past two decades has run parallel to that of Edelman and has been concerned with exploring a hypothesis outlined most influentially by the Montreal psychologist Donald Hebb in his book *The Organization of Human Behaviour*, which was published in 1949. What Hebb proposed, in effect, is that whenever conditioned reflexes are established in an organism by a process of learning, a new anatomical substratum is laid down in the brain by a physiological process in which weak or even non-functional synapses are strengthened by biochemical modification or by permanent changes in their electrical properties. Learning, in other words, is not simply something which is impressed upon a passive brain. The process of learning might actually be cognate with a process in which the cellular structure of the brain is permanently modified.

Donald Hebb's theory has proved to be a classic scientific hypothesis – comparable, perhaps to Harvey's prediction that microscopic examination of the body would reveal that an exchange of blood took place between veins and arteries by way of invisible 'pores'. For just as Harvey's hypothetical pores eventually became real capillaries, so recent research into the neurophysiology of learning has established beyond doubt that the kind of structural changes in the brain which Hebb hypothesised do in fact take place. Steven Rose has summarised the results of the neuroscientific research into this problem over the last two or three decades:

When an animal learns – that is, when it confronts some novel environment, some new experience which requires it to change its behaviour so as to achieve some goal – specific cells in its central nervous system change their properties. These changes can be measured morphologically, in terms of persistent modifications to the structure of the neurons and their synaptic connections as observed in the light or electron microscope. They can be measured dynamically, in terms of localised, transient changes in blood flow and oxygen uptake by the neurons during the processes of learning or recall. They can be measured biochemically, in terms of a cellular cascade of processes which begins with the opening of ion channels in the synaptic membranes and proceeds by way of complex intercellular signals to the synthesis of new proteins which, inserted into the synaptic and dendritic membranes, are responsible for these morphological changes. And they can be measured physiologically, in terms of the changed electrical properties of the neurons that also result from their altered membrane structures.[15]

What applies to animals, and the way in which they modify their behaviour in response to novel situations, also applies to human beings and the manner in which we build mental maps or theories. Because our intellectual habits – our habits of belief, and our habits of thought – are, no less than our muscular habits, physically encoded in complex patterns of interconnecting neuronal groups within the brain, patterns which become stronger each time they are used, it is extremely difficult for us to *unthink* our orthodox assumptions and to rethink old problems in terms of radically new categories and assumptions. *Unlearning* cultural responses, orthodoxies and theories to which we have been habituated since the cradle is something which comes no more naturally than dancing the foxtrot backwards or systematically inverting the word-order of every sentence that we speak.

If, lapsing back into the creationist world-view, we say, as I have done here, that we find it *psychologically* difficult to think about human nature other than in creationist terms, we exemplify the very problem we seek to analyse. It is because this psychological difficulty is actually a *physiological* difficulty, determined ultimately by the structure of the human brain, and the biological changes which take place in the human brain as a result of any form of learning, that our predicament is so general and that we, like Gerald Edelman (and indeed like Darwin himself), tend to relapse into pre-Darwinian categories whenever we discuss that part of nature we have theorised about most extensively and with the greatest emotional involvement – ourselves.

TWENTY-FOUR

Beyond Psychoanalysis

ONE OF THE OBSTACLES which stands in the way of the Darwinian or neo-Darwinian programme to construct an adequate theory of human nature is science itself. For modern science is, as Bacon conceived it in the seventeenth century, and as it has subsequently developed, 'a legitimate, chaste and severe form of inquiry'.[1] In these words we can see the influence of Puritanism on scientific thought at its most direct. An attitude of chastity is certainly fitting for the scientist probing into the secrets of mother nature. It is, however, in no way appropriate to the study of carnal humanity. When we confuse the pursuit of knowledge with the pursuit of virtue it is usually at the expense of truth.

Historians of science inadvertently point to the religious fault which runs beneath the epistemology of modern science when they talk of the 'mathematical empiricism' of Kepler and Galileo, or the 'rational empiricism' of Boyle and Newton. For a rational empiricist is no more a true empiricist than a vegetarian omnivore is truly omnivorous. Although rational or mathematical empiricists are bound to disavow idealism, they remain crypto-idealists. For they are committed to accepting the testimony of their senses and their experience only to the extent that this can be formulated according to rationalist or mathematical models. Any experience which cannot be assimilated in this manner into a universe of rationality is tacitly denied or repudiated.

Throughout the scientific revolution, Christian scientists such as Descartes, Newton and Boyle not only repudiated or ignored a great deal of evidence in this manner, they also divided nature into different areas and focused on particular aspects or properties of it in order that they might more easily measure and thus mathematise it. In adopting these partial approaches they effectively broke the complex unity of nature into tiny fragments which could not easily be reassembled into any coherent picture. But whereas Christian rationalism had led to this *microscopic* approach to science, in which nature was divided and dissected before it was analysed, Darwin's own much larger conception of empiricism led him to recognise that any truly scientific theory of nature could not be formulated from any other point of view than a *macroscopic* one. His own task was therefore clear. It was to develop a theory which would itself help him to laboriously piece together the fragments of the vast picture which had been broken up by Christian rationalism. Only by disregarding artificial disciplinary boundaries between botany and zoology, between geology and biology, and by viewing the whole of nature in a historical perspective, was Darwin able to theorise himself into a position where he could reclaim nature from rationalistic abstraction and see the entire coherent picture. It was this holistic approach which enabled him to discern for the first time the complex and subtle relationships which existed between the structure of every organic being and that 'of all other organic beings with which it comes into competition for food or residence, or from which it has to escape, or on which it preys'.[2]

The difference between the *microscopic* analysis of Christian scientists and the *macroscopic* approach adopted by Darwin was both dramatic and radical. Whereas microscopic analysis was essentially transcendental and creationist in its conclusions, Darwin's macroscopic approach was, in almost all cases, truly scientific and truly empirical. The revolutionary significance of Darwin's shift in perspective can be summed up in a single example. Abstracting a flower from the dark tangle of its earthy roots and the sticky sex of its stigmata, the nineteenth-century theologising botanist would point to the symmetry of its petals as evidence for the existence of a pure-minded, pattern-loving deity. It took a Darwinian perspective to establish that the flower was crucial to the plant's reproductive cycle and had evolved its particular form in response to the sexual preferences and anatomical proportions of pollen-bearing insects.[3]

As Freud himself came near to perceiving, it is Darwin's regenerate science, rather than the fragmented theologising science of Bacon or Newton, which must serve as a model for those who study human nature. For truly scientific empiricism, of the kind which is necessary to the construction of any adequate neo-Darwinian theory of human nature, cannot be chaste. Nor can it allow itself to restrict its attention merely to those aspects of human nature which can be construed in narrow, rationalistic terms. But although Freud challenged the chastity of science in a more interesting manner than any other thinker who has claimed, and sometimes been accorded, the title of 'scientist', his challenge was broken in its very conception both by his mentalism and by his parallel compulsion to subject emotional and erotic behaviour to a process of purificatory rationalisation.

Freud's rationalism is directly reflected in his evident intellectual disdain for the most ordinary levels of human behaviour. Any naturalistic account of the process which Freud labelled as 'repression' would be likely to conclude that it is not something which is mysterious or elusive, something which may be conveyed only in the Latinate doxologies elaborated by psychoanalysis. Repression seems on the contrary to be something which is wrought amid the shoe-scuffing and the hurt pride, the tantrums and the slammed doors, the dirty word and the black look, the red eyes and the smarting face, the stinging rebuke and the averted gaze which we have all experienced as child-victim or parent-perpetrator, or parent-victim or child-perpetrator, and in which there is nothing ennobling, nothing numinous or distinguishing, nothing which will confer upon the investigator the aura of holiness or the halo of the transcendental. By virtue both of his mentalism and his biologism, however, Freud was able to sweep almost all such ordinary behaviour beneath the psychological carpet and discourse instead on the metaphysical mysteries associated with the internal and invisible transactions of the 'mind'.

Because of the power of theories, whether they be of the psychoanalytic type or of the kind we conceal in 'common-sense', to eclipse human behaviour, and because of the rationalistic dullness of our own imagination, we have, to a quite extraordinary degree, actually failed to notice how little childhood behaviour is considered in psychoanalytic theory (including supposedly empirical theories like Bowlby's), and how much is genially – or contemptuously – ignored. Academic psychologists, who are often themselves wedded to rationalistic theories of various kinds, have for the most part been reluctant to recognise this. But some have applied the most profound lesson of empiricism to their own discipline. One outstanding example of such research is to be found in the work of John and Elizabeth Newson. In their studies of modern child-rearing behaviour they have documented in rich detail 'those aspects of child-rearing which *parents themselves* take to be important'. Their books, which quote generously and extensively from interviews conducted with parents, have every claim to be regarded as one of the most valuable of all pieces of modern sociological research. The Newsons' implicit assumption that 'ordinary mothers' are theoretically innocent should be treated sceptically. But their research has unusual strength. This can be seen above all in their freedom from the psychologist's customary arrogance, and the respect which they show for the insight and understanding of those who are not psychologists:

> Fundamentally our principle is that the mother is the expert on her own child. She knows more about him than anyone else; she knows about him in more situations than anyone else. Much of her knowledge is available from no other source . . . The function of this research, then, is simply to tap a rich source of information which already exists but which is too often ignored: the ordinary mother's ability to examine her own behaviour and her own feelings . . .

As the Newsons themselves observe elsewhere, 'so far very few theories of child-rearing have been subject to the inconvenience of being reconciled with the empirical evidence.' Such is the magnitude of their achievement that any empirically based theory of human nature is likely to be indebted to them.[4]

The close study of child-rearing behaviour, while undoubtedly important, is by no means the only significant area of investigation. Indeed it is only if we set childhood development back into a much larger context that we are likely to avoid the kind of abstractionist fallacies which are characteristic of Freudian thinking. In this respect we should recognise that a holistic approach to the problem of human nature is not a Romantic indulgence but a scientific necessity. It is also entirely in accord with the approach to the mind–body problem which I have already outlined. For if we follow the radical anti-Cartesianism of Ryle, we must assume that the whole range of human behaviour, from winning wealth to waging war, from poetry to prostitution, is a legitimate subject for neo-Darwinian theory. Nor can there be any reason why theorists should not draw freely upon the works of other observers of human nature, from priests, playwrights and propagandists to anthropologists, historians and feminists. Those theorists who succeed in overcoming the intellectual's disdain for the ordinary and the unclean are also likely to draw on more vulgar sources. Not only will they accord much more significance to observable sexual *behaviour* than psychoanalysis does, but they will also give due attention to the obscene folk-humour of our culture and to the realm of sexual fantasy.[5]

It might be objected that, by widening the range of admissible evidence in this way, we will only succeed in making our task hopelessly difficult and ensuring that any conclusions we draw will be impossibly complex. If empiricism were actively hostile to all forms of theory then this might well be the case. Investigators would simply be bewildered by the sheer weight and variety of evidence available to them. But it is because empiricism at its best does not disdain the organisational power of theory that it can afford to remain open to the evidence provided by the full range of human behaviour and to accommodate even the most unruly facts of human nature. Indeed, by refusing such openness, and by treating artificial disciplinary boundaries as though they corresponded to the real structure of intellectual problems, we have, up to now, effectively ensured that the problem of human nature cannot even be formulated, let alone approached with a coherent theory. Like pre-Darwinian botanists we have studied people as though they were autonomous organisms which can be analysed by dissection. Because our unacknowledged purpose has been to preserve the creationist view of human nature which was so profoundly threatened by Darwin's theory of evolution, we have insisted on adopting a microscopic approach to human nature rather than a macroscopic one. In an effort to simplify our task and lend a spurious precision to our hypotheses, we have studied not our own nature but certain aspects of it which we have artificially abstracted and delimited. We have studied not human beings but human beings without one or several of their most vital dimensions – without a history or without a significant religious tradition, without dependent family relationships or without sexuality, without emotions or without a mammalian nature, without a sense of humour or without a determining physical and economic environment. Above all we have often written about human beings in a language which no man or woman speaks and which few are expected to understand. At a certain extreme we have surrounded our beliefs with a difficult scientific prose whose secret purpose is not to communicate, but to intimidate and impress.

In modelling our approach to human nature not on the holistic perspective of Darwinian biology, but on the fragmented approach of rationalistic science, we have effectively removed the object of analysis from our field of vision. At the same time, in attempting to substitute for the richness, subtlety and complexity of ordinary language an artificial scientific or technical-sounding language, we have renounced the most accurate and the most sensitive instrument we have for analysing our own nature.

If we have indeed mistaken the part for the whole, then far from easing our task we have made it much more difficult. Instead of solving real problems we have frequently created non-existent ones. Adopting the posture of the rational and dispassionate observer in order to clear our vision, we have sometimes ended by converting human nature into a replica of our own rationalistic ideals; form, structure, rationality – these become the deodorised and hygienic abstractions to which human nature must be reduced. In the end we do not divide human nature in order to understand it. We divide it because secretly we do not want to understand it. If we did we might make the terrible discovery that we are only human after all, the only animals in the whole of evolution who like to pretend that they are not animals.

In this we resemble the seventeenth-century Puritans whose scientific ethos we have adopted as our intellectual ideal. For it was in order to avoid making this terrible discovery that they turned their eyes upwards in order to study the mathematics of the heavens, after which they began to discern the rational plan of God in every part of nature. The evidence which could have confuted their creationist belief in an omniscient and benevolent God was not, for the most part, either abstruse or hidden. It teemed in every village pond, grew quietly in every meadow and every orchard, swarmed in every hive, and decayed on every autumn fruit tree. It was written in blood on every page of every history book, carved on every gallows, and screamed out in agony from every engine of torture. Yet so powerful was the doctrine of creation, and so subtle and complex the concepts of 'evil' and of 'Original Sin' which had been elaborated by Christian theologians, that seventeenth-century natural philosophers could perceive these rich stores of evidence only by viewing them through creationist theory. Since this particular theory defined almost all the most puzzling phenomena of nature and of human nature as being without ultimate significance, they were almost universally treated by natural philosophers as being irrelevant or insignificant, with the result that these same philosophers ceased to 'see' them in any important sense at all.

Many of the most puzzling phenomena of the natural world were eventually explained by Darwin. But although Darwin attempted to include human beings in his theory of evolution, he did so only by excluding from consideration some of the most refractory problems of human nature and human behaviour. We have not needed to build any new theories to hide these problems, for they had been quite adequately hidden centuries ago by the theory of creationism. Our own intellectual achievement has been to hide this theory. We have hidden it in psychoanalysis and in Marxism, in existentialism and in structuralism. We have even hidden it in some aspects of Darwinian thought itself. Failing to recognise the religious origins of the very rationalism we continue to idealise, we have bewitched ourselves with reason. Having hidden God inside our theories without noticing that we have done so we have tried to use those theories to eliminate the last traces of God from the universe.

The most convenient method of accounting for our failure to do this satisfactorily is to blame our theories. A much more radical approach, however, is to consider sceptically the very notion we have of 'reason'. One explanation of why rationalism might be the wrong method to use for exorcising religion is offered by the philosopher Mary Midgley. Noting the rationalist denigration of all forms of feeling, she writes that 'it is the admission, not the ignoring, of the part played by feeling in thought that still alarms the academic mind.'

> We need to say firmly and repeatedly, against Hume, and also against the tide of our times, that the mere presence of an emotional factor in any kind of decision does not take it out of the realm of thought. All our thinking involves emotional factors as well as rational ones, just as every physical object has size as well as shape. These are not alternatives. The presence of one does not mean the absence of the other. The kind of emotional need that we have to see the universe as ordered is not something alien to thought, nor is it only its biological cause. It is also its conceptual condition. The need is a single need with two aspects.
>
> More deeply, this whole cleft between reason and feeling – this official division of our nature into radically distinct emotional and rational elements – with which European philosophy long worked and which Hume sharpened to the point of suicide, is a disastrous error. It hides essential organic connections in the middle ground, structures common to our thoughts and feelings. And this middle ground is specially important for very large metaphysical questions concerning things like the kind of order we need to believe in.[6]

One way of developing Midgley's insight is to note that, although modern rationalists are usually unable to give any satisfactory definition of reason or any explanation of why it should be opposed to feeling, religious rationalists, with whom they seem to have something in common, have no such difficulty. Traditionally, from the time of Paul and Plato to the time of St Augustine and beyond, reason was imagined as a part of the soul, and one of its main functions, as we have already noted, was to chastise concupiscence. This is implicit in Paul and explicit in Augustine. Concupiscence was not imagined exclusively as the arena of sexual lust, but it was also the whole of man's impulsive, fallen being, which was frequently understood to include the feelings – especially unreligious 'bodily' feelings and 'earthly' affections which might distract the mind from God. The role of the rational chastisement advocated by the early Christians was to overcome this lower nature. 'And they that are Christ's,' as St Paul put it, 'have crucified the flesh with its affections and lusts' (Galatians 5: 24, Authorised Version). If we inquire how it was that a part of 'man' was imagined as being able to 'chastise', or 'crucify' another part, we will find that the ancients were actually thinking in metaphors, as they frequently did, and that this metaphor sometimes involved personifying both the rational soul and the body (or the analogous elements). 'Reason' in this respect was imagined as a god or angel who had taken up residence in the human body which was itself sometimes imagined as an animal or a beast in need of control and discipline.

The implications of this go very deep indeed. For, at the very heart of the historical concept of reason, we find concealed nothing other than the view of human psychology which is central to creationist theory; we find what should perhaps be known as 'beast–angel dualism'.[7] According to this view the purpose of reason is not to accommodate or understand or explain human nature. It is to control or subjugate the more unruly aspects of it – or even to deny or negate them.

Alex Comfort, uttering the battle-cry of all campaigning rationalists, has urged that 'we cannot leave any patches of straw unthreshed because God happens to be nesting in them.'[8] Comfort's words are bracing indeed and summon us to perform even sterner feats of reason than we have in the past. What Comfort has evidently not considered, however, is the possibility that God has proved so elusive and so difficult to eliminate from our theories because he has been nesting all the time in the threshing-machine itself. He has been hiding in the very instrument of reason.

If we are indeed to thresh every patch of straw systematically and scientifically we need to employ a more sensitive instrument than that which has been bequeathed to us by rationalism. For rationalist epistemologies, of the kind which were originally developed by Plato and eventually employed by the Puritan scientists who carried through the scientific revolution of the seventeenth century, cannot accommodate human feelings and, indeed, are actively hostile to many aspects of human nature. If we seek to enlarge the scope of science to deal with the problems of human nature which have traditionally been excluded from it, we need an epistemology which does not repudiate or deny significance to any aspect of reality merely because it is emotionally laden, erotically charged or considered to be degraded by its ordinariness or its association with common humanity.

Many would question whether any theory of human nature constructed in terms of such an epistemology could ever be regarded as truly 'scientific'. Behind such scepticism there usually lies the idea that any attempt to deal with human feelings is traditionally not science and probably not true.[9] If we were to allow the tradition of Christian or post-Christian rationalism to maintain a monopoly on the use of the term 'science' – a term which simply means 'systematic knowledge' – then this kind of scepticism would inevitably triumph. We would do well to note, however, that every scientific discipline must, if it is to remain a genuine science, recognise the level of mathematical abstraction which is appropriate to its subject matter, and not engage in abstractions which go beyond this level. It is entirely possible to think systematically, coherently *and* scientifically about aspects of nature without resorting to mathematics at all. Darwin's theory of evolution is an example of such thinking. There is no good reason why human nature cannot be studied in the same way, providing we eschew mentalism and adopt a truly biological epistemology.[10]

One further objection which is sometimes raised against such views is that all science depends on scientists' ability to remove their own nature and their own feelings from the objects which they study. In the words of the quantum physicist Erwin Schrödinger:

> Without being aware of it and without being rigorously systematic about it, we exclude the Subject of Cognizance from the domain of nature that we endeavour to understand. We step up with our own person back into the part of an onlooker who does not belong to the world, which by this very procedure becomes an objective world.

The point has been interestingly developed by Bryan Appleyard. 'Galileo's discovery,' he writes, '. . . was that an extraordinarily effective way of understanding the world is to pretend that we do not exist':

> Few faiths, cults or institutions can have made such a bizarre and extreme demand of their adherents. It is precisely as if some sect had insisted only that its followers believe they were invisible and all else would

follow. Such a faith would be confined, we assume, to a few eccentrics and inadequates. Yet science's demand is even more extreme, and we do not notice our own acquiescence, our own eccentricity. And we do not notice because, astonishingly, the demand produces results. It works.[11]

It is because any science in which theorists treat themselves as both the subjects *and* objects of their thinking goes against the entire renunciatory pattern of the kind of puritanical ethos which Appleyard describes, that the very idea of a science of human nature is sometimes resisted so fiercely.

The suspicion which 'hard' scientists often show towards psychologists in this respect is understandable. For one of the things which is problematic about psychology is that, as well as sharing with the natural sciences the aim of solving problems, and divining the significance behind the apparently arbitrary, it also shares with poetry and art something of their capacity both to arouse the pleasure of recognition and to work powerfully on individual feelings. For while physicists and chemists focus attention on aspects of matter which are far removed from everyday experience and emotional involvement, psychologists do not – or rather should not. The more closely and accurately a physicist describes the structure of a particle of matter, the more remote will the terms of that description be from his or her own emotions and nature. As a true believer in the ethos of scientific objectivity wrote in the 1940s, 'The stars have no sentiments, the atoms no anxieties which have to be taken into account. Observation is objective with little effort on the part of the scientist to make it so.'[12]

When psychologists confront human nature, however, they are dealing with something in which they themselves participate. Their own desires, anxieties, inhibitions and fantasies are a part of human nature. To the degree to which these are not merely individual and idiosyncratic, the more closely they approach human nature, the more they will find that they confront their own nature. The objective study of others which ostensibly leads outwards in impersonal terms thus simultaneously leads inwards in terms that are intimately personal. In a science where the knower is, in a sense, cognate with the known, this pattern is natural and inevitable. The task of psychologists – or of theorists of human nature – is eternally to hold in balance the intimately personal nature of their science with its more objective, problem-solving aspects. They must above all resist that hard-centred mysticism which would import into the science of human nature ideals of remoteness, impersonality and mathematical abstraction which are appropriate only to the science of matter. The love of impersonality and mathematical rigour is entirely appropriate to physics and chemistry, which eschew the study of organisms and their behaviour in favour of studying the relatively simple structure of matter, but any attempt to transfer to the study of human beings that love of mathematical abstraction which is the necessary attribute of the physical scientist brings with it the risk – one might better say the certainty – that the science which results will be in some way hostile to its subject; the rich complexity of human nature will be reduced to formulations appropriate only to the simplicity of matter.

That the dangers of applying mathematics to human beings and human culture are not always recognised can be seen from the proliferation of pseudo-mathematical equations, algorithms and abstractions which are now commonly encountered in post-structuralist or post-modernist writing about literature or human nature. The lack of moral scruples shown by many literary critics about such false science contrasts interestingly with the moral sensitivity of one of the mathematicians who has thought most carefully about the 'mathematical spirit':

Human suffering must not be abstracted. This should be the first law of ethics, the Golden Rule.
    An absurd commandment, when you think about it. If it could conceivably be carried out, it would destroy, in one blow, all applications of mathematics to the human sphere. Gone would be money, economics, laws of damages, insurance, operations research, statistics, medicine, social planning, military technology, and strategy. Our lives would be primitive and naive, unrecognisable.
    In my mind it is no accident that the great evils of the period 1933–1945 were perpetrated in a country that was the world leader in theoretical science and mathematics. It was not necessary for the policy makers to have understood mathematics; it sufficed that a certain spirit – part of which was mathematical – was in the air . . .
    If the major unsolved problem of the history of Western civilisation is to account for the collapse of the Roman Empire, then surely the major problem of contemporary history is to account for the Holocaust. The narrative aspects of the events in Germany during 1933–1945 are still being assembled. Alongside the narratives have been many attempts at interpretive histories. Such interpretations have been organised along a few dominant themes. Jung suggested the resurgence of the 'Wotan

Archetype'. Wilhelm Reich suggested the suppression of genital sexuality. Jean-Paul Sartre suggested intellectual jealousy. Erich Fromm pointed to the desire to control, and to the necrophilism of Hitler. Elias Canetti suggested that the German inflation of the early 1920s, which introduced huge, unreal numbers, disturbed the relationship between the abstract and the concrete. George Steiner suggested that Jewish monotheism, Christian piety, and Marxist messianism set perfectionist goals which mankind found impossible to achieve, and that the Holocaust was a violent reaction against these ideals.

I will add one more vision of perfection to Steiner's list: the Greek idea of a perfect truth attainable through mathematical abstraction. I should like to suggest that advanced mathematization, through abstraction and subsequent loss of meaning, played a role. It is a possibility that merits the collection of evidence, merits speculation and argumentation; for, of course, the full story does not only involve Germany alone, nor does it stop with the events of 1933–45.[13]

Philip J. Davis, the mathematician who writes these words, stresses that he is not suggesting 'that a high degree of mathematization necessarily leads to a holocaust'. But his words are disturbing partly because they accord closely with the obsessive scientism of Hitler's own outlook. As Daniel Gasman has observed, one of the words most frequently employed by Hitler in his *Tabletalk* is '*Wissenschaft*', 'science'. 'From the content of his conversations it is patently clear that he thought of himself as rooted in the rational and scientific tradition of modern European civilisation, and that he was certain that there was a basis in science for all the beliefs and policies which he espoused.'[14]

It is because of the dangers which always attend any attempt to fit human beings into the narrow categories of 'hard' rationalistic science that we need to develop a more sensitive, more flexible scientific instrument than rationalism. As the literary critic L. C. Knights has written: 'What we need is not to abandon reason, but simply to recognise that reason in the last three centuries has worked within a field which is not the whole of experience, that it has mistaken the part for the whole and imposed arbitrary limits on its own working.'[15]

These words were written almost exactly fifty years ago, just after the end of the Second World War. But the kind of narrow and defensive rationalism which Knights describes still dominates our contemporary intellectual culture. Fifty years ago the most obvious remedy for this problem was to attempt to apply psychoanalytic modes of explanation. By now, it has become reasonably clear that this remedy has not worked. Today, if we are to follow the truly reasonable course which Knights recommends, we need, I believe, to lay aside psychoanalysis, together with its rationalism and its mentalism. We need in its place to develop a more Darwinian understanding of reason which is in keeping with the kind of neo-Darwinian theory of human nature whose development is already under way.

One of the most attractive aspects of Gerald Edelman's approach to this problem is that, as a professional scientist, trained in an objective and to some extent rationalistic tradition, he recognises that the biologically based epistemology which must undergird any neo-Darwinian theory of human nature cannot exclude questions of value, or, indeed, questions of morality:

> In addition to qualifying our realism, we must consider questions of history and culture and ones related to value and purpose. This may seem strange in a discussion of science, which is supposed to be value-free. But the science touted as value-free is that based on the Galilean position, a physical science that quite deliberately and justifiably removed the mind from nature. A biologically based epistemology has no such luxury.[16]

The fact that any neo-Darwinian theory of human behaviour is obliged to consider questions of value, morality and feeling does not mean that reason no longer has any part to play. What we need, as I have already suggested, is to exercise our scepticism about the way reason has been used in the past and re-adjust our present practice accordingly.

One of my main purposes in writing this book has been to engage in just such an exercise in constructive scepticism. What I have tried to show, by looking in depth at one modern theory of human nature, is that our modern intellectual culture, for all its secularism and its rationalism, remains largely theological or crypto-theological in its nature. This is why psychoanalysis, with its subtle reworking of Judaeo-Christian orthodoxies and its almost completely invisible reliance on the creationist theory of human nature, has proved so deeply appealing. In seeking to explain how the psychoanalytic movement achieved the medical prestige which has been accorded to it during our own century (particularly in the United States) I have found it necessary to dig deep into medical history and to reconstruct, in the spirit of an archaeologist, a stage in the development of modern neurology and modern psychiatry which has been almost completely obscured by modern medical mythology. The conclusion which I have reached, namely that the illness supposedly suffered by Freud's early patients has never existed, is a very significant part of my argument. But my main concern, as will be evident, is not with the *medical* reasons for Freud's diagnostic mistakes, so much as with the *psychological* reasons. This is why I have focused so much attention on Freud's massive idealisation of his own medical heroes – particularly Charcot, Breuer and Fliess. In suggesting that Freud's susceptibility to hero-worship was an expression of his own messianic complex, I am not offering a wholly new approach. I hope, however, that the particular account I have given of Freud as the leader of a messianic movement will help to illuminate both psycho-analysis itself and its place in our cultural history.

There will almost inevitably be some readers of this book who see, in the portrait of Freud which I have offered, not an upset for rational-ism, but another victory for it. The messianic confusions of psycho-analysis will be seen by such doubly determined rationalists as but an odd, regressive phenomenon, of the kind we will soon leave behind us for ever as reason extends its dominion. Or they will be seen merely as symptoms of weak will, proving the need for yet more determined atheism, yet sterner rationalism.[17] That is certainly one possible way of reacting to the critique of psychoanalysis which I have presented. It is not, however, my own intention to offer any such simple comfort to rationalism. For, as should by now be clear, I have chosen to examine psychoanalysis at such length not because I regard it as an aberration but because I see it as merely a special case of an intellectual predica-ment which is much more general. It is not only Freud and his fol-lowers who have deeply internalised creationist assumptions about human nature and human psychology, but our intellectual culture as a whole.

One of the assumptions on which my entire argument is based is that we cannot free ourselves from our own creationist assumptions simply by recognising them in others. Intellectually it may well be that many thinkers long ago discarded the concept of God and simul-taneously embraced the theory of natural selection. But to the extent that we continue to imagine human beings as consisting of a non-physical 'mind' which is in some way attached to, but separate from, our animal body, and continue to see evolution as teleological and hierarchical, we remain cryptic creationists. Merely recognising the intellectual vagaries of psychoanalysis will not in itself release us from this intellectual predicament. We need, as I have already suggested, to focus our scepticism not simply upon psychoanalysis or upon Marxism, or upon structuralism or deconstruction, but upon the very concept of reason itself.

In seeking a more sensitive instrument of investigation than that which is idealised by rationalism, my own preference is for a view of reason similar to that which has been outlined by Nicholas Humphrey. As we saw earlier, Humphrey suggests that we have evolved the behavioural capacities which we tend to refer to as 'the intellect' primarily in order to enable us to predict and respond to the enormously complex behaviour of other human beings and of our own family and social groups. This functional view of the intellect is not a rationalistic concept of 'mind', for it implicitly includes the various capacities which we tend to abstract from our political, social and intimate behaviour and label as 'sympathy', 'insight', 'reason', 'intuition' or 'feeling'. I would prefer to designate this aspect of human behaviour, although Humphrey himself does not do so, as our 'imaginative intellect', or even simply as 'imagination'.

Once we accept this account of the evolution of the human intellect we cannot also maintain that intelligent behaviour is rigidly determined by genetic factors, or even governed by some innate 'biogrammar'. For because of the infinitely various forms taken by societies and by social interaction, and above all because of the various degrees of renunciation which may be biologically appropriate in a given situation, the adaptive effectiveness of our intellect may very well depend on its possessing a corresponding flexibility. So long as we allow ourselves to exercise this flexibility fully, then we give ourselves at least a chance of ordering our affairs reasonably. It would seem, however, that large parts of modern educational practice and of more ancient religious principles have had the effect of constraining imaginative flexibility, and severely limiting our imaginative range. To the extent to which we submit to such constraints and artificially invest our imagination with the rigidities of our social and economic structure, and the asceticism on which this structure is built, to that extent is it likely that we will mismanage our affairs.

We cannot, given our present social structures, ever revert to living intuitively, according to the unverified and unchecked conclusions of our most impulsive insights. It would be both foolish and dangerous even to hold out that as a utopian possibility. For this reason we still need all the sceptical, systematic and evidence-demanding conventions which have been established as one of the most valuable elements in our scientific tradition. At the same time, however, we cannot afford to empty our full imaginative intellects of those capacities which we call 'sympathy', 'compassion', 'feeling' – or even of 'anger' and 'hatred'. Nor can we afford to renounce the most extraordinary of all our imaginative capacities – our ability to form images, to translate these into language, and to use a complex grammar of images in order to think deeply, richly and coherently about human relationships and human society. If, in deference to authority or to the spirit of our times, we renounce these imaginative and emotionally rich aspects of our intellect, we only succeed in creating that artificial and profoundly dangerous capacity which is the 'rational intellect', and do so by discarding the very elements of our intellect which are most adaptive – which bear most directly on the way we understand and shape both our own behaviour and the behaviour of others.

Unless we use the full range of our imaginative intellect, we cannot even begin to define the problems which are posed by human behaviour. This is so whether we are dealing with literature, with religion and ritual, with sexual love, with the behaviour of parents and children, or, indeed, with any aspect of behaviour normally treated by anthropologists or psychologists. It is also true in the case of that discipline which underlies all others – history.

We need to take back our imaginative powers from the artists, novelists and poets to whom we have delegated them. For there is a danger in delegating imaginative powers just as there is a danger in delegating any powers. We need our own imagination. For the imagination is not something which God gave us so that a few men and women might write poetry and a few others read it. It is a capacity of the human animal which has evolved its rich complexity through all the millennia of our mammalian evolution. By far the most probable explanation for its intricate and extraordinary power is that it has survival-value. If this is so it would be no more sensible to renounce its full power than it would be to forgo the use of our legs or of our hands. It is only when we have learnt again how to use our imagination – to use it not impulsively or whimsically, but systematically, consistently and coherently – and when we have applied the full resources of our imaginative intellect to the construction of an adequate theory of human history, that we will ever begin to grasp the realities of our own nature and our own historical predicament.

Until we have done this it seems likely that we will remain in thrall to the dissociated, intellectual culture which we inhabit today, where an austere and politically influential scientific and technological culture, devoid of human sympathy and understanding, exists side by side with a weak literary and artistic culture which, because it has unconsciously internalised the image of its own superfluity, is prepared both to stand back from the political process and to concede to the natural sciences the exclusive right to explore reality systematically and to pronounce authoritatively upon it. Such a dissociated intellectual culture, together with the riven sensibility which belongs to it, is one which, whatever its members may consciously profess, exists in unconscious complicity with those political strategies which seek to subordinate human needs to technological progress, which defer meekly to imaginary economic laws, and which are committed to squandering human wealth in the compulsive pursuit of material riches. It is an intellectual culture which, by its very nature, tacitly endorses the assumption that human feelings, human fulfilment and the wealth of our intimate and community relations should be discounted as factors in the equations of politics, and that men and women should submit willingly, pacifically and even eagerly to government by the cruel junta of the rational and the quantifiable.

This assumption has by now become the ruling and almost undisputed orthodoxy of our technocentric, growth society. It has been able to achieve such a position of dominance because it is associated with a theory of human nature which, far from being some recent outgrowth of our modern technological environment, lies at the very heart of our most ancient and revered religious traditions. It is a theory which enjoys the almost universal assent not only of priests and politicians but also of psychologists and philosophers, and which has been endorsed by practically every significant movement in the history of Western rationalism, including psychoanalysis. This theory, which is entirely false, is the one whose epistemological consequences I have been trying to trace in this chapter – and, indeed, throughout this book. It is the theory which, in its most common form, maintains that human beings are compounded of two separate but interconnected entities – a mind which is pure and a body which is relatively impure. It further maintains that the mind constitutes the essential reality of the individual and that the more securely it can assert its dominance and control over the body, the more surely the cause of human knowledge and human progress will be advanced. This theory might be given a number of different names. It might be known as Cartesian dualism, Platonic idealism, Aristotelian rationalism, apocalyptic reductionism, beast–

angel dualism, or even Christianity. All these names, however, tend misleadingly to localise a theory which has a much wider scope. It is more helpful to designate it simply as Western rationalism – either in its religious or its post-religious form.

Because psychoanalysis attempts to deal with the realm of human feelings and human sexuality, Freud has sometimes been seen as an opponent of rationalism. Freud himself was under no such illusion. He saw himself, rather as Ernst Haeckel did, as a militant opponent of religion, who sought to supplant superstition with reason. 'The more the treasures of our knowledge become accessible to people,' he wrote, 'the more the defection from religious belief will spread, at first only from its obsolete, offensive vestments, but then from its fundamental presuppositions as well.' This, as Peter Gay has accurately observed,

> is the heart of Freud's argument: the very premises of science are incompatible with those of religion ... 'The warfare between science and religion', that militant slogan of the eighteenth century so fervently echoed in the nineteenth, continued to represent an axiomatic truth for Freud right into the middle of the twentieth century. As he said more than once, in more than one text, religion was, quite simply, the enemy ... Freud's rationalist stance resembles, and follows, nineteenth-century anti-clerical thought ... His view of religion as the enemy was wholly shared by the first generation of psychoanalysts.[18]

Although Freud set out to defeat this enemy, he failed. He failed because, like other campaigning rationalists, he was unable to grasp that the very rationalism which, in the eighteenth and nineteenth centuries, militantly opposed itself to religion, was itself born out of the superstitions it sought to sweep away.

One of the many things signified by Freud's failure is that the enterprise on which our scientific culture embarked in 1859 with the publication of *The Origin of Species* remains unfinished. The goal of completing that enterprise is not necessarily an unattainable one. But it is remote. Before it can be reached the outward forms of human culture and the entire realm of human behaviour must be sceptically reviewed. They must be reviewed not from the narrow perspective of rationalism but with the full resources of the imaginative intellect. The voyage of the *Beagle* must, in other words, be made over again, and this time its course must be set so that it leads not towards remote and sometimes uninhabited islands, but towards the populous shores of human history, where alone it is possible to examine the most significant forms of religious, political and economic behaviour.

The voyage in question is a hazardous one and, like all voyages of discovery, its success depends not upon the speed of the departure but upon the thoroughness of the preparations which have been made for it.[19] This book is intended as a contribution to those preparations. What I have tried to show, by relating the psychoanalytic movement to the cultural and religious context out of which it grew, is that, to the extent that they accept the cryptic creationism of 'rationalism', to that same degree do modern intellectuals follow in the footsteps of priestly elites throughout history. For when thinkers accept the ethos of rationalism uncritically, their function is not so much to discover naturalistic truths about human evolution, but to suppress, transcend or in some other way evade such truths. In structuralism, in Marxism and in psychoanalysis itself – all theories of human nature which begin by repudiating the evidence offered by human behaviour – the cultural function of the intellectual as an agent of mystification has been carried to unprecedented extremes. We might well invoke the words of Nietzsche:

> How much does learning hide these days, or, at least, how much does it wish to hide! The solidity of our best scholars, their automatic industry, their heads smoking night and day, their very skill and competence: all these qualities betoken more often than not a desire to hide and suppress something.[20]

One of the most effective means which intellectuals have always used in order to advance their role as agents of mystification has been the promulgation of what might be called the 'myth of difficulty'. Traditional Christian thinkers were always doctrinally committed to the view that the ultimate secrets of human history and human nature were mysterious, that they were known only to God himself, and that they would be revealed only in the fullness of time when the apocalyptic moment finally came. This belief was held not only by pre-scientific Christian thinkers but also by such Christian scientists as Isaac Newton and Robert Boyle. Our modern intellectual culture has preserved this apocalyptic view of human nature and human knowledge in a secularised form. We still tend to believe that the 'laws' of human nature are secret, mysterious, cryptic and inaccessible, and that they can be formulated only by means of abstruse theories, or through the construction of abstract models of 'mind'.

It would, on the whole, be more reasonable to assume that the 'laws' of human nature, far from being secret or cryptic, are written openly across the pages of our history books, and across the very face of human behaviour, in letters so bold and characters so bloody that we, in our love of the refined and the mysterious, have never even dreamed of trying to read them. This does not mean that we should replace the 'myth of difficulty' with its opposite and claim that human nature is transparent, or explicable merely by reference to 'common sense'. But there is no reason to accept the common view that the mystery of human nature is destined to remain eternally beyond our grasp or that it cannot be approached at all.

For one of the most serious limitations of intellectuals in Judaeo-Christian culture has always been their readiness to accept that some of the greatest problems of human existence are impenetrable. Although this view has recently been taken down from the attic of history, dusted off and presented as one of the central doctrines of postmodernism, its origins are recognisably ancient. For it derives ultimately from the belief that large mysteries are the preserve of God and that his creatures have a right to delve only into smaller ones.

So familiar are we with the biblical story of the Fall that we sometimes forget that the foundation-myth of our entire religious culture places a taboo against knowledge at the very centre of human history. The boundaries of this taboo have been perpetually shifted and it is no longer enforced, as it once was, by torture and terror. But we should not succumb to the illusion that we have ever escaped the taboo altogether. Many of our contemporary attitudes towards knowledge and towards the investigation of human nature suggest that the terror still remains long after the apparatus of religious torture which maintained it was dismantled. To the extent that this is so our intellectual life is still largely governed by fear and taboo. Only if we identify the taboos which still constrain our intellectual imagination and openly transgress them are we likely to create in reality a modicum of that intellectual freedom which we constantly idealise, but do not in practice possess.

In the largeness of his ambitions at least, Freud may serve as an example to those theorists who come after him. For this reason, if for no other, any wholly negative assessment of his achievement would be mistaken. As I wrote in my introduction, I have devoted a whole book to a theory I believe to be mistaken partly because I think it is mistaken in a particularly interesting way, and partly in order to establish the need for an alternative theory of human sexuality and human nature.

What we should recognise, I believe, is that although Freud himself failed to construct an adequate theory of human nature, his attempt was more significant than many, not least because he did seek to find a place for aspects of human nature which other theorists, yet more rigorously rationalistic than him, have sought to exclude from their theoretical outlook or even to excise from human nature altogether. It is because Freud's rationalism is less icy and less cold than many other kinds, that we, in the dying moments of our emaciated and shrunken humanism, have sometimes followed the example of Anna Freud, and huddled for warmth within the ample folds of Freud's green *Lodenmantel*.

The fact that we have done this as a culture should not be a cause for shame, or for guilt, or for the wringing of scholarly hands. Neither should it be an occasion for chastising Freud for deceiving us, or ourselves for being deceived. It should, if we are to continue on the path of exploration, be the occasion for analysis. In this book I have tried to undertake that task, replying to the individualistic ethos of Freud's 'psychoanalysis' with an essay in cultural analysis. Although this essay is frequently critical both of Freud and of his theories, I have tried to qualify my criticism throughout its considerable length and I end by qualifying it again. For the intellectual estate of psychoanalysis is a large and complex one which contains, amidst much theoretical poverty and worthless intellectual bric-à-brac, a small quantity of the gold of true psychological insight. It is only, I believe, if we accept this small but precious legacy with gratitude that we will be in a position to pass beyond psychoanalysis in order to construct the kind of neo-Darwinian theory of human nature which does possess the explanatory power psychoanalysis lacks.

The task of constructing that theory has already begun, and a number of neo-Darwinian biologists have already made fundamental contributions to it. If, religiously, we place our entire trust in science and obediently follow all its precepts, which is what we have tended to do in the last three centuries, there is little likelihood of any adequate theory of human nature ever emerging from these contributions. If, following the inner logic of science itself, we submit our theories of knowledge to the rationalistic scepticism of the *mind*, we will almost inevitably end, as many postmodernist thinkers do, by entering into collusion with the most tyrannical and repressive aspects of the intellectual tradition we seek to criticise. If, however, seeking not to reject science but to regenerate it, we examine the problems of human nature with the almost infinitely rich intelligence of the body, and bring to our attempt all the wealth and resources of the human imagination, the task which Darwin left unfinished may yet be completed.

AFTERWORD

Freud's False Memories

Psychoanalysis and the Recovered Memory Movement

THE OBSERVATION THAT Freud's writings, and in particular his theory of repression, are the ultimate source of the recovered memory movement which has flourished in the United States in the last decade, has been made on a number of occasions already. The subject is a huge one and in order to avoid becoming ensnared by the present I have only touched upon it briefly in this attempt to review the psychoanalytic past. But because the recovered memory movement has assumed such an extraordinary importance in contemporary psychotherapy, no attempt to estimate the influence of Freud upon our century would be complete if it did not offer some account of this movement and of the phenomenon of 'false memory' which, in the view of many, is associated with it.

One of the obstacles which stands in the way of any realistic appraisal of the recovered memory movement is the difficulty most people have in imaginatively grasping the sheer scale of it, and the extraordinary speed with which it has come to dominate the mental health debate in North America and to move rapidly up mental health agendas in many other countries. As Frederick Crews has written, 'during the past decade or so a shockwave had been sweeping across North American psychotherapy and in the process causing major repercussions in our families, courts and hospitals. A single diagnosis for miscellaneous complaints – that of unconsciously repressed sexual abuse in childhood – has grown in this brief span from virtual non-existence to epidemic frequency.'[1]

Quite what the frequency of this diagnosis now is in the United States is impossible to say with any accuracy. But it is possible to make informed estimates. Crews himself relays the conservative estimate that a million people have been helped by their psychotherapists to recover putative 'memories' of child sexual abuse since 1988 alone. Tens of thousands of families have been torn apart by allegations of incest springing from these 'recovered memories'. So massive and disruptive have the effects of this kind of therapy been that there seems little doubt that in a hundred years time historians and sociologists will still be studying one of most extraordinary episodes in twentieth century history, and that in all probability they will still be arguing about its causes.

It seems reasonably clear, however, that one of the crucial factors associated with the rise of the recovered memory movement is the extensive denial of the reality of child sexual abuse which has reigned both among lawyers and among mental health professionals through-out most of the twentieth century. In the realm of the law a particularly powerful influence was exercised by John Henry Wigmore, whose monumental *Treatise on Evidence* (1934) was one of the most famous legal texts ever published in the United States. In it Wigmore sets forward his own views on the reliability of women and children as witnesses in cases of sexual abuse. The doctrine he expounds impeaches the credibility of any female – especially if she is a child – who complains of a sexual offence. Wigmore warns that women and girls are in his view predisposed to bringing accusations against men of good character. He therefore recommends that any female complainant, but especially a girl who accuses her father of incest, should be examined by a psychiatrist to determine her credibility.[2]

For the next forty years at least it was extremely difficult for women, and above all for children, to gain a hearing for accusations of sexual assault or incest made against men. This applied not only to the court-room but also to the clinic. Again and again women found that their own entirely genuine memories of sexual abuse were discounted or denied by psychotherapists. Again and again the factual accounts of distraught and distressed children were dismissed as fantasies.

This massive denial of the experience of women and children who genuinely had been victims of sexual abuse provided the essential con-ditions without which the recovered memory movement could never have grown and flourished in the way that it did. John Henry Wigmore clearly played a significant role in bringing about this state of affairs. But, as should already be clear, his doctrine could never have become established without the support of the psychiatric establishment. There can be no doubt at all that it received this support in America largely because of the influence of one man – Freud.

The reason that Freud's influence in this area was so pernicious is readily apparent. In the theory of the Oedipus complex Freud had, in effect, invented a perfect theoretical instrument for explaining away allegations of sexual abuse and undermining their credibility. Since Freud's theory held that all children might fantasise about sexual relations with their parents, it followed that recollections of sexual abuse by parents could be construed as fantasies. Even though Freud himself specifically pointed out on a number of occasions that memories of childhood seductions sometimes *did* correspond to real events, the overwhelming tendency of the psychoanalytic profession throughout most of the twentieth century has been to construe recollections of incest as fantasies. In this respect, at least, psychoanalysis in general and the theory of the Oedipus complex in particular have caused untold harm.[3]

The harm which they have caused would not be so surprising if it were widely known how Freud came to formulate the Oedipus complex in the first place. As I have already noted, the generally accepted version, related by Ernest Jones, is that during his self-analysis Freud unearthed a 'memory' of an occasion when, as a child, he had been sexually aroused by seeing his mother naked. It may well be that Jones was faithfully recording what Freud himself had told him. But there is no evidence whatsoever that the scene ever took place. For, as we have already seen, what Freud actually wrote at the time was that he remembered a train journey – a long train journey from whose duration he *deduced* that he might have had the opportunity of seeing his mother naked. He then speculated further that he might have been sexually aroused by this entirely hypothetical sight. Although Freud may eventually have come to experience the scene he had ingeniously constructed as a 'memory', it would seem that it was almost certainly a false memory.[4]

Freud's false memory, however, was instrumental in creating a climate of tyrannical scepticism about incest and child abuse which would remain almost unchallenged throughout most of the century. Only in the last twenty years has it become possible to oppose this climate effectively. This is almost entirely due to the influence of feminism. For during the late 1970s and the early 1980s many feminist writers and therapists began to recognise the frequency with which real cases of sexual abuse were subject to denial. Quite deliberately they started to draw back the veil of patriarchy and to reveal the reality which had been concealed behind it.

Women who had been sexually abused by their fathers, who had always remembered this, but who had kept the shameful secret to themselves, began to talk about their experience, or to recount their stories in books. Some women also began to disclose their histories of sexual abuse to psychotherapists who, almost for the first time, were prepared to listen to their stories and to believe them. This new development in American psychotherapy in its turn generated more books. In 1981 the Harvard University Press published *Father–Daughter Incest* by the psychiatrist Judith Herman, in which she persuasively argued that the incidence of this form of incest was much greater than had ever been suspected.

These were immense positive gains and they were brought about almost entirely by women – by women who were rebelling against the patriarchal straitjacket of Freud and psychoanalysis. It should be noted that most of these early pioneers were not seeking to recover *repressed* memories of child sexual abuse. They were seeking to create a safe space in which memories which had always been present could be disclosed by women, without being met by scepticism and denial.

If that is so we might well ask how it was that a movement which had its origins in a feminist rebellion against Freud, in an attempt to draw the veil of silence from memories which had never been repressed, should eventually have come to rely more and more on the most sacred of all Freudian doctrines – that of repression.

One answer to this question is provided by Judith Herman in her 1981 book. In this book she makes her quarrel with Freud's patriarchalism and with the tyranny of his Oedipus complex abundantly clear. Yet, like countless critics of Freud both before and after her, she is unable to resist the massive potency of the Freud legend. Instead of escaping entirely from the influence of Freud, Herman actually found the authority for her rebellion against orthodox psychoanalysis in the writings of Freud himself. For she believed that she had discovered another, unknown Freud. This Freud, the Freud of 1896 and of the seduction theory, could be seen as a kind of proto-feminist. Instead of rejecting stories of incest as fantasies, he had listened to the women who had told these stories with respect and understanding:

> The patriarch of modern psychology stumbled across the incest secret in the early and formative years of his career. It was Freud's ambition to discover the cause of hysteria, the archetypal female neurosis of his time. In his early investigations, he gained the trust and confidence of

many women, who revealed their troubles to him. Time after time, Freud's patients, women from prosperous, conventional families, unburdened painful memories of childhood sexual encounters with men they had trusted: family friends, relatives and fathers. Freud initially believed his patients and recognised the force of their confessions.

But Freud, according to Herman's account, eventually recoiled from the implications of his seduction theory, and chose to incriminate daughters for their incestuous fantasies rather than fathers for their incestuous deeds. 'At the moment that Freud turned his back on his female patients and denied the truth of their experience,' writes Herman, 'he forfeited his ambition to understand the female neurosis. Freud went on to elaborate the dominant psychology of modern times. It is a psychology of men.'[5]

Judith Herman was not the first person to put forward this view of Freud. She herself refers back to the very similar view taken by the social worker, Florence Rush, in an article written in 1974. Another version of the same argument would, of course, soon be put forward in 1984 amidst massive publicity and controversy by Jeffrey Masson in his book *The Assault on Truth*.

Masson, as we know, had trained as a psychoanalyst and was himself seeking to escape from orthodox Freudian doctrine. The abiding temptation for those caught in this kind of predicament is to submit to the authority of a new messiah in order to find the strength to rebel against the tyranny of the old one. That, in a sense, is what Jeffrey Masson, in spite of all his best intentions, found himself doing. Except that in this case the messiah through which he sought liberation from the patriarchal doctrines of Freud was none other than Freud himself.

For, like Judith Herman, Masson too discovered a proto-feminist Freud apparently unmarked by the patriarchalism of orthodox psychoanalysis. In words which have already been quoted, he wrote of this early period in Freud's career that 'Freud's female patients had the courage to face what had happened to them in childhood – often this included violent scenes of rape by a father – and to communicate their traumas to Freud . . . Freud listened and understood and gave them permission to remember and speak of these terrible events.' Masson of course went on to argue, as Judith Herman had before him, that Freud eventually turned his back on the 'truth' he had discovered because of the fear, distaste and outrage of his colleagues.[6]

This argument about Freud and the abandonment of the seduction theory has, especially in Masson's well-known version of it, exerted an enormous influence over the way American psychotherapy has developed over the last ten years. Yet, as I have suggested in the main body of this book, it is an argument which fundamentally misrepresents the actual course of Freud's development and the entire nature of his early 'discovery'.

For the proto-feminist Freud which both Judith Herman and Jeffrey Masson thought they had discovered never existed. Both Herman and Masson imply that Freud's early patients – those he discusses in his paper 'The Aetiology of Hysteria' – came to consult him burdened with memories of incest which they then spontaneously disclosed. There is no mystery about why Herman and Masson should have assumed this, because Freud himself said that this was what had happened. As we have already seen, on several occasions, many years after he had abandoned his seduction theory, Freud described how his early patients had come to him and told him stories of sexual abuse and how he had begun by believing these stories.

It may well be that Freud had, by the time thirty years or so had elapsed, come to believe in this version of events himself. He may have 'remembered' this happening. But if this was Freud's memory of events then, once again, we are forced to recognise that it was a 'false memory'. For in his original 1896 paper Freud had made it abundantly clear that when his early patients came to him they had no memories of incest at all. Since they are so crucial, Freud's exact words should perhaps be quoted again: 'Before they come for analysis,' he writes, 'the patients know nothing about these scenes.'[7]

How then, did these patients know what kind of scenes they were expected to reproduce? Freud himself, it will be recalled, implicitly answers this question. 'They are indignant as a rule,' he writes, 'if we warn them that such scenes are going to emerge.' It was thus evidently Freud's habit to inform his patients of the kind of scenes he expected to emerge. But if his patients were indignant when they were told they were going to reproduce scenes of child sexual abuse, how did Freud persuade them to do this? Once again Freud himself gives us the answer. 'Only the strongest compulsion of the treatment can induce them to embark on a reproduction of them.' The phrase 'the strongest compulsion of the treatment' is a telling one. We have all experienced 'the strongest compulsion of the treatment' at one time or another, if only when we have been forced to take medicine whose taste we did not like. Freud, we must recall once again, was not originally a psychotherapist. He was a physician. He believed – especially at this point in his career – that he was dispensing a kind of medicine. His theoretical speculations had led him to the conclusion that 'hysteria' was a single disease, and that the 'pathogen' which caused it was repressed sexual abuse. His task was to persuade patients to reproduce the pathogenic memories which, according to his theories, were lodged in a submerged part of their minds. Freud's duty, then, was not to treat the patient. It was to cure the disease. The way to do this was to persuade the patient to 'remember' scenes of childhood sexual abuse. If they declined, it was his job, as a conscientious physician, to use his 'pressure technique' and to make sure that they followed the treatment he pre-scribed. For, as he writes, 'We must insist on this, we must repeat the pressure and represent ourselves as infallible, till at least we are really told something.'[8]

There is no evidence that any of the patients who came to Freud without memories of sexual abuse had ever suffered from such abuse. But, as a growing number of Freud scholars have recognised in recent years, and as I have argued in this book, there is a great deal of evidence, most of it in Freud's own frank and astonishing words, that he went out of his way to persuade, encourage, cajole and sometimes bully his female patients to reproduce scenes of child sexual abuse which he himself had reconstructed from their symptoms or their associations. Freud's manner of treating his early women patients was not essentially different from the manner he treated his later ones. For in both cases his theories denied women autonomy and declined to validate their own experiences and their own memories. Whereas his later theories led countless psychoanalysts to persuade women who had been abused to believe that they had not, Freud himself had, under the influence of his early theories, frequently tried to persuade women who had not been abused to believe that they had. In short, in his disregard for his female patients' autonomy and their right to psychological self-determination, Freud was just as much the nineteenth-century patri-arch *before* he abandoned the seduction theory as he was afterwards.

In failing to understand the deep consistency of Freud's patriar-chalism and, in implicitly (and sometimes explicitly) holding up the early Freud as a model of therapeutic wisdom and sensitivity, Masson, Herman and all those who shared their views were in effect com-mending not a decisive break with Freud's patriarchalism but a return to its earliest form.

*　　　*　　　*

It has sometimes been suggested by commentators on the incest survivors' movement that the concept of repression was a relatively late
ingredient. In as much as this movement appears to have started outside
the realm of psychotherapy, there may be some truth in this. But
although both Herman and Masson give the impression that Freud's
early patients were able quite spontaneously to gain access to their
memories of being sexually abused, they appear *simultaneously* to accept
Freud's original assumption that such memories might be entirely
repressed. It is clear that in 1981, when her book *Father–Daughter
Incest* first appeared, Judith Herman was already placing some reliance
on psychotherapeutic reconstructions of sexual abuse, as opposed to
spontaneous memories. She describes how one woman patient was
helped during therapy to reconstruct 'previously repressed memories'
of sexual assaults by her father. According to the account we are given,
from the age of six until mid-adolescence her father had repeatedly
exhibited himself to her and insisted that she masturbate him. It is
implied that she had entirely lost any memory of almost ten years of
repeated sexual abuse until it was pieced together in psychotherapy.⁹

Even before the publication of Jeffrey Masson's book in 1984, a
number of psychotherapists in the Boston area and elsewhere began
to form therapy groups for incest survivors. It would seem that in
these very early days of the incest survivors' movement, most of those
who enrolled in these therapy groups were victims of incest who had
always remembered their abuse. In their groups they shared their
experience with others, and undoubtedly felt stronger and more secure
as a result of doing so.

But the very fact that Freud, and Freud's early theories, had played
such a crucial role in shaping the incest survivors' movement during
this period meant that the possibility of *repressed* memories of incest
could never be ruled out. From the descriptions we have of them, it
is clear that some of these early therapy groups also included women
who had no memories of incest but who had been diagnosed by their
psychotherapists or psychiatrists as suffering from repressed memories
of incest. In their pursuit of the hidden memories which supposedly
accounted for the symptoms of these women, therapists sometimes
used a form of time-limited group therapy. At the beginning of the
ten or twelve weekly sessions, patients would be encouraged to set
themselves goals. For many patients without memories of incest the
goal was to recover such memories. Indeed they evidently felt under
considerable group-pressure to do so and thus prove their right to

belong to the group. 'Women who wished to recover memories, were often preoccupied with obsessive doubt about ... whether they belonged to the group at all.' Some of them actually defined their goal by saying 'I just want to be in the group and feel I belong.' After the fifth session the therapist would remind the group that they had reached the middle of their therapy, with the clear implication that time was running out. As pressure was increased in this way women with no memories would often begin to see images of sexual abuse involving fathers or other adults, and these images would then be construed as memories or 'flashbacks'.[10]

One need not be particularly sceptical about the recovered memory movement in order to recognise that what was happening here was that distressed and vulnerable women with no memories of sexual abuse, and no reason to believe they had been abused other than their therapist's diagnosis, were being placed under immense psychological pressure to produce 'memories' which would confirm that diagnosis. It is equally clear, however, that the therapists running the group were quite unable to see that they, like the pre-psychoanalytic Freud on whom they had modelled themselves, were actually dispensing an extremely coercive form of therapy. Instead they evidently saw each instance of a woman recovering putative memories of sexual abuse as a vindication of their original diagnosis, and as scientific proof of the theory of massive repression – a form of repression which was first named by Judith Herman in a speech made to the American Psychiatric Association in 1985.[11]

Group therapy sessions of the kind I have described here were ostensibly designed to empower the women who joined them as patients. We should not rule out the possibility that, in some cases, this is exactly what they did, or appeared to do. It would seem, however, that one of their other effects was to induce a massive sense of empowerment in the psychiatrists and psychotherapists who ran them. This sense of empowerment was spread rapidly through informal networks of psychotherapists at the same time that it began to be disseminated formally through seminars, books and academic papers. A movement which appears to have begun in the Boston area thus soon started to spread throughout the entire United States.

There can be little doubt that its spread was very significantly accelerated by the appearance of Jeffrey Masson's book *The Assault on Truth* in 1984. For, in the concluding pages of this book, Masson suggested that psychoanalysts had spent the twentieth century progressively erasing what he took to be Freud's original insight. Consequently most American psychoanalysts did not now recognise what, according to Masson, was implicit in Freud's 1896 paper. They did not therefore accept that 'many (probably most) of their patients had violent and unhappy childhoods, not because of some defect in their character, but because of something terrible which had been done to them by their parents.' Masson went on to make clear that he was talking specifically about the sexual abuse of children by their parents. He suggested that sexual abuse might 'form the core of every serious neurosis', and that if this is so, 'it would not be possible to achieve a successful cure of a neurosis if this central event were ignored.' What Masson comes very near to saying here is that all, or nearly all, serious cases of neurosis have one single underlying cause – child sexual abuse – and that orthodox psychoanalysts were collectively engaged in a massive denial of this reality. By implication Masson now calls for an equally massive collective effort to retrieve these painful memories of incest. 'Free and honest retrieval of painful memories,' he writes, 'cannot occur in the face of scepticism and fear of the truth.'

In the thunderous closing paragraphs of his book Masson makes his appeal quite explicit:

> The time has come to cease hiding from what is, after all, one of the great issues of human history . . .
> If it is not possible for the therapeutic community to address this serious issue in an honest and open-minded manner, then it is time for their patients to stop subjecting themselves to needless repetition of their deepest and earliest sorrow.[12]

By writing this, Masson was issuing an ideological ultimatum to the entire American psychotherapeutic community. What he was saying, in effect, was this: 'Face up to the reality of incest and to the fact that, as Freud himself originally maintained, hidden memories of child sexual abuse are the root cause of your patients' symptoms, and allow your patients to retrieve these memories in therapy. Otherwise your patients will leave you.' The corollary of this view was implied but never stated: 'If you do not have the courage and honesty to allow repressed memories of incest to emerge, your patients will leave you and find other psychotherapists who do.'

If Jeffrey Masson had been the only person preaching this new understanding of Freud to the psychotherapeutic community his ultimatum might have had relatively little effect. But Masson, as can now be seen, was in reality part of a broad historical movement. A number of writers and therapists, including Judith Herman in Boston and other therapists and psychiatrists elsewhere, were preaching a very similar gospel.

The best way to understand the immensely powerful dynamic of this new psychotherapeutic movement is, I believe, to translate its battle-cry out of its modern secular register and into an older register which is more deeply rooted in our culture. For what Judith Herman, Jeffrey Masson and others were saying was something like this: 'Woe to you orthodox psychoanalysts, you Pharisees. For you have whitened the sepulchre of your patients' unconscious and you have turned your eyes away from the evil and corruption which lie within. Woe to you psychoanalysts, you generation of vipers! Repent of your ways and be saved. For only those who follow the one true Freud, whom others have concealed, but whom I have revealed, will be healed and redeemed at the end. But all those who do not believe will suffer for their disbelief. For their patients shall leave them. And they shall be flung into the burning lake of therapeutic despair, where they will be tormented for all eternity.'

Quite how this gospel was spread will probably never be known with accuracy. For it was spread not only by books but in the way that new gospels often are – by word of mouth, and by example. It was spread through informal networks of psychotherapists, and by therapists who met in coffee-breaks, in conferences or in workshops. As a result it spread rapidly. What made its progress initially uncheckable was the ease with which it proved possible to implant, or create through suggestion, 'memories' of incest in women who had previously had no recollection of being abused. Therapists unfamiliar with the malleability of human memory, treated the extraordinary and vivid 'memories' which their patients now began to construct as proof that 'massive repression' could and did take place.

Before very long the belief that repressed memories of child sexual abuse were the cause of most serious neuroses, especially in women, began to be embraced by particular groups and sub-cultures of psychotherapists and psychiatrists all over the United States. It was embraced not only by many new-wave therapists, hypnotherapists and bodyworkers, but by some old-wave psychoanalytically trained therapists and by a number of young psychoanalysts. It was also sometimes embraced by reputable psychiatrists and even neurologists. A number of psychiatric conditions whose aetiology remained obscure were now held by some clinicians to be the result of sexual abuse during childhood. Seemingly sophisticated studies appeared purporting to demonstrate this aetiology.[13]

Nor was the diagnosis of child abuse invoked only to explain psychiatric disorders. One recent academically serious contribution to what might be called post-Massonian psychoanalytic theory presents a table entitled 'Childhood Symptoms of Sexual Abuse'. This includes a section headed 'Changes in School Performance', which specifies the following possible indicators of sexual abuse:

> Falling grades
> Decreased interest in school
> Difficulty concentrating
> School Phobia[14]

This is only a small example of the manner in which symptom lists, offered as aids to the diagnosis of repressed memories of sexual abuse, have proliferated within certain sub-cultures of American psychotherapy in recent years. The only certain conclusion which can be drawn from studying such lists is that there is by now practically no form of negative or mildly anxious human behaviour, from fear of the dark to neglecting to brush your teeth, which has not been cited by American therapists in recent years as a possible indicator or symptom of the existence of repressed memories of child sexual abuse.[15]

Once it began to be accepted by some therapists and counsellors during the mid 1980s that *millions* of people in the United States were suffering from repressed memories, the incest recovery movement was well and truly under way, and before very long patients who had never had any recollection of being abused were emerging from therapy with detailed and graphic 'memories' of how they had been sexually abused in childhood.[16]

Many large bookshops in America have entire sections devoted to 'Recovery'. A growing proportion of the books in such sections deal with incest and many are about repressed memories and the therapeutic recovery of such 'memories'. By far the most important of these is *The Courage to Heal: A Guide for Women Survivors of Child Sexual Abuse*, written by Ellen Bass and Laura Davis. One way of conveying the sheer size and power of the recovery movement in America is simply to register the fact that *The Courage to Heal*, published in 1988, has now sold more than 750,000 copies in the United States alone.

The Courage to Heal has been described as the Bible of the recovered memory movement. If we are to understand the enormous impact that this book has had on North American history in the last decade I believe that this description should be treated very seriously indeed. Because ultimately, as I have tried to show in this brief appendix to my central argument, the recovered memory movement, although it may be supported by some feminists, does not belong to the cause of liberation. It is essentially a patriarchal movement, which can be traced back to the sternest patriarch and prophet of modern psychology – Freud. Its doctrines are remarkably similar to those of other movements of Puritan revivalism, and it is largely because of this that it has swept through Puritan North America, not *against* the tide of Christian fundamentalism but in alliance with it. For in some communities women have been encouraged to recover 'memories' of incest almost as frequently by ministers of religion or Christian counsellors as they have by secular psychotherapists.

As is the case with the leading figures in almost all revivalist movements, there can be no doubting the genuineness of Ellen Bass and Laura Davis, and the utter sincerity of their belief that their book will facilitate healing and psychological wholeness. But just as more traditional revivalists have always proceeded by vitalising the anxieties and the sense of sin of those they seek to convert, so Bass and Davis encourage their readers to search their own memories for dark and shameful secrets which, they are told, may have been completely hidden by the power of repression.

Sexual abuse in childhood has, in effect, become the new Original Sin in Puritan America, and one of the aims of *The Courage to Heal* is to help women who have no memories of being sexually abused in childhood to 'find' such memories. The entire book is in one respect a literary surrogate for, or supplement to, the kind of time-limited survivor group therapy sessions which I have already described. With the help of *The Courage to Heal* and of therapists who believe in the possibility of 'massive repression', hundreds of thousands of women have recovered 'memories' of being raped, or sexually abused repeatedly and for long periods during their childhood. As yet no external evidence has been produced which convincingly demonstrates that any therapeutically recovered 'memory' of repeated and sustained sexual abuse actually corresponds to real episodes of sexual abuse. In early editions of *The Courage to Heal*, however, readers are never cautioned about the dangerous inaccuracy of most recovered 'memories'. Instead proper caution is replaced by credulity. 'If you think you were abused,' write Ellen Bass and Laura Davis, 'and your life shows the symptoms, then you were.'[17]

Bass and Davis encourage women to engage in fantasies of vengeance against the people they believe they were abused by. 'You may dream of murder or castration,' they write. 'It can be pleasurable to fantasize such scenes in vivid detail.' What is perhaps even more significant is that, disregarding the need for corroborative evidence, *The Courage to Heal* encourages women to consider using their artificially constructed 'memories' as grounds for confronting their supposed abusers and denouncing them – even, if necessary, accusing their own parents or grandparents on their death-beds.[18]

The deep hostility towards the family and towards family relationships which is expressed in certain parts of *The Courage to Heal* has sometimes been construed as evidence of the liberating and truly 'radical' nature of the doctrines espoused by its authors. To take this view, however, is to betray the very innocence of cultural and religious history on which the recovered memory movement thrives. For it is one of the most notable features of repressive patriarchal ideologies that, in their original revivalist phases, they have tended to show a contemptuous disregard for the bonds of affection which exist within even the most troubled families. The clearest example of such an attitude is that which is found in the New Testament itself, in the words attributed in Luke's gospel to Jesus:

> If any man come to me, and hate not his father, and mother, and wife, and children, and brethren, and sisters, yea, and his own life also, he cannot be my disciple (Luke 14:26 AV).

The literal sense of these words has frequently been repudiated by Christians, especially in modern times. Yet the particular form of *contemptus mundi* which they express has helped to sustain the entire Western monastic tradition. Partly because of the strength of this tradition, and the subsequent secularisation of the monastic virtues by Puritanism, the sentiments expressed in Luke's words have been deeply internalised into our culture. The resulting climate of feeling has always tended to facilitate the growth of repressive cults and revivalist movements which actively disseminate hostility to the family. *The*

Courage to Heal is perhaps best understood as the central text of one such revivalist movement.

Like any other movement of patriarchal revivalist Puritanism the effect of the recovered memory movement has been not to liberate women but to subjugate them, and to encourage dependence and deference to doctrines they are expected to accept unquestioningly – in this case to doctrines derived directly or indirectly from Freud – the true Freud which others had concealed, but which a number of modern scholars claim to have revealed.

The most disturbing feature of the recovered memory movement is the manner in which it encourages an attitude of emotional coldness and cruelty between different generations. Almost as disturbing as this, however, is the role it has played in the deepening sex war which has been fought out with increasing bitterness in recent years, particularly in America. Although some observers who are unsympathetic to feminism see the issues in this war as entirely synthetic, I cannot share this view. It is clear that many women have suffered immensely as a result of orthodox psychoanalysts construing real episodes of sexual abuse as Oedipal fantasies. To this extent the recovered memory movement was actually born out of a reaction against some of the tyrannical assumptions of psychoanalysis. The terrible irony, as I have tried to show, is that some of the key doctrines in this attempt to rebel against the patriarchalism of psychoanalysis have themselves been drawn from the original oppressor. For the notion that Freud based his seduction theory on real instances of sexual abuse has become the foundation myth of the entire recovered memory movement.[19] Proponents of this movement are, in effect, fighting Freud's second delusion by taking refuge in his first delusion. In some cases at least they are doing something very similar to what Freud was doing to his own patients during the period he formulated his seduction theory – they are forcing their own theoretical preconceptions onto young and psychologically vulnerable women in a way which creates dependence in the patient and feelings of empowerment in the therapist. Freud's patriarchal bullying can, when viewed sceptically, be recognised quite easily for what it is. It is much more difficult for us to recognise that the same kind of misogyny has now actually been taken over by a small section of the feminist movement and is being deployed *by women against women*, in the name of liberation and 'healing'.

It does, however, seem reasonably clear that those who support the recovered memory movement either in its 'low-church' self-help form, or in its more scholarly and academic form, are currently playing into the hands of precisely those whom they ostensibly oppose – the repressive men (and women) who seek to deny that child abuse occurs at all. In 1992, in a preface to a new edition of his *The Assault on Truth* Jeffrey Masson wrote that 'society has, even if reluctantly and belatedly, come to recognise that the sexual abuse of children is real, widespread, serious, and long-silenced.'[20] If that recognition has indeed been made it is undoubtedly a good thing. Yet the great danger is that whatever progress has been made in this direction will be undone by the reaction against the recovered memory movement and the multiple injustices which it has helped to perpetrate. For although this reaction has frequently been both critical *and* constructive there has inevitably also been a more destructive effect. In this respect the recovered memory movement itself poses a threat to the victims of genuine sexual abuse, who may now once again find themselves disbelieved. It also threatens the many thousands of psychotherapists and counsellors who treat their patients with genuine sensitivity and understanding. For the great danger posed by any form of misguided therapy is that it may bring the entire profession of psychotherapy into disrepute, and lead those who make mental health policy to starve psychotherapists of the resources they need in order to maintain a vital and constructive presence in the lives of those who sometimes desperately need their help.

The social and sexual conflict which has been caused by this particular issue is already considerable. My impression is that this kind of conflict is likely to deepen inexorably unless we can as a culture face up to the depth of the patriarchalism which has shaped Judaeo-Christian history. For only if we do this is it likely that we can begin to grasp how pervasive and powerful patriarchial attitudes are, and how easy it is for those who genuinely and courageously seek liberation from them to become ensnared by them themselves.

BIBLIOGRAPHICAL NOTE

The only consolation which can be drawn from one of the most tragic and distressing episodes in twentieth-century history is that the recovered memory movement in the United States has not been unopposed, and that, indeed, it has inspired some compelling writing on the part of its critics. Frederick Crews's trenchant two-part article in the New York Review of Books *(November/December 1994) reviews some of the most important books on the subject. This article, and the exchanges which followed it, themselves constitute a very significant contribution to the debate. Crews's warning against what he calls 'middle-of-the-road extremism' is, I believe, particularly apt. For the idea that in every fierce debate the truth must lie 'somewhere in the middle' is always dangerous – doubly so in the case of the debate about recovered memory.*

Fortunately there are a number of works which either implicitly or explicitly recognise this. Lawrence Wright's disturbing and immensely valuable book, Remembering Satan, *in which he recounts one of the strangest cases of recovered memory in recent years, is a work of extraordinary power which ought to become a classic. Richard Ofshe, a key figure in Wright's book, has himself worked with Ethan Watters to produce, in* Making Monsters, *a lucid, detailed and powerful critique of the entire recovered memory movement. Meanwhile Elizabeth Loftus and Katherine Ketcham have written in* The Myth of Repressed Memory *a book which is no less powerful, and which, while constantly informed by Loftus's own research into the manufacture of false memories, never loses sight of the human dimensions of the problem and of the need for bridge-building and conciliation.*

Both Richard Ofshe, a social psychologist, and Elizabeth Loftus, a cognitive psychologist, have been drawn into the recovered memory debate by their professional interests rather than their personal involvement. Mark Pendergrast, the author of Victims of Memory, *which is perhaps the most comprehensive study of the recovered memory movement, writes as an accused parent who is also an investigative journalist. His book, richly documented, and informed throughout by a sense of history, is both wise and profound. Perhaps the most striking testimony to its power is that of Joan Kennedy Taylor, National Coordinator of the Association of Libertarian Feminists in America. Reading Pendergrast's book as somebody who believed that memories of sexual abuse were often repressed until unearthed by special therapeutic techniques, she found this assumption turned upside down. 'I cannot remember ever before,' she writes, 'both admiring the research in a book and being moved to tears by it.'*[21]

Joan Kennedy Taylor's words convey the unusual character of Mark Pendergrast's book well. You do not need to be a king who has divided his kingdom between two of his daughters in order to appreciate the tragedy of King Lear. *You do not need to be a father who has been accused of unspecified sexual abuse by his daughters in order to appreciate the tragedy of* Victims of Memory. *Although it may seem inconsiderate of an author to end a very long book by recommending to his readers that they read another long book,* Victims of Memory *is such an unusual book that I feel I should not refrain from doing just this.*

The Diagnosis of 'Hysteria'*

ELIOT SLATER'S VIEWS have exercised considerable influence on psychiatrists and neurologists over the past thirty years and the use of the term 'hysteria' has declined in consequence. In the United States the diagnosis has, in theory at least, disappeared from mainstream psychiatry. Yet there appears to be a significant gap between theory and practice. If we are to believe the psychiatrist Philip Slavney, writing in 1990, the term still enjoys some currency even in American medical practice: 'Despite condemnation from physicians and feminists . . . the concept of "hysteria" is alive and well in the practice of medicine. No term so vilified is yet so popular; none so near extinction appears in better health.'[1]

As these words suggest, the questions raised by Slater's argument are very far from having been resolved. While this is not the place for a complete review of the problem, the continued confusion which surrounds the concept of 'hysteria' makes an abbreviated account seem necessary.

It should already be evident that Slater's position is not new or revolutionary. A small anthology of agnostic reactions to the concept of 'hysteria' is contained in Aubrey Lewis's paper 'The Survival of Hysteria' (1975). As early as 1874, W. B. Carpenter objected to the view that hysteria was a specific illness the grounds that 'there is no . . . fixed tendency to irregular action as would indicate any positive disease.' In 1899 J. A. Ormerod suggested that the objections to 'hysteria' were obvious: 'not only that it has become etymologically meaningless but also that to many minds it has the disagreeable connotation of a certain moral feebleness in the patient, and of unreality in the symptoms'. In 1904 the Swiss psychiatrist Dubois wrote that 'hysteria' should not be regarded as a disease entity, and in 1908 Steyerthal pronounced the unequivocal rejection of the idea that hysteria was a disease which has already been quoted (see above, Chapter 6). In 1911 Gaupp summarised the reaction which had by then taken place against Charcot: 'Nowadays the cry is ever louder: away with the name and concept of hysteria: there is no such thing, and what we call hysteria is either an artificial, iatrogenic product, or a melange of

---

* This appendix continues the discussion of hysteria which will be found at the beginning of Chapter 6.

symptoms which can occur in all sorts of illnesses and are not patho-
gnomonic of anything.' In 1925 Bumke looked back on the history of
psychiatry and wrote 'There was once a disease hysteria, just as there
was hypochondria, and neurasthenia. They have disappeared. The syndrome has replaced the disease entity.' In 1953 Kranz put forward his
view that

> hysterical phenomena are only modes of reaction which fundamentally are
> available to everybody and are not in themselves abnormal, but become so
> in that they last unduly long, become fixed or are excessive ... It is reasonable
> to ask that we should at least drop the word 'hysteria' in favour of 'hysterical
> reaction', and in the end give up this term too, loaded as it is with moral
> value judgments: we can make ourselves understood by psychiatrists without
> it. But in spite of all that 'hysteria' will not disappear altogether from psychi-
> atric vocabulary for a long time to come.[2]

Kranz's prophecy has proved accurate, especially with regard to the
situation in Britain. Although Eliot Slater's subsequent attempt to dislodge
the concept of 'hysteria' was probably as influential as any of the earlier
interventions, neither his arguments nor the conclusions he drew from
his research have been universally accepted. Aubrey Lewis, having anthol-
ogised the views quoted above, describes how he conducted his own follow-up inquiry on patients diagnosed as hysterical at the Maudsley
Hospital. He reports that he did not find any significant incidence of
misdiagnosis, and that therefore his study did not bear out Slater's conclusions. He notes that a significant divergence between the results of a
study based on a neurological hospital, and those of a study made at a
psychiatric hospital was only to be expected. Lewis still draws the conclusion, however, that the diagnosis of 'hysteria' is legitimate, 'so long as
it is regarded as a reaction'. He ends his paper by observing that 'the
majority of psychiatrists would be hard put to it if they could no longer
make a diagnosis of "hysteria" or "hysterical reaction"; and in any case,
a tough old word like hysteria dies very hard. It tends to outlive its obituarists.'

Even before Lewis's reply, the neurologist Sir Francis Walshe, writing
in the *British Medical Journal* in December 1965, sought to rebut Slater's
argument, seeing in it 'a challenge to neurologists once again to justify
the concept of hysteria as a nosological entity in its own right'. In a
remarkable paper Walshe passionately restates many of the central doctrines associated with the traditional concept of 'hysteria', some of them
dating back to Sydenham and beyond. Thus he reiterates the ancient
view that 'hysteria' often takes the form of 'a mimesis or ... caricature of
disturbances on the physiological and morphological levels' and goes on

to stress, again in traditional terms, that 'in view of the polymorphic manifestations of hysteria, diagnosis and psychological study present peculiar difficulties'. Although generally commending the views of Babinski, Walshe expresses regret that he declined to see hysteria as compatible with deception and 'pathological lying' on the patient's part – 'for it has long been acknowledged that the hysteric is a master, or a mistress of this upon occasion, and it may be an integral element in what is essentially a psychical illness. Lhermitte has said that "hysteria is the mother of deceit and trickery." '

Although Walshe stresses at several points in his article that physicians are fallible and prone to make mistakes, he simultaneously upholds a view of medicine in which it is implicitly regarded as a perfect science. He thus sees as one of the crucial characteristics of hysteria the presence in the patient of patterns of disorder that 'plainly arise from mental dispositions' and 'which are not congruous with nature's laws as observed in the physical and biological sciences . . .' Walshe's final words about what he terms 'the unity of hysteria' maintain the traditional view expounded throughout his paper:

> Whatever the kaleidoscope of its manifestations, I submit that its essential difference from somatic disease is that it constitutes *a behaviour disorder*, a human act, on the psychological level. An hysterical paraplegia is exactly this, but a compression paraplegia is not this at all.
>
> Apart from the mimesis of somatic disease hysteria may present, the dramatizations, the exaggerations and the pathological lying are also behavioural disorders, part of the total expression of the abnormal psychical state which is hysteria.[3]

Some of the other contributions to the debate have taken a similarly conservative view, and a number of psychiatrists seem surprisingly untroubled by the possibility that such a confused concept might increase the risk of misdiagnosis which is always faced by patients with obscure cerebral or neurological disorders. In other areas of psychiatry, however, the extraordinary variety of meanings which the word 'hysteria' has traditionally been made to bear, and the bewildering array of physical symptoms and mental states it has been invoked to explain, has given rise to concern. One response to such concern has been to attempt to resolve the problem through the adoption of new terminology. It was this approach which was taken by the American Psychiatric Association when the diagnosis of 'hysteria' disappeared from their *Diagnostic and Statistical Manual of Mental Disorders* in 1952. The shift away from traditional terminology has been consolidated in later editions. But although the concept of 'hysteria' is conspicuously absent from the list of recognised diagnoses, the manual does give criteria for the diagnosis of three disorders which are clearly derived from the traditional concept – 'conversion disorder', 'somatization disorder' and 'histrionic personality disorder'. The research criteria for the diagnosis of 'conversion disorder' as given by the third edition (*DSM III*) in 1980 were as follows:

A. The predominant disturbance is a loss of or alteration in physical functioning suggesting a physical disorder. It is involuntary and medically unexplainable...
B. One of the following must also be present:
    (1) A temporal relationship between symptom onset and some external event of psychological conflict.
    (2) The symptom allows the individual to avoid unpleasant activity.
    (3) The symptom provides opportunity for support which may not have been otherwise available.[4]

There are at least two apparent advantages of this approach. In the first place the disappearance of the label 'hysterical', with its pejorative and morally censorious overtones, is a considerable gain. In the second place the insistence that the physical symptom should be involuntary has the effect of separating this putative psychiatric disorder from deliberately feigned or simulated illnesses – a category which the traditional concept of 'hysteria' tends confusingly to embrace.

The *DSM III* definition of conversion order, however, is far from satisfactory. One major problem is that, although it excludes *consciously* simulated illness, it does not exclude the unconscious simulation of illness. What this means in practice is that patients with imaginary symptoms which have no apparent physiological basis have to be placed in the same category as patients whose symptoms seem real, but are not susceptible to medical explanation. The dangers of this approach should become evident if we consider the subsidiary indicators given for the disorder. Criterion (2) – that the symptom allows the individual to avoid unpleasant activity – is, it will be noted, scarcely specific to emotionally based disorders. Most forms of illness, from broken legs to acute appendicitis, create just such opportunities. Criterion (2) is thus rather like saying that a specific name may be given to a plant providing that its leaves are green. Though the restriction may create the illusion of rigour, the field of definition is not very much reduced. Something similar can be said about the next criterion. For since most illnesses provide an opportunity for seeking support – if only from a physician – criterion (3) is almost as empty as criterion (2). Among the subsidiary criteria this leaves only (1), which demands that there should be some kind of temporal relationship between the onset of the illness and 'some external event of psychological conflict'. The most fitting response to this is perhaps Slater's, in the words which are quoted in the main body of my text: 'Unfortunately we have to recognise that trouble, discord, anxiety and frustration are so prevalent at all stages of life that their mere occurrence near to the time of onset of an illness does not mean very much.'[5]

In view of the fact that the subsidiary criteria (1), (2) and (3) are objectively empty, or very nearly empty, it would seem that, in *DSM III*, the diagnosis of 'conversion disorder' relies almost entirely on the main condition and that therefore the only strict criterion is that the patient's symptoms should be medically inexplicable.

It is difficult not to draw the conclusion that, in formulating its criteria in this particular instance, the American Psychiatric Association did little more than take an old diagnostic error and give it a new name together with a new aura of respectability. Since the very concept of 'conversion' is specifically psychoanalytic, and since it is historically indivisible from Freud's own idiosyncratic theories of 'hysteria', it further seems that the creation of the category 'conversion disorder' was a politically astute way of preserving the old concept of 'hysteria' in euphemistic disguise.

To say this is not to rule out the possibility that there can be a direct relationship between prolonged stress or severe emotional trauma and *some* physical symptoms. Many common disorders do seem to be stress-related. In most cases, however, we do not yet understand the precise physiological mechanism of such a relationship. To confer medical respectability on a label originally invented by a nineteenth-century nerve-doctor who put forward as a scientific fact an entirely fictional account of the pathology of 'hysteria' seems, on the face of it, an unsatisfactory way of dealing with medical uncertainty. To allow the resulting syndrome, which has supposedly been carefully delimited, to be equally applicable to real physical symptoms and imaginary or spectral ones (providing they are not consciously produced) is merely to compound the original confusion.

Since 1980, *DSM III* has itself been revised and the definition of conversion disorder has been modified yet again. But the underlying concept has remained unaltered. Meanwhile relatively new terms such as 'conversion disorder' and 'somatization' have not entirely succeeded in ousting the older terminology. As Aubrey Lewis predicted, the term 'hysteria' has outlived its obituarists, and is still sometimes used as a diagnosis.

The dangers of this situation feature prominently in one of the most searching contributions to the entire debate, C. D. Marsden's paper 'Hysteria – a Neurologist's View', which was published in *Psychological Medicine* in 1986. After reviewing the concept of 'hysteria', Marsden gives careful consideration to the problem of misdiagnosis. He cites Slater's finding

that 58 per cent of his series of 'hysterical' patients had an underlying
organic illness and then quotes the work of Tissenbaum who, in a paper
published in 1951, specifically warned of the danger of misdiagnosing
patients with neurological disorders. No less than 53 (13.4 per cent) of a
series of 395 patients with organic neurological disorders were originally
wrongly diagnosed as suffering from psychiatric illness. This tendency
towards misdiagnosis was particularly marked in the field of movement
disorders, and among Tissenbaum's patients as many as 40 per cent of
those with Parkinson's disease were initially diagnosed as suffering from
psychiatric disorders. Since about half of all patients who are diagnosed
as 'hysterical' have some kind of movement disorder as their main symptom, such a high rate of misdiagnosis is extremely significant. Marsden's
own experience, as a neurologist specialising in movement disorders, bears
this out. He notes that in a standard diagnostic manual published in 1970
Engel lists a wide range of such disorders as symptoms of hysteria, including spasmodic torticollis, writer's cramp, blepharospasm and spasmodic
dysphonia.[6] He goes on to observe that all these conditions are now
thought to be manifestations of a physical disorder, namely torsion dys-
tonia. In his experience, however, '50% or more of such patients are still
initially misdiagnosed as hysterics.' Marsden goes on to endorse one of
the most significant of the arguments put forward by Slater:

> There can be little doubt that the term 'hysterical' is often applied as a
> diagnosis to something that the physician does not understand. It is used
> as a cloak for ignorance. In addition we can still recognise new neurological
> diseases. Not only can a patient's symptoms be dismissed as hysterical
> because the physician makes a mistake out of inexperience, but also because
> the illness has only recently been identified.
>
> Neurology has never been and is not static. Many neurological diseases
> are still not widely recognised ... No doubt there are many other neurologi-
> cal conditions still undiscovered. History tells us that there must be illnesses
> which presently we do not recognise but dismiss as 'hysterical'.

At this point in his argument, however, Marsden makes it clear that he
does not believe that medical progress is likely to remove altogether the
small percentage (1 per cent) of patients who make up the category which
has tended in the past to be labelled 'hysteria'. Since there are still likely
to be at least some patients who 'exhibit symptoms and/or signs that
cannot be explained by organic or functional disease' the question which
arises is how such patients are to be described. For, as Marsden writes,

> It is essential for communication between doctors and other health workers
> to have some form of shorthand to explain the state of affairs. Consider
> the paralysed patient who cannot walk, who may or may not have a mild

paraparesis, but whose major problem is weakness or even total paralysis not due to organic or functional disease. How are we to convey this concept?

Having noted Slater's plea for the abandonment of the diagnosis of 'hysteria' he goes on to observe that neurologists have sometimes fallen into the trap of calling such symptoms 'functional' – 'he had a functional paraplegia'. As Marsden points out, however, this common usage of 'functional' is actually a misuse of a word which correctly designates an illness which is presumed to be a real organic disorder but which has no visible pathology. Another alternative sometimes resorted to is 'psychogenic', as in 'he has a psychogenic paraplegia'. But Marsden brusquely, and I believe quite justly, dismisses this usage by referring to the view of Aubrey Lewis. According to Lewis the word 'psychogenic' is 'at the mercy of inconsistent theoretical positions touching on the fundamental problems of causality, dualism and normality. It would be as well at this stage to give it a decent burial, along with some of the fruitless controversies whose fire it has stoked.'[7]

Next Marsden considers the alternative 'conversion disorder' which, as we have seen, has been endorsed by the American Psychiatric Association. He finds this slightly more palatable than 'psychogenic' but nevertheless goes on to reject it on grounds very similar to those which I have already given. For as he points out, this ostensibly neutral term presumes a particular pathogenesis which was described by Freud, a pathogenesis which Marsden finds unconvincing.

Having temporarily renounced use of the term 'hysteria', and having declined for good reasons to adopt the most readily available substitutes, Marsden now recounts his own quest for an alternative. After experimenting with 'feigned' or 'simulated', as in 'a simulated paraplegia', he eventually rejects this usage on the grounds that the words suggest deceit where none may be meant. 'Most patients with neurological hysteria are not malingerers, and do not appear to be consciously pretending or trying to deceive.' He considers and rejects 'fictitious' on similar grounds and finally toys with another possibility: 'A fable is a fictitious tale, so why not "Aesop's syndrome" – he has an Aesoplegia (Aesopsia, Aesothesia, etc.).' This suggestion is perhaps not made entirely seriously, and Marsden goes on to suggest that the term 'hysteria' should be reconsidered. As he recognises, and as Slater cogently argues, one of the central objections to the medical use of the term is that is liable to be treated as a diagnosis rather than as a description. Marsden refers us back to Slater's original (1965) paper in which this distinction was discussed by reference to Brain's (1963) distinction between the adjectival and substantival views of hysteria, where the adjective was seen as implying a description of the symptom and

the noun a disease. Marsden goes on to quote the relevant passage from
Slater:

> I shall endeavour to persuade you that, to use Brain's terminology, the
> adjectival view can be maintained with some qualifications, whereas the
> substantival view cannot ... it would be legitimate, I believe, in a given
> instance to say that a particular symptom was 'hysterical'; ... however one
> should be aware of the possibilities of error. There is no 'hysterical' symptom
> which cannot be produced by well-defined, non hysterical cause ... With
> such a caveat, then, the adjectival use may be allowed to pass. However, to
> suppose that one is making a diagnosis when one says that a patient is
> suffering from 'hysteria' is, as I believe, to delude oneself. The justification
> for accepting 'hysteria' as a syndrome is based entirely on tradition and
> lacks evidential support. No closely definable meaning can be attached to
> it; and as a diagnosis it is used at peril. Both on theoretical and on practical
> grounds it is a term to be avoided.[8]

After making some adventurous detours to explore the possibility of new
terminology, Marsden thus returns almost to the place where he first
started and arrives at the conclusion that ' "hysterical" remains the historical and the best choice to describe such symptoms, provided that the term
is not used to imply a disease.'

It must be said that, occurring as it does in the course of one of the
most thoughtful and constructive contributions to the debate, this view is
disappointing. All the more so in view of the fact that, as we shall see,
Marsden goes on to make a number of extremely cogent suggestions about
how the symptoms he deems 'hysterical' should be treated.

The problem with his reversion to 'hysterical' is that it is nowhere
defended by argument and is supported only by the invocation of Slater.
Yet the passage which Marsden quotes smacks of a compromise which
Slater makes in order to deflect criticism from an argument which some
might consider extreme but which, if maintained consistently, ought to be
recognised as moderate and reasonable. The central objection to Slater's
attempt to split the concept of 'hysteria' into an illegitimate noun signifying a (non-existent) disease and a legitimate adjective which can be used
to describe some symptoms is that it introduces a crucial inconsistency
into his argument, while at the same time it defies ordinary language-use.
It is rather like licensing the use of the adjective 'canine' while denying
the existence of dogs. Under such a semantic regime it would, of course,
be perfectly possible for somebody who heard what he thought was a dog
barking to talk of having heard a canine noise. But it would, strictly
speaking, be illegitimate to draw the conclusion that this particular canine
noise indicated the existence of a dog. The case of the dog who did not

bark in the night is difficult enough. But it must be said that the case of the non-existent dog who repeatedly does bark is even more mysterious and more confusing.[9]

In taking over Slater's ill-considered linguistic compromise Marsden makes it quite clear that, in his new usage, the word 'hysterical' will not mean the same thing as it traditionally meant in the past. The standard dictionary definitions of the adjective will therefore no longer apply. For, rather than implying a positive characterisation of a symptom, or clutch of symptoms, 'hysterical' will now be used simply as a way of referring, in medical shorthand, to 'disturbances of function that cannot be explained fully by organic or functional neurological disease'. No emotional aetiology will initially be presumed and indeed the entire question of aetiology and pathology will remain an open question.

There can be no doubt that if in practice the term 'hysterical' could indeed be used in this radically new way a great deal of confusion would be cleared up. The difficulty is that Marsden's usage depends essentially on his own private redefinition of the word. The fact that he seeks, in his paper, to launch this private usage into the high seas of public medical discourse is likely to make very little difference. For although Marsden has redesigned the word 'hysterical' internally and loaded it with new meaning, outwardly it remains identical to older vessels bearing the same name. It is therefore liable to the presumption that it carries the same cargo. Repeated use of the term, however much it has been privately redefined, will tend to strengthen the concept of 'hysteria' in all of its diverse traditional meanings – just as repeated use of the word 'divine' tends to strengthen the concept of God and, in some contexts at least, implies the real existence of such a being.

The immense difficulties of maintaining the adjectival form 'hysterical' while renouncing the substantive from which it is derived are illustrated by Marsden himself. For no sooner has this policy been formulated than a table is introduced entitled 'The Six Rules of Hysteria'. Elsewhere in his paper Marsden uses the term 'neurological hysteria' without any reservations.

In view of this it is perhaps not surprising that Marsden's attempt to invest the term 'hysterical' with a radically new meaning should eventually be invoked by a physician who seeks to endorse one of the old meanings. This is what happens when Marsden's argument is referred to by the Freudian neuropsychologist Laurence Miller in his study of the neurological dimensions of psychoanalysis, *Freud's Brain: Neuropsychodynamic Foundations of Psychoanalysis*.[10] Miller follows Marsden by presenting to the reader a fascinating series of misdiagnoses in which a wide variety of genuine organic diseases have been misconstrued as hysteria. Some of these case histories are taken directly from Marsden's paper. Miller also draws on many other sources. A particularly striking aspect of the case histories he presents is the frequency with which epileptic seizures are misdiagnosed as hysterical even though EEGs have been administered between episodes. What often happens is that, because electrodes are applied only to the scalp, deep seizure activity is not registered. In these cases the patient is rescued from the diagnosis of hysteria only by depth electrode recordings which confirm the presence of epileptic seizure activity.[11]

Yet, having presented all the evidence necessary to mount a massively sceptical attack on the concept of 'hysteria', Miller declines to submit to this evidence. Updating Freud's conceptual vocabulary slightly, he puts forward a 'neuropsychodynamic model' of hysteria which

> asserts that the psychical impetus provided by the person's personality takes advantage of brain dynamics that are usually only seen in their boldest form in structural organic disorders of the brain but that may occur more transiently, more subtly, and in more complexly organised ways, interwoven with ordinary aspects of behaviour, when expressed in the form of 'functional,' or 'hysterical' symptoms. [12]

With considerable daring, Miller now treads even closer to the brink of scepticism only to draw back again at the last moment. 'If symptoms that were yesterday called hysterical,' he writes, 'are today considered to be (at least partly) organic because our modern knowledge of pathophysiology is greater than in the past, might not today's hysterical symptoms just as naturally become tomorrow's medical syndromes as our knowledge continues to grow?' The question, as Miller acknowledges, was originally posed by Marsden. Marsden's answer is one that he echoes and endorses: 'Not necessarily ... because the discovery of new diseases probably cannot go on for ever, and such new diseases certainly will not account for many of the one percent (Marsden's figure) of neurological patients presenting with *bona fide* hysterical symptoms.'[13] From these words it should be reasonably clear what has happened to Marsden's careful attempt to redefine the term 'hysterical'. Without doing any significant violence to the words which Marsden himself uses, Miller has managed to convert *bona fide* hysterical symptoms which do not indicate the existence of hysteria into *bona fide* symptoms which do.

Miller's appropriation of Marsden's sceptical argument for his own unsceptical purposes should be set alongside an even more remarkable reading of his argument which is offered in Mark Micale's survey of recent literature on the subject of 'hysteria'. Having noted that Slater's attack on the concept of hysteria was energetically resisted in some quarters, he cites as an example of such resistance 'a prominent London neurologist' who, we are told, 'has reaffirmed the value of the diagnosis in neurological practice.' In a footnote the neurologist is identified as C. D. Marsden and we are referred to the same article which I have discussed here.[14]

One reason why this whole argument continues to trouble physicians and other interested parties is that the questions of medical ignorance and medical progress raised by Miller are extremely important ones. One of the main problems in this area is that, as the history of medicine eloquently demonstrates, soundings taken by physicians of the depths of their own ignorance are notoriously unreliable. Whenever such soundings are taken it is almost invariably claimed that the waters are already shallow and that the dry land of absolute physiological knowledge will soon be in reach. In reality, however, the ocean of medical ignorance has remained both dark and deep and has concealed numberless shoals of undiscovered pathologies and physiological mechanisms. Writing in 1993 the psychiatrist Graeme Taylor pointed out that the tradition of identifying a disease as organic by the presence of structural lesions has been challenged more and more strongly in recent times 'as it is now evident that many medical, psychiatric and neurological patients have complex dynamic disorders of function in the brain and/or other physiological systems.' He goes on to suggest that medical research is likely to reveal many supposed psychogenic conditions as ' "legitimate" disorders of physiological function'.[15]

Marsden himself is exceptionally alert to the possibilities of future research shedding light on symptoms which today remain unexplained. At the same time, perhaps because of his own specialism, he is also exceptionally aware of the high proportion of confirmed misdiagnoses which are associated with the traditional concept of 'hysteria'. If we can for a moment disregard the question of terminology it is well worth considering the specific recommendations he makes regarding the treatment of those symptoms he classifies as 'hysterical'.

Since Marsden uses the term 'hysterical' to signify not a homogeneous class of symptoms but merely those signs which are not currently susceptible to medical explanation, he recognises that patients may manifest them for a variety of quite different reasons. The main purpose of classifying disparate symptoms as 'hysterical' is not to profess understanding of their nature but to emphasise that further investigations need to be made. The aim of these investigations, according to the scheme which Marsden offers, will be to come to at least a provisional conclusion as to whether the symptoms fall into any one of a number of different categories.

It may prove, on further investigation, that the initially unexplained symptoms are actually the signs of a recognised physical illness which is little known or whose symptoms are ambiguous. Alternatively they may be real symptoms of a disease which is not recognised. They may also be the product of some underlying psychiatric disorder such as schizophrenia or depression. For all these reasons Marsden emphasises that patients with inexplicable physical symptoms should be given further psychiatric and physical examinations. It is conceivable that these tests may lead the examining physician to conclude that the patient is exhibiting 'abnormal illness behaviour'. Some patients, Marsden suggests, are driven by a desire to help the doctor make a diagnosis: 'Their anxiety leads to elaboration or exaggeration of their real deficit.' Another group of patients may enjoy puzzling or outwitting the doctor, while others benefit from 'their so-called illness' in financial, social or personal terms. Such 'abnormal illness behaviour' may be motivated 'by fear of disease or death, or by reward as a result of the advantages of the invalid role, or both'. It may be adopted without any conscious awareness of its real motivation. In some cases, however, as in the case of malingering or simulation, it is acted out at a fully conscious level of the mind.

Marsden goes on to observe that those who consciously simulate illness, or who exaggerate or elaborate real physical illness because of their fear, clearly employ normal brain mechanisms to produce their signs and symptoms:

> But what of those who appear to believe in their loss or distortion of neuro-logical function, quite unconscious of the fact that their nervous system is operating normally, or at least much better than they think. In what way has their brain managed to dissociate conscious awareness from the mechanisms of sensation, movement, or even memory?
>
> Is there a nervous mechanism that can suppress, for example, the conscious appreciation of sensory experience from the reception of sensory information by the brain, or the will to move from the cerebral mechanisms responsible for generating movements?

He goes on to point out that both sensory appreciation and willed voluntary movement involve consciousness and suggests that it is here that contemporary neurobiology faces a major challenge, for 'the cerebral mechanisms of consciousness are not understood.' Having discussed this problem he suggests that future research may eventually illuminate this entire field: 'Exploitation of advanced neurophysiological techniques in those with hysteria may provide one way of studying the mechanisms involved in the generation of hysterical symptoms.'

Marsden thus ends his paper on a genuine note of scientific openness, showing himself refreshingly willing to admit the depths of current neuro-physiological ignorance, as well as refreshingly determined that those depths should eventually be plumbed. It must be pointed out, however, that at the very same time that he does this, he inadvertently allows the illegitimate substantival form 'hysteria' back into the closing paragraph of the very paper in which he announces its banishment. The moral of this story should be clear: If non-existent dogs are encouraged to bark, it will not be long before they bound back from their quarantine-pen bringing non-existent diseases with them.

Both the pathology and the remedy for this particular outbreak of linguistic confusion can be traced, I believe, if we examine the relevant step in Marsden's own argument. For it will be recalled that his decision to re-adopt the term 'hysterical' is made in response to his quest for suitable medical shorthand to convey the concept of symptoms which have no apparent organic cause. Shorthand should, by common consent, be succinct, objective and unambiguous. 'Hysterical' is certainly succinct. But it is neither an objective nor an unambiguous way of *suspending* judgement on the pathology of puzzling physical symptoms. If such symptoms are indeed to be described as accurately and objectively as possible, then perhaps they should be formally referred to as 'unexplained physical symptoms'. This description may not add greatly to the scientific self-esteem of those physicians and psychiatrists who are obliged to utter it. But scientific self-esteem is not everything. Those medical practitioners who, suffering from 'physics-envy', attempt to invest medicine with more precision and certainty than the current state of medical knowledge allows, do a disservice to their profession and to their patients.

The fact that few doctors and few patients would be likely to rest content with such a formula is a point in its favour. 'Hysterical', though offered by Marsden merely as an interim label, sounds far too much like a diagnostic conclusion and might easily discourage further investigation. 'Unexplained physical symptoms' is patently not a diagnosis and invites – and indeed almost compels – further efforts towards understanding.

If further investigation shows that there is strong, irrefutable evidence that the symptom is simulated then this verdict should be perhaps be stated by explicitly calling attention to the *conscious* process – 'a consciously simulated paraplegia' is unambiguous, whereas 'a simulated paraplegia' might be construed as unconscious. If the symptom is apparently real to the patient, but cannot be confirmed by medical tests, and therefore seems in some sense *unreal*, we are confronted by the same problem with which Marsden wrestles unsuccessfully in the course of his paper. One possibility which Marsden does not consider is the one suggested by Molière when he called his play about hypochondria *Le Malade Imaginaire*. Patients might be described as suffering from 'an imaginary illness' or 'an imaginary symptom'. The problem with this usage is that it does not correspond to the experience of patients who genuinely believe that their symptoms are real.

For normally we recognise the products of our imagination as such; a novelist does not usually ask his characters to dinner or invite them to stay for the weekend. It is because the term 'imaginary' is deficient in this respect that it might well be worth considering an alternative: 'spectral'. The advantage of this term is that it does correspond to the experience of many patients, and to the observations of many physicians. A 'spectral' symptom is a kind of physiological ghost. Like a ghost it can seem completely real to the person who experiences it, and for this reason it can generate strong emotional reactions, such as fear. But, like a ghost, a 'spectral' symptom *appears* to have no physiological substance. This may be because it is indeed the product of the patient's imagination. But it might also be a kind of physiological hallucination – a product of exactly the kind of subtle neurophysiological disorder of consciousness on whose existence Marsden speculates at the close of his own paper.

There may well be good reasons for not adopting the term 'spectral'. But it would be difficult to claim that the adequacy of current medical terminology should be counted among them. For even where the concept of 'hysteria' has been discarded as old-fashioned, a great deal of confusion still seems to be associated with the terms which have been adopted in its place. One example of such confusion is provided by the increasingly widespread use of the term 'somatization'. In 1980 *DSM III* adopted 'somatization disorder' as a recognised psychiatric diagnosis, characterising the disorder as a syndrome of multiple somatic symptoms that cannot be explained medically. The revised edition of *DSM III*, produced in 1987, requires a history of several years' duration beginning before the age of thirty. The patient must have at least thirteen symptoms from a list of thirty-five. According to the most recent edition of the most authoritative American psychiatric textbook, Kaplan and Sadock's *Comprehensive Textbook of Psychiatry V*, 'A symptom need only be reported by the patient in order to be counted; it is not necessary to establish that the patient actually had the symptom.'[16] Among the symptoms included in the list of thirty-five are diarrhoea, nausea, back pain, chest pain, trouble walking (sic), difficulty urinating, sexual indifference, and menstrual periods which are judged by the patient concerned to be more irregular or more painful than is normal.

There can be no doubt that physicians do frequently encounter patients who report multiple physical symptoms which they have imagined or exaggerated because of their anxiety, insecurity or need for attention, and that many such patients believe themselves to be genuinely ill. The problem posed by such patients is an extremely serious one, partly because they can use up a disproportionate amount of a country's health services, and partly because their tendency to take refuge in illness often masks serious psychological distress.[17] But describing such patients as 'somatisers' or judging that they suffer from 'somatization disorder' merely adds another layer of confusion to a situation which is already confused enough. For the term somatization has at least two different, mutually contradictory meanings. In Kaplan and Sadock's *Comprehensive Textbook of Psychiatry V* we are offered the following definition of the term in the section devoted to 'Somatoform Disorders': '*Somatization* is the tendency to experience, to conceptualise and to communicate mental states and personal distress as bodily complaints and medical symptoms.' We are told that somatization is a general psychological disposition and that it is not in itself a psychiatric disorder although it can become one in extreme manifestations. We are further told that whereas the concept of a conversion reaction was elaborated in the psychoanalytic tradition, 'somatization disorder originated in the phenomenological and descriptive approach'.[18]

Yet if we turn from the section on 'Somatoform Disorders' to that devoted to classical psychoanalysis, we find that the concept of somatization makes its appearance in a list of 'Immature Defence Mechanisms'. In somatization, we are told, 'psychic derivatives are converted into bodily symptoms and there is the tendency to react with somatic rather than psychic manifestations.'[19] On this view, then, somatization, far from being distinct from conversion, appears to be cognate with the process of hysterical conversion which Freud himself postulated and which was adopted as a key aetiological assumption in the first edition of the *DSM*, which defined a conversion reaction as a functional symptom resulting from the conversion of anxiety into bodily sensations. The psychiatrist Z. J. Lipowski, who has had a major influence on popularising the term, actually confirms its origin in psychoanalytic terminology when he writes that the term 'was introduced by Stekel early in this century to refer to a hypothetical process whereby a "deep-seated" neurosis could cause a bodily disorder.' As Lipowski notes, the term somatization 'was thus related to, if not identical with, the concept of conversion'.[20] Having acknowledged its psychoanalytic origins, Lipowski then goes on to use the term in the non-psychoanalytic sense given above.

The confusion as to what somatization actually means, and where the concept comes from, is significant. For while it may well be the case that it has been redefined in terms of phenomenology, it must be suggested that its strongest appeal to psychiatrists, and the reason it has been adopted so widely, springs from the fact that it is both congruent with psychoanalytic assumptions and, ostensibly at least, independent of them. In its 'strong' sense, which also coincides with its etymological sense, the word 'somatization' refers to a process whereby real physical symptoms are supposedly created by transforming psychological or emotional energy into somatic form. In its 'weak' sense the word refers to a process in which patients use a multiplicity of physical symptoms, which may be imaginary or non-existent, in order to mask depression or anxiety or in order to establish a particular kind of relationship with doctors. A major problem stemming from this conceptual double-life is that, as is the case with 'hysteria', the widespread use of the 'weak' form of the word actually tends to reinforce the psychosomatic fundamentalism of those wedded to the 'strong' form of the word and to the psychoanalytic aetiologies associated with it.[21]

The greatest practical danger of this state of affairs is that it encourages physicians to entertain in a somewhat inchoate form the extreme Charcotian or Freudian assumption that almost any physical symptom can be produced psychosomatically. This assumption is sometimes actively encouraged by careless and historically ill-informed discussions of topics like 'hysteria' which sometimes find their way into influential medical textbooks. In one of the most highly regarded and commonly used British textbooks on clinical neurology, which was first published in 1989, and from which many future general practitioners and hospital doctors learn the principles of neurological diagnosis, Sir Francis Walshe's attempt to rebut Eliot Slater is cited in positive terms and we find the following discussion of hysteria:

> Hysteria involves a state of dissociation or conversion, unconsciously determined for emotional gain ... The gain is usually not a simple desire to manipulate others or obtain a financial reward, it is often an attempt to reduce intolerable anxiety ...
>
> Conversion is a concept whereby anxiety is 'converted' to a physical symptom and anxiety is relieved in the process ... Conversion symptoms can be motor, such as disturbance of gait, loss of speech, muscle weakness or paralysis and abnormal movements. Sensory symptoms include pain anaesthesias, blindness and deafness...
>
> *Hysterical symptoms may mimic almost any medical condition*, and the diagnosis is even more difficult when there is an 'hysterical overlay' [italics added].[22]

The extraordinary claim that 'hysterical symptoms may mimic almost any medical condition' derives ultimately not from any body of medical knowledge, but from centuries-old medical lore which, even though it is based on physiological fallacies, has been accepted on trust by generations of physicians. Although the author of the passage which is quoted above goes on to warn his readers of the dangers of misdiagnosis, he seems not to understand that many of these dangers are a direct product of formulations such as the one he has given.

The capacity of such formulations to mislead is perhaps best understood if we place them alongside an extreme version of psychosomatics such as that of Freud's follower Georg Groddeck. Groddeck believed (or sometimes behaved as though he believed) that illnesses performed a psychological function and that specific illnesses could actually be produced by the unconscious, which he called the 'It':

> Sometime or other in the course of the treatment I am accustomed to call my patient's attention to the fact that from the human semen there is born, not a dog, nor a cat, but a human being, that there is some force within the germ which is able to fashion a nose, a finger, a brain, [and] that accordingly this force, which carries out such marvellous processes, might well produce a headache or diarrhoea or an inflamed throat, that indeed I do not consider it unreasonable to suppose that it can even manufacture pneumonia or gout or cancer. I dare to go so far with my patients as to maintain that the force really does such things, that according to its pleasure it makes people ill for specific ends...

In this particular case Groddeck writes that he never worries himself in the least 'as to whether I believe what I am saying or not'. But he does appear to endorse the view that all diseases have a psychological function:

> May I repeat what I am saying? Illness has a purpose; it has to resolve the conflict, to repress it, or to prevent what is already repressed from entering consciousness; it has to punish a sin against a commandment ... Whoever breaks an arm has either sinned or wished to commit a sin with that arm, perhaps murder, perhaps theft or masturbation; whoever goes blind desires no more to see, has sinned with his eyes or wishes to sin with them; whoever gets hoarse has a secret and dares not tell it aloud. But the sickness is also a symbol, a representation of something going on within, a drama staged by the It, by means of which it announces what it could not say with the tongue. In other words, sickness, every sickness, whether it be called organic or 'nervous', and death too, are just as purposeful as playing the piano, striking a match, or crossing one's legs. They are a declaration from the It, clearer, more effective than speech could be, yes, more than the whole of the conscious life can give.[23]

It would be easy to dismiss Groddeck's paeans to the purposefulness of disease as a historical curiosity with no relevance to the present. Yet Groddeck's views are still taken seriously by many people today, including some mainstream physicians.[24]

It would seem that one of the reasons his theories continue to exercise an appeal some seventy years after they were first published is that, like Freud's theories with which they are closely associated, they translate into a persuasive (and highly poetic) register a popular folk-theory of medicine which has a very wide appeal. It is from this perspective, I believe, that we should view the claim that hysteria may 'mimic almost any medical condition'. When such careless claims are made by experienced physicians in textbooks which credulous medical students are expected to treat with respect, they tend to confer academic respectability on this kind of folklore. This, in turn, can all too easily result in dangerous or even fatal misdiagnoses.

In an article dealing with the tendency of doctors to misdiagnose real organic conditions as psychological disorders, Linda Gamlin relates the case of a woman who, by the time she was taken to hospital, was so ill that she nearly died. 'For over two weeks she had been feverish and extremely weak, with typical signs of liver disease: yellow skin, dark brown urine, and putty-coloured stools.' The woman's general practitioner, however, had diagnosed post-natal depression and had associated her illness with an emotional breakdown which she had suffered seven years earlier. This view was repeated by no less than four other doctors in her group practice. Only when her husband rang a hospital consultant in desperation was the proper diagnosis of viral hepatitis made and the woman rushed to hospital.[25]

Such anecdotes can be multiplied almost indefinitely. A common feature of many of them is the credulous and perhaps not always fully conscious acceptance by some physicians of extreme theories of psychosomatic illness for whose correctness there exists no evidence whatsoever, and which are ultimately derived from ancient medical fallacies about the nonexistent disease of hysteria.

The careless use of the term 'somatization', and, indeed, the very fact that this medically tendentious word is used at all, almost certainly contributes to sustaining this climate of credulity. It also suggests that modifications of terminology alone will not solve any problems. It is the concept of 'hysteria' and not merely the external label which needs to be discarded.

This does not mean that we should deny that emotional experiences can have neurological or other physiological consequences. What we should recognise, however, is that emotional events (such as stress, trauma or shock) are themselves experienced by the human organism as *physiological* changes. It is in these changes, and not in some putative, purely psychological realm, that we should seek the cause of *real* symptoms which, after exhaustive investigation, *do* seem to be correlated with intense emotions. If 'hysteria' has indeed functioned for centuries as a diagnostic dustbin into which physicians have tossed a huge and ill-assorted selection of diseases, syndromes, symptoms, and responses, there may well be one or several discrete syndromes within it which do have this kind of complex relationship to the physiology of human emotions. This does not mean, however, that the term 'hysteria' should be retained, any more than recognition of the reality of, say, catamenial epilepsy, indicates that 'lunacy' ought to be retained as a serious psychiatric category.[26]

In those quite different cases where it can be proved beyond doubt that we are dealing with *unreal* symptoms, which involve no organic dysfunction, then we are by definition dealing not with a disease but with a behavioural problem. There is therefore no reason why a term which is still associated with a disease-concept, and whose currency is owed almost entirely to the prevalence of misdiagnosis and medical ignorance in the past, should be invoked.

The crux of the problem is that medicine has, for very many centuries, framed its discussions of symptoms in terms of a creationist ontology. Medical practitioners have, in other words, accepted the dualistic proposition that human beings are made up of two separate but interconnected entities – a physical body and a non-physical mind or soul. Such dualism has actually been institutionalised in the profession. For, originally at least, 'psychiatry' was understood as a branch of medicine which was not concerned with diseases of the body or any organic dysfunction, but solely with diseases of the mind or soul. The very complexity which has been traditionally attributed to the soul has sometimes actually encouraged physicians to accept or tolerate an impoverished notion of the body and its extraordinary neurological and biochemical complexity. It is the fact that orthodox medicine has tended historically to underestimate the neurophysiological complexity of the human body that has enhanced the credibility not only of therapeutic systems such as psychoanalysis but also of a whole range of 'alternative' approaches to medicine. For although many of these therapies may be entirely spurious, there can be little doubt that those who proclaim 'the power of the soul to heal' are *in some cases* dealing with quite genuine physiological phenomena which orthodox medicine has accidentally defined out of its model of the body.[27]

During the 'medical dark ages', from which we only began to emerge at the beginning of this century, and during which physicians remained extraordinarily ignorant about countless aspects of human physiology and human pathology, dualistic models of the human organism were inevitable and perhaps even necessary. In our present post-Darwinian era we will only cause confusion if we persist in using them. For when physicians continue to use terms such as 'hysteria', 'somatization', 'psychogenic' and even 'psychosomatic', they merely perpetuate the very kind of creationist dualism which I have tried to analyse in the last part of this book. Such dualism is no more conducive to clear thinking about medicine than it is to clear thinking about any form of human behaviour.

Babinski's Test for 'Hysteria'

PERHAPS THE MOST distinguished of all of those of Charcot's pupils who, unlike Freud and Janet, elected to continue their career as neurologists, was Joseph Babinski. Babinski was Charcot's chief assistant for many years. In 1896, three years after his master's death, he discovered the toe reflex which was named after him, and which is still known by physicians as 'Babinski's sign'. (The reflex is elicited by firmly stroking the outer border of the whole of each foot. Normally the big toe will turn down. If the toe turns up – a movement which is often accompanied by fanning out of the toes – this is usually taken to indicate the presence of an upper motor neurone lesion.)

After Charcot's death and even before his discovery of the plantar reflex, Babinski began to take issue with the doctrine of hysteria which he had, up until that point, been obliged to accept. He did not dispense with the concept altogether but restricted it to conditions which could, in his view, be induced by 'suggestion'. In this way he managed, at a single stroke, to exclude a large number of the diagnostic absurdities which had begun to proliferate under the influence of Charcot – such as the tendency to diagnose hysteria in cases of paralysis accompanied by exaggerated reflexes, ulceration, haemorrhage or even gangrene. He even attempted to displace the traditional label of 'hysteria' with his own coinage – 'pithiatism' – which was formed from the Greek term for 'suggestion'.

Some of Babinski's criticisms of Charcot were sound. But it would be quite wrong to suggest that Babinski was himself immune to diagnostic error or that he ever understood the real nature of Charcot's mistakes. He too, it should be remembered, learned his neurology long before the advent of the electro-encephalogram and, like all his contemporaries, did not have the help either of this or of other non-invasive investigatory techniques which have been invented since. Partly because of this, and partly because neurology was such a young science at the time he practised, Babinski's revised concept of 'hysteria' or 'pithiatism' was based on a number of misconceptions. Some of these misconceptions were implicitly endorsed by Sir Francis Walshe, who, as we have seen, invoked Babinski's authority in support of his own attempt to defend the diagnosis of 'hysteria' against Eliot Slater's critique (see above, Appendix I).

Perhaps the clearest example of the manner in which neurological misconceptions were carried over by Babinski from the nineteenth century
into the twentieth is provided by what I have called 'Babinski's Test for
Hysteria'. The test was supposed to enable physicians to discriminate
reliably between fits which were 'genuinely' epileptic and those which
were caused by 'hysteria'. Like many nineteenth-century neurologists (and
a good many twentieth-century ones), Babinski believed it was possible
to recognise hysterical attacks by looking for certain seizure patterns and
maintained that hysterical attacks 'are ... distinguished by the form which
they assume (wide-ranged movements, gesticulations and opisthotonos
[extreme backwards arching of the spine as in the arc-de-cercle position])'.
As we have already seen, the seizure pattern which Babinski describes here
corresponds closely to that encountered in some cases of frontal lobe
epilepsy, and Babinski's confident assumption that such florid symptomatology proclaimed the hysterical nature of the fit in question has been
shown to be mistaken.

Babinski, however, was not content to apply merely one criterion. For
he believed that a hysterical fit could be recognised by another characteristic which was conclusive – 'the possibility of reproducing it exactly by
suggestion, and causing it to disappear immediately by counter-sugges-
tion'. Although the term 'suggestion' might very reasonably be construed
as signifying merely an oblique hint given to the patient by the physician,
this is not how Babinski and his colleague and co-author Froment understood it. They describe their 'test' in the following terms:

> We first of all announce in the patient's hearing that we are going to try
> to reproduce the attack, this being indispensable to enable us to lay down
> the treatment and to get a proper understanding of the case. We add that
> electricity is almost infallible in such cases, especially when the electrodes
> of the faradic machine are placed on a definite spot. It is not necessary to
> employ strong currents; sometimes, even, we content ourselves with merely
> applying the electrodes without passing the current.
>
> Shortly after we have put the electrodes in position, we declare that the
> attack is going to begin and that the patient will struggle. To prevent his
> falling we put him at full length on the ground or on a bed. As a rule, in
> cases of hysteria the effects of suggestion appear rapidly; the legs become
> stiff, the body is thrown into contortions, and the fit proceeds with special
> modifications according to the individual. As soon as the attack is fully
> developed, we declare that we have an infallible method for arresting it. We
> then apply the electrodes to another region, or we exercise a pressure on
> the abdomen or trunk, saying in a confident tone that the attack will be
> over in a few moments. In fact, an hysterical attack produced in this way
> does stop, and the subject is at once able to answer questions put to him
> and to leave the room where the examination has taken place.[1]

What is perhaps most remarkable about these words is the clear implication that Babinski did not simply feign giving electric shocks to his patients, but that, on some occasions at least, he actually administered *real* shocks. Since electro-convulsive therapy itself consists in using electric shocks in order to provoke 'artificial' attacks of epilepsy, we cannot rule out the possibility that Babinski may inadvertently have done exactly this in some of his 'tests'.

In view of the low currents which were apparently used this is perhaps less likely than might first appear to be the case. But even in those instances where no current was passed at all, the procedure which Babinski describes is unsuitable as a means of discriminating between epileptic and non-epileptic convulsions. This is because it might quite easily have triggered genuine epileptic seizures.

For by announcing his intention to administer an electric shock to his patients and by predicting that this will provoke a seizure, Babinski was subjecting them to a quite considerable level of stress. Research carried out in 1971 suggested that emotional stress precipitated fits in 21 per cent of patients with temporal lobe epilepsy. Citing this finding, C. D. Marsden and E. H. Reynolds specifically note that 'even minor medical manipulations, such as blood-letting, dental treatment or ear syringing, may provoke a fit in a susceptible subject'.[2] At the same time, as T. A. Betts has noted, 'some people with self-induced epilepsy seem able to produce an attack at will, or on request, but without any realization of how they do it; some unconsciously hyperventilate; others do it by an effort of concentration.'[3] The conclusion we must draw from these and many similar observations is that Babinski's supposedly 'conclusive' test for epilepsy was unreliable, and – particularly in view of the fact that those simulating fits might well see through Babinski's deception – just as likely to lead to an incorrect diagnosis as a correct one.

The point is not simply a historical one. For, even though it seems highly unlikely that Babinski's specific test survived much beyond the 1950s, variations on it have been described in relatively recent times. I have already referred to a paper by R. P. Lesser and his colleagues, in which they report the case of a patient in whom a genuine seizure appears to have been triggered by 'suggestion' (see above, pp. 85–6). What was *not* noted was the kind of 'suggestion' which was being used. In summarising the paper in his book *Freud's Brain*, Laurence Miller refers to a process of 'hypnotic suggestion'. Yet the paper itself does not use the term 'hypnotic' at all, and indeed it actually fails to report the method which Lesser used. One clue to this minor medical mystery is perhaps provided in a slightly earlier paper by Lesser and his colleagues. A note in this paper provides a cross-reference to a third paper. The authors of *this* paper describe a procedure very similar to that used by Babinski and Froment in 1914, except that in this case the place of the electric shock is taken by an intravenous saline injection.[4] This version of the test is, of course, open to many of the objections already levelled against what would appear to be its prototype. That Babinski should have made this mistake in the early years of the century is at least understandable. That Lesser and his colleagues should have repeated it in 1983, and that they should then subsequently have failed to describe the procedure they were using in a paper in which they themselves questioned its reliability, is rather less so.

Notes and References

THE FULLEST SOURCE for Freud's ideas is the twenty-four-volume *Standard Edition of the Complete Psychological Works of Sigmund Freud* edited by James Strachey. Much more widely available is the fifteen-volume Penguin Freud Library edited by Angela Richards and Albert Dickson. This edition contains most of Freud's major writings, but excludes some essays and a number of papers – such as 'The Aetiology of Hysteria' – which have become increasingly important to Freud scholars in recent years.

I have often worked from the Penguin edition but, wherever possible, I have given references both to the Standard Edition (abbreviated as SE followed by the volume number) and to the Penguin Freud Library (abbreviated as PF followed by the volume number). The task of converting these references was made immeasurably easier by one of the most useful achievements of modern psychoanalytic scholarship, *The Concordance to the Standard Edition of the Complete Psychological Works of Sigmund Freud*, edited by Samuel A. Guttman, Randall L. Jones and Stephen M. Parrish (6 volumes, Boston: G. K. Hall, 1980).

One minor but irksome problem for Freud scholars is that the pagination of two key texts – Ernest Jones's three-volume biography of Freud, and the standard selection of Freud's letters (*The Letters of Sigmund Freud, 1873–1939*, ed. Ernst L. Freud) – is different in the British and American editions. In the face of this problem I have adopted two different solutions. In the case of Freud's letters all references are to the British edition, but I have included details of the recipient and date of the letter so that the corresponding passage in the American edition may be located with relative ease. In the case of Ernest Jones's biography I have followed the example of Ronald Clark and given both sets of references. The page numbers to the British edition are given first. The page numbers to the American edition are italicised and given second. I have also included, wherever possible, the page reference to the Penguin edition of the one-volume abridged version of Jones's biography.

For ease of reference the works repeatedly cited (and therefore most frequently abbreviated in the notes) are as follows, preceded by their abbreviation:

Clark:	Ronald W. Clark, *Freud: The Man and the Cause*, Jonathan Cape/Weidenfeld and Nicolson, 1982
Ellenberger:	Henri Ellenberger, *The Discovery of the Unconscious: The History and Evolution of Dynamic Psychiatry*, New York: Basic Books, 1970.
Freud, SE:	Sigmund Freud, *The Standard Edition of the Complete Psychological Works of Sigmund Freud*, ed. James Strachey, Hogarth Press and the Institute of Psycho-Analysis, 24 volumes, 1953–74.
PF:	Angela Richards and Albert Dickson (ed.), *The Penguin Freud Library*, Penguin, 15 volumes, 1973–86.
FF:	Jeffrey Mousaieff Masson (ed.), *The Complete Letters of Sigmund Freud to Wilhelm Fliess 1887–1904*, Harvard University Press, 1985.
Letters:	Ernst L. Freud (ed.), *Letters of Sigmund Freud, 1873–1939*, Hogarth Press, 1961. (Pagination of American edition differs, see above.)
Gay:	Peter Gay, *Freud: A Life for Our Time*, Dent, 1988.
Jones:	Ernest Jones, *Sigmund Freud: Life and Work*, 3 volumes, London: Hogarth Press (1953–7); *The Life and Work of Sigmund Freud*, 3 volumes, New York: Basic Books (1953–7). (On pagination of and references to the British and American editions, see above.) All references to volumes 1 and 2 of the Hogarth edition are to the second editions (1954 and 1958 respectively). All other references are to the first editions. Penguin edition, *The Life and Work of Sigmund Freud*, edited and abridged by Lionel Trilling and Steven Marcus, Penguin, 1964.
Macmillan:	Malcolm Macmillan, *Freud Evaluated: The Completed Arc*, Amsterdam: New Holland, 1991.
Roazen:	Paul Roazen, *Freud and His Followers*, Penguin, 1979.

Sulloway: Frank Sulloway, *Freud, Biologist of the Mind: Beyond the Psychoanalytic Legend*, Burnett Books/André Deutsch, 1979.

Thornton: E. M. Thornton, *The Freudian Fallacy: Freud and Cocaine*, Paladin, 1986. (First published in Britain by Blond and Briggs Ltd, 1983, under the title *Freud and Cocaine*. All references are to the revised British paperback edition.)

INTRODUCTION · THE LEGACY OF FREUD

1. Gershon Legman, quoted in Gay Talese, *Thy Neighbour's Wife*, Pan, 1980, p. 389.
2. Lucy Freeman, *Freud Rediscovered*, 1980, New York: Arbor House, pp. 1−2.
3. Walter Kendrick, review of Jeffrey Masson's *Freud: The Assault on Truth*, *Voice Literary Supplement*, June 1984.
4. Phyllis Grosskurth, *The Secret Ring: Freud's Inner Circle and the Politics of Psychoanalysis*, Jonathan Cape, 1991, p. 14.
5. Paul Robinson, *Freud and His Critics*, University of California Press, 1993, p. 269.
6. Harold Bloom, 'Freud, the Greatest Modern Writer', *New York Times Book Review*, 23 March 1986, quoted in Robinson, p. 270.
7. Freud, *Minutes of the Vienna Psychoanalytic Society*, ed. Herman Nunberg and Ernst Federn, vol. II, New York: International Universities Press, 1967.
8. Erik H. Erikson, *Young Man Luther*, New York: W. W. Norton, 1958; Norman O. Brown, *Life Against Death*, Routledge and Kegan Paul, 1959.
9. John Updike, in his introduction to F. J. Sheed (ed.), *Soundings in Satanism*, Mowbrays, 1972, p. vii. The best-known modern example of this attitude will be found in Bishop John Robinson's *Honest to God* (SCM Press Ltd, 1963), in which the traditional doctrines and beliefs of Christianity are systematically repudiated. John Robinson's position is very close to that outlined by the Anglican lay-theologian John Wren-Lewis, whose words he quotes:

> I cannot emphasise too strongly that acceptance of the Christian faith became possible for me *only* because I did not have to go back on my wholesale rejection of the superstitious beliefs which surrounded me . . . There is a misplaced sense of loyalty which makes many Christians feel reluctant to come out in open opposition to anything that calls itself by the same name, or uses words like 'God' and 'Christ'; even Christians who in practice dislike superstition as much as I do still often treat it as a minor aberration to be hushed up rather than a radical perversion to be denounced . . . In fact a very large part of what passes for religion in our society is exactly the sort of neurotic illness which

Freud describes, and the first essential step in convincing people that Christianity can be true in spite of Freud is to assert outright that belief based on the projection mechanisms he describes is false, however much it may say 'Lord, Lord.' It is not enough to describe such beliefs as childish or primitive, for this implies that the truth is *something* like them, even though more 'refined' and 'enlightened', whereas in reality *nothing like* the 'God' and 'Christ' I was brought up to believe in can be true. It is not merely that the Old Man in the Sky is only a mythological symbol for the Infinite Mind behind the scenes, nor yet that this Being is benevolent rather than fearful; the truth is that this whole way of thinking is wrong, and if such a Being did exist he would be the very devil (quoted in *Honest to God*, p. 43).

The theology of John Robinson and John Wren-Lewis is by no means as novel as might be supposed. Historically speaking this kind of theology has its origins in extreme Puritanism. In 1650 the Leveller Gerrard Winstanley wrote that the traditional Christian, who 'thinks God is in the heavens above the skies, and so prays to that God which he imagines to be there and everywhere ... worships his own imagination which is the devil' (quoted in Christopher Hill, *The World Turned Upside Down*, Penguin, 1975, p. 140). It is both interesting and significant that while Wren-Lewis and Winstanley both decry 'superstitions' neither of them can dispense with the concept of 'devil' and both end by eschewing reasoned criticism of the beliefs they oppose in favour of a kind of exasperated demonology.

10. Although I have included in this list psychoanalytic writers who have, in my view, made interesting contributions to psychology, the inclusion of any particular writer should not be construed as an unqualified endorsement of his or her work. In the case of John Bowlby, for example, it remains my impression that, for all the immense value of his work in changing hospital practice, his theoretical contribution tends to be accepted uncritically by too many writers (particularly those who are out of sympathy with Freud), simply because it *appears* to have empirical foundations and a sounder relation to Darwinian theory than can be claimed by classical psychoanalysis. For an interesting view of Bowlby, see Jeremy Holmes, *John Bowlby and Attachment Theory*, Routledge, 1993. See also Michael Rutter's *Maternal Deprivation Reassessed*, 2nd edition, Penguin, 1981. Rutter's criticisms of Bowlby, though mildly put, add up to a significant repudiation of the lofty estimate which Bowlby formed of his own theories.

I yoke together Lawrence Kubie and Joel Kovel because of Kovel's *White Racism: A Psychohistory*, Allen Lane, 1972, in which Kovel acknowledges his debt to Kubie's 'The Fantasy of Dirt', *Psychoanalytic Quarterly*, vol. VI, 1937. Kovel is one of the few psychoanalysts to have appreciated something of the value and profundity of Kubie's paper.

11. Chesterton, quoted in Frank Cioffi (ed.), *Freud: Modern Judgments*, Macmillan, 1973, p. 24.

12. Gide, quoted by Cioffi, p. 23.

13. Dreiser, quoted in Ronald W. Clark, *Freud: The Man and the Cause*, Paladin, 1982, p. 421.

14. Although he makes no such sweeping claim as I have made here, it is interesting that Paul Roazen has written that 'whereas others have taken pains to differentiate their work from Freud's, Erikson actually ascribed his own ideas to Freud. Erikson does not always seem to want to acknowledge his own originality' (*Freud and His Followers*, Penguin, 1979, p. 500).

PROLOGUE · IMAGES, MYTHS AND LEGENDS

1. Thomas Mann, in Frank Cioffi (ed.), *Freud: Modern Judgments*, Macmillan, 1973, pp. 58–9.

2. See in particular Frank J. Sulloway, *Freud: Biologist of the Mind: Beyond the Psychoanalytic Legend*, Burnett Books, 1979, *passim*. Also Henri Ellenberger, *The Discovery of the Unconscious: The History and Evolution of Dynamic Psychiatry*, New York: Basic Books, 1970, pp. 418–570.

3. Ernest Jones, *Sigmund Freud: Life and Work*, 3 vols, Hogarth Press, 1953–7. This quotation from the author's first preface, p. vii, *US, p. xi*; Penguin edition (*The Life and Work of Sigmund Freud*, edited and abridged by Lionel Trilling and Steven Marcus, Penguin, 1964), p. 25.

4. Freud, 'Leonardo da Vinci and a Memory of His Childhood', SE11, p. 130.

5. Trilling, introduction to Jones, Penguin edition, pp. 11–24.

6. Ellenberger, pp. 547–8.

7. Roazen, pp. 34–5.

8. Sulloway, p. 5. On Sulloway, Crews and Cioffi, see below, note 12.

9. In the Bibliographical Essay which is appended to his 1988 biography of Freud, Peter Gay concedes that Roazen's book 'includes much usable material' but describes it as 'a maddening mixture of hard digging, extensive interviewing, snap judgments and uncertain tone' which 'must be used cautiously'. He goes on to quote approvingly from Richard Wollheim's review of the book in *The Times Literary Supplement*:

> Professor Roazen has many criticisms to make of Freud. Freud, he tells us on different occasions, was cold, snobbish, excessively interested in money, indifferent to his family; he never fed his children bottles nor did he once change their diapers; he was a respecter of persons but not of the truth, over-controlled, resentful, narrow-minded, authoritarian. Yet alongside all these different criticisms, and there are few that do not surface on one page or another, there is one reiterated eulogy: Freud was a great man; we must not forget to praise him for his bravery and his genius. Freud has as good a friend in Professor Roazen as ever Brutus found in Mark Antony.

Wollheim has written elsewhere in similarly dismissive terms of Frank Sulloway's contribution to Freud scholarship. Nor has his critical voice been a solitary one. With his controversial account of the association between Victor

Tausk and Freud, which ended in Tausk's suicide, Roazen even launched one major figure in the psychoanalytic movement, Kurt Eissler, into more than a decade of rebuttals and rearguard actions which resulted in the publication of two books. See K. R. Eissler, *Talent and Genius: The Fictitious Case of Tausk Contra Freud*, New York: Grove Press, 1971; *Victor Tausk's Suicide*, New York: International Universities Press, 1983.

10. Roazen, pp. 40–41.
11. Sulloway, p. 503.
12. In an essay which appeared in 1991, 'Reassessing Freud's Case Histories. The Social Construction of Psychoanalysis', Sulloway comes to the conclusion that the erroneous biological assumptions on which Freud based his theories 'were more lethal to his enterprise than I had previously concluded'. He goes on to write that 'Freud erected his psychoanalytic evidence on a kind of intellectual quicksand, a circumstance that consequently doomed many of his most important intellectual conclusions from the outset' ('Reassessing Freud's Case Histories. The Social Construction of Psychoanalysis', *Isis*, vol. 82, pp. 245–75). A similar view is put forward in the preface to the 1992 edition of *Freud, Biologist of the Mind*, Harvard University Press, 1992, pp. xi–xv.

Frank Cioffi, 'Freud and the Idea of a Pseudo-Science' in Robert Borger and Frank Cioffi (ed.), *Explanation in the Behavioural Sciences*, Cambridge University Press, 1970, pp. 471–99.

Frederick Crews, 'The Freudian Way of Knowledge', *New Criterion*, 1984. Reprinted in *Skeptical Engagements*, New York: Oxford University Press, 1986, pp. 43–74. See also Crews's other essays on Freud which are collected in the same volume. 'Beyond Sulloway's *Freud*: Psychoanalysis Minus the Myth of the Hero' (pp. 88–111), is particularly relevant to the argument presented in this chapter. It contains the following passage:

> Of all Sulloway's reviewers only one, Frank Cioffi, fully understood that *Freud: Biologist of the Mind* not only exposes psychoanalytic myths but also exemplifies 'how difficult it is, even for an aspiring iconoclast, to stand upright in the presence of the Freud legend . . .' And it was Cioffi again who imposed the following important challenge, which carries us even beyond Sulloway's present assessment of Freud's stand-ing: 'Although much of what he recounts undermines it, Sulloway does not directly address the most potent and strategically necessary myth of all – the myth of Freud's superlative integrity. For the Freud myths were not devised by Freud's followers; they are no more than reiter-ations of accounts Freud himself had given. To depart from these would have been to impugn Freud's veracity and who, with the exception of one or two noble spirits, has been willing to do that? Certainly not Sulloway, who mealy-mouthedly concludes: "The myths were merely [Freud's] historical due and they shall continue to live on protecting his brilliant legacy to mankind." Carry on lying' (Cioffi, 'Freud – New Myths to Replace the Old', *New Society*, 1979, 50, pp. 5034).

Ernest Gellner, *The Psychoanalytic Movement*, Paladin, 1985.

13. Paul Robinson, *Freud and His Critics*, University of California Press, 1993, pp. 12–13.

E. M. Thornton, *Freud and Cocaine*, Blond and Briggs, 1983. Published in America as *The Freudian Fallacy*, 1984. All references are to the revised British paperback edition, *The Freudian Fallacy: Freud and Cocaine*, Paladin, 1986. Thornton's main argument, namely that Freud's long-standing use of cocaine played a central role in shaping his theories, should certainly not be dismissed out of hand as it is by some Freud scholars. One recent critic of Freud who has allotted a significant role to the part played by cocaine in psychoanalysis is Robert Wilcocks (see below, note 17). The problem with Thornton's argument about cocaine is that she claims far too much for it. As Frederick Crews has noted, 'To ascribe psychoanalysis entirely to cocaine . . . would be an act of reductionism comparable to Freud's own crude explanatory overreaching' (*Skeptical Engagements*, New York: Oxford University Press, 1986, p. 65).

Jeffrey Masson, *The Assault on Truth: Freud's Suppression of the Seduction Theory*, New York: Farrar, Straus and Giroux, Inc., 1984; published with a new preface and afterword by Penguin Books, 1985. Reissued with a new preface under the title *The Assault on Truth: Freud and Child Sexual Abuse*, HarperCollins, 1992.

14. The reception accorded to E. M. Thornton's book was remarkable. In Britain Thornton's claims about Freud's addiction to cocaine generated a small amount of sensational and shallow coverage in *The Sunday Times Magazine*. But her book was virtually ignored in the review sections of the quality press. One exception was a hostile review in *The Times Literary Supplement* in which the reviewer, after making some reasonable criticisms of Thornton's thesis, went on to enumerate a number of misspellings of proper names and proceeded to the conclusion that 'this ill-conceived, slovenly, dogmatic book should never have been published' (*TLS*, 18 November 1983, p. 1266). Meanwhile the *London Review of Books* had published an equally hostile review whose author poured scorn on what he called 'Thornton's bizarre, monomaniacal thesis', complained that her references to current medical research were 'anachronistic' and went on to write that he suspected her of 'a harmless, if dislikeable, anti-semitism' (*LRB*, 20 October–2 November 1983, p. 19). This latter accusation, for which there were no grounds whatsoever, was eventually withdrawn and an apology given. By this time, however, a great deal of damage had already been inflicted on the book. According to Thornton's own account, *The Times Literary Supplement* declined to publish any reply to their review and one London bookshop unofficially remaindered her book shortly after its publication on the grounds that they did not wish to give shelf-space to 'that kind of book'. The book was received with little more enthusiasm in America. One significant exception was Frederick Crews, who gave some recognition both to the book's faults and to its many merits in his essay 'The Freudian Way of Knowledge'. Another reviewer who wrote positively about the book was Carol Tavris in *Discover – The Newsmagazine of Science*, April 1984, pp. 45–51.

15. Adolf Grünbaum, *The Foundations of Psychoanalysis: A Philosophical Critique*, University of California Press, 1984.

16. Frank Cioffi, '"Exegetical Myth-Making" in Grünbaum's Indictment of Popper and Exoneration of Freud', in Peter Clark and Crispin Wright (ed.), *Mind, Psychoanalysis and Science*, Oxford: Blackwell, 1988, pp. 61–87. See also 'Psychoanalysis, Pseudo-Science and Testability' in G. Currie and A. Musgrave (ed.), *Popper and the Human Sciences*, Dordrecht: Nijhoff, pp. 13–44.

Grünbaum's *The Foundations of Psychoanalysis* contains many insights and much pertinent criticism of Freud's approach. But it is scarcely the monumental achievement it has sometimes been acclaimed as. The overvaluation of Grünbaum's work by some of the very critics who have written most penetratingly about psychoanalysis is one of the most interesting phenomena in recent Freud scholarship. In part it can be accounted for by the intimidatory nature of Grünbaum's style. For he mounts his attack on Freud from an extraordinarily high theoretical altitude. Many of Grünbaum's readers clearly regard this as an advantage. My own impression is that the intellectual altitude at which Grünbaum operates tends to distract attention from his almost complete neglect of Freud's character, and of the historical and human dimensions of the culture in which he developed his ideas. For a useful introduction to the debate on Grünbaum's ideas, see Paul Robinson, *Freud and His Critics*, 1993, pp. 179–266. A very strong case against Grünbaum is made in an unpublished paper by Allen Esterson, 'Grünbaum's Tally Argument'. I am grateful to Allen Esterson for supplying me with a copy of this paper.

17. See Frank Cioffi, '"Exegetical Myth-Making" . . .' in *Mind, Psychoanalysis and Science*, pp. 61–87; 'Was Freud a Liar?', *Listener*, 7 February 1974, pp. 172–4; 'The Cradle of Neurosis', *The Times Literary Supplement*, 6 July 1984, pp. 743–4; Morton Schatzman, 'Freud: Who Seduced Whom?', *New Scientist*, 21 March 1992, pp. 34–7; Han Israëls and Morton Schatzman, 'The Seduction Theory', *History of Psychiatry*, vol. IV, 1993, pp. 23–59; Malcolm Macmillan, *Freud Evaluated: The Completed Arc*, Amsterdam: New Holland, 1991. Macmillan's book, although relatively little known, contains a wealth of material which will not be found in earlier works such as Sulloway's. My most significant disagreement with Macmillan is over Charcot, hysteria and related medical matters. On such issues Macmillan seems sometimes too ready to accept psychogenic theories of illness. My own view gives a great deal more weight to the extraordinary neurological (and neuropathological) complexity of the human organism. Macmillan's book remains, however, an immensely valuable resource, full of meticulous readings and close study of the development of Freud's ideas. His closing section on the appeal of psychoanalysis is particularly perceptive. It includes the simple but profound observation that 'Psychoanalysis concentrates on precisely those things in which people have the greatest interest and about which no other discipline says anything very much' (p. 603). What Macmillan has in mind above all is Freud's 'emphasis on sexuality':

> There is no doubt that this was part of the attraction which psychoanalysis exercised in its early days. While it is alleged that a sexual revolution has occurred, that same emphasis on sexuality seems to me to appeal to young people today (i.e. the undergraduate students I know) as

strongly as it did to those two or three generations ago. Even among
those who have some knowledge of the revolt of the object-relations
theorists like Fairbairn and Winnicott, or perhaps just a dim understanding that Freud's sexual theories are out-of-date, psychoanalysis
continues to license public interest in a matter in which almost everyone
is still curious (p. 607).

Allen Esterson, *Seductive Mirage: An Exploration of the Work of Sigmund
Freud*, Chicago: Open Court, 1993. Reviewed in Frederick Crews, 'The
Unknown Freud', *New York Review of Books*, 18 November 1993. Robert
Wilcocks, *Maelzel's Chess Player: Sigmund Freud and the Rhetoric of Deceit*,
Lanham, Maryland: Rowman and Littlefield, 1994.

18. A discussion of 'the heroic model of science' and the manner in which, during
the eighteenth and nineteenth centuries, science became 'the absolute model
for all knowledge in the West' will be found in an extremely valuable book
by three of America's foremost historians, *Telling the Truth About History*, by
Joyce Appleby, Lynn Hunt and Margaret Jacob, New York: W. W. Norton,
1994. pp. 15–51 and *passim*.

19. Walter Kendrick, *Voice Literary Supplement*, June 1984.

20. In this respect it is interesting to note the way in which the 'new theology'
of psychoanalysis is beginning to replace what might be called its 'old demonology'. As will be seen clearly in later chapters, one of the original functions
of Freud's theory of resistance was to allow psychoanalysis to defend itself
against its critics by imputing to them not simply unconscious resistance but
neurosis. In extreme cases this medicalised version of demonology actually
gave way to traditional demonological rhetoric, as when Freud accused one
of his critics, Albert Moll, of 'having stunk up the room like the devil himself'
(see above, Chapter 17).

It is highly unlikely that such language would now be used by any modern
apologist for psychoanalysis. Even the notion of resistance is sometimes
repudiated by such apologists. In *Freud and His Critics*, Paul Robinson quotes
Freud's own explanation of why so many people reject his teachings:

> Psycho-analysis is seeking to bring to conscious recognition the things
> in mental life which are repressed; and everyone who forms a judgment
> on it is himself a human being, who possesses similar repressions and
> may perhaps be maintaining them with difficulty. They are therefore
> bound to call up the same resistance in him as in our patients; and that
> resistance finds it easy to disguise itself as an intellectual rejection and
> to bring up arguments like those which we ward off in our patients by
> means of the fundamental rule of psycho-analysis.

So deeply has this reaction to criticism become established in the psychoanalytic movement that it comes as something of a shock to read Robinson's
own comments on the passage from Freud which he has just quoted. 'The
only proper response to this kind of reasoning,' he writes, 'is to insist that it
is entirely out of bounds: it undermines the very possibility of intellectual life
... Ad hominem arguments – of which the appeal to resistance is a classic

example – simply have no place in reasoned debate.' In this remarkable pronouncement by a leading defender of psychoanalysis we may find a classic
example of the tendency of Freud's apologists to take over the scepticism of
their opponents and make it their own. A striking act of irreverence towards
Freud's own words becomes part of a larger act of homage to his teachings.
In this particular case, however, Robinson cannot resist the temptation to
piece together the fragments of the icon he has just broken:

> That having been said, one must also concede that, empirically speak-
> ing, Freud was probably right: his ideas disturb us as do those of no
> other important thinker, and many of our objections to them, whatever
> their intellectual validity, spring from deep emotional sources ...
> There remains, I'm convinced, an underground reservoir of resentment
> to [Freud's] troublesome ideas. Granted this perennial anti-Freudian
> sentiment cannot alone explain the specific criticisms of Frank Sullo-
> way, Jeffrey Masson, and Adolf Grünbaum. But it assures them of a
> receptive audience. Apparently there are always people eager to believe
> the worst about Freud (p. 10).

It is difficult to escape the impression that Robinson is here employing a
modified version of the very same argument whose illegitimacy he has just
announced.

21. Quoted in Andrew Billen, 'Freudians' Slips Are Showing', *Observer*, 30 January
    1994, p. 21.
22. Peter Gay, *Freud: A Life for Our Time*, Dent, 1988.
23. Peter Swales, *The Times Literary Supplement*, Letters, 3 August 1990, p. 823.
24. Frederick Crews, 'The Freudian Way of Knowledge' (1984). Reprinted in
    Crews, *Skeptical Engagements*, New York: Oxford University Press, 1986,
    p. 47.
25. After welcoming Gay's biography, Robinson goes on to point to the work of
    two younger scholars, Jonathan Lear's *Love and its Place in Nature: A Philosophi-
    cal Interpretation of Freudian Psychoanalysis* and Mark Edmundson's *Towards
    Reading Freud*, both published in 1990. Lear, writes Robinson,

    > is a philosopher and Edmundson a literary critic, and although they
    > offer contrasting readings of Freud, they agree about his stature. Lear
    > places him in the mainstream of Western philosophical thought, an
    > heir to Socrates, and the most important modern theorist of the indi-
    > vidual. For Edmundson he belongs in the great tradition of imaginative
    > writers whose principal subject has been the self: Shakespeare, Milton,
    > Wordsworth and Emerson (Robinson, p. 270).

26. Candia McWilliam, 'The Importance of Writing to Ernest', *Independent on
    Sunday*, 23 May 1993.
27. In making this comment I have in mind the following observation by Donald
    Bannister, who argues that one of the distinctive features of the discipline of
    psychology, which sets it apart from the natural sciences, is the duty it has
    to account for its own construction:

Of the requirements which make a concretistic imitation of the natural sciences unprofitable in psychology, probably the most serious is that of reflexivity. Formulating theories, conducting experiments and modifying explanatory concepts in terms of outcome is a part of human behaviour and any discipline which purports to be 'the science of human behaviour' should account for its own construction (in Borger and Cioffi (ed.), *Explanation in the Behavioural Sciences*, p. 416).

A psychological theory which is derived from therapeutic practice must also account for this aspect of its nature. It therefore follows that only if psychoanalysis could provide a satisfactory explanation of the motivation of its practitioners in offering therapy, of the reasons why they habitually elicit – but never offer – confessions of an intimate or sexual nature, of the clinical code which enables orthodox analysts to place their patients in a situation of emotional vulnerability while they themselves retain a god-like remoteness and inviolability, of the messianic behaviour of the founder of psychoanalysis and of the ecclesiastical behaviour of its members in unconsciously obscuring or rewriting the history of the movement to which they belong – only if all these and other similar conditions could be met would the requirement of reflexivity be complied with. The other passage which lies behind my remark about Freud remaining a psychological enigma is taken from a discussion of the attitude adopted by a number of followers towards the leader of a movement which has a great deal in common with psychoanalysis:

> Since they thought of him as essentially a supernatural figure . . . his humanity would not in itself interest them very much, They recognised it of course as the means through which his work had been accomplished, but it never occurred to them to think of him as receiving anything essential from his human environment; and so they made no attempt to trace the effects of his environment upon him or the working of his mind – what led him to the conclusions he arrived at or what influenced him in forming his plans. Indeed, if they could have understood the term at all, they would no doubt have denied that the Son of God, for all his humanity, had any 'psychology' in this sense at all . . . One is reminded of the hyper-orthodox student, described by H. J. Cadbury, who, 'when asked of a certain narrative in the gospels what Jesus had in mind, replied simply that Jesus had no mind' (D. E. Nineham, *The Gospel of St Mark*, Pelican New Testament Commentaries, 1963, p. 20).

CHAPTER ONE · FROM CAUL TO COCAINE

1. Trilling, see above, Prologue, note 5.
2. Ernst L. Freud (ed.), *Letters of Sigmund Freud, 1873–1939*, Hogarth Press, 1961, pp. 152–3 (to Martha Bernays, 28.4.1885).
3. Jones, I, p. 21, *US, pp. 18–19*; Penguin edition, p. 47.

4. Freud, SE17, p. 156.
5. D. W. Winnicott, *Collected Papers: Through Paediatrics to Psychoanalysis*, Hogarth, 1975, p. 165.
6. Jones, I, pp. 17–18, *US, pp. 15–16*; Penguin edition, p. 44.
7. Jones, I, pp. 18–19, *US, pp. 16–17*; Penguin edition, p. 45.
8. Jones, I, p. 20, *US, pp. 17–18*; Penguin edition, p. 46.
9. See Jones, I, p. 32, *US, p. 29*; Penguin edition, p. 55. The essay is reprinted as Goethe's in *The Oxford Book of German Prose*, Oxford, 1943, pp. 178–80. It has also been attributed to Goethe's friend, Georg Christoph Tobler (see Ronald Clark, p. 28).
10. Jones, I, p. 72, *US, p. 65*; Penguin edition, p. 79.
11. Jones, I, pp. 21–2, *US, p. 19*; Penguin edition, pp. 47–8.
12. Frank Manuel, *The Religion of Isaac Newton*, Oxford: The Clarendon Press, 1974, p. 23. In the same book Manuel writes: 'That Newton was conscious of his special bond to God and that he conceived of himself as the man destined to unveil the ultimate truth about God's creation does not appear in so many words in anything he wrote. But peculiar traces of this inner conviction crop up in unexpected ways. More than once Newton used *Jeova sanctus unus* as an anagram for *Isaacus Neuutonus*' (p. 19).
    See also Anthony Storr's illuminating essay on Newton in his *Churchill's Black Dog*, Collins, 1989.
13. The enduring power and psychological significance of Jewish messianic hope has not always been recognised. This is perhaps due in part to the way in which Jewish eschatological hope has tended increasingly to be pushed out of the public realm into the realm of private prayer and fantasy. This process has been particularly strong ever since the trauma suffered by European Jews as a result of the wave of eschatological excitement caused by the false-messiah Sabbatai Sevi in the seventeenth century. But even Reformed and secularised Jews have tended to keep alive more intimate forms of eschatological hope. This is perhaps best illustrated by the religious language which is frequently used by secular Zionists. When Theodor Herzl took the platform at the First Zionist Congress in 1897, one of the delegates wrote that 'It seemed as if the dream cherished by our people for two thousand years had come true at last, and Messiah the son of David, was standing before us' (Karen Armstrong, *Holy War: The Crusades and Their Impact on Today's World*, Macmillan, 1988, p. 58).
    On Sabbatai Sevi, see Paul Johnson, *A History of the Jews*, Weidenfeld and Nicolson, 1987, pp. 268–74. For some interesting comments on Freud's messianic view of his own role, see the chapter entitled 'Freud's Messianic Identification' in David Bakan, *Sigmund Freud and the Jewish Mystical Tradition*, Princeton: D. Van Nostrand Co., 1958, pp. 169–83.
14. Jones, I, p. 88, *US, p. 80*; Penguin edition, p. 90.
15. Quoted in Jones, I, p. 89, *US, p. 81*; Penguin edition, p. 92.
16. Jones, pp. 93, 90, *US, pp. 84, 82*; Penguin edition, pp. 95, 93.
17. Jones, I, p. 91, *US, p. 82*; Penguin edition, p. 93. See Robert Byck (ed.), *Cocaine Papers by Sigmund Freud*, New York: Stonehill, 1974, p. 60.
18. Freud, *The Interpretation of Dreams*, SE4, pp. 115, 117; PF4, pp. 192, 194.

19. Freud 'On the General Effect of Cocaine' (paper read before the Psychiatric Society, March 1885), p. 117; see also p. 154. Freud endorsed the use of hypodermic injections in writing as early as November 1884, when he actively recommended this method. He wrote that: 'Dr E. v. Fleischl … has determined that cocaine, by hypodermic injection, has proved itself to be an invaluable adjuvant against the continued use of morphia. This fact alone should give the remedy an enduring place among the treasures of the physician' ('Cocaine and Its Salts', November 1884, in Byck (ed.), pp. 78–9).

20. Jones, I, p. 106, *US*, *p. 96*; Penguin edition, pp. 105–6.

21. Byck, p. 71; see also Jones, I, p. 91, *US*, *pp. 82–3*; Penguin edition, p. 94. E. M. Thornton, pp. 45–6.

22. Byck, p. 154; Thornton, p. 50.

CHAPTER TWO · HYPNOTISM AND HYSTERIA

1. Jones, I, p. 227, *US*, *p. 207*; Penguin edition, p. 191.

2. Quoted by Jones, I, p. 84, *US*, *p. 76*; Penguin edition, p. 87.

3. Raymond Hierons, 'Charcot and His Visits to Britain', *British Medical Journal*, vol. 307, December 1993, p. 1589.

4. Hierons, p. 1589; Edward Shorter, *From Paralysis to Fatigue: A History of Psychosomatic Illness in the Modern Era*, New York: Free Press, 1992, p. 170. Shorter's book contains a wealth of fascinating insights into medical history and an interesting chapter on Charcot on which I have drawn with gratitude here. It must also be said, however, that Shorter's model of psychosomatic illness is one which begs a great many more questions than it answers. He postulates that the 'unconscious' selects plausible organic-seeming symptoms from a culturally determined 'symptom-pool' in such a way that these symptoms will be taken seriously by physicians. This leads Shorter to some strange conclusions such as his claim that 'paralysis as a response to loss, mourning and trauma was not often seen in the eighteenth or the twentieth centuries. It was a culturally specific nineteenth-century mode of processing extreme emotion' (p. 114). For a severely critical and, in my view, just assessment of the book's central argument, see the review by Graeme J. Taylor in *Psychosomatic Medicine*, 1993, vol. 55, no. 1, pp. 88–9. See also the critical review by Theodore M. Brown, *Journal of the History of the Behavioural Sciences*, vol. XXIX, 1993, pp. 241–5. Further comment on Shorter's central argument will be found below in note 21 to Appendix I, 'The Diagnosis of "Hysteria"'.

5. Quoted in Shorter, pp. 166–7.

6. Shorter, p. 175.

7. Shorter, p. 176.

8. Robert Brudenell Carter, *On the Pathology and Treatment of Hysteria*, London, 1853, p. 1; Weir Mitchell, quoted in Barbara Sicherman, 'The Uses of a Diagnosis' in *Journal of the History of Medicine*, vol. 32, 1977, p. 41; Charles Lasèque, 'Des hystéries périphériques', *Archives Générales de médicine*, série 7, i (1878), p. 655, quoted in Mark S. Micale, 'Hysteria and Its Historiography' in *History of Psychiatry*, vol. 1, 1990, p. 42 (note).

9. 1766 is the date given by Lord Brain in his article 'The Concept of Hysteria in the time of William Harvey', the reference being to William Cullen's Clinical Lectures of that year (*Proceedings of the Royal Society of Medicine*, vol. 56, 1963, pp. 317–24).

10. Quoted in Brain, p. 318.

11. J. M. Charcot and Pierre Marie, 'Hysteria' in D. Hack Tuke (ed.), *Dictionary of Psychological Medicine*, Churchill, 1892, pp. 627–41; A. R. G. Owen, *Hysteria, Hypnosis and Healing: The Work of J.-M. Charcot*, Dobson, 1971, pp. 66–9.

12. Sydenham, see Thornton, p. 72.

13. Owen, p. 63.

14. Shorter, p. 179.

15. Shorter, p. 179.

16. Owen, pp. 64–6.

17. J. M. Charcot, *Clinical Lectures on Diseases of the Nervous System*, vol. III, trans. Thomas Savill (1887), New Sydenham Society, 1889, p. 278.

18. I borrow this example from Malcolm Macmillan, who uses it in a different but related context – a discussion of Freud's theories of symptom formation. See Macmillan, p. 150.

19. Macmillan, p. 150.

20. Anne Harrington, *Medicine, Mind and the Double Brain*, Princeton University Press, 1987, pp. 167–8; on Charcot's concept of functional lesions see also Mark S. Micale, 'Charcot and the Idea of Hysteria in the Male', *Medical History*, 1990, vol. 34, pp. 382–3.

21. On Richet, see Georges Guillain, *J. M. Charcot, 1825–1893: His Life, His Work* (1955), New York: Hoeber, 1959, p. 166; Ellenberger, pp. 750–51; on the connection with Burq see Harrington, pp. 184–5. The same suggestion is made independently by Alan Gauld, *A History of Hypnotism*, Cambridge University Press, 1992, pp. 310–11. The third suggestion is made by E. M. Thornton, p. 97.

22. This view is taken, for instance, by Shorter.

23. For James Braid's account of his first experiments in hypnosis, see Charles E. Goshen (ed.), *Documentary History of Psychiatry*, Vision, 1967, p. 832ff.

24. In Goshen, pp. 833–4.

25. A. Gamgee, 'Demonstration on the Phenomena of Hystero-Epilepsy', *British Medical Journal*, 12 October 1878, vol. 2. Quoted in Thornton, p. 100.

26. Anonymous account, 'Charcot on the Somnambulic and Cataleptic Condition in Hysteria', *Medical Record*, 1879, vol. 35, p. 82. Quoted in Thornton, pp. 100–101.

27. W. J. Morton, 'Induced Hysterical Somnambulism and Catalepsy', *Medical Record*, 1880, vol. 33, p. 467. Quoted in Thornton, p. 102 .

28. G. Robertson, 'Hypnotism at Paris and Nancy: Notes of a Visit', *Journal of Mental Science*, 1892, vol. 38, p. 494.

29. Thornton, p. 99.

30. Freud, 'Report on my Studies in Paris and Berlin' (1886), SE1, p. 3.

31. Sulloway, pp. 38–9.

32. This argument is put forward by one of Charcot's former assistants Gilbert

Ballet, in 'Le Domaine de la Psychiatrie', *Presse médicale*, 10 May 1911, p. 377–80. See Shorter, p. 375 (note).

33. Charcot, III, p. 289. I have used Malcolm Macmillan's translation; see Macmillan, p. 64.
34. Charcot, III, p. 305; Macmillan's translation.
35. Charcot, III, p. 222.
36. Charcot, III, p. 289.
37. See Charcot and Marie, article on 'Hysteria, Mainly Hystero-Epilepsy' in D. H. Tuke (ed.), *A Dictionary of Psychological Medicine*, 1892, pp. 627–41. Quoted in Macmillan, p. 65.
38. Freud, SE3, p. 22.
39. Freud, Letters, p. 196 (to Martha Bernays, 21.11.1885).
40. Quoted in Jones, I, p, 99, *US, p. 90*; Penguin edition, p. 100.

CHAPTER THREE · CHARCOT'S MISTAKE

1. Sulloway, p. 59. Sulloway does devote a footnote to the problem in which he refers to the speculative psychosociological account of the diminution of hysteria put forward by Carroll Smith Rosenberg in her 'The Hysterical Woman: Sex Roles and Role Conflict in 19th-Century America', *Social Research*, vol. 39, pp. 652–78; Anthony Storr, *Freud*, Oxford University Press, 1989, p. 8.
2. The remarks of Jacques Lacan and Etienne Trillat are both quoted in Mark S. Micale, 'Hysteria and its Historiography: The Future Perspective', *History of Psychiatry*, vol. 1, 1990, p. 101. See also Roberta Satow, 'Where Has All the Hysteria Gone?', *Psychoanalytic Review*, I, lxvi, 1979, pp. 463–77, and Micale's own discussion of 'The Disappearance of Hysteria', pp. 101–9. Micale's argument in his 1990 paper is worked out at much greater length and many new and valuable components are added to it in an essay which appeared only when my own chapters on hysteria were virtually completed. 'On the "Disappearance" of Hysteria: A Study in the Clinical Deconstruction of a Diagnosis', *Isis*, September 1993, vol. 84, pp. 496–526. See below, note 23.
3. See Thornton, p. 85.
4. Thornton, p. 86.
5. Mark S. Micale, 'Charcot and the Idea of Hysteria in the Male', *Medical History*, vol. 34, 1990, p. 390.
   A quite different and much more substantial example of a psychogenic interpretation of Le Log–'s case is offered by Malcolm Macmillan in his *Freud Evaluated: The Completed Arc*. In that Macmillan quotes a long section from the beginning of Charcot's case history, he gives a much more detailed picture of the early stages of Le Log–'s illness. But he appears to accept Charcot's psychologising almost entirely and does not consider at any point the possibility that Le Log– may have sustained internal injuries. While 'traumatic hysteria' usually followed a physical injury, he writes 'it had no physical basis' (p. 61). It is perhaps for this reason that Macmillan does not give any account

of the later stages of the illness. He therefore does not mention either the profuse nose-bleeds which Le Log– suffered or the violent seizure which led to his second period of unconsciousness. As should by now be clear, most modern physicians would see these as two of the most revealing of all Le Log–'s symptoms.

6. Charcot, *Clinical Lectures on Diseases of the Nervous System*, vol. III (1887), trans. Thomas Savill, New Sydenham Society, 1889, III, p. 374–9.

Charcot's case history goes on to describe a significant and dramatic improvement in Le Log–'s condition. For at the same time that the seizures were becoming more severe, Le Log–'s nose-bleeds became rarer and less profuse. Up to this point Le Log–'s lower limbs remained quite immovable. On the morning of 15 August 1886, however, the patient 'had a convulsive seizure of great severity'. During the attack his legs began to be thrown about and his feet struck the bar at the end of the bed with so much force that it became displaced. The attack ended; the patient got up from his bed and began to walk, at first with a certain amount of hesitation, supporting himself along the wall and by means of surrounding objects, but at the end of a few hours his ability to walk normally had almost returned. Le Log–'s recovery continued but was very far from being complete. He still suffered from seizures although they became much less frequent and severe. His anaesthesia and contraction of the visual field continued, as did a degree of 'cerebral torpor'. All these symptoms were still present when the case history ended on 1 November 1886.

The specific pathology of Le Log–'s illness cannot be reconstructed with any certainty, but the details which Charcot does give make a conjectural re-diagnosis possible. The patient's initial period of unconsciousness was clearly caused by the original accident. This may have produced either a basal skull fracture or the kind of lesions associated with closed head injury. The nose-bleeds subsequently suffered by Le Log– may have been a sign of gross injury accompanied by internal bleeding. Bleeding into the cerebral ventricles can itself cause an obstruction of the circulation of cerebrospinal fluid, which would lead to a rise in pressure inside the skull. Raised intracranial pressure is associated with a reduced blood-flow to the brain. Overall blood-pressure would then rise in order to compensate and this might lead to even more profuse nose-bleeds.

The severe seizure which Le Log– suffered in January is a common sequel of such a head injury. In this case, however, it gave rise to an unusually long period of unconsciousness. One possible explanation is that the oxygen supply to the brain was interrupted during or following the seizure resulting in further brain damage.

After his second admission to hospital following this seizure, Le Log– exhibits signs and symptoms of raised intracranial pressure. These include severe headache, vomiting, restriction of visual field and weakness of the lower limbs combined with an inability to move them. In Le Log–'s case the left-sided facial spasm and tremor of the lips indicates focal epileptic activity as a result of focal brain damage. The more generalised seizures would probably have been caused by the same pathology. Le Log–'s eventual and dramatic

recovery of the use of his legs after his most severe seizure suggests a significant fall in intracranial pressure. Modern physicians would produce such a
fall artificially by draining the cerebrospinal fluid. In the case of Le Log– it
is possible that a similar effect was produced spontaneously. The sudden fall
in intracranial pressure may itself have been brought about by the exceptionally severe seizure which Charcot describes.

In considering the relevance of the case of Le Log– to psychoanalysis it
should be noted that Charcot encountered this particular patient about a
month *after* Freud's visit to Paris, and the case is not included in Freud's
translation of Charcot's *Lectures*. But, as Malcolm Macmillan has noted, other
similar cases had already been described (see Macmillan, p. 61, note). It is
also almost certain that Freud would have become acquainted with Le Log–'s
case history, and he may have known it well.

7. Charcot, III, p. 246.
8. Some of these scholars do make the conventional criticism of Charcot in
which, following Bernheim and numerous others, they refer to the atmosphere
of suggestion which prevailed at the Salpêtrière. See, for example,
Ellenberger, p. 785. Charcot's more fundamental mistakes, however, are not
alluded to. Ironically it is perhaps Charcot himself who has offered the best
description of the tyranny of those familiar assumptions which sometimes
prevent us from seeing what is in front of our eyes:

> How is it that one fine morning Duchenne discovered a disease that
> probably existed in the time of Hippocrates? Why do we perceive things
> so late, so poorly and with such difficulty? Why do we have to go over
> the same set of symptoms twenty times before we understand it? Why
> does the first statement of what seems a new fact always leave us cold?
>
> Because our minds have to take in something that deranges our
> original set of ideas, but we are all of us like that in this miserable
> world.

For this quotation I am indebted to Harold L. Klawans, who uses it as an
epigraph to one of the chapters in his remarkable *Toscanini's Fumble and Other
Tales of Clinical Neurology*, The Bodley Head, 1989, p. 73.

9. W. G. Lennox, 'Bernard of Gordon on Epilepsy', *Annals of Medical History*,
1941, vol. 3, p. 374. Quoted by Gilbert H. Glaser, 'Epilepsy, Hysteria and
"Possession": A Historical Essay', *Journal of Nervous and Mental Disease*, 1978,
vol. 166, p. 269.
10. Hughlings Jackson, quoted in Thornton, p. 92.
11. For an account of a case of complex partial seizures in which the aura began
with intense, pleasurable sensations in the vagina, which subsequently rose
upwards towards the throat, see T. A. Betts, 'Neuropsychiatry', in John Laidlaw, Alan Richens and Jolyon Oxley (ed.), *A Textbook of Epilepsy*, 3rd edition,
Churchill Livingstone, 1988, pp. 372–3. The case is an interesting one
because the aura in question is probably under-reported, but may well have
been one of the phenomena which originally gave rise to the ancient association between 'hysteria' and the womb.

12. Quoted in Thornton, p. 76.
13. Quoted in Thornton, p. 76.
14. K. Henner, in J. Chorobski (ed.), *Neurological Problems*, London, 1967. Quoted in E. M. Thornton, *Hypnosis, Hysteria and Epilepsy: An Historical Synthesis*, Heinemann Medical, 1976.

    Henner's view is valuable but it oversimplifies the problem of 'globus hystericus'. Where this symptom is preceded by a rising epigastric sensation and appears to be part of a seizure, there can be little doubt that Henner's view holds good. But the term 'globus hystericus' has frequently been applied to a different symptom – to a *persistent* sensation of a lump in the throat. This sensation can have a number of organic causes, including cancer, pharyngeal pouch, post-cricoid web, and thyroid goitre. Yet even after all these conditions were identified a number of patients complaining of feeling a lump in the throat continued to be diagnosed as neurotics suffering from 'globus hystericus'. In a paper published in 1968, Kenneth Malcolmson pointed out that a surprisingly high percentage of these patients suffered from hiatus hernia, and, to a lesser extent, peptic ulceration. He suggested that the term 'globus hystericus' should be abandoned, since the feeling of a lump in the throat was usually a real symptom caused by an irritative lesion in the foregut, and sometimes produced by a 'referred' sensation. See Kenneth G. Malcolmson, 'Globus Hystericus Vel Pharyngis', *Journal of Laryngology and Otology*, vol. 82, 1968, pp. 219–30. See also J. E. Delahunty and G. M. Ardran, 'Globus Hystericus – A Manifestation of Reflux Oesophagitis?', *Journal of Laryngology and Otology*, vol. 84, 1970, pp. 1049–54. Once again I am grateful to Elizabeth Thornton for drawing my attention to these articles (see Thornton, p. 297).
15. Pierre Marie, quoted in Shorter, p. 182.
16. George Robertson, 'Hypnotism at Paris and Nancy: Notes of a Visit', *Journal of Mental Science*, vol. 38, 1892. Quoted in Thornton, *Freudian Fallacy*, p. 118.
17. Jackson, *Selected Writings of John Hughlings Jackson*, 2 vols, Hodder and Stoughton, 1931–2. Quoted in Thornton, p. 99. On the relationship of 'hysteria' to post-epileptic phenomena, see also Mark S. Micale, 'On the "Disappearance" of Hysteria', *Isis*, 1993, vol. 84, pp. 505–6.
18. D. Yellowlees, 'Notes of a Visit to Professor Charcot's Wards', *Journal of Mental Science*, vol. 26, p. 131. Quoted in Thornton, pp. 101–2.
19. W. G. Lennox, *Epilepsy and Related Disorders*, Churchill, 1966; see Thornton, p. 105.
20. Thornton, p. 107.
21. See Mark S. Micale, 'Hysteria and its Historiography: The Future Perspective', *History of Psychiatry*, vol. 1, 1990, pp. 101–9.
22. Henri Gastaut, *The Epilepsies: Electro-Clinical Correlations*, Springfield, Illinois: Charles C. Thomas, 1954. Quoted in Thornton, p. 70.
23. Shorter, p. 356 (note). For a discussion of the difficulty surrounding the diagnostic differentiation of 'hysteria' and multiple sclerosis, see William Alwyn Lishman, *Organic Psychiatry: The Psychological Consequences of Cerebral Disorder*, 2nd edition, Oxford: Blackwell, 1987, pp. 596–7. Lishman evidently believes in the reality of 'hysteria'. The discussion is inconclusive and it should

perhaps be read as an illustration of the deep medical confusion which still reigns in this area.

For Mark Micale's discussion of the diagnostic mistakes associated with syphilis, see Micale, 'On the "Disappearance" of Hysteria: A Study in the Clinical Deconstruction of a Diagnosis', *Isis*, September 1993, vol. 84, pp. 507–9. In this essay Micale also recognises the extent to which the epilepsy diagnosis was refined and enlarged throughout the early part of the twentieth century and the account he offers is almost entirely compatible with that which I have given here. One of his most penetrating observations, significantly different in tone from the credulity he displays towards the hysteria diagnosis in his early work, is contained in the following paragraph:

> Hysteria, it is often said today, is a 'diagnosis of exclusion'. By definition, it can be applied only when all possible anatomical and physiological explanations for the symptoms have been ruled out. As a consequence, the legitimate sphere of the diagnosis (some critic would say of psychodynamic psychiatry as a whole) may be fated continually to contract as the understanding of organic illness expands. In the ongoing appropriation of the mental by the physical, the early twentieth century was a highly active period. The most astute observers were aware of the change and its implications. In 1914 Paul Guirard of Tours wrote, 'When we have completed the clinical analysis of all the hysterical symptoms, when we have given to each malady what belongs to it, who knows if anything will still remain of hysteria?' (p. 510)

It should be noted, however, that Micale still treats the diagnosis of 'hysteria' as 'legitimate' in some circumstances. Towards the end of his essay he maintains the position of medical relativism found in his early work, and declares that 'the intention of this essay is not to establish the scientific error of past diagnostic practices or to prove the superiority of present-day diagnostics' (p. 523). In one sense Micale is quite right. Modern diagnostics are not 'superior' to ancient diagnostics, for they do not belong to a 'higher' civilisation. But they are more accurate.

24. R. P. Lesser, H. Lueders, J. P. Conomy, A. J. Furlan and D. S. Dinner, 'Sensory Seizure Mimicking a Psychogenic Seizure', *Neurology*, vol. 33, pp. 800–802. See Laurence Miller, *Freud's Brain: Neuropsychodynamic Foundations of Psychoanalysis*, New York: The Guilford Press, 1991, pp. 67–8.

25. C. D. Binnie, 'Electroencephalography' in Laidlaw, Richens and Oxley (ed.), *A Textbook of Epilepsy*, pp. 268, 264. The first intimations of the existence of a distinct syndrome of frontal lobe epilepsy seem to go back to the 1950s and the work of Wilder Penfield. But it would appear that it was only in the 1980s that an attempt was made to define the syndrome by P. D. Williamson and his colleagues (see P. D. Williamson, D. D. Spencer, S. S. Spencer, R. A. Novelly and R. H. Mattson, 'Complex Partial Seizures of Frontal Lobe Origin', *Annals of Neurology*, vol. 18, 1985, pp. 497–504). A summary of some of the hysterical-seeming symptoms displayed by the patients with frontal lobe epilepsy who are discussed in this paper is given in Laurence Miller,

Freud's Brain, pp. 64–5. It should be noted, however, that Williamson and his colleagues make no reference in their original paper to the arc-de-cercle posture as being associated with frontal lobe epilepsy. This insight is evidently a later one.

Before the general introduction of EEG tests earlier this century one of the main problems surrounding the diagnosis of epilepsy was the lack of any test which could reliably confirm this diagnosis. Since the introduction of the EEG, however, a quite new problem has been the tendency of some physicians to overestimate the sensitivity of EEG scans. A negative EEG result simply signifies that no epileptic activity *has been registered*. It does not signify that no epileptic activity is present. This being the case, negative EEG results should never in themselves be taken to indicate that a patient is not suffering from epilepsy. In the past such negative results have all too frequently been used to support a diagnosis of 'hysteria' or 'hysterical seizures'. Commenting on the general problem of diagnosis, Professor Alan Richens, one of the editors of the standard textbook on epilepsy in which Binnie's case history appears, writes as follows:

> As you are well aware, our knowledge about epilepsy has advanced considerably since Charcot's day, with the advent of EEG and various imaging techniques. However, there is still a small proportion of patients in whom the diagnosis remains elusive because the clinical presentation is atypical and the investigations are normal, even the EEG recorded during a seizure. The term 'hysterical seizures' is now seldom used for these patients, most neurologists preferring to call these attacks 'non-epileptic seizures'. *I suspect, however, that like Charcot we are failing to recognise organic pathology in the absence of sufficiently sensitive techniques.* Colin Binnie's patient in our *A Textbook on Epilepsy* was fortunate in showing an ictal abnormality in the EEG. *I believe that a number of patients are less fortunate in that they have a deep seated focal abnormality which does not reveal itself even in an ictal recording* [i.e. one taken during a seizure] ... I do recognise, however, that occasionally feigned attacks can occur, often in those who have or have had true epileptic seizures, and who are attention-seeking in some form or other. But they should not be labelled 'hysterical' [italics added] (Letter to the author, December 1993).

26. Binnie, in Laidlaw, Richens and Oxley (ed.), *A Textbook* . . ., p. 276; C. D. Binnie, C. E. Darby, R. A. De Korte and A. J. Wilkins, 'Self-induction of Epileptic Seizures by Eyeclosure: Incidence and Recognition', *Journal of Neurology, Neurosurgery, and Psychiatry*, 1980, vol. 43, p. 387.

One intriguing way in which this argument might be extended is suggested by Mark Pendergrast in his account of the recovered memory movement in the United States, *Victims of Memory: Incest Accusations and Shattered Lives* (Hinesberg, Vermont: Upper Access, 1995). Commenting on what appears to be an organic underlay in some cases of the seemingly spurious psychiatric diagnosis of 'Multiple Personality Disorder', he quotes the view of Herbert

Spiegel that a number of the patients who are given this diagnosis have a symptom described as 'high eye-roll in which someone can look up so far that only the whites of the eyes are showing'. Without referring either to Binnie's research or to the Evans–Mulholland effect, of which he is evidently unaware, Pendergrast goes on to observe that 'it is possible, though quite hypothetical at this point, that abnormally high electrical activity in the temporal lobe of the brain may have something to do with the high eye-roll.' Citing the work of experimental psychologist Michael Persinger, he relays the theory that there is a continuum of temporal lobe activity within the population, ranging from very low activity to those diagnosed as having temporal lobe epilepsy. 'Regardless of whether they experience real seizures, those with high electrical activity display an interesting set of phenomena: 'visual hallucinations, the sense of a presence, mystical (paranormal) experiences, unusual smells, anomalous voices or sounds, vestibular movements and anxiety.' According to Persinger about a third of the population display 'temporal lobe signs'. As Pendergrast himself makes clear, however, abnormal temporal lobe activity is certainly not a precondition of multiple personality disorder. The beliefs and behaviour associated with the multiple personality role 'can be instilled in anyone, given the right circumstances and mindset' (see Pendergrast, pp. 182–7; see also note 13 to Afterword, 'Freud's False Memories', below).

27. Gay, pp. 48–53. Paul Robinson, *Freud and His Critics*, University of California Press, 1993, pp. 24–35. Robinson dismisses Thornton's book in his introduction as one 'purporting to show that Freud's ideas were the "direct outcome" of his use of cocaine'. This is true in one respect, but as a description of Thornton's extraordinarily complex and wide-ranging argument it is also completely inadequate.

28. Strictly speaking Gall was the originator of 'organology' while his collaborator Spurzheim developed 'phrenology'. For a review of the work of these two pioneers in relation to contemporary neurology, see Edwin Clarke and L. S. Jacyna, *Nineteenth Century Origins of Neuroscientific Concepts*, University of California Press, 1987, index entries under 'phrenology' and 'organology'.

29. Ann Harrington, *Medicine, Mind and the Double Brain*, Princeton University Press, 1987, p. 172.

30. This argument was often put forward by Charcot's critics. See Arthur F. Hurst, *The Psychology of the Special Senses and Their Functional Disorders*, London, 1920, pp. 6–7. It is also possible, as is implicit in Micale's 1993 paper, that many of Charcot's cases of partial anaesthesia were actually cases of undiagnosed syphilis.

31. See Harrington, p. 183.

32. Harrington, pp. 179–81.

33. A. A. Liébeault, *Ebauche de Psychologie*, Paris: Masson, 1873, p. 176. Quoted by Ellenberger, p. 149.

34. Guillain, pp. 178–9.

35. Féré, quoted in Shorter, p. 196. I should stress here that my explanation of the psychological motives behind Charcot's excursion into confabulatory science is speculative. It could quite plausibly be argued that Charcot was not

exposed to the full force of Bernheim's criticisms until after he had first begun to work out his new synthesis. This would not affect the overall argument of the chapter, however, since Charcot's confabulations remain, suggesting that, for whatever ultimate reason, he was unable to tolerate the uncertainty which a less Napoleonic investigator might have accepted.

36. Eissler, quoted in John E. Gedo and George H. Pollock, *Freud: The Fusion of Science and Humanism*, New York: International Universities Press, 1976, p. 127.

37. L. J. Rather, *Mind and Body in Eighteenth Century Medicine*, Berkeley: University of California Press, 1965. Quoted in Z. J. Lipowski, 'What Does the Word "Psychosomatic" Really Mean? A Historical and Semantic Inquiry', *Psychosomatic Medicine*, 1984, vol. 46, p. 162.

38. Lipowski, p. 163.

39. Jones, I, p. 253, *US, pp. 230–31*; Penguin edition, p. 207.

40. It is interesting that Ellenberger reports this episode in terms which, although they do not belong to any larger analysis, are fully compatible with the account which I offer here. In seeking to explain Freud's seeming insensitivity to his colleagues' reaction, he writes:

> One reason was that Freud, who had always been subject to prompt and strong enthusiasms, was now under the spell of Charcot. Another reason was Freud's craving for the great discovery that would bring him fame. He was still aching with the disappointment caused by the cocaine episode, and he apparently thought that *the revelation he had received at the Salpêtrière* [italics added] could be the starting point for further discoveries (Ellenberger, p. 441).

CHAPTER FOUR · ANNA O. AND THE BIRTH OF PSYCHOANALYSIS

1. Freud, SE20, p. 19.
2. *Studies on Hysteria*, SE2 pp. 30–32; PF3, pp. 83–5.
3. SE2, p. 34; PF3, p. 88.
4. SE2, p. 35; PF3, p. 89.
5. Sulloway, pp. 56–7.
6. Ellenberger, p. 773.
7. Quoted by Clark, p. 135. It should be noted that this parallel is acknowledged by Breuer in *Studies on Hysteria* (see SE2, p. 211; PF3, p. 288). Breuer and Freud also refer to the relevant works of Benedikt and Janet, without explicitly acknowledging any debt to them.
8. SE2, p. 6; PF3, p. 57. Malcolm Macmillan has argued persuasively that the idea that the expression of *emotions* was crucial to the therapeutic process was not part of Breuer's original conception, and that he retrospectively adjusted his case history of Anna O. in order to bring it into conformity with a theory of emotional dynamics which he and Freud did not adopt until much later – possibly as late as 1893 (see Macmillan, pp. 26–31).

9. Frank Cioffi stresses what he calls the 'felt continuity' of Freud's explanatory modes and intuitions with literary culture and folk-wisdom'. My own argument here is derived in part from his. See Cioffi (ed.), *Freud: Modern Judgments*, Macmillan, 1973, pp. 4–5.

10. William Sargant, *Battle for the Mind*, Pan, 1959; W. S Sadler, *Theory and Practice of Psychiatry*, Henry Kimpton, 1936, quoted in Sargant, p. 54.

11. Sargant, p. 61. Sargant's own observation is made in a book where he seeks to explain some of the psychological strategies which are intuitively employed by charismatic religious leaders in order to gain converts. The observation also seems particularly relevant to some modern therapies such as Janov's Primal Therapy, and to 'therapy cults' such as est and Exegesis, which all depend heavily on producing emotional excitement. This parallel in itself suggests that the positive results of abreaction should be treated with some scepticism. A shrewd cautionary note is sounded by Anthony Storr:

> Abreaction, the explosive expression of powerful emotions of love, hate or fear, may cure certain cases of traumatic neurosis. Indeed most of us feel better for giving vent to emotions which we have had to control, or by which we are alarmed, and acknowledgement and expression of emotion is certainly one valuable feature of the psychoanalytic process. Every analyst, however, will have had patients who continue for long periods to express violent emotions at every session, but who do not show improvement as a result ('The Concept of Cure', in Charles Rycroft (ed.), *Psychoanalysis Observed*, Penguin, 1968, p. 62).

For a critique of psychotherapeutic 'ventilationism' see below, note 12.

12. Carol Tavris, *Anger: The Misunderstood Emotion* (1982), New York: Simon and Schuster, revised Touchstone edition, 1989, pp. 130–38 and *passim*.

13. Ellenberger, p. 44.

14. Ellenberger, p. 46. On Benedikt see also Ellenberger's essay 'Moritz Benedikt (1835–1920): An Insufficiently Appreciated Pioneer of Psychoanalysis' (1973), in Ellenberger, *Beyond the Unconscious: Essays of Henri F. Ellenberger in the History of Psychiatry*, ed. Mark S. Micale, Princeton University Press, 1993, pp. 104–18.

15. Ellenberger, pp. 361–4.

16. Gaub, quoted in Z. J. Lipowski, 'What Does the Word "Psychosomatic" Really Mean? A Historical and Semantic Inquiry', *Psychosomatic Medicine*, 1984, vol. 46, p. 163.

17. *Studies on Hysteria*, SE2, pp. 40–41; PF3, p. 95.

18. Quoted by Thornton, p. 129.

19. Jones, I, p. 247, *US, pp.* 224–5; Penguin edition, p. 203. On the accuracy of this story, see below.

20. Ellenberger, 'The Story of "Anna O.": A Critical Review with New Data', *History of the Behavioural Sciences*, vol. 8, 1972, p. 279. This essay is reprinted in Ellenberger, *Beyond the Unconscious*.

21. SE2, p. 23; PF3, p. 75.

22. SE2, p. 23; PF3, p. 76.

23. SE2, p. 23; PF3, pp. 75–6.

24. Thornton, p. 133.

25. Thornton, p. 78.

26. Thornton, p. 134. It would appear that Thornton is referring to the following passage from Macdonald Critchley's *Parietal Lobes*, 1953: 'One patient with a right parieto-occipital lesion would seek to limit the number of surrounding visual stimuli, as the sight of "many things at once" somehow distressed her. Large bunches of flowers, and bowls of fruit, caused visual embarrassment, and she would select one or two blossoms and put them in a vase, and place one or two apples on a plate' (p. 389). It should be noted that this patient's symptoms, while resembling those of Anna O., do not correspond to them exactly.

27. SE2, p. 25; PF3, p. 77.

28. Laurence Miller, *Freud's Brain: Neuropsychodynamic Foundations of Psychoanalysis*, New York: The Guilford Press, 1991, p. 42; Miller's account appears to be taken from Henri Hecaen and Martin A. Albert, *Human Neuropsychology*, Wiley, 1978, p. 80.

29. Miller, p. 42. Miller himself writes as an advocate of the Freudian model of hysteria and would presumably not accept the argument advanced in this chapter.

It should be noted that there are a number of other features of Anna O.'s symptoms which, while they may seem bizarre and inexplicable to the lay observer, are susceptible to neurological explanation. Thornton's chapter on the Anna O. case deals persuasively with a number of these, including the Anna O.'s 'negative hallucination' of the physician who accompanies Breuer on one of his visits. The following passage from a section on perceptual manifestations of cerebral disorders in a standard textbook of 'organic psychiatry' may help to show how many points of similarity there are between Anna O.'s behaviour and common neurological symptoms:

> Early on the patient may be aware that accurate perception requires unusual effort, particularly where vision is concerned. Sometimes, by contrast, perceptions may appear subjectively to be hyper acute. Disturbance of vision may lead to micropsia, macropsia or distortions of shape and position. Disordered auditory perception may hinder clear communication. There may be distortions of weight and size, or bizarre disorders of the body image in which body parts feel shrunken, enlarged, misplaced or even disconnected … Depersonalisation and derealisation are common … Perceptual abnormalities readily lead on to misinterpretations and illusions which are usually fleeting and changeable. The visual modality is affected more than any other. Difficulty with visual recognition combines with faulty thinking and memory to lead to false recognition and faulty orientation in place. The unfamiliar tends to be mistaken for the familiar, or may be interpreted as hostile and persecutory. Thus the patient may misidentify a nurse as a relative, or a doctor as a close friend or enemy … Personally

meaningful fantasies may be projected, as when a tabletop is misperceived as a coffin . . .

Hallucinations are also commonest in the visual modality, though tactile and auditory hallucinations occur as well. They are probably derived partly from failure to distinguish inner images from outer percepts, and partly from vivid dreams and hypnagogic phenomena which are carried over into the waking state as consciousness waxes and wanes . . . (William Alwyn Lishman, *Organic Psychiatry: The Psychological Consequences of Cerebral Disorder*, 2nd edition, Oxford: Blackwell, 1987, pp. 11–12).

30. Thornton, p. 134.
31. Thornton, pp. 136–7.
32. Since published in Albrecht Hirschmüller, *The Life and Work of Josef Breuer*, New York University Press, 1989, pp. 277–91.
33. Thornton, p. 139.
34. Malcolm Robson Parsons, letter to the author, October 1991. See Alfred E. Martin, 'The Occurrence of Remissions and Recovery in Tuberculous Meningitis: A Critical Review', *Brain*, 1909, pp. 209–31. E. M. Thornton refers to this paper in the revised paperback edition of her book in an attempt to meet the criticisms levelled against the first edition of her book. Commenting on this paper, Malcolm Robson Parsons writes: 'most of Martin's "definite" cases either lack the very long follow-up necessary to confirm that permanent recovery has occurred or fall into the category of serous meningitis (in which, of course the tubercle bacilli can be found).' He agrees, however, that at least one of Martin's cases is 'very impressive'. He goes on quote the words of two near contemporaries of Breuer who

> certainly did not lack experience of the disease: Osler says: 'I have neither seen a case which I regard as tuberculous meningitis recover nor have I seen post mortem evidence of past disease of this nature. Cases of recovery have been reported by reliable authorities but they are extremely rare and there is always a reasonable doubt as to the correctness of the diagnosis' (1892). Gowers – the famous neurologist of the period – expresses similar sentiments, although again he admits 'It is probable that cases of tuberculous meningitis do sometimes recover' (1888).

Robson Parsons's own view remains that 'genuine and untreated tuberculous meningitis is for all practical purposes a lethal condition.'

Thornton would reply to this argument by pointing out that, until the introduction of the lumbar puncture, it was not possible to confirm a diagnosis of tuberculous meningitis, and that the prevailing belief that the disease was invariably fatal was therefore self-confirming, since patients who did recover were held to have been misdiagnosed. She would further point out that since the introduction of modern chemotherapy the phenomenon of untreated tuberculous meningitis has itself become a clinical rarity with the result that modern physicians are both unfamiliar with the symptoms of the untreated disease and unlikely ever to encounter cases of spontaneous remission. Thornton's solution to the problem, nevertheless, remains highly improbable, as Robson Parsons suggests.

It should perhaps be noted that Thornton's argument, though widely ignored by Freud scholars, has been embraced uncritically by Hans Eysenck in his *Decline and Fall of the Freudian Empire* (Penguin, 1986). Eysenck's book contains many criticisms of Freud which are both cogent and interesting. But his unequivocal and unqualified announcement that Anna O. was suffering from tuberculous meningitis seems to indicate that his scepticism, so active when Freud's theories are in question, is sometimes suspended when it comes to assessing the arguments of Freud's critics (see Eysenck, p. 32).

35. Lindsay Hurst, 'What Was Wrong with Anna O.?', *Journal of the Royal Society of Medicine*, vol. 75, 1982, pp. 129–31. The other suggestions have been made informally by physicians and neurologists with whom I have discussed the case.

Albrecht Hirschmüller, in his biography of Josef Breuer, suggests that the various attempts at re-diagnosis of Anna O.'s illness which have been made only serve to illustrate the dangers of something which he calls 'palaeo-diagnosis':

> Psychiatric case histories, even such comprehensive accounts as Breuer's, should not be assimilated to timeless pathological or anatomical descriptions. We are not free to wrench symptoms and diagnosis from their own temporal and sociocultural contexts. The question of 'correct' diagnosis (or of 'correct' treatment indeed!) is hardly fruitful. The interpretation of this case, as of others, is stamped with the thought schemata of a given period, as well as being influenced by current institutional conditions. The identification and description of categories appropriate to a particular time would be a most difficult task. (p. 132)

In the face of an argument like this it must immediately be conceded that if we were discussing symptoms which had been consciously or unconsciously simulated by patients, Hirschmüller might have a point. But in so far as the most pressing questions raised by Anna O.'s illness are concerned with whether Breuer failed to recognise the signs of organic, neurological disease, his argument is curiously beside the point. For whatever may be the case with regard to our emotional foibles, the pathology and symptoms of organic trauma and disease are remarkably constant. Even Edward Shorter, who appears to share many of Hirschmüller's assumptions, concedes this point: 'There is very little cultural shaping of the symptoms of organic disease, and people presumably turned yellow with liver failure in the fourteenth century just as they do in the twentieth' (*From Paralysis to Fatigue*, p. 2). It should be noted that, if we were to accept Hirschmüller's argument, we would be obliged to accept every diagnostic error ever made by a psychiatrist (or a physician). We would also be similarly obliged to reject psychoanalysis itself as a therapeutic fossil of no relevance to our changed sociocultural circumstances. While this last conclusion may be true, it is true for reasons quite other than those advanced by Hirschmüller, whose argument seems designed more to protect precious illusions than to advance the cause of knowledge. It is undeniably the case that whenever we attempt to re-diagnose individual patients retrospectively we are liable to make mistakes and that no certain conclusion is likely to be reached. But exactly this can be said of the practice of history itself and it has not yet been advanced as a reason for renouncing historical research altogether.

36. Alison Orr-Andrawes, 'The Case of Anna O.: A Neuropsychiatric Perspective', in *Journal of the American Psychoanalytic Association*, 1987, vol. 35, p. 399.

37. N. Geschwind, 'Aphasia', *New England Journal of Medicine*, 1971, vol. 284, p. 654–6. Cited in Orr-Andrawes, p. 407.

38. O. Hommes, 'Psychomotor Epilepsy: A Neurological Approach to Hysteria', in *Psychiat. Neurol. Neurochir.*, 1964, vol. 67, pp. 497–519. Cited in Orr-Andrawes, p. 409.

39. Orr-Andrawes, p. 406.

40. Orr-Andrawes writes that chloral hydrate, a non-barbiturate sedative, was introduced as a hypnotic agent in 1869. It was

> commonly abused in the past century before its addictive potential was fully recognised. It is cross-tolerant with barbiturates and produces a similar abstinence syndrome, marked by lowering of the seizure threshold due to rebound hyperexcitability of the nervous system, and by a delirium which is particularly difficult to reverse. The intoxication state also produces delirium, which . . . may be euphoric or dysphoric depending on the situational context.

Orr-Andrawes's specific suggestion is that, unknown to Breuer, Anna O. secretly took chloral hydrate in the early stages of her illness, having got into the habit of sharing her father's supply in order to ensure her 'nurse's nap'. Her 'afternoon somnolence, followed by deeper sleep and an autohypnotic state, might then be viewed as a manifestation of chloral intoxication . . .' caused by 'the mild withdrawal symptoms that developed as the day progressed' (pp. 397–8).

As I have suggested here, one of the most interesting aspects of this argument is to be found in its more general implications. In his *From Paralysis to Fatigue*, for example, Edward Shorter cites the case of a Mlle X., who suffered from a number of epileptoid symptoms and used massive doses of chloral hydrate – up to six grams daily. According to Shorter's account, it was only after she was moved to a private clinic in the South of France that she began to have fully developed 'Charcot-style' seizures. Shorter treats her as a hysteric who was affected by the 'climate of suggestion in this provincial sanatorium'. This view is entirely plausible. It seems possible, however, that what actually happened is that she developed full epileptic seizures in response to the withdrawal or reduction of her doses of chloral hydrate (see Shorter, p. 189).

41. SE2, p. 35; PF3, p. 89.

42. Hirschmüller, p. 288.

43. Hirschmüller, p. 288.

44. SE2, p. 34; PF3, p. 88.
45. SE2, p. 35; PF3, p. 89.
46. Hirschmüller, p. 289.
47. SE2, pp. 39-40; PF3, p. 94.
48. SE2, p. 35; PF3, p. 89.
49. SE2, p. 35; PF3, pp. 89-90.
50. SE2, p. 36; PF3, pp. 90-91.
51. SE2, p. 44; PF3, pp. 99-100.
52. Sulloway, p. 56.
53. Gay, p. 63.
54. Jones, I, p. 247, US, p. 225; Penguin edition, p. 203.
55. Jeffrey Mousaieff Masson (ed.), *The Complete Letters of Sigmund Freud to Wilhelm Fliess 1887-1904*, Harvard University Press, 1985, p. 435.
56. Freud, *Letters*, pp. 408-9; 'On the History of the Psychoanalytic Movement', SE14, p. 12; PF15, pp. 68-9; 'An Autobiographical Study', SE20, p. 26; PF15, p. 210.
57. Freud, *Letters*, p. 409.
58. Hirschmüller, p. 127.
59. Gay, p. 67.

CHAPTER FIVE · FREUD'S FIRST CASE

1. Breuer, quoted in John E. Gedo and George H. Pollock (ed.), *Freud: The Fusion of Science and Humanism*, New York: International Universities Press, 1976, p. 147.

2. This list of the symptoms reported by Freud's early patients is compiled for the most part from two sources – the index to the Penguin edition of *Studies on Hysteria* (entries under 'hysterical symptoms'), and the list which Freud and Breuer themselves give in their 'On the Psychical Mechanism of Hysterical Phenomena: Preliminary Communication' (1893), Penguin edition, p. 54. It is in the latter paper that Freud and Breuer refer to 'epileptoid convulsions' and '*petit mal*'.

3. In the last twenty years an alternative, relativistic approach to medical history has come into being. Reacting against Whiggish views, and failing to recognise that scepticism about the ideology of 'progress' is entirely compatible with acceptance of the reality of 'medical progress', adherents of the relativistic approach seem sometimes to be embarrassed by the very possibility that modern physicians might know more than ancient ones. As a result they tend to decline on principle to judge past medical practice against current medical knowledge. See the quotation from Hirschmüller and discussion, Chapter 4, note 35.

   My comments about the tendency of medical historians to ignore medical mistakes and misdirections have their origin in a conversation with Elizabeth Thornton. Much more recently, after I had written the words which occur in the main text, Frank Cioffi drew my attention to a paper by the psychiatrist E. H. Hare which contains the following passage:

It may be argued that historians ought to pay more attention than they have done to scientific hypotheses which proved to be failures. The trouble with the history of science, and of scientific medicine, is that it has too often been presented as one long success story; whereas, in fact, a striking feature of the history of science (particularly where science overlaps with medical and social matters) has been the tenacious persistence of supposedly scientific ideas long after they ought to have been abandoned. I think the historical study of scientific failures is important, not only because it is likely to give us a keener insight into the nature of the scientific process, but also because it may lead us to examine more closely the soundness of some of our own pet ideas' (E. H. Hare, 'Medical Astrology and its Relation to Modern Psychiatry', *Proceedings of the Royal Society of Medicine*, vol. 70, 1977, pp. 105–10).

One medical historian who has given an unusual amount of attention to the role of misdiagnoses in the history of psychiatry is Richard Hunter. See Richard A. Hunter, 'Psychiatry and Neurology: Psychosyndrome or Brain Disease', *Proceedings of the Royal Society of Medicine*, vol. 66, April 1973; Richard A. Hunter and Ida Macalpine, *Three Hundred Years of Psychiatry, 1535–1860*, Oxford University Press, 1983. See also Roy Porter, 'Ida Macalpine and Richard Hunter' in Mark S. Micale and Roy Porter (ed.), *Discovering the History of Psychiatry*, New York: Oxford University Press, 1994, pp. 83–94.

4. A. Steyerthal, *Was ist Hysterie?*, 1908, Halle a S., Marhold. Quoted by Aubrey Lewis, 'The Survival of Hysteria' in Alec Roy (ed.), *Hysteria*, Wiley, 1982, p. 22.

An interesting sociological perspective on the creation of spurious diagnostic categories is offered by Susan Leigh Starr in her study, *Regions of the Mind: Brain Research and the Quest for Scientific Certainty*, Stanford University Press, 1989:

> The creation of 'garbage categories' is a process familiar to medical sociologists. When faced with phenomena which do not fit diagnostic or taxonomic classification schemes, doctors often make residual diagnoses. One function of such diagnoses is to shunt unmanageable, incurable or undiagnosable patients into other spheres of care where they will not interfere with the ongoing work. Hysteria, senility and depression, for example, have been criticised as such categories . . .
>
> Localizationists created such categories for problems that did not have an identifiable localised referent or the possibility of a physical treatment. These patients were diagnosed as hysteric or neurasthenic. (p. 173)

5. Eliot Slater, 'What is Hysteria?', in A. Roy (ed.), *Hysteria*, 1982, p. 40.
6. Eliot Slater, 'Diagnosis of "Hysteria"', *British Medical Journal*, 29 May 1965, p. 1399.
7. Thomas Willis, *Affectionum Quae Dicuntur Hystericae* (1670), trans. R. G. Latham, London, 1848. Quoted in Ilza Veith, *Hysteria: The History of a Disease*, University of Chicago Press, 1965, p. 134.

8. *The Psychopathology of Everyday Life*, SE6, p. 146 (note); PF5, pp. 197–8 (note). See Thornton, p. 298.

9. Although Emmy von. N. is generally seen as Freud's first psychoanalytic patient, Freud's treatment of the patient he refers to as Frau Cäcilie M., who has since been identified by Peter Swales as Anna von Lieben, began around the same time. Whereas Frau Emmy's treatment began in May of 1889, Swales suggests that Freud may have begun employing the cathartic method to treat Frau Cäcilie in July 1889. See Peter J. Swales, 'Freud, His Teacher and the Birth of Psychoanalysis' in Paul E. Stepansky (ed.), *Freud: Appraisals and Reappraisals*, Contributions to Freud Studies, vol. 1, New Jersey: The Analytic Press, 1986, pp. 3–82. Malcolm Macmillan's suggestion that 'in neither case was any kind of cathartic method used' appears to be based on the observation that Freud was not yet using the technique of emotional abreaction. It is interesting, however, that both Swales and Macmillan refer to Freud's reading of Edward Bellamy's novel *Dr Heidenhoff's Process*. This remarkable novel describes a process in which Dr Heidenhoff uses an electrical machine in order to offer a kind of redemptive therapy which cleanses away guilt. Swales writes that 'the theme of Bellamy's extraordinary book is the medicalisation – one might say the "psychiatrisation" – of morals and values' (p. 36). This is an accurate description of the novel. More interestingly still, it might be claimed that what is actually being 'medicalised' in Bellamy's novel is nothing other than the apocalyptic promise that the sins of mankind will be washed 'in the blood of the Lamb'. The therapy offered by Dr Heidenhoff, then, is itself 'cathartic' – in that it offers *purification* – as the imagery of the novel repeatedly suggests. Bellamy offers a kind of medicalised, secularised apocalypse which had a deep appeal not only to Freud, but also to Sydney Webb, who adopted the book as a kind of personal bible and evidently felt it had relieved him of his own crippling sense of guilt. On Webb and Bellamy see Stanley Pierson, *Marxism and the Origins of British Socialism: The Struggle for a New Consciousness*, Cornell University Press, 1973, p. 117.

10. Freud, SE2, p. 49; PF3, p. 104.

11. I have used the rather unusual phrase 'provisional fact' in preference to 'hypothesis' since it seems to reflect Freud's unsceptical attitude towards his speculative constructions more accurately.

12. Freud himself seems implicitly to concede as much in the footnotes he progressively added to his case history; see below.

13. L. Kanner, *Child Psychiatry*, 3rd edition, Oxford: Blackwell, 1957. Quoted in William Alwyn Lishman, *Organic Psychiatry: The Psychological Consequences of Cerebral Disorder*, 2nd edition, Oxford: Blackwell Scientific, 1987, p. 581.

14. Arthur K. Shapiro and Elaine Shapiro, 'Tic Disorders' in Harold I. Kaplan and Benjamin J. Sadock (ed.), *Comprehensive Textbook of Psychiatry V*, 5th edition, Baltimore: Williams and Wilkins, 1989, p. 1867.

15. Shapiro, p. 1867; SE2, pp. 50, 71; PF3, pp. 106, 127–8. Whether or not these feelings possessed the recurrent pattern of 'sensory tics' is not clear from Freud's case history.

16. Else Pappenheim, 'Freud and Gilles de la Tourette: Diagnostic Speculations

on "Frau Emmy von N." ', *International Review of Psychoanalysis*, 1980, vol. 7, pp. 265, 274; Thornton, pp. 208–13.

Pappenheim writes that 'Shapiro *et al.* mentions that "Freudian scholars" occasionally suggest that Frau Emmy suffered from Tourette's syndrome, but they find the clinical description insufficient to make this diagnosis' (p. 265). See A. K. Shapiro, E. S. Shapiro, R. L. Bruun and R. D. Sweet, *Gilles de la Tourette's Syndrome*, New York: Raven Press, 1978. One issue which is crucial here is the power which is still exercised by the diagnosis of 'hysteria' (or 'conversion') over modern neurologists and psychiatrists. So long as this label is allowed a degree of medical legitimacy it means that modern physicians are not obliged to leave a patient like Emmy von N. without a diagnosis at all. We will only be in a position to consider her case and similar cases objectively when it is accepted that 'hysteria' is indeed a chimaera, and that that whatever Frau Emmy was suffering from, she was not suffering from this non-existent disease.

17. For a discussion of this issue which considers both sides of the argument, see Lishman, pp. 582–7. For a remarkable description of a 'Touretter' written from a strongly organic point of view by a neurologist well known to be sympathetic to psychoanalysis, see Oliver Sacks's 'Witty Ticcy Ray' in *The Man Who Mistook His Wife for a Hat*, Picador, 1986, pp. 87–96.

18. Lishman, p. 586.

19. SE2, p. 79; PF3, p. 138.

20. SE2, p. 74 (note); PF3, p. 133 (note).

21. SE2, p. 101; PF3, p. 163.

22. SE2, p. 96; PF3, pp. 156–7.

23. SE7, p. 40; PF8 pp. 72–3.

24. SE2, p. 105 (note); PF3, p. 167 (note).

25. SE2, p. 103; PF3, p. 165.

26. SE2, p. 105; PF3, pp. 167–8.

27. See 'L'histoire d' "Emmy von N." ' , *L'Evolution psychiatrique*, vol. 42, 1977, p. 519–40; Lisa Appignanesi and John Forrester, *Freud's Women*, Weidenfeld and Nicolson, 1992, pp. 101–3; English translation in Ellenberger, *Beyond the Unconscious*, 1993, pp. 273–90.

CHAPTER SIX · MORE MEDICAL MISTAKES

1. Freud, *Studies on Hysteria*, SE2, pp. 145, 153–4; PF3, pp. 213–14, 222–3. See also the discussion of the pressure technique in Freud's case history of Lucy R., PF3, pp. 173–5. On Freud's use of the pressure technique, see Macmillan pp. 90–91; Mark Pendergrast, *Victims of Memory: Incest Accusations and Shattered Lives*, Hinesberg, Vermont: Upper Access Inc., 1995, pp. 409–11.

2. SE2, pp. 125, 126; PF3, pp. 190, 192.

3. See, for example, the section on 'Blackouts, Fits and Faints', in C. David Marsden and Timothy J. Fowler (ed.), *Clinical Neurology*, Edward Arnold, 1989, pp. 28–32.

4. Karen Armstrong, *Beginning the World*, Pan, 1983, especially pp. 231–8.

5. SE2, p. 106; PF3, p. 169.
6. Hughlings Jackson, quoted in Thornton, pp. 214–15; Henri Gastaut, *The Epilepsies: Electro Clinical Correlations*, Springfield: Thomas, 1954, p. 15; Doris A. Trauner, 'Seizure Disorders' in Wigbert C. Wiederholt (ed.), *Neurology for Non-Neurologists*, Philadelphia: Grune and Stratton, 1988, p. 245.
7. SE2, pp. 106–7; PF3, pp. 169–70.
8. As is suggested by Thornton, pp. 214–15.
9. SE2, p. 135; PF3, p. 202.
10. SE2, p. 135; PF3, p. 202.
11. SE2, p. 150; PF3, p. 219.
12. SE2, p. 151; PF3, p. 220.
13. SE2, p. 152; PF3, p. 222.
14. SE2, p. 154; PF3, p. 223.
15. SE2, pp. 154–5; PF3, p. 224.
16. SE2, p. 156; PF3, p. 226.
17. SE2, p. 295; PF3, p. 382.
18. SE2, p. 157; PF3, p. 227.
19. SE2, p. 158; PF3, p. 227.
20. Quoted in Gay, p. 72.
21. See Macmillan's excellent discussion, Macmillan, pp. 111–19.
22. SE2, p. 160; PF3, p. 231.
23. Eliot Slater, 'Diagnosis of "Hysteria"', *BMJ*, 29 May 1965, p. 1399.

CHAPTER SEVEN · MYSTERIOUS MECHANISMS

1. Freud, 'The Neuro-Psychoses of Defence', SE3, pp. 60–61; see Sulloway, pp. 61–2.
2. See Freud and Breuer, 'On the Psychical Mechanism of Hysterical Phenomena', SE2, pp. 3–17; PF3, pp. 53–69; Sulloway, pp. 62–3.
3. SE2, pp. 203–14; PF3, 279–91; Sulloway, p. 63.
4. Freud, 'The Neuro-Psychoses of Defence', SE3, p. 87.
5. See Macmillan, pp. 98–103; 111–19.
6. Sulloway, p. 114.
7. Sulloway, p. 113; Freud, *The Origins of Psychoanalysis: Letters to Wilhelm Fliess, Drafts and Notes, 1887–1902*, ed. Marie Bonaparte, Anna Freud, Ernst Kris, Imago, 1954, p. 118. See FF, p. 127.
8. FF, p. 146.
9. FF, p. 152.
10. For this simplified description of Freud's extraordinarily complex system, see Clark, p. 153, and Sulloway, p. 117.
11. Richard Wollheim, *Freud*, Fontana, 1971, p. 65.
12. Sulloway, pp. 102–31.
13. Ellenberger, p. 218.
14. Sulloway, pp. 66–7. Although most of Sulloway's references to Fechner are respectful, he should be given due credit for quoting the splendid verdict which William James delivered on 'the great Fechner'. 'It would be terrible,'

wrote James in 1890, 'if even such a dear old man as this could saddle our Science forever with his patient whimsies, and, in a world so full of more nutritious objects of attention, compel all future students to plough through ... his own works ... Those who desire this dreadful literature can find it ... but I will not even enumerate it in a footnote' (*The Principles of Psychology*, vol. I, New York, 1890, p. 549, quoted in Sulloway, p. 290).

15. Ellenberger, p. 21.
16. Ellenberger, pp. 202ff, 434, 535–41.
17. Ellenberger, p. 535.
18. Thornton, pp. 223–7; I am once again indebted to Elizabeth Thornton for her insight into the historical genealogy of Freud's model of nervous energy.
19. Robert R. Holt, *Freud Reappraised: A Fresh Look at Psychoanalytic Theory*, New York: The Guilford Press, 1989, pp. 128–9.

CHAPTER EIGHT · SEX, MASTURBATION AND NEURASTHENIA

1. FF, p. 141.
2. SE2, p. 200; PF3, p. 276.
3. William McGuire (ed.), *The Freud/Jung Letters*, Hogarth Press and Routledge and Kegan Paul, 1974, pp. 140–41 (Letter 84F); see Sulloway, p. 90.
4. SE14, p. 13.
5. SE14, pp. 14–15.
6. Clark, p. 126.
7. Freud, SE1, p. 51. Most accounts of Freud's views on sexual aetiology appear to have missed this statement. Inexplicably Richard Wollheim quotes the same encyclopaedia article in an attempt to demonstrate his view of the late emergence of Freud's views on sexuality. He appears not to have noticed the passage quoted here. I am grateful to Frank Cioffi for drawing my attention both to the article and to Wollheim's misleading citation of it.
8. G. M. Beard, 'Neurasthenia or Nervous Exhaustion', *Boston Medical and Surgical Journal*, vol. 3, pp. 217–21. See Macmillan, p. 126; Ellenberger p. 243.
9. G. M. Beard, *A Practical Treatise of Nervous Exhaustion*, New York, 1880; *American Nervousness*, New York, 1881. See Barbara Sicherman, 'The Uses of a Diagnosis: Doctors, Patients and Neurasthenia', *Journal of the History of Medicine*, vol. XXXII, 1977, p. 33.
10. Ellenberger, p. 243; Macmillan, pp. 128–9.
11. Some elements of this argument are put forward by Barbara Sicherman, whose list of organic ills 'caught' by the diagnosis I have borrowed and extended. Sicherman, however, takes what seems to me an overly positive view of the neurasthenia diagnosis, suggesting that it was a means used by doctors to provide necessary psychological therapy to their patients. In some cases this may be true. In many others, as Sicherman's own observation about misdiagnosed organic conditions implies, it evidently was not.
12. Quoted in Macmillan, p. 130.
13. J. M. López Piñero, *Historical Origins of the Concept of Neurosis* (1963), Cambridge University Press, 1983. Quoted in Macmillan, p. 131.

14. See Macmillan, p. 131.
15. FF, p. 25.
16. Macmillan, pp. 124–5.
17. FF, p. 39.
18. FF, p. 41.
19. FF, p. 41; Freud, 'On the Grounds for Detaching a Particular Syndrome from Neurasthenia Under the Description "Anxiety Neuroses"' (1895), SE3 pp. 90–117. The best accounts of Freud, neurasthenia and the anxiety neuroses is Malcolm Macmillan's, see Macmillan pp. 122–143. On Freud's warning to one of his sons about the dangers of masturbation, see Roazen, p. 41.
20. FF, p. 104.
21. FF, p. 57.
22. Seneca, *Fragments*, ed. Friedrich G. Haase, Leipzig, 1897, no. 84. For commentary on this passage and on the background to Christian doctrine on marriage, see John T. Noonan, Jr., *Contraception: A History of Its Treatment by the Catholic Theologians and Canonists*, Harvard University Press, 1965, pp. 37–49 and *passim*.
23. Quoted in Arthur Calder-Marshall, *Havelock Ellis*, Hart-Davis, 1959, p. 158.
24. Alex Comfort, *The Anxiety Makers*, Panther, 1968, p. 81. See also E. H. Hare, 'Masturbatory Insanity: The History of an Idea', *Journal of Mental Science*, 1962, vol. 108, pp. 1–25; Jean Stengers and Anne Van Neck, *Histoire d'une grande peur: la masturbation*, Editions de l'Université de Bruxelles, 1984.
25. Comfort, *Anxiety Makers*, pp. 81–5.
26. FF, p. 96.

CHAPTER NINE · THE SEDUCTION THEORY

1. SE2, p. 6; PF3, p. 56.
2. SE2, pp. 246–8; PF3, pp. 327–9.
3. Sulloway, p. 85.
4. SE2, p. 79; PF3, p. 138; see above, Chapter 5.
5. SE2, p. 279; PF3, p. 364.
6. SE2, pp. 273–4; PF3, p. 358. SE3, p 57.
7. Sulloway, p. 95.
8. Janet Malcolm, *Psychoanalysis: The Impossible Profession* (1982), London: Karnac Ltd, 1988, p. 97.
9. Malcolm, p. 73.
10. 'Dora', SE7, pp. 76–8; PF8, pp. 112–14.
11. SE7, p. 80; PF8, p. 118.
12. FF, p. 144.
13. Masson, *The Assault on Truth*, pp. 9–10.
14. Freud, 'The Aetiology of Hysteria', SE3, pp. 204. (This paper is reprinted as an appendix to Masson's *The Assault on Truth*; see pp. 272–3.)
15. SE3, p. 201; Masson, p. 269.
16. SE3, pp. 195–6; Masson, p. 264.
17. SE3, p. 204; Masson, p. 273.

18. John E. Gedo and George H. Pollock (ed.), *Freud: The Fusion of Science and Humanism*, New York: International Universities Press, pp. 204, 273. See Clark, p. 159.
19. 'Heredity and the Aetiology of the Neuroses', SE3, p. 154.
20. SE3, p. 203; Masson, p. 272.
21. FF, p. 266.
22. SE3, p. 199; Masson, pp. 267–8.
23. SE3, p. 200; Masson, p. 268.
24. FF, pp. 194, 218, 220, 230, 232. See Thornton, pp. 245, Han Israëls and Morton Schatzman, 'The Seduction Theory', *History of Psychiatry*, vol. IV, 1993, p. 54.
25. Israëls and Schatzman, p. 54.
26. FF, p. 220.
27. FF, p. 218.
28. FF, p. 223.
29. FF, p. 222.
30. SE20, p. 34; PF15, p. 218.
31. SE22, p. 120.
32. Schatzman, 'Freud: Who Seduced Whom?', *New Scientist*, 21 March 1992, p. 37.
33. Masson, *The Assault on Truth*, p. 144.
34. Ferenczi, quoted in Masson, *Against Therapy*, pp. 129–30.
35. This chapter, like the book as a whole, was completed before I had read Robert Wilcocks's excellent *Maelzel's Chess Player: Freud and the Rhetoric of Deceit*, Lanham, Maryland: Rowman and Littlefield, 1994. Wilcocks makes a very similar point about Freud's lack of interest in his patients' feelings, noting that Freud was never interested in the feelings of emotional shock, hurt or distress which might reasonably be imputed to the victims of sexual abuse:

> Notice, once again, that it is the physiological site of the interference (mouth, anus) that may cause 'deferred *internal disgust*', rather than the psychological significance of the experience and the affective atmosphere that accompanied it. The notion that it is frightening to the child, or incomprehensible, or that it profoundly disturbed his or her sense of autonomy or self-worth is *never* considered by Freud, beyond the 'bogeyman' comments of Part III of the 'Aetiology' lecture, which seem more and more an exercise in rhetoric and less a genuine plea from a concerned doctor who is maturely in charge of his own sexuality, and maturely aware of the emotional hurt that such adult molestation may incur (p. 152).

On a different front it should be noted that, although Freud's change of mind over the seduction hypothesis undoubtedly led to the widespread therapeutic denial of real instances of sexual abuse by the majority of Freud's followers, Freud himself did not completely rule out seduction as a possible cause of neurosis even after he had repudiated his general theory (see Gay, p. 95). On this question, however, see Masson's discussion in his Afterword to *The Assault on Truth*, pp. 195–200, and my own Afterword, 'Freud's False Memories'.

CHAPTER TEN · FREUD, FLIESS AND THE THEORY OF INFANTILE
SEXUALITY

1. FF, p. 264.
2. FF, p. 264.
3. FF, p. 264.
4. A similar view is taken by Frank Sulloway (see Sulloway, p. 421). Frederick Crews cites Sulloway in the course of making the same criticism of Freud's intellectual style: '. . . Freud's supporters and detractors alike have been bemused by the "empirical" window-dressing of his ideas and have underestimated their actual deductive, speculative, and derivative origins. In other words, they have failed to grasp that "the structure of Freud's published arguments is often the exact reverse of the actual genesis of his ideas" ' (Frederick Crews, 'The Freudian Way of Knowledge', in *Skeptical Engagements*, p. 47).
5. Walter Kendrick, *Voice Literary Supplement*, June 1984.
6. FF, p. 184.
7. SE14, p. 22.
8. Freud to Ferenczi, 9 July 1913, *The Letters of Sigmund Freud 1873–1939*, Hogarth Press, 1961, p. 301.
9. Sulloway, p. 136.
10. FF, p. 7.
11. FF, p. 8; see also M. Schur (ed.), *Drives, Affects, Behaviour*, vol. 2, New York: International Universities Press, 1965.
12. Thornton, unpublished letter to *The Times Literary Supplement*, 9 December 1983, text kindly supplied by the author. See also Thornton, pp. 162–4.
13. Thornton, p. 165.
14. Fliess, *The Relations between the Nose and the Female Sex Organ from the Biological Aspect*, 1897. Quoted in Sulloway, p. 141.
15. See Sulloway, p. 140.
16. Ry's review is quoted in a footnote appended by Masson to Freud's letter to Fliess of 14 April 1898, FF, p. 310.
17. Sulloway, p. 144.
18. Schur, *Freud: Living and Dying*, Hogarth Press, 1972.
19. FF, pp. 116–17.
20. FF, p. 186.
21. FF, p. 125.
22. FF, pp. 320, 323.
23. Sulloway, pp. 135–70.
24. Jones, I, pp. 316–50, *US*, pp. 287–318; Penguin edition, pp. 249–75.
25. Jones actually goes so far as to invent a 'psychoneurosis' supposedly suffered by Freud throughout the 1890s in order to account for his attitude towards Fliess. Jones, I, p. 334, *US, p. 304*; Penguin edition, p. 263.

26. FF, p. 193, p. 51; Jones, I, pp. 330–31, US, p. 300; Penguin edition, pp. 260–61. The resonance of Freud's reference to the Messiah, caught well in Jones's translation, is lost in Masson's (FF, p. 51). The original German reads: '. . . *drittens hoffe ich noch auf dich als auf den Messias, der das von mir aufgezeigte Problem durch eine technische Verbesserung löst'* (J. Masson (ed.), *Sigmund Freud: Briefe an Wilhelm Fliess 1887–1904*, Frankfurt am Main: Fischer, 1986, p. 43).

27. Freud, *An Autobiographical Study* (1925), PF15, p. 194.

28. Von Uexküll on Robert Bunsen, quoted by Ellenberger, p. 449.

29. FF, p. 254.

30. Sulloway, p. 171.

31. Sulloway, pp. 199–201, 259–64; on Piaget and Spock, see Stephen Jay Gould, *Ontogeny and Phylogeny*, Harvard University Press, 1977.

32. Ernst Haeckel, *The Riddle of the Universe* (1899), Watts, 1929, p. 117. See also Haeckel, *The Evolution of Man* (1874), Watts, 1906.

33. On this aspect of Haeckel's work, see Daniel Gasman's *The Scientific Origins of National Socialism: Social Darwinism in Ernst Haeckel and the German Monist League*, Macdonald, 1971. But see also Alfred Kelly, *The Descent of Darwin: The Popularization of Darwin in Germany, 1860–1914*, University of North Carolina Press, 1981. Kelly's book contains a great deal of valuable research on the dissemination of Darwin's ideas in Germany. He also criticises Gasman's work (see pp. 120–21). Some criticism of Gasman's argument may well be justified. To discern in Haeckelian monism the intellectual *origins* of National Socialism is to claim too much. But the case Kelly argues is both historically and politically unpersuasive, and his attempt to dispose of Gasman's book in a paragraph fails to grapple with the very complex and, I believe, crucial issues which Gasman raises.

34. Haeckel, *Riddle*, p. 119.

35. George Romanes, *Mental Evolution in Animals*, London, 1883; *Mental Evolution in Man: Origin of Human Faculty*, London, 1888. See Sulloway, pp. 248–9.

36. Sulloway, p. 247. The theory in question is not expounded explicitly in the text of *Mental Evolution in Man*, but it is made quite clear in the diagram which forms its frontispiece. This is reproduced by Sulloway (p. 249). Romanes's project of writing a series of studies on the development of the intellect, of emotions, volition and morality was cut short by his death in 1894. See Sulloway, p. 248 (note).

37. FF, p. 223; where the meaning is clearer I have sometimes used the earlier translation of these letters from Freud, *The Origins of Psycho-Analysis, Letters to Wilhelm Fliess, Drafts and Notes, 1887–1902*, ed. Marie Bonaparte, Anna Freud and Ernst Kris, New York: Basic Books, 1950.

38. FF, p. 279 (translation from *Origins*).

39. Macmillan, p. 285.

40. Macmillan, pp. 286–7.

41. On Bölsche, see Sulloway, pp. 262–3. See also Kelly, *The Descent of Darwin*, *passim*.

42. Bölsche, quoted in Sulloway, p. 263.

43. Freud, *Introductory Lectures on Psychoanalysis*, SE16, p. 354; PF1, p. 400.

44. Freud, *Three Essays on Sexuality*, SE7, p. 241; PF7, pp. 166–7.

45. SE16, p. 354; PF1, p. 400.

46. Chief among the factors which interfered with sexual development were, according to Freud, 'the innate variety of sexual constitutions' (*Three Essays*, SE7, p. 235; PF7, p. 160).

47. For a more complex exposition of Freud's biological thinking in this and related areas, see Sulloway, pp. 388–90.

48. SE7, p. 177; PF7, p. 93.

49. SE7, p. 162; PF7, p. 76 (footnote, added 1915).

50. 'A Child is Being Beaten', SE17, p. 188; PF10, p. 174.

51. SE7, p. 199; PF7, p. 118. Freud also writes of the oral organisation and the sadistic-anal organisation of sexual life that they are stages 'which almost seem as though they were harking back to early forms of animal life' (SE7, p. 198; PF7, p. 116).

52. SE7, p. 131; PF7, pp. 40–41.

53. Sulloway, p. 445–6.

54. Erik Erikson, *Childhood and Society*, Penguin, 1967, p. 59.

55. Sulloway, p. 430.

56. Alex Comfort, *Darwin and the Naked Lady*, Routledge and Kegan Paul, 1961, p. 5.

57. Philip Rieff, *Freud: The Mind of the Moralist*, University of Chicago Press, 1959, p. 33.

58. Sulloway, p. 275

59. Jones, III, p. 336, *US, p. 313*.

CHAPTER ELEVEN · EXPLORING THE UNCONSCIOUS: SELF-ANALYSIS AND OEDIPUS

1. Jones, I, p. 316, *US, p. 287*; Penguin edition, p. 249.

2. Jones, I, p. 351, *US, p. 319*; Penguin edition, p. 276.

3. Sulloway, p. 209.

4. Ernest Gellner, *The Psychoanalytic Movement*, Paladin, 1985, p. 163. By making this concession it seems to me that Gellner undermines his spiky, interesting and entertaining critique of Freud, placing himself in the position, almost, of the atheist who concedes the existence of heaven.

5. See Lancelot Law Whyte, *The Unconscious Before Freud*, Social Science Paperbacks, 1967, pp. 79–80.

6. Quoted in Whyte, p. 99; p. 161.

7. Freud, 'Introductory Lectures', SE15, p. 212; PF1, p. 249. Freud later adopted the term 'id' to describe the putative psychological system which he had initially designated as the Unconscious. See 'New Introductory Lectures', PF2, p. 101ff (Lecture 31).

8. *Studies on Hysteria*, SE2, pp. 269, 268; PF3, pp. 353, 352.

9. Thomas Hobbes, *Leviathan* (1651), Fontana, 1962, p. 101 (Part I, Chapter 8).

10. Jones, I, p. 358, *US, p. 326*; Penguin edition, p. 282.
11. FF, p. 268,
12. See Sulloway, p. 191.
13. FF, p. 272.
14. *An Outline of Psychoanalysis*, SE23, p. 189; PF15, pp. 423-4.
15. George Devereux, 'Why Oedipus Killed Laius. A Note on the Complementary Oedipus Complex in Greek Drama', *International Journal of Psychoanalysis*, 1953, vol. 34, p. 132. This passage is quoted in Morton Schatzman's *Soul Murder: Persecution in the Family*, Allen Lane, 1973, p. 103. The entire chapter in which this passage is cited is relevant to the argument advanced here (see Schatzman, pp. 93-115).
16. Schatzman, *Soul Murder*, p. 112. On Freud's systematic disregard of the evidence of human behaviour, see below, Chapter 22, 'The Ghost in the Psychoanalytic Machine'.
17. Erich Fromm, *Sigmund Freud's Mission*, Unwin, 1959, p. 15.
18. 'Outline', SE23, p. 193; PF15, p. 428.

CHAPTER TWELVE · DREAMS AND SYMPTOMS

1. 'An Autobiographical Study', SE20, p. 34; PF15, p. 217-19.
2. SE16, p. 337.
3. FF, p. 140; see Macmillan, pp. 232-5.
4. FF, p. 25.
5. SE5, p. 589.
6. FF, p. 189; see Macmillan, p. 238.
7. FF, pp. 217-18.
8. FF, p. 251; Macmillan, p. 239.
9. FF, pp. 338, 345.
10. Freud, *The Interpretation of Dreams*, SE5, p. 569; PF4, pp. 723-4.
11. SE5, p. 570; PF4, p. 724.
12. SE5, p. 608; PF4, p. 769.
13. Clark, p. 184.
14. SE4, p. 151; PF4, p. 254.
15. SE4, p. 152; PF4, p. 235.
16. SE4, p. 159; PF4, p. 243.
17. SE4, p. 158; PF4, pp. 242-3.
18. SE5, p. 355; PF4, p. 472.
19. SE4, pp. 183-5; PF4, pp. 270-73.
20. SE5, p. 355; PF4, p. 472.
21. Wittgenstein, 'Conversations on Freud', noted by Rush Rhees in Richard Wollheim and James Hopkins (ed.), *Philosophical Essays on Freud*, Cambridge University Press, 1982, pp. 5-6.
22. Orwell, quoted in Bernard Crick, *George Orwell: A Life*, Penguin, 1982, p. 574.
23. Gomperz, quoted in FF, p. 388 (note).
24. SE7, p. 9. In 'A Case of Hysteria' Freud also writes as follows:

I have certainly heard of some people – doctors and laymen – who are scandalised by a therapeutic method in which conversations of this sort occur, and who appear to envy either me or my patients the titillation which, according to their notions, such a method must afford. But I am too well acquainted with the respectability of these gentlemen to excite myself over them. I shall avoid the temptation of writing a satire upon them (SE7, p. 49; PF8, p. 82).

25. Freud, *Introductory Lectures on Psychoanalysis*, SE16, p. 252; PF1, p. 291.
26. SE16, p. 252; PF1, p. 291.
27. The charge that Freud had an affair with his sister-in-law, Minna Bernays, was made in private by Jung in an interview in 1957 with his friend John M. Billinsky, who published it in 1969: 'Jung and Freud (The End of a Romance)', *Andover Newton Quarterly*, X. The idea has been developed in considerable detail by Peter Swales in his essay 'Freud, Minna Bernays and the Conquest of Rome: New Light on the Origins of Psychoanalysis' in *New American Review*, I, 1982, pp. 1–23. Swales's essay is a meticulously argued and persuasive attempt to unearth disguised autobiographical episodes in Freud's writings – particularly in his *On Dreams* and in *The Psychopathology of Everyday Life* where Swales focuses on the 'Aliquis' episode in Chapter 2. In this portion of his book Freud describes a travelling companion whose failure to remember accurately a quotation from Virgil is traced back to his fear that his mistress has become pregnant. Swales suggests that the travelling companion is a literary invention and that both the failure to remember a line from Virgil and the fears about a mistress becoming pregnant were those of Freud himself. The mistress was none other than Minna, with whom Freud was travelling abroad (alone) at the relevant time.

The issue has been discussed by Peter Gay in the bibliographical essay appended to his biography of Freud. Gay is sceptical about Jung's story and implies that he may have made it up. But he does seem to recognise reluctantly the force of Peter Swales's arguments, and concedes that 'Freud may have had an affair with Minna Bernays' (p. 752). Gay, however, is clearly deeply uneasy with this possibility.

By far the best discussion of this issue by a writer who is not personally involved in the scholarly arguments is to be found in John Kerr's *A Most Dangerous Method*, which appeared in 1994 when my own book had been almost completed. Pointing to a phenomenon which, in any other context, most psychoanalysts would instantly (and perhaps correctly) identify as 'resistance', Kerr observes that the publication of Billinsky's shattering revelation in 1969 was met, for the most part at least, with disbelieving silence. The main problem here seems to be the difficulty that most scholars appear to have firstly in *imagining* this particular kind of sexual transgression, and secondly in believing that such a sublime and heroic figure as Freud could actually have engaged in it.

Kerr weighs the evidence carefully and is duly impressed by Swales's published work. As he writes of the 'Aliquis' episode: 'Not only do the imagined interlocutor's attitudes and situation fit exactly with Freud's own, but *every association* he gives in Freud's description can be convincingly traced to some event, person, or book with which Freud was personally familiar, this to the point where all bounds of coincidence completely collapse.' He is also impressed by unpublished work by both Swales and another Freud scholar, Anthony Stadlen. His conclusion is that the weight of evidence suggests that Freud *did* have such a sexual affair with his sister-in-law. This view seems to me as plausible as Kerr's qualifications are prudent. 'Ultimately, of course,' he writes, 'it is not in anyone's power to advance incontrovertible proof for the thesis. As Rosemary Dinnage has remarked in another connection, "Later generations who try to find out who did what to whom sexually are always on a losing wicket." ' See John Kerr, *A Most Dangerous Method: The Story of Jung, Freud and Sabina Spielrein*, Sinclair Stevenson, 1994, pp. 135–40.

28. In his account of the 'Rat Man', 'Notes on a Case of Obsessional Neurosis' (1909), Freud suggests that some obsessive patients go to great lengths in order to avoid certainty and remain in doubt. Some of them supposedly 'give a vivid expression to this tendency in a dislike of clocks and watches' which Freud goes on to describe as 'doubt-removing instruments' (SE10, p. 232; PF9, p. 112).

29. SE16, p. 267; PF1, p. 306.

CHAPTER THIRTEEN · DEVELOPING THE DOCTRINE

1. FF, p. 403.
2. FF, p. 404.
3. Many of the arguments I have advanced about Freud's style of explanation in *The Interpretation of Dreams* are equally applicable to this later work, and for this reason I have not examined it in any detail. An account of the book which treats Freud's ideas with due scepticism can be found in Sebastiano Timpanaro, *The Freudian Slip: Psycho-Analysis and Textual Criticism*, New Left Books, 1976.
4. Sulloway, p. 465.
5. Sulloway, p. 466.
6. FF, p. 456.
7. FF, p. 457.
8. FF, p. 456.
9. FF, p. 457.
10. FF, p. 457.
11. SE7, p. 135; PF7, p. 45.
12. SE7, p. 151; PF7, p. 64.
13. SE7, pp. 152–3; PF7, p. 65.
14. SE9, p. 175; PF7, p. 215.
15. An equally valid 'organic analogy' would, of course, be with the mouth and the breast. Indeed this analogy had already been pointed out by Havelock Ellis: 'The analogy is indeed very close, though I do not know, or cannot recall, that it has been pointed out: the erectile nipple corresponds to the erectile penis, the eager watery mouth of the infant to the moist and throbbing

vagina, the vitally albuminous milk to the vitally albuminous semen . . .' (Ellis, 'The Analysis of the Sexual Impulse' in *The Alienist and Neurologist*, 21, p. 250. Quoted by Sulloway, p. 309.)

That Freud was acquainted with this passage we know from the fact that he refers to it in a footnote to his *Three Essays* of 1905 (see Sulloway's discussion, pp. 308–10). But when, in 1917, Freud himself used the idea of an 'organic analogy' he neither acknowledged the debt to Ellis nor used his example – which, as Ellis's enthusiastic description makes clear, is a much better piece of body-mysticism than Freud's. The reason is clear enough. One of the main explanatory functions of anal-erotism in Freud's scheme was to account for the origins of anal intercourse and in particular the role played by this in homosexual relationships. Because of the architecture of his theory, any acknowledgement of Ellis's original 'organic analogy' would have meant abandoning his entire explanation of homosexuality and starting again.

16. SE17, p. 128; PF7, p. 297.
17. SE17, p. 129; PF7, p. 297.
18. SE17, p. 133; PF7, p. 302.
19. SE17, p. 133; PF7, pp. 301–2.
20. PF7, p. 302.
21. Allen Esterson, *Seductive Mirage: An Exploration of the Work of Sigmund Freud*, Chicago: Open Court, 1993, p. 230.
22. Freud, SE22, p. 60; see Esterson, p. 230.
23. Macmillan, pp. 328–506; Freud, SE19, p. 37; see Sulloway, pp. 374–5.
24. Freud, SE20, p. 94; see Sulloway, p. 375, Macmillan, p. 541.
25. Esterson, p. 230–31. The reference is to William McDougall, *Psychoanalysis and Social Psychology*, Methuen, 1936.
26. Knight Dunlap, 'The Pragmatic Advantage of Freudo-analysis', *Psychoanalytic Review*, I, 1913, p. 151. Quoted in Frank Cioffi (ed.), *Freud: Modern Judgments*, Macmillan, 1973, p. 18.
27. Frank Cioffi, 'Freud and the Idea of a Pseudo-Science', in R. Borger and F. Cioffi (ed.), *Explanation in the Behavioural Sciences*, Cambridge University Press, 1970. p. 497.

CHAPTER FOURTEEN · 'FREUD, WHO WAS MY CHRIST!'

1. Freud to Eitingon, 10 December 1906, quoted by Gay, p. 179.
2. Freud, quoted in Jones, II, p. 168, *US, p. 148*; Penguin edition, p. 413.
3. Clark, p. 226.
4. Frank Manuel, *The Religion of Isaac Newton*, Oxford: Clarendon Press, 1974, p. 24.
5. The most familiar example of this pattern is the story of the crucifixion as related by the gospels. The underlying messianic fantasies associated with this story are perhaps still best understood by way of Albert Schweitzer's *The Quest of the Historical Jesus* (1906), Macmillan, 1961. Another instructive example of messianic psychology is provided by the story of the seventeenth-century Jewish Messiah Sabbatai Sevi. For one version of this story see Léon

Poliakov, *The History of Anti-Semitism*, vol. II, Routledge and Kegan Paul, 1974, pp. 261-8; see also Paul Johnson, *A History of the Jews*, Weidenfeld and Nicolson, 1987, pp. 268-74. More recently, on 26 September 1994, the *Guardian* reported the case of a twenty-four-year-old man who had survived being mauled by two lions at London Zoo. The man 'said . . . that he had been trying to prove that he was the Son of God because his pastor would not believe him'. After being mauled for some twenty minutes he had been rescued by 'people coming and hitting things to distract the lions'. He attributed his survival to divine intervention: 'I realised God had saved my life. Now I believe I can't ever die. I am indestructible. I want to move forward now and make people believe who I am. I can heal Aids and cancer. I want people to believe there is a living God.'

6. See Manuel, *passim*. See also J. M. Roberts, *The Pelican History of the World*, Pelican, 1980, p. 648.

7. Quoted in Adrian Desmond and James Moore, *Darwin*, Michael Joseph, 1991, p. 477.

8. Desmond and Moore, p. 475.

9. Desmond and Moore, pp. 324, 448.

10. Emil A. Gutheil (ed.), *Autobiography of Wilhelm Stekel: The Life Story of a Pioneer Psychoanalyst*, New York: Liveright, 1950, p. 116.

11. Quoted by Gay, p. 179.

12. Stekel, *Autobiography*, p. 106.

13. Max Graf, 'Reminiscences of Professor Sigmund Freud', *Psychoanalytic Quarterly*, XI, 1942, p. 470-71.

14. Roazen, p. 193.

15. Sachs, p. 57.

16. Quoted in Sulloway, p. 481.

17. Roazen, pp. 330-31.

18. Roazen, p. 306.

19. Wollheim, *Freud*, Fontana Modern Masters (1971), 2nd edition, 1991, Supplementary Preface, p. xxiii.

20. Sulloway, p. 480.

21. Weisz, 'Scientists and Sectarians: The Case of Psychoanalysis', *Journal of the History of the Behavioural Sciences*, vol. 11, pp. 350-364. Quoted in Sulloway, pp. 482.

22. Gay, p. 145.

23. Fritz Wittels, *Sigmund Freud: His Personality, His Teaching and His School*, Unwin, 1924.

24. Jung, *Memories, Dreams, Reflections*, Routledge and Kegan Paul, 1963.

25. Graf, p. 473.

26. Darwin, *The Descent of Man* (1871), Watts, 1930, p. 244.

27. Havelock Ellis, *Selected Essays* ('St Francis'), Dent, 1936, p. 97.

28. Freud, SE10, p. 276.

29. Freud, *Minutes of the Vienna Psychoanalytic Society*, ed. Herman Nunberg and Ernst Federn, vol. II, New York: International Universities Press, 1967, p. 89.

30. Freud, 'The Future of an Illusion', SE21, p. 48.

31. Thomas Szasz in *The Myth of Mental Illness* (Paladin, 1972) has advanced what

is perhaps the best-known argument against the tendency of psychiatrists to label people who are 'disabled by living' as mentally ill. In a number of significant respects our arguments are similar. The account Szasz gives of Charcot and hysteria, however, is quite different from the one which I have offered here, with Szasz assuming that 'hysteria' was an emotional problem and that therefore Charcot's patients were not really ill at all. See, for example, *The Myth of Mental Illness*, pp. 37–43.

32. David Bakan, *Sigmund Freud and the Jewish Mystical Tradition*, Boston: Beacon Press, 1958, p. 170.

33. Freud, *Introductory Lectures on Psychoanalysis*, PF1, p. 326; SE16, p. 285.

34. Pascal, quoted in T. O. Wedel, 'On the Philosophical Background of *Gulliver's Travels*' (1926) in Richard Gravil (ed.), *Swift: Gulliver's Travels*, Macmillan, 1974, p. 88.

35. Wedel, pp. 88–9. This account of the decline of the doctrine of Original Sin might well be considered alongside Ernest Gellner's succinct summary of one of the most important dimensions of Western intellectual history in his *The Psychoanalytic Movement*:

> The great pre-industrial and pre-scientific civilisations, especially perhaps the Western ones, tend to see man as half-angel, half-beast . . . This dualistic vision caused great torment to those condemned to live with it . . .
>
> None the less, anguished though it may have been, this vision had one or two marked advantages. It provided a validation for the rules and values towards which men were obliged to aspire. They contained an answer to the question – why must we strive and suffer so? These higher values were tied to the better parts of the total cosmic order, and to the better elements within man . . .
>
> But there was a further and very important advantage: the picture also provided an idiom and an explanation for all the forces within man which were opposed to the higher and purer elements. However much the Lower Aspects of our nature might have been reprobated, their very existence was not denied. Quite the reverse: the devil had a recognised place in the scheme of things. His power was treated with respect. No one who found him within his own heart had any reason to feel surprised. We had been warned.
>
> However, with the coming of modernity, the total dualistic picture, of which divided man was a part, lost its authority. The twin currents of empiricism and materialism destroyed it, and replaced it with a unitary vision both of nature and man (pp. 12–13).

36. Wesley, quoted in Wedel, p. 89.

37. See Wedel. See also Roland Mushat Frye, 'Swift's Yahoos and the Christian Symbols for Sin', *Journal of the History of Ideas*, vol. XV, 1954, pp. 201–17.

38. Swift, *Gulliver's Travels*, Penguin, 1967, p. 345 (Part 4, 'A Voyage to the Houyhnhnms', Chapter 12.

39. Deane Swift, quoted in Frye, p. 203.

40. William Morton Wheeler, 'On Instincts', *Journal of Abnormal Psychology* (1917), vol. 15, pp. 295–318. Quoted in Sulloway, p. 4.
41. SE16, pp. 304–6; PF1, pp. 346–8.
42. SE15, pp. 142–3.
43. SE10, p. 177.
44. *A Short Account of Psychoanalysis*, SE19, p. 197; PF15, p. 168.
45. SE22, p. 221; SE21, pp. 7–8.

CHAPTER FIFTEEN · FREUD, SATAN AND THE SERPENT

1. John Wren-Lewis, 'Love's Coming of Age' in Charles Rycroft (ed.), *Psychoanalysis Observed*, Penguin, 1968, p. 84; Ernest Gellner, *The Psychoanalytic Movement*, Paladin, 1985, p. 36.
2. R. S. Lee, *Freud and Christianity* (1948), Penguin, 1967, p. 144.
3. David C. McClelland, *The Roots of Consciousness*, Princeton: D. Van Nostrand Co., 1964, pp. 127–8. This passage occurs in McClelland's essay 'Psychoanalysis and Religious Mysticism' (1960), which contains one of the best descriptions of the crypto-religious nature of psychoanalysis ever given. As a Christian himself, McClelland is one of those commentators who finds the Judaeo-Christian dimensions of psychoanalysis a positive asset rather than a reason for criticism. But his discussion of the issue is subtle and perceptive and ought to be much better known than it is. His description of psychoanalysis as the faculty religion in American universities during the 1950s is particularly interesting:

    Psychoanalysis stands in striking contrast to Christianity in intellectual circles. It is enthusiastically accepted, or at least taken very seriously, by the very same men who ignore or despise Christianity. Unfortunately I have no precise figures, but it is my strong impression that an influential minority among both faculty and students in our great urban universities have either been psychoanalysed or would like to be. It has been seriously proposed in one university department known to me, that a psychoanalyst be added to the permanent staff of the department whose function would be largely to analyse his fellow staff members. In Cambridge where I live it is as difficult to spend an evening with friends without discussing some aspect of psychoanalysis as it was perhaps a hundred years ago to spend the same kind of evening without discussing Christianity (p. 120).

    McClelland also has an unusual perspective when it comes to explaining the dual affinity of psychoanalysis with both Judaism and Christianity, and concludes his essay with the following remarkable words:

    Christianity was itself initially a response of mystical, individualistic elements within Judaism to the Pharisaic orthodoxy of the times. If Goodenough's evidence is to be believed, it was spread all over the

Mediterranean world by Hellenized Jews; by Jews like Paul who were in contact with Greek mysticism and rationality. Are we witnessing a similar development today? Has the Christian Church become so petri-fied, so insensitive to the needs of our times, that a new religious movement has again arisen out of Judaism, opposed to orthodoxy and spread by secularized Jews? Certainly psychoanalysis has all these characteristics. It is essentially individualistic, mystical and opposed to religious orthodoxy. It originated in Judaism and it has been spread by Jews who had lost their faith by contact once again with the spirit of Greek rationalism as represented by modern science. Would it not be the supreme irony of history if God had again chosen his People to produce a new religious revolt against orthodoxy, only this time [ortho-doxy] of Christian making? It is an interesting question, but time and the response of the Christian Church alone can give the answer (pp. 144–5).

This passage might be seen as offering a revealing analysis of the historical significance of psychoanalysis, for the account McClelland gives of the relationship of psychoanalysis to both Judaism and Christianity is, I believe, broadly correct. But if we are to appreciate the full significance of what are, perhaps, the most extraordinary words which have ever been written about Freud by an academic psychologist, we need to read McClelland's essay, which originally appeared in a Christian anthology of essays entitled *The Ministry and Mental Health*, with the utmost care and with due attention to McClelland's own intended meaning. He himself goes to some lengths to speak out against the secularist taboos of American academia and what he calls 'the conspiracy of silence on religion'. He does so by boldly declaring his own religious background and convictions:

Let me confess at the outset that my remote ancestors were Huguenots and strict Presbyterians from Scotland and Northern Ireland, that my mother was reared a Covenanter – one of the most radical forms of Presbyterianism, that my father is a Methodist minister and that I am a convinced Quaker, whose approach to religion is primarily mystical. It would be hard to find a background of more 'radical' Christianity. Its relevance to my theme will become clearer as I proceed (p. 119).

McClelland's unusually full statement of his own religious assumptions should help to make it clear that when he talks in the concluding words of his essay about the possibility of God having again 'chosen his People to produce a new religious revolt against orthodoxy', he is not talking loosely or figuratively. He appears actually to be considering the possibility that psychoanalysis may be a divinely inspired movement and (by implication) that Freud himself might be, for all his ostensible hostility to religion, a *real* prophet or messiah, chosen by the God of the New and the Old Testaments to inaugurate a new radical covenant, replacing those of Moses and Jesus. Psychoanalysis, on this view, is part of God's ultimate plan and Freud, without knowing it himself, was actually carrying out the will of the very God he forbore to worship.

So bizarre will this reading of modern intellectual history seem to some that there is a temptation to dismiss it as entirely eccentric and irrational. I think that it would be wrong to give in to this temptation. For in this particular case a religious view provides a much better understanding of history than that sometimes shown by non-Christian intellectuals. Secure in his faith in the reality of a God who exercises ultimate control over history, McClelland is able to recognise, as modern secularised intellectuals usually cannot, that the course of Western history has been shaped and determined at practically every point by people who share such a faith. This, together with his own deep familiarity with the biblical tradition, enables him to acknowledge the many points of resemblance between psychoanalysis and Judaeo-Christian doctrine and to offer a subtle, and in many respects profound explanation of phenomena which secular intellectuals frequently ignore. If the rationality of a hypothesis is measured according to its ability to explain odd resemblances and other puzzling phenomena, then any hypothesis which represents psychoanalysis as a scientific theory of human behaviour which is unrelated to religious orthodoxies is far more 'irrational' than one which, like Mc-Clelland's, sees it as part of a divine plan.

4. SE11, p. 54.
5. SE11, p. 54.
6. The mythology of modern literary scholarship has often made Swift into a misanthropist. Swift himself, however, saw the matter more clearly than his critics: 'I tell you after all that I do not hate Mankind, it is vous autres who hate them because you would have them reasonable Animals, and are Angry for being disappointed.' What Swift implicitly recognises here is that the philosophy of rationalism, which begins with the greatest optimism, can only lead to the cruellest kind of disappointment. For those who refuse to acknowledge 'animality' or 'unreason' as elements in their own identity, and who seek to banish these elements from their consciousness, can only end by hating those other men and women who continue to display them. This view of rationalism lies at the heart of *Gulliver's Travels*. See T. O. Wedel, 'On the Philosophical Background of *Gulliver's Travels*' (1926) in Richard Gravil (ed.), *Swift, 'Gulliver's Travels': A Casebook*, Macmillan, 1974, p. 86.
7. Freud, *Letters*, pp. 419–20 (Letter to Anon., 9.4.1935).
8. Quoted in Weiss, *Sigmund Freud as a Consultant*, p. 28. On Freud's concept of 'worthiness', see Paul Roazen's excellent discussion, to which I am indebted (Roazen, pp. 160–65).
9. See Roazen, p. 163.
10. Heinrich Meng and Ernst Freud (ed.),*Psychoanalysis and Faith: The Letters of Sigmund Freud and Oskar Pfister*, New York: Basic Books, 1963, pp. 61–2.
11. *Studies on Hysteria*, SE2, p. 265; PF3, p. 348.
12. On the relationship between Christian demonology and anti-semitic stereotypes, see Joshua Trachtenberg, *The Devil and the Jews*, Yale University Press, 1943.
13. Owen Berkley-Hill, 'The Anal-Erotic Factor in Hindu Religion', *International*

Journal of Psychoanalysis, 1921, p. 336. For a lively attack on this paper, see Reginald Reynolds, *Cleanliness and Godliness*, Allen and Unwin, 1943, pp. 154–9.

14. Ben Karpman, 'Neurotic Traits of Jonathan Swift', in *Psychoanalytic Review*, vol. 29, 1942, p. 182.
15. Erich Fromm, *The Anatomy of Human Destructiveness*, Penguin, 1977, p. 549, p. 488.
16. Léon Poliakov, *The History of Anti-Semitism*, vol. 1, Routledge and Kegan Paul, 1974, p. 274.
17. See Norman Cohn, *Europe's Inner Demons*, Paladin, 1976, p. xiv.
18. *Introductory Lectures*, SE15, p. 210; PF1, pp. 247–8.
19. Erik Erikson, *Childhood and Society*, Penguin, 1967, p. 59.
20. Melanie Klein, *The Psychoanalysis of Children*, Hogarth Press, 1975, p. 129.
21. Ernst Nolte, *Three Faces of Fascism*, New York: Mentor, 1969, p. 368.
22. Keith Thomas, *Religion and the Decline of Magic*, Penguin, 1978, p. 40.
23. Cleaver and Dod, *A Godly Form of Household Government*, London, 1621. Quoted in Michael Walzer, *The Revolution of the Saints*, Weidenfeld and Nicolson, 1979, p. 190.
24. More, quoted in Lawrence Stone, *The Family, Sex and Marriage in England 1500–1800*, Penguin, 1979, p. 294.
25. *Interpretation of Dreams*, SE4, p. 250; PF4, p. 350.

CHAPTER SIXTEEN · PRIESTS, PENITENTS AND PATIENTS

1. Jones, II, p. 15, *US, pp. 13–14*; Penguin edition, p. 316.
2. Quoted in Gay, p. 178.
3. Jones, *Free Association: Memories of a Psycho-Analyst*, 1959, pp. 169–70. Quoted in Gay, p. 178.
4. Gay, p. 177.
5. Freud to Abraham, quoted in Roazen, p. 183.
6. Roazen, p. 183.
7. *Studies on Hysteria*, SE2, p. 282; PF3, p. 368.
8. John T. Noonan, Jr., *Contraception: A History of Its Treatment by the Catholic Theologians and Canonists*, Harvard University Press, 1965, pp. 271–2.
9. Freud, *Two Short Accounts of Psychoanalysis*, Penguin, 1962, p. 131 (SE20, p. 218).
10. Freud, *Introductory Lectures*, SE15, p. 17; PF1, p. 42.
11. Rabelais, *Gargantua and Pantagruel*, trans. J. M. Cohen, Penguin, 1955, p. 220 (Book II, Chapter 15).
12. Quoted in James Cleugh, *Love Locked Out*, Tandem, 1964, p. 260.
13. Noonan, *Contraception*, pp. 271–2.
14. C. Sydney Carter and G. E. Alison Weeks, *The Protestant Dictionary*, revised edition, 1933, Article on 'Confession, Auricular', p. 140.
15. Quoted in D. Felicitas Corrigan, *Helen Waddell: A Biography*, Gollancz, 1986, p. 149.

16. Quoted in O. John Rogge, *Why Men Confess*, New York: Da Capo, 1975, pp. 168–9.
17. Quoted in Rogge, p. 169.
18. Lawrence Kubie, 'The Fantasy of Dirt', *Psychoanalytic Quarterly*, vol. VI, 1937, p. 402.
19. Quoted in R. D. Laing, *The Divided Self*, Pelican, 1965, p. 172.
20. Rogge, p. 227.
21. On the subject of confession and adulterous relationships see Annette Lawson's excellent *Adultery: An Analysis of Love and Betrayal*, Oxford University Press, 1990, pp. 224–63 and *passim*.
22. John Donne, Sermon preached at Lincolns Inne [? Easter Term, 1620], in John Donne, *Collected Prose*, ed. Neil Rose, Penguin, 1987, p. 166.
23. 'Recommendations to Physicians Practising Psychoanalysis', SE12, pp. 118, 115. See Roazen, p. 166.
24. SE12, p. 115; see Roazen, p. 148.
25. *Two Short Accounts*, pp. 139–40 (SE20, p. 225).
26. *Two Short Accounts*, pp. 140–41 (SE20, p. 226). In suggesting that patients' emotional reactions to their analysts sometimes have their source in the one-sided relationship which orthodox therapists are obliged to establish with their clients, I am not implying that all emotional reactions during psychoanalysis necessarily have the same source. The idea that patients do sometimes 'transfer' emotional reactions from earlier deep relationships and displace them onto their therapists seems almost beyond dispute. For in so far as the patterns of emotional interaction which tend to be followed by any individual are likely to have been strongly shaped by their earliest relationships, patterns of reaction formed at this stage will almost inevitably recur in all later deep emotional relationships, whether or not these involve a psychotherapist.
27. Ernest Jones, *Psycho-Myth, Psycho-History: Essays in Applied Psychoanalysis*, vol. 2, New York: Stonehill Publishing, 1974, pp. 248–53.
28. *Two Short Accounts*, p. 85 (SE11, p. 53).
29. Quoted in Jeffrey Masson, *Against Therapy*, p. 122. See Ferenczi, *The Clinical Diary of Sandor Ferenczi*, ed. Judith Dupont, Harvard University Press, 1988, p. 199.
30. *Against Therapy*, p. 122; *Clinical Diary*, p. 199.
31. *Against Therapy*, p. 122; *Clinical Diary*, p. 199.
32. *Against Therapy*, pp. 129–30; *Clinical Diary*, pp. 92–3.

CHAPTER SEVENTEEN · CRITICS AND DISSIDENTS

1. Jones, II, p. 36, *US, p. 32*; Penguin edition, p. 328.
2. Quoted in Janet Malcolm, *Psychoanalysis: The Impossible Profession*, Pan, 1982, pp. 166.
3. Malcolm, p. 166.
4. Sulloway, pp. 470–71.
5. Sulloway, p. 471.
6. Sulloway, p. 473.

7. Pfister, *Letters*, p. 48.
8. Fritz Wittels, *Sigmund Freud: His Personality, His Teaching, and His School*, Allen and Unwin, 1924, p. 151.
9. Gay, p. 223.
10. Gay, p. 224.
11. Sachs, p. 51.
12. Jones, III, p. 223, *US, p. 208*.
13. Gay, p. 214.
14. Jones, II, p. 154, *US, p. 136*; Penguin edition, p. 404. Joseph Wortis, *Fragment of an Analysis with Freud*, New York: Simon and Schuster, 1954, p. 30.
15. Hilda C. Abraham and Ernst L. Freud (ed.), *A Psychoanalytic Dialogue: The Letters of Sigmund Freud and Karl Abraham, 1907–1926*, New York: Basic Books, 1965, p. 125.
16. Freud, *Letters*, p. 352 (Freud to Stekel, 13.1.1924).
17. Quoted in Roazen, p. 254.
18. Roazen, p. 254.
19. Graf, 'Reminiscences', p. 473.
20. Gay, p. 463.
21. Quoted in Gay, p. 491.
22. Roazen, p. 308.
23. Quoted by Gay, p. 191.
24. Pfister to Freud, 29 October 1918; see Gay, p. 192.
25. Quoted in Roazen, p. 306.
26. Roazen, p. 306.
27. Roazen, p. 202.
28. Roazen, p. 199.

CHAPTER EIGHTEEN · JUNG: CROWN PRINCE AND BELOVED SON

1. C. G. Jung, 'Freud and Psychoanalysis', *The Collected Works of C. G. Jung*, Princeton University Press, 1953–1974, vol. IV, p. 7.
2. CW IV, p. 4.
3. Jung, *Memories, Dreams, Reflections*, Flamingo, 1967, p. 172.
4. Hilda C. Abraham and Ernst L. Freud (ed.), *A Psychoanalytic Dialogue: The Letters of Sigmund Freud and Karl Abraham, 1907–1926*, New York: Basic Books, 1965, p. 34.
5. MDR, p. 13.
6. MDR, pp. 27, 56, 55, 57.
7. MDR, pp. 57, 58, 57.
8. William McGuire (ed.), *The Freud/Jung Letters*, Hogarth Press and Routledge and Kegan Paul, 1974, p. 97 (Letter 51).
9. F/J, p. 491 (Letter 303).
10. Jones, II, p. 37, *US, p. 33*.
11. F/J, p. 218 (Letter 139); pp. 196–7 (Letter 125).
12. Wittels, p. 140.
13. Sachs, p. 120.

14. *On the History of Psychoanalysis*, PF15, p. 102.
15. FF, pp. 158–9.
16. Wittels, p. 138.
17. Jones, *Psycho-Myth, Psycho-History: Essays in Applied Psychoanalysis*, vol. 2, p. 244.
18. Roazen, p. 353.
19. Jones, *Essays*, vol. 2, pp. 253–6.
20. Jones, *Essays*, vol. 2, pp. 263–4.
21. F/J, p. 95 (Letter 49); p. 275 (Letter 168).
22. F/J, pp. 25–6 (Letter 17).
23. F/J, p. 30 (Letter 19).
24. F/J, pp. 322–5 (Letters 195–6).
25. MDR, p. 173.
26. MDR, p. 181.
27. John M. Billinsky, 'Jung and Freud (The End of a Romance)', *Andover Newton Quarterly*, X, 1969, p. 43. On Freud's putative sexual affair with his sister-in-law, see Chapter 12, note 27.
28. MDR, p. 182.
29. Jung, 'Freud and Psychoanalysis' in CW IV, pp. 107, pp. 164–5. pp. 153–6.
30. MDR, p. 174.
31. F/J, p. 476 (Letter 290).
32. F/J, pp. 526–7 (Letter 330).
33. F/J, pp. 534–5 (Letter 338).
34. Freud to Jones, 26 December 1912, quoted in Gay, p. 234.
35. Ferenczi/Freud, 26 December 1912, quoted in Phyllis Grosskurth, *The Secret Ring: Freud's Inner Circle and the Politics of Psychoanalysis*, Jonathan Cape, 1991, p. 50.
36. F/J, pp. 538–9 (Letter 342).
37. Jones to Freud, 25 April 1913, quoted by Clark, p. 330.
38. François Roustang, *Dire Mastery: Discipleship from Freud to Lacan*, Washington: American Psychiatric Press, 1986, p. 4.
39. Grosskurth, p. 62.
40. Gay, p. 241.
41. Freud and Abraham, p. 160.
42. Freud and Abraham, p. 168.
43. Freud and Abraham, p. 186.
44. Roazen, p. 235.
45. Victor White, *God and the Unconscious*, Fontana, 1960, p. 69.
46. White, p. 67ff.
47. F/J, pp. 427–9 (Letters 259–60).
48. Jung, *Modern Man in Search of a Soul*, p. 264.
49. Basel Seminar, 1934, in C. G. Jung, *Psychological Reflections*, Routledge and Kegan Paul, 1953, pp. 341–2.
50. Jung, *Psychological Reflections*, pp. 224–5.
51. Quoted in Jones, II, p. 396, US, p. 353.
52. 'On the History of the Psychoanalytic Movement', SE14, p. 62ff; PF15, p. 120ff.

CHAPTER NINETEEN · THE SECRET COMMITTEE:
FROM FORMATION TO FAILURE

1. François Roustang, *Dire Mastery: Discipleship from Freud to Lacan*, Washington: American Psychiatric Press, 1986, p. 54.
2. Quoted in Roazen, pp. 328–9.
3. Freud to Jones, 1 August 1912, quoted in Phyllis Grosskurth, *The Secret Ring: Freud's Inner Circle and the Politics of Psychoanalysis*, Jonathan Cape, 1991, p. 47.
4. Jones to Freud, 7 August 1912, quoted in Grosskurth, pp. 47–8.
5. Freud to Ferenczi, 30 September 1918, quoted in Grosskurth, p. 78.
6. 'On the History of the Psychoanalytic Movement', SE14, p. 25; PF15, p. 82; Gunther Stuhlmann (ed.), *The Diary of Anaïs Nin*, vol. I, New York: Harcourt Brace and World, 1966, p. 279. Quoted in Roazen, p. 390.
7. Jones to Abraham, 8 April 1924, quoted in Grosskurth, p. 154.
8. Jones, III, p. 72, *US*, pp. 69–70.
9. Rank, quoted in Grosskurth, p. 166.
10. Grosskurth, p. 167.
11. Ferenczi to Freud, 9 January 1927, quoted in Grosskurth, p. 184.
12. Freud to Ferenczi, 6 October 1910, quoted in Gay, p. 576.
13. Ferenczi to Freud, 15 May 1922, quoted in Gay, p. 576.
14. Freud to Ferenczi, 13 December 1931, quoted in Gay, p. 579.
15. Ferenczi, *The Clinical Diary of Sandor Ferenczi*, ed. Judith Dupont, Harvard University Press, 1988.
16. Masson, *The Assault on Truth*, p. 147.
17. Quoted in Masson, *The Assault on Truth*, p. 147.
18. 'Confusion of Tongues between Adults and the Child' in Masson, *The Assault on Truth*, pp. 295–6.
19. Masson, *The Assault on Truth*, pp. 170–71.
20. Jones, III, p. 190; Penguin edition, p. 615.
21. Balint, quoted in Clark, p. 459.
22. Wittels, quoted in Clark, p. 460.
23. Szasz, 'Freud as Leader', *Antioch Review*, 1963, p. 153.

CHAPTER TWENTY · ANNA FREUD: DAUGHTER AND DISCIPLE

1. Elisabeth Young-Bruehl, *Anna Freud*, Macmillan, 1989, p. 27.
2. Uwe Henrik Peters, *Anna Freud*, Weidenfeld and Nicolson, 1985, p. xii.
3. Young-Bruehl, p. 37.
4. Peters, p. 10.
5. Roazen, p. 433.
6. Young-Bruehl, pp. 52–3.
7. Heinrich Heine, *Poetry and Prose*, ed. Jost Herman and Robert C. Holub, trans. Louis Untermeyer, New York: Continuum, 1982. See Peters, pp. 17–18.
8. See Norman Cohn, *The Pursuit of the Millennium*, Paladin, 1970, pp. 31–3.
9. Young-Bruehl, p. 51.

10. Gay, p. 431; Young-Bruehl, p. 55.
11. Quoted in Peters, pp. 13–14.
12. Quoted in Young-Bruehl, p. 59.
13. Freud, SE12, p. 301.
14. Phyllis Grosskurth, *Melanie Klein: Her World and Her Work*, Hodder and Stoughton, 1986, p. 99 (note).
15. Young-Bruehl, p. 103.
16. Peters, p. 49.
17. *The Writings of Anna Freud*, New York: International Universities Press, 1966–80, vol. I, p. 151.
18. In her own account of how the original beating fantasies supposedly intruded on her daydreams when she was an adolescent, Anna Freud does not explicitly associate them with the act of masturbation, writing obscurely that 'the sexual gratification connected with [the beating scene] had obtained full discharge for the dammed-up excitation' (*International Journal of Psychoanalysis*, IV, 1923, p. 98). In her authorised biography of Anna Freud, Elisabeth Young-Bruehl glosses this to mean 'masturbation' (see Young-Bruehl, p. 105).
19. 'A Case of Hysteria', SE7, p. 80; PF8, p. 117.
20. Nancy Friday, *Women on Top*, Arrow, 1992, pp. 28–9.
21. These quotations are taken from the first English translation of Anna Freud's paper, *International Journal of Psychoanalysis*, IV, 1923, pp. 90, 93.
22. Young-Bruehl, pp. 110–11.
23. Gay, p. 441.
24. *International Journal of Psychoanalysis*, vol. VI, 1925, p. 106.
25. *The Writings of Anna Freud*, I, pp. 166–7.
26. *Writings*, I, p. 65.
27. Young-Bruehl, p. 118.
28. Gay, p. 442 (note).
29. See Young-Bruehl, p. 128; my translation.
30. *Writings*, II, p. 131.
31. Young-Bruehl, p. 133.
32. Young-Bruehl, p. 134.
33. Young-Bruehl, p. 136.
34. Young-Bruehl, p. 137.
35. Gay, p. 621.
36. Jones, III, p. 234, *US, p. 219*; Penguin edition, p. 636.
37. Gay, pp. 622–5; Clark pp. 503–9.
38. Young-Bruehl, p. 226.
39. Gay, p. 629.
40. Gay, p. 640.
41. Gay, p. 650.
42. Young-Bruehl, p. 239.
43. Gay, p. 631.
44. Anna Freud, *Introduction to the Technique of Child Analysis* (1927), in *Writings*, I, pp. 37–8.
45. The truth about Klein's early patients was disseminated widely only with the publication of Phyllis Grosskurth's biography in 1986. Grosskurth notes that

several commentators had already read the signs correctly, but that when she identified 'Fritz', Klein's first 'patient', as her son Erich, to a number of English Kleinians, they expressed shock and dismay.

> One said that she had always had the impression that 'the mother' in the background left something to be desired. Another said that he did not know what name to apply to this kind of analysis but that it had nothing to do with mothering. A third confessed rather poignantly that the revelation would make him re-examine the work he had been doing for thirty years since he now saw in a new light why Melanie Klein had underestimated the role of the mother (Grosskurth, p. 79).

46. Young-Bruehl, p. 450.
47. The incident which follows is related by Elisabeth Young-Bruehl and I have drawn directly and with gratitude on her beautifully written account here.

CHAPTER TWENTY-ONE · PSYCHOANALYSIS, SCIENCE AND HUMAN NATURE

1. P. B. Medawar, review of Irving S. Cooper's The *Victim Is Always the Same*, *New York Review of Books*, 23 January 1975.
2. E. H. Hare, 'Medical Astrology and Its Relation to Modern Psychiatry', *Proceedings of the Royal Society of Medicine*, vol. 70, 1977, p. 106.
3. Hare, p. 108.
4. Thomas S. Kuhn, *The Structure of Scientific Revolutions*, University of Chicago Press, 1970, p. 56.
5. On Lacan see Raymond Tallis's luminous discussion in his *Not Saussure: A Critique of Post-Saussurean Literary Theory*, Macmillan, 1988. See also my article, 'The Cult of Lacan', *Quarto*, May 1981. There is, so far as I am aware, no adequate critique of Melanie Klein's contribution to psychoanalytic theory. Phyllis Grosskurth's biography, excellent in its way, uncritically assumes the value of Klein's theories (*Melanie Klein: Her World and Her Work*, Hodder and Stoughton, 1986). Alice Miller's *Thou Shalt Not be Aware: Society's Betrayal of the Child* (Pluto Press, 1985) contains, alongside a fundamental misreading of Freud's seduction theory, some very acute criticisms of Klein (see, for example, pp. 216–19).
6. Kuhn, p. 77.
7. Medawar, *The Limits of Science*, Oxford University Press, 1985, pp. 59, 66, 88, 93, 96.
8. See Brian Easlea, *Science and Sexual Oppression: Patriarchy's Confrontation with Woman and Nature*, Weidenfeld and Nicolson, 1981, pp. 163–9.
9. Berlin, quoted in Ramin Jahanbegloo, *Conversations with Isaiah Berlin*, Peter Halban, 1992, p. 70; Berlin, *Against the Current: Essays in the History of Ideas*, ed. Henry Hardy, Hogarth Press, 1980, p. 248.
10. *Against the Current*, p. 160; Keith Thomas, review of *Against the Current*, *Observer*, 1980.

11. Gilbert Adair, *The Sunday Times*, 9 May 1993. As Adair's words imply, the moderate scepticism implicit in pluralism has, in recent years, increasingly been overshadowed by the more extreme forms of scepticism associated with structuralism and post-structuralism. One of the most comprehensive and astute critiques of postmodern theory and its effects on modern intellectual culture is provided by Brian Vickers in his *Appropriating Shakespeare: Contemporary Critical Quarrels*, Yale University Press, 1993.

12. Frederick Crews, *Skeptical Engagements*, New York: Oxford University Press, 1986, p. xi.

13. Crews, p. xviii.

14. Ted Hughes, 'Myth and Education' (1976) in Ted Hughes, *Winter Pollen: Occasional Prose*, Faber, 1994, p. 146.

15. R. Hooykaas, *Religion and the Rise of Modern Science*, Scottish Academic Press, 1972, p. xi

16. On the specific association between Puritanism and modern science, see Robert K. Merton, 'Puritanism, Pietism and Science' (1936), reprinted in C. A. Russell (ed.), *Science and Religious Belief: A Selection of Recent Historical Studies*, University of London Press Ltd, 1973. For a discussion of the same issue see also A. Rupert Hall's 'Merton Revisited' (1963) and Douglas S. Kemsley's 'Religious Influences in the Rise of Modern Science' (1968), reprinted in the same volume; R. Hooykaas, *Religion and the Rise of Modern Science*, Scottish Academic Press, 1972; P. M. Rattansi, 'The Social Interpretation of Science in the Seventeenth Century' in Peter Mathias (ed.), *Science and Society 1600–1900*, Cambridge University Press, 1972. These essays reveal considerable areas of disagreement among historians. Many of these disagreements, however, arise out of over-specific claims which disregard the fact that seventeenth-century Puritanism was merely one manifestation of a particular form of Judaeo-Christian rigorism which finds expression elsewhere both in the Jewish and in the Catholic tradition. It is perhaps Max Weber who, looking back on the history of monasticism from the perspective of the Reformation, focuses the issues best and illuminates the essentially religious origins of the frame of mind idealised by Western rationalism:

> The life of the saint was directed solely towards a transcendental end, salvation. But precisely for that reason it was thoroughly rationalised in this world and dominated entirely by the aim to add to the glory of God on earth . . . Only a life guided by constant thought could achieve conquest over the state of nature. Descartes' *cogito ergo sum* was taken over by the contemporary Puritans with this ethical reinterpretation. It was this rationalisation which gave the Reformed faith its peculiar ascetic tendency, and is the basis both of its relationship to and its conflict with Catholicism. For naturally similar things were not unknown to Catholicism.
>
> Without doubt Christian asceticism, both outwardly and in its inner meaning, contains many different things. But it has had a definitely rational character in its highest Occidental forms as early as the Middle Ages, and in several forms even in antiquity. The great historical

significance of Western monasticism, as contrasted with that of the Orient, is based on this fact, not in all cases, but in its general type. In the rules of St Benedict, still more with the monks of Cluny, again with the Cistercians, and most strongly the Jesuits, it had become emancipated from planless otherworldliness and irrational self-torture. It had developed a systematic method of rational conduct with the purpose of overcoming the *status naturae*, to free man from the power of irrational impulses and his dependence on the world and on nature. It attempted to subject man to the supremacy of a purposeful will, to bring his actions under constant self-control with a careful consideration of their ethical consequences. Thus it trained the monk, objectively, as a worker in the service of the kingdom of God, and thereby further, subjectively, assured the salvation of his soul. This active self-control, which formed the end of the *exercitia* of St Ignatius and of the rational monastic virtues everywhere, was also the most important practical ideal of Puritanism . . . The Puritan, like every rational type of asceticism, tried to enable a man to maintain and act on his constant motives, *especially those which it taught him itself, against the emotions . . .* Contrary to many popular ideas, the end of this asceticism was to be able to lead an alert, intelligent life: *the most urgent task the destruction of spontaneous, impulsive enjoyment*, the most important means was to bring order into the conduct of its adherents. All these important points are emphasised as strongly in the rules of Catholic monasticism as in the principles of conduct of the Calvinists [italics added] (Max Weber, *The Protestant Ethic and the Spirit of Capitalism*, Allen and Unwin, 1930, pp. 118–19).

On the ethos of Puritanism one of the best sources is R. H. Tawney's classic *Religion and the Rise of Capitalism*, Penguin, 1938. On the general question of the psychological correlates of intellectual specialisation, there can be no better introduction than the work of Liam Hudson. Hudson's first two books in particular are rich storehouses of evidence, insight and careful inference. See Liam Hudson, *Contrary Imaginations: A Psychological Study of the English Schoolboy*, Methuen, 1966, *Frames of Mind: Ability, Perception and Self-Perception in the Arts and the Sciences*, Methuen, 1968. See also Liam Hudson (ed.), *The Ecology of Human Intelligence*, Penguin, 1970, and David C. McClelland, *The Roots of Consciousness*, Princeton: D. Van Nostrand Co., 1964, especially Chapter 7, 'The Psychodynamics of Creative Scientists', pp. 146–81.

17. Bryan Appleyard, *Understanding the Present: Science and the Soul of Modern Man*, Picador, 1992.
18. Raymond Tallis, *Not Saussure: A Critique of Post-Saussurean Literary Theory*, Macmillan, 1988; Philip J. Davis and Reuben Hersh, *Descartes' Dream: The World According to Mathematics*, Penguin, 1990, p. 283.
19. Huxley, quoted in Adrian Desmond and James Moore, *Darwin*, Michael Joseph, 1991, p. 491.
20. Medawar, *Limits*, p. 66.
21. Medawar, *Limits*, p. 66.
22. Richard Dawkins, *The Selfish Gene*, Paladin, 1978, p. 1.

23. Dawkins, p. 1.
24. Stephen Hawking, *A Brief History of Time*, Bantam, 1988, pp. 13, 175.
25. Gerald Edelman, *Bright Air, Brilliant Fire: On the Matter of the Mind*, Penguin, 1992.
26. See Steven Rose, *The Making of Memory*, Bantam, pp. 88, 317.

CHAPTER TWENTY-TWO · THE GHOST IN THE PSYCHOANALYTIC MACHINE

1. C. D. Darlington, quoted in T. H. Dobzhansky, *Mankind Evolving: The Evolution of the Human Species*, Yale University Press, 1962, p. 54.

It should be said that one of the factors which has made it easier for some theorists to put forward extreme versions of genetic determinism successfully has been the biological naïvety of many social scientists in the first half of the twentieth century. In what has been called the 'Standard Social Science Model', championed by many influential anthropologists, psychologists and sociologists, including Margaret Mead and J. B. Watson, human nature was held to be almost infinitely malleable. Human beings were treated as though they were biologically empty, their behaviour and temperament being almost entirely the product of culture. It was the extremism of this argument, and its steadfast disregard for the biological evidence, which made it much easier for sociobiologists such as Edward O. Wilson to gain a hearing for their theories in the 1970s and 1980s. Partly because of the fierceness with which these theories were in turn attacked by other biologists, the extreme varieties of genetic determinism common a few decades ago are now much less prominent. They have been replaced, in part at least, by the arguments of evolutionary psychologists and other Darwinians – arguments which are both more moderate-seeming and, sometimes at least, more sophisticated.

An excellent example of this more nuanced approach has been provided by the cognitive psychologist Steven Pinker. In his book *The Language Instinct* he argues cogently for the view that the human capacity for language is a part of our genetic endowment and that it is associated with the evolution through natural selection of specialised neural networks within the brain. Not only does he argue this position powerfully and persuasively, but he also mounts an effective attack on the 'Standard Social Science Model' of human nature. All but the most sceptical readers of his book are likely to be persuaded that the capacity for language has, at least in some respects, been genetically programmed into the human brain throughout the many millennia of the evolution of our species. All but the most recalcitrant will concede that Pinker's broadside against the 'Standard Social Science Model' has some justification. For it would seem almost beyond question that twentieth-century social scientists have, for ideological or rationalistic motives, tended to underestimate grossly the extent to which human nature is shaped and constrained by genetic factors.

To say all this, however, is not to accept Pinker's argument in its entirety. One of the most questionable parts of his book is that in which he uses his carefully worked out argument about language as the basis for a series of speculations about other specialised neural networks which he believes may have evolved within the human brain. He suggests that there may be 'innate modules' or 'families of instincts' for many facets of human behaviour includ-ing 'intuitive mechanics: knowledge of the motions, forces, and deformations that objects undergo' and 'intuitive biology'. He even suggests that there may be a brain module for 'justice' through which human beings inherit a specific neural basis for a 'sense of rights, obligations and deserts' (p. 420).

Not all Pinker's guesses about the genetic make-up of human nature should, I believe, be dismissed out of hand. But the suggestion that there may be something which resembles a 'gene for justice' is one which many will find alarming. One of the great dangers of indulging in this kind of genetic guesswork is that what Pinker presents as speculation will be treated by others as science. Unsubstantiated speculations such as those he presents only play into the hands of those who advocate the kind of extreme genetic determinism whose excesses Pinker himself generally manages to avoid. In particular they are liable to lend support to a tendency which seems to be widespread among biologically orientated thinkers who make pronouncements about human nature – the tendency to assume that the aspects of human behaviour which can be shown to be genetically determined are the 'real' substratum of human nature, and that what is added by nurture is little more than a superficial cultural 'dressing'.

One of the characteristics of thinkers who adopt this approach is that they tend to manifest considerable interest in any feature of human nature which could be deemed instinctual while simultaneously showing an almost complete disregard for the complexities of human behaviour and cultural history which are not susceptible to this kind of explanation. In this respect the more extreme proponents of genetic determinism resemble the navigator who decides to delete the land from his charts on the grounds that he is interested only in the ocean. Where the navigator goes wrong is in failing to recognise that the ocean is actually defined by land. Similarly the influence of genetic factors on human behaviour can be studied and assessed properly only by including a detailed and meticulous exploration of the role which is played by *nurture*. The main reason we can be confident that, however much our capacity for language is shaped by biological inheritance, there is no 'gene for German' (or for Japanese), is not because we have any knowledge of the particular genes which facilitate language. It is because we are intimately acquainted with the way in which people learn languages, and with the manner in which 'nurture' completely determines which particular languages individuals acquire. It follows that, paradoxically, the study of the role of 'nurture' – of the complex effects of child-rearing behaviour, education and social con-ditioning – is actually a precondition of understanding the role of 'nature'. To engage in such a study is not in any sense to neglect the realm of biology. For what many thinkers have failed to recognise is that 'nurture', far from being opposed to 'nature', is itself a part of nature. It is itself a biological process with a rich and complex natural history of its own which has yet to be fully investigated.

Those thinkers who neglect to study the role of nurture sometimes attempt to justify their approach by characterising it as 'scientific'. Yet the attempt to explain human nature by directing attention away from the observable details of human behaviour and towards invisible and largely inscrutable entities is not the monopoly of modern genetic determinists. Something very similar was done for centuries by priests, prophets, theologians and other 'spiritual determinists' working within the mainstream of the Judaeo-Christian tradition. One of the reasons that sociobiology, like psychoanalysis before it, has found such an enthusiastic following in Puritan America is that it possesses many of the characteristics of the religious ideology which preceded it. It too frequently seeks to explain the visible by reference to the invisible. It too can be used to justify the economic, political or sexual *status quo* by appealing to unseen powers which supposedly control our destiny. Not only this but it also frequently provides what some have seen in religious faith – an excuse to evade the need to think and evaluate evidence. Sociobiology, in all these respects at least, is perhaps best seen as one of the new spiritualisms of our age – a form of hard-centred mysticism which, like that created by Freud himself, has managed to reintroduce a traditional religious ideology in a disguised form, safe from the criticism of scientists (or some scientists at least) precisely because it is itself offered as a contribution to science. Although some forms of 'evolutionary psychology' may be more subtle than the sociobiology they derive from, others merely continue the same kind of biological reductionism under another name.

   For expositions of the tenets of sociobiology, see E. O. Wilson, *Sociobiology: The New Synthesis*, Harvard University Press, 1975 and David Barash, *Sociobiology: The Whisperings Within*, Souvenir Press, 1979. See also E. O. Wilson, *On Human Nature*, Harvard University Press, 1978. For a critique of sociobiology and genetic determinism which is, for the most part, much more subtle and valuable than the Marxism which frequently informs it, see Steven Rose, R. C. Lewontin and Leon J. Kamin, *Not in Our Genes: Biology, Ideology and Human Nature*, Penguin, 1984. For the argument about language referred to above, see Steven Pinker, *The Language Instinct: The New Science of Language and Mind*, Penguin, 1994. For one example of dual allegiance to sociobiology and psychoanalysis, see Frank Sulloway's *Freud: Biologist of Mind*. For a recent attempt to marry Freud and Darwin which illustrates how meagre are the arguments of some 'evolutionary psychologists', see Christopher Badcock, *PsychoDarwinism: The New Synthesis of Darwin and Freud*, HarperCollins, 1994.

2. Alex Comfort, *Darwin and the Naked Lady: Discursive Essays on Biology and Art*, Routledge and Kegan Paul, 1961, p. 8.
3. Gerald Edelman, *Bright Air, Brilliant Fire: On the Matter of the Mind*, Penguin, 1992, p. xiii.
4. Edelman, p. 145.
5. Gilbert Ryle, *The Concept of Mind* (1949), Penguin, 1963.
6. Patricia Churchland, for example, in her *Neurophilosophy* (MIT Press, 1986), has characterised the mind as 'essentially a kind of logic-machine that operates on sentences'. These words are quoted by Raymond Tallis in his *The Explicit Animal: A Defence of Human Consciousness*, Macmillan, 1991, p. 103. Tallis

goes on to offer an extended critique of computational models of the mind in which he sees such models as defying logic while at the same time traducing 'the rich plenitude of experience' (p. 140).

7. Colin McGinn, 'Can We Solve the Mind–Body Problem?', *Mind*, vol. XCVII, no. 891, July 1989. This essay is reprinted in McGinn's *The Problem of Consciousness*, Oxford: Blackwell, 1991, pp. 1–22.

8. W. M. O'Neill, *The Beginnings of Modern Psychology*, Penguin, 1968, p. 11.

9. Ryle, p. 301.

10. Ryle, pp. 302–3.

11. Wheeler, see above, Chapter 14, note 40.

12. Freud, *New Introductory Lectures on Psychoanalysis*, PF2, p. 90.

13. Charles Rycroft, *A Critical Dictionary of Psychoanalysis*, Penguin, 1972, p. xxi.

14. Elisabeth Roudinesco, *Jacques Lacan & Co.: A History of Psychoanalysis in France, 1925–1985*, Free Association Books, 1990, p. 424.

15. Adam Kuper, *Anthropologists and Anthropology: The British School 1922–72*, Penguin, 1973, p. 206.

16. Claude Lévi-Strauss, *Totemism*, Penguin, 1969, pp. 140, 142.

17. Edmund Leach, *Lévi-Strauss*, Fontana, 1970, p. 42.

18. Stanley Diamond, 'The Myth of Structuralism' in Ino Rossi (ed.), *The Unconscious in Culture: The Structuralism of Claude Lévi-Strauss in Perspective*, New York: E. P. Dutton, 1974, p. 315. See also Simon Clarke's *The Foundations of Structuralism: A Critique of Lévi-Strauss and the Structuralist Movement*, Harvester Press/ Barnes and Noble, 1981.

A view of Lévi-Strauss which is strikingly similar to the one I have taken here was offered recently by John Carey in a review of the paperback edition of Brian Vickers's *Appropriating Shakespeare: Contemporary Critical Quarrels*, Yale University Press, 1994. After praising Vickers's critique of modern critical theory, Carey writes the following:

> In setting out theory's assumptions, [Vickers] reveals, inadvertently it seems, its resemblance to certain ancient ways of thought that may account for its residual appeal. Theory's preference for the immaterial over the things of this world, which it pronounces unreal, recalls the anti-materialist strain in Christianity and other religions. Lévi-Strauss, reducing all social systems to abstract models, located in the unconscious, sounds curiously like St Paul: 'In my mind, models are real, and I would say that they are the only reality . . . They do not correspond to the concrete reality of empirical observation. It is necessary, in order to reach the model which is the true reality, to transcend the concrete-appearing reality.' When St Paul talked like that, he had spiritual things in mind, not anthropological models. But the contempt for material fact and observation (shared by all the Paris intellectuals) is identical, and constitutes a sort of godforsaken Christianity (*The Sunday Times*, 7 August 1994, Books, p. 3).

1. Gilbert Ryle, *The Concept of Mind* (1949), Penguin, 1963, p. 302.
2. See Anthony Kenny, *The Metaphysics of Mind*, Oxford University Press, 1989, p. 3.
3. In *The Concept of Mind*, Ryle observes that the general trend of his book 'will undoubtedly, and harmlessly be stigmatised as "behaviourist"'. It seems to me, however, that Ryle's implicit willingness to accept this characterisation actually misrepresents his own much more nuanced and sophisticated position, and that the stigma of behaviourism which has indeed been placed upon his arguments is very far from being as harmless as he suggests. Ryle himself certainly does not seek to deny the reality of what we frequently term 'internal' sensations, thoughts or imaginings. He merely denies that these belong to a realm which is *logically* distinct from, and independent of, the 'external' realm of ordinary human behaviour:

> Certainly there are some things which I can find out about you only, or best, through being told of them by you. The oculist has to ask his client what letters he sees with his right and left eyes and how clearly he sees them; the doctor has to ask the sufferer where the pain is and what sort of a pain it is; and the psycho-analyst has to ask his patient about his dreams and daydreams. If you do not divulge the contents of your silent soliloquies and other imaginings, I have no sure way of finding out what you have been saying or picturing to yourself. But the sequence of your sensations and imaginings is not the sole field in which your wits and character are shown; perhaps only for lunatics is it more than a small corner of that field. I find out most of what I want to know about your capacities, interests, likes, dislikes, methods and convictions by observing how you conduct your overt doings, of which by far the most important are your sayings and writings. It is a subsidiary question how you conduct your imaginings, including your imagined monologues (p. 60).

4. Traherne, *Poetical Works*, London, 1903, p. 49. Quoted in Kenny, p. 86.
5. Quoted in Phyllis Grosskurth, *Havelock Ellis: A Biography*, New York University Press, 1985, Introduction, p. xvi.
6. Nicholas Humphrey, 'The Function of the Intellect', in P. P. G. Bateson and R. A. Hinde (ed.), *Growing Points in Ethology*, 1976.
7. Ryle, p. 28.
8. Ryle, p. 190ff.
9. Blackburn, quoted in Raymond Tallis, *The Explicit Animal: A Defence of Human Consciousness*, Macmillan, 1991, p. 9.
10. Colin McGinn, 'Can We Solve the Mind–Body Problem?' (1989) in McGinn, *The Problem of Consciousness*, Oxford: Blackwell, 1991, pp. 1–2.
11. Nicholas Humphrey, *A History of the Mind*, Chatto and Windus, 1992.
12. McGinn, *London Review of Books*, 1992, vol. 17.
13. Julian Dibbell, *Voice Literary Supplement*, 1992.
14. The metaphors of models, maps and charts which I use here in an attempt

to describe the relationship of the brain to the rest of the body are clearly inadequate. In 1911 the Swiss neurologist, Carl von Monakow offered a much more complex image, itself no doubt inadequate, but a great deal more intricate and suggestive:

> The connections between a local anatomical lesion [of the brain] and the residual functional disturbance [of the body, including speech, perception, movement etc.] are similar to that of a music box out of whose cylinder a locally circumscribed series of pegs has been taken (local defect) and the disturbance of the melody ... The error of tunes will be, even by the most experienced person, deduced only with difficulty from the number and place of the lacking pegs (Von Monakow, 1911, quoted in Anne Harrington, *Medicine, Mind and the Double Brain*, Princeton University Press, 1987, p. 263).

15. Steven Rose, *The Making of Memory: From Molecules to Mind*, Bantam, 1993, p. 313. Although I write that Rose's research has run 'parallel' to the work of Edelman, these words should not be construed as implying either an identity of scientific interests or complete agreement. In particular Rose is sceptical about the process of putative neuronal selection which Edelman calls 'neural Darwinism':

> Although his phrase is catchy, I do not find it apt. Darwinian evolution is a process of preservation of favoured genotypes as a consequence of differential survival and reproduction of phenotypes. Neuronal ensembles do not survive and reproduce in this way – indeed they don't even replicate. Evolution and selection are poor metaphors to describe the processes of interaction, feedback, stabilization and growth of cells and synapses occurring during development – and indeed throughout an entire lifetime. What is to be welcomed, however, is Edelman's insistence on just that dynamic and developmental nature of biological processes which the computer analogy suppresses ... (p. 317).

CHAPTER TWENTY-FOUR · BEYOND PSYCHOANALYSIS

1. Bacon, *Works*, ed. Spedding, Ellis and Heath, London, 1857-9, IV, p. 66.
2. Darwin, *The Origin of Species* (1859), ed. J. W. Burrow, Penguin, 1968, p. 127.
3. Darwin, pp. 139-42.
4. John and Elizabeth Newson, *Seven Years Old in the Home Environment*, Penguin, 1978, p. 13; *Four Years Old in an Urban Community*, Penguin, 1970, pp. 25-6; *Patterns of Infant Care in an Urban Community*, Penguin, 1965, p. 14.
5. One example of the immensely rich resources which are already available to theorists is provided by the work of the historian Norman Cohn on the role played by collective fantasies in European history. In three widely acclaimed books, *The Pursuit of the Millennium*, *Warrant for Genocide*, and *Europe's Inner*

Demons, Professor Cohn has explored one of the most enduring of the irrational impulses which lie behind Judaeo-Christian history – 'the urge to purify the world through the annihilation of some category of human beings imagined as agents of corruption and incarnations of evil'. In studying what are, in effect, some of the practical historical consequences of the Judaeo-Christian apocalyptic tradition, he has thrown more light on the history and dynamics of persecution and prejudice than perhaps any other historian either in Europe or America. It should be noted that, like many who have worked on the history of human irrationalism, Cohn has both invoked psychoanalytic theories, and implicitly endorsed their value – holding a view of history and psychoanalysis which bears some resemblance to that of E. R. Dodds (see below, note 15). Cohn's own richly empirical approach, however, overbrims this theoretical vessel and seems itself to call for a much more capacious and historically sensitive theoretical framework than psychoanalysis can provide. The major question raised by his work, but not answered satisfactorily, concerns the relationship between the supposedly 'aberrant' or 'regressive' apocalypticism which he analyses to the orthodox apocalypticism of New Testament Christianity – or indeed of seventeenth-century Puritanism.

In a quite different area of cultural history the extraordinary body of research which has been produced by Gershon Legman on obscene humour is one of the most useful and least celebrated of all recent scholarly achievements. Legman's work shows how fruitful an ostensibly psychoanalytic approach can be in the hands of a natural investigator, whose impulse towards empiricism constantly enriches his impoverished conceptual framework and repeatedly confutes his own psychoanalytically inspired theoretical pronouncements.

Whereas Legman has concentrated his attention on sexual humour, the realm of sexual fantasy has been reviewed in some detail by Nancy Friday. Friday has been criticised by some feminists, sometimes justifiably. Read critically, however, her work, like that of Legman, is an invaluable resource, and she frequently writes of both sexual behaviour and emotional relationships with great insight and perceptiveness.

The single greatest problem with Friday's approach is her quasi-Freudian tendency to assume that the themes of sexual fantasy are somehow intrinsic to human sexuality. This approach goes hand in hand with her implied view that the most healthy response to all forms of fantasy is that of acceptance. At times this attitude of extreme libertarianism seems to lead to the implicit endorsement not only of fantasies which celebrate the sexual bodies of men and women but also of fantasies in which women (or men) are hurt, humiliated or degraded. In this respect Friday's work is perhaps best understood, for all its seeming emancipation from cultural taboos, as the expression of a particular kind of Puritanism. Behind her libertarianism and her reluctance to criticise sexual fantasies, we may discern something of the Puritan idealisation of the individual conscience, and the Puritan tendency to transfer the doctrine of scriptural inerrancy from the Bible-without to the 'Bible-within' of the individual human imagination.

Friday herself is by no means completely in thrall to this kind of puritan libertarianism, but it does colour her work with the result that she seems at times to enter into uncritical complicity with the misogynistic culture which is reflected in some of the fantasies she collects.

Friday's work, broadly focused though it is, offers only one perspective on sexual fantasy. Since pornography itself is one of the major forms of sexual fantasy, any attempt to survey the entire realm of fantasy must consider the pornographic imagination in all its complexity. The literature on this subject is huge and some of the most illuminating perspectives have been offered by feminist critics. It is my own impression, however, that while feminist critics have rightly drawn attention to the role played by misogynistic fantasies in modern pornography, they have sometimes tended to understate the role played by such fantasies in Judaeo-Christian orthodoxy and in Western history as a whole. At the same time, some feminist critics of pornography appear themselves to underestimate the extent to which modern attitudes towards pornography and to the portrayal of sexual intimacy continue to be shaped by Puritanism. They too are sometimes reluctant to discriminate between different aspects of the sexual imagination. The indiscriminate acceptance of sexual fantasies which characterises some extreme forms of libertarianism thus sometimes appears to be met with an indiscriminate rejection of all sexual themes which may be deemed pornographic. Among those most zealously opposed to pornography there appears to be very little appreciation of the extraordinary psychological and imaginative wealth which has been locked up in the realm of the obscene, or of the need to liberate this wealth.

The battle now being fought over pornography in the United States, Britain and elsewhere is an extremely complex one in which there are many different positions. Yet it is difficult to avoid the impression that at the heart of this battle is a clash not between two radical alternatives, but between two different kinds of cultural puritanism, neither of which is in a position to deliver the liberation which both unfailingly promise.

See Norman Cohn, *Europe's Inner Demons: An Enquiry Inspired by the Great Witch-Hunt*, Paladin, 1976, p. xiv; *The Pursuit of the Millennium: Revolutionary Millenarians and Mystical Anarchists of the Middle Ages*, Paladin, 1970; *Warrant for Genocide: the Myth of the Jewish World Conspiracy and the Protocols of the Elders of Zion*, Penguin, 1970. Gershon Legman, *Rationale of the Dirty Joke*, first series, London: Jonathan Cape, 1969; *No Laughing Matter: Rationale of the Dirty Joke*, second series, London: Granada Publishing, 1978. Nancy Friday, *My Secret Garden: Women's Sexual Fantasies*, Quartet, 1976; *Men in Love, Men's Sexual Fantasies: The Triumph of Love over Rage*, Hutchinson, 1980; *Women on Top*, Hutchinson, 1991; *My Mother/My Self*, Fontana, 1986. Andrea Dworkin, *Pornography: Men Possessing Women*, Women's Press, 1981; Susan Griffin, *Pornography and Silence*, Women's Press, 1981; John Stoltenberg, *Refusing to Be a Man*, Fontana, 1990. On the association between Puritanism and libertarianism see my *A Brief History of Blasphemy: Liberalism, Censorship and 'The Satanic Verses'*, The Orwell Press, 1990, pp. 19–67. See also my essay 'The Body Politic and the Politics of the Body: The Religious Origins of Western Secularism' in John Keane (ed.), *The Decline of Secularism? New Perspectives*, in press.

6. Mary Midgley, *Science as Salvation: A Modern Myth and Its Meaning*, Routledge, 1992, p. 129.

   For those who are sympathetic to the view that the traditional dichotomy between reason and feeling is both artificial and damaging, perhaps the most encouraging sign is the appearance of a book written by a neurologist which contests the traditional division on the basis of clinical experience and the findings of modern neuroscience. In *Descartes' Error: Emotion, Reason and the Human Brain* (New York: G. P. Putnam's, 1994), Antonio R. Damasio recounts how he began writing his book in order 'to propose that reason may not be as pure as most of us think it is or wish it were, that emotions and feelings may not be intruders in the bastion of reason at all: they may be enmeshed in its networks, for worse *and* for better' (p. xii). His entire argument is relevant to the point of view which I have put forward in the last part of this book.

7. Credit for this vivid and extremely useful way of characterising Western dualism should go to Ernest Gellner, who uses the term 'beast–angel dualism' in his *The Psychoanalytic Movement*, Paladin, 1985, p. 11.

8. Alex Comfort, *Darwin and the Naked Lady*, Routledge and Kegan Paul, 1961, p. 8.

9. Comfort, p. 8.

10. A question which is frequently raised in response to the kind of arguments I put forward here is how rival theories of human nature can be 'rigorously tested'. The question is an interesting one in that it reflects the deep need felt by many of those working in the human sciences to conform to the criteria of knowledge which tend to be applied in the natural sciences – and above all in the physical sciences. One way of answering the question is to point out that, although some scientific hypotheses can be rigorously tested in laboratory conditions, many cannot. Hypotheses produced by physicists or chemists can generally be submitted to rigorous tests. Since most philosophies of science, including complex and interesting ones like that put forward by Karl Popper, tend to treat physics as a paradigm of scientific knowledge, testability has come to be widely viewed as an essential feature of any scientific hypothesis. But, as has been pointed out by many, if this criterion had been accepted and applied to Darwin's hypothesis of natural selection when it was first outlined in 1859, that theory would never have been regarded as a scientific hypothesis at all, since it was not the kind of theory which could be submitted to rigorous testing. Popper himself was aware of this, and, at first at least, declined to regard the theory of natural selection as a genuine scientific theory.

    The question of the intellectual differences between theories in the physical sciences and theories in the biological sciences is a large one and cannot be treated adequately in a note. I would suggest here, however, that the reason why most modern biologists now regard the theory of natural selection as a genuine scientific theory is not primarily because of the numerous experiments which have been performed with fruit-flies, interesting and valuable though these may be. It is because of the huge explanatory power which Darwin's theory possesses. In practice what evolutionary scientists have found is that the best way of 'testing' Darwin's theory has been to search out system-atically the most difficult, complex and 'miraculous' phenomena of the natural world and show how, contrary to the frequently expressed incredulity of modern creationists and anti-evolutionists, these can be explained in terms of the theory of natural selection. It is precisely this approach which is adopted with wonderful cogency by Richard Dawkins in his book *The Blind Watch-maker*. What his arguments demonstrate is that the explanatory power of the God-hypothesis is severely limited and can be used to account for the natural world only if we are prepared to tolerate repeated, theologically determined, leaps and lapses of reason. The explanatory power of the hypothesis of natural selection, however, is immense and has yet to be defeated by *any* significant problem posed by organic structures. If another theory were to be formulated which appeared to possess the same explanatory power as natural selection, *when applied to the same range of problems*, the status of Darwin's theory would be called into serious question. For the moment no such theory exists, or seems likely to be formulated, and the theory of natural selection is generally, and quite reasonably, regarded as a scientific theory *even though it cannot be subjected to rigorous testing in a laboratory*.

In the case of evolution, it might be said, the almost infinite variety of living experiments which are part of the process of nature itself obviates the need for scientists to set up artificial experiments in laboratories. Nature is its *own* laboratory and the only experiments which can ultimately test the theory have already been underway for many millions of years. The primary task of the scientist is not to set up new experiments, but to observe the existing ones with scrupulous care, focusing minutely on any aspects of nature which appear to be at odds with the theory. Given the sheer scale and com-plexity of life on earth, no more extensive method of testing a theory could be conceived, and so far Darwin's theory, which was originally worked out on the basis of data drawn from thousands of the earth's 'natural laboratories', has passed all the tests. Any theory which seeks to extend Darwin's theory into the realm of human nature and human history must ultimately be tested in a similar way. Given the huge number of problems posed by human behaviour and human history, problems which current sociobiological theories do not even begin to deal with, there is likely to be no shortage of such tests. Because such tests are not experiments carried out in laboratory conditions there are some who will continue to insist that theories of human nature can never be 'scientific'. This view, however, suggests more a scientistic outlook than a scientific one. For if science were to be restricted to investigat-ing that which can be tested in laboratories, then it would be an impoverished instrument indeed, and the intellectual wealth contained in Darwin's theories could not be counted part of it.

Although these remarks do not provide a complete answer to the question about testing, they should perhaps help to make it clear that attempts to transfer the epistemological criteria of the physical sciences to the life sciences, however rigorous-seeming they may be, are profoundly unscientific.

11. Schrödinger, quoted by Bryan Appleyard, *Understanding the Present*, p. 208; for Appleyard's discussion, see pp. 208–10.

12. The original source for this quotation from an unidentified sociologist is the *Bulletin of the American Association of University Professors* (1948). My source for it is *Telling the Truth about History* by Joyce Appleby, Lynn Hunt and Margaret Jacob (W. W. Norton, 1994, p. 16). They in turn cite Robert N. Proctor's use of the quotation in *Value-Free Science? Purity and Power in Modern Knowledge* (Cambridge, Mass., 1991, p. 176).

13. Philip J. Davis and Reuben Hersh, *Descartes' Dream: The World According to Mathematics*, Penguin, 1990, pp. 290–91.

14. Daniel Gasman, *The Scientific Origins of National Socialism: Social Darwinism in Ernst Haeckel and the German Monist League*, Macdonald, 1971, p. 162.

15. L. C. Knights, *Explorations*, London, 1946, p. 111. This passage is quoted by E. R. Dodds in a note appended to the last chapter of his *The Greeks and the Irrational* (1951), University of California Press, 1968, p. 269. In the same note Dodds writes that

> The late R. G. Collingwood held that 'irrational elements . . . the blind forces and activities in us, which are part of human life . . . are not parts of the historical process.' This agrees with the practice of nearly all historians, past and present. My own conviction . . . is that our chance of understanding the historical process depends very largely on removing this quite arbitrary restriction upon our notion of it.

Dodds's judgements are frequently perceptive, as they are here, but it should be noted that, for all his interest in the irrational, he has a fundamentally rationalist outlook. For Dodds in 1949, which is when the lectures making up his book were originally delivered at Berkeley, psychoanalysis is understood as an instrument for understanding *and controlling* the 'irrational' so that the rational intellect may triumph at last and usher in the Open Society. So eloquently does Dodds, in the closing paragraphs of his book, picture psycho-analysis as the essential instrument of political and historical progress, and so closely does his view correspond with Freud's own prophetic, rational apocalypticism, that it seems worth reproducing those paragraphs here. In them Dodds draws a parallel between his own times and those of classical Greece, where a movement towards rationalism and science had recoiled, as Dodds sees it, into unreason and superstition. It should be noted that he refers to psychoanalysis only obliquely as an 'instrument' but that the context makes it reasonably clear the instrument he has in mind is a specifically Freudian one:

> We too [like the Greeks] have experienced a great age of rationalism, marked by scientific advances beyond anything that earlier times had thought possible, and confronting mankind with the prospect of a society more open than any it has ever known. And in the last forty years we have also experienced something else – the unmistakable symp-toms of a recoil from that prospect. It would appear that, in the words used recently by André Malraux, 'Western civilisation has begun to doubt its own credentials.'
>
> What is the meaning of this recoil, this doubt? Is it the hesitation

before the jump, or the beginning of a panic flight? I do not know. On such a matter a simple professor of Greek is in no position to offer an opinion. But he can do one thing. He can remind his readers that once before a civilised people rode to this jump – rode to it and refused it. And he can beg them to examine all the circumstances of that refusal.

Was it the horse that refused, or the rider? That is really the crucial question. Personally, I believe it was the horse – in other words those irrational elements in human nature which govern without our know-ledge so much of our behaviour and so much of what we think is our thinking. And if I am right about this, I can see grounds for hope. As these chapters have, I trust, shown, the men who created the first European rationalism were never – until the Hellenistic Age – 'mere' rationalists: that is to say they were deeply and imaginatively aware of the power, the wonder and the peril of the Irrational. But they could describe what went on below the threshold of consciousness only in mythological or symbolic language; they had no instrument for under-standing it, still less for controlling it; and in the Hellenistic Age too many of them made the fatal mistake of thinking they could ignore it. Modern man, on the other hand, is beginning to acquire such an instrument. It is still very far from perfect, nor is it always skilfully handled; in many fields, including that of history, its possibilities and its limitations have still to be tested. Yet it seems to offer the hope that if we use it wisely we shall eventually understand our horse better; that, understanding him better, we shall be able by better training to overcome his fears; and that through the overcoming of fear horse and rider will one day take that decisive jump, and take it successfully (pp. 254–5).

Few passages could illustrate more clearly the manner in which an essentially creationist and fundamentally superstitious form of dualism (beast–angel dualism being here replaced by horse–rider dualism) is presented by an intellectual as though it were the most reasonable thing in the world. Dodds's confidence that the rider (or angel) will triumph over the horse (or beast) is entirely orthodox. Given the argument already advanced in this book, it should not be the occasion of surprise that psychoanalysis is seen by Dodds as the intellectual means by which a rational heaven-on-earth is eventually to be brought about. It should perhaps also be noted that this kind of orthodox rationalist dream is also similar in some respects, though the similarity is not often remarked, to the sublime optimism of the apocalyptist John as he con-jured up his revelatory vision of the End in which the Beast, after being bound for a thousand years, is finally vanquished, and the Chosen reign with Christ and his angels for all eternity.

16. Edelman, *Bright Air, Brilliant Fire*, p. 1.
17. I borrow some of my terms here from Mary Midgley's stimulating discussion of what she calls 'The Unexpected Difficulties of Deicide' (see Midgley, p. 92ff).

18. Gay, *Freud: A Life for Our Time*, Dent, 1988, p. 533 (and note).

19. It might well seem that to write in these terms is to tempt fate and to invite the response that the ship of discovery, as I have presented it here, is very far from being well caulked and that, in a number of respects, it remains intellectually unseaworthy. Such a response, however, far from constituting an objection to the project I have described, is exactly the kind of reaction on which its success depends. For, as Joyce Appleby, Lynn Hunt and Margaret Jacob write in the last sentence of their recent book, 'Telling the truth takes a collective effort' (*Telling the Truth about History*, p. 309). The preparations for any intellectual project of the kind I have described need to be wide-ranging indeed and that is why I have described this book merely as a 'contribution' to them. Fortunately many other contributions have already been made and I have tried to indicate, both in my text and in my notes, where some of the most helpful of these are to be found. Other contributions have yet to be made and if these do not contain searching criticism of all philosophies of science, including the one outlined in this chapter, little progress is likely to result.

   The ideals of critical debate and discussion which I endorse here are very similar to those which are held by most defenders of rationalism. It would be wrong to assume, however, that such ideals are always maintained consistently by those who most frequently appeal to them. Karl Popper has contrasted the rationalist intellectual cultures of 'open societies' with the doctrinaire intellectual schools of 'closed societies'. In such schools, he observes, full debate of crucial doctrines is usually outlawed and 'in the main it is with assertion and dogma and condemnation rather than argument that the doctrine is defended' (*Conjectures and Refutations*, Routledge and Kegan Paul, 1972, p. 149). We should perhaps note, however, that neither liberals nor rationalists are immune to behaving in the same narrow doctrinaire way as Popper's 'schools', especially on those occasions when the doctrinal foundations of liberal individualism or of rationalism are themselves under attack. They themselves, in an attempt to defend an intellectually indefensible position, sometimes replace argument and reasoned criticism with dogma, condemnation and abuse. (For one of the most perceptive commentaries on the manner in which intolerance sometimes undergirds doctrines of intellectual toleration, see John Stuart Mill, *On Liberty*, Penguin, pp. 93–4.)

20. Nietzsche, *The Genealogy of Morals*, Third Essay, XXIII.

AFTERWORD · FREUD'S FALSE MEMORIES

1. See Frederick Crews, 'The Revenge of the Repressed', *New York Review of Books*, 17 November 1994, pp. 54–60; 1 December 1994, pp. 49–58. See also the ensuing correspondence in issues up to 20 April 1995. These essays together with selections from published and unpublished correspondence, will form part of Frederick Crews's forthcoming book *The Memory Wars: Freudian Science in Dispute*, New York Review Imprints, 1995. The best treatment of the history of the recovered memory movement will be found in

Mark Pendergrast's *Victims of Memory: Incest Accusations and Shattered Lives*, Hinesburg, Vermont: Upper Access, Inc., 1995, pp. 41–83 and *passim*.

2. See Judith Lewis Herman, *Father–Daughter Incest*, Harvard University Press, p. 11.

3. See Jeffrey Masson, *The Assault on Truth: Freud and Child Sexual Abuse* (1984), HarperCollins, 1992, Afterword (1985), pp. 195–200.

4. See above, Chapter 11.

5. Herman, pp. 9–10.

6. See above, Chapter 9. See also the article by Russell A. Powell and Douglas P. Boer, 'Did Freud Mislead Patients to Confabulate Memories of Abuse?', *Psychological Reports*, vol. 74, 1994, pp. 1283–98. This article is excellent in many ways. But it should be noted that its authors, whilst justly critical of much recovered memory therapy, appear to take a more positive view of recent aetiological speculations concerning trauma, incest and repression than I have done here, or than I believe is warranted by the evidence. Their implicit approval of memory-retrieval therapy so long as patients are warned by their therapists that the traumatic 'memories' they recover may be false, seems to me misguided. (see p. 1295.)

7. 'The Aetiology of Hysteria' in Masson, p. 273.

8. Freud, PF3, p. 364. It should be noted that Freud is referring here to his 'pressure technique'.

9. Herman, p. 8.

10. Judith Herman and Emily Schatzow, 'Time-Limited Group Therapy for Women with a History of Incest', *International Journal of Group Psychotherapy*, 1984, vol. 43, pp. 605–16; 'Recovery and Verification of Memories of Childhood Sexual Trauma', *Psychoanalytic Psychology*, 1987, vol. 4, pp. 1–14. See the discussion of these papers in Richard Ofshe and Ethan Watters, *Making Monsters: False Memories, Psychotherapy and Sexual Hysteria*, New York: Scribner's, 1994, Appendix, pp. 309–12. See also Pendergrast, pp. 95–6

11. Pendergrast, p. 50.

12. Masson, pp. 192–3.

13. See, for example, Ofshe and Watters, pp. 69–81.

The psychiatric diagnosis most closely associated with the recovered memory movement is 'multiple personality disorder'. This diagnosis was only accepted 'officially' by the American Psychiatric Association with the publication of *DSM III* in 1980. A mere ten years earlier the disorder had been so rare as to be little more than a curiosity. Ten years later it appeared to have become epidemic, and by 1992, according to one observer, 'there were hundreds of multiples in treatment in every sizable town in North America' (Hacking, p. 8, see below). The partisans of the multiple personality movement are often overtly critical of Freud. According to Colin Ross, a leading advocate of the diagnosis, 'Freud did to the unconscious mind with his theories what New York does to the ocean with its garbage.' Yet beneath its ostensible hostility to psychoanalysis, the multiple personality movement has deep affinities with the Freud of 1896, not least through the work of the psychoanalyst Cornelia Wilbur and her case history of Sybil, which she related to the journalist Flora Rheta Schreiber. It was Schreiber's book, *Sybil* (Chicago:

Regnery, 1973), which popularised 'multiple personality disorder' and its putative origins in repressed memories of childhood sexual abuse.

As the 'disorder' has spread like an epidemic across North America an increasing number of reputable psychiatrists, psychologists and other observers have come to the conclusion that it is not a genuine psychiatric syndrome at all, and that the alternate personalities, or 'alters', which therapists call out of their patients are nothing more than the products of expectant therapeutic attention and suggestion (see Pendergrast, pp. 155–94; Ofshe and Watters, pp. 205–24).

If multiple personality disorder is indeed an 'iatrogenic' disorder, produced by the therapy which purports to cure it, one of the most intriguing questions about its history is how it ever came to be seen as a genuine psychiatric disorder in the first place. One possible answer to this question was suggested in 1994 with the publication of *DSM IV*. In this extensively revised edition of the American bible of psychiatric diagnosis, multiple personality disorder was renamed 'dissociative identity disorder'. More interestingly still, the criteria for making the diagnosis now stipulated for the first time that the disturbance of personality should not be produced 'by a general medical condition (e.g. complex partial seizures)'. As this stipulation clearly implies, effects similar to those now associated with multiple personality disorder can be produced by certain forms of epilepsy. It would therefore seem reasonable to suggest that this particular modern psychiatric diagnosis had its origin in the historical *mis*diagnosis of an organic condition – in this case, as in so many others, of some of the more bizarre-seeming manifestations of epilepsy. Although the fragmentary nature of the case histories renders their interpretation difficult, Elizabeth Thornton long ago suggested that many of the classic historical cases of double personality (now frequently cited in the literature of the modern multiple movement) were unrecognised cases of complex partial seizures, or temporal lobe *status epilepticus*. It seems equally clear, however, that other cases, including some of Janet's, were early instances of therapeutic suggestion. (On the phenomenon of double personality, see Thornton, pp. 254–60; on Janet, see Pendergrast, pp. 420–21). If this is so, what is now termed 'multiple personality disorder' would perhaps best be understood as a therapeutically synthesised 'imitation' of a real organic disorder which has only been properly recognised in the latter part of the twentieth century.

It is both interesting and, I believe, extremely significant, that one of the leading figures in the modern multiple personality movement, the psychiatrist Frank Putnam, has rediagnosed one of the most celebrated of all psychoanalytic patients as a case of multiple personality. The case which he chooses to reinterpret in this way is none other than that of Anna O., who, as we have seen, was almost certainly suffering from complex partial seizures (see above, Chapter 4).

On the criteria for dissociated identity disorder, see *Diagnostic and Statistical Manual of Mental Disorders*, 4th edition, Washington, DC: American Psychiatric Association, 1994, p. 487. On the ambivalent attitude of the modern multiple movement towards Freud, and on Frank Putnam's particular contribution to the rediagnosis of Anna O., see Ian Hacking, *Rewriting the Soul:*

Multiple Personality and the Sciences of Memory, Princeton University Press, 1995, pp. 136–7, 286–7. It should be noted that Ian Hacking writes, apparently, as a sophisticated but credulous believer in the accuracy of many (though not all) recovered memories. His moderate-seeming but highly tendentious account of the history of multiple personality disorder, and of the 'sciences of memory', reflects this point of view.

14. Jody Messler Davies and Mary Gail Frawley, *Treating the Adult Survivor of Childhood Sexual Abuse: A Psychoanalytic Perspective*, New York: Basic Books, 1994.

15. On symptom lists, see Ofshe and Watters, pp. 65–80.

16. See Renée Frederickson, *Repressed Memories: A Journey to Recovery from Sexual Abuse*, New York: Simon and Schuster, 1992. 'Finally,' writes Frederickson, 'I realised the size of the problem. Millions of people have blocked out frightening episodes of abuse. They want desperately to find out what happened to them and they need the tools to do so' (p. 15).

17. Ellen Bass and Laura Davis, *The Courage to Heal: A Guide for Women Survivors of Child Sexual Abuse*, Reed Consumer Books, 1990, p. 22.

18. Bass and Davis, p. 128.

19. To describe the account of the seduction theory given by Rush, Herman and Masson as the 'foundation myth' of the entire recovered memory movement is not, I believe, an exaggeration. This myth not only plays a key role in Herman and Masson's early texts but is also prominent in many of the other most important texts of the movement. Versions of it will be found in *The Courage to Heal* (p. 347), in Davies and Frawley's *Treating the Adult Survivor . . .* (pp. 12–16), and in Judith Herman's *Trauma and Recovery* (New York: Basic Books, 1992). In this book Herman writes of Freud's 1896 paper, 'The Aetiology of Hysteria', in the following terms: 'A century later, this paper still rivals contemporary clinical descriptions of the effects of childhood sexual abuse. It is a brilliant, compassionate, eloquently argued, closely reasoned document' (p. 13).

Perhaps the most remarkable of all the redactions of the foundation myth which have appeared in the literature of the recovered memory movement is what might be termed the 'satanised' version given in the opening paragraphs of Valerie Sinason's introduction to Valerie Sinason (ed.), *Treating Survivors of Satanist Abuse*, Routledge, 1994, pp. 1–2.

20. Masson, p. xix.

21. For full references to Crews's work on the recovered memory moment, see above, note 1; Lawrence Wright, *Remembering Satan*, Serpent's Tail, 1994; Elizabeth Loftus and Katherine Ketcham, *The Myth of Repressed Memory: False Memories and Allegations of Sexual Abuse*, New York: St Martin's Press, 1994; Richard Ofshe and Ethan Watters, *Making Monsters: False Memories, Psychotherapy, and Sexual Hysteria*, New York: Scribner's, 1994; and Mark Pendergrast, *Victims of Memory: Incest Accusations and Shattered Lives*, Hinesburg, Vermont: Upper Access, Inc., 1995.

On the general problem of therapists inadvertently guiding their patients' thoughts in a particular direction, see Malcolm Macmillan's excellent discussion of 'Unintentional Influences in Psychotherapy' in his *Freud Evaluated* (pp. 213–18). Macmillan's discussion includes details of research into how Karl Rogers, the founder of 'client-centred', 'non-directive' therapy, unwittingly directs the course of his clients' treatment. It also deals with the creation of pseudo-memories, drawing an interesting parallel between psychoanalysis and scientology 'auditing', which involves the supposedly therapeutic recovery of memories of previous lives.

APPENDIX I · THE DIAGNOSIS OF 'HYSTERIA'

1. Phillip R. Slavney, *Perspectives on 'Hysteria'*, Johns Hopkins University Press, 1990, p. 3. At the end of his book Slavney puts forward what may turn out to be a more realistic view:

> This could well be the last book with *hysteria* in its title written by a psychiatrist. Although the word is used daily in the practice of medicine, 'those who would like to drop it once and for all' seem to have won the battle for control of psychiatric nomenclature, and the next generation of physicians will no longer find it indispensable when they wish to indicate certain traits and behaviours. *Hysteria, hysteric,* and *hysterical* are on the verge of becoming anachronisms (p. 190).

Slavney, it should be noted, is describing the situation as he sees it in the United States, where he is Director of Resident Education in the Department of Psychiatry at the Johns Hopkins University School of Medicine. In Britain it is probably true to say that the term 'hysteria', while clearly waning, still enjoys a degree of official recognition. See below, note 22.

2. A. Lewis, 'The Survival of Hysteria', *Psychological Medicine*, 1975, vol. 5, pp. 9–12. This paper is reprinted in Alec Roy (ed.), *Hysteria*, John Wiley, 1982, pp. 21–6. The quotations here are all taken from Lewis's paper, where full references are given.

3. Sir Francis Walshe, 'The Diagnosis of Hysteria', *British Medical Journal*, 1965, 2, pp. 1451–4.

4. American Psychiatric Association, *Diagnostic and Statistical Manual of Mental Disorders (DSM)*, 3rd edition, Washington, DC: APA, 1980. The fourth edition of this manual was published in 1994. For an excellent brief critique of the approach of *DSM* to the problem of mental 'illness', see Carol Tavris, *The Mismeasure of Woman*, New York: Simon and Schuster, 1992, pp. 176–92. For a sceptical view of the background to *DSM*, the 'psychiatrists' bible', see Stuart A. Kirk and Herb Kutchins, *The Selling of DSM: The Rhetoric of Science in Psychiatry*, New York: A. de Gruyter, 1992. This book, of whose salutary existence many workers in the field of 'mental health' evidently remain unaware, has been described by Thomas Szasz as 'a well-documented exposé of the pretence that psychiatric diagnoses are the names of genuine diseases, and of the authentication of this fraud by an unholy alliance of the media, the government and psychiatry.' In his endorsement of the book Szasz goes on to recommend it 'to anyone concerned about the catastrophic

economic and moral consequences of psychiatrizing the human predicament'.

5. Eliot Slater, 'Diagnosis of "Hysteria"', *British Medical Journal*, 29 May 1965, p. 1399. See above, Chapter 6, final paragraph.

6. G. L. Engel, 'Conversion Symptoms' in C. M. MacBryde and R. S. Blacklow (ed.), *Signs and Symptoms*, 5th edition, Pitman Medical, 1970, pp. 650–68. Quoted in C. D. Marsden, 'Hysteria – A Neurologist's View', *Psychological Medicine*, 1986, vol. 16, pp. 277–88.

7. A. Lewis, '"Psychogenic": A Word and its Mutations', *Psychological Medicine*, 1985, vol. 2, pp. 209–15.

8. Slater, *British Medical Journal*, p. 1396.

9. The same objection is made by Walshe, who writes that 'one cannot accept hysteria adjectivally and deny it substantively' (p. 1452).

10. Laurence Miller, *Freud's Brain: Neuropsychodynamic Foundations of Psychoanalysis*, New York: The Guilford Press, 1991.

11. A similar point is made by Thornton in relation to the phenomenon of hypnosis. See *The Freudian Fallacy*, revised edition, Paladin, 1986, pp. 95–6.

12. Miller, p. 26.

13. Miller, p. 80.

14. Mark S. Micale, 'Hysteria and Its Historiography: The Future Perspective', *History of Psychiatry*, vol. 1, 1990, p. 108.

15. Graeme J. Taylor, review of Edward Shorter's *From Paralysis to Fatigue: A History of Psychosomatic Illness in the Modern Era*, published in *Psychosomatic Medicine*, vol. 55, no. 1, pp. 88–9.

    For one recent contribution to the study of 'hysteria' which seems to bear out Taylor's suggestion, see Peter Eames, 'Hysteria Following Brain Injury', *Journal of Neurology, Neurosurgery and Psychiatry*, 1992, 55, pp. 1046–53. This paper contains an account of work in a unit treating severe behaviour disorders after brain injury. Fifty-four patients in this unit showed clinical features which also occur in some descriptions of 'hysteria'. It was discovered that the appearance of such symptoms was closely correlated with diffuse insults to the brain, including hypoxia and hypoglycaemia (oxygen starvation and abnormal reduction of sugar levels in the blood). One case of 'hysteria' was caused when a patient undergoing a routine operation was accidentally placed on nitrous oxide rather than oxygen, and suffered chronic brain damage as a result.

    Although Eames's paper contains a misleading account of Charcot's research into 'hysteria' it remains an interesting and extremely valuable contribution to the subject.

16. Harold I. Kaplan and Benjamin J. Sadock, *Comprehensive Textbook of Psychiatry V*, 5th edition, Baltimore: Williams and Wilkins, 1989, p. 1009.

17. Much of the work which has been done on 'somatization' is clearly of value. See, for example, Z. J. Lipowski, 'Somatization: The Concept and Its Clinical Application', *American Journal of Psychiatry*, vol. 145:11, November 1988, pp. 1358–68; Wayne Katon, Elizabeth Lin, Michael Von Korff, Joan Russo, Patricia Lipscomb and Terry Bush, 'Somatization: A Spectrum of Severity', *American Journal of Psychiatry*, vol. 148:1, January 1991, pp. 34–40; Donna

E. Stewart, 'The Changing Face of Somatization', *Psychosomatics*, vol. 31, no. 2, 1990, pp. 153-8.

18. Kaplan and Sadock, p. 1009.

19. Kaplan and Sadock, p. 375.

20. Lipowski, p. 1359.

21. A striking, book-length example of this process at work is provided by Edward Shorter's *From Paralysis to Fatigue: A History of Psychosomatic Medicine*. The main authority which Shorter cites in support of his own arguments is the psychiatrist Z. J. Lipowski, who has written a great deal about 'somatization'. Yet whereas Lipowski promotes a complex and 'weak' form of the concept, which eschews psychoanalytic notions of conversion, Shorter invokes his authority in support of his own theories, according to which the unconscious mind freely converts the 'stress of psychological problems into physical symptoms'. The relationship between Shorter's ideas and Lipowski's is discussed acutely by Theodore M. Brown in his review of Shorter in *Journal of the History of the Behavioral Sciences*, vol. XXIX, 1993, pp. 243-5.

22. C. David Marsden and Timothy J. Fowler (ed.), *Clinical Neurology*, Edward Arnold, 1989, p. 428. The section on hysteria from which I quote is part of the chapter entitled 'Psychiatric Disorders' which was written by Paul Bridges, Consultant Psychiatrist at Guy's and the Brook Hospital. Bridges cites the papers by Eliot Slater and Sir Francis Walshe, but he makes no reference to Marsden's own contribution to the debate.

23. Georg W. Groddeck, *The Book of the It* (1923), Vision Press, 1979, pp. 100-101.

24. In his book *Migraine*, for example, Oliver Sacks suggests that there is a certain kind of migraine which should be approached not only as a physical event 'but as a peculiar form of symbolic drama into which the patient has translated important thoughts and feelings'. The symptoms of this kind of migraine can constitute 'a bodily alphabet or proto-language' and must be interpreted, he suggests, 'as if they were palimpsests in which the needs and symbols of the individual are inscribed . . .' One of the main authorities invoked in order to justify this approach is Georg Groddeck. Sacks also explicitly draws a parallel between his own speculative account of 'situational migraines' and Freud's theory of hysteria, which he appears to accept (Oliver Sacks, *Migraine: Evolution of a Common Disorder*, revised edition, Pan, 1981, pp. 223-4).

25. Linda Gamlin, 'All in Whose Mind?', *Guardian*, 16 July 1991. This article draws some examples from a paper by Erwin K. Koranyi, 'Morbidity and Rate of Undiagnosed Physical Illnesses in a Psychiatric Clinic Population', *Archives of General Psychiatry*, vol. 36, April 1979, pp. 414-19. I am grateful to Linda Gamlin for supplying me with a copy of this paper.

26. The suggestion that 'hysteria' should be understood as a 'residual diagnosis' – or a diagnostic dustbin – is made by Susan Leigh Starr in her book, *Regions of the Mind: Brain Research and the Quest for Scientific Certainty*, Stanford University Press, 1989.

27. The implication of my own remarks here is that the entire discipline of psychiatry still bears the marks of its birth out of what I have called the 'medical dark ages', and that the misdiagnosis of 'genuine' organic illnesses

and their construal as psychological syndromes has played a major part in its development. For Susan Leigh Starr's acute and, I believe, accurate analysis of the historical and practical status of the hysteria diagnosis, and for references to work by Richard Hunter and Mark S. Micale which bears on this problem, see above, Chapter 5, notes 3 and 4, pp. 580–1.

APPENDIX II · BABINSKI'S TEST FOR 'HYSTERIA'

1. J. Babinski and J. Froment, *Hysteria or Pithiatism and Reflex Nervous Disorders in the Neurology of War*, University of London Press, 1918, p. 51.
2. C. D. Marsden and E. H. Reynolds, 'Seizures in Adults', in John Laidlaw, Alan Richens and Jolyon Oxley (ed.), *A Textbook of Epilepsy*, 3rd edition, Churchill Livingstone, 1988, pp. 156–7.
3. T. A. Betts, 'Epilepsy and Behaviour', *A Textbook of Epilepsy*, p. 374.
4. R. P. Lesser, H. Lüders and D. S. Dinner, 'Evidence for Epilepsy is Rare in Patients with Psychogenic Seizures', *Neurology*, 1983, vol. 33, pp. 502–4. For an account of the form of 'suggestion' used by Lesser and his colleagues, see R. J. Cohen and C. Suter, 'Hysterical "Seizures" – Suggestion as a Provocative EEG Test', *Annals of Neurology*, 1982, vol. 11, pp. 391–5.

Bibliography

Abraham, Hilda C., and Freud, Ernst L. (ed.), *A Psychoanalytic Dialogue: The Letters of Sigmund Freud and Karl Abraham, 1907–1926*, New York: Basic Books, 1965

Adair, Gilbert, 'Freud Slips into the Shadows', *The Sunday Times*, 9 May 1993

American Psychiatric Association, *Diagnostic and Statistical Manual of Mental Disorders (DSM)*, Washington, DC: 3rd edition, 1980; 3rd edition (revised), 1987; 4th edition, 1994

Appignanesi, Lisa, and Forrester, John, *Freud's Women*, Weidenfeld and Nicolson, 1992

Appleby, Joyce, Hunt, Lynn, and Jacob, Margaret, *Telling the Truth about History*, New York: W. W. Norton, 1994

Appleyard, Bryan, *Understanding the Present: Science and the Soul of Modern Man*, Picador, 1992

Armstrong, Karen, *Beginning the World*, Pan, 1983

– *Holy War: The Crusades and Their Impact on Today's World*, Macmillan, 1988

Babinski, J., and Froment, J., *Hysteria or Pithiatism and Reflex Nervous Disorders in the Neurology of War*, University of London Press, 1918

Bacon, Francis, *Works*, ed. Spedding, Ellis and Heath, London, 1857–9

Badcock, Christopher, *PsychoDarwinism: The New Synthesis of Darwin and Freud*, HarperCollins, 1994.

Bakan, David, *Sigmund Freud and the Jewish Mystical Tradition*, Princeton: D. Van Nostrand Co., 1958

Barash, David, *Sociobiology: The Whisperings Within*, Souvenir Press, 1979.

Bass, Ellen, and Davis, Laura, *The Courage to Heal: A Guide for Women Survivors of Child Sexual Abuse* (1988), Reed Consumer Books, 1990; 3rd edition, New York: HarperCollins, 1994

Bateson, P. P. G., and Hinde, R. A. (ed.), *Growing Points in Ethology*, Cambridge University Press,1976

Beard, G. M., *A Practical Treatise of Nervous Exhaustion*, New York, 1880

– *American Nervousness*, New York, 1881

Berkley-Hill, Owen, 'The Anal-Erotic Factor in Hindu Religion', *International Journal of Psychoanalysis*, vol. 2, part 3–4, 1921

Berlin, Isaiah, *Against the Current: Essays in the History of Ideas*, ed. Henry
  Hardy, Hogarth Press, 1980
Billen, Andrew, 'Freudians' Slips Are Showing', *Observer*, 30 January
  1994
Billinsky, John M., 'Jung and Freud (The End of a Romance)', *Andover
  Newton Quarterly*, X, 1969, pp. 3–34
Binnie, C.D., 'Electroencephalography' in John Laidlaw, Alan Richens
  and Jolyon Oxley (ed.), *A Textbook of Epilepsy*, 3rd edition, Churchill
  Livingstone, 1988
Binnie, C. D., Darby, C. E., De Korte, R. A., and Wilkins, A. J.,
  'Self-induction of Epileptic Seizures by Eyeclosure: Incidence and
  Recognition', *Journal of Neurology, Neurosurgery, and Psychiatry*, vol.
  43, 1980, pp. 386–9
Bonaparte, Marie, Freud, Anna, Kris, Ernst (ed.), *The Origins of
  Psychoanalysis: Letters to Wilhelm Fliess, Drafts and Notes, 1887–1902*,
  Imago, 1954
Borger, Robert, and Cioffi, Frank (ed.), *Explanation in the Behavioural
  Sciences*, Cambridge University Press, 1970
Brain, Russell, 'The Concept of Hysteria in the Time of William
  Harvey', *Proceedings of the Royal Society of Medicine*, vol. 56, 1963,
  pp. 321–3
Brown, Norman O., *Life Against Death: The Psychoanalytical Meaning of
  History*, Routledge and Kegan Paul, 1959
Brown, Theodore M., review of Edward Shorter's *From Paralysis to
  Fatigue*, *Journal of the History of the Behavioral Sciences*, vol. XXIX, 1993,
  pp. 241–5
Byck, Robert (ed.), *Cocaine Papers by Sigmund Freud*, New York:
  Stonehill, 1974
Calder-Marshall, Arthur, *Havelock Ellis*, Hart-Davis, 1959
Carter, C. Sydney, and Weeks, G. E. Alison, *The Protestant Dictionary*,
  revised edition, The Harrison Trust, 1933
Charcot, J. M., *Clinical Lectures on Diseases of the Nervous System*, vol. III,
  trans. Thomas Savill (1887), New Sydenham Society, 1889
– *Charcot the Clinician: The Tuesday Lessons*, ed. Christopher G. Goetz,
  New York: Raven Press, 1987
Charcot, J. M., and Marie, Pierre, 'Hysteria, Mainly Hystero-Epilepsy'
  in D. H. Tuke (ed.), *A Dictionary of Psychological Medicine*, 1892,
  pp. 627–41
Cioffi, Frank (ed.), *Freud: Modern Judgments*, Macmillan, 1973
Cioffi, Frank, 'Freud and the Idea of a Pseudo-Science' in Robert Borger
  and Frank Cioffi (ed.), *Explanation in the Behavioural Sciences*,
  Cambridge University Press, 1970, pp. 471–99

– 'Was Freud a Liar?', *Listener*, 7 February 1974, pp. 172–4
– 'Freud – New Myths to Replace the Old', *New Society*, vol. 50, 1979,
pp. 503–4
– 'The Cradle of Neurosis', *The Times Literary Supplement*, 6 July 1984,
pp. 743–4
– 'Psychoanalysis, Pseudo-Science and Testability' in G. Currie and A
Musgrave (ed.), *Popper and the Human Sciences*, Dordrecht: Nijhoff,
1985, pp. 13–44
– '"Exegetical Myth-Making" in Grünbaum's Indictment of Popper and
Exoneration of Freud' in Peter Clark and Crispin Wright (ed.), *Mind,
Psychoanalysis and Science*, Oxford: Blackwell, 1988, pp. 61–87
Clark, Peter, and Wright, Crispin (ed.), *Mind, Psychoanalysis and Science*,
Oxford: Blackwell, 1988
Clark, Ronald W., *Freud: The Man and the Cause*, Jonathan Cape/
Weidenfeld and Nicolson, 1980
Clarke, Edwin, and Jacyna, L. S., *Nineteenth Century Origins of
Neuroscientific Concepts*, University of California Press, 1987
Clarke, Simon, *The Foundations of Structuralism: A Critique of Lévi-Strauss
and the Structuralist Movement*, Harvester Press/Barnes and Noble, 1981
Cleugh, James, *Love Locked Out: A Survey of Love, Licence and Restriction
in the Middle Ages*, Tandem, 1964
Cohen, R. J., and Suter, C., 'Hysterical "Seizures" – Suggestion as a
Provocative EEG Test', *Annals of Neurology*, vol. 11, 1982, pp. 391–5
Cohn, Norman, *The Pursuit of the Millennium: Revolutionary Millenarians
and Mystical Anarchists of the Middle Ages*, Paladin, 1970
– *Warrant for Genocide: the Myth of the Jewish World Conspiracy and the
Protocols of the Elders of Zion*, Penguin, 1970
– *Europe's Inner Demons: An Enquiry Inspired by the Great Witch-Hunt*,
Paladin, 1976
Comfort, Alex, *Darwin and the Naked Lady: Discursive Essays on Biology
and Art*, Routledge and Kegan Paul, 1961
– *The Anxiety Makers*, Panther, 1968
Crews, Frederick, *Skeptical Engagements*, New York: Oxford University
Press, 1986
– 'The Unknown Freud', *New York Review of Books*, 18 November 1993,
pp. 55–66
– 'The Revenge of the Repressed', *New York Review of Books*, Part I, 17
November 1994, pp. 54–60; Part II, 1 December 1994, pp. 49–58
– *The Memory Wars: Freudian Science in Dispute*, New York Review
Imprints, in press, 1995
Corrigan, D. Felicitas, *Helen Waddell: A Biography*, Gollancz, 1986
Crick, Bernard, *George Orwell: A Life*, Penguin, 1982

Currie, G., and Musgrave, A. (ed.), *Popper and the Human Sciences*,
   Dordrecht: Nijhoff, 1985
Damasio, Antonio R., *Descartes' Error: Emotion, Reason and the Human
   Brain*, Macmillan, 1995
Darwin, Charles, *The Origin of Species* (1859), ed. J. W. Burrow, Penguin,
   1968
– *The Descent of Man* (1871), Watts, 1930
Davies, Jody Messler, and Frawley, Mary Gail, *Treating the Adult
   Survivor of Childhood Sexual Abuse: A Psychoanalytic Perspective*, New
   York: Basic Books, 1994
Davis, Philip J., and Hersh, Reuben, *Descartes' Dream: The World
   According to Mathematics*, Penguin, 1990
Dawkins, Richard, *The Blind Watchmaker*, Longman, 1986
– *The Selfish Gene*, Paladin, 1978
Delahunty, J. E., and Ardran, G. M., 'Globus Hystericus – A
   Manifestation of Reflux Oesophagitis?', *Journal of Laryngology and
   Otology*, vol. 84, 1970, pp. 1049–54
Desmond, Adrian, and Moore, James, *Darwin*, Michael Joseph, 1991
Diamond, Stanley, 'The Myth of Structuralism' in Ino Rossi (ed.), *The
   Unconscious in Culture: The Structuralism of Claude Lévi-Strauss in
   Perspective*, New York: E. P. Dutton, 1974
Dobzhansky, T. H., *Mankind Evolving: The Evolution of the Human
   Species*, Yale University Press, 1962
Dodds, E. R., *The Greeks and the Irrational* (1951), University of
   California Press, 1968
Donne, John, *Collected Prose*, ed. Neil Rose, Penguin, 1987
Dworkin, Andrea, *Pornography: Men Possessing Women*, Women's Press,
   1981
Eames, Peter, 'Hysteria Following Brain Injury', *Journal of Neurology,
   Neurosurgery and Psychiatry*, 55, 1992, pp. 1046–53
Easlea, Brian, *Science and Sexual Oppression: Patriarchy's Confrontation with
   Woman and Nature*, Weidenfeld and Nicolson, 1981
Edelman, Gerald, *Bright Air, Brilliant Fire: On the Matter of the Mind*,
   Penguin, 1992
Eissler, K. R., *Talent and Genius: The Fictitious Case of Tausk Contra Freud*,
   New York: Grove Press, 1971
– *Victor Tausk's Suicide*, New York: International Universities Press, 1983
Ellenberger, Henri, *The Discovery of the Unconscious: The History and
   Evolution of Dynamic Psychiatry*, New York: Basic Books, 1970
– *Beyond the Unconscious: Essays of Henri F. Ellenberger in the History of
   Psychiatry*, ed. Mark S. Micale, Princeton University Press, 1993
Ellis, Havelock, *Selected Essays*, Dent, 1936

Erikson, Erik H., *Young Man Luther*, New York: W. W. Norton, 1958
– *Childhood and Society*, Penguin, 1967
Esterson, Allen, *Seductive Mirage: An Exploration of the Work of Sigmund Freud*, Chicago: Open Court, 1993
Eysenck, Hans, *Decline and Fall of the Freudian Empire*, Penguin, 1986
Ferenczi, Sandor, *The Clinical Diary of Sandor Ferenczi*, ed. Judith Dupont, Harvard University Press, 1988
Frederickson, Renée, *Repressed Memories: A Journey to Recovery from Sexual Abuse*, New York: Simon and Schuster, 1992
Freeman, Lucy, *Freud Rediscovered*, New York: Arbor House, 1980
Freud, Anna, 'The Relation of Beating-Phantasies to a Day-Dream', *International Journal of Psychoanalysis*, IV, 1923, pp. 89–102
– *The Writings of Anna Freud*, New York: International Universities Press, 8 volumes, 1966–80
Freud, Ernst L. (ed.), *Letters of Sigmund Freud, 1873–1839*, Hogarth Press, 1961
Freud, Sigmund, *The Standard Edition of the Complete Psychological Works of Sigmund Freud*, ed. James Strachey, Hogarth Press and the Institute of Psycho-Analysis, 24 volumes, 1953–74:

    I *Pre-Psycho-Analytic Publications and Unpublished Drafts* (1886–99)
    II *Studies on Hysteria* (1893–5)
    III *Early Psycho-Analytic Publications* (1893–9)
    IV *The Interpretation of Dreams* (I) (1900)
    V *The Interpretation of Dreams* (II) and *On Dreams* (1900–1901)
    VI *The Psychopathology of Everyday Life* (1901)
    VII *A Case of Hysteria, Three Essays on Sexuality and Other Works* (1901–5)
    VIII *Jokes and their Relation to the Unconscious* (1905)
    IX *Jensen's 'Gradiva', and Other Works* (1906–8)
    X *The Cases of 'Little Hans' and the 'Rat Man'* (1909)
    XI *Five Lectures on Psycho-Analysis, Leonardo and Other Works* (1910)
    XII *Case History of Schreber, Papers on Technique, and Other Works* (1911–13)
    XIII *Totem and Taboo and Other Works* (1913–14)
    XIV *On the History of the Psycho-Analytic Movement, Papers on Metapsychology and Other Works* ((1914–16)
    XV *Introductory Lectures on Psycho-Analysis* (Parts I and II) (1915–16)
    XVI *Introductory Lectures on Psycho-Analysis* (Part III) (1916–17)
    XVII *An Infantile Neurosis and Other Works* (1917–19)
    XVIII *Beyond the Pleasure Principle, Group Psychology and Other Works* (1920–22)
    XIX *The Ego and the Id and Other Works* (1923–5)

   xx *An Autobiographical Study, Inhibitions, Symptoms and Anxiety, Lay Analysis and Other Works* (1925–6)
   xxi *The Future of an Illusion, Civilization and its Discontents and Other Works* (1927–31)
   xxii *New Introductory Lectures on Psycho-Analysis and Other Works* (1932–6)
   xxiii *Moses and Monotheism, An Outline of Psycho-Analysis and Other Works* (1937–9)
   xxiv *Indexes and Bibliographies*

– *Two Short Accounts of Psychoanalysis*, Penguin, 1962
– *Minutes of the Vienna Psychoanalytic Society*, ed. Herman Nunberg and Ernst Federn, vol. II, New York: International Universities Press, 1967
– *The Penguin Freud Library*, ed. Angela Richards and Albert Dickson, Penguin, 15 volumes, 1973–86:

    1. *Introductory Lectures on Psychoanalysis*
    2. *New Introductory Lectures on Psychoanalysis*
    3. *Studies on Hysteria*
    4. *The Interpretation of Dreams*
    5. *The Psychopathology of Everyday Life*
    6. *Jokes and their Relation to the Unconscious*
    7. *On Sexuality*
    8. *Case Histories I*
    9. *Case Histories II*
   10. *On Psychopathology*
   11. *On Metapsychology* – The Theory of Psychoanalysis
   12. *Civilization, Society and Religion*
   13. *The Origins of Religion*
   14. *Art and Literature*
   15. *Historical and Expository Works on Psychoanalysis*

– *Cocaine Papers by Sigmund Freud*, ed. Robert Byck, New York: Stonehill, 1974
Freud – Letters
  Collections of letters are listed under their editors, i.e.:
  Sigmund Freud, see Freud, Ernst L. (ed.)
  with Karl Abraham, see Abraham, Hilda C., and Freud, Ernst L. (ed.)
  with Wilhelm Fliess, see Bonaparte, Marie, Freud, Anna, and Kris, Ernst (ed.); Masson, Jeffrey
  with C. G. Jung, see McGuire, William (ed.)
  with Oskar Pfister, see Meng, Heinrich, and Freud, Ernst L. (ed.)

Friday, Nancy, *My Secret Garden: Women's Sexual Fantasies*, Quartet, 1976

– *Men in Love, Men's Sexual Fantasies: The Triumph of Love over Rage*, Hutchinson, 1980

– *My Mother/My Self*, Fontana, 1986

– *Women on Top*, Arrow, 1992

Fromm, Erich, *Sigmund Freud's Mission*, Unwin, 1959

– *The Anatomy of Human Destructiveness*, Penguin, 1977

Frye, Roland Mushat, 'Swift's Yahoos and the Christian Symbols for Sin', *Journal of the History of Ideas*, vol. XV, 1954. pp. 201–17

Gamlin, Linda, 'All in Whose Mind?', *Guardian*, 16 July 1991

Gasman, Daniel, *The Scientific Origins of National Socialism: Social Darwinism in Ernst Haeckel and the German Monist League*, Macdonald, 1971

Gastaut, Henri, *The Epilepsies: Electro Clinical Correlations*, Springfield, Illinois: Charles C. Thomas, 1954

Gauld, Alan, *A History of Hypnotism*, Cambridge University Press, 1992

Gay, Peter, *Freud: A Life for Our Time*, Dent, 1988

Gedo, John E., and Pollock, George H. (ed.), *Freud: The Fusion of Science and Humanism*, New York: International Universities Press, 1976

Gellner, Ernest, *The Psychoanalytic Movement or the Cunning of Unreason*, Paladin, 1985

Glaser, Gilbert H., 'Epilepsy, Hysteria and "Possession": A Historical Essay', *Journal of Nervous and Mental Disease*, vol. 166, 1978, pp. 268–74

Goshen, Charles E. (ed.), *Documentary History of Psychiatry*, Vision, 1967

Gould, Stephen Jay, *Ontogeny and Phylogeny*, Harvard University Press, 1977

Graf, Max, 'Reminiscences of Professor Sigmund Freud', *Psychoanalytic Quarterly*, XI, 1942, pp. 465–76

Gravil, Richard (ed.), *Swift, 'Gulliver's Travels': A Casebook*, Macmillan, 1974

Griffin, Susan, *Pornography and Silence*, Women's Press, 1981

Groddeck, Georg W., *The Book of the It* (1923), Vision Press, 1979

Grosskurth, Phyllis, *Havelock Ellis: A Biography*, New York University Press, 1985

– *Melanie Klein: Her World and Her Work*, Hodder and Stoughton, 1986

– *The Secret Ring: Freud's Inner Circle and the Politics of Psychoanalysis*, Jonathan Cape, 1991

Grünbaum, Adolf, *The Foundations of Psychoanalysis: A Philosophical Critique*, University of California Press, 1984

Guillain, Georges, *J. M. Charcot, 1825–1893: His Life, His Work* (1955), New York: Hoeber, 1959

Gutheil, Emil A. (ed.), *Autobiography of Wilhelm Stekel: The Life Story of a Pioneer Psychoanalyst*, New York: Liveright, 1950

Guttman, Samuel A., Jones, Randall L., and Parrish, Stephen M. (ed.), *The Concordance to the Standard Edition of the Complete Psychological Works of Sigmund Freud*, 6 volumes, Boston: G. K. Hall, 1980

Hacking, Ian, *Rewriting the Soul: Multiple Personality and the Sciences of Memory*, Princeton University Press, 1995

Haeckel, Ernst, *The Evolution of Man* (1874), Watts, 1906

– *The Riddle of the Universe* (1899), Watts, 1929

Hare, E. H., 'Masturbatory Insanity: The History of an Idea', *Journal of Mental Science*, vol. 108, 1962, pp. 1–25

– 'Medical Astrology and Its Relation to Modern Psychiatry', *Proceedings of the Royal Society of Medicine*, vol. 70, 1977, pp. 105–9

Harrington, Anne, *Medicine, Mind and the Double Brain*, Princeton University Press, 1987

Hawking, Stephen, *A Brief History of Time*, Bantam, 1988

Hecaen, Henri, and Albert, Martin A., *Human Neuropsychology*, Wiley, 1978

Heine, Heinrich, *Poetry and Prose*, ed. Jost Herman and Robert C. Holub, trans. Louis Untermeyer, New York: Continuum, 1982

Herman, Judith Lewis, *Father–Daughter Incest*, Harvard University Press, 1981

– *Trauma and Recovery*, New York: Basic Books, 1992

Herman, Judith, and Schatzow, Emily, 'Time-Limited Group Therapy for Women with a History of Incest', *International Journal of Group Psychotherapy*, vol. 34, 1984, pp. 605–16

– 'Recovery and Verification of Memories of Childhood Sexual Trauma', *Psychoanalytic Psychology*, vol. 4, 1987, pp. 1–14

Hierons, Raymond, 'Charcot and His Visits to Britain', *British Medical Journal*, vol. 307, December 1993, pp. 1589–91

Hill, Christopher, *The World Turned Upside Down*, Penguin, 1975

Hirschmüller, Albrecht, *The Life and Work of Josef Breuer*, New York University Press, 1989

Hobbes, Thomas, *Leviathan* (1651), Fontana, 1962

Holmes, Jeremy, *John Bowlby and Attachment Theory*, Routledge, 1993

Holt, Robert R., *Freud Reappraised: A Fresh Look at Psychoanalytic Theory*, New York: The Guilford Press, 1989

Hooykaas, R., *Religion and the Rise of Modern Science*, Scottish Academic Press, 1972

Hudson, Liam, *Contrary Imaginations: A Psychological Study of the English Schoolboy*, Methuen, 1966

– *Frames of Mind: Ability, Perception and Self-Perception in the Arts and the Sciences*, Methuen, 1968

Hudson, Liam (ed.), *The Ecology of Human Intelligence*, Penguin, 1970
Hughes, Ted, *Winter Pollen: Occasional Prose*, Faber, 1994
Humphrey, Nicholas, *A History of the Mind*, Chatto and Windus, 1992
– 'The Function of the Intellect' in P. P. G. Bateson and R. A. Hinde
  (ed.), *Growing Points in Ethology*, Cambridge University Press, 1976
Hunter, Richard A., 'Psychiatry and Neurology: Psychosyndrome or
  Brain Disease', *Proceedings of the Royal Society of Medicine*, vol. 66, April
  1973, pp. 359–64
Hunter, Richard A., and Macalpine, Ida, *Three Hundred Years of
  Psychiatry, 1535–1860*, Oxford University Press, 1983
Hurst, Arthur F., *The Psychology of the Special Senses and Their Functional
  Disorders*, London, 1920
Hurst, Lindsay, 'What Was Wrong with Anna O.?', *Journal of the Royal
  Society of Medicine*, vol. 75, 1982, pp. 129–31
Israëls, Han, and Schatzman, Morton, 'The Seduction Theory', *History
  of Psychiatry*, vol. IV, 1993, pp. 23–59
Jackson, John Hughlings, *Selected Writings of John Hughlings Jackson*, 2
  vols, Hodder and Stoughton, 1931–2
Jahanbegloo, Ramin, *Conversations with Isaiah Berlin*, Peter Halban, 1992
Johnson, Paul, *A History of the Jews*, Weidenfeld and Nicolson, 1987
Jones, Ernest, *Sigmund Freud: Life and Work*, 3 vols, Hogarth Press
  (1953–7); vol. 1, 2nd edition, 1954; vol. 2, 2nd edition, 1958; vol. 3,
  1st edition, 1957. *The Life and Work of Sigmund Freud*, 3 vols, New
  York: Basic Books, 1953–7
– *Free Associations: Memories of a Psycho-Analyst*, 1959
– *The Life and Work of Sigmund Freud*, edited and abridged by Lionel
  Trilling and Steven Marcus, Penguin, 1964
– *Psycho-Myth, Psycho-History: Essays in Applied Psychoanalysis*, vol. 2, New
  York: Stonehill Publishing, 1974
Jung, C. G., *The Collected Works of C. G. Jung*, Princeton University
  Press, 1953–74
– *Psychological Reflections*, Routledge and Kegan Paul, 1953
– *Memories, Dreams, Reflections*, Routledge and Kegan Paul, 1963
– *Modern Man in Search of a Soul*, Routledge and Kegan Paul, 1960
Kaplan, Harold I., and Sadock, Benjamin J. (ed.), *Comprehensive Textbook
  of Psychiatry V*, 5th edition, Baltimore: Williams and Wilkins, 1989
Karpman, Ben, 'Neurotic Traits of Jonathan Swift', *Psychoanalytic Review*,
  vol. 29, 1942, pp. 165–84
Katon, Wayne, Lin, Elizabeth, Von Korff, Michael, Russo, Joan,
  Lipscomb, Patricia, and Bush, Terry, 'Somatization: A Spectrum of
  Severity', *American Journal of Psychiatry*, vol. 148: 1, January 1991,
  pp. 34–40

Kelly, Alfred, *The Descent of Darwin: The Popularization of Darwin in Germany, 1860–1914*, University of North Carolina Press, 1981

Kendrick, Walter, 'Not Just Another Oedipal Drama: The Unsinkable Sigmund Freud', *Voice Literary Supplement*, June 1984, pp. 12–16

Kenny, Anthony, *The Metaphysics of Mind*, Oxford University Press, 1989

Kerr, John, *A Most Dangerous Method: The Story of Jung, Freud and Sabina Spielrein*, Sinclair Stevenson, 1994

Kirk, Stuart A., and Kutchins, Herb, *The Selling of DSM: The Rhetoric of Science in Psychiatry*, New York: A. de Gruyter, 1992

Kitcher, Patricia, *Freud's Dream: A Complete Interdisciplinary Science of Mind*, MIT Press, 1992

Klawans, Harold L., *Toscanini's Fumble and Other Tales of Clinical Neurology*, The Bodley Head, 1989

Klein, Melanie, *The Psychoanalysis of Children*, Hogarth Press, 1975

Koranyi, Erwin K., 'Morbidity and Rate of Undiagnosed Physical Illnesses in a Psychiatric Clinic Population', *Archives of General Psychiatry*, vol. 36, April 1979, pp. 414–19

Kovel, Joel, *White Racism: A Psychohistory*, Allen Lane, 1972

Kubie, Lawrence, 'The Fantasy of Dirt', *Psychoanalytic Quarterly*, vol. VI, 1937, pp. 388–425

Kuhn, Thomas S., *The Structure of Scientific Revolutions*, University of Chicago Press, 1970

Kuper, Adam, *Anthropologists and Anthropology: The British School 1922–72*, Penguin, 1973

Laidlaw, John, Richens, Alan, and Oxley, Jolyon (ed.), *A Textbook of Epilepsy*, 3rd edition, Churchill Livingstone, 1988

Laing, R. D., *The Divided Self*, Pelican, 1965

Lawson, Annette, *Adultery: An Analysis of Love and Betrayal*, Oxford University Press, 1990

Leach, Edmund, *Lévi-Strauss*, Fontana, 1970

Lee, R. S., *Freud and Christianity* (1948), Penguin, 1967

Legman, Gershon, *Rationale of the Dirty Joke*, first series, Jonathan Cape, 1969; *No Laughing Matter: Rationale of the Dirty Joke*, second series, Granada Publishing, 1978

Lennox, W. G., *Epilepsy and Related Disorders*, Churchill, 1966

Lesser, R. P., Lüders, H., and Dinner, D. S., 'Evidence for Epilepsy is Rare in Patients with Psychogenic Seizures', *Neurology*, vol. 33, 1983, pp. 502–4

Lesser, R. P., Lüders, H., Conomy, J. P., Furlan, A. J., and Dinner, D. S., 'Sensory Seizure Mimicking a Psychogenic Seizure', *Neurology*, vol. 33, 1983, pp. 800–802

Lévi-Strauss, Claude, *Totemism*, Penguin, 1969

Lewis, A., ' "Psychogenic": A Word and Its Mutations', *Psychological Medicine*, vol. 2, 1985, pp. 209–15

Lipowski, Z. J., 'What Does the Word "Psychosomatic" Really Mean? A Historical and Semantic Inquiry', *Psychosomatic Medicine*, vol. 46, 1984, pp. 153–71

– 'Somatization: The Concept and Its Clinical Application', *American Journal of Psychiatry*, vol. 145: 11, November 1988, pp. 1358–68

Lishman, William Alwyn, *Organic Psychiatry: The Psychological Consequences of Cerebral Disorder*, 2nd edition, Oxford: Blackwell, 1987

Loftus, Elizabeth, and Ketcham, Katherine, *The Myth of Repressed Memory: False Memories and Allegations of Sexual Abuse*, New York: St Martin's Press, 1994

Macmillan, Malcolm, *Freud Evaluated: The Completed Arc*, Amsterdam: New Holland, 1991

Malcolm, Janet, *Psychoanalysis: The Impossible Profession* (1982), London: Karnac Ltd, 1988

– *In the Freud Archives*, Jonathan Cape, 1984

Malcolmson, Kenneth G., 'Globus Hystericus Vel Pharyngis', *Journal of Laryngology and Otology*, vol. 82, 1968, pp. 219–30

Manuel, Frank, *The Religion of Isaac Newton*, Oxford: Clarendon Press, 1974

Marsden, C. D., 'Hysteria – A Neurologist's View', *Psychological Medicine*, vol. 16, 1986, pp. 277–88

Marsden, C. David, and Fowler, Timothy J. (ed.), *Clinical Neurology*, Edward Arnold, 1989

Martin, Alfred E., 'The Occurrence of Remissions and Recovery in Tuberculous Meningitis: A Critical Review', *Brain*, 1909, pp. 209–31

Masson, Jeffrey, *The Assault on Truth: Freud's Suppression of the Seduction Theory*, New York: Farrar, Straus and Giroux, Inc., 1984; published with a new preface and afterword, Penguin, 1985; reissued with new preface under the title *The Assault on Truth: Freud and Child Sexual Abuse*, HarperCollins, 1992

– *Against Therapy: Emotional Tyranny and the Myth of Psychological Healing*, Fontana, 1990

– *Final Analysis: The Making and Unmaking of a Psychoanalyst*, Fontana, 1992

Masson, Jeffrey (ed.), *The Complete Letters of Sigmund Freud to Wilhelm Fliess 1887–1904*, Harvard University Press, 1985; *Sigmund Freud: Briefe an Wilhelm Fliess 1887–1904*, Frankfurt am Main: Fischer, 1986

Mathias, Peter (ed.), *Science and Society 1600–1900*, Cambridge University Press, 1972

McClelland, David C., *The Roots of Consciousness*, Princeton: D. Van Nostrand Co., 1964

McDougall, William, *Psychoanalysis and Social Psychology*, Methuen, 1936

McGinn, Colin, *The Problem of Consciousness*, Oxford: Blackwell, 1991

McGuire, William (ed.), *The Freud/Jung Letters*, Hogarth Press and Routledge and Kegan Paul, 1974

McWilliam, Candia, 'The Importance of Writing to Ernest', *Independent on Sunday*, 23 May 1993

Medawar, P. B., review of Irving S. Cooper's *The Victim Is Always the Same*, *New York Review of Books*, 23 January 1975

– *The Limits of Science*, Oxford University Press, 1985

Meng, Heinrich, and Freud, Ernst (ed.), *Psychoanalysis and Faith: The Letters of Sigmund Freud and Oskar Pfister*, New York: Basic Books, 1963

Merskey, Harold, *The Analysis of Hysteria*, Baillière Tindall, 1979

– *Does Hysteria Still Exist?*, Welwyn Garden City: SK&F Publications, Smith Kline and French Laboratories Ltd, 1983

Micale, Mark S., 'Hysteria and Its Historiography: A Review of Past and Present Writings', *History of Science*, vol. 27, 1989, pp. 223–61, 319–51

– 'Charcot and the Idea of Hysteria in the Male', *Medical History*, vol. 34, 1990, pp. 363–411

– 'Hysteria and Its Historiography: The Future Perspective', *History of Psychiatry*, vol. 1, 1990, pp. 33–124

– 'On the "Disappearance" of Hysteria: A Study in the Clinical Deconstruction of a Diagnosis', *Isis*, vol. 84, September 1993, pp. 496–526

Micale, Mark S., and Porter, Roy (ed.), *Discovering the History of Psychiatry*, New York: Oxford University Press, 1994

Midgley, Mary, *Science as Salvation: A Modern Myth and Its Meaning*, Routledge and Kegan Paul, 1992

Mill, John Stuart, *On Liberty*, Penguin, 1985

Miller, Alice, *Thou Shalt Not be Aware: Society's Betrayal of the Child*, Pluto Press, 1985

Miller, Laurence, *Freud's Brain: Neuropsychodynamic Foundations of Psychoanalysis*, New York: The Guilford Press, 1991

Newson, John and Elizabeth, *Patterns of Infant Care in an Urban Community*, Penguin, 1965

– *Four Years Old in an Urban Community*, Penguin, 1970

– *Seven Years Old in the Home Environment*, Penguin, 1978

Nietzsche, Friedrich, *The Birth of Tragedy and the Genealogy of Morals*, trans. Francis Golffing, New York: Doubleday, 1956

Nineham, D. E., *The Gospel of St Mark*, Pelican New Testament Commentaries, 1963

Nolte, Ernst, *Three Faces of Fascism*, New York: Mentor, 1969
Noonan, John T., Jr., *Contraception: A History of Its Treatment by the Catholic Theologians and Canonists*, Harvard University Press, 1965
O'Neill, W. M., *The Beginnings of Modern Psychology*, Penguin, 1968
Ofshe, Richard, and Watters, Ethan, *Making Monsters: False Memories, Psychotherapy and Sexual Hysteria*, New York: Scribner's, 1994
Orr-Andrawes, Alison, 'The Case of Anna O.: A Neuropsychiatric Perspective', *Journal of the American Psychoanalytic Association*, vol. 35, 1987, pp. 387–419
Owen, A. R. G., *Hysteria, Hypnosis and Healing: The Work of J.-M. Charcot*, Dobson, 1971
Pappenheim, Else, 'Freud and Gilles de la Tourette: Diagnostic Speculations on "Frau Emmy von N."', *International Review of Psychoanalysis*, vol. 7, 1980, pp. 265–77
Pendergrast, Mark, *Victims of Memory: Incest Accusations and Shattered Lives*, Hinesberg, Vermont: Upper Access Inc., 1995
Peters, Uwe Henrik, *Anna Freud: Her Father's Daughter*, Weidenfeld and Nicolson, 1985
Pierson, Stanley, *Marxism and the Origins of British Socialism: The Struggle for a New Consciousness*, Cornell University Press, 1973
Piñero, J. M. López, *Historical Origins of the Concept of Neurosis* (1963), Cambridge University Press, 1983
Pinker, Steven, *The Language Instinct: The New Science of Language and Mind*, Penguin, 1994.
Poliakov, Léon, *The History of Anti-Semitism*, vols 1–3, Routledge and Kegan Paul, 1974–5; vol. 4, Oxford University Press, 1985
Popper, Karl, *Conjectures and Refutations*, Routledge and Kegan Paul, 1972
Powell, Russell A., and Boer, Douglas P., 'Did Freud Mislead Patients to Confabulate Memories of Abuse?', *Psychological Reports*, vol. 74, 1994, pp. 1283–98
Rabelais, François, *Gargantua and Pantagruel* (1532–52), trans. J. M. Cohen, Penguin, 1955
Rather, L. J., *Mind and Body in Eighteenth Century Medicine*, Berkeley: University of California Press, 1965
Reynolds, Reginald, *Cleanliness and Godliness*, Allen and Unwin, 1943
Rieff, Philip, *Freud: The Mind of the Moralist*, University of Chicago Press, 1959
Roazen, Paul, *Brother Animal: The Story of Freud and Tausk*, Penguin, 1973
– *Freud and His Followers*, Penguin, 1979
Roberts, J. M., *The Pelican History of the World*, Pelican, 1980

Robinson, J. A. T., *Honest to God*, SCM Press Ltd, 1963

Robinson, Paul, *Freud and His Critics*, University of California Press, 1993

Rogge, O. John, *Why Men Confess*, New York: Da Capo, 1975

Romanes, George, *Mental Evolution in Animals*, London, 1883

– *Mental Evolution in Man: Origin of Human Faculty*, London, 1888

Rose, Hilary, *Love, Power and Knowledge: Towards a Feminist Transformation of the Sciences*, Polity Press, 1994

Rose, Steven, *The Making of Memory: From Molecules to Mind*, Bantam, 1993

Rose, Steven, Lewontin, R. C., and Kamin, Leon J., *Not in Our Genes: Biology, Ideology and Human Nature*, Penguin, 1984

Rossi, Ino (ed.), *The Unconscious in Culture: The Structuralism of Claude Lévi-Strauss in Perspective*, New York: E. P. Dutton, 1974

Roudinesco, Elisabeth, *Jacques Lacan & Co.: A History of Psychoanalysis in France, 1925–1985*, Free Association Books, 1990

Roustang, François, *Dire Mastery: Discipleship from Freud to Lacan*, Washington: American Psychiatric Press, 1986

Roy, Alec (ed.), *Hysteria*, John Wiley, 1982

Russell, C. A. (ed.), *Science and Religious Belief: A Selection of Recent Historical Studies*, University of London Press Ltd, 1973

Rutter, Michael, *Maternal Deprivation Reassessed*, 2nd edition, Penguin, 1981

Rycroft, Charles, *A Critical Dictionary of Psychoanalysis*, Penguin, 1972

Rycroft, Charles (ed.), *Psychoanalysis Observed*, Penguin, 1968

Ryle, Gilbert, *The Concept of Mind* (1949), Penguin, 1963

Sacks, Oliver, *Migraine: Evolution of a Common Disorder*, revised edition, Pan, 1981

– *The Man Who Mistook His Wife for a Hat*, Picador, 1986

Sargant, William, *Battle for the Mind*, Pan, 1959

Satow, Roberta, 'Where Has All the Hysteria Gone?', *Psychoanalytic Review*, I, lxvi, 1979, pp. 463–77

Sayers, Janet, *Mothering Psychoanalysis: Helene Deutsch, Karen Horney, Anna Freud and Melanie Klein*, Hamish Hamilton, 1991

Schatzman, Morton, *Soul Murder: Persecution in the Family*, Allen Lane, 1973

– 'Freud: Who Seduced Whom?', *New Scientist*, 21 March 1992, pp. 34–7

Schreiber, Flora Rheta, *Sybil*, Chicago: Regnery, 1973

Schur, Max (ed.), *Drives, Affects, Behaviour*, vol. 2, New York: International Universities Press, 1965

Schur, Max, *Freud: Living and Dying*, Hogarth Press, 1972

Schweitzer, Albert, *The Quest of the Historical Jesus* (1906), Macmillan, 1961

Shapiro, A. K., Shapiro, E. S., Bruun, R. L., and Sweet, R. D., *Gilles de la Tourette's Syndrome*, New York: Raven Press, 1978

Shapiro, Arthur K., and Shapiro, Elaine, 'Tic Disorders' in Harold I. Kaplan and Benjamin J. Sadock (ed.), *Comprehensive Textbook of Psychiatry V*, 5th edition, Baltimore: Williams and Wilkins, 1989

Sheed, F. J. (ed.), *Soundings in Satanism*, Mowbrays, 1972

Shorter, Edward, *From Paralysis to Fatigue: A History of Psychosomatic Illness in the Modern Era*, New York: Free Press, 1992

Sicherman, Barbara, 'The Uses of a Diagnosis: Doctors, Patients and Neurasthenia', *Journal of the History of Medicine*, vol. XXXII, 1977, pp. 33–54

Sinason, Valerie (ed.), *Treating Survivors of Satanist Abuse*, Routledge, 1994

Slater, Eliot, 'Diagnosis of "Hysteria"', *British Medical Journal*, 29 May 1965, pp. 1395–9

– 'What Is "Hysteria"?' (1976) in Alec Roy (ed.), *Hysteria*, John Wiley, 1982, pp. 37–40

Slavney, Phillip R., *Perspectives on 'Hysteria'*, Johns Hopkins University Press, 1990

Smith-Rosenberg, Carroll, 'The Hysterical Woman: Sex Roles and Role Conflict in 19th-Century America', *Social Research*, vol. 39, 1972, pp. 652–78

Spurling, Laurence (ed.), *Sigmund Freud: Critical Assessments*, 4 volumes, Routledge, 1989

Stadlen, Anthony, 'Was Dora "Ill"?' in Laurence Spurling (ed.), *Sigmund Freud: Critical Assessments*, vol. 2, Routledge, 1989, pp. 196–203

Starr, Susan Leigh, *Regions of the Mind: Brain Research and the Quest for Scientific Certainty*, Stanford University Press, 1989

Stengers, Jean, and Van Neck, Anne, *Histoire d'une grande peur: la masturbation*, Editions de l'Université de Bruxelles, 1984

Stepansky, Paul E. (ed.), *Freud: Appraisals and Reappraisals*, Contributions to Freud Studies, vol. 1, New Jersey: The Analytic Press, 1986

Stewart, Donna E., 'The Changing Face of Somatization', *Psychosomatics*, vol. 31, no. 2, 1990, pp. 153–8

Stoltenberg, John, *Refusing to Be a Man*, Fontana, 1990

Stone, Lawrence, *The Family, Sex and Marriage in England 1500–1800*, Penguin, 1979

Storr, Anthony, *Churchill's Black Dog*, Collins, 1989

– *Freud*, Oxford University Press, 1989

Sulloway, Frank J., *Freud, Biologist of the Mind: Beyond the Psychoanalytic Legend*, Burnett Books/André Deutsch, 1979

– 'Reassessing Freud's Case Histories. The Social Construction of
   Psychoanalysis', *Isis*, vol. 82, 1991, pp. 245–75
Swales, Peter, 'Freud, Minna Bernays and the Conquest of Rome: New
   Light on the Origins of Psychoanalysis', *New American Review*, I, 1982,
   pp. 1–23
– 'Freud, His Teacher and the Birth of Psychoanalysis' in Paul E.
   Stepansky (ed.), *Freud: Appraisals and Reappraisals*, Contributions to
   Freud Studies, vol. 1, New Jersey: The Analytic Press, 1986, pp. 3–82
– Letter to *The Times Literary Supplement*, 3 August 1990
Swift, Jonathan, *Gulliver's Travels*, Penguin, 1967
Szasz, Thomas S., 'Freud as Leader', *Antioch Review*, vol. XXIII, 1963,
   pp. 133–44
– *The Myth of Mental Illness*, Paladin, 1972
Talese, Gay, *Thy Neighbour's Wife*, Pan, 1980
Tallis, Raymond, *Not Saussure: A Critique of Post-Saussurean Literary
   Theory*, Macmillan, 1988
– *The Explicit Animal: A Defence of Human Consciousness*, Macmillan, 1991
Tavris, Carol, 'Assault on Freud', *Discover – The Newsmagazine of Science*,
   April 1984, pp. 45–51
– *Anger: The Misunderstood Emotion* (1982), New York: Simon and
   Schuster, revised Touchstone edition, 1989
– *The Mismeasure of Woman*, New York: Simon and Schuster, 1992
Tawney, R. H., *Religion and the Rise of Capitalism*, Penguin, 1938
Taylor, Graeme J., review of Edward Shorter's *From Paralysis to Fatigue:
   A History of Psychosomatic Illness in the Modern Era*, *Psychosomatic Medicine*,
   vol. 55, no. 1, 1993, pp. 88–9
Thomas, Keith, *Religion and the Decline of Magic*, Penguin, 1978
– review of *Against the Current*, *Observer*, 1980
Thornton, E. M., *Hypnosis, Hysteria and Epilepsy: An Historical Synthesis*,
   Heinemann Medical, 1976
– *The Freudian Fallacy: Freud and Cocaine*, Paladin, 1986 (first published
   in Britain by Blond and Briggs Ltd, 1983, under the title *Freud and
   Cocaine*)
Timpanaro, Sebastiano, *The Freudian Slip: Psycho-Analysis and Textual
   Criticism*, New Left Books, 1976
Trachtenberg, Joshua, *The Devil and the Jews*, Yale University Press,
   1943
Trauner, Doris, 'Seizure Disorders' in Wigbert C. Wiederholt (ed.),
   Neurology for Non-Neurologists, Philadelphia: Grune and Stratton,
   1988
Trilling, Lionel, Introduction to Ernest Jones, *The Life and Work of
   Sigmund Freud*, edited and abridged by Lionel Trilling and Steven
   Marcus, Penguin, 1964

Tuke, D. Hack (ed.), *Dictionary of Psychological Medicine*, Churchill, 1892

Updike, John, Introduction to F. J. Sheed (ed.), *Soundings in Satanism*, Mowbrays, 1972

Veith, Ilza, *Hysteria: The History of a Disease*, University of Chicago Press, 1965

Vickers, Brian, *Appropriating Shakespeare: Contemporary Critical Quarrels*, Yale University Press, 1993

Walshe, Sir Francis, 'The Diagnosis of Hysteria', *British Medical Journal*, 2, 1965, pp. 1451–4

Walzer, Michael, *The Revolution of the Saints*, Weidenfeld and Nicolson, 1979

Weber, Max, *The Protestant Ethic and the Spirit of Capitalism*, Allen and Unwin, 1930

Webster, Richard, 'The Cult of Lacan', *Quarto*, May 1981

– *A Brief History of Blasphemy: Liberalism, Censorship and 'The Satanic Verses'*, The Orwell Press, 1990

– 'The Body Politic and the Politics of the Body: The Religious Origins of Western Secularism' in John Keane (ed.), *The Decline of Secularism? New Perspectives*, in press

Weiss, Edoardo, *Sigmund Freud as a Consultant: Recollections of a Pioneer in Psychoanalysis*, New York: Intercontinental Medical Book Corp., 1970

White, Victor, *God and the Unconscious*, Fontana, 1960

Whyte, Lancelot Law, *The Unconscious Before Freud*, Social Science Paperbacks, 1967

Wiederholt, Wigbert C. (ed.), *Neurology for Non-Neurologists*, Philadelphia: Grune and Stratton, 1988

Wilcocks, Robert, *Maelzel's Chess Player: Sigmund Freud and the Rhetoric of Deceit*, Lanham, Maryland: Rowman and Littlefield, 1994

Williamson, P. D., Spencer, D. D., Spencer, S. S., Novelly, R. A., and Mattson, R. H., 'Complex Partial Seizures of Frontal Lobe Origin', *Annals of Neurology*, vol. 18, 1985, pp. 497–504

Wilson, E. O., *Sociobiology: The New Synthesis*, Harvard University Press, 1975

– *On Human Nature*, Harvard University Press, 1978

Winnicott, D. W., *Collected Papers: Through Paediatrics to Psychoanalysis*, Hogarth Press, 1975

Wittels, Fritz, *Sigmund Freud: His Personality, His Teaching and His School*, Allen and Unwin, 1924

Wittgenstein, Ludwig, 'Conversations on Freud', noted by Rush Rhees in Richard Wollheim and James Hopkins (ed.), *Philosophical Essays on Freud*, Cambridge University Press, 1982

Wollheim, Richard, *Freud*, Fontana, 1971; 2nd edition with
   Supplementary Preface, 1991
Wollheim, Richard, and Hopkins, James (ed.), *Philosophical Essays on
   Freud*, Cambridge University Press, 1982
Wortis, Joseph, *Fragment of an Analysis with Freud*, New York: Simon
   and Schuster, 1954
Wren-Lewis, John, 'Love's Coming of Age' in Charles Rycroft (ed.),
   Psychoanalysis Observed, Penguin, 1968
Wright, Lawrence, *Remembering Satan*, Serpent's Tail, 1994
Young-Bruehl, Elisabeth, *Anna Freud*, Macmillan, 1989

Index

References to Freud's works are to be found grouped under the entry for Freud.

Abraham, Karl, 335, 361, 369, 382, 391, 393–4
abreaction, 107–8, 169, 575
abuse, *see* sexual abuse
Académie des Sciences, 92, 96
actual neuroses, 188, 261
Adair, Gilbert, 445, 608
Adler, Alfred, 367, 379, 392, 399
    diverges from Freud, 358–9
    ejected as 'heretic', 310, 362
    Freud leads attack on, 359–60
    Jung on, 380
    'terrorism and *Sadismus*' of, 360
    and Wednesday Society, 304, 335
adultery, 275, 341, 343, 602
affection, 36, 38, 406
    Paul on crucifixion of, 496
    Puritan contempt for, 449
agoraphobia, 23, 186, 262
'Aliquis' episode, 592–3
algorithmic compression, 261
American Psychiatric Association, 519, 531, 533, 535, 626
American Psychoanalytic Association, 395
amnesia, 57, 128
anaesthesia, 64, 65, 91
anal character, 325
anal-erotism, development of concept, 233–4, 287–9, 291, 317, 325–6
anal sadism, 237, 325
anal stage, 233–4, 286
Andreas-Salomé, Lou, 324, 360, 415, 423
animal spirits, 179
Anna O. case (Breuer), 103–135, 147, 150–2, 155, 228
    absences, 104

contractures, 113–114
hallucinations, 104, 110–1
hysteria diagnosis, 104, 112, 121–2, 137
language disorder, 110–1, 115–7, 120
myth of cure, 51, 110–12, 122–5, 136, 144, 205, 228
'phantom pregnancy', 133–5
rediagnosis by Hurst, 119
rediagnosis by Orr-Andrawes, 119–21
rediagnosis by Putnam, 627
rediagnosis by Thornton, 114–8, 577–8
rediagnoses rejected by Hirschmüller, 578–9
role in Freud legend, 132–5
spontaneous remission and therapy, 125–31
stocking caprice, 122–4
symptoms, 104–5, 106–7, 110, 112–13
wish fulfilment, case as example of, 131
anorexia, 66, 95, 186, 294, 407–8
anti-semitism:
    and Christianity, 325, 326–7, 329, 427, 617
    and Freud's academic career, 279
    Freud's encounters with, 16, 369, 427
    Freud's internalisation of, 360
    Jung's, 375, 389
    role of projection in, 326–7, 329, 600
anus, 208–9, 232–3, 283, 285–6, 289

anxiety:
  attacks, 156–7, 197
  children's play and, 432
  confession and, 343
  in Katharina case, 156–7
  neurasthenia and, 186
  neurosis, 188, 586
  Original Sin and, 321
aphasia, 116, 120
apocalypticism:
  and fantasy of purity, 311, 377, 477, 617
  Anna Freud and secularised, 405
  Jewish, 20
  'medicalised', 582
  rational apocalypticism and Freud, 622–3
  sheep-and-goats habit of mind, 324
  see also demonology, Freud, Jesus, Judaeo-Christian tradition, messianism
Appleby, Joyce, 561, 621, 624
Appleyard, Bryan, 450, 497–8
Aquinas, Thomas, 445
arc-de-cercle (arc-en-ciel), 58, 86, 87, 573, see also epilepsy, frontal lobe
Archer, John, 98
Aristotle, 106, 505
Armstrong, Karen, 158, 564
Arnoux, Danièle, 469
Aschaffenburg, Gustav, 368
associationism, physiological, 165, 170, 171
astrology, 166, 385, 438
atheism, 443, 502
Auden, W. H., 10
Augustine, St, 243, 314, 316, 321, 495–6
authority:
  Adler's claims to, 359
  Charcot's, 99, 101
  Freud and Breuer, 134
  Freud's, 304, 359, 378
  role in medicine, 132
auto-eroticism, 233, 415

babies, 36
  as penises, 289–90
Babinski, Joseph, 85, 92, 531, 549–52
Bacon, Francis, 489, 490
Bakan, David, 314, 564
Balint, Michael, 398

Bannister, Donald, 562–3
Barthes, Roland, 477
Bass, Ellen, 522–4
Beard, George M., 138, 185–7
behaviour, study of:
  in relation to brain, 486–8
  theological aversion to, 465–8, 474
  versus theory of mind, 460–76
behaviourism, 479, 615
Bellamy, Edward, 582
Benedikt, Moritz, 17, 109, 574
Bentham, Jeremy, 485
Berger, Alfred, 106
Berkley-Hill, Owen, 326
Berlin, Isaiah, 443–5, 451
Berlin Psychoanalytic Society, 423
Bernard of Gordon, 77–8
Bernays, Jacob, 106
Bernays, Martha, see Freud
Bernays, Minna (Freud's sister-in-law), 428
  Anna's relationship with, 406, 407, 424
  Freud's possible affair with, 275, 378, 592–3
Bernheim, Hippolyte, 81–2, 92–3, 94–6, 155, 161
Bettelheim, Bruno, 8
Betts, T. A., 551, 569
Billen, Andrew, 562
Billinsky, John M., 592, 604
Binnie, Colin, ix, 86–8, 572, 573
Binswanger, Ludwig, 238, 362, 369
biogenetic law, 229–32, 234, 236–7, 239–40
biology:
  biologists 'all wrong', 240
  evolutionary theory, 310–11, 453
  Fliess's periodicity theory, 222–3, 225
  Haeckel's biogenetic law, 229–32, 234, 236–7, 239–40
  importance of heredity to Freud, 293
  Lamarckian theory, 4, 236, 240, 388
  neural Darwinism, 454
  as origin of Freud's theories, 17, 179, 240
  theory of human nature, 457
birth:
  theory of anal, 289–91
  trauma, 393

Blackburn, Simon, 483
Blake, William, 107
Bleuler, Eugen, 182, 300, 368
Bloom, Harold, 3
body:
 behaviour and, 486–8
 consciousness and, 484–5
 evolutionary biology and, 484
 and impurity, 342, 461–6, 505
 intelligence of, 485, 510
 mind and, 461–6, 502
 mind as cause of bodily disease,
  66–7, 82, 97–9
 soul and, 461–6
 spirit and, 4, 311, 461–6
 unity of brain and, 485–6, 616
Boer, Douglas P., 625
Bohr, Niels, 449
Bölsche, Wilhelm, 233–4, 294
Bonaparte, Marie, 218–19, 427
Bowlby, John, 8, 556, 491
Boyle, Robert, 442, 489, 508
Braid, James, 62, 87–8
Brain, 106
Brain, Russell, 535
brain:
 associationism and, 165
 brain-body dualism, 486
 cocaine and, 221
 Damasio on emotions and, 619
 Edelman's work on, 454, 459–60,
  475
 'Hysteria Following Brain Injury',
  630
 imaging, 73, 137
 injury, 73, 76, 116, 117
 learning and structural change in,
  487–8
 lesions, 42, 59–60, 67, 68, 73, 80,
  84, 90, 115, 121, 201
 mythology, 178, 213
 study of, 42, 89, 178, 478
 tumour, 86, 141, 152, 159
 unity of body and, 485–6, 616
 visceral brain, 79
 see also Edelman, epilepsy
breast-feeding, 36, 285, 402
Breuer, Josef, 51, 102, 103–135
 Anna O. *see* Anna O. case
 befriends Freud, 103
 cathartic method, 106–9, 117,
  122–3, 135, 136, 143, 163, 195–6

collaboration with Freud, 104–10
Freud breaks with, 217, 361
on Freud's excessive generalisation,
  218, 261
influence on Freud, 102, 103, 134,
  183–4, 217–18, 226, 228, 251,
  313, 502
lacks 'Faustian' ambition, 133
'On the Psychical Mechanism of
  Hysterical Phenomena', 195
Studies on Hysteria, 106, 110, 113,
  115–16, 122, 131–2, 137, 155,
  168–9, 182
 see also Anna O. case
Breughel, Pieter, 318
Bridges, Paul, 631
Brill, A. A., 335
Briquet, Paul, 57
British Medical Journal, 530
British Psycho-Analytical Society,
  356
Brown, Norman O., 5, 284, 477
Brown, Theodore M., 565, 631
Brücke, Ernst: 41–2, 103
 influence on Freud, 41–2, 69, 102,
  178, 183, 367
 zeal for physicism and mechanism,
  41
Bullitt, William, 427
Bultmann, Rudolf Karl, 18
Bumke, 530
Bunsen, Robert, 227
Burchard, Bishop of Worms, 339
Burghölzli hospital, 368, 369
Burlingham, Bob, 421–2, 425
Burlingham, Dorothy, 421, 426–7,
  428
Burlingham, Mabbie, 422, 425
Burlingham, Robert, 426
Burq, Victor, 61, 90–2, 94

Cäcilie M., Frau, 582
Canetti, Elias, 500
Carey, John, 614
Carpenter, Edward, 384
Carpenter, W. B., 529
Carter, Robert, 56
case histories, *see* Anna O., Dora and
  Freud: case histories
castration anxiety, 267, 419
 castration, threat of, 255
catalepsy, 63–4, 82, 83, *see also* epilepsy

cathartic method:
    abreaction, 107–8
    Anna O. case, 117, 122–3
    development of, 106–9, 135, 136,
        153, 195
    Emmy von N. case, 143, 148–9
    origins of, 106
Charcot, Jean Martin, 52–102
    and anatomical-clinical method, 53
    Anna O. case, 105, 136
    anorexia treatment, 66, 95, 407–8
    artistic and theatrical talents, 54
    and confabulatory science, 96–7,
        573–4
    criticised by Bernheim, 81–2
    and 'dynamic lesions', 59–60, 68, 90
    elasticity of hysteria diagnosis, 72
    experiments in hypnosis, 61–5,
        67–8, 80–3, 92–4
    and faith-healing, 95
    fear of ignominy, 94
    Fliess studies under, 218
    Freud studies under, 51, 218, 312
    Freud identifies with, 97
    Freud worships, 97
    Freud 'wrecked' by Charcot's
        revelation, 69
    Freud's new gospel and, 100
    hysteria theory, 55–61, 65–8,
        71–102, 119, 138, 142, 145, 165,
        170, 195, 200–1, 313, 529, 549
    on hysterical crisis, 58
    ideas as pathogens, 67, 68
    influence on Freud, 69–70, 96–102,
        103, 135, 152, 157, 165, 183–4,
        195, 200–1, 226, 228, 242, 251,
        260, 279, 313, 367, 502, 574
    intellectual amour-propre, 95
    internalises scepticism of critics, 95
    'iron laws of hysteria', 94
    Le Log– case, 74–7, 82, 567–9
    metallotherapy, 91–2
    and misdiagnosis, 71–81, 83–87
    as 'Napoleon of the neuroses', 94
    on neurasthenia, 187
    'paralyses by imagination', 68
    'star pupil' of Nancy school, 96
    and suggestion, 81–2, 92–4, 95, 96
    Thornton on, 22–3, 77, 79–86, 119
    on tyranny of assumptions, 569
    unconscious symptom-formation,
        67–8, 77, 86

Chaufford, Anatole, 72
chemistry, 41, 385, 498
Chesterton, G. K., 9
childhood, 327–30
child-rearing, 36–7, 257, 491–2, 612
children:
    analysis of, 418–23
    development of, 236, 246–7, 332–3
    as 'evil', 327, 330, 332
    and Original Sin, 330–3
    play as sexual soliloquy, 431–2
    projection of 'badness' onto,
        327–33
    sadism, 328
    sexual abuse of, 23, 193, 204, 396,
        512–13, 516–17
    see also infantile sexuality, Original
        Sin
chloral hydrate, 121, 579
Chodorow, Nancy, 8
Christ, 275, 405
    'Freud, who was my Christ!', 305
    see also Jesus, messianism
Christianity:
    attitudes to masturbation, 189–92
    Christian psychology, 461–5
    Christian rationalism, 489, 497
    creationist theory of human nature
        6, 462, 474–6, 495–7, 502,
        505–6
    Jung on, 387
    'medicalised' Christianity, 192
    portrayal of Jews, 325
    Rabelais' obscene parable, 338–9
    sexual doctrines, 192, 322
    sexualism of, 192
    sin, see Original Sin
    treatment of Jews, 329
    see also apocalypticism, God, Jesus,
        Judaeo-Christian tradition,
        Original Sin, messianism
Chrobak, Rudolf, 183, 184
Churchland, Patricia, 613
Cioffi, Frank, vii, 575
    critique of psychoanalysis, 21–2, 24,
        454
    on Freud's interpretative style, 294,
        575
    on Grünbaum's work, 25
    on seduction theory, 25, 202, 210
    on Sulloway, 558
Clark, Ronald, 77, 184, 300

Clark University, 377
Clarke, Michell, 106
Cleaver, Robert, 331
clitoral sexuality, Freud's theory, 415
clitoris, 276
cocaine:
  Fliess's theories, 220–1, 223–4
  Freud's advocacy of, 45–7
  Freud's paper on, 49–50, 278
  Freud's use of, 22, 45–50, 223–4
cocaine episode, 45–51
  and Freud's intellectual
    independence, 102, 227
  Freud's misreporting of, 47–50,
    565
  Thornton on, 22, 49–50
Cohn, Norman, 600, 617, 619
coitus interruptus, 188, 189, 190, 192,
  337
Collingwood, R. G., 622
Comfort, Alex, 239, 458, 496
common sense, 229, 447, 508
community and co-operation
  ideological hostility to, 449
complex partial seizures, 119–20, 121,
  159, 569
  and multiple personality disorder,
    626–7, see also epilepsy
compromise formation, 262
computed tomography (CT) scan, 137
concupiscence, chastised by reason,
  495–6
Condorcet, Marquis de, 443
confession, 106, 163, 336
  of 'pathogenic secret'
  Protestant version of, 109
  and psychoanalysis, 106, 197,
    336–46, 352, 355, 563
conscience, 5–6, 293, 321, 417
conscious mind, 246–8, 271
consciousness, 67, 243–4, 249, 483–4
contemptus mundi, 524
conversion, 543
  disorder, 532–3, 535
  hysteria, 71, 84, 141
  hysterical, 179, 196
  process of, 169, 262
  somatization and, 543
Copernicus, Nicolas, 438, 439, 449
correspondences, Freud's theory of,
  289–92
counter-transference, 212

counter-wish dreams, 266
The Courage to Heal, 522–5
creationist theory of human nature, see
  Judaeo-Christian tradition
Crews, Frederick, viii–ix
  critique of psychoanalysis, 21–2, 26,
    446–7, 454
  on Freud's empirical window-
    dressing, 588
  as rational empiricist, 446–7, 451
  on recovered memory movement,
    511, 526–7, 625
  on Thornton's work, x, 559
Critchley, Macdonald, 115
cultural analysis, 8, 509
Cure of Souls, 109

Dallas, E. S., 243
Damasio, Antonio R., 619
Darlington, C. D., 458
Darwin, Charles:
  Dawkins on, 453
  Descent of Man, 311
  embraces Christian teleology, 311,
    468
  holistic science of, 490, 493
  influence on Fliess, 228
  influence on Freud, 21, 239–40,
    314, 317, 322
  influence on Haeckel, 229, 239
  macroscopic science, 490, 492–3
  'neural Darwinism', see Edelman
  Origin of Species, 2, 12, 302–4,
    451–2, 486
  regenerate empiricism of, 303–4,
    490–1
  Romanes' work, 231
  and Royal Society, 430
  Social Darwinism, 310–11
  testability of his theory, 620–1
  and theory of human nature, 454,
    456, 457–9, 475, 497, 501
  and Wallace's work, 442
Daudet, Alphonse, 54
Daudet, Léon, 54
Davis, Laura, 522–4
Davis, Philip J., 450, 500
Dawkins, Richard, 453, 620
de Beauvoir, Simone, 22
death instinct, 335
defence, 168, 170
deferred action, 204

degeneracy, 282
demonology:
    and anti-semitism, 326–7, 329, 600
    Christian, 6, 324, 600
    Freud's private, 358–9, 365, 377,
        561
    mediaeval, 328, 600
    psychoanalytic, 324–7, 399, 561
    see also apocalypticism, devil, evil
Descartes, René:
    concept of mind, 461, 486
    his dream, 173
    dualism, 505
    and Puritanism, 609
    rationalism, 448
    'reversible rationalism', 442
Deutsch, Helene, 366
Devereux, George, 256
devil:
    in apocalyptic fantasies, 324
    children possessed by, 330
    Freud, Jung and Beelzebub's stench,
        377
    Gellner on dualism and the, 597
    and irrational fantasies in history, 5
    Moll as devil, 358
    in psychoanalytic demonology,
        325–6, 399, 561
    in Rabelais' parable, 339
    see also apocalypticism, demonology,
        evil
Diagnostic and Statistical Manual of
    Mental Disorders (DSM), 531–3,
        542–3
    criticisms of DSM and scientism, 629
diagnostic techniques, 137–8, 186
Diamond, Stanley, 474
Dibbell, Julian, 484
Dickens, Charles, 341
Diderot, Denis, 443
difficulty, myth of, 507–8
Dinnage, Rosemary, 593
dirt, 37, 39, 249, 316–17, 341,
    'The Fantasy of Dirt', 556
    scatology and sin, 344
    see also purity, uncleanness
disease:
    Freud enlarges concept of, 313
    functional, 534, 535
    germ theory of, 66, 98, 187, 201, 260
    psychological causation, 97–8, 109
    sin and, 345

    see also illness
dissociative identity disorder, 626–7,
    see also multiple personality
        disorder
Dod, John, 331
Dodds, E. R., 617, 622–3
Donne, John, 344
Doolittle, Hilda (H. D.), 357
Dora case:
    Aschaffenburg's attack on, 368
    dreams in, 272
    Freud's interrogation technique,
        198–200
    Freud's sexual fantasies, 272, 276, 411
    Janet Malcolm on, 197–8
    patient runs away, 414
    'somatic compliance' theory, 151
Dostoevsky, Fyodor, 341
dreams:
    counter-wish dreams, 266
    in Freud's analysis of Anna, 409
    in Freud's self-analysis, 251–2
    Freud's theory of, 258, 260–77, 294,
        334, 409
    Jung's and Freud's, 377–8
    sexual explanations of, 269–72
    sexually explicit dreams ignored, 270
    and symptoms, 262–4, 273–7
Dreiser, Theodore, 10
drug-based therapies, 107–8
Du Bois-Reymond, Emil, 41
dualism:
    beast-angel, 496, 505, 596, 619–20
    brain-body, 486
    Cartesian, 505
    Freud's adaptation of, 465
    Gellner on the devil and, 596–7
    Humphrey's dissolution of, 484
    and hysteria, 547
    Judaeo-Christian, 244, 465
    Lévi-Strauss and, 475
    mind-body, 461–76
Dubois, 529
Dunlap, Knight, 294
Dworkin, Andrea, 619

Eames, Peter, 630
Easlea, Brian, 608
Eckstein, Emma, 224–5
Edelman, Gerald:
    neural Darwinism, 454, 459–60,
        475–6, 501, 616

on 'mind', 486, 488
Edmundson, Mark, 562
ego, 67, 170, 292, 335, 466
Einstein, Albert, 326, 449, 485
Eissler, Kurt, 23, 97, 558
Eitingon, Max, 300, 335, 395, 397, 399, 415, 425, 426
  Freud's analysis of, 356
  visits Vienna, 356, 368
electricity as metaphor, 179, 186
electroencephalogram (EEG), 79, 80, 86–7, 137, 158, 538, 572
electrotherapy, 136
Elisabeth von R., 151, 155, 160–7, 171
Ellenberger, Henri:
  Anna O. case, 111–12, 117, 131
  on brain mythology, 178
  on Charcot, 569
  and Charcot's mistake, 77
  on confession, 109
  Discovery of the Unconscious, 16–17, 109, 174
  on Fechner, 175
  on Freud legend, 16–17, 100
  on reception of Freud's hysteria paper, 574
Ellis, Havelock, 190–1, 282, 283, 311, 594
Emmy von N., Frau, 143–54, 155, 160
emotions:
  and brain, 619
  and 'inner life', 480–1
  Lévi-Strauss's dismissal of, 470–1
  as pathogens, 97, 109, 169
  rationalist denigration of, 449, 495–6, 504–6
  therapeutic ventilationism, 575
see also reason, rationalism, affection
empiricism
  and child-rearing behaviour, 492
  dangers of, 447
  Darwin's regenerate, 303–4, 490–1
  Freud's disregard for, 15, 215, 257
  Freud's pseudo-empiricism, 252, 257, 270. 386, 588
  Freud's rhetoric of, 206
  rational empiricism, 442, 489–90
  religious origins of Newton's, 302
  and the role of theory, 93–4, 493
  value of, 448
encephalitis, 119

energy:
  conservation of, 175
  in Freud's model of mind, 168, 173–5
  nervous, 169, 179
  sexual, 183
Engel, 534
Enlightenment, 332
  Isaiah Berlin on, 443,
  Freud as child of, 180
  rationalism, 244, 322, 442–3, 451–2
  Swift's view of, 322–3
epilepsy:
  in Anna O. case, 119–20, 137
  arc-de-cercle, (*arc-en-ciel*), 86–7, 571–2
  aura of, 77, 78, 79–80, 569
  Babinski and, 551
  Bernard of Gordon on, 77–8
  brain injury and, 73
  catalepsy as form of, 83
  a Charcot-like case of, 86–7
  and Charcot's 'hysterical' patients, 55–6, 79–81, 83–4, 90
  complex partial seizures, 119–20, 121, 159, 569
  difficulty in diagnosing, 158, 538, 572
  focal, 77, 78, 568
  Freud's sexual theories of, 209
  frontal lobe, 86–7, 550, 571–2
  'hystero-', 55, 63, 84, 119
  Hughlings Jackson on, 78–9, 82–3, 158–9
  Katharina case, 157
  and Le Log–, 74–7, 82, 567–9
  Lucy R. case, 159
  'numerous epilepsies', 77–8
  post-seizure phenomena, 83, 570
  'quasi-trifling signs' of, 83
  reflex epilepsy, 81, 120
  self-induced seizures, 87–8, 551
  a symptom, not a disease, 120
  and syphilis, 85
  temporal lobe, 79–80, 83–4, 90, 119–20, 137, 157, 158–9, 551, 573
  and vagina, 79, 569
epistemology, 450, 489, 497
  Edelman on biological, 501
Erasmus, Desiderius, 18, 338
Erb, Wilhelm, 220

Erikson, Erik, 5, 11, 238, 284, 327, 557
Erlenmeyer, Albrecht, 47
erotogenic zones, 209
  a proposed addition to theory of, 286–7
Esquirol, Jean, 192
Esterson, Allen, viii, 25, 292, 293, 454
Evans-Mulholland effect, 87
evil, 494, 521, 617
  children as, 327, 330, 332
  confession and, 341–2
  Freud on good and, 325
  psychoanalytic doctrine of, 321, 326, 332
  the Unconscious as, 311, 319
  see also apocalypticism, demonology, devil, Original Sin
evolutionary psychology, 611–3
excrement, 284, 317, 344
Exner, Sigmund, 175, 178, 279, 367
Eysenck, Hans, 578

faeces, 289–91, 342
  as baby, 290
  penis, 289
Falconer, Hugh, 303
Falconer, Murray, 80
false memory, x, 415, 511–27, 572, 625–8
fantasy, sexual, 247, 248–9, 284, 343, 492
  Freud fantasises about patients, 272, 276, 411
  Freud ignores, 271, 283
  Nancy Friday and, 617–9
  projection onto children, 328
father–daughter relationship, 416–17
Fechner, Gustav, 17, 175–81
  on anatomy of angels, 176,
  holds chair of physics, 175
  William James on whimsies of, 584–5
  as mystic and messiah, 181
  and Naturphilosophie, 176–7
Federn, Paul, 334, 335
feelings, see emotions, affection
fellatio, 198, 208, 210, 262, 272, 294
feminism, 22, 514, 523, 525, 527, 617–8
Féré, Charles, 96
Ferenczi, Sandor, 217, 300, 335, 394

criticisms of analysis, 353–5
  on Freud, 211–12, 354, 396
  illness and death, 398
  Nuremberg Congress, 372
  relationship with Freud, 395–9
  Secret Committee, 391
  seduction theory, 211–12, 396–7
fetishistic behaviour, 282
fits, see seizures, epilepsy, hysteria
fixation, 234, 284, 288, 327
Fleischl-Marxow, Ernst von, 46, 47–9, 69, 132, 205
Fliess, Robert, 254
Fliess, Wilhelm, 132, 172–3, 182, 185, 187, 188, 200, 206–7, 209, 214, 215, 218–20, 232, 253–4, 255, 260, 262, 278, 280
  Emma Eckstein case, 224–5
  explanatory style parallels Freud's, 264, 277, 288–9, 291–2, 294, 304
  and 'gobbledygook', 223
  Haeckel's influence on, 229, 231
  infantile sexuality, 228–9, 231–3, 284, 286, 288–9, 291
  influence on Freud, 69, 102, 213, 218, 223–8, 241–2, 281, 291, 293–4, 305, 309, 313, 361, 373, 386, 389, 502
  as 'Kepler of biology', 225
  masturbation theory, 198, 221, 224
  mathematical theories, 222–3, 225, 264, 270, 288–9, 292, 294, 385
  medical career, 217–18, 220
  nasal reflex neurosis theory, 220–1, 223–4, 229
  periodicity theory, 222–3, 225
  Ry's criticism of, 223, 225
  'Teutonic crackpottery', 222
  tonsil-eye theory, 223
foot-fetishism, 282, 286
Fordham University, 378
Forel, Auguste Henri, 103
Frederickson, Renée, 627
free-association, 136, 196, 251, 346
Freeman, Lucy, 1–2
French Revolution, 444
Freud, Anna (Freud's daughter), 402–434
  and altrusitic surrender, 424
  analysis by Freud, 409–18

'Beating Fantasies and Daydreams', 409–11
as Black Devil, 403, 418
and Dorothy Burlingham, 426–7
'A Child is Being Beaten', 409–10
as Cordelia, 408
death of, 434
emperor faith of, 404–5, 430
Freud weeps for, 428
and Freud's death, 429–30
and Freud's *Lodenmantel*, 430, 434, 509
and Freud's papers, 219, 433
and Freud's sexual curiosity, 416
Gestapo arrests, 428
and idea of incest, 416–7
on Jung's quarrel with Freud, 390
lack of self-esteem, 425
and Masson's work, 23, 219
and masturbation, 410–5, 416, 419, 420, 422, 606
as psychoanalyst, 409, 418–23, 425–6, 431–3
Secret Committee, 399
seeks Freud's affection, 406
Freud, Ernst (Freud's son), 406
Freud, Jakob (Freud's father), 35, 39, 43, 44, 253
Freud, Martha (née Bernays, Freud's wife), 46, 49, 52, 69, 97, 98, 101
children, 402, 407
engagement, 42, 45
and Freud's illness, 424, 428
marriage, 99
Freud, Martin (Jean Martin, Freud's son), 97, 427, 428
Freud, Oliver (Freud's son), 406
Freud, Sigmund:
life
birth in caul, 34
childhood, 34–9
education, 40–1
Brücke Institute, 41–2
engagement, 42, 45
Vienna General Hospital, 42, 45
researcher in neurological anatomy, 42
cocaine episode, 45–50
Privatdozent in Neuropathology, 52, 279, 281
destroys papers, 33–4
visits Charcot's hospital, 52, 65, 68–9, 96–7

marriage, 99
opens medical practice, 99, 136
reputation as neuroanatomist, 227
reads Charcot paper to Viennese Society of Physicians, 99–101
cases, *see* case histories
model of mind, 168, 172–5, 179–80, 182
seduction theory, 200–16
self-analysis, 215–16, 241–2
correspondence with Fliess, 218–20
relationship with Fliess, 226–8
theory of unconscious, 242–53
Associate Professorship, 279–81
lectures, 304, 307
fiftieth birthday presentation, 334
Secret Committee, 390–5
analysis of daughter, 409–18
illness, 423–4, 427, 428–9
leaves Vienna, 427–8
arrives in England, 428
closes medical practice, 429
death, 429–30
relationships
with Anna, 400–1, 403–18, 423–5, 427–31
with followers, 11, 299, 305–8, 335–6, 356–7, 360, 365–6
with parents, 34–40, 43, 44, 48, 253–8, 513
with mother, 253–5, 257–8
possible affair with sister-in-law, 275, 378, 592
treatment of critics and dissidents, 357–62, 365–7, 377
see also Adler, Breuer, Charcot, Ferenczi, Anna Freud, Fliess, Jung, Rank, Stekel
case histories
Cäcilie M., 582
Dora, 151, 197–200, 272, 276, 368, 411, 414, *see also* Dora case
Elisabeth von R., 151, 155, 160–7, 171
Emma Eckstein, 224–5
Emmy von N., 143–54, 155, 160
Katharina, 156–7, 159
Little Hans, 257
Lucy R., 155, 158–9, 171
M-l, 142–3, 152, 159
Rat Man, 593
Wolf Man, 289
see also Anna O. case (Breuer)

Freud, Sigmund: – *cont.*
character and personality
aetiological monotheism, 201, *see also* single key, search for
ambition, 15, 33, 34, 38–41, 42–3, 48–9, 52, 132, 216, 227–8, 278, 509
Anna O. legend, use of, 134–5
asceticism, 403
avoids emotional intensity, 257–8
credulity, 48, 96–7, 98–9, 220, 225, 226, 386
charisma, 304, 306
'conversion' by Charcot, 99, 100–1
election, feeling of, 43–4, 148–9, 164, 227
exaggerates therapeutic success, 49–50, 148–50, 164, 205–7
excessive generalisation, love of, 218, 261
explanatory style parallels Fliess's, 264, 277, 288–9, 291–2, 294, 304
failure, Freud's sense of, 44, 278
fame, Freud's need for, 34, 39, 205, 227, 279, 406, 430
generosity and moral courage, 324
honesty and dishonesty, 50, 132, 133, 149, 150, 206–7, 437
idealisation of teachers, 69, 97, 101
identification with Charcot, 97
intellectual dependence, 101, 102, 104
intellectual conformity, 35
intellectual rebelliousness, 1
intellectual submissiveness, 70
isolation, myth of Freud's, 13, 15, 16–7, 101, 217, 220
'kingdom' of, 40–1, 70, 430
and legend-weaving, 16–21, 27, 28, 132, 134–5, 220, 434
'mendacity', charge of, 50, 132
messianic identity, *see* Freud: roles and images, *see also* messianism
need for revelation, 45, 48, 205, 228, 385
need to dominate, 366
need to be loved, 39, 305, 357, 363–4, 366–7
parental expectations, 43, 44, 406
patriarchalism, 514, 517
scepticism, 226, 282
single key, search for 187, 196, 261

stoicism, 428
tenderness towards Anna, 429
roles and images
as adventurer, 2, 306
as apostle, 99
as Christ, 305, 365
as confessor, 197, 336
as conqueror, 35
as *conquistador*, 102
as despot, 399
as 'dirty child', 39
as disciple, 226, 367, 373
as emperor, 405
as explorer, 1, 220
as father, 407–8
as 'fisher of men', 305
as founder of religion, 300, 599
as 'gallant knight', 13
as genius, 15, 33
as giant, 19
as god, 16, 29, 167, 307, 350–1, 354–5, 374–5, 376, 378, 395
as 'good hater', 367
as great man, 39, 334
as head of church, 300
as healer, 98, 308, 313–4
as hero, 9, 13, 19, 21, 29, 33, 376, 392
as hero-worshipper, 42, 69, 373, 502
as king, 40–1, 70, 227, 430
as leader, 304–5, 306, 367, 373, 399–400
as messiah, 9, 44, 69, 134, 181, 226, 228, 299, 304–5, 314, 502, 515, 563, 599,
as moralist, 275
as miracle-worker, 134–5
as Moses, 9, 132, 372
as police inspector, 197–200, 204
as Pope, 362
as prophet, 305, 306, 308, 324, 599
as prosecuting attorney, 197
as redeemer, 308, 355
as sage, 308
as scientist, 13, 215, 430
as solitary, 13
works
'The Aetiology of Hysteria', 202–3, 205, 207, 516, 628
An Autobiographical Study, 133, 134, 210, 259
'Character and Anal Erotism', 288

'A Child is Being Beaten', 409–10
Delusions and Dreams in Jensen's Gradiva, 406
The Ego and the Id, 292
Group Psychology and the Analysis of the Ego, 367
The Interpretation of Dreams, 253, 260, 263–6, 269–71, 278, 299, 304, 331, 368, 385
Introductory Lectures on Psychoanalysis, 273, 327
Moses and Monotheism, 428, 429
'Mourning and Melancholia', 166
'The Neuro-Psychoses of Defence', 168
'Notes on a Case of Obsessional Neurosis', 593
'On Male Hysteria', 99
On the History of the Psychoanalytic Movement, 133
'On the Psychical Mechanism of Hysterical Phenomena', 195
'On Transformations of Instinct as Exemplified in Anal Erotism', 289
Outline of Psychoanalysis, 428
Project for a Scientific Psychology, 172–5, 178, 179–80, 182, 183, 200, 242, 466
The Psychopathology of Everyday Life, 142, 278, 334
'The Psychotherapy of Hysteria', 163
A Short Account of Psychoanalysis, 319
Studies on Hysteria, 106, 110, 113, 115–16, 122, 131–2, 137, 163, 168–9, 172, 182, 183, 184, 205, 217, 336
Three Essays on the Theory of Sexuality, 215, 237, 253, 277, 281–2, 299, 594
Freud, Sophie (Freud's daughter), 403, 406, 407–8
Friday, Nancy, 4,
  on masturbation, 412
  and sexual fantasies, 617–619
Friedan, Betty, 22
Friedell, Egon, 427
Friedländer, Hofrat, 377
Friedmann, Manna, 434
Froment, J., 552
Fromm, Erich, 8, 11, 284

critique of Freud, 11, 239
on Hitler, 326, 500
on Oedipus complex, 257–8
Frye, Roland Mushat, 597

Galen, 97
Galileo, 438, 439, 442, 489, 497
Gall, Franz Joseph, 89
Galton, Francis, 368
Gamgee, Arthur, 63
Gamlin, Linda, 546, 631
Gandhi, Mahatma, 307
Gardner, Martin, 222
Gasman, Daniel, 230, 500, 589
Gastaut, Henri, 84, 119, 159
Gaub, Hieronymus David, 110
Gaupp, 529
Gay, Peter:
  on Anna O. case, 131, 135
  on Freud's followers, 335–6, 360
  Freud: A Life for Our Time, 27–8, 29
  ignores Charcot's error, 77, 88
  on infantile sexuality theory, 309
  on religion and psychoanalysis, 362, 506
  on Roazen's work, 557
Gellner, Ernest, 22
  on beast-angel dualism, 596–7, 619–20
  on Unconscious, 242, 320, 590
genetic determinism, 458, 610–13
genitals, 183, 199, 270,
  mouth and anus as, 283–4
genital sexuality, 415–6
germ theory, 66, 98, 187, 201, 260
Geschwind, N., 120
Gide, André, 10
globus hystericus, 57, 58, 79, 80, 570
Goad, John, 438
God, 495, 502
  image of in confession and analysis, 350–1
  Freud's father and, 43
  habit of worshipping, 15–16
  hypothesis of, 441–2
  Jung's relationship to, 369–70
  Lacan as 'God the Father', 469
  messiah's relationship to, 363–4
  psychoanalysis chosen by, 598–9
  Puritan relationship to, 494
  rationality of, 442
  and secrets of universe, 507

see also Christianity, Freud, God complex, Jesus, Jung, Judaeo-Christian tradition, messianism
God complex, 350, 355, 374–6
Goethe, Johann Wolfgang von, 41, 106, 219
Gomperz, Heinrich, 271
Gothic novel, 244
Gould, Stephen Jay, 229
Graf, Max, 305–6, 310, 335, 362
Greece, classical, 622
Greer, Germaine, 22
Griffin, Susan, 619
Groddeck, Georg, 545, 631
Grosskurth, Phyllis, 2, 395, 409, 607
Grünbaum, Adolf, 24, 25, 560
Guillain, Georges, 566
guilt, 199, 343, 432, 352, 321
    Hawthorne's work and, 341
    as outcome of analysis 352
    parents' feelings of, 36–7
    see also Original Sin, confession
Gulliver's Travels, 316–7, 322–3, 600

Hacking, Ian, 627
Haeckel, Ernst:
    biogenetic law, 229–31, 236, 239
    influence on Fliess, 229, 231
    influence on Freud, 231, 236, 239, 284, 294, 317, 465
    influence on Hitler, 230
    opposition to religion, 230, 506
    'scientific religion' of, 230
    theory of soul, 230
Hall, A. Rupert, 608
hallucinations:
    in Anna O. case, 104, 110–11, 112, 132
    in cerebral disorders, 576–7
    Katharina case, 156
    olfactory (Lucy R.), 155, 158–9
Hare, E. H., 580–1, 586
Harrington, Anne, 60
Harvey, William, 60, 93, 487
Hawking, Stephen, 453–4
Hawthorne, Nathaniel, 341
head injury, 73, 76–7
    closed head injury, 73, 568, *see also* brain
Hebb, Donald, 487
Heine, Heinrich, 404–5

Heitler, 46
Helmholtz, Hermann, 41, 261
Helvétius, Claude-Adrien, 443
hemianaesthesia, 66, 91
Henner, K., 80, 84, 570
Heraclitus, 1
Herbart, Johann Friedrich, 17
Hering-Breuer reflex, 103
Herman, Judith, 514–16, 517–19, 521, 625
Hersh, Reuben, 450
Hess, Moses, 444
Hierons, Raymond, 565
Himmler, Heinrich, 427–8
Hinduism, 326
Hippocrates, 89, 97
Hirschmüller, Albrecht, 134, 578–9
Hitler, Adolf, 16, 218, 445
    Freud's flight from, 427–8, 430
    Fromm on necrophily of, 326
    Haeckel's influence on, 230
    Nolte on infantilism of, 329–30
    scientism of, 500
Hoare, Samuel, 427
Hobbes, Thomas, 249–50
Holbach, Baron d', 443
holistic science, *see* Darwin
Holmes, Jeremy, 556
Holt, Robert, 180
Hommes, O., 120
homosexuality, 4, 282, 323–4, 325, 395, 594
Hooykaas, R., 608
Horney, Karen, 8, 11, 239
Hostiensis, Cardinal, 336
Hudson, Liam, 610
Hughes, Ted:
    on puritanism of science, 448–9
human nature:
    construction of theory of, 441, 455–6, 457, 509–10
    creationist theory of, 6, 462, 474–6, 493, 495–7, 502, 505–6
    Edelman's work, 459–60
    formal and informal theories of, 249–50, 486
    'laws' of, 444, 456, 508
    modern theories of, 6
    psychological study of, 498
    science and, 440–456
    'Standard Social Science Model' of, 610–11

humoral theory, 179–80
Humphrey, Nicholas:
 mind-body problem, dissolution of,
  484, 486
 on evolutionary function of intellect,
  481, 503–5
hunger and 'repression', 246–7
Hunt, Lynn, 561, 621, 624
Hunter, Richard, 581
Hurst, Arthur F., 573
Hurst, Lindsay, 119
Huxley, Thomas, 303, 452
hypnosis:
 animal magnetism and, 61, 92
 Braid's work on, 62
 Breuer's use of, 196
 Charcot's use of, 61–5, 67–9, 80–3,
  92–4
 Freud's use of, 136, 148, 196
 Thornton on, 80–1
hysteria:
hysteria, general
 agnosticism about, 138–9, 529–30
 Babinski's test for, 549–52
 Charcot's theory of, 55–61, 65–8,
  71–102, 138, 142, 145, 165, 170,
  195, 200–1, 313, 529, 549
 concept of, 56–7, 138–9
 as diagnosis, 139–42, 529–47
 disappearance of, 71–2, 84, 529–30
 and dualism, 547
 'dynamic lesions' and, 59–60, 68
 as 'garbage category', 581
 globus hystericus, 57, 58, 79, 80, 570
 'Hysteria Following Brain Injury',
  630
 ideas, causal role of, 66–7
 major and *minor*, 59
 male, 66, 67, 100
 Marsden on, 533–42
 Micale on, 74, 75, 76, 85, 538, 565,
  566, 571, 573
 mimicry of other diseases, 58, 85,
  145, 530, 544, 546
 as misdiagnosis, *see below*
 non-existence of, 141, 198n, 502,
  546, 583
 as sham-diagnosis, 139, 529–47
 Slater on, 139–42, 167, 529, 533,
  535–7
 as 'syndrome of convenience',
  138–9

 and somatization, 542–4
 Thornton on, 22, 77, 79–86
 traumatic, 66–8, 74, 80, 93, 106–7,
  170, 195, 200–1, 212, 261–2
 Walshe's defence of, 530–1, 544,
  549
 womb theory of, 57, 78–9, 139, 141,
  569
hysteria and psychoanalysis:
 'Aetiology of Hysteria', 202–3, 205,
  207, 516
 Anna O. case, 104, 106, 112, 119,
  135
 Dora case, 198n
 Elisabeth von R. case, 161, 165
 Emmy von N. case, 152–3
 Freud–Breuer disagreement, 196
 Freud's theory, appeal of, 356
 as Freud's diagnostic *idée fixe*, 143
 Jung's approach to, 368
 Katharina case, 157
 Lucy R. case, 155, 158–9, 171
 M-l case, 142–3, 152, 159
 'On Male Hysteria', 99–101
 non-sexual traumas and, 195, 196
 'On the Psychical Mechanism of
  Hysterical Phenomena', 195
 and sexual abuse, 23, 193, 200–1,
  516–17
 somatic compliance, theory of,
  114n, 151
 Studies on Hysteria, 106, 110, 113,
  115–16, 122, 131–2, 137, 163,
  168–9, 172, 182, 183, 184, 205,
  217, 336
 Thornton on, 22, 77, 79–86
'hysteria' as misdiagnosis: 22–3, 72, 80,
  139–43, 534–5, 537–9, 544–7,
  571
 and cancer, 570
 and blepharospasm, 534
 and brain injury, 630, 74–7, 567–9
 and brain tumour, 140, 141
 and complex partial seizures,
  119–20
 and frontal lobe epilepsy, 86–7, 550,
  571–2
 and hiatus hernia, 570
 and multiple sclerosis, 85, 140
 and Parkinson's disease, 534
 and pelvic appendicitis, 198n
 and peptic ulceration, 570

hysteria' as misdiagnosis: – cont.
    and pharyngeal pouch, 570,
    and post-cricoid web, 570,
    and reflux oesophagitis, 570
    and sarcoma, 142–3
    and spasmodic dysphonia, 534
    and syphilis, 85, 571, 573
    and temporal lobe epilepsy, 79–80,
        83–4, 90, 119–20. 158–9
    and thyroid goitre, 570
    and torsion dystonia, 534
    and Tourette's syndrome, 145–7
    and vascular disease, 140
    and viral hepatitis, 546
    and writer's cramp, 534
    Gastaut on, 84
    Guirard (1914) on, 571
    Henner on, 80, 84
    Marsden on, 533–4
    Micale on, 85, 571
    Miller on, 537–8
    Slater on, 139–42
    Thornton on, 79–86
    Willis (1648) on, 141
hysterical conversion, 71, 84, 141, 179,
    see also conversion
hysterical fits, 57–9, 66–7, 78, see also
    seizures, epilepsy
hysterical paralysis, 57, 65–8,
    73–6
hystero-epilepsy, 55, 63, 84, 119

iconoclasm:
    as expression of orthodoxy, 18
id, 292, 319, 335, 466
Ignatius Loyola, 609
illness, 348
    Freud enlarges concept of, 312–14,
        315, 596
    Groddeck on purpose of, 545
    psychogenic views of, 74, 75, 76, 85,
        87, 90, 98, 115, 129, 139, 195, 535,
        560, 567
    see also disease
imagination, 503–4, 510
incest, 512–4
    father–daughter, 416–7, 514
    Freud–Jung disagreement, 379
    Freud's seduction theory, 514–16
    recovered memories of, 518–19
    taboo, 236, 256, 416–7
individualism, 454

infantile sexuality, theory of:
    biological origins, 228–40
    as catch-all hypothesis, 287
    development of theory, 228–9, 233,
        238–9, 241, 277, 284–9, 334
    Fliess and, 213, 228–9, 231–3, 284,
        286, 288–9, 291
    Freud's attitude to his theory,
        309–10, 379
    Freud's self-analysis and, 215, 216
    Jung and, 378–9
    and Original Sin, 312–9
    a proposed addition to, 286–7
    sacredness of, 309–10
    Three Essays, 215, 237, 253, 277,
        281–2, 299
instincts, component, 284
intellect, 470–1, 481, 503–4
International Psychoanalytic
    Congresses, 299, 372, 381, 391,
    399, 409
International Psychoanalytical
    Association, 359, 381–2, 399
Islam, 6
Israëls, Han, 25, 202, 207, 210

Jackson, John Hughlings, 78, 79,
    82–3, 158, 170
Jacob, Margaret, 561, 621, 624
Jakobson, Roman Osipovich, 473
James, Henry, 480
James, William, 584–5
Janet, Pierre, 17, 109, 119, 574, 549
    on Charcot, 92–3
    cures by confession, 109
    and suggestion, 627
Janov's Primal Therapy, 575
Jenyns, Leonard, 303
Jesuits, 609
Jesus:
    on adultery and fantasy, 275
    Freud and, 305, 563
    Freud compares Jung to, 374
    history and legend of, 18, 20–1
    Jung and, 371
    and messianic behaviour, 301–2,
        314, 595
    as phallus in Jung's dream, 370
    and psychoanalysis, 5, 366
    as psychologist, 462
    and Rabelais' obscene parable, 339
    Schweitzer on, 20–1

see also apocalypticism, Christianity, Freud, Judaeo-Christian tradition, Jung, messianism

Jewish culture, 44, 322, 325, 329, *see also* anti-semitism, Judaeo-Christian tradition, Judaism

John XXIII, Pope, 326

John the Baptist, 301–2

Johnson, James, 185

Johnson, Paul, 564, 595

jokes, 334

Jones, Ernest, 8, 28, 39, 42, 52, 77, 100, 334, 356, 359, 360, 361, 381, 372, 382, 395, 428
  on Anna O. case, 111, 131, 133, 134
  biography of Freud, 14–16, 19, 27–9, 33, 424
  on cocaine episode, 46, 48, 49
  on Ferenczi, 398–9
  and Fliess correspondence, 219
  on Freud–Fliess relationship, 226, 241
  Freud warns Anna about, 408
  on God complex, 349–50, 374–5
  on origins of Oedipus complex, 253–4, 513
  on psychoanalysis as a religion, 362
  relationship with Freud, 240, 335, 390–1, 393, 408, 428
  suggests Secret Committee, 390–1

Jorden, Edward, 56

Joyce, James, 3

Judaeo-Christian tradition:
  apocalyptic, *see* apocalypticism
  creationist theory of human nature 6, 462, 474–6, 495–7, 502, 505–6
  dualism, 244, 311, 465
  eschatology, 5, 324
  Fechner's relation to, 181
  Freud's relation to, 332, 351, 386, 439, 465, 468, 475
  Fromm's relation to, 326
  iconoclasm as part of, 18
  morality, 275, 318, 351
  misogynistic fantasies and, 618
  psychological assumptions, 471–2, 475
  and psychoanalysis, 4–7, 330, 362, 366, 597–600
  sexual ideology, 275, 310, 321–2
  sheep-and-goats habit of mind, 324

and sociobiology, 612
and structuralism, 469–75
see also apocalypticism, Christianity, Freud, God, human nature, Jesus, Jung, messianism, psychoanalysis

Judaism, 6, 18, 598–9, *see also* Jewish culture

Jung, Carl Gustav, 368–89, 335, 358, 360, 365, 404, 499
  on Anna O. case, 111, 133, 134
  and Bleuler, 182, 368
  breaks with Freud, 362, 367, 379–89, 390–2, 399
  as Christ type, 375–6
  on Christianity, 387
  and Eitingon, 300
  on Freud's affair with sister-in-law, 378, 592
  and God, 369–70, 376
  hatred of in psychoanalytic movement, 382–3
  'The Jung Cult', 389n
  messianic identity of, 370–1, 376–7, 384
  occult interests, 385–6
  religious 'crush' on Freud, 376
  religious identity, 377, 386–9
  on theory of infantile sexuality, 309–10, 378–9
  see also Freud, messianism, psychoanalysis

Kafka, Franz, 3

Kamin, Leon J., 613

Kanner, L., 582

Kaplan, Harold, 542–3

Karpman, Ben, 326

Katharina, 156–7, 159

Kelly, Alfred, 589

Kemsley, Douglas S., 608

Kendrick, Walter, 2, 26, 216

Kepler, Johann, 489

Kerr, John, 592–3

Ketcham, Katherine, 527

Kirk, Stuart A., 629

Klawans, Harold L., 569

Klein, Erich, 607

Klein, Melanie, 284, 327–8, 431–2, 439, 613

Knights, L. C., 500–1

Koch, Robert, 66, 98, 187, 201, 260

Kohut, Heinz, 11

Koller, Carl, 47
Kovel, Joel, 8, 556
Krafft-Ebing, Richard von, 201, 217,
    279–80, 282
  seduction theory as 'fairy-tale', 280
Kranz, 530
Kris, Ernst, 219
Kubie, Lawrence, 8, 342
  'The Fantasy of Dirt', 556
Kuhn, Thomas, 440
Kuper, Adam, 470
Kutchins, Herb, 629

Lacan, Jacques, 28, 71, 439, 466, 477
  as 'God the Father', 469
Laing, R. D., 342
Laius complex, 256
Lamarck, Jean de, 4, 236, 240, 388
language, 473, 482, 493, 504
Lasèque, Charles, 56
Lavoisier, Antoine Laurent, 439
Lawrence, D. H., 4, 384
Lawson, Annette, 602
Leach, Edmund, 471
Lear, Jonathan, 562
Lee, R. S., 320
Legman, Gershon, 1, 4, 617–18, 619
Leibniz, Gottfried Wilhelm, 243
Leidesdorf, Professor, 99
Le Log– (Charcot's patient), 74–7, 82,
    567–9
Lenin, Vladimir Ilich, 16, 384–5, 444,
    485
Lennox, W. G., 83
lesions, 'dynamic', 59–60, 68, see also
    brain
Lesser, R. P., 85–6, 551–2
Lévi-Strauss, Claude, 7, 445, 460,
    469–75, 478
  as apocalyptic thinker, 474
  and dualism, 475
  and St Paul, 614
Lewis, Aubrey, 529, 530, 533, 535
Lewontin, R. C., 613
Lhermitte, 531
libido, 234, 286, 309–10, 335, 415
Library of Congress, 219, 433
Liébeault, Auguste, 81, 92, 95–6, 98
Lieben, Anna von, 582
Lipowski, Z. J., 543, 630–1
Lishman, William Alwyn, 147, 570,
    576, -577, 583

Little Hans, 257
localisation, cerebral, 54, 78
Loftus, Elizabeth, 527
love:
  of Christ for penitent, 345
  Freud's need to be loved, 39, 305,
    357, 363–4, 366–7
  followers' need for Freud's, 365–6
  'like a young girl on a date', 365
  in messianic movements, 362–3,
    364–5
  parental love as rejection, 38–9
  psychoanalysis as gospel of, 5, 366
  unrequited love as pathogen, 110, 163
Lucy R., 155, 158–9, 171
lumbar puncture, 137, 577
Luther, Martin, 5, 101, 338
Lyell, Charles, 303

M-l case, 142–3, 152, 159
McClelland, David, 321, 610
  Freud's religious mission, 597–600
McGinn, Colin, 461, 483–5
Macmillan, Malcolm, 60, 262, 292,
    293, 567–8, 569, 582, 586
  on appeal of psychoanalysis, 560–1
  on ego and id, 292
  on emotional catharsis, 574
  on Freud and heredity, 293
  Freud Evaluated, 25, 454, 560
  on William Harvey, 60
  on unintentional influences in
    therapy, 628
McWilliam, Candia, 28–9
Malcolm, Janet, 197–9, 357
Malcolmson, Kenneth, 570
Malinowski, Bronislaw, 287
Malraux, André, 622
Mann, Thomas, 10, 11, 13, 15, 29, 230
'manual-erotism', 286–7
'manual stage', 286–7
Manuel, Frank, 44, 300–2, 564
  on messianic doubt, 301
Marcus, Steven, 14
Marcuse, Herbert, 477
Marie, Pierre, 81–2
Marsden, C. D., 533–42, 551
Martin, Alfred E., 577
Marx, Karl, 7, 11, 384–5
  Darwin's influence, 452
  influence and status, 3, 16, 26
  theory of human nature, 445, 455

Marxism, 6, 446, 495, 507
  embraces Judaeo-Christian
    orthodoxy, 447
masochism, 282, 342, 409, 411
Masson, Jeffrey:
  Against Therapy, 23, 353
  Assault on Truth, 22, 23, 201, 515,
    519–20, 526
  Final Analysis, 23, 24
  and Freud–Fliess letters, 219
  reception of work, 23–4, 26
  and recovered memory movement,
    515–16, 517–18, 519–21,
    627–8,
  on seduction theory, 23–4, 25, 201,
    210, 211–12, 515–16, 517–18,
    519–21, 627–8
masturbation, 188–194, 196, 420, 422,
  and Anna Freud's analysis, 409–14
  Catholic confessional and, 337
  as cause of death, 192
  and Christian doctrine, 189–92
  in Dora case, 198–9, 411
  Fliess's theories, 198, 221, 224
  Freud's attitude to, 4, 188, 411, 586
  Freud's theories, 188–9, 192–3,
    196, 221, 411–12
  Freud warns son about, 586
  and insanity, 192
  'medicalised' Christianity and, 192
  neurasthenia and, 188–9
  Stoic attitude to, 189–90
  women and, 411–13
materialism, 177, 383, 597
mathematics:
  dangers of, 450, 499–500
  Fliess' theories, 222–3, 225, 264,
    270, 288–9, 292, 294, 385
  Newtonian, 222, 261
Maudsley Hospital, 140, 530
Mead, Margaret, 610
Medawar, Peter, 437–42, 445, 450,
  452–3
'medicalisation' of Christianity, 192,
  582
medicine, history of, 565
  and relativism, 571, 578–9, 580
  technical progress in 137–8
  Whig approach to, 137–8, 580–1
memory:
  Anna O's, 127–8
  false memories, x, 415, 511–27, 513

lapses of, 278
malleability of, 521
pathogenic memory structure, 165
pressure technique, 155, 161
recovered, 414n, 511–27
repressed, 107, 109, 247, 518
seduction theory and, 202–5
traumatic, 247
unconscious memory, 136, 250
Mendel, Gregor, 291, 458
meningitis, tuberculous, 117–18
menstruation, 221–2
Merton, Robert K., 608
Mesmer, Franz Anton, 61, 90, 109
mesmerism, 62, 98, *see also* hypnosis
messianism:
  Freud as messianic leader, 9, 300,
    304–14, 367, 502, 597–600
  Fechner as mystic and messiah, 181
  Fliess seen as messiah by Freud, 226,
    228, 373, 589
  Freud's account of Anna O. case as
    example of his, 134
  Freud and followers, 305–8, 365–6,
    439
  Freud's messianic identity, 9, 44, 69,
    134, 181, 226, 228, 299, 304–5,
    314, 502, 515, 563, 599,
  Freud's projection of his messianic
    identity onto Fliess, 69, 228, 373
  Jewish, 44, 564, 595
  Jung's messianic identity, 370–1,
    376–7
  Jung and Freud as messiahs, 384
  Manuel on, 44, 300–2, 564
  the messiah as 'worm', 364
  messianic cults, 362–5, 439
  messianic fantasies, 39
  messianic personality, 9–10, 38–9,
    40, 43–4, 363–5
  Newton's messianic personality,
    43–4, 301–3, 304, 564
  parental expectations and, 38–9, 40,
    43–4
  pattern of doubting conviction,
    300–1, 595
  and projection by followers, 11
  Sabbatai Sevi, the 'false messiah',
    564, 595
  uncleanness and, 364, 370–1
  see also apocalypticism, Fechner,
    Fliess, Freud, God, God complex,

Jesus, Jung, Judaeo-Christian tradition, Newton
metallotherapy, 91, 92
Meynert, Theodor, 17, 42, 53
  brain mythology, 178
  influence on Freud, 42, 69, 102, 367
  physiological associationism, 165, 170
Micale, Mark, 85, 538–9, 565, 566, 571
  on disappearance of hysteria, 567, 571
  on Le Log– case, 74, 75, 76
  on misdiagnosis of syphilis, 85, 573
Midgley, Mary, 624
  on cleft between reason and feeling, 495, 619
migraines, 220–1, 224, 631
Mill, John Stuart, 624
Miller, Alice, 607
Miller, Laurence, 115, 537–9, 551, 571
Millet, Kate, 22
mind:
  and body, 461–6, 483–4, 502, 505
  Cartesian concept of, 461, 486
  as cause of illness, 82, 97–9, 177, 545–7
  Edelman on, 460, 475–6, 486, 488
  Exner's psychomechanical model of, 175
  Freud's model of, 168–9, 172–5, 182, 319, 460
  Freud's theory of, 168–75, 179–80, 460, 465–7
  Lévi-Strauss on, 460
  'private theatre' concept of, 482
  problem of, 460–1, 465, 484
  and purity, 505
  Gilbert Ryle on, 460–1, 481–3, 615
  traditional doctrine of, 475
  see also behaviour, body, brain, brain mythology, creationist theory of human nature, dualism, soul, spirit, unconscious
Ministry of Education, 279–80
misdiagnosis, see hysteria
misogyny, 22, 153, 525, 618
Mitchell, Juliet, 27
Mitchell, Silas Weir, 56
Moebius, 282
Molière, 541

Moll, Albert, 232, 282, 357–8, 365, 561
Monakow, Carl von, 616
monism, 230
More, Hannah, 331
morphine, 45, 47, 49–50, 112
Morton, W., 64
Moser, Fanny, 154, see also Emmy von N.
Moses, 9, 18, 100, 132, 372, 374
mother
  eclipse of in psychoanalysis, 400,
  Freud's relationship to his, 253–5, 257–8
  as expert on children, 490
  see also, children, Oedipus complex, parent–child relationship
motor neurone disease, 53–4
mouth, 208–9, 232–3, 234, 283, 285–6
multiple personality disorder, 572–3, 625–6
multiple sclerosis, 53, 85, 119, 140, 570

Nancy, University of, 81, 82
Nancy school, 94, 96
nasal reflex neurosis, see Fliess
National Hospital for Nervous Diseases, 140
Naturphilosophie, 176–7
nervous energy, 179
Neue Freie Presse, 106
neurasthenia, 138, 185–9, 196, 201, 337
  and masturbation, 187–9, 193
  non-existence of, 193
  as refuge from diagnostic uncertainty, 138, 186
  symptoms of, 185–6
neurology:
  Charcot's work, 52–3, 103
  Freud's career, 42, 95, 103, 227
  nineteenth-century, 179, 186
  present-day, 180, 501
neurones, 173–4
neuroscience, 454, 487, see also brain, Edelman
neurotic illness, 273, 313
New Testament, 189, 371, 524, 599
Newson, John and Elizabeth, 491–2
Newton, Isaac, 176
  and mathematics, 222, 261

messianic identity, 43–4, 301–3, 304, 564
religious beliefs, 442, 449, 464, 489, 490, 507
Royal Society, 430
Nietzsche, Friedrich Wilhelm, 13, 17, 507
Nin, Anaïs, 392
Nineham, D. E., 563
Noll, Richard, 389n
Nolte, Ernst, 329–30
Noonan, John T., Jr, 586, 601
Nothnagel, Hermann, 280

object-choice, 425
obsessional neurosis, 182
obscenity, 4, 145, 192, 248, 271, 277
Oedipus complex:
  criticisms of theory, 256–8
  and denial of sexual abuse, 513, 525
  development of theory, 211, 253–6, 259–60, 513
  Fromm on 257–8
  Herman on, 514
  and infantile sexuality, 286
  Jung on, 379
  Klein's revision of, 431
  Mitchell on, 27
  origins of theory, 253–4, 513
  as pathogen, 259, 260
  resonance of, 255–6, 277
Ofshe, Richard, 527, 625–6
Ojemann, George, 117
ontogeny, 234. 237, 282
Ophuijsen, van, 399
oral-erotism, 287–8, 317
oral-genital contact, 283
oral sexual system, 209
oral stage, 286
orgasm, 192, 285
orgasmic potency, 247
Original Sin, 6
  and 'affirmation-in-negation', 344
  attempts to revive doctrine, 318
  Christian psychology and, 463, 471
  compared to psychoanalysis, 320–2
  creationist theory and, 494
  elaboration of doctrine, 314–15
  Freud's reinvention of, 319, 336
  Freud's view of childhood and 330–3, 355
  Gulliver's Travels and, 316–8, 322–3

Lévi-Strauss and, 471–2
Rabelais on, 339
and recovered memory movement, 523
Unconscious as, 320
scatological rhetoric of, 344
see also apocalypticism. Christianity, Jesus, messianism, infantile sexuality, creationist theory of human nature
organic analogy, 289–91, 594
Ormerod, J. A., 529
Orr-Andrawes, Alison, 119–21, 579
orthodoxy, 5, 7, 11, 399, 447, 505
  opium of, 447
Orwell, George, 270, 271
Ovid, 291
Owen, A. R. G., 58

Page, Herbert, 66
panerotic rituals, 287
Pappenheim, Bertha, 111–12, see also Anna O. case
Pappenheim, Else, 146
paralysis, 57, 65–8, 73–6, 104, 110
  'paralysis by imagination', 68
parent–child relationship, 35–40, 256–7
Parkinson's disease, 53, 534
Parsons, Malcolm Robson, ix, 118, 577–8
Pascal, Blaise, 243, 315
Pasteur, Louis, 66, 98, 187, 201, 260
patriarchalism, 400, 424, 514, 517, 525, 526
Paul, St, 100, 101
  and crucifixion of the 'flesh', 496
  flesh-spirit dichotomy, 462, 463, 474, 496, 614
  and function of reason, 495–6
  Lévi-Strauss compared to, 614
  and unregenerate man, 316
'pedal-erotism', 287
'pedal stage', 286
Pendergrast, Mark, 527, 572–3, 625, 627
Penfield, Wilder, 571
penis, 183, 208, 234, 267, 287, 289–91
  as baby, 290
  as faeces, 289
penis-envy, 290, 425
Persinger, Michael, 573

perversion, sexual, 208, 231–2, 234–5, 282, 318
Peters, Uwe Henrik, 410
Pfister, Oscar, 5, 325, 359, 366
phallic stage, 254, 286
phallic sexuality, 416
Phillips, John, 303
phlogiston theory, 295, 438, 440
phrenology, 89
phylogeny, 234–5, 236, 237, 282
physics, 41, 385, 442, 453, 463, 498
Piaget, Jean, 229, 409
Piñero, J. M. López, 585
Pinker, Steven, 611–13
pithiatism, 549
Pitres, 116
Planck, Max, 449
Plato, 1, 57, 219
    attitude to empiricism, 445, 448
    dualism in, 461, 462, 495, 505
    rationalism of, 496
    theory of human nature, 445
Plotinus, 243
pluralism, 443, 444–6, 451, 459, 608
Poliakov, Léon, 326, 595
Pope, Alexander, 1
Popper, Karl, 620, 624
Porter, Roy, 581
Powell, Russell A., 625
pornography, 6, 248, 328, 618–19
postmodernism, 445, 469, 499, 508, 510, 608
post-structuralism, 444, 469, 499, 608
positivism, 177–8, 385
preconscious, 247
pressure technique, 155, 161, 196–7, 517
Preyer, William, 230
pride, human, 320, 321
Professorship, Freud's, 279–81
projection:
    and demonology, 325, 326–7, 364
    and displacement, 424–5
    in anti-semitism, 326–7
    onto messiah, 11, 69, 228, 373
    in psychoanalysis, 326–7, 329, 348, 364, 388
prosopagnosia, 120
Protestantism:
    attitude to confession, 109, 336, 338, 340
    Cure of Souls, 109
    and demythologisation, 18–19
    and psychoanalysis, 5
    and rationalism, 6, 244–5, 315–16
    role of sinner in, 350
    see also Puritanism
Proust, Marcel, 3
pseudo-science, 12, 21, 24, 88–9, 178, 180, 277, 300, 438
pseudo-seizures, 87–7, 572
psychiatry, 138, 165
    Charcot shapes development of modern, 68, 90
    role of misdiagnosis in history of, 581
psychical analysis, 149
psychoanalysis:
    and astrology, 165–6, 438–9
    attacks on, 2–3, 8, 440
    as confessional ritual, 336–55
    as confidence trick, 437–8
    demonology of, 358, 365, 377, 561
    E. R. Dodds on, 622–3
    and emotional coldness, 346, 349
    evaluation of, 438, 509
    as Fliessian science, 264, 277, 288–9, 291–2, 294, 304
    Freud directs development of movement, 299
    as Freud's 'frail child', 391–2
    as Freud's 'kingdom', 40–1, 430
    as Freud's revelation, 365
    as gospel of love, 5, 366
    Jewish origins of, 369, 598–9
    legend of origins, 16
    new theology of, 27
    as part of divine plan, 599–600
    and 'permissiveness', 332
    protected by sexual taboos, 277
    and pseudo-explanations of sexual behaviour, 288
    as pseudo-science, 12, 21, 24, 180, 277, 300, 438
    as religious cult, 308–9, 362, 366
    and resistance, 3, 295, 561–2
    sacredness of libido theory in 309–10
    as science and art, 498
    success of, 26
    see also Freud, messianism
psychogenic, see illness
psychology, Freud's move to, 103

psychosomatic medicine, 98n,
  Charcot, Freud, Groddeck and,
    544–7
psychotherapy, 108, 110, 122, 352,
  440, 526
Puritanism:
  iconoclasm as expression of, 18
  libertarianism, Puritan, 618
  and monasticism, 524, 609
  and psychoanalysis, 321, 330–1
  and rationalism, 449
  and recovered memory movement,
    523–5
  and science, 449, 489, 494, 608–9
  secularised, 345
  and sociobiology, 612
  see also Protestantism
purity:
  apocalypticism and, 311, 377, 477,
    617
  Havelock Ellis on evolution and, 311
  human impulse towards, 236
  Jung, Freud and, 377
  mind and, 505
  spirit and, 462–5, 470, 474–5
  see also apocalypticism, dirt,
    uncleanness
Pusey, Edward Bouverie, 340
Putnam, Frank, 627

'Q', Freud's theory of, 173–4

Rabelais, François, 337–41, 344
railway accidents, 65–6, 73
Rank, Otto, 8, 306, 335, 382, 392–5
  break with Freud, 393–6, 400
  Rank's 'grovelling' letter, 394–5
  and Secret Committee, 391, 393–5
  Trauma of Birth, 393
Rat Man, 593
Rather, L. J., 97
rationalism:
  Aristotelian, 505
  Isaiah Berlin on dangers of, 443–4,
  born out of superstition, 5–6, 506
  Cartesian, 442, 448
  Christian, 489, 497
  continuity of religious and secular
    rationalism, 6–7, 469
  dominates Western culture, 448
  Enlightenment, 244, 322, 442–3,
    451–2

epistemology of, 496–7
Freud and, 10, 491, 506, 509
hostility to feelings, 495–5, 504–6
irrationality of, 7, 456
power of secular, 5
Plato and, 496
Protestant, 6, 244–5, 315–16, 449
religious origins of, 495, 506–7,
  608–9
religious rationalism, 18
response to attacks on, 624
'reversible rationalism', 442, 443,
  445, 449–51, 455
and revolution, 444
twentieth-century, 9
Max Weber on, 608–9
Western, 506
Rattansi, P. M., 608
reaction-formation, 288
reason, 449, 500–1,
  instrument of, 496, 503
  chastises concupiscence, 495–6
  psychoanalysis as magical use of, 4
  and subjugation of feelings, 495–6,
    619
  see also emotions, rationalism
recapitulation, 234, 236, 237, 238
recovered memory movement, x, 414n,
  511–27, 572, 625–8
Reformation, 5, 18, 191, 315, 322
regression, 234, 288, 327
Reich, Wilhelm, 8, 500
Reik, Theodor, 308, 365
religion:
  Darwin, 468
  Freud's rejection of, 179, 383, 389,
    506
  Gay on, 362, 506
  Haeckel's opposition to, 230, 506
  need of twentieth-century
    intellectuals for, 384, 433
  as neurotic illness, 555–6
  see also Christianity, Judaeo-
    Christian tradition, Judaism,
    messianism, God, Jesus, Freud,
    Jung
repression, 11
  and condemning judgement, 351
  of coprophilia, 237
  'massive repression', 519, 521, 523
  and parent–child relationship,
    491

repression – *cont.*
  and memories of sexual abuse, 514, 518
  primal, 293
  process of, 170, 235, 245–8, 491
  secondary, 293
  the Unconscious and, 245–8
resistance, 3, 409, 414n
  as ally of psychoanalysis, 295
  Freud on, 561
  Paul Robinson on, 561–2
revelation, 45, 48, 100, 173
Reynolds, E. H., 551
Reynolds, J. Russell, 66
Reynolds, Reginald, 600
Ribot's Law, 116
Richens, Alan, ix, 572
Richet, Charles, 61
Rieff, Philip, 239
Rilke, Rainer Maria, 424, 425
Rivers, W. H. R., 264–5
Riviere, Joan, 424
Roazen, Paul, x
  as admirer of Freud, 19–20
  as *enfant terrible*, 19
  on Erikson, 557
  Freud and His Followers, 17–20, 21, 29, 433
  on Anna Freud, 403–4, 432–3
  on Freud's attitude to masturbation, 586
  on Freud's disciples, 307–8, 366
  on God complex, 374
  on Jung, 383
  Wollheim's review of, 557
Robertson, G., 64
Robinson, Heath, 173
Robinson, John, 555–6
Robinson, Paul, 3, 22, 88, 560, 561–2, 573
Rogers, Karl, 628
Rogge, O. John, 343
Rolland, Romain, 10
Roman Catholic Church:
  confession, 106, 337–8, 344–5, 352, 356
  doctrine of Original Sin, 315
  role of penitent, 350
  teaching on sexuality, 190–1
Romanes, George, 231, 589
Romanticism, 177, 179, 244–5, 332
Roosevelt, Franklin D., 427

Rosanes, Ignaz, 224
Rose, Steven, 487, 613, 616
Rosenberg, Carroll Smith, 567
Rosenfeld, Eva, 421
Rosenfeld, Minna, 421
Rosenthal, Moritz, 35
Ross, Colin, 626
Roustang, François, 381
Royal Society, 430
Rush, Benjamin, 192
Rush, Florence, 515
Russian Revolution, 444, 452
Rutter, Michael, 556
Ry, Benjamin, 223, 225
Rycroft, Charles, 414n, 468
Ryle, Gilbert:
  anti-Cartesianism, 460–1, 482, 492
  and charge of 'behaviourism', 615
  Concept of Mind, 460–1, 481–3, 615
  on 'mental phenomena', 478, 615
  on study of psychology, 464

Sachs, Hans, 9, 306, 391, 395
  on Adler schism, 360, 366–7
  on Freud and Jung, 373
  Freud's remoteness from, 307
Sacks, Oliver, 454, 583, 631
Sade, Marquis de, 328
sadism, 237, 282, 325, 328
Sadler, W. S., 107
Sadock, Benjamin, 542–3
Salpêtrière, La, 52, 53, 55–6, 63, 82–3, 86, 90–1, 99
  establisment of outpatients' department, 65
  as 'Mecca of neurologists', 52
  see also Charcot
Sargant, William, 107–8, 575
Sartre, Jean-Paul, 7, 500
Satan, 5, 325–6, 330, *see also* devil
Satanism, 6
Satow, Barbara, 567
Savonarola, Girolamo, 18
Schatzman, Morton, viii, 25, 202, 207, 210, 211, 257, 591
Schaudinn, Fritz, 72
Schopenhauer, Artur, 13
Schreiber, Flora Rheta, 626
Schrödinger, Erwin, 497
Schubert, von, 260
Schur, Max, 219, 223, 429–30
Schweitzer, Albert, 18, 20–1, 326, 595

science:
  appropriation of term by
    rationalism, 497
  Darwinian revolution, 451–2, 490
  empiricism and, 447–8
  good theories displace bad, 440
  heroic model of, 26, 561
  history of modern, 88, 449, 451–2
  holistic, 490–3
  Ted Hughes on puritanism of,
    448–9
  and human nature, 441–2
  macroscopic, 490, 492–3
  and 'mind of God', 453
  objectivity and impersonality of,
    497–8
  and rationality of God, 442
  religion and, 442, 449–50, 608–10
  and 'reversible rationalism', 442,
    443, 445, 449–51, 455
  and superstition, 319, 336, 386
  value-free, 501
  see also Darwin, empiricism,
    Newton, pseudo-science,
    rationalism, theory
Secret Committee, 390–401
  finally disbanded, 399
  Freud dissolves, 394
  Jones proposes, 390–1
  re-established, 395
seduction theory:
  abandonment of, 25, 200, 210–13,
    214–16, 233, 259, 310, 396
  cases, 206–10
  Ferenczi's view of, 211–12, 396–7
  formulation of, 182, 193, 200–6
  Freud's misrepresentation of, 194
  Freud's misrepresentation of as
    foundation myth of recovered
    memory movement, 525, 627–8
  Freud's reconstruction technique,
    208–9, 211, 516–17, 625
  Herman's return to, 514–15,
    516
  Masson on, 23–4, 25, 201, 210,
    211–12, 515–16, 517–18,
    519–21, 627–8
  Oedipus complex and, 253
  and recovered memory movement,
    514–27, 626, 627–8
  'a scientific fairy-tale', 280
  as 'source of the Nile', 205, 214

seizures, 62, 63
  'akinetic', 83
  complex partial, 119–20, 121, 159.
    569, 626–7
  Le Log– case, 75, 568–9
  olfactory, 159
  pseudo- (non-epileptic), 86–7, 572
  see also epilepsy, fits, hysteria
self-analysis, Freud's, 215–16, 241–2,
    253, 277, 381
Seneca, 190
Sevi, Sabbatai, 564, 595
sexual abuse:
  denial of, 512–13
  false memories of, 204, 516–17
  Ferenczi's approach, 212, 396–7
  see also incest, Masson, recovered
    memory movement, seduction
    theory
sexual behaviour, 2, 12, 458, 492, see
    also masturbation
sexual energy, 183
sexual fantasies, see, fantasy, sexual
sexual 'noxae', 188–9, 192, 196, 201
sexual perversion, see perversion,
    sexual
sexuality, theory of, 181–5, 204, 359,
    378–9, see also infantile sexuality,
    Oedipus complex, women
Shakespeare, William, 243
Shapiro, Arthur K., 145, 146
Shapiro, Elaine, 145
Shorter, Edward, 58, 85, 565, 578, 579,
    630–1
Sicherman, Barbara, 585
Sigmund Freud Archives, 23, 433
sin, 190–1, 336
  carnal, 316–17
  coitus interruptus as, 190
  concept of, 322
  and Judaeo-Christian doctrine, 7
  masturbation as, 190
  original, see Original Sin
Sinason, Valerie, 628
sinners, 350
Slater, Eliot:
  on hysteria, 139–42, 167, 529, 533,
    535–7
  reception of work, 530, 538, 544,
    549
Slavney, Philip, 529
slips of the tongue, 278

smell, 158–9
Social Darwinism, 311
Société de Biologie, 91, 92
sociobiology, 21, 239, 458–9, 611–13
somatic compliance, theory of, 114n,
    151
somatization, 532, 542–3, 546
somnambulism, 57, 61
Sophocles, 334
soul, 177, 179, 230, 461–6, 472–4
    'complete incontamination', 465
Spiegel, Herbert, 572–3
spirit, 4, 177, 179, 311, 461–6, 470–5
    'spiritualist' views, 175, 177, 178
Spitzka, Edward, 187
Spock, Benjamin, 229
Spurzheim, Johannes, 573
Stadlen, Anthony, 198n, 593
Stalin, Joseph, 16, 327, 383, 444, 445
'Standard Social Science Model' of
    human nature, 610–11
Starr, Susan Leigh, 581, 631
Steiner, George, 500
Steiner, Rudolf, 229
Stekel, Wilhelm, 287, 335, 359,
    360–1, 380
    Freud abuses as 'pig', 'louse' and
      'pea', 361
    relationship with Freud, 304–5,
      360–1, 365, 367, 379
    on somatization, 543
Stengers, Jean, 586
Steyerthahl, A., 138, 529
Stoicism, 189–90
Stoltenberg, John, 619
Storr, Anthony, 8, 71, 564, 575
Strachey, James, 172, 356–7
structuralism, 6–7, 444, 446, 469–75,
    507, 608, 614
sublimation, 288, 312
submission, 362–3, 367
suggestion, 85–6
    Babinski and, 549–52
    Bernheim's work, 81–2, 92–3,
      95–6
    Charcot's experiments and, 61–2,
      64, 67, 95–6, 569
    Freud's use of, 136
    Janet's use of, 627
Sulloway, Frank, x
    approach to Freud legend, 17–19,
      20–1, 29, 279–80

Freud, Biologist of the Mind, 20–1
    on Anna O. case, 131
    on biological influences, 237–9, 558
    Cioffi on, 558
    on Charcot, 77, 88
    on Fechner, 175, 176
    on Fliess's mathematics, 225
    on Freud as 'prosecuting attorney',
      197
    on Freud–Fliess relationship,
      228–9
    on Freud's biological thinking, 590
    on Freud's 'brilliant legacy to
      mankind', 558
    on Freud's career, 279–80
    on Freud's 'discoveries', 588
    on Freud's hysteria paper reception,
      100
    on Freud's model of mind, 168,
      174–5
    on Freud's self-analysis, 242
    on Haeckel's influence, 237, 239
    on hysteria, 71, 567
    as iconoclast, 18–19, 20–21
    on religion and psychoanalysis, 308
    revises estimate of Freud, 21, 558
    and sociobiology, 21, 239, 613
    Wollheim on, 557
superego:
    Ferenczi on Freud, 212
    Freud's concept, 292–3, 335, 466
    and Original Sin, 320–1
    and theory of repression, 235, 293
Swales, Peter, x, 28, 582, 592–3
Swift, Deane, 316
Swift, Jonathan, 316–19, 322–3, 326,
    339, 600
Sydenham, Thomas, 58, 530
symptom-formation, unconscious, 68,
    77, 86
symptoms:
    Anna O. case, 104–5, 106–7, 110,
      112–21, 125–31, 147, 578
    dreams and, 262–4, 273–7
    Elisabeth von R. case, 160–1
    Emmy von N. case, 144–7, 149–50
    formation, 68, 77, 86
    Freud's changing theories of, 261–4
    in Freud's early cases, 137, 580
    Freud's mixed aetiological theory of,
      150–1
    hysterical, 95, 106–7

Katharina case, 156
Lucy R. case, 155, 158–9
M-l case, 142–3, 152, 159
of neurasthenia, 185–6
and seduction theory, 206
and 'somatic compliance', 114n, 151
spontaneous remission of 125, 128, 130–1
transfer of, 92
syphilis, 54, 72, 85, 266, 571, 573
Szasz, Thomas, 399, 596, 629

taboo:
  against knowledge, 508
  desire to transgress, 9
  incest, 236, 256
  individual differences in response to, 248
  internalisation of, 248
  parent–child relationship and, 36, 416–7
  phylogentic transmission of, 236
  power of, 1, 9, 244
  sexual, 247, 248
  taboos serve to protect psychoanalysis, 277
'talking cure', 104–5, 106, 123, 336
Tallis, Raymond, vii-viii, 450, 607, 613
Tausk, Victor, 8, 361, 433, 557–8
Tavris, Carol, x, 108, 559, 629
Tawney, R. H., 609–10
Taylor, Graeme, 539, 565
Taylor, Joan Kennedy, 527
temporal lobe epilepsy, see epilepsy
Ten Commandments, 18
Tennyson, Alfred, Lord, 107
theory:
  creationist theory of human nature 6, 462, 474–6, 495–7, 502, 505–6
  Carey on literary theory, 614
  Darwin's use of, 303–4, 489–90,
  explanatory theories, 3
  Freud's use of 252–3, 491
  function in science, 60, 93–4, 96
  'grand theory', viii, 6
  William Harvey and, 60
  of human nature, 2, 7, 249–50, 440–56, 457–60, 509–10, 620–1
  internalisation of Judaeo-Christian theory, 7, 471–2, 486, 488

invention of facts to fit, 276
Newton and, 302
pluralist distrust of, 443–448, 454–5
role in empirical science, 93–94, 448, 493
see also Darwin, empiricism, Fliess, Freud, human nature, Lévi-Strauss, mind, pseudo-science, science
Thomas, Keith, 601
Thornton, Elizabeth M., ix-x
  on Anna O. case, 114–20
  on Charcot's diagnosis of hysteria, 77, 79–80, 82–6
  on Charcot and hypnosis, 64–5, 80–1, 83
  on cocaine episode, 49
  on double personality, 626–7
  on Emmy von N. case, 146
  on Fliess's theories, 221
  on Freud's hysteria paper reception, 100
  on Freud's use of cocaine, 22, 49, 559
  The Freudian Fallacy, 22–3, 114
  hostile reception of work, 26, 84, 88, 559, 573
  Hypnosis, Hysteria and Epilepsy, 80
  on organic illnesses, 22–3
  on seduction theory, 202, 207, 210
Timpanaro, Sebastiano, 593
Tissenbaum, 534
Tissot, Samuel Auguste David, 191–2
Tourette, Gilles de la, 145
Tourette's syndrome, 144–7, 582–3
Trachtenberg, Joshua, 600
Traherne, Thomas, 479–80
training analysis, 336, 356–7
transcendentalism, 477
transference, 134, 409, 602
  as reality, 602
  as theoretical fiction, 348–9, 353–4
trauma:
  of birth, 393
  hysteria and, 66–8, 74, 80, 93, 106–7, 170, 195, 200–1, 212, 261–2
  in Lucy R. case, 171

trauma – *cont.*
  sexual, 188, 200–1, 203, 206, 209, 212
Trauner, Doris, 159
Trillat, Etienne, 71
Trilling, Lionel, 14–15, 33
Trotsky, Leon, 16, 383

uncleanness:
  and annihilation of human beings, 327
  apocalypticism and, 311, 324, 377, 477, 617
  and confession, 341–2, 344–5
  confession of in analysis, 347, 350, 351
  and dualism, 244, 316
  Jung's feelings of, 371
  physicality and, 464, *see also* body
  rejection by messianic personality, 364
  of Swift's Yahoos, 316
  see also apocalypticism, body, dirt, purity
unconscious:
  concept of, 242–6, 249–53, 257–8, 279, 313–14, 319, 320, 383, 386, 465
  dreams and, 252
  as evil self, 311, 319
  importance of, 215
  Jung's attitude to, 383–4
  memories, 136, 163
  pathogenic role of, 246, 313
  as repository of pseudo-empirical evidence, 251–3, 257
  repression processes, 248
  symptom-formation, 68, 77, 86, 565
  traumatic hysteria, 74
Updike, John, 6

vagina, 79, 234, 267, 338, 569
vaginal sexuality, Freud's theory, 416
Van Neck, Anne, 586
Vickers, Brian, 608, 614
Vienna General Hospital, 42, 45
Vienna Neurological Society, 207
Vienna Psychoanalytic Society, 305, 306, 358–61, 403–4, 409, 418
Vienna University, 334, 392
Viennese Society of Physicians, 99–101

Voltaire, 443
Vulpian, Félix, 53

Waddell, Helen, 341
Wallace, Alfred, 442
Walle, 47
Walshe, Francis, 530–1, 544, 549, 629
Watson, J. B., 610
Watters, Ethan, 527, 625–6
Webb, Sydney, 582
Weber, Max, 608–9
Wedel, T. O., 315
Wednesday Psychological Society, 304–6
Weisz, George, 308
Wesley, John, 315–16, 318, 339
Westphal, 220
Wheeler, William Morton, 317–18, 465
White, Victor, 383
Whyte, Lancelot Law, 590
Wigmore, John Henry, 512
Wilbur, Cornelia, 626
Wilcocks, Robert, 25, 454, 559, 587
Williamson, P. D., 571–2
Willis, Thomas, 141–2
Wilson, Edward O., 611
Wilson, Woodrow, 427
Winnicott, Donald, 8, 36
Winstanley, Gerrard, 556
wish-fulfilment, 131, 260, 261, 262–6, 271–2
Witchhunt, Great European, 327
Wittels, Fritz:
  on Adler split, 359
  on Freud's attitude to libido theory, 309
  on Freud's despotism, 399
  on Freud's followers, 307
  on Freud's relationship with Jung, 374
  Wednesday Society, 335
Wittgenstein, Ludwig, 24, 270
Wolf Man, 289
Wollheim, Richard, 174, 308, 557, 585
women:
  contribution to psychoanalytic theory, 400
  feminism, 22, 514, 523, 525, 527, 617–9

Freud's treatment of women
    patients, 515–18
and masturbation, 411–13
misogyny, 22, 153, 525, 618
phallic and genital sexuality in,
    416
psychoanalytic denigration of, 22
sexual abuse and recovered memory,
    512–26
sexuality of, Freud's distaste for,
    4
Woolf, Leonard, 429
Woolf, Virginia, 429
word-association tests, 368
World War I, 107

World War II, 107–8
worthiness, concept of, 324, 600
Wren-Lewis, John, 320, 555–6
Wright, Lawrence, 527

X-rays, 137

Yeats, W. B., 15
Yellowlees, D., 570
Young-Bruehl, Elisabeth, 404, 405,
    410, 424, 434, 606, 607

Zentralblatt, 361
Zweig, Arnold, 430
Zweig, Stefan, 133, 134, 360